D1035592

For my sister Thelma with
the compliments of the Editor

Chester H. Topp

Donated by

**The Editor, in memory of
His sister, Thelma Gretchen
Topp Ferguson,
wife of Ivan Ferguson.**

© DEMCO, INC. 1990 PRINTED IN U.S.A.

Victorian Yellowbacks & Paperbacks,
1849–1905

Victorian Yellowbacks & Paperbacks, 1849–1905

VOLUME IV
FREDERICK WARNE & CO.

SAMPSON LOW & CO.

by Dr. Chester W. Topp

HERMITAGE ANTIQUARIAN BOOKSHOP
Denver, Colorado
1999

Published by
The Hermitage Bookshop
290 Fillmore Street
Denver, Colorado 80206-5020
(303) 388-6811

Printed and bound in the United States of America

First edition 1999, limited to 500 copies

This book was designed by Polly Christensen, edited by Michelle Asakawa, and photographed by John Youngblut.

Typesetting was done by the patient and impeccable crew of Wilsted & Taylor, Oakland, California.

⊗ The paper used in this publication meets the minimum requirements of American National Standard for Information Sciences—Permanence of Paper for Printed Library Materials, ANSI Z39.48-1984.

International Standard Book Number 0-9633920-3-4
Library of Congress Catalog Card Number: 92-073200

Contents

*A 32-page section of color photos appears
in the approximate middle of the book.*

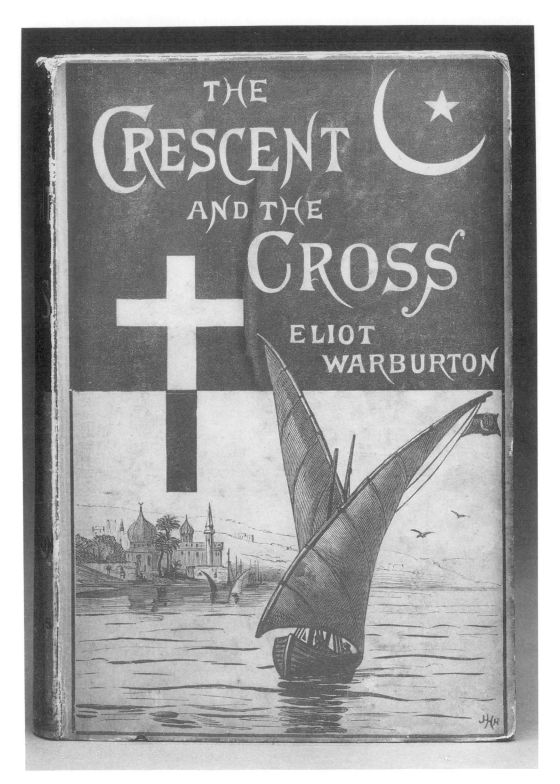

961   *The Crescent and the Cross*

Victorian Yellowbacks & Paperbacks, 1849–1905

VOLUME IV
FREDERICK WARNE & CO.

Short Titles and Abbreviations

Acad	*The Academy*
ALG&PC	*American Literary Gazette and Publishers' Circular*
Am Cat	*The American Catalog*
APC&LG	*American Publishers' Circular and Literary Gazette*
Ath	*The Athenaeum*
BAL	*Bibliography of American Literature*
Bks	*The Bookseller* (London)
BM	*The British Library Catalogue*
Eng Cat	*The English Catalogue*
Glover &	
Greene	*Victorian Detective Fiction*
Ind	*The Independent* (New York)
Lit W	*Literary World* (New York and Boston)
PC	*The Publishers' Circular and Booksellers' Record* (London)
PW	*Publishers' Weekly*
Roorbach	*Bibliotheca Americana*
Sat Rev	*The Saturday Review* (London)
Sadleir	Michael Sadleir's *Nineteenth Century Fiction*, 2 volumes
Spect	*The Spectator*
TLS	*The Times Literary Supplement* (London)
TWEd	*The Times Weekly Edition* (London)
U Cat	*The National Union Catalog*
Wolff	Robert Lee Wolff's *Nineteenth-Century Fiction*, 5 volumes
Wright	Lyle H. Wright's *American Fiction*, 3 volumes

Introduction

The present work attempts to list all the yellowbacks and paperbacks and cheap cloth issues of children's books issued by Frederick Warne & Co. from 1865 to 1905. They are listed chronologically by year and to the extent possible within the year. I have used my modest collection of over 40 yellowbacks and over 40 paperbacks issued by Warne and over 2,000 editions of pirated Victorian works in paper, issued by American publishers. The listings are fully coordinated with Sadleir and Wolff. In most cases the first English edition and the first American edition, if any, are given as well as important later editions and the first yellowback edition, if any. Fine points of first editions are, of course, not attempted.

The date of issue is given, where possible, as the date of listing in an important literary periodical; or, lacking such information, as given by the *Eng Cat*, the *BM*, or the *U Cat*. In some instances I've had to give the year of issue only as ascertained from internal evidence from the book or from my knowledge of the publisher's practice. Following the title of each entry, a date along with the title of a periodical means a listing in that periodical on that date.

I have used "wrappers" or "sewed" to indicate paperbacks and "boards" to indicate yellowbacks or other cheap boards issues. I have given the height of the bound book in centimeters if it is known to me and have otherwise indicated the height as gleaned from ads and references as 16mo, Fcp 8vo, 12mo, Cr 8vo, Demy 8vo, 8vo, or 4to. In general these terms indicate lengths of about 15 cm., 16.8 cm. (Sadleir's small format), 17.5 cm. (Sadleir's large format), 19 cm., 21 cm., 23 cm., and 29 cm. respectively. The number of pages refers to the last page of text. In some cases only the price is given, the binding being unknown to me. Prices are given in pounds, shillings, and pence. Thus 2/6 means 2 shillings and 6 pence; 0/6 means 6 pence; 1/0 means 1 shilling, and so on. When a notation as to edition is given in brackets after the title in an entry, it means that notation describes the issue—although the words may or may not appear on the title page (as I am unable to say). When no brackets appear, the given notation appeared on the title page.

The address or addresses of the publishers in the imprint are important to collectors in dating undated books, and the various changes in such are here recorded.

Michael Sadleir gives a discussion of yellowbacks in *Collecting Yellowbacks*, Constable, 1938, a 38-page pamphlet. His comments in the preliminary notes to *XIXth Century Fiction*, volume 2 is also of value. A brief history of yellowbacks and paperbacks is given in volume 1 of the present series.

Frederick Warne started his company about June 24, 1865, having left the firm of Routledge, Warne & Routledge, where he had been a partner since 1851. He and his brother William H. Warne (the latter taken in as a Routledge partner in 1848) were both brothers-in-law of George Routledge. The firm of Frederick Warne & Co. consisted of Frederick Warne and partners Edward J. Dodd and A. W. Duret. The catalog of Routledge, Warne & Routledge was divided up; Warne's first ad in the *Spect* appeared on July

1, 1865, and the first Warne catalog was issued June 30, 1865. The address of the firm was Bedford Street, Covent Garden, London, and it so remained through 1905. Duret retired in 1870, and Warne and Dodd retired in 1895, leaving the firm in the hands of Warne's three sons. Frederick Warne died on Nov. 7, 1901, at the age of 77.

The imprint of the firm from 1866 to 1867 was Frederick Warne & Co., London; Scribner & Co., New York. From 1868 to 1871 it was joined with Scribner, Welford & Co., New York; and from 1872 to 1877 it was joined with Scribner, Welford & Armstrong, New York. The imprint was Frederick Warne & Co., Bedford Street, London, from 1881 to 1885, and a New York office of the company was opened at 20 Lafayette Place and was there from 1885 to 1887. It moved to 3 Cooper Union, Fourth Avenue, where it remained from 1888 to 1894 and probably later. By 1897 it was at 103 Fifth Avenue and probably remained there from 1897 to 1905.

Warne certainly ranks as one of the prominent issuers of yellowbacks and paperbacks; it was primarily a reprint house. The niche it carved out for itself was in the issuance of juvenile works in cloth at o/6, o/9, 1/0, 1/6, 2/0, and 2/6. It ranked with Nelson & Sons, the Religious Tract Society, Gall & Inglis, and others in this respect. Because Warne was such a prominent publisher of cheap cloth juveniles, I have departed from the practice used in volumes 1–3 of listing only yellowbacks, cheap boards editions, and paperbacks and have here included the cheap cloth issues of children's literature.

At the very beginning of the firm in 1865 the *Shilling Juvenile Series* at 1/0 cloth, with colored illustrations, was started, along with the *2/6 Gift Series* in cloth, illustrated, and the *Eighteenpenny Juveniles* in cloth, illustrated. There followed dozens of juvenile series, mostly in cloth, by such authors as Aunt Louisa (Laura Valentine), Frances H. Burnett, Anna and Susan Warner, Elizabeth Prentiss, Annie Keary, Mrs. Henry H.B. Paull, Aunt Friendly (Sarah S. Baker), A.L.O.E. (Charlotte Tucker), Matilda Planche, Holme Lee (Harriet Parr), Caroline Bell, and Caroline Hadley.

Warne issued several long series of reprints, both fiction and nonfiction. The *Companion Library*, mainly fiction, beginning with No. 1 at 1/0 sewed in 1865, shortly to be issued at 2/0 boards, reached No. 146 in 1884. They issued the *Star Series* for young people, starting with No. 1 at 1/0 sewed in 1875 (shortly advanced to 1/6 sewed and also in cloth) and ending with No. 130 in 1893, although a few unnumbered issues followed sporadically. A series of reprinted novels, *Notable Novels*, at o/6 sewed, 1/0 cloth, began with No. 1 in 1867 and shortly was issued at o/6 sewed only, ending with No. 154 in 1894. *Chandos Classics*, a series of primarily nonfiction reprints, began with No. 1 in 1868 at 1/0 sewed, 1/6 and 2/0 cloth, and continued at various prices in paper and cloth, reaching No. 148 in 1893. As the above series indicate, paperbacks formed a substantial part of Warne's output, and they issued many other series in paper throughout the period covered by the present bibliography.

Warne published 20 titles of Frances H. Burnett, both first and early editions. They published 22 titles of Susan Warner, both first and early editions.

Victorian Yellowbacks & Paperbacks,
1849–1905

Frederick Warne & Co.
Bedford Street, Covent Garden
1865

Frederick Warne left the firm of Routledge, Warne & Routledge, where he was a partner, and started his own publishing house about June 24, 1865. The catalog of Routledge, Warne & Routledge was divided up. The first Warne ad in the Spect *appeared on July 1, 1865, and their first catalog was issued on June 30 of that year.*

1 CHARLOTTE LANKESTER **Marian and Her Pupils.** [Second edition.] Fcp 8vo. Illustrated. 2/6 cloth   June 24 (*Ath* ad)

2/6 Gift Books. This was assigned to Warne in the breakup of Routledge, Warne & Routledge. It has 300 pp. The first edition was issued by Routledge, Warne & Routledge, 1864 [1863], 12mo, illustrated, 2/6.

2 ANONYMOUS **Eildon Manor.** Fcp 8vo. Illustrated. 2/6 cloth   June 24 (*Ath* ad)

2/6 Gift Books. This was assigned to Warne in the breakup of Routledge, Warne & Routledge. The first edition was issued by Routledge, Warne & Routledge in 1861, Fcp 8vo, 2/6, noticed in the *Spect* on Dec. 28, 1861.
Also 1881

3 (H. E. SCUDDER) **Tales from Dreamland.** 18mo. Illustrated. 1/6 cloth
July 8 (*Ath* ad)

Eighteenpenny Juveniles. This is 1865, 183 pp. It wasn't listed in the *Reader* until Oct. 2. The first edition was *Dream Children*, issued by Sever & Frances, Cambridge, Mass., 1864, 16.5 cm., anonymous, 241 pp., illustrated.

4 HANS C. ANDERSEN **Tales for the Young.** [New edition.] 18mo. Illustrated. 1/6 cloth   July 8 (*Ath* ad)

Eighteenpenny Juveniles. This has 216 pp. and was listed by the *Reader* on Dec. 23, 1865. It was issued with this title by James Burns, London, 1847, 230 pp., with partly colored illustrations; and issued by Lumley, London, in 1857, 18mo, 2/6. There was an edition listed in the *Ath* on Dec. 16, 1865, 1/6, probably the same title as was listed in the *Reader* on Dec. 23. Andersen's fairy stories were first issued as *Eventyr*, in 3 collections, in Denmark, 1835–37, and translations were issued in England and America in 1846. For a fuller discussion of the first editions see the entry in 1874.
Also 1874, 77, 97. See 1883

5 ANONYMOUS **Truth and Falsehood.** 18mo. Illustrated. 1/6 cloth   July 18 (*Ath* ad)

Eighteenpenny Juveniles. This is 1865, 188 pp., probably a first edition. It was listed in the *Reader* on Oct. 21. Warne issued it as *The Lost Heir* in 1871 in the *Birthday Series*, a new name for the *Eighteenpenny Juveniles*, 18mo, illustrated, 1/6 cloth. It was reissued in the *Birthday Series* in 1879, the same; and was placed in the *Oakleaf Library* at 1/0 in the 1890s.

6 ANONYMOUS *Patient Henry.* 18mo. Illustrated. 1/6 cloth   July 18 (*Ath* ad)
This is 1865, 188 pp., and is probably the first edition. It was listed in the *Reader* on Oct. 21. It is in the *Eighteenpenny Juveniles.*

7 (MIRIAM C. HARRIS) (MRS. SIDNEY S. HARRIS) *The Sutherlands.* 12mo. 2/0 sewed   July 29 (*Ath*)
Companion Library No. 1. This is 1865, 326 pp. This series was started by Gall & Inglis, Edinburgh and London, and was taken over by Warne. The present title was No. 84 in the Gall & Inglis issue. I have a copy of *Walter Goring* issued by Warne, no date, with Gall & Inglis ads on the endpapers giving titles in the *Companion Library* through No. 94, many of which were not even published until long after Warne started their series. *Walter Goring*, by Annie Thomas, was issued by Warne in the *Companion Library* as No. 29 in July 1867. I surmise that the reissue with the Gall & Inglis ads was circa 1885 and that the list of the *Companion Library* for Gall & Inglis was actually issued by Warne and, apparently, was for sale by Gall & Inglis. The first edition of the present title was issued by G. W. Carleton, New York, 1862, 12mo, anonymous, 474 pp., $1.25 cloth, advertised in the *New-York Times* on Dec. 12, 1861, as "On Dec. 14." A new edition was advertised on Dec. 22 as "Today." Warne reissued it as *Companion Library* No. 43, at 2/0 boards, in Apr. 1871, with publisher's ads for Florence Marryat's novels on the back cover.

8 (MIRIAM C. HARRIS) *Rutledge.* 12mo. 1/0 sewed   July 29 (*Ath* ad)
Companion Library No. 2. The *BM* gives this as 1866, which possibly was a second edition. The present edition was also

listed in the *Reader* on Aug. 12 and in the *Bks* as published in Aug. The first edition was issued by Derby & Jackson, New York, 1860, anonymous, 504 pp., $1.25, advertised in *Harper's Weekly* on May 19 as "On May 19" and listed in *APC&LG* (weekly) on May 26. The second edition was advertised in the *New-York Times* on May 31 as "Now ready"; the third edition was advertised on June 14, and the fourth edition on June 22, all at $1.25. G. W. Carleton, New York; Frederick Warne & Co., London, issued the 20th edition, 1866, 18.5 cm., anonymous, 504 pp., $1.25, advertised in the *New-York Times* on Dec. 12, 1861, new edition, "On Dec. 14"; the ad stated that the title had passed through more than 20 editions. Warne issued a new edition, 12mo, anonymous, 2/0 boards, as *Companion Library* No. 44, listed by the *Bks* as published in Apr. 1871.

9 (MIRIAM C. HARRIS) *Christine; or, St. Philip's.* 12mo. 1/0 sewed   July 29 (*Ath*)
Companion Library No. 3. The *BM* gives only a new edition, 1866, 297 pp., but the present edition was also listed in the *Reader* on Aug. 5 and by the *Bks* as published in Aug. The first edition was issued by G. W. Carleton, New York, *St. Philip's*, 1865, anonymous, 340 pp. Warne issued a new edition, 12mo, anonymous, 2/0 boards, as *Companion Library* No. 45, listed by the *Bks* as published in Apr. 1871.

10 LOUISA L. CLARKE *The Common Seaweeds of the British Coast and Channel Islands.* Fcp 8vo. Illustrated. 1/0 boards   Aug. 5 (*Ath*)
Household Books. Country and Sea-Side Library. This is the first edition, no date, 16.5 cm., 140 pp., tinted plates, in white pictorial boards, printed in red, green, and black, with publisher's ads on the endpapers, on the back cover, and on 4 pp. at the back. It was also issued in cloth at 2/0 about Sept. 23, 1865. It was reissued in 1881, at 1/0, given by the *Eng Cat.*

11 JOHN G. WOOD **The Common Shells of the Sea-Shore.** Fcp 8vo. Illustrated. 1/o boards   Aug. 5 (*Ath*)

Household Books. Country and Sea-Side Library. This is the first edition, 1865, 16.5 cm., 132 pp. It was also issued in cloth at 2/o about Sept. 23, Warne issued the third edition, 1/o, 2/o, in 1869, given by the *Eng Cat.*

12 ANONYMOUS *Major Jack Downing.* Fcp 8vo. 1/o sewed   Aug. 12 (*Ath*)

This is 1865, 286 pp. Warne advertised a second edition in the *Ath* on Sept. 30, 1865. It is a reissue of *Letters of Major Jack Downing of the Downingville Militia*, published by Bromley & Co., New York, 1864, listed in *ALG&PC* (fortnightly) on Sept. 15. Ward & Lock, London, also issued the Bromley edition at o/6 sewed, about Mar. 17, 1866. George Routledge & Sons, London, also issued the Bromley edition, Cr 8vo, o/6 sewed, 100 pp., in 1867. The Jack Downing writings were first issued in the *Portland Courier* of Portland, Maine, 1830–33, written by (Seba Smith), and were issued for the publisher, Philadelphia, 1834, 17.5 cm., 212 pp., frontispiece, *The Select Letters of Major Jack Downing of the Downingville Militia*, etc.; and were issued by Lilly, Wait, Colman & Holden, Boston, 1833, 260 pp., illustrated, *The Life and Writings of Major Jack Downing of Downingville, etc.*, listed in the *American Monthly Magazine*, New York, for Jan. 1834. It was advertised by a Washington, D.C., bookstore in the *Globe* on Dec. 6, 1833, $1.25, "Just received"; a second edition was advertised at $1.00 on Feb. 13, 1834, "Just received," and the sixth edition was advertised on July 30. This edition was imported into England by Kennett, London, and listed in the *Ath* on Mar. 15, 1834. Harper & Brothers, New York, issued *The Letters, etc.*, 1834, 19.5 cm., 240 pp. illustrated, by (Charles A. Davis), listed by the *North American Review* (quarterly) for Apr.

1834. This Harper text was probably that issued by John Murray, London, 1835, 14 cm., 223, 207–215 pp., advertised in the *Spect* on May 9 as "This day," anonymous; and the second edition with 3 added letters, 18mo, anonymous, 3/o, was advertised on June 20.

13 ALBANY FONBLANQUE *How We Are Governed.* Revised to the Present Date. [Popular edition.] 12mo. 1/o boards   Aug. 12 (*Spect*)

The first edition was issued by George Routledge & Co., London and New York, 1858, 17 cm., 216 pp., 2/6 cloth, listed in the *Spect* on Sept. 25. Routledge, Warnes & Routledge issued it, 1859, new edition, 12mo, 226 pp., 2/6 cloth, listed by *PC* as published Jan. 1–15, 1859; they reissued it, the same, listed as published May 14–31. Routledge, Warne & Routledge issued it, 1861, new edition, 2/6 cloth, advertised in the *Spect* on Feb. 2. Warne reissued it, revised to the present date by W. A. Holdsworth, 1867, 17 cm., 214 pp; and they issued it, 1869, further revised by A. D. Ewald, 18 cm., 158 pp., 2/6 cloth, listed in the *Ath* on Sept. 9, 1868. Apparently this latter edition was reissued in 1869, as the *Eng Cat, BM*, and *U Cat* all give it only as 1869. The 12th edition, revised and enlarged, was issued in 1872, 12mo, 188 pp., 2/6 cloth, listed by *PC* as published Aug. 16–31. The 13th edition was issued in 1879, revised by a barrister, listed in the *Spect* on June 7; and the 14th edition was issued in 1880, revised by Smalman Smith, 12mo, 2/6 cloth, listed in the *Spect* on Aug. 7. The 16th edition, 1889, revised by W. J. Gordon, p 8vo, 208 pp., 1/6 cloth, is given by the *Eng Cat*; it was issued by Warne in New York, at $.75, listed in the *Nation* on Sept. 19, 1889. The 17th edition, the same, was advertised in the *Times Weekly Edition* (London) on Mar. 7, 1890, as "Now ready."

14 MAYNE REID **Croquet.** [New edition.] 1/o cloth sewed   Aug. 12 (*Reader*)

Beeton's Shilling Handbooks. The first English edition was issued by Charles J. Skeet, London, 1863, 8vo, 46 pp., illustrated, 2/6 limp cloth, listed in the *Ath* on Sept. 12. The second edition was issued by Houlston, London, in 1865, Fcp 8vo, 95 pp., 1/o cloth sewed, listed in the *Reader* on Apr. 29. The first American edition was issued by J. Redpath, Boston, 1863, $.50, advertised in the *New-York Times* on Oct. 22 as "Just published."

15 FREDERICK WOOD **Beeton's Cricket Book.** 18mo. o/6 boards   Aug. 19 (*Reader*)

The first Warne ad in the *Ath* on June 24, 1865, advised that after July 1 Warne would have the exclusive sale of S. O. Beeton books. This has 86 pp. The *BM* gives it with "A Match I Was in" by (J. Pycroft), S. O. Beeton (1866), 18mo, 116 pp., and it was listed in the *Spect* on Apr. 21, 1866, but probably as issued by Warne. It was noticed in the *Spect* on Mar. 23, 1867, as issued by Warne.
See also 1866

16 J. E. CARPENTER, ed. **Penny Readings in Prose and Verse.** Fcp 8vo. 1/o boards Sept. 2 (*Ath*)

This is vol. 1 of a first edition of these readings. There were 6 vols., each vol. made up of 2 fortnightly o/6 sewed parts. Vol. 3 was listed in the *Reader* on Nov. 4, 252 pp.; vol. 4 on Dec. 2, 248 pp.; vol. 5 on Dec. 30, 244 pp.; and vol. 6 on Feb. 3, 1866, all given as 1/o sewed. The vols. were also issued at 1/6 cloth each.

17 (MIRIAM C. HARRIS) (MRS. SIDNEY S. HARRIS) **Frank Warrington.** [New edition.] Fcp 8vo. 1/o sewed   Sept. 2 (*Ath*)

The first American edition was issued by G. W. Carleton & Co., New York, 1863, 12mo, anonymous, 478 pp., $1.50 cloth, advertised in the *New-York Times* on May 30 as "Next week."

18 (SUSAN & ANNA WARNER) **Carl Krinken: His Christmas Stocking.** 18mo. Colored illustrations. 1/o cloth   Sept. 9 (*Reader*)

Shilling Juveniles. This has 128 pp. It is vol. 1 of *Ellen Montgomery's Bookshelf.* Warne reissued it in their *Round the Globe Library* No. 12, 12mo, 1/o cloth, colored frontispiece, probably in 1869. The first edition was issued by G. P. Putnam, New York, 1854, 18 cm., anonymous, 308 pp., illustrated, with a preface signed by Amy Lothrop (Anna Warner), in red or green cloth, yellow endpapers, various stampings, edges plain or gilt, $.75 and $1.25, both in cloth. It was deposited on Dec. 16, 1853, and advertised in the *New York Daily Times* on Dec. 19 as "On Dec. 22." In England it was issued by James Nisbet & Co., etc., London, 1854, 16 cm., anonymous, 255 pp., illustrated, with a preface signed by Amy Lothrop and dated New York, Dec. 13, 1853, with the present title on the title page but with *The Christmas Stocking* on the cover. It was deposited at the *BM* on Jan. 24, 1854, and listed by *PC* on Jan. 2. They issued a later edition, listed by *PC* on Jan. 17, 1865. Clarke, Beeton & Co., London, issued *The Christmas Stocking,* 1855 (1854), 12mo, 155 pp., 1/o; and the same, with a different title page, was issued by Piper, Stephenson & Spence, London, 1855 (1854), listed by *PC* on Dec. 16, 1854. George Routledge & Co., London and New York, issued it with the present title, listed by *PC* on Dec. 16, 1854. Warne issued *Ellen Montgomery's Bookshelf,* complete, in 1865, Fcp 8vo, anonymous, 516 pp., colored illustrations, 3/6 and 4/o, listed in the *Ath* on July 29. They issued it in 1886, colored illustrations, 2/o boards, listed in the *Reader* on May 19; and they issued it in 1877 as *Star Series* No. 43, 16mo, 1/6 sewed, 2/o cloth, listed in the *Spect* on

Sept. 22. I have a copy of the *Star Series* issue in green cloth, elaborately stamped in black and gilt, inscribed date of Christmas 1902, 19 cm., 592 pp., with the authors' names, S. & A. Warner, on the cover only. It contains *Mr. Rutherford's Children*; *Carl Krinken; or, The Christmas Stocking*; *Casper*; and *Happy Days; or, Holly Farm*.

19 PETROLEUM V. NASBY (D. R. LOCKE) *The Nasby Papers*. Fcp 8vo. 1/o sewed Sept. 16 (*Ath*)

This or the Beeton issue below was the first English edition. The present edition has 124 pp., and Warne issued a second edition, advertised in the *Ath* on Sept. 30. S. O. Beeton, London, issued it, 1865, 16 cm., 124 pp., 1/o, with a preface signed S.O.B., issued in Sept. Ward, Lock & Tyler, London, issued it in 1865, an original stereotyped edition, 18 cm., 88 pp., introduction by George A. Sala (Oct. 1865) and a dedication (Aug. 1, 1864), in white pictorial wrappers, listed in the *Reader* on Nov. 11, 1865. The first edition was issued by C. O. Perrine & Co., Indianapolis, 1864, 19.5 cm., 64 pp., listed in *ALG&PC* (fortnightly) on Nov. 1.

20 ANONYMOUS *The Boy's Shilling Book of Sports, Games, Exercises, and Pursuits*. Fcp 8vo. Illustrated. 1/o sewed Sept. 23 (*Ath*)

This has 228 pp. The *U Cat* gives Warne, 1866, 228 pp., illustrated, probably a second edition. Warne issued it in 1903, Fcp 8vo, 1/o, advertised in the *Times Literary Supplement* on May 8.

21 ELIZABETH WATTS *Poultry: An Original and Practical Guide to Their Breeding, etc*. Fcp 8vo. Illustrated. 1/o boards Sept.?

Country Library and Family Circle Books. This is the first edition, 192 pp. It was reissued in 1867, the same, listed in the *Spect* on

Mar. 16; and in 1870, a new edition, illustrated, at 1/o sewed, listed by the *Bks* as published in Mar.

22 ELIZABETH WATTS *Flowers and the Flower Garden*. Fcp 8vo. Illustrated. 1/o boards Oct. 14 (*Ath*)

Country Library and Family Circle Books. This is the first edition, 188 pp. There is a known copy, no date, in light blue pictorial boards, printed in red, green, and black, with series ads on the endpapers and a commercial ad on the back. This was also listed in the *Reader* on Oct. 21 and in the *Bks* for Oct. Thus it seems strange that the *Eng Cat* and the *BM* give 1866 only. It was advertised in the *Spect* on Nov. 11 at 1/o, Fcp 8vo, stiff covers and 2/6, square 12mo. The *U Cat* gives Warne, 1867, 16.5 cm., 188 pp.

23 (MIRIAM C. HARRIS) (MRS. SIDNEY HARRIS) *Louie Atterbury*. 12mo. 1/o sewed Oct. 21 (*Ath*)

Companion Library No. 5. I think this is the first edition in England, reissued, the same, in Dec., listed in the *Spect* on Jan. 13, 1866. The present edition was also listed in the *Reader* and in the *Bks* as published in Oct., and thus it seems strange that the *BM* gives only 1866, 232 pp. Warne advertised the present title in the *Ath* on Mar. 24, 1866, as a new, large-type Sunday book, with colored illustrations. It was placed in the 2/o *Gift Books* series in 1866, 12mo, illustrated, 2/o cloth, and was advertised in this series in the *Ath* on Nov. 27, 1869, as a new publication. It was placed in the *Home Circle Gift Books* series, illustrated, 2/o cloth, after 1871.

24 S. O. BEETON *Beeton's Book of Chemistry*. 12mo. Illustrated. 1/o sewed Nov. 4 (*Reader*)

This is a first edition, 1865, 18 cm., 123 pp. Warne advertised in the *Spect* on Sept. 30, 1865, that they were the sole wholesale agents for the books written by Beeton.

25 S. O. BEETON **Beeton's Book of Jokes
and Jests.** 12mo. 1/0 sewed   Nov. 11
(*Reader*)
I think this is the first edition. The *BM*
gives Warne, 1866 (1865), 140 pp.

26 L. V. **In and Out of School.** Roy 8vo.
Illustrated. 2/6 boards   Nov. 11 (*Reader*)
This is the first edition, no date, in verse. It
was also listed in the *Ath* on Nov. 4 but was
advertised there on July 8 as a new publication and advertised on Oct. 14 as a new
book. It was also issued at the same time as
the present edition at 4/0 with colored
illustrations.

27 AUNT LOUISA (LAURA VALENTINE)
Aunt Louisa's Sunday Books. 4to. Colored
illustrations. 1/0 sewed each   Nov. 11
(*Reader*)
This contains the two titles: *Joseph and His
Brethren* and the *Proverbs of Soloman*. The
only reference to this I've found was given
by the *U Cat* as New York, 188-?. 1 vol., unpaged, 27 cm., colored plates, with the title on the cover, *Aunt Louisa's Sunday Book.*

28 HENRY C. ADAMS **Sundays at
Encombe.** 12mo. Illustrated. 2/0 cloth
Nov. 18 (*Ath*)
2/0 Gift Books. This is probably the first edi-
tion, 1866, 184 pp. as both the *BM* and the
U Cat give only 1866. It was placed in the
Home Circle Gift Books series after 1871. It
was advertised in the present series in the
Ath on Nov. 27, 1869. *Encombe Stories*
(Adam to Saul) was listed in the *Spect* on
June 13, 1868, 12mo, 3/6.

29 ANNA L. BARBAULD & DR. AIKIN
Evenings at Home. [New edition.] Fcp
8vo. Illustrated. 1/6 boards, 2/0 cloth
Nov. 18 (*Reader*)
Juvenile Library. The first edition was issued in 6 vols. by J. Johnson, London,
1792–96. The first three vols. were reviewed in the *Critical Review*, London

(monthly) for Dec. 1793, 12mo, 4/6
boards, Johnson, 1793; vol. 4 was reviewed in Jan. 1795, 1/6 boards, Johnson,
1794; vols. 5 and 6 were reviewed in Aug.
1796, 3/0, Johnson, 1796. *The Works of
Mrs. Anna L. Barbauld* was issued by David
Reed, Boston, 3 vols., 1826; and by G. & C.
Carvill, New York, 2 vols., 1826. Longmans, London, issued it in 1863. Warne
repeatedly reissued this in their various
juvenile series. It was issued in the *Juvenile
Library*, Fcp 8vo, 357 pp., illustrated, 1/0
sewed, listed in the *Reader* on Jan. 20,
1866; in *2/0 Gift Books*, 12mo, 2/0 cloth, advertised in the *Ath* on Nov. 7, 1869; in *National Books*, Imp 32mo, 2 plates, 0/6 stiff
wrappers at 1/0, 1/6 cloth with colored
plates, still advertised in 1895 at 1/0 picture boards or 1/6 cloth; in *Incident and Adventure Library*, Fcp 8vo, illustrated, 2/0
cloth, issued in 1881, given by the *Eng Cat*;
in the *Village Library*, Cr 8vo, 1/0 cloth,
listed in *PC* on May 9, 1891.

30 DANIEL DEFOE **Life and Adventures of
Robinson Crusoe.** Fcp 8vo. Illustrated. 1/6
boards, 2/0 cloth   Nov. 18 (*Reader*)
Juvenile Library. The *U Cat* gives Warne,
1865, 17 cm., illustrated, 308 pp., 2 parts.
The first edition was issued by W. Taylor,
London, 3 vols., anonymous. Vol. 1, *The
Life and Strange Surprizing Adventures of
Robinson Crusoe*, 1719, in Apr.; vol. 2, *The
Farther Adventures of Robinson Crusoe*, 1719;
vol. 3, *Serious Reflections During the Life and
Surprising Adventures of Robinson Crusoe*,
1720; both the latter 2 vols. issued in Aug.
The Brigham bibliography of the Ameri-
can editions, Worcester, 1958, gives the
earliest unlocated edition as *Serious Re-
flections During the Life and Surprizing Adventures of Robinson Crusoe* . . . , Samuel
Keimer, Philadelphia, 1725. He gives the
earliest located edition as *The Wonderful
Life and Surprizing Adventures of the Re-
nowned Hero, Robinson Crusoe*, issued by
Hugh Caine, New York, 1774, 138 pp.,
frontispiece and 6 illustrations and 4 pp.

of ads at the back. He also gives the same title but with "surprising," N. Coverly, Boston (ca. 1779), 32 pp., frontispiece and 4 illustrations, with Coverly spelled "Coveely." He next gives the same, Charles Cist, Philadelphia, 1787, (164) pp. and 6 illustrations. It was also issued as *The Travels of Robinson Crusoe by Himself*, issued by Issac Thomas, Worcester, 1786, 31 pp., frontispiece and 7 illustrations, with the text on pp. 25–31 not by Defoe. *The Life and Most Surprizing Adventures of Robinson Crusoe . . .* was issued by Peter Stewart, Philadelphia, 1789, 3 parts in 1 vol., 180 pp., frontispiece and 5 illustrations, condensed. *The Most Surprising Adventures and Wonderful Life of Robinson Crusoe . . .* was issued by Thomas P. Wait, Portland, 1789, 130 pp., frontispiece and 8 illustrations, with a portrait on page (131). Warne issued it as a *2/o Gift Book*, 12mo, illustrated, 2/o cloth, 1867, 17 cm., 332 pp., parts 1 & 2, given by the *U Cat*; and it was listed in the *Reader* on Oct. 20, 1866, at 3/6 cloth. It was issued as *National Books* No. 3., 16mo, colored illustrations. o/6 sewed, 1/o, 1/6 cloth, 13 cm., 284 pp. abridged, with the series title on the cover, with the joint imprint of Scribner, Welford & Co., New York. It was given by the *BM* and the *U Cat* as 1869. It was reissued in *2/o Gift Books*, advertised in the *Ath* on Nov. 27, 1869, with 1870 on the titlepage. Warne issued it in the *Incident and Adventure Library*, 1871, 17 cm., 332 pp., illustrated, 2/o cloth, with the series title on the cover, given by the *U Cat*.

Also 1873, 79

31 THOMAS DAY *The History of Sandford and Merton*. Fcp 8vo. Illustrated. 1/6 boards, 2/o cloth   Nov. 18 (*Reader*)

Juvenile Library. The first edition was in 3 vols., issued by J. Stockdale, London, 3/o each: vol. 1, small 8vo, noticed in the *Critical Review*, London (monthly), for Mar. 1874, anonymous; vol. 2 noticed in June 1876, 12mo; vol. 3 noticed in Oct. 1789,

12mo; both the latter two also anonymous. In the United States it was issued by W. Young, Philadelphia, 2 vols.-in-1, 1788, the fifth edition corrected, and a third vol. was issued by Young, 1791. George Routledge & Sons, London, issued it at 2/o boards about Oct. 28, 1865, in their *Railway Library*. Warne reissued it in the *Juvenile Library* in 1866, Fcp 8vo, 366 pp., illustrated, 1/o sewed, listed in the *Reader* on Jan. 27, 1866. It was issued in the *2/o Gift Book* series in 1869, 12mo, illustrated, 2/o cloth, advertised in the *Ath* on Nov. 27; and it was issued in the *National Books* series No. 13 in 1879, 16mo, 2 plates, o/6 stiff wrappers, 1/o, 1/6 cloth with colored plates, advertised in the *Ath* on Nov. 15. It was issued in the *Incident and Adventure Library* in 1881, Fcp 8vo, illustrated, 2/o cloth, given by the *Eng Cat*; and issued in the *Village Library* in 1892, Cr 8vo, 1/o cloth, listed in *PC* on July 16, and reissued in Oct.

32 EDWARD LEAR *A Book of Nonsense*.
3 vols. Oblong 8co. Illustrated. 1/o sewed each   Dec. 9 (*Ath*)

Warne advertised this in the *Ath* on Oct. 14, 1865, 18th thousand, Demy oblong 8vo, illustrated, 3/6 boards, colored cover; colored plates, 6/o; 3 parts, 1/o each, colored cover. The first edition was issued by Thomas McLean, London, 2 vols., 1846, 36 leaves and illustrated title page in each, paper-covered pictorial boards with bright red linen spines; the second edition was issued in 1856. They published it as 2-vols.-in-1 on Feb. 20, 1846, Fcp folio, 74 pp., 14.5 cm. high and 21 cm. wide. In the United States it was issued by William P. Hazard, Philadelphia, no date, long 8vo, 113 leaves, illustrated, $1.00, from the tenth London edition, listed in the *Atlantic Monthly* for July 1863. M. Doolady, New York, issued it from the same plates, the *U Cat* copy having an inscribed date (Jan. 1863). Warne issued it in 4 parts in 1870, 4to, 1/o stiff fancy wrappers each, advertised in the *Spect* on Oct. 22, and the same ad gave Demy 8vo, 11 colored illustrations, 5/0 cloth, 1 vol. The *Eng Cat* gives 6 parts, 4to, 1/0 each, Warne, in 1875; and the Osborne Collection had a copy, imprinted jointly with Scribner, Welford & Armstrong, New York (ca. 1875), Fcp folio, 54 pp., 26×22 cm., with "130 colored illustrations" on the cover, bound in blue pictorial cloth. Warne issued it in 1881, 4to, 7/6, listed in the *Spect* on Dec. 24; and issued it in 1888, the 26th edition, oblong 4to, illustrated, $2.00 cloth, advertised in the *New-York Times* on May 20, as issued by Warne, New York, "Now ready." *Nonsense Drolleries* was issued in 1889, small 4to, 30 pp., illustrated, 1/6 boards, advertised in the *Ath* on Aug. 24.

33 HARRIET MYRTLE (LYDIA F. MILLER) *The Pet Lamb, and Other Tales.* [New edition.] 18mo. Colored illustrations. 1/0 cloth   Dec. 9 (*Ath*)

Shilling Juveniles. The first edition was issued by George Routledge, London, in 1848, 2/6, 3/6. It was issued in the United States by Sheldon, New York, 1866, 63 pp., *The Pet Lamb*.

34 HARRIET MYRTLE *Little Amy's Birthday, and Other Tales.* [New edition.] 18mo. Colored illustrations. 1/0 cloth Dec. 9 (*Ath*)

Shilling Juveniles. The *BM* gives London, 1846, and the *Eng Cat* gives George Routledge, London, 1849, 2/6, 3/6.

35 HARRIET MYRTLE *The Little Foundling, and Other Tales.* [New edition.] 18mo. Colored illustrations. 1/0 cloth Dec. 9 (*Ath*)

Shilling Juveniles. This has 119 pp. The first edition was issued by George Routledge, London, 1850, 2/6, 3/6.

36 HARRIET MYRTLE *The Man of Snow, and Other Tales.* [New edition.] 18mo. Colored illustrations. 1/0 cloth   Dec. 9 (*Ath*)

Shilling Juveniles. This has 122 pp. The *U Cat* gives J. Cundall, London, 1848, 17.5 cm., 124 pp.; and the *Eng Cat* gives George Routledge, London, 1848, 2/6, 3/6.

37 (SUSAN WARNER) *Little Nettie.* [New edition.] 32mo. Colored frontispiece. 0/6 cloth   Dec. 9 (*Ath* ad)

The Dec. 9 ad gave 16 titles in this series beginning with this title. Warne issued it in *Round the Globe Library* in 1872, 12mo, colored frontispiece, 1/0 cloth, listed in the *Ath* on Oct. 19, 128 pp. This is No. 7 of the stories illustrative of the 8 beatitudes. Nisbet & Co., London, issued the *Golden Ladder*, 1863, containing all 8 stories; No. 7 was "Drops of Oil." It was 17 cm., 479 pp., frontispiece and 7 plates, with 7 pp. of ads, in green cloth with red-brown endpapers. It was listed in the *Ath* on Nov. 29, 1862, 476 pp.; a new edition with 480 pp. was listed on Jan. 31, 1863. George Routledge, London, issued it as *The Carpenter's Daughter*, listed in the *Bks* on May 31, 1864. Carleton and Porter, Sunday-School Union, New York, issued the stories separately (1862, i.e., 1863), No. 7 being *The Carpenter's House*, which was 15 cm., 168 pp., frontispiece and 2 plates, in lavender cloth with yellow endpapers, deposited on Mar. 9, 1863.

38 CATHERINE D. BELL *Self-Mastery; or, Kenneth and Hugh.* [New edition.] Fcp 8vo. Illustrated. 2/6 cloth Dec. 9 (*Ath* ad)

2/6 Gift Books. The first edition was issued by W. P. Kennedy, Edinburgh, 1857, 12mo, 351 pp., apparently in a joint issue with Hamilton, London, at 5/0 cloth, Warne issued it as *Kenneth and Hugh* as a *3/6 Gift Book*, illustrated, advertised in the *Spect* on Dec. 8, 1866. They issued it in the

Star Series in 1876, 16mo, 1/0 sewed, *Kenneth and Hugh*, listed in the *Spect* on Mar. 25. In the United States it was issued by A.D.F. Randolph, New York, no date, 419 pp., frontispiece as *Kenneth and Hugh*; and was also issued with date 1865.

39 CATHERINE D. BELL *Lily Gordon.* Fcp 8vo. Illustrated. 2/6 cloth Dec. 9 (*Ath* ad)

2/6 Gift Books. The first edition was issued by W. P. Kennedy, Edinburgh, 1853, 348 pp., by Cousin Kate, probably at 4/6 issued jointly with Hamilton, London. It was issued in the United States by A.D.F. Randolph, New York, 1856, 16mo, 371 pp., frontispiece. Warne issued it in their *Star Series* No. 82, 16mo, 1/0 sewed, 1/6 cloth, probably in 1883.

40 CATHERINE D. BELL *The Huguenot Family; or, Help in Time of Need.* [New edition.] Fcp 8vo. Illustrated. 2/6 cloth Dec. 9 (*Ath* ad)

2/6 Gift Books. This has 270 pp. The first edition was issued by W. P. Kennedy, Edinburgh, 1856, 270 pp., with an added title page dated 1857, *Help in Time of Need*, probably issued jointly with Hamilton, London, at 3/6 cloth. It was reissued by Warne in 1866, listed in the *Reader* on May 19; and Warne issued it in their *Star Series* with the present title, 16mo, 1/0 sewed, 1/6 cloth, No. 69, listed in the *Spect* on Mar. 5, 1881.

41 CATHERINE D. BELL *Last Hours with Cousin Kate.* [New edition.] 12mo. Illustrated. 2/0 cloth Dec. 9 (*Ath* ad)

2/0 Gift Books. This is a collection of Miss Bell's stories and was first issued by W. P. Kennedy, Edinburgh, jointly with Hamilton, London, 1862, 240 pp., 3/6 cloth.

42 ANONYMOUS *Easy Rhymes and Simple Poems for Young Children.* 18mo. Colored illustrations. 1/0 cloth Dec. 9 (*Ath* ad)

Shilling Juveniles. The first edition was issued by Routledge, Warne & Routledge, London, 1864, 160 pp., illustrated. Warne reissued it in 1870, new edition, 18mo, 1/0.

43 ANONYMOUS *Ruth Clayton.* 18mo. Colored illustrations. 1/0 cloth Dec. 9 (*Ath*)

Shilling Juveniles. The *BM* gives London (1856), 18mo, and the *Eng Cat* gives Knight & Son, London, 1860, new edition, 18mo, 1/0, and also Knight, 1865, 18mo, 1/0. Warne issued it, 1869, 15 cm., 120 pp., colored frontispiece, a known copy.

44 ANNE BOWMAN *Poetry: Selected for the Use of Schools and Families from the Most Approved Authors.* 12mo. Illustrated. 2/0 cloth Dec. 9 (*Ath* ad)

2/0 Gift Books. Warne advertised this as the ninth edition. The first edition was issued by George Routledge & Co., London and New York, 1856, 16mo, 292 pp. Warne reissued it in the present series, the same, advertised in the *Ath* on Nov. 27, 1869; and they issued a new edition, 750 pp., 2/0 cloth, listed by *PC* as published Apr. 1–15, 1872.

45 AMY LOTHROP (ANNA WARNER) *Caspar and His Friends.* 18mo. Colored illustrations. 1/0 cloth Dec. 9 (*Ath* ad)

Shilling Juveniles. This has 128 pp. This is a vol. in *Ellen Montgomery's Bookshelf* (see item 18 above). The first edition was issued by G. P. Putnam, New York, as vol. 4 of *Ellen Montgomery's Bookshelf*, listed in the *Ind* on Dec. 27, 1855. It was also issued by Robert Carter & Brothers, New York, 1864 as one of 5 vols. in the *Bookshelf*, listed in the *Ind* on Nov. 24. In England it was issued in 1856 by Nisbet, London, at 1/6, probably jointly with Houlston, Edinburgh. Warne issued it in their *Round the Globe Library* No. 11, 12mo, colored frontispiece, 1/0 cloth, probably in 1869. The Putnam first edition was 1856, 17 cm., 262 pp., illustrated, in brown or blue cloth, deposited on Dec. 18, 1855, and listed in *APC&LG* on Dec. 29, 1855. The Nisbet edition was listed in the *Ath* on Jan. 19, 1856, and in *PC* on Feb. 1. Knight & Son, London, issued it, listed in *PC* on Feb. 1, 1856; and George Routledge & Co., London and New York, issued it, listed in *PC* on Feb. 15, 1856.

46 SUSAN WARNER *Mr. Rutherford's Children.* 2 vols., 18mo. Colored illustrations. 1/o cloth each   Dec. 9 (*Ath* ad)

Shilling Juveniles. This is a vol. in *Ellen Montgomery's Bookshelf* (see item 18 above). The first American edition was issued by George P. Putnam & Co., New York, 2 vols., 17 cm., illustrated: vol. 1, 1853, 265 pp. in red, blue, or green cloth, yellow endpapers, deposited Nov. 4, 1853, and listed in *Norton's Literary Gazette . . .* on Nov. 15, 1853; vol. 2, 1855, 212 pp., in red, blue, green, or salmon cloth, yellow endpapers, listed in *Norton's Literary Gazette . . .* on Dec. 15, 1854. The first edition was issued by James Nisbet & Co., London (1853), 17 cm., 216 pp., illustrated, in pink or red cloth, pale yellow endpapers, deposited Oct. 21, 1853, and listed in the *Ath* on Oct. 29, vol. 1. Vol. 2 was listed in *PC* on Jan. 1, 1855. It was also issued in 2 vols. by George Routledge & Co., London and New York; vol. 1 listed in *PC* on Dec. 16, 1854, and vol. 2 listed there on June 15, 1855. The preface of the Putnam edition was signed E. Wetherell. Warne issued it as an *Eighteenpenny Juvenile*, 18mo, illustrated, 1/6 cloth, advertised in the *Ath* on Nov. 2, 1867, as the last title in a list of 13 titles in the series.

47 HARRIET MYRTLE (LYDIA F. MILLER) *Country Scenes, and Tales of the Four Seasons.* 18mo. Colored illustrations. 1/o cloth   Dec. 9 (*Ath* ad)

Shilling Juveniles. This has 128 pp. This was listed in the *Reader* on Dec. 30, and

both the *BM* and the *U Cat* give it as 1866. The first edition was issued by George Routledge, London, in 1846, colored illustrations, 3/6. Warne issued it in Nov. 1865, Square Fcp 8vo, colored illustrations, 3/6, 4/o. Warne also issued it in 1868, *2/6 Gift Books*, new edition, Fcp 8vo, illustrated, 2/6 cloth, given by the *Eng Cat*.

48 ANONYMOUS *Ada Brenton.* 18mo. Colored illustrations. 1/o cloth   Dec. 9 (*Ath* ad)

Shilling Juveniles. The first edition was issued by Knight & Son, London, no date, 108 pp., 1/o, probably in 1860 or 1861. Warne issued it in their *Ninepenny Juveniles* series in 1869, new edition, 18mo, colored frontispiece, o/9 cloth, given by the *Eng Cat*.

49 ELLEN L. BROWN *Master Gregory's Cunning, and Other Tales.* 18mo. Colored illustrations, 1/o cloth   Dec. 9 (*Ath* ad)

Shilling Juveniles. This is the first edition, 1865, 118 pp. Warne reissued it in this series in 1869, given by the *Eng Cat*. They issued it in the *Round the Globe Library* in 1872, 118 pp., 12mo, colored frontispiece, 1/o cloth, advertised in the *Ath* on Nov. 9. It had no date.

50 (JOHANN C. VON SCHMID) *The Basket of Flowers.* [Revised edition.] 18mo. Colored illustrations. 1/o cloth   Dec. 9 (*Ath* ad)

Shilling Juveniles. The first edition was *Das Blumenkörbchen*, Landshut, 1823. The first edition in English was issued by Perkins, Philadelphia, etc., in 1833, 16mo, 148 pp., translated from the French version by G. T. Bedell, listed in the *North American Review* (quarterly) for Jan. 1834. The first English edition was issued in 1839, Fcp 8vo, 3/6, listed in the *Edinburgh Review* as published July–Oct. 1839 and listed in the *Spect* on June 29, no publisher given. It was issued by T. Nelson, London and Edinburgh, 1853, 192 pp. According to Eric Quayle in *Early Children's Books*, the first translation directly from the German was issued by Warne in 1868, no date, 19 cm., 191 pp., colored illustrations, in cloth, noticed in the *Spect* on Dec. 19, 1868. He states that earlier English editions were translations from the French version by Bedell or were modified Bedell translations taken from American editions. Routledge, Warne & Routledge, London, issued it in 1862, no date, according to the *BM*, new edition, 16mo, 128 pp., translated by Bedell. They also issued it in 1865, no date, new edition, 32mo, o/6 limp cloth, listed in the *Reader* on Mar. 11; and George Routledge & Sons issued it in 1866, 32mo, 128 pp., o/6 cloth sewed, listed in the *Reader* on Jan. 27, 1866. Warne issued it in their *National Books* series (or possibly the *Sixpenny 32mo Books* series) in 1871, colored frontispiece, o/6 sewed, 1/6 cloth, given by the *Eng Cat*.

They issued it in the *Home Circle Gift Books* series in 1875, 12mo, colored illustrations, 2/0 cloth, listed in the *Ath* on Oct. 23. They issued it in the *National Books* series in 1879, Imp 32mo, 2 plates, o/6 stiff wrappers and 1/0, 1/6 cloth, with colored plates, advertised in the *Ath* on Nov. 15. They issued it in *Home Circle Gift Books* in 1881, 12mo, illustrated, 2/0 cloth, with colored illustrations. It was later placed in the *Round the Globe Library*, illustrated, 1/0 cloth, given by the *Eng Cat*.

51 J. E. CARPENTER, ed. *Carpenter's New Military Song Book.* 24 mo. 1/0 boards Dec. 30 (*Reader*)

This is the first edition, 1865, which the *U Cat* gives as 283 pp. and the *BM* gives as 276 pp.

52 J. E. CARPENTER, ed. *Carpenter's New Naval Song Book.* 24mo. 1/0 boards Dec. 30 (*Reader*)

This is the first edition, 1865, 276 pp.

Frederick Warne & Co.
Bedford Street, Covent Garden
1866

53 CATHERINE D. BELL *Hope Campbell.*
Fcp 8vo. Illustrated. 2/6 cloth   Dec. 9,
1865 (*Ath* ad)

2/6 Gift Books. This has 331 pp., and the
Eng Cat gives it as issued in 1866. The first
edition was issued by W. P. Kennedy, Edinburgh; Hamilton, Adams, London, 1854,
Fcp 8vo, 354 pp., 4/6 cloth, advertised in
the *Spect* on Dec. 30, 1854, by Cousin Kate,
as "Just published." Warne issued it in *3/6
Gift Books*, 1866, 331 pp., in cloth, listed in
the *Reader* on May 5 and advertised in the
Spect on Dec. 8, 1866. They issued it in
their *Star Series* in 1876, new edition,
16mo, 1/0 sewed, listed in the *Spect* on Apr.
15, No. 18 in the series. The first American edition was issued by A.D.F. Randolph, New York, 1855, 17.5 cm., 369 pp.,
$.75, advertised in the *New-York Times* on
Mar. 21 as "Next week."

54 CATHERINE D. BELL *Cousin Kate's
Story.* 18mo. Illustrated. 1/6 cloth
Dec. 9, 1865 (*Ath* ad)

Eighteenpenny Juveniles. I've put this here
although it could have been issued at the
end of 1865. The *Eng Cat* gives it as issued
in 1866. The first edition was issued in Edinburgh, 1847, 12mo, anonymous, as *Set
About It at Once; or, Cousin Kate's Story*. It was
issued by W. P. Kennedy, Edinburgh;
Hamilton, Adams, London, in 1863, 7th
thousand, 18mo, by Bell, 237 pp., 2/6,
listed in the *Reader* on Aug. 15.
See No. 556 in 1876.

55 CATHERINE D. BELL *Mary Elliot.*
[New edition.] 12mo. Illustrated.
2/0 cloth   Dec. 9, 1865 (*Ath* ad)

2/0 Gift Books. The *Eng Cat* gives this as issued in 1866, but it could have been issued
at the end of 1865. It was listed in the
Reader on May 12, 1866, at 2/0, with 242
pp. The second edition was issued by W. P.
Kennedy, Edinburgh; Hamilton, Adams,
London, no date, by Cousin Kate, 247 pp.,
4/0, listed in the *Spect* on Oct. 13, 1855;
and the third edition, by Bell, was listed on
Dec. 13, 1856. It was reissued in the present series, advertised in the *Ath* on Nov.
27, 1869, and issued in the *Star Series* No.
15, 16mo, 1/0 sewed, listed in the *Spect* on
Mar. 25, 1876.

56 CATHERINE D. BELL *Arnold Lee.*
[New edition.] 18mo. Illustrated.
1/6 cloth   Dec. 9, 1865 (*Ath* ad)

Eighteenpenny Juveniles. The *Eng Cat* gives
this as issued in 1866, and it was listed
in the *Reader* on May 19, 1866, 186 pp.,
1/6. The first edition was issued by W. P.
Kennedy, Edinburgh; Hamilton, Adams,
London, 1852, 18mo, by Cousin Kate,
3/0. Warne issued it, new edition, square
16mo, 1/0, 1/6, uniform with the *Star
Series* but not in that series, given by
the *Eng Cat* as issued 1876–79. It was
placed in the *Oakleaf Library* at 1/0, in the
1890s.

57 CATHERINE D. BELL **The Douglas Family.** [New edition.] 18mo. Illustrated. 1/6 cloth   Dec. 9, 1865 (*Ath* ad)

Eighteenpenny Juveniles. The *Eng Cat* gives it as issued in 1866, and it was listed in the *Reader* on May 19, 1866, 182 pp., 1/6. The first edition was issued by W. P. Kennedy, Edinburgh; Hamilton, Adams, London, 1851, 12mo, by Cousin Kate. It was issued, new edition, square 16mo, 1/o, 1/6, uniform with the *Star Series* but not in it, given by the *Eng Cat* as published 1876–79. It was in the *Oakleaf Library* at 1/o in the 1890s.

58 CATHERINE D. BELL **An Autumn at Karnford.** [New edition.] 18mo. Illustrated. 1/6 cloth   Dec. 9, 1865 (*Ath* ad)

Eighteenpenny Juveniles. The *Eng Cat* gives it as issued in 1866, and it was listed in the *Reader* on May 26, 1866, 186 pp., 1/6. The first edition was issued by W. P. Kennedy, Edinburgh; Hamilton, Adams, London, 1847, 12mo, by Cousin Kate, 2/6 cloth. Warne issued it in the *Birthday Series*, 1874, 16mo, 186 pp., illustrated, 1/6 cloth, given by the *U Cat.*

59 CATHERINE D. BELL **Georgie and Lizzie.** [New edition.] 18mo. Illustrated. 1/6 cloth   Dec. 9, 1865 (*Ath* ad)

Eighteenpenny Juveniles. The *Eng Cat* gives it as published in 1866, and it was listed in the *Reader* on May 26, 1866, 186 pp., 1/6. The first edition was issued by W. P. Kennedy, Edinburgh; Hamilton, Adams, London, 1849, 12mo, by Cousin Kate, 3/o. It was issued in the *Birthday Series* at 1/6 cloth in the mid 1870s.

60 L. V., ed. (LAURA VALENTINE) **Warne's Victoria Picture Spelling-Book.** 8vo. Illustrated. 1/o cloth   Jan. 13 (*Spect*)

This is the first edition, 1866. It was reissued, the same, in 1868, given by the *Eng Cat*; a new edition was issued in 1869, the same, given by the *Eng Cat*. There was a new edition, the same, in 1876 and in Sept. 1899, by Valentine as editor, both given by the *Eng Cat.*

61 FREDERICK HARVEY **Ventriloquism Made Easy.** 48mo. Illustrated. o/6 cloth sewed   Jan. 20 (*Reader*)

Illustrated Bijou Books No. 1. The first edition was issued by F. Pitman, London, 1865, 24mo, 32 pp. The present edition has no date and 94 pp. and colored illustrations. This series, Nos. 1–15, was imported by Scribner, Welford & Co., New York, and issued 48mo, colored frontispiece, diagrams, etc., $.30 cloth, gilt edges each, advertised in the *Nation* on Sept. 20, 1866.

62 ANONYMOUS **Fun and Flirtation, Forfeits.** 48mo. Illustrated. o/6 cloth sewed   Jan. 20 (*Reader*)

Illustrated Bijou Books No. 2. This is the first edition, 1866, 96 pp., colored illustrations.

63 ANONYMOUS **Etiquette for Ladies in Public and Private.** [New and revised edition.] 48mo. Illustrated. o/6 cloth sewed   Jan. 20 (*Reader*)

Illustrated Bijou Books No. 3. This has colored illustrations. *Etiquette for Ladies and Gentlemen* was issued with colored plates at 1/o cloth, listed in the *Spect* on Dec. 25, 1875, which could have been in the *Handy Manual Series* or the *Boquet Series*. It was advertised in an 1883 book as in the *Boquet Series*, Imp 16mo, 1/o cloth, colored plates. Scribner, Welford & Armstrong, New York, imported it and issued it in the *Boquet Series*, no date, 13 cm., 126 pp., colored illustrations. *Etiquette for Ladies and Gentlemen* was reissued in 1893, new edition, 32mo, 1/o, listed in *PC* on Dec. 9.

64 ANONYMOUS *Etiquette for Gentlemen.* [New edition.] 48mo. Illustrated. o/6 cloth sewed   Jan. 20 (*Reader*)

Illustrated Bijou Books No. 4. This has colored illustrations. It was reissued in this series, the same, no date, 96 pp., in 1887, given by the *Eng Cat*. See the preceding item.

65 ANONYMOUS *The Ball-Room Guide.* 48mo. Illustrated. o/6 cloth sewed Jan. 20 (*Reader*)

Illustrated Bijou Books No. 5. This is the first edition, 1866, 96 pp., colored plates, with an added title page in colors with the title *The Ball-Room Companion*. This was reissued in 1874, 32mo, 96 pp., colored frontispiece, 1/o cloth, listed in the *Ath* on Jan. 24. It was issued jointly with Scribner, Welford & Armstrong, New York, no date, 13 cm., 128 pp., colored frontispiece, illustrated, in the *Handy Manual* series. The present title was reissued in Jan. 1876; it was issued in the *Boquet Series*, 32mo, 128 pp., colored frontispiece, 1/o, in 1877, given by the *Eng Cat*, and advertised in the *Times Weekly Edition* (London) on Jan. 19, 1877.

66 SYDNEY WHITING *Heliondé.* Third edition. 12mo. Illustrated. 2/6 boards Jan. 27 (*Reader*)

This was issued in Leipzig, 1855, Heliondé, oder, Abenteuer auf der Sonne. The first English edition was issued by Chapman & Hall, London, 1855, 22 cm., anonymous, 424 pp.

67 ANONYMOUS *Friendly Truths for Working Homes.* [New edition.] 12mo. 1/o boards   Jan. 27 (*Ath*)

I haven't located the first edition. There was a second edition issued by Knight & Son, London, in 1861, Fcp 8vo, anonymous, 1/6; and there was an issue in 12 parts, London, 1863.

68 ANONYMOUS *Kindly Hints on Woman's Cottage Life.* [New edition.] 12mo. 1/o boards   Jan. 27 (*Ath*)

This was issued in 12 parts, London, 1863.

69 ELIZABETH WATTS *Vegetables, and How to Grow Them.* Fcp 8vo. 1/o boards Feb. 10 (*Ath*)

The Country Library and Family Circle Books. This is the first edition, 1866, 188 pp. It was reissued in 1867 at 1/o, noticed in the *Spect* on Mar. 30.
See 1876

70 CATHERINE D. BELL *How to Be Happy.* [New edition.] 12mo. Illustrated. 2/o cloth   Feb. 10 (*Reader*)

2/o Gift Books. This has 240 pp. and was also listed in the *Reader* on Feb. 24, the same. The first edition was probably T. Nelson & Sons, London, 1859, 16mo, 62 pp., *The Way to Be Happy*; reissued 1871. The *U Cat* gives an edition, 1867. It was reissued in the present series in 1869, the same, advertised in the *Ath* on Nov. 27.

71 (S. M. FRY) *The Lost Key.* 32mo. o/6 limp cloth   Feb. 10 (*Reader*)

This has 128 pp. The first edition was issued by the Religious Tract Society, London (1855), 18mo, 1/6. In the United States it was issued by the Presbyterian Board of Publication, Philadelphia (1860), 15.5 cm., anonymous, 253 pp., illustrated; and by Carleton & Porter, New York, no date, 24mo, 178 pp., illustrated, probably in the 1860s.

72 CHARLOTTE ADAMS *Laura and Lucy.* Fcp 8vo. Illustrated. 2/6 cloth   Feb. 17 (*Ath*)

2/6 Gift Books. This is the first edition, 275 pp. It was reissued in this series in 1869, the same, advertised in the *Ath* on Nov. 27. Warne issued it in the *Golden Links Series* in 1882, 12mo, illustrated, 2/6 cloth, given by the *Eng Cat*.

73 ANONYMOUS *The Toilette.* 48mo. Illustrated. o/6 cloth sewed   Feb. 17 (*Reader*)

Illustrated Bijou Books No. 6. This has 96 pp. The *BM* gives only London, 1854, 12mo.

74 JOSEPH E. CARPENTER *Sunday Readings.* Fcp 8vo. 1/o cloth boards Mar. 24 (*Ath*)

This is the first edition, vol. 1, with 256 pp. Vol. 2, *Sunday Readings in Prose and Verse*, Fcp 8vo, 220 pp., 1/o boards, was listed in the *Ath* on Apr. 30, 1866; and *Penny Readings in Prose and Verse*, 3 vols., was listed in the *Spect* on Apr. 21, 1866.

75 L. V., ed. (LAURA VALENTINE) *The Language of Flowers.* 48mo. Illustrated. o/6 cloth sewed Apr. 7 (*Reader*)

Illustrated Bijou Books No. 7. This has 96 pp. The first edition was issued by Warne, 1866, 16mo, 160 pp., colored illustrations, 2/6 cloth, *The Language and Sentiment of Flowers*, listed in the *Spect* on Jan. 27, 1866. The *Eng Cat* gives a new edition, 18mo, 2 colored plates, 1/o, issued in 1866. It was issued jointly with Scribner, Welford & Co., New York (1866), completely revised, 14 cm., colored frontispiece, with the longer title. A new and revised edition of the longer title was advertised in the *Ath* on May 29, 1869, 6 colored plates, 2/6 cloth; and it was advertised there on Jan. 29, 1876, as a *Shilling Handy Manual*. The longer title was issued in the *Boquet Series* (1883), 13 cm., 154 pp., colored plates, 1/o cloth, 1/6 imitations ivory, given by the *Eng Cat*.

76 ELIZABETH WATTS *Fish: and How to Cook It.* Fcp 8vo. 1/o boards   Apr. 7 (*Reader*)

The Country Library and Family Circle Books. This is the first edition, 1866, 16.5 cm., 140 pp. It was imported by Scribner, Wel-

ford & Co., New York, and issued in 1866, 16mo, $.50 limp cloth, listed in the *Nation* on Sept. 20.

77 JOSEPH & JOHN GAMGEE *Plain Rules for the Stable.* 12mo. 1/o boards   Apr. 7 (*Ath*)

This is the first edition, 1866, 59 pp. The second edition, revised and enlarged, was issued 1866, 72 pp., listed in the *Spect* on May 26. It was imported by Scribner, Welford & Co., New York, in 1866, and issued at $.50 limp cloth, listed in the *Nation* on Sept. 20.

78 BENJAMIN DISRAELI *The Young Duke.* Fcp 8vo. 1/o sewed   Apr. 7 (*Reader*)

Companion Library No. 6. The first edition was issued by Henry Colburn & Richard Bentley, London, 3 vols., 19 cm., anonymous, 31/6 in boards, half cloth and labels (Sadleir's copy) or all-over boards (Wolff's copy). It was published Apr. 21 according to the Bentley private catalog. Colburn paid £500 for it. It was issued by David Bryce, London, 17 cm., 304 pp., 1/6 boards, in Oct. 1853. Warne issued it in their *Notable Novels* series No. 116, p 8vo, o/6 sewed, listed by the *Bks* as published in Apr. 1888. Warne issued a complete edition in 5 vols., Fcp 8vo, 12/6 cloth, advertised in the *Spect* on Sept. 29, 1866; and 5 vols., p 8vo, 21/o, were listed there on Mar. 21, 1868. The first American edition of the present title was issued by J. & J. Harper, New York, 2 vols., 1831, 16.5 cm., anonymous, *Library of Select Novels* Nos. 5 and 6, advertised by a Washington, D.C., bookstore in the *Globe* (daily) on Aug. 3, 1831, as "Just received"; this is a very accurate source of the date of issue. It was listed in the *North American Review* (quarterly) for Oct. 1831.

79 BENJAMIN DISRAELI *Tancred.* Fcp 8vo. 1/o sewed   Apr. 7 (*Reader*)

Companion Library No. 7. The first edition was issued by Henry Colburn, London, 3 vols., 1847, 20.5 cm. in paper boards, half cloth, paper labels, white endpapers, with a 12-page catalog at the back of vol. 3. It was advertised in the *Ath* on Mar. 13 as "On Mar. 15" and advertised in the *Spect* on Mar. 27 as "Now ready." He issued a second edition, 3 vols., 1847, in boards and labels. It was issued by David Bryce, London, at 1/6 boards about Sept. 30, 1853. It was reissued in the *Companion Library*, no date, my copy, 16 cm., 342 pp. buff wrappers, printed and decorated in green and black, with a portrait of the author on the front cover, cut flush. There are ads on the back cover and inside covers, and 4 pp. of publisher's ads at the back. The series title appears only on the spine. It was advertised in the *Ath* on Oct. 22, 1870. The first American edition was advertised in *Lit W* on Apr. 24, 1847, 8vo, 127 pp., as "Just ready," Carey & Hart, Philadelphia, 1847; it was listed in the *United States Magazine* (monthly) as published in May 1847, Burgess & Stringer, New York; Carey & Hart, Philadelphia.

80 BENJAMIN DISRAELI **Venetia.** Fcp 8vo. 1/o sewed   Apr. 7 (*Reader*)
Companion Library No. 8. This has 336 pp. The first edition was issued by Henry Colburn, London, 3 vols., 1837, 19.5 cm., anonymous. It was in paper boards, half cloth, paper labels, with white endpapers, listed in the *Spect* on May 20. It was issued by David Bryce, London, new edition, 16.5 cm., 1/6 boards, in Mar. 1853. Warne issued it in their *Notable Novels* series No. 117, p 8vo, o/6 sewed, in 1888. The first American edition was issued by Carey & Hart, Philadelphia, 2 vols., 1837, 12mo, anonymous.

81 BENJAMIN DISRAELI **Contarini Fleming.** Fcp 8vo. 1/o sewed   Apr. 7 (*Reader*)
Companion Library No. 9. This has 311 pp. The first edition was issued by John Mur-

ray, London, 4 vols., 1832, 18 cm., anonymous, 24/o in paper boards, half cloth, paper labels, white endpapers, advertised in the *Spect* on May 5 as "This day" and listed on May 19. Edward Moxon, London, issued the second edition, 4 vols., 1834, by Disraeli, in glazed pink linen with paper labels. Colburn issued *Contarini Fleming and Alroy,* 3 vols., 1846, second edition (third edition of the first title and second edition of the second title). It had a frontispiece (portrait) and was in boards and labels, with a 24-page catalog at the back of vol. 3. It had new prefaces (July 1845) and was advertised in the *Spect* on Dec. 22, 1845. The present title was issued by David Bryce, London, 277 pp., 1/6 boards, in June 1853. Warne issued the present title in their *Notable Novels* series No. 118, p 8vo, o/6 sewed, in 1888. The first American edition was issued by J. & J. Harper, New York, 2 vols., 1832, 18.5 cm., anonymous, listed in the *North American Review* (quarterly) for Jan. 1833.

82 BENJAMIN DISRAELI **Coningsby.** Fcp 8vo. 1/o sewed   Apr. 7 (*Reader*)
Companion Library No. 10. This has 316 pp. The first edition was issued by Henry Colburn, London, 3 vols., 1844, Cr 8vo, paper boards, half cloth, paper labels, white endpapers, advertised in the *Spect* on May 11 as "Now ready"; the second edition, the same, was advertised June 8 as "Now ready"; and the third edition was advertised July 27, the same, "Now ready." Colburn issued a popular edition in 1849, the fifth edition, Fcp 8vo, 472 pp., frontispiece (portrait), at 6/o in dark green cloth. It had a new preface (May 1849) and was advertised in the *Spect* on May 5,1849, as "Immediately." It was issued by David Bryce, London, at 1/6 boards, in Aug. 1853. Warne issued a new edition in 1870, 1/o sewed, advertised in the *Ath* on Oct. 22; and they issued it in their *Notable Novels* series No. 119, p 8vo, o/6 sewed, in 1888. In the United States it was issued by Carey

& Hart, Philadelphia, 1844, 22.5 cm., 159 pp.; and by William H. Colyer, New York, 1844, 24 cm., 136 pp., with the cover dated 1845.

83 BENJAMIN DISRAELI *Sybil.* Fcp 8vo. 1/0 sewed   Apr. 7 (*Reader*)

Companion Library No. 11. This has 336 pp. The first edition was issued by Henry Colburn, London, 3 vols., 1845, 19.5 cm., paper boards, half cloth, paper labels, white endpapers, advertised in the *Spect* on Apr. 26 as "Just ready." Sadleir's copy has a 32-page Longmans catalog at the back of vol. 1, but it is not in Wolff's copy. The second edition, in 3 vols., was advertised in the *Spect* on June 28 as "Now ready," and Sadleir had a copy of the third edition, 3 vols., 1845, the same. The first American edition was issued by Carey & Hart, Philadelphia, 1845, 24 cm., 125 pp., $.25 in buff wrappers with a cover title, noticed in *Graham's American Monthly Magazine* for Sept. 1845. Warne issued it in 1888 in their *Notable Novels* series No. 120, p 8vo, 0/6 sewed.

84 BENJAMIN DISRAELI *The Wondrous Tale of Alroy.* Fcp 8vo. 1/0 sewed   Apr. 7 (*Reader*)

Companion Library No. 12. This has 320 pp. The first edition was *The Wondrous Tale of Alroy. The Rise of Iskander*, issued by Saunders & Otley, London, 3 vols., 1833, 20 cm., anonymous, in paper boards with paper labels and white endpapers, listed in the *Spect* on Mar. 9. Sadleir's copy had a 12-page catalog of William Curry, Jr. & Co. at the back of vol. 1, not in Wolff's copy. It was issued by David Bryce, London, at 1/6 boards, in July, 1853. Warne issued it in their *Notable Novels* series No. 121, p 8vo, 0/6 sewed, in 1888. The first American edition was issued by Carey, Lea & Blanchard, Philadelphia, 2 vols., 1833, 20.5 cm., anonymous, $1.25, advertised in the *Globe* (daily) in Washington, D.C., on May 29, 1833, as "Received this day," a

very accurate indicator of the American publication date. It was listed in the *Knickerbocker* for July as lately published or in the press.

85 BENJAMIN DISRAELI *Ixion in Heaven.* Fcp 8vo. 1/0 sewed   Apr. 7 (*Reader*)

Companion Library No. 13. This has 303 pp. The first edition was *Ixion in Heaven—The Infernal Marriage—The Voyage of Captain Popanilla. The Tragedy of Count Alarcos*, issued by David Bryce, London, 1853, 17 cm., 303 pp., 1/6 pink paper boards, issued the first half of Sept. This was the first book edition of the first two titles, which had appeared in the *New Monthly Magazine* in 1829 and 1830.

86 BENJAMIN DISRAELI *Henrietta Temple.* Fcp 8vo. 1/0 sewed Apr. 7 (*Reader*)

Companion Library No. 14. This has 316 pp. The first edition was issued by Henry Colburn, London, 3 vols., 1837, 19 cm., anonymous, 31/6 in paper boards, half cloth, paper labels and white endpapers. It was advertised in the *Spect* on Nov. 26, 1836, as "On Dec. 1" and listed Dec. 10. David Bryce, London, issued it in Apr. 1853, 331 pp., 1/6 in pink paper boards; and Warne issued it in their *Notable Novels* series No. 122, p 8vo, 0/6 sewed, in 1888. The first American edition was issued by Carey & Hart, Philadelphia; Wiley & Putnam, New York, 1837, advertised by a Washington, D.C., book dealer in the *Globe* (daily) on Feb. 16, 1837, as "Received this day," and this is a very accurate source for the date of American issue. It was noticed in the Mar. issue of the *Knickerbocker*.

87 BENJAMIN DISRAELI *Vivian Grey.* Fcp 8vo. 1/0 sewed   Apr. 7 (*Reader*)

Companion Library No. 15. This has 416 pp. The first edition was issued by Henry Colburn, London, 5 vols.: vols. 1 and 2, 1826, about Apr. 22, and vols. 3–5, 1827, about

Feb. 23, the dates given by Sadleir. It was in paper boards with paper labels and white endpapers and was anonymous. David Bryce, London, issued it in Dec. 1853, new edition, 17 cm., by Disraeli, 416 pp., at 1/6 pink paper boards. Warne issued it in their *Notable Novels* series No. 123, p 8vo, o/6 sewed, in 1888. The American issues were by Collins & Hannay, etc., New York, 1826, 19.5 cm., listed in the *North American Review* (quarterly) for Oct. 1826; and by Carey, Lea & Carey, Philadelphia, 2 vols., 1827, 21 cm.

88 MRS. HAWTREY *Alphabet of Fruits for Good Children.* Square 16mo. o/6 sewed Apr. 14 (*Reader*)

This is the first edition (1866), illustrated and in verse.

89 HENRY STACKE *The Story of the American War. 1861–65.* Fcp 8vo. 1/6 boards, 5/0 Apr. 21 (*Reader*)

This is the first edition, 1866, 16 cm., 264 pp., with a folding map. Both prices were listed in the *Reader*, but the *Eng Cat* gives only the 1/6 issue. The *U Cat* states that this was republished in 1867 as *Heroism and Adventure in the Nineteenth Century*, anonymously, and it was listed in the *Ath* on Aug. 10, 1867, 2/0.

90 ANONYMOUS *The Companion Letter Writer.* Fcp 8vo. 1/0 boards May 5 (*Reader*)

This is the first edition, no date, 180 pp., *Useful Books.*

91 ANONYMOUS *London in Miniature.* 48mo. o/6 May 12 (*Reader*)

The *Reader* indicates this as a *Bijou* Book, and the *BM* gives (1875), 32mo, 86 pp., map, *Bijou Books*; and also (1878), the same, with 83 pp. However, it was not among the first 15 titles in the series.

92 CHARLES SPENCER *The Modern Gymnast.* Fcp 8vo. Illustrated. 1/0 boards May 19 (*Spect*)

Useful Books. This was advertised in the *Ath* as in cloth boards at 1/0. Warne issued a third edition, no date, 17 cm., 125 pp., illustrated. It was imported by Scribner, Welford & Co., New York, in 1866 and issued, 16mo, $.50 limp cloth, illustrated, listed in the *Nation* on Sept. 20, *Useful Books.*

93 ANNIE WEBB, later WEBB-PEPLOE *The Stitch in Time.* 18mo. Colored frontispiece. o/9 cloth May 19 (*Reader*)

Ninepenny Juveniles. This is the first edition, 1866.

94 A.L.O.E. (CHARLOTTE TUCKER) *The Straight Road Is Shortest and Surest.* 18mo. Colored frontispiece. o/9 cloth May 19 (*Reader*)

Ninepenny Juveniles. This is the first edition, 1866. The *U Cat* gives no date, 104 pp., 17 cm., colored frontispiece. A.L.O.E. stands for A Lady of England, and she published over 160 books and booklets, issued mainly by Gall & Inglis, London, and Thomas Nelson & Sons, London, from 1852 on.

95 MRS. SAMUEL A. WINDLE *Home Pleasures and Home Failings.* 18mo. Colored frontispiece. o/9 cloth May 19 (*Reader*)

Ninepenny Juveniles. This is the first edition, 1866, 15 cm., 104 pp.

96 EMMA MARSHALL *The Crofton Cousins.* 18 mo. Colored frontispiece. o/9 cloth May 19 (*Reader*)

Ninepenny Juveniles. This is the first edition, 15 cm., 100 pp.

97 ANONYMOUS *Tales for Village Schools.* 18mo. Colored frontispiece. o/9 cloth May 19 (*Reader*)

Ninepenny Juveniles. I cannot trace this.

98 MARY E. MILLS **Truth.** 18mo. Colored frontispiece. o/9 cloth May 19 (*Reader*)

Ninepenny Juveniles. This is the first edition, 1866. In a Nov. 2, 1867, *Ath* ad there were ten titles in this series and the present title was No. 6.

99 H.J.B. HANCOCK **Archery.** 48mo. Illustrated. o/6 cloth sewed June 2 (*Reader*)

Illustrated Bijou Books No. 8. The *BM* gives Warne, 1868, 32mo, 89 pp., illustrated, *The Bijou Book of Out-Door Amusements, etc.*

100 JOHN G. WOOD **The ABC of Swimming.** 48mo. Illustrated. o/6 cloth sewed June 2 (*Reader*)

Illustrated Bijou Books No. 10. This is the first edition, no date, 95 pp., colored illustrations.

101 MRS. BAYLE BERNARD **Our Common Fruits.** Fcp 8vo. Illustrated. 2/o boards June 30 (*Reader*)

Useful Books. This is the first edition, 1866, 16.5 cm., 294 pp. Waren issued it also with colored plates at 3/6 cloth.

102 ANONYMOUS **The Business Letter Writer.** Fcp 8vo. o/6 June 30 (*Reader*)

I can't trace this. It was given by the *Eng Cat* as issued in 1866 by Warne.

103 HENRY NOEL-FEARN (HENRY CHRISTMAS) **The Money Market . . .** Fcp 8vo. 1/o June 30 (*Reader*)

Useful Books. This is a first edition, 1866, 192 pp. It was imported by Scribner, Welford & Co., New York, and issued in 1866, Imp 16mo, *Useful Books*, listed in the *Nation* on Aug. 20 at $.50 cloth boards and listed on Sept. 20 as $.50 limp cloth! It was issued jointly with Scribner, Welford & Armstrong, New York, 1873, revised and corrected by a city man, 17 cm., 171 pp., *Useful Books*, listed in the *Ath* on June 21, the third edition.

104 ANONYMOUS **The Lover's Correspondent.** Fcp 8vo. o/6 June 30 (*Reader*)

Useful Books. This has no date, 63 pp.

105 ANONYMOUS **The Children's Harp.** 18mo. Illustrated. 1/o cloth July 14 (*Ath* ad)

Shilling Juveniles. This has colored illustrations. The first edition was issued by Knight & Son, London (1860), 12mo, anonymous, 162 pp.; reissued by them in 1865, new edition, 18mo, anonymous, illustrated, 1/6, listed in the *Reader* on May 20. The *Eng Cat* gives a new edition from Warne, 1/o, in 1869.

106 JOSEPH T. BURGESS **Elementary Gymnastics for the Young and Sedentary.** 48mo. Illustrated. o/6 cloth sewed July 21 (*Reader*)

Illustrated Bijou Books No. 11. This is the first edition, 1866, 9 cm., 95 pp.

107 JOHN G. WOOD **Croquet.** 48mo. Illustrated. o/6 cloth sewed July 21 (*Reader*)

Illustrated Bijou Books No. 13. This is the first edition, 1866, 9 cm., 94 pp., one colored plate. It was contained in *The Bijou Book of Out-Door Amusements, etc.*, issued in 3 parts, 1868, 32mo.

108 P. A. NUTTALL, ed. **Walker's Pronouncing Dictionary of the English Language.** Fcp 8vo. 1/o boards Sept. 8 (*Reader*)

Warne also issued this in 1869, o/6. George Routledge & Co., London and New York, issued the 18th thousand in 1856, 2/o cloth, advertised in the *Ath* on Mar. 22, 1856, as "Now ready"; they issued a new edition in 1866, Fcp 8vo, 288 pp.,

1/0 cloth boards, advertised in the *Ath* on Feb. 3; and issued a new edition in 1867, 12mo, 1/0, listed in the *Spect* on Aug. 10. The first edition was *A Critical Pronouncing Dictionary* . . . by John Walker, issued by Robinsons, London, 1791, 28.5 cm., 71, (499) pp. The first American edition was issued by H. & P. Rice, M. Carey, etc., Philadelphia, 1803, 22 cm., (990) pp. The *U Cat* gives an edition by Warne, no date, thoroughly remodeled, 16mo, 284 pp., illustrated.

109 JOSEPH E. CARPENTER, ed. *Penny Readings.* Vols. 7 and 8. Fcp 8vo. 1/0 boards each   Sept. 22, Oct. 27 (*Ath*)

These are first editions. Vol. 7 has 256 pp., and vol. 8 has 208 pp. Vol. 9 was listed in the *Ath* on Nov. 24, and vol. 10 on Dec. 22, completing the present series. See 1876 for a continuing series.

110 (HELEN C. WRIGHT) *Richard Harvey, or Taking a Stand.* 32mo. Frontispiece. 0/4 sewed, 0/6 limp cloth   Sept. 29 (*Reader*)

Sixpenny 32mo Books. The 0/4 issue has a plain frontispiece, and the 0/6 issue has it colored. A Dec. 9, 1865, ad in the *Ath* listed 16 titles in this series, and a Nov. 2, 1867, ad listed 26 titles. The *U Cat* gives S. A. Howland, Worcester (circa 1848), anonymous, 62 pp.; it gives *Taking a Stand* issued by H. Hoyt, Boston (1860), 16mo, 94 pp., illustrated. The present edition has 108 pp.

111 AUNT FRIENDLY (SARAH BAKER) *Kate Darley.* 32mo. Frontispiece. 0/4 sewed, 0/6 limp cloth   Sept. 29 (*Reader*)

Sixpenny 32mo Books. This has 108 pp., with a plain frontispiece in the 0/4 issue and colored in the 0/6 issue. I cannot trace it.

112 MRS. G. H. CURTEIS *The Children's Hour. Twelve Songs for the Little Ones.* Obl Demy 8vo. 1/0 stiff wrappers Sept. 29 (*Spect* ad)

The *U Cat* gives Warne, 1867, 21.3×27.6 cm. The *Eng Cat* gives it as issued in 1866.

113 AUNT FRIENDLY (SARAH BAKER) *Caroline Eaton.* 32mo. Frontispiece. 0/6 cloth sewed   Sept. 29 (*Reader*)

This is probably in *Sixpenny 32mo Books*, the first edition.

114 AUNT FRIENDLY (SARAH BAKER) *Little Josie.* 32mo. Frontispiece. 0/6 cloth sewed   Sept. 29 (*Reader*)

This is probably in *Sixpenny 32mo Books*. I can't trace it.
Also 1872

115 ANONYMOUS *Timid Lucy.* 32mo. Frontispiece. 0/6 cloth sewed Sept. 29 (*Reader*)

This is probably in *Sixpenny 32mo Books*. The first edition was issued by the Protestant Episcopal Sunday School Union, New York, 1851, 238 pp., noticed in the *Southern Literary Messenger* for Feb. 1852. They reissued it, 1869, 15.5 cm., 238 pp., illustrated. The *Eng Cat* gives Warne, 32mo, 0/6, issued in 1869.

116 HENRY C. ADAMS *The Judges of Israel; or, Tales for Sunday Reading.* 12mo. Illustrated. 2/0 cloth   Oct. 20 (*Ath*)

2/0 Gift Books. This is the first edition, 1866, 184 pp. It was advertised in the *Reader* on Nov. 3, 1866, as *Tales for Sunday Reading*, 12 books in a packet, 18mo, 1/0. It was reissued in the present series in 1869, the same, advertised in the *Ath* on Nov. 27. It was placed in *Home Circle Books* after 1871, illustrated, 2/0 cloth.

117 CAROLINE GASCOYNE *Aunt Prue's Railway Journey.* Fcp 8vo. 1/0 sewed Oct. (*Bks*)

Companion Library No. 18. Nos. 16 and 17 in this series were apparently never issued. I think this is the first edition. It was reissued as a *2/o Gift Book*, illustrated, 2/o cloth, listed in the *Ath* on Aug. 20, 1870; it was reissued in the *Companion Library* No. 73, 12mo, 2/o boards, listed in the *Spect* on July 10, 1875.

118 ANONYMOUS *Willis the Pilot.* Fcp 8vo. Illustrated. 1/o sewed   Oct. (*Bks*)

Juvenile Library. This has no date, 342 pp. The first edition was *Le Pilote Willis* by Adrien Paul, Tours, 2 vols., 1855. The first English edition was issued by C. H. Clarke, London, 1857, 2/o, 3/6. The 2/o was in boards and was listed in *PC* as published Apr. 14–30, 1857. Warne also issued the present edition at 2/o cloth in the *2/o Gift Book* series, listed in the *Reader* on Nov. 10, 1866; they reissued it in that series in 1869, advertised in the *Ath* on Nov. 27. It was issued in the *Daring Deeds Library* in 1882, 12mo, illustrated, 2/6 cloth, given by the *Eng Cat*; and reissued in that series in 1895, listed by *PC* on Nov. 16. It was issued in the United States by Mayhew & Baker, Boston, 1858, 17.5 cm., 350 pp., illustrated, listed in *APC&LG* (weekly) on Dec. 5, 1857.

119 (JOHANN D. WYSS) *The Swiss Family Robinson.* Fcp 8vo. Illustrated. 1/o sewed   Nov. 3 (*Reader*)

Juvenile Library. This has 288 pp. The first edition was *Der Schweizersche Robinson*, Zurich, 2 vols., 1812–13. The first French edition was *Le Robinson Suisse*, Paris, 1814, with 12 plates. The first English edition was issued by M. J. Godwin & Co., London, 2 vols., 1814, *The Family Robinson Crusoe*, with 4 plates. Darton states that there was a fuller version in 1816 and a second edition, 1818, double the length of the first edition. The most familiar editions are based on the French version of Mme. de Montholieu, who had permission from Wyss's son to expand it. She issued a version in 1814 according to Percy

Muir; she issued it in 5 vols., 1824–26, according to Darton. Vol. 1 of the first English edition was listed in the *Edinburgh Review* at 6/o, as published Aug.–Nov. 1814. The seventh London edition at 7/o was listed in the *Monthly Review* (London) for Aug. 1828 as recent. Warne issued it in 1868 at 1/o boards, listed in the *Bks* for Sept.; and they issued it in the *2/o Gift Books* series in 1869, advertised in the *Ath* on Nov. 27. They issued it in their *National Books* series, 16mo, colored illustrations, o/6 sewed, 1/6 cloth, listed by *PC* as published Nov. 16–30, 1872; and in their *Chandos Classics* No. 22, Cr 8vo, illustrated, 1/6 sewed, 2/o cloth, a translation by Mrs. Paull in the unabridged version of the Wyss-Montholieu edition in its completest form, 562 pp., issued probably in Nov. 1873 and reissued in the same series, advertised in the *Ath* on Dec. 1, 1877. It was reissued in *National Books* with colored plates, 1/o, 1/6 cloth and with 2 plates at o/6 in stiff wrappers, advertised in the *Ath* on Nov. 15, 1879. It was issued in the *Incident and Adventure Library*, Fcp 8vo, illustrated, 2/o cloth, given by the *Eng Cat* as issued in 1881. The Paull translation with colored plates at 7/6 was listed in the *Spect* on Aug. 25, 1888. The first American edition was issued by J. & J. Harper, New York, 2 vols., 1832, 12mo, frontispiece and engraved title page in each vol., printed boards. It was from the seventh London edition, greatly improved, vols. 2 & 3 in the *Boy's and Girl's Library of Useful and Entertaining Knowledge*. Warne issued the Paull translation in New York in 1888, large 8vo, colored plates, $3.00, listed in the *Nation* on Nov. 15.

120 ANONYMOUS *Nursery Rhymes, Tales, and Jingles.* [New edition.] Square Cr 8vo. 2/6 boards   Nov. 3 (*Reader*)

This has 109 pp. The first edition was issued by James Burns, London (1844), 19.2 cm., 102 pp.

121 MRS. HENRY B. PAULL *Lucy West.*
12mo. Illustrated. 2/0 cloth Nov. 10
Spect

2/0 Gift Books. This is probably the first
edition, 208 pp. It was reissued in this series in 1869, advertised in the *Ath* on
Nov. 27; reissued in 1873, 12mo, 2/6 cloth,
listed in the *Ath* on Oct. 25. It was issued in the *Golden Links Series* in 1881,
12mo, illustrated, 2/6 cloth, given by the
Eng Cat; and in the *Star Series* No. 122,
16mo, 1/6 sewed?, listed in *PC* on June
27, 1891.

122 TOM HODD, ed. *Warne's Christmas
Annual. The Five Alls.* Roy 8vo. Colored
illustrations. 1/0 sewed Nov. 10 (*Ath*)

This has no date, 96 pp. The 50th thousand was advertised in the *Spect* on Nov. 10
as "Now ready." It was reissued in 1868
with the joint imprint of Scribner & Co.,
New York, 25 cm., 2 colored plates,
colored wrappers. It was imported by
Scribner, Welford & Co., New York, in
1866. It contains 41 stories, etc., by
A. Ward, Dutton Cook, Tom Hood,
Arthur Sketchley, et al., advertised in
the *New-York Times* on Dec. 17 as "Just
received."

123 ALICE SOMERTON *The Torn Bible.*
[Third edition.] 18mo. Illustrated. 1/6
cloth Nov. 24 (*Reader*)

Eighteenpenny Juveniles. This has 174 pp.
The *BM* gives London, 1862, 12mo.
It was listed in the *Spect* on Jan. 4, 1868,
as issued by Warne, new edition, 18mo,
1/6. Warne issued it in the *Birthday Series*
in 1879, 18mo, illustrated, 1/6 cloth,
with the joint imprint of Scribner, Welford & Armstrong, New York, no date,
174 pp., with the series title on the spine,
given by the *Eng Cat*. It was issued in the
Star Series No. 81, no date, 16mo, 175 pp.,
1/0 sewed, 1/6 cloth, listed by the *Bks* for
Dec. 1882.

124 EL EDEN, ed. *The Life of a Navvy.*
[New edition.] 1/0 sewed Nov. or Dec.
(*Bks*)

The *Bks* gives this as issued by Hodges &
Warne, which I cannot understand.
Warne reissued it in 1867 at 0/6 sewed,
listed in the *Bks* for July.

125 JANE PORTER *The Scottish Chiefs.*
p 8vo. 0/6 sewed Nov. or Dec. (*Bks*)

Notable Novels No. 1. This has 256 pp. in
double columns. The first edition was issued by Longmans, London, 5 vols., 1810,
in blue-gray paper boards, with labels and
with white paper spines, given by the *Edinburgh Review* as published at 25/0, Feb.–
May; and given by the *Eng Cat* as published at 35/0 in Apr. There was a revised
and illustrated edition, 2 vols., 8vo, 21/0,
listed in the *Edinburgh Review* (quarterly)
as published Oct. 1841–Jan. 1842. It was
issued as *Colburn & Bentley's Standard Novels*
Nos. 7 & 8, 1831, with a new introduction
and notes written especially for that edition, 6/0 each: No. 7 advertised in the *Spect*
on Aug. 28 as "On Sept. 1," and No. 8 advertised as "On Oct. 1." George Routledge
& Co., London, issued it in their *Railway
Library* No. 68, Fcp 8vo, 2/0 boards, 2/6
cloth, listed in the *Ath* on Oct. 29, 1853. In
the United States it was issued by Bradford & Inskeep, Philadelphia, 3 vols.,
1810, 21 cm.; by D. Longworth, New
York, 1810, from the 1810 London edition; and by W. L. Allison, New York, no
date, 671 pp., illustrated, which the *U Cat*
gives as (1809) (incorrectly, I think). It was
reissued in *Notable Novels* in 1867, 0/6
sewed, 1/0 cloth, listed by the *Bks* in June.
See 1874

126 (SARAH S. BAKER) *First Steps
in the Better Path.* Fcp 8vo. Colored
illustrations. 2/6 cloth Dec. 8 (*Ath*)

2/6 Gift Books. This is 1867. It was issued by
Warne in 1866 as *Hatty and Marcus*, 32mo,
96 pp., 0/6 cloth sewed, probably as a *32mo
Sixpenny Book*, listed in the *Reader* on Sept.

29. It contains 4 stories. The first edition was in New York, 1860, *Hatty and Marcus*, 16 cm., 97 pp., frontispiece, by Aunt Friendly.

127 (SARAH S. BAKER) **Golden Links.**
Fcp 8vo. Colored illustrations. 2/6 cloth
Dec. 15 (*Ath*)

2/6 Gift Books. This is probably the first English edition, 1867. It was placed in the *Golden Links* series, illustrated, 2/6 cloth, in the 1870s. I have not found an American edition.

128 ELIZA A.K. OGILBY **Sunday Acrostics.**
Fcp 8vo. 1/0 cloth boards   Dec. 15
(*Ath* ad)

Useful Books. This is the first edition, 1867. The *Eng Cat* gives it as 2/0.

129 MISS E. R. BABINGTON **Hidden Sense. Seek and Find; or, Double Acrostics.**
Fcp 8vo. Illustrated. 1/0 cloth boards
Dec. 15 (*Ath* ad)

Useful Books. This is the first edition, 1867, 112 pp. A new edition at 2/0 was issued in 1868, given by the *Eng Cat.*

130 ANONYMOUS **Christmas Cheer; or, Every Day Cookery for Families of Moderate Income.** Fcp 8vo. 1/0 boards
Nov. or Dec. (*Bks*)

This is probably the first edition. It was reissued for Christmas 1867, new edition, 0/6 sewed, listed in the *Bks* for Jan. 1868; it was reissued, the same, for Christmas 1870, no date, given by the *Eng Cat.*

131 GEORGE T. HOARE, ed. **Dare and Endure! or, True Stories of Brave Deeds.**
Part 1. Fcp 8vo. 0/6 limp cloth   Dec. 15
(*Ath* ad)

This is the first edition. Part 2, the same, was listed in the *Bks* for Apr. 1868, 0/6 sewed. The Warne ads give 0/6 limp cloth. The *BM* gives 4 parts, edited by Hoare, with the last three parts written by E.E.D.

and others. I have found only 2 parts. *True Stories of Brave Deeds* was issued in *2/6 Gift Books,* Fcp 8vo, illustrated, cloth, listed in the *Spect* on Nov. 12, 1870, no date. The same title was issued in the *Daring Deeds Library,* 12mo, illustrated, 2/6 cloth, in 1881, given by the *Eng Cat*; it was reissued in this latter series in 1895, the same, listed in *PC* on Nov. 16.

132 JAMES GREENWOOD **Reminiscences of a Raven.** Fcp 8vo. Illustrated. Wrappers 1866

This is my copy, 1866, 16 cm., 215 pp., yellow wrappers cut flush, pictorially printed on the front in black, with Beeton ads on the back cover and plain white endpapers and inside covers. There are 8 full-page illustrations. The imprint on the front cover is S. O. Beeton, and on the title page it is Warne with a Beeton device. The first edition was issued by Warne in 1865, Fcp 8vo., 215 pp., illustrated, 2/0 cloth, listed in the *Ath* and the *Spect* on Nov. 4, 1865.

133 FREDERIC HARDY **ABC of Billiards.**
48mo. Illustrated. 0/6 cloth sewed   1866
(*Eng Cat*)

Illustrated Bijou Books No. 9. This is the first edition, 9 cm., 95 pp., colored frontispiece, illustrations. It was reissued in 1868.

134 FREDERICK WOOD **Cricket.** 48mo.
0/6 cloth sewed   1866 (*Eng Cat*)

Illustrated Bijou Books No. 12. This is 1866. Also 1865

135 ANONYMOUS **The Etiquette of Courtship and Marriage, etc.** 48mo.
0/6 cloth sewed   1866 (*Eng Cat*)

Illustrated Bijou Books No. 14. This is 9 cm. The first edition was issued by Kent, London, 1843, *The Etiquette of Courtship and Matrimony,* 32mo, 1/0; reissued by David Bogue, London, 1852, 13 cm., 95 pp.; and issued by George Routledge & Sons, London (1865), new edition, 32mo, 0/6. The

Kent edition was issued in New York by Burgess and Stringer, New York, 1844, 15 cm., 57 pp. as by the Countess of Blessington.

136 FREDERIC HARDY **Chess for Beginners, etc.** 48mo. o/6 cloth sewed 1866 (*Eng Cat*)

Illustrated Bijou Books No. 15. This is 9 cm., possibly the first edition, with 92 pp. Warne reissued it, 1869, 94 pp., colored frontispiece.

137 ANONYMOUS **The Model Letter Writer.** 48mo. o/6 cloth sewed 1866

Illustrated Bijou Books. 48mo. o/6 cloth sewed. This is 9 cm., and it was advertised in the *Ath* on July 14.

138 ALEXANDER F. FOSTER **History of England for Schools and Families.** 12mo. 2/o 1866 (*Eng Cat*)

The *BM* gives only London, 1861.

139 ANONYMOUS **All About It.** [New edition.] 12mo. 1/o 1866 (*Eng Cat*)

The first edition was issued by Hamilton, Adams, London, 1858, 258 pp., 2/6; reissued in 1861, new edition, 1/6, and they also issued a second edition, 1858. In the United States it was issued by W. A. Townsend & Co., New York, 1859, 19 cm., 369 pp.

140 ANONYMOUS **Clara Woodward and Her Day Dreams.** 18mo. Colored illustrations. 1/o cloth 1866?

Shilling Juveniles. The first edition was issued by Knight & Son, London, 1857, anonymous. There was a reissue, new edition, 18mo, 1/6, and a reissue in 1865, 18mo, illustrated, 1/6, listed in the *Reader* on May 20, 1865.

141 ANONYMOUS **Frank Russell.** 18mo. Illustrated. 1/o cloth 1866?

Shilling Juveniles. The first edition was issued by Knight & Son, London (1857), 18mo, 1/6. There was a new edition, the 6th thousand, the same, listed in the *Reader* on May 20, 1865.

142 ANONYMOUS **My Earnings.** 18mo. Illustrated. 1/o cloth 1866?

Shilling Juveniles. The first edition was issued by Knight & Son, London, in 1859, 18mo, 1/6; it was reissued, the same, in 1865.

143 ANONYMOUS **Every-Day Cookery for Families of Moderate Income.** Fcp 8vo. 1/o 1866?

This was noticed in the *Spect* on Mar. 30, 1867, and the *U Cat* gives it as 1867, 16.5 cm., illustrated, 156 pp. The *Eng Cat* gives it only in an 1870 edition, 1/o.

Frederick Warne & Co.
Bedford Street, Covent Garden
1867

144 HENRY COCKTON *Sylvester Sound.*
12mo. 2/0 boards Jan. (*Bks*)

Companion Library No. 20. Warne reissued it in this series, my copy, new edition, 12mo, 2/0 boards. It has no date, with the Warne imprint on the cover and a joint imprint with Scribner, Welford & Armstrong, New York, on the title page, with publisher's ads on the endpapers, back cover, and on a leaf at the back. It has the series title on the spine. Warne issued it at 6/0 in 1873, 8vo, listed in the *Spect* on July 5. Warne issued it in *Readable Books* No. 19, no date, 191 pp., given by the *U Cat* as 1882, Fcp 8vo, 1/0 sewed; reissued as *Notable Novels* No. 72, Cr 8vo, 0/6 sewed, in 1884. It was issued in the *Library of Fiction* No. 3, 12mo, 2/0 boards, in 1885.

145 JAMES F. COOPER *The Water-Witch.*
0/6 sewed Jan. (*Bks*)

The first edition was issued by Walther, Dresden, 1830, before Sept. 18. The first English edition was issued by Colburn and Bentley, London, 3 vols., 1830, 18.5 cm., anonymous, 31/6, listed in the *Ath* on Oct. 16. It was issued as *Bentley's Standard Novels* No. 36, 1834, 429 pp., revised, corrected with a new preface. George Routledge & Co., London, issued it in their *Railway Library* No. 9, 1850, 17.3 cm., by Cooper, my copy, 324 pp., 1/0 green boards, listed by *PC* as published Nov. 14–29, 1849. The first American edition was issued by Carey & Lea, Philadelphia, 2 vols., 1831, 21 cm.,

anonymous, published Dec. 11, 1830, and mentioned in an editorial note in the *Globe*, Washington, D.C. (semi-weekly), on Dec. 22 as "This morning."

146 JAMES F. COOPER *The Pathfinder.*
0/6 sewed Jan. (*Bks*)

The first edition was issued by Bentley, London, 3 vols., 1840, 20.5 cm., anonymous, 31/6, reviewed in the *Ath* on Feb. 22 and listed on Mar. 7, and advertised in the *Spect* on Feb. 22 as "On Feb. 26." It was issued as *Bentley's Standard Novels* No. 90, 1843, in Dec. 1842. It was issued by George Routledge & Co., London and New York, 1855, 335 pp., 1/6 boards, listed in the *Ath* on Sept. 23, 1854. The first French edition was issued by Baudry, Paris, 1840, 386 pp., in English. The first American edition was issued by Lea & Blanchard, Philadelphia, etc., 2 vols., 1840, 18 cm., anonymous, on Mar. 14 and advertised by three Washington, D.C., bookstores in the *Globe* (daily) on Mar. 17 as "Just published."

147 JAMES F. COOPER *The Prairie.*
0/6 sewed Feb. (*Bks*)

The first printing was by Hector Bossange, Paris, 3 vols., 1827, anonymous, in wrappers. An agreement between Cooper and Colburn stated that advance sheets were to be sent to Colburn and that he had the right to publish 1 to 3 days before the Paris edition. he issued it in 3 vols., 1827,

18 cm., Anonymous, 24/0, listed in the *Literary Gazette* on Apr. 28 and given by the *Eng Cat* as published in Apr. It was issued in *Colburn and Bentley's Standard Novels* No. 17, 1832, 443 pp., revised, corrected, and with a new introduction. George Routledge & Co., London, issued it at 1/0 boards, *Railway Library* No. 5, listed in the *Ath* on Nov. 24, 1849. The first American edition was issued by Carey, Lea, and Carey, Philadelphia, 2 vols., 1827, 19 cm., anonymous, 5,000 copies, advertised in the *National Gazette and Literary Record* on May 17 and listed in the *United States Literary Gazette* for June. Cooper received $5,000 for it.

148 WYKEHAMICUS FRIEDRICH, ed. (FREDERICK GALE) *Anno Domini 1867. The History of the English Revolution of 1867. By Lord Macaulay's New Zealander.* Cr 8vo. o/6 sewed   Mar. 2 (*Ath* ad)

The *BM* gives P. S. King, London, A.D. 3867 (1867), 18 cm., 31 pp. The *U Cat* gives Warne, A.D. 3867 (1859?), 17.5 cm., 32 pp. Warne advertised a third edition in the *Ath* on Mar. 23, 1867, Fcp 8vo, o/6 sewed.

149 (JOHN B. HARWOOD) *Lord Lynn's Wife.* New edition. 12mo. 1/0 sewed Apr. 13 (*Ath*)

Companion Library No. 19. This is my copy, no date, 16.5 cm., 250 pp., in pictorial glazed wrappers cut flush, printed in red and black. There are Warne ads on the back cover and the endpapers and on the insides of the covers, with a page of ads at the back. The list of the *Companion Library* on the back cover ends with No. 35, which was issued in Sept. 1868. The first edition was issued by Bentley, London, 2 vols., 1864, p 8vo, anonymous, 21/0, advertised in the *Ath* on Oct. 15 as "On Oct. 28" and listed on Oct. 29. They issued the second edition, 2 vols., p 8vo, advertised in the *Reader* on Dec. 10, 1864. They issued it as

a *Globe Novel*, 1865, 12mo, 250 pp., 2/0 boards, listed in the *Ath* on June 10. It ran in *Chambers's Journal*, complete in 1864 (there were 9 chapters in the May issue). Warne reissued it as *Companion Library* No. 46, 12mo, 2/0 boards, listed in the *Ath* on Sept. 16, 1871; they issued it as *Readable Books* No. 13, Fcp 8vo, 1/0 sewed, listed in the *Spect* on Sept. 27, 1879; and in the *London Library* No. 39, 12mo, 1/0 sewed, listed in the *PC* on May 23, 1891. This latter edition was issued by Warne in New York, anonymous, $.30 paper, listed in the *Literary Digest* on July 25, 1891.

150 FREDERICK CHAMIER *The Saucy Arethusa.* 12mo. 2/0 boards   May (*Bks*)

Companion Library No. 27. This has a joint imprint with Scribner & Co., New York, 1867, 17.5 cm., 443 pp. The first edition was issued by Bentley, London, 3 vols., 1837, p 8vo, *The Arethusa*, by Chamier. It was published May 11 according to the Bentley private catalog and was advertised and listed in the *Spect* on May 13 as "Just published." Bentley issued it at 2/0 boards, 1860, in Sept., *The Saucy Arethusa*. The first American edition was issued by Carey & Hart, Philadelphia, etc., 2 vols., 1837, 20 cm., *The Arethusa*. It was advertised by a Washington, D.C., bookstore in the *Globe* (daily) on Dec. 5, 1837, 2 vols., anonymous, "Added during the last 2 weeks." These *Globe* ads give a very reliable date of issue of the American editions. It was reviewed in the *Knickerbocker* for Dec. 1837. Warne issued it as *Notable Novels* No. 55, Cr 8vo, o/6 sewed, no date, 191 pp., listed in the *Bks* for Mar. 1881.

151 CHARLES CLARKE *Tom Crackenthorpe; or, Hunting and Steeple Chasing Adventures.* New edition. 12mo. 1/0 sewed   May (*Bks*)

Companion Library No. 24. This is 1867. The first edition was *A Box for the Season*, issued by Chapman & Hall, London, 2 vols.,

1864, p 8vo, 21/0 rose-madder cloth with cream endpapers, listed in the *Ath* on Jan. 16, 1864. They issued it in 1 vol., 1865, second edition, 19 cm., 346 pp., 5/0 cloth, listed in the *Reader* on Dec. 17, 1864. They issued it as *Select Library of Fiction* No. 207, 1873, 12mo, 17.9 cm., 247 pp., my copy in yellow pictorial boards, printed in red and blue, listed in the *Ath* on Mar. 22, 1873.

152 ELIZABETH WATTS *The Orchard and Fruit Garden.* Fcp 8vo. Colored frontispiece. 1/0 boards June 1 (*Ath*)
Country Library. This is the first edition, 1867, 16.5 cm., 188 pp. There is a known copy, no date, 16.5 cm., in yellow pictorial boards, printed in red, blue, and black with a series ad on the back cover and publisher's ads on the endpapers and 1 leaf of ads at the front, also issued in limp cloth. It was advertised in the *Times Weekly Edition* (London) on Mar. 7, 1890, Fcp 8vo, illustrated, 1/0 pictorial boards or cloth, and advertised in the *TLS* on May 8, 1903, Fcp 8vo, 1/0.
See 1876

153 JOSEPH T. BURGESS *Angling: A Practical Guide.* Fcp 8vo. Illustrated. 1/0 boards June 15 (*Ath*)
Country Library and Family Circle Books. This has no date, 182 pp., the first edition. I have a reissue in *Useful Books*, no date, 182 pp., in yellow pictorial boards, printed in red and black, with a preface (May 1867). It has a frontispiece and 3 plates and textual illustrations, and the series title is on the front cover. There are publisher's ads on the endpapers and an ad on the back cover, and with the rear paste-down dated Apr. 17, 1886. *Angling and How to Angle* was reissued in *Useful Books*, in 1895, Cr 8vo, illustrated, 1/0 sewed, 2/6 cloth, revised and brought up to date by R. B. Marston, 212 pp., 1895, listed in *PC* on Aug. 31. It was mentioned in editorial matter in the *New-York Times Book Review* on Apr. 2,

1898, 12mo, illustrated, $1.00, with an illustrated cover. A new edition was advertised in the *TLS* on May 8, 1903, revised by Marston, Fcp 8vo, illustrated, 1/0, containing a new chapter on pike fishing and one on dry fly fishing.

154 MORDECAI C. COOKE *A Fern Book for Everybody.* Fcp 8vo. Illustrated. 1/0 boards June 15 (*Spect*)
Country Library & Family Circle Books. This is the first edition, my copy, 1867, 124 pp., series title on the front cover, buff boards pictorially printed in black, red, and green, all edges cut. It has publisher's ads on the back cover and on the endpapers. The *Bks* gives a new edition in Sept. 1867, 1/0 boards; and the *U Cat* gives an edition, 1868, 17 cm., 124 pp., colored plates, and a New York edition, no date. I have a reissue, no date, Fcp 8vo, 124 pp. in pale yellow boards, decoratively printed on the front cover in red, blue, and green, with *Useful Books* on the front cover. There are publisher's ads on the back cover and endpapers and 12 full-page colored plates with plain illustrations in the text, probably issued in 1879. The *Eng Cat* gives an edition with colored illustrations, 1/0, issued in 1881; and an edition, 1889, 124 pp., illustrated, 1/0. It was advertised in the *TWEd* on Sept. 11, 1891, Cr 8vo, plain and colored illustrations, 1/0 cloth; and in the *TLS* on May 8, 1903, Fcp 8vo, 1/0.

155 JAMES B. BORLASE *The Night Fossickers, and Other Australian Tales of Peril and Adventure.* Fcp 8vo. 1/0 sewed June 29 (*Ath*)
Companion Library No. 28. This is the first edition, 1867, 248 pp. *Australian Tales of Peril and Adventure* was issued at 2/0 cloth, listed in the *Ath* and *Spect* on Feb. 19, 1870.
See 1868, 80, 94

156 HENRY COCKTON **The Love Match.**
[New edition.] 12mo. 2/0 boards
June (*Bks*)
Companion Library No. 26. This is 1867. It
was first issued in 12 monthly 1/0 parts by
W. M. Clark, London, No. 1 advertised in
the *Illustrated London News* as "On Oct. 1,"
1844. The first book edition was issued by
Clark, 1845, 373 pp., illustrated. Warne issued it as *Notable Novels* No. 73, Cr 8vo,
0/6 sewed, in 1884, probably in Mar. In the
United States it was issued in parts by Burgess & Stringer, New York, Nos. 1 and 2
listed in *Godey's Lady's Book* for June 1845.

157 EMMA MARSHALL **Theodora's
Childhood.** 18mo. Colored illustrations.
1/0 cloth   July 13 (*Ath*)
Shilling Juveniles. This is the first edition,
1867. The *BM* has a copy, 1868, with a second title page bearing the date 1867. A
Nov. 2, 1867, ad in the *Ath* gave 30 titles in
this series.

158 ANNIE THOMAS, later MRS. CUDLIP
Walter Goring. [New edition.] 12mo. 2/0
boards   July (*Bks*)
Companion Library No. 29. It was later put
in this series as No. 70. I have a copy, no
date, probably after 1878, a yellowback
with the Warne imprint on the title page
and front cover and with a Warne ad on
the back cover. It has Gall & Inglis, Edinburgh and London, ads on the endpapers,
with the front endpapers listing the present series through No. 94, with the present title being No. 70. Warne took over the
series from Gall & Inglis according to Sadleir, but many of the titles in the Gall & Inglis ad weren't even published until after
1873, long after Warne started their *Companion Library.* I think the endpaper listing
of the series was actually the Warne issues.
The first edition was issued by Chapman
& Hall, London, 3 vols., 1866, p 8vo, 31/6,
listed in the *Ath* on Jan. 27. The first
American edition was issued by Harper &

Brothers, New York, 1866, 8vo, 155 pp.,
$.75 paper, *Library of Select Novels* No. 265,
advertised in the *New-York Times* on Apr. 2
as "This day" and listed in the *Nation* on
Apr. 5, anonymous. Leypoldt & Holt, New
York, issued the Tauchnitz edition, 2 vols.,
listed in the *Nation* on July 5, 1866, $.75
each.

159 HARRIET B. STOWE **Uncle Tom's
Cabin.** Cr 8vo. 0/6 sewed, 1/0 cloth
July (*Bks*)
Notable Novels No. 2. It was reissued in this
series, listed in the *Bks* for Apr. 1869. It
was issued in the *Star Series* No. 61, 16mo,
1/0 sewed, 1/6 cloth, listed in the *Spect* on
Aug. 2, 1879. It was issued in *National
Books*, Imp 32mo, 0/6 stiff wrappers with 2
plates, and 1/0, 1/6 cloth with colored
plates, as No. 12 in the series, advertised in
the *Ath* on Nov. 15, 1879. It was issued in
the *Incident and Adventure Library*, Fcp 8vo,
illustrated, 2/0 cloth, given by the *Eng Cat*;
and in the *Chandos Classics* No. 140, Cr
8vo, 1/6 sewed, 2/0 cloth, 2/6 imitation
Roxburghe, listed in the *Ath* on Apr. 19,
1890. The first edition was issued by John
P. Jewett, Boston, etc., 2 vols., 1852, in tan
printed wrappers or black, purple, brown,
or blue cloth, noticed in the *Ind* on Mar.
25, giving Mar. 20 as the date of issue; deposited Apr. 1; advertised in *Lit W* on Mar.
13 as "On Mar. 20" and listed as published
Mar. 20–Apr. 10. A June 5 ad for 2 vols.,
$1.50 or $2.00 cloth, stated that 50,000
copies had been sold in 8 weeks. In England the *PC* for Oct. 15, 1852, announced 10 different editions in one fortnight, and at least 12 different editions
(not reissues) were published in England
in 1852; there were 40 editions from 18
houses in England within a year of the first
edition. The first English edition was
probably Henry Vizetelly; Clarke & Co.,
London, 1852, 19 cm., 329 pp., 2/6 cloth,
in an edition of 2,500 copies, the American preface signed "G," reprinted verbatim from the tenth American edition. It

was advertised in the *Ath* on Apr. 24 as "On Apr. 30" and advertised on May 15 as "Now ready," and it was listed in the *Literary Gazette* on May 15 and in the *Spect* on May 22.

160 ELIZABETH HELME **St. Clair of the Isles.** Cr 8vo. o/6 sewed, 1/o cloth July (*Bks*)

Notable Novels No. 3. This is 1867, 138 pp. in double columns. The first edition was issued by T. N. Longman & O. Rees, London, 4 vols., 1803, 12mo, 14/0, listed by the *Edinburgh Review* as published Oct. 25, 1803–Jan. 20, 1804, and given by the *Eng Cat* as published in Nov. 1803. It was issued in the United States by Perry, Philadelphia, 4 vols., 1856.
See also 1874

161 M. M. BELL (MARY L. MARTIN?) **Dr. Weld.** [New edition.] 12mo. 2/o boards Aug. 17 (*Ath*)

Companion Library No. 31. This is 1867. The first edition was issued by Warne, 2 vols., 1866, 12/0, advertised in the *Ath* on Jan. 20 as "This day" and listed Jan. 13, 1866. It is not given by either the *BM* or the *U Cat*!

162 ROBERT ST. JOHN CORBET **Sir Harry and the Widows.** 12mo. 1/o sewed Sept. 18 (*Ath*)

Companion Library No. 32. This is the first edition, 1868, 187 pp. It was reissued in this series at 1/o, listed in the *Spect* on July 10, 1875; it was issued in *Readable Books* in 1876 or 1877, Fcp 8vo, 1/o sewed.

163 MATILDA C. HOUSTOUN **Zoe's "Brand."** [New edition.] 12mo. 2/o boards Sept. (*Bks*)

Companion Library No. 21. The first edition was issued by Chapman & Hall, London, 3 vols., 1864, p. 8vo, anonymous, 31/6, listed in the *Ath* on May 28.

164 REGINA M. ROCHE **The Children of the Abbey.** Cr 8vo. o/6 sewed. 1/o cloth Sept. (*Bks*)

Notable Novels No. 4. The first edition was William Lane, London, 4 vols., 1796. In the United States it was issued by W. A. Leary, Philadelphia, 3 vols.-in-1, no date, 14 cm., frontispiece, with a preface (1796). The first American edition was issued by H. Caritat, New York, 4 vols.-in-2, 1798, 16.5 cm., separate pagination, from the second London edition. Another American edition was issued at Exeter, 3 vols., 18mo, listed in the *North American Review* (quarterly) for July 1826. Warne reissued it in *Notable Novels*, p 8vo, o/6 sewed, listed in the *Bks* for May 1885.
See 1874

165 LAURA VALENTINE **Sea Fights from Sluys to Navarino.** Fcp 8vo. Illustrated. 2/6 cloth Oct. 19 (*Ath*)

2/6 Gift Books. This is the first edition, 1868. A Nov. 2, 1867, ad in the *Ath* gave this as the last title in a list of the series, Nos. 1–3, 5, 6, 14–17. It was issued jointly with Scribner, Welford & Co., New York, 1869, 17 cm., illustrated, 279 pp., advertised in the *Ath* for Nov. 27. It was issued in the *Daring Deeds Library* in 1880, 12mo, illustrated, 2/6 cloth, given by the *Eng Cat*; and reissued in that series, the same, in an updated version, *Sea Fights from Sluys to the Bombardment of Alexander*, listed in *PC* on Nov. 16, 1895.

166 ALEXANDER C. EWALD **Warne's Bijou Dictionary of the English Language.** 32mo. Portrait. 1/o limp cloth, 1/6 roan Oct. 19 (*Ath*)

This is the first edition, probably dated 1868, 640 pp.

167 ANONYMOUS **The Little Miner.** 18mo. Colored illustrations. 1/o cloth Nov. 2 (*Ath*)

Shilling Juveniles. This is also given by the *Eng Cat*, but otherwise I cannot trace it.

168 LAURA VALENTINE *Nursery Tales.*
A New Version. 18mo. Illustrated.
1/6 cloth   Nov. 2 (*Ath*)

Eighteenpenny Juveniles. This is the first edition, probably dated 1868, 15.5 cm., 184 pp. A Nov. 2 *Ath* ad listed 13 titles in this series with this title being No. 15. This was put in the *Illustrated Fairy Library* No. 3, 12mo, 182 pp., illustrated, 1/0 sewed, 1/6 cloth, given as issued in 1877 by the *Eng Cat* and listed in the *Bks* on Jan. 4, 1878.

169 ANONYMOUS *My Market Table.*
32mo. 1/0 cloth   Nov. 2 (*Spect*)

This is the first edition. It was reissued at 1/0, advertised in the *Ath* on June 14, 1873, and reissued at 0/6 boards, given by the *Eng Cat* as issued in 1876.

170 AUNT FRIENDLY (SARAH S. BAKER)
Cousin Annie. 18mo. Illustrated. 1/6 cloth   Nov. 2 (*Ath*)

Eighteenpenny Juveniles. This is the first edition, 1868, 191 pp. It was reduced to 1/0, listed by *PC* on Nov. 2, 1895.

171 JOHN BUNYAN *The Pilgrim's Progress.* Unabridged. Imp 16mo. Colored illustrations. 0/6 stiff wrappers Nov. 2 (*Spect* ad)

The *Spect* ad gave 0/6 stiff wrappers, 4 colored plates; 1/0 cloth, 20 colored plates; 1/6 cloth, 32 colored plates. It was issued in the *Chandos Classics* No. 65, new edition, no date, Cr 8vo, 349 pp., illustrated, 1/6 sewed, 2/0 cloth, listed in the *Ath* on Nov. 9, 1878, and reissued in this series in the 1880s. It was issued in *National Books* No. 1, Imp 32mo, 2 plates, 0/6 stiff wrappers, 1/0, 1/6 colored plates, advertised in the *Ath* on Nov. 15, 1879. The first edition was issued by Nathaniel Ponder, London, part 1, 1678, 15 cm., 232 pp.; part 2, 1684, 224 (i.e., 210) pp., illustrated. In the United States it was issued by Thomas Fleet, Boston, 1744, 17th edition, 166 (176) pp.; and

by John M'Culloch, Philadelphia, 3 parts in 1 vol., 1789, 12mo, part 3 being spurious.

172 CATHERINE D. BELL *Every Saturday.*
[New edition.] 12mo. Illustrated. 2/0 cloth   Nov. 2 (*Ath* ad)

2/0 Gift Books. This is also given by the *Eng Cat*, but otherwise I cannot trace it. The *Ath* ad listed 14 titles in this series, No. 1–3 and 7–17. I think it was reissued in this series in 1869, advertised in the *Ath* on Nov. 27.

173 W.H.G. KINGSTON *Ralph Clavering.*
18mo. Colored frontispiece. 0/9 cloth Nov. 2 (*Ath* ad)

Ninepenny Juveniles. This is the first edition, 1867.

174 (MATILDA A. PLANCHE, later MACKARNESS) *Example Better than Precept.* 18mo. Colored frontispiece. 0/9 cloth   Nov. 2 (*Ath* ad)

Ninepenny Juveniles. This is the first edition, 1867.

175 EDWARD C. TAINSH *Mr. Johnston's School; or, The New Master.* 18mo. Colored frontispiece. 0/9 cloth Nov. 2 (*Ath* ad)

Ninepenny Juveniles. This is the first edition, 1867. In the United States it was issued by Dutton & Co., New York, 1870, 104 pp.

176 MARGARET HOWITT *Birds of a Feather.* 18mo. Colored frontispiece. 0/9 cloth   Nov. 2 (*Ath* ad)

Ninepenney Juveniles. This is the first edition, 1867.

177 (CLARA F. GUERNSEY) *The Silver Cup.* 12mo. Illustrated. 2/0 cloth Nov. 16 (*Ath*)

2/0 Gift Books. The first edition was issued by the American Sunday-School Union,

Philadelphia and New York (1865), 16
cm., anonymous, 316 pp., illustrated. The
present edition is the first English edition,
1868, 243 pp. This was probably reissued
in the present series, the same, advertised
in the *Ath* on Nov. 27, 1869. It was issued
in the *Incident and Adventure Library*, Fcp
8vo, illustrated, 2/0 cloth, probably before
1880, and it was issued in the *Daring and
Doing Library*, Cr 8vo, illustrated, 1/6 cloth,
in the 1890s.

178 (CHARLES H. SMITH) **Tom Butler's
Trouble.** 18mo. Colored illustrations.
1/0 cloth   Nov. 23 (*Ath*)

Shilling Juveniles. This is the first edition,
1868, 123 pp., with only the Warne imprint. It was also issued with the joint imprint of Scribner, Welford & Co., New
York, 1869, but retaining the 1868 title
page also.

179 OTTILIE WILDERMUTH **A Queen.**
18mo. Colored illustrations. 1/0 cloth
Nov. 23 (*Ath*)

Shilling Juveniles. This has 1868 on the title
page, and is a translation from the German, *Eine Königin.* It was issued in the
United States by E. P. Dutton, Boston,
1867, 129 pp., illustrated. Warne issued it
in their *Round the Globe Library*, 12mo, colored frontispiece, 1/0 cloth, by Wildermuth, in 1871, given by the *Eng Cat*; and
as *Home Queen*, by Wildermuth, 18mo, 1/0,
in 1879, given by the *Eng Cat.*

180 AUNT FRIENDLY (SARAH S. BAKER)
Charlie Clement. 18mo. Colored
illustrations. 1/0 cloth   Nov. 23 (*Ath*)

Shilling Juveniles. This is probably the first
English edition, 1868. It was issued in
Philadelphia, 1862, 12mo, as *The Boy
Friend*; and by Martien, Philadelphia,
1873, copyright 1865, 150 pp., as *Boy
Friend; or, All Can Help*, by Aunt Friendly.

181 LADY B.C.G. **Lizzie Johnson.**
18mo. Colored illustrations. 1/0 cloth
Nov. 23 (*Ath*)

Shilling Juveniles. This is the first edition,
1868. This was the last of 30 titles in this
series given in an ad in the *Ath* on Nov. 2,
1867.

182 MARIA CUMMINS **The Lamplighter.**
Cr 8vo. 0/6 sewed, 1/0 cloth
Nov. or Dec. (*Bks*)

Notable Novels No. 5. The first edition was
issued by John P. Jewett & Co., Boston;
Jewett, Proctor & Worthington, Cleveland, 1854, 12mo, anonymous, 523 pp.,
advertised in the *New York Daily Times* on
Feb. 23 as "On Feb. 25," and it was received at the Library of Congress on Mar.
16. It was advertised in the *Ind* on Feb. 23
as "About Mar. 1." They issued the 20th
thousand, noticed in the *Merchant's Magazine*, New York (monthly) for May 1854,
and the 35th thousand was noticed in *Godey's Lady's Book* for July. The first English
edition was either by Clarke, Beeton &
Co., London, (1854), Fcp 8vo, anonymous, 412 pp., 1/6 boards or p 8vo, 7/6,
listed in the *Ath* on Apr. 15 and listed by
PC as published Apr. 14–29; or by George
Routledge & Co., London, 1854, Fcp 8vo,
anonymous, 350 pp., 1/6 boards, advertised on Apr. 15 and listed by *PC* as published Apr. 14–29. The House of Lords
decided on Aug. 1 that there was no copyright in American works, and by Sept. 9,
1854, there were at least 7 reprints of this
work in England, including Nelson, London, and Cassell, London. Warne issued it
in their *Star Series* No. 36, 16mo, 1/6
sewed, 2/0 cloth, probably in early 1877;
they issued it at 2/6, Cr 8vo, colored illustrations, listed in the *Spect* on July 12,
1879.
See 1874

183　LAURA VALENTINE **Gold, Silver, Lead.** Roy 8vo. Colored illustrations. 1/0 sewed　Dec. 7 (*Ath* ad)

This is Warne's Christmas Annual for 1867. The ad said most of the first printing has been sold, and I think it was issued in Nov. It had pieces by Dutton Cook, Henry Kingsley, Charlotte Yonge, F. W. Robinson, et al. It was imported by Scribner, Welford & Co., New York, and issued in 1867, Imp 8vo, colored and plain illustrations, $.50 picture cover, advertised in the *New-York Times* on Dec. 4, 1867.

184　FREDERIC HARDY **Cribbage and Dominoes.** 32mo. Illustrated. o/6 cloth 1867 (*Eng Cat*)

Illustrated Bijou Books No. 17. This is the first edition.

185　ANONYMOUS **Etiquette of the Dinner Table: with the Art of Carving.** 32mo. Illustrated. o/6 cloth　1867 (*Eng Cat*)

Illustrated Bijou Books No. 18. This is the first edition, 1867, 10 cm., 95 pp.

186　FREDERIC HARDY **Parlour Magic.** 32mo. Illustrated. o/6 cloth 1867 (*Eng Cat*)

Illustrated Bijou Books No. 19. This is the first edition, 94 pp.

187　FREDERIC HARDY **Draughts and Backgammon.** 32mo. Illustrated. o/6 cloth　1867 (*Eng Cat*)

Illustrated Bijou Books No. 20. This is the first edition, 1867. *The Bijou Book of In-Door Amusements* by Hardy was issued by Warne, 1868, 3 parts in 1 vol., 2-¾ × 3-¾ inches, colored illustrations, containing the *Illustrated Bijou Books* No. 1, 19, and 20.

188　J.R.W **Handbook of Whist.** 32mo. Illustrated. o/6 cloth　1867 (*Eng Cat*)

Illustrated Bijou Books No. 21. This is the first edition.

189　JOHN C. JEAFFRESON **Olive Blake's Good Work.** 12mo. 2/0 boards　1867

Companion Library No. 22. The first edition was issued by Chapman & Hall, London, 3 vols., 1862, p 8vo, 31/6. They issued it at 5/0 in 1862. The first American edition was issued by Harper & Brothers, New York, 1862, 24 cm., *Library of Select Novels* No. 222, noticed in *Harper's New Monthly Magazine* for July.

190　CHARLES KENT (WILLIAM C. M. KENT) **Footprints on the Road.** [New edition.] 12mo. 2/0 boards　1867 (*Eng Cat*)

Companion Library No. 23. The first edition was issued by Chapman & Hall, London, 1864, 420 pp.

191　ALBERT SMITH **Paris and London: Humorous Sketches of Life in France and England.** 12mo. 1/0 sewed 1867 (*Eng Cat*)

Companion Library No. 25. This is 1867, 182 pp. The first edition was issued by Bentley, London, 1852, *Pictures of Life at Home and Abroad.* Warne issued a new edition in 1868, 12mo, 1/0 sewed, listed by the *Bks* in Aug.

192　ANNIE THOMAS, later CUDLIP **On Guard.** [New edition.] 12mo. 2/0 boards　1867 (*Eng Cat*)

Companion Library No. 30. The first edition was issued by Chapman & Hall, London, 3 vols., 1865, p 8vo, 31/6, listed in the *Ath* on Mar. 25. The first American edition was issued by Harper & Brothers, New York, 1865, 8vo, $.50 paper, *Library of Select Novels* No. 254, advertised in the *New-York Times* on June 14 as "This day."

193　J. T. AKERMAN **The Recovery of Debts.** [New edition.] 12mo. o/6 1867 (*Eng Cat*)

The first edition was issued by T. Pettitt & Co., London (1864), 55 pp.

194 H. B. INGRAM *Executors', Administrators', and Trustees' Guide.* [New edition.] Fcp 8vo. 1/o boards 1867 (*Eng Cat*)

Useful Books. I cannot trace this.

195 ANONYMOUS *Nellie Grey.* [New edition.] 18mo. Colored illustrations. 1/o cloth 1867 (*Eng Cat*)

Shilling Juveniles. The first English edition was issued by Knight & Son, London, 1857, 18mo, 1/6. They reissued it in 1865, sixth edition, illustrated, 1/6, listed in the *Reader* on May 20. It was issued in the United States by the American Sunday-School Union, Philadelphia, New York, etc. (copyright 1855), 15.5 cm., anonymous, 216 pp., illustrated.

196 CAROLINE HADLEY *Stories of Old; or, Bible Narratives Limited to the Capacity of Young Children.* Old Testament. 18mo. Illustrated. 1/6 cloth 1867?

Eighteenpenny Juveniles. This was 1868, 15.5 cm., with "Juvenile Illustrated Library" on the cover. The first edition of this and the next item was *Stories of Old: or Bible Narratives*, 2 vols., 1862, 3/6 each, old and new testament respectively, listed in the *Spect* on Dec. 6, 1862, Smith, Elder & Co., London. They issued *Stories of Old and Stories of the Apostles*, 2 vols., listed in the *Spect* on Dec. 3, 1864. Warne issued *Stories of Old*, both series, 1 vol., 3/6, listed in the *Spect* on Apr. 11, 1868. Smith, Elder & Co. issued both series, new editions, 18mo, 4 illustrations each, 2/6 cloth each, the old testament with 311 pp. and the new testament with 255 pp., listed in the *Reader* on Dec. 3, 1864. In the United States Sheldon & Co., New York, issued both series of *Stories of Old*, 2 vols., 16mo, illustrated, $1.00 each, advertised in the *New-York Times* on Oct. 29, 1863, as "This week."

197 CAROLINE HADLEY *Stories of Old; or, Bible Narratives, etc. New Testament.* 18mo. Illustrated. 1/6 cloth 1867?

Eighteenpenny Juveniles. See the preceding item.

Frederick Warne & Co.
Bedford Street, Covent Garden
1868

198 THOMAS GRIFFITHS *The Modern Fencer.* Fcp 8vo. Illustrated. 1/o boards Jan. 18 (*Ath*)

Useful Books. This is the first edition, 1868, 17 cm., 91 pp., probably with the joint imprint of Scribner, Welford & Co., New York. This went through at least 8 editions, one being issued in 1879.

199 HOLME LEE (HARRIET PARR) *Legends from Fairy Land.* Fcp 8vo. Illustrated. 2/6 cloth   Feb. 1 (*Spect*)

2/6 Gift Books. The first edition was issued by Smith, Elder & Co., London, 1860, Fcp 8vo, plates by H. Sanderson, 3/6 gilt pictorial violet cloth, listed in the *Spect* on Dec. 15, 1860. Warne issued it in their *Illustrated Fairy Library* No. 4, 12mo, 238 pp., 1/o sewed, 1/6 cloth, 238 pp., 1/o sewed, 1/6 cloth, listed in the *Bks* on Jan. 4, 1878; they reissued it in this library at 1/6 cloth, listed by *PC* on Sept. 11, 1897.

200 CAROLINE HADLEY *Stories of the Apostles.* 18mo. Illustrated. 1/6 cloth Feb. 15 (*Spect*)

Eighteenpenny Juveniles. The first edition was issued by Smith, Elder & Co., London, 1864, 18mo, 243 pp., 2/6 cloth, listed in the *Spect* on Dec. 3, 1864. It was issued in the United States by Sheldon & Co., New York, listed in the *Christian Examiner* (bimonthly) for Jan. 1866. It was also issued by E. P. Dutton, New York, 1870, 15.5 cm., 243 pp., frontispiece.

201 LEITCH RITCHIE *Wearyfoot Common.* [New edition.] Fcp 8vo. 1/o sewed Feb. 29 (*Spect*)

Companion Library No. 33. The first English edition was issued by David Bogue, London, 1855 (1854), Fcp 8vo, 6 illustrations, 5/o cloth, listed in the *Ath* on Dec. 9, 1854. The first American edition was issued by Stringer & Townsend, New York, 1854, $.37½, advertised in the *New York Daily Times* on July 12 as "This morning" and advertised there on July 22, the third edition in 10 days. It was listed in the *Ind* on July 27. Warne issued it in 2/o *Gift Books*, 12mo, illustrated, 2/o cloth, listed in the *Ath* on May 9, 1868; they probably reissued in the series in 1869, advertised in the *Ath* on Nov. 27, and reissued again in the series in 1873, given by the *Eng Cat*. It was issued in the *Star Series* No. 28, 16mo, 1/o sewed, 1/6 cloth, in late 1876 or early 1877.

202 LOUISA L. GREENE *Cushions and Corners.* [New edition.] 12mo. Illustrated. 2/o cloth   Feb. 29 (*Spect*)

2/o Gift Books. The first edition was issued by Smith, Elder & Co., London, 1864, 12mo, 190 pp., 3/6 cloth, listed in the *Spect* on Dec. 24, 1864. The first American edition was issued by E. P. Dutton, Boston, in 1865, 16mo, anonymous, illustrated, $1.25, advertised in the *Nation* on Dec. 21, 1865. I think it was reissued in this series, advertised in the *Ath* on Nov. 27, 1869. It was reissued by Warne in 1881, new edition, Cr 8vo, 2/6 cloth, listed in the *Spect* on Aug. 6. It was issued, no date, p 8vo, illustrated, 2/6 cloth, 229 pp., listed in *PC* on Dec. 19, 1891.

203 MARIA CUMMINS *Mabel Vaughan.*
Cr 8vo. 0/6 sewed, 1/0 cloth   Mar. (*Bks*)
Notable Novels No. 6. The first American edition was issued by John P. Jewett & Co., Boston; Henry P. B. Jewett, Cleveland; Sampson Low, London, 1857, anonymous, 508 pp., listed in *APC&LG* (weekly) on Sept. 26 and in the *Ind* on Oct. 8. Crosby, Nichols & Co., Boston, advertised a new edition on Oct. 29, 1857, as "Now ready," stating that the publisher of the first edition of 15,000 copies was embarrassed and couldn't continue so new arrangements had been made with the authoress. The first English edition was issued by Sampson Low, London, 1857, edited by Mrs. Gaskell, 18 cm., anonymous, 310 pp., 1/6 yellow pictorial boards, with a frontispiece in red and black and an inside front cover ad (Sept. 19, 1857); and 3/6 cloth, 459 pp., frontispiece. It was advertised in the *Ath* on Sept. 5 as "On Sept. 20" and listed Sept. 19. Sadleir's copy had an inscribed date (Sept. 19). George Routledge & Co., London and New York, issued it, 1857, Fcp 8vo, 369 pp., 1/6 boards, listed by *PC* as published Nov. 14–30. Warne reissued it in *Notable Novels* No. 6, p 8vo, 0/6 sewed, listed by the *Bks* for Oct. 1887.
See 1874

204 E. H. (M. HIBBERD) *The Silver Trumpet, and Other Allegorical Tales.*
16mo. Illustrated. 1/6 cloth   Apr. 4 (*Ath*)
Large Type Book for Children. This is a first edition, no date. This was issued in 1871, 18mo, 1/0, given by the *Eng Cat*, and issued in the *Illustrated Fairy Library*, probably in 1878, 12mo, illustrated, 1/0 sewed,

1/6 cloth, given as 1878 by the *Eng Cat.*; it also was issued in 1882, 16mo, 1/6, given by the *Eng Cat.*

205 CHARLES J. SMITH *History of England for Young Students.* [New edition.] 12mo. 1/0 boards
Apr. 11 (*Spect*)
The first edition was issued by Warne, 1867, 12mo, 2/0.

206 GEORGE ARMATAGE *The Horse.*
Fcp 8vo. 1/0 boards   Apr. 11 (*Spect*)
Useful Books. This is the first edition, 1868, 116 pp. It was issued in the *Country Library*, Fcp 8vo, illustrated, 1/6 boards, in 1873, listed in the *Ath* on May 31; it was reissued, Fcp 8vo, 1/0, listed in the *Bks* for Sept. 1890. It was advertised in the *TWed* on May 2, 1890, illustrated, condensed from Stonehenge (John H. Walsh), but there was no mention of Armatage. It was issued in New York by Warne, $.50 cloth, by Armatage, listed in *Literary Digest* on Nov. 22, 1890.

207 BENJAMIN DISRAELI *Vivian Grey.*
[New edition.] Fcp 8vo. 1/0 sewed
Apr. (*Bks*)
Also 1866

208 MARY JEWRY, ed. *Warne's Model Cookery and Housekeeping Book. People's Edition.* Cr 8vo. Colored illustrations.
1/0 boards, 1/6 half-bound   May 9 (*Ath*)
This is an abridgement of the first edition, the latter noticed in the *Spect* on Feb. 22 1868, Cr 8vo, 7/6, 10/6 half morocco. The present edition has a joint imprint with Scribner, Welford & Co., New York, dated 1868, 19 cm., 156 pp. Warne issued the people's edition in 1870, Cr 8vo, colored illustrations, 1/6 half-bound, given by the *Eng Cat*, and advertised it in the *Ath* on Sept. 25, 1880, Cr 8vo, colored illustrations, 1/0, 1/6 half-bound. Warne reissued

it in 1892, Cr 8vo, 156 pp., illustrated, colored frontispiece, o/6, listed by *PC* on July 2.

209 MARTHA M. LAMONT *The Gladiator.* 12mo. 1/0 sewed   May 9 (*Spect*)
The first edition was issued by Longmans, London, 1840, 12mo. It was reissued by them, 1849, 12mo, 3/6, with a new title page.

210 (ELIZABETH S. SHEPPARD) *Willie's Rest.* 16mo. Illustrated. 1/6 cloth Before May 16
Large Type Book for Children. A May 16 ad in the *Ath* said that it had already been issued. The first edition was issued by Smith, Elder & Co., London, 1857, 16mo. Warne issued a new edition in the *Round the Globe Library*, 12mo, colored frontispiece, 1/0 cloth, in 1871, given by the *Eng Cat.*

211 STONEHENGE (JOHN H. WALSH) *Pedestrianism; Health and General Training.* 32mo. Illustrated. o/6 cloth May 16 (*Ath* ad)
Illustrated Bijou Books No. 22. This is a first edition as a separate book, but Walsh had sections on pedestrianism in earlier Routledge publications; this may be excerpted from them.

212 MARK H. ROBINSON *La Crosse.* 32mo. Illustrated. o/6 cloth May 16 (*Ath* ad)
Illustrated Bijou Books No. 23. This is the first edition.

213 AUNT FRIENDLY (SARAH S. BAKER) *The Babes in the Basket.* 18mo. Colored illustrations. 1/0 cloth   June 6 (*Ath*)
Shilling Juveniles. This has no date, 128 pp. The first American edition was issued by A. D. F. Randolph, New York, 1859, 17 cm., 216 pp., frontispiece. The first English edition was issued by T. Nelson & Sons, London, 1859, 16mo. This title should not be confused with a book with the same title by Mrs. C. E. Brown.

214 JOSEPH T. BURGESS *Old English Wild Flowers.* Fcp 8vo. Illustrated. 1/0 boards June 13 (*Ath*)
Country Library. This is the first edition, 1868, 291 pp. Warne also issued it at 3/6 with colored illustrations, listed in the *Ath* on Aug. 22, 1868. Warne issued a new edition, *English Wild Flowers*, no date, 181 pp., colored illustrations, 2/0 boards, listed in the *Ath* on Mar. 11, 1871. Ruari McLean in *Victorian Publishers' Book-Binding in Paper*, 1983, shows a picture of this, no date, 17 cm., in pink boards showing flowers on the cover in red, blue, and green, with "Warnes's Useful Books" on the front cover. A new and improved edition, 12mo, colored illustrations, 3/6 cloth, was advertised by Warne in the *Spect* on May 10, 1873. It was advertised in the *Ath* on July 13, 1878, 1/0 boards, colored frontispiece; a new edition was listed in the *Spect* on May 21, 1881, 12mo, 3/6; and it was advertised by Warne in the *TWed* (London) on Mar. 7, 1890, Fcp 8vo, illustrated, 1/0 picture boards or cloth.

215 WILLIAM SHAKESPEARE *Shakespeare's Works.* Cr 8vo. 1/0 sewed, 1/6, 2/0 cloth   June 27 (*Spect*)
Chandos Classics No. 1. This begins the long run of this series, which had over 150 titles. It has 768 pp. It was advanced in price to 1/6 sewed, 2/0 cloth, listed by *PC* as published Feb. 16–29, 1872. Warne issued it in *Chandos Poets* at 7/6, listed in the *Spect* on Aug. 8, 1874; they issued the Bedford edition, 12 vols., 32mo, 21/0, listed in the *Spect* on Nov. 24, 1888. It was imported by Scribner, Welford & Co., New York, and issued with the joint imprint, 1868, 12mo, 763 pp., $.50, *Chandos Classics*, advertised in the *New-York Times* on Aug. 8 as "Now ready."

216 HENRY W. LONGFELLOW *Poetical Works.* Cr 8vo. 1/0 sewed, 1/6 cloth July 4 (*Ath*)

Chandos Classics No. 2. This has 640 pp. Warne issued it in *Chandos Poets*, Cr 8vo, 627 pp., portrait, illustrations, 6/0, listed in the *Reader* on Nov. 24, 1866, and the third edition, the same, 7/6, was advertised in the *Spect* on June 20, 1868, as "Now ready." It was reissued in *Chandos Classics*, new edition, Cr 8vo, 1/0 sewed, 1/6 cloth, advertised in the *Spect* on July 20, 1872, 672 pp., and listed by *PC* as published July 16–Aug. 1, 656 pp. The first edition was *Ballads and Other Poems*, issued by John Owen, Cambridge, 1842, 132 pp., yellow boards, reviewed in the *Knickerbocker* for Feb. 1842. Carey & Hart, Philadelphia, issued the *Poetical Works*, 1845, 23 cm., 387 pp., portrait, called the first collected edition, with all previous poems plus 8 additional ones. It was deposited Oct. 29. Harper & Brothers, New York, issued the complete poetical works in 1846, 8vo, 117 pp., $.50, listed in the *United States Magazine* for July 1846. In England *Longfellow's Ballads, Poems and Drama* were issued by Edward Moxon, London, 1843, from American sheets. T. Allman, London, issued the poetical works, 1845, 13 cm., 192 pp., frontispiece. George Routledge & Co., London, issued the *Poetical Works*, 1850, 13.5 cm., 399 pp., at 2/0 cloth, advertised in the *Ath* on Feb. 9 as "Now ready" and issued editions in 1853, 65, 68 and in at least 8 later years.

217 CHARLOTTE RIDDELL *George Geith of Fen Court.* New edition. 12mo. 2/0 boards July 11 (*Spect*)

Companion Library No. 34. This has 423 pp. The first edition was issued by Tinsley Brothers, London, 3 vols., 1864, p 8vo, 31/6, by F. G. Trafford, listed in the *Ath* on Dec. 10, 1864. They issued the second edition, 3 vols., advertised in the *Spect* on Jan. 28, 1865, as "On Feb. 1"; and issued the

third edition, 3 vols., advertised in the *Spect* on Mar. 18, 1865, as "This day." They issued it in a new edition, p 8vo, 469 pp., 6/0, listed in the *Spect* on Sept. 23, 1865. Skeet, London, issued it in 1868, 8vo, 2/0 sewed, listed in the *Spect* on June 13. The first American edition was issued by T. O. H. P. Burnham, Boston, etc., 1865, 12mo, 555 pp., $2.00 cloth, by Trafford, advertised in the *New-York Times* on Mar. 4 as "Now ready" and listed in *ALG&PC* (fortnightly) on Mar. 15. It was reissued as *Companion Library* No. 57, new edition, 12mo, 2/0 boards, by Riddell, listed in the *Ath* on Apr. 17, 1875.

218 LORD BYRON *Poetical Works.* Cr 8vo. 1/0 sewed, 1/6 cloth Aug. 22 (*Ath*)

Chandos Classics No. 3. This has 640 pp. Warne issued it in 1869, large Cr 8vo, portraits, illustrations, 3/6 cloth, advertised in the *Spect* on Sept. 4; and advertised there on Oct. 9, large Cr 8vo, 640 pp., 1/0 stiff wrappers, 2/0 cloth. Warne issued it at 7/6, listed in the *Spect* on Nov. 28, 1874; they advertised it in *Chandos Classics*, 1/6 sewed, 2/0 cloth, in the *Ath* on July 24, 1875. The first edition of the collected works was issued by John Murray, London, 8 vols., Fcp 8vo, 56/0, vols. 1–4 listed in the *Edinburgh Review* as publisher Mar. 10–June 10, 1815; vol. 5, Sept.–Dec. 1815; vol. 6, Nov. 1817–Mar. 1818; vol. 8, Jan.–Apr. 1820. Murray issued the poems, 5 vols., 35/0, in Jan. 1821, given by the *Eng Cat*. In the United States the *Poetical Works* was issued by Cummings & Hilliard, Boston, listed in the *North American Review* (quarterly) for Oct. 1820 as "Lately published." *The Works*, 4 vols., 18mo, $5.00, published in New York, was listed in the same for Oct. 1820.

219 JANE PORTER *Thaddeus of Warsaw.* Cr 8vo. 0/6 sewed, 1/0 cloth Aug. 22 (*Ath*)

Notable Novels No. 7. The first edition was issued by T. N. Longman & O. Rees, Lon-

don, 4 vols., 1803, 17 cm., 14/0 boards, noticed in the *Critical Review* for Sept. 1803. They issued the second edition, the same, listed by the *Edinburgh Review* as published Apr. 18–July 7, 1804; and they issued the third edition, the same, revised, listed as published July 6–Oct. 10, 1805. They issued the 11th edition, 3 vols., 18/0, advertised in the *Spect* on Dec. 25, 1830 as "This day." It was issued in *Colburn and Bentley's Standard Novels* No. 4, revised and corrected, 1831, 440 pp. In the United States it was issued by Lemuel Blake, Boston, 2 vols., 1809, 20.5 cm., the first American edition from the fourth English edition. It was also issued by I. Riley, Flatbush, 4-vols.-in-2, 1809, 18 cm.
See 1874

220 FLORENCE WILFORD *Nigel Bartram's Ideal.* 12mo. 1/0 sewed   Sept. 12 (*Ath*)
Companion Library No. 35. This is 1869, probably the first edition. Warne issued it in their *Household Novels*, Cr 8vo, illustrated, 5/0, listed in the *Spect* on Nov. 12, 1870, and it was advanced to 6/0 cloth in Nov. 1872. They issued it in 1880, p 8vo, 2/6 boards, listed in the *Spect* on May 15, and issued it as *Companion Library* No. 134, 12mo, 2/0 boards, listed in the *Ath* on Apr. 21, 1883. The first American edition was issued by D. Appleton & Co., New York, 1871, 8vo, 126 pp., illustrated, $.50. Advertised in the *New-York Times* on May 20 as "This day" and listed in the *Nation* on June 8.

221 MISS C. E. DYSON *Bird-Keeping.* Fcp 8vo. Illustrated. 1/0 boards
Sept. 12 (*Ath*)
Country Library. This is the first edition. Warne issued a revised and enlarged edition, no date, 262 pp., at 1/6 picture boards and 3/6 with colored illustrations in the latter. The 3/6 was advertised in the *Ath* on Oct. 12, 1878, and the 1/6 was listed in the *Spect* on Apr. 5, 1879. the *Eng Cat*

gives an edition issued in 1884, illustrated, 1/0. Warne issued it in 1890, Fcp 8vo, 1/0 picture cover, and in Cr 8vo, colored plates at 2/6, advertised in the *TWed* on Mar. 7.

222 FLORENCE MARRYAT (MRS. ROSS CHURCH, later LEAN) *Love's Conflict.* [New edition.] 12mo. 2/0 boards
Sept. 19 (*Ath*)
Companion Library No. 36. The first edition was issued by Bentley, London, 3 vols., 1865, p 8vo, 31/6, listed in the *Ath* on Jan. 28. It was reissued, the same, in 1872, listed in the *Ath* on Apr. 13. I have a copy, a reissue in the *Companion Library*, no date, 17.4 cm., 432 pp., in yellow pictorial boards, printed in red, blue, and black, with the series title at the foot of the spine. It has the Warne imprint on front and Warne, Scribner, Welford & Armstrong, New York, on the title page. There are publisher's ads on the endpapers and back cover. I think it was issued in 1877, according to the lists in the endpaper ads, where the present series ends with No. 91. The first American edition was issued by A. K. Loring, Boston, advertised in the *New-York Times* on May 12, 1866, $.75, in their *Railway Library.* This was the authoress's first novel, submitted to Bentley as "The Struggle for Life." His reader, Miss Jewsbury, submitted 10 pp. of suggestions for improving vol. 3.

223 FLORENCE MARRYAT (MRS. ROSS CHURCH, later LEAN) *Woman Against Woman.* [New edition.] 12mo. 2/0 boards   Sept. 26 (*Ath*)
Companion Library No. 37. This is 1869 with 442 pp. The first edition was issued by Bentley, London, 3 vols., 1865, p 8vo, 31/6, listed in the *Ath* on Dec. 23, 1865. It was reissued in this series in 1872, listed in the *Ath* on Apr. 13. The first American edition was issued by A. K. Loring, Boston, listed in the *Nation* on Apr. 2, 1866.

224 FLORENCE MARRYAT (MRS. ROSS CHURCH, later LEAN) *For Ever and Ever.* [New edition.] 12mo. 2/0 boards Sept. 26 (*Ath*)

Companion Library No. 40. This is 1869. The first edition was issued by Bentley, London, 3 vols., 1866, p 8vo, 31/6, listed in the *Ath* on Sept. 22. It was reissued in this series, the same, in 1877, in May I think. The first American edition was issued by A. K. Loring, Boston, listed in *Godey's Lady's Book* for May 1867.

225 FLORENCE MARRYAT (MRS. ROSS CHURCH, later LEAN) *The Confessions of Gerald Estcourt.* [New edition.] 12mo. 2/0 boards Oct. 3 (*Ath*)

Companion Library No. 38. There is a known copy, dated 1868, and the *BM* gives 1869. The first edition was issued by Bentley, London, 3 vols., 1867, p 8vo, 31/6, listed in the *Ath* on Aug. 3 and in the *Spect* on Aug. 10. The first American edition was issued by Loring, Boston, 1867, listed in *ALG&PC* (fortnightly) on Sept. 3. The authoress was the sixth daughter of Frederick Marryat.

226 FLORENCE MARRYAT (MRS. ROSS CHURCH, later LEAN) *"Too Good for Him."* 12mo. 2/0 boards Oct. 17 (*Ath*)

Companion Library No. 39. This has 444 pp. A known copy has no date, whereas the *BM* and the *U Cat* give 1868. The first edition was issued by Bentley, London, 3 vols., 1865, p 8vo, 31/6, listed in the *Ath* on June 3. They issued the second edition, 3 vols., advertised in the *Spect* on Aug. 26, 1865, as ready. The first American edition was issued by A. K. Loring, Boston, 1865, listed in the *Nation* on Nov. 1.

227 SIR WALTER SCOTT *Poetical Works.* Cr 8vo. 1/0 sewed, 1/6 cloth Oct. 17 (*Ath*) *Chandos Classics* No. 4. This has 640 pp. Warne issued it also in *Chandos Poets*, large Cr 8vo, portrait, illustrated, 7/6, adver-

tised in the *Spect* on July 15, 1871, but possibly issued earlier. The same ad gave the *Popular Poet's Edition*, small Cr 8vo, portrait, illustrated, 3/6. *Ballads and Lyrical Pieces* was issued by Longmans, London, 1806, 8vo, reviewed in the *Critical Review* for Dec. 1806. *The Poetical Works of Walter Scott, Esq.: Now First Collected* was issued in 12 vols. by Constable, Edinburgh; Hurst, London, Fcp 8vo, portrait, 72/0, listed by the *Edinburgh Review* as published July–Oct. 1819. It was issued in 10 vols., 8vo, 120/0, listed in the same as published Aug.–Nov. 1820.

228 HENRY C. ADAMS *Short Tales for Sunday Reading.* 18mo. Illustrated. 1/6 cloth Oct. 17 (*Ath*)

Eighteenpenny Juveniles. The *BM* gives *Tales for Sunday Reading*, 12 parts (1868). It consists of *Sundays at Encombe* (see 1865) and *The Judges of Israel* (see 1866). *The Encombe Stories; or, Tales for Sunday Reading*, 1868, 12mo, 3/6, stories from Adam to Saul, was listed in the *Spect* on June 13, 1868. A new edition of *Tales for Sunday Reading*, 18mo, in packets, 1/6, was issued in 1870 according to the *Eng Cat.*

229 MARY M. BUTT, later SHERWOOD *The History of Susan Gray.* 18mo. Illustrated. 1/0 cloth Oct. 31 (*Ath*)

Shilling Juveniles. It was issued by Hazard, Bath, in 1802, anonymous. The *BM* gives a new edition, by a clergyman, issued by J. White, Wisbech, 1815, 164 pp. The *Eng Cat* gives Houlston, London, 18mo, 1/6, circa 1820, and they issued it, 18mo, at 1/0 in 1857. The present edition was reissued by Warne in 1871, given by the *Eng Cat*. In the United States it was issued by E. Bacon, Philadelphia, 1825, by a clergyman, 24mo, 144 pp.; and by Shirley & Edwards, Portland, 1825, 14 cm., 174 pp.

230 GEORGE ARMATAGE *The Horseowner and Stableman's Companion.* Fcp 8vo. 1/o boards Nov. 7 (*Ath*)

This is the first edition, 1869, 16.5 cm., 120 pp., with the joint imprint of Scribner, Welford & Co., New York. The third edition, Fcp 8vo, 1/o, was listed in the *Bks* for Sept. 1890; the fifth edition was issued around 1904, 17 cm., 120 pp. The fourth and enlarged edition was advertised in the *TWEd* on Apr. 17, 1891.

231 HENRY F. WILKINSON *Modern Athletics.* Fcp 8vo. 1/o boards Nov. 7 (*Ath*)

Useful Books. This is the first edition, 1868, 17 cm., 120 pp.

232 MORDECAI C. COOKE *One Thousand Objects for the Microscope.* Fcp 8vo. Illustrated. 1/o boards Nov. 7 (*Ath*)

Country Library and Family Circle Books. This is the first edition, 1869, 17 cm., 123 pp. It was reissued, the same, in 1891, advertised in the *TWEd* on Sept. 11.

233 HENRY C. ADAMS *Falconshurst.* 16mo. Illustrated. 2/o cloth Nov. 7 (*Ath*)

2/o Large Type Books. This is a first edition, 1869, 156 pp. *Falconshurst; or, Meta's Birthday* was issued in *Home Circle Gift Books*, new edition, 12mo, illustrated, 2/o cloth, probably in Dec. 1873. There was a review in the *Ath* on Jan. 31, 1874, of *The Falcon Family; or, Meta and Willy: Tale of Two Birthdays.* The *Eng Cat* gives this new edition of *Falconshurst* as issued in 1873. Actually *Gannet Island; or, Willie's Birthday*, was issued in 1873. Actually *Gannet Island; or, Willie's Birthday*, was issued in *Home Circle Gift Books*, listed in the *Ath* on Oct. 18, 1873, and thus *The Falcon Family* consisted of the two birthday books.

234 WILLIAM E. COGHLAN *St. George's Key.* 12mo. Illustrated. 2/o cloth Nov. 14 (*Ath*)

2/o Gift Books. This is the first edition, 1869, 240 pp. It was reissued in this series in 1869, advertised in the *Ath* on Nov. 27. It was issued in the *Incident and Adventure Library* in 1881, Fcp 8vo, illustrated, 2/o cloth, given by the *Eng Cat*; and it was placed in the *Daring and Doing Library*, Cr 8vo, illustrated, 1/6 cloth, in the 1890s.

235 JAMES S. BORLASE *Daring Deeds and Tales of Peril and Adventure.* Fcp 8vo. Illustrated. 2/6 cloth Nov. 14 (*Ath*)

2/o Gift Books. This is also given by the *Eng Cat.* It is possibly a reissue of *The Night Fossickers, and Other Australian Tales of Peril and Adventure* (see 1867). The present title was reissued in the *Daring and Adventure* (see 1867). The present title was reissued in the *Daring Deeds Library* in 1880, 12mo, illustrated, 2/6 cloth, given by the *Eng Cat*; and there was an edition in 1894, new edition, Cr 8vo, illustrated, 2/o, listed in *PC* on Nov. 17.

236 LOUISA L. GREENE *Filling Up the Chinks.* 12mo. 2/o cloth Nov. 21 (*Ath*)

This was also reviewed in the *Ath*, on Dec. 5, 1868, but I cannot place it in any of the myriad Warne series. It was issued as a 2/6 *Gift Book*, Fcp 8vo, illustrated, 2/6 cloth, advertised in the *Ath* on Nov. 27, 1869; it was shortly thereafter placed in the *Golden Links Series*, Square Fcp 8vo, illustrated, 2/6 cloth, and this edition was reissued, the tenth edition, advertised in the *Ath* on Dec. 4, 1875. It was again issued in the *Golden Links Series* in 1880, given by the *Eng Cat*, and it was issued in the *Bedford Library*, 12mo, illustrated, 1/6 cloth, listed in the *PC* on Oct. 5, 1895. In the United States it was issued by Dutton & Co., New York, 16mo, 232 pp. $1.00, listed in *Putnam's Monthly* as published Sept.–Nov. 1869.

237 ÉLISE DE PRESSENSÉ *Two Years of School Life.* Fcp 8vo. Illustrated. 2/6 cloth Nov. 21 (*Ath*)

2/6 Gift Books. This is the first English edition, translated from the French, edited by

Charlotte Yonge, 1869. The present edition has the joint imprint with Scribner, Welford & Co., New York. The second French edition was *Deux Ans au Lycée*, Paris, 1868, 340 pp. Warne issued a new edition, Cr 8vo, illustrated, 2/0, listed in *PC* on Feb. 15, 1896.

238 LAURA VALENTINE *Warne's Home Annual.* Imp 8vo. Illustrated. 1/0 sewed Nov. 28 (*Ath*)

This has no date, 25 cm.

239 LAURA VALENTINE *Land Battles from Hastings to Inkermann.* Fcp 8vo. Illustrated. 2/6 cloth Dec. 5 (*Ath*)

2/6 Gift Books. This is also given by the *Eng Cat* and was reviewed in the *Ath* on Jan. 9, 1869. *Sea Fights and Land Battles (Alfred to Victoria)*, edited by Valentine, Cr 8vo, 5/0, 6/0, was listed in the *Spect* on Dec. 5, 1868. *Land Battles from Hastings to the War in Aoudan*, new edition, Cr 8vo, illustrated, 2/0, was issued in 1894, listed in *PC* on Nov. 17.

240 MRS. HENRY H.B. PAULL *Pride and Principle.* 18mo. Colored illustrations. 1/0 cloth Dec. 12 (*Ath*)

Shilling Juveniles. This is the first edition, 1869, 128 pp., colored frontispiece and an added title page, illustrated in color.

241 MRS. HENRY H.B. PAULL *Mary Elton.* 18mo. Colored illustrations. 1/0 cloth Dec. 12 (*Ath*)

Shilling Juveniles. This is the first edition, 1869.

242 GEORGE T. HOARE, ed. *Choice Readings; or, True Stories of Brave Deeds.* Fcp 8vo. 1/0 sewed (boards?) Dec. 26 (*Ath*)

See 1870, 81, 95 and *Dare and Endure*, 1866

243 J. T. AKERMAN *The Legal Guide, or Instructions to Landlords, Tenants, and Lodgers.* [New edition.] 12mo. 0/6 1868 (*Eng Cat*)

The first edition was issued by T. Pettitt & Co., London, 1855, 52 pp., reissued by them, 15th edition, revised (1864), 56 pp.

244 FRANCIS WALKINGHAME (FRANCIS WALKINGAME) *Walkinghame's Tutor's Assistant.* [New edition.] 12mo. 0/9 1868 (*Eng Cat*)

The first edition was printed for the author by D. Browne, London, 1751, 17 cm., 176 pp. *A New and Complete Master Key*, edited by C. Pearson, was issued by L. Nichols, London, 1816, 8vo, 244 pp., noticed in the *Critical Review* for July 1816. Rivingtons, etc., London, issued the 70th edition, improved by John Fraser, 2/0, advertised in the *Spect* on Jan. 23, 1830. It was issued by Armour & Ramsey, Montreal, 1837, and by Sadleir, New York and Boston, 1851.

245 ANONYMOUS *Warne's Ready Reckoner.* 18mo. 0/6 limp cloth 1868 (*Eng Cat*)

The Model Ready Reckoner, 18mo, 288 pp., 1/0, was listed in the *Spect* on Mar. 17, 1866, issued by Warne. The *U Cat* gives *Ready Reckoner*, no date, 24mo, 70 leaves; *Warne's Bijou Ready Reckoner*, 32mo, 156 pp. 0/6 cloth, was listed in the *PC* as published May 16–31, 1872. *Warne's Ready Reckoner*, 12mo, 0/6 was issued in 1875, given by the *Eng Cat*.

246 LAURA VALENTINE *Warne's Everlasting Victoria Primer.* 8vo. Illustrated. 1/0 cloth 1868 (*Eng Cat*)

This is the first edition, no date.

247 ANONYMOUS *Willie's Birthday.* [New edition.] 16mo. Illustrated. 1/6 cloth 1868 (*Eng Cat*)

Large Type Book for Children. A May 16, 1868, ad in the *Ath* said that this had already been issued. It was eventually placed in the *Round the Globe Library*, 12mo, colored frontispiece, 1/0 cloth. The first edition was issued by Smith, Elder & Co., London, 1857, 16mo, 2/6.

248 HOLME LEE (HARRIET PARR) *Tuflongbo's Life and Adventures*. Fcp 8vo. Illustrated. 2/6 cloth   1868 (*Eng Cat*)

2/6 Gift Books. This has a joint imprint with Scribner, Welford & Co., New York, 1868, 17 cm., 240 pp. The first edition was *Tuflongbo's Journey in Search of Ogres*, issued by Smith, Elder & Co., London, 1862, 19 cm., 240 pp., illustrated. The present edition was reissued by Warne in the *Illustrated Fairy Library* No. 5, 12mo, illustrated, 1/0 sewed, 1/6 cloth, listed by the *Bks* on Jan. 4, 1878; and it was reissued in this library in 1897, 12mo, 1/6 cloth, listed in *PC* on Sept. 11.

249 (ELIZABETH S. SHEPPARD) *Round the Fire. Six Stories*. [New edition.] 16mo. Illustrated. 2/0 cloth   1868 (*Eng Cat*)

2/0 Large Type Books. The first edition was issued by Smith, Elder & Co., London, 1856, 16mo, anonymous, 172 pp., illustrated, 2/6. This title and *Old Gingerbread* were issued by Robert Carter, New York, 1861, 16 cm., anonymous, 189, 93 pp., illustrated. Warne reissued the present edition in 1873, new edition, 12mo, 2/0 cloth, listed in the *Ath* on Oct. 18. Warne issued it in their *Birthday Series* in 1878 or 1879, 18mo, illustrated, 1/6 cloth. The *Eng Cat* gives 1/0, 1/6, 1878–79.

250 GERALDINE STEWART *The Laird's Return*. [New edition.] 18mo. 1/6 1868 (*Eng Cat*)

The first edition was issued by Hogg, London (1861), 16mo, illustrated, 2/0.

251 (ELIZABETH S. SHEPPARD) *Uncle Jack the Fault-Killer*. [New edition.] 16mo. Illustrated. 2/0 cloth   1868 (*Eng Cat*)

2/0 Large Type Books. The first edition was issued by Smith, Elder & Co., London,

1857, 16mo, anonymous, 2/6. It was issued in the United States by D. D. Merrill, St. Paul, no date, anonymous, 143 pp. Warne issued it in the *Birthday Series*, new edition, 18mo, illustrated, 1/6 cloth, in 1873, given by the *Eng Cat*.

252 CHARLES VINES *Mother and Child*. 12mo. 0/6   1868 (*Eng Cat*)

Useful Manuals. This is the first edition, 1868.

253 JOHN G. EDGAR *The Wars of the Roses*. [New edition.] Fcp 8vo. Illustrated. 2/6 cloth   1868 (*Eng Cat*)

2/6 Gift Books. This may be a reissue by Warne, as their lists seem to place it in 1866. The first edition was issued by W. Kent & Co., London, 1859, 17 cm., 432 pp., frontispiece, 5/0, advertised in the *Ath* on Dec. 18, 1858, and listed in the *Spect* on Jan. 8, 1859. The *BM* gives a duplicate of the preceding with a new title page, London (1860), *Stories of the Struggle of York and Lancester; or, The Wars of the Roses*. The *Eng Cat* gives *The Wars of the Roses*, C. H. Clarke, London, 1860, Fcp 8vo, 3/6. Warne issued it in the *Daring Deeds Library*, no date, 12mo, 291 pp., illustrated, 2/6 cloth, given by the *Eng Cat* as issued in 1880. Warne issued a new edition, Cr 8vo, illustrated, 2/0, listed in *PC* on Feb. 15, 1896. The first American edition was issued by Harper & Brothers, New York, 1859, 17.5 cm., 470 pp., illustrated, advertised in the *New-York Times* on June 17, $.60 muslin, as "This day."

254 ANONYMOUS *Fanny Lincoln*. 18mo. Colored frontispiece. 0/9 cloth   1868 (*Eng Cat*)

Ninepenny Juveniles. The first edition was issued by Knight & Son, London (1861), 18mo, 1/0. They reissued it in 1865, new edition, the same, listed in the *Reader* on May 20.

255 LADY ELEANOR FENN *Cobwebs to Catch Flies.* [New edition.] 18mo. Illustrated. o/9 cloth 1868 (*Eng Cat*)

Ninepenny Juveniles. The first edition was issued by J. Marshall & Co., London, 2 vols. (1783), anonymous. It was issued in the United States by Coale, Baltimore, revised and enlarged, 1825, 112 pp., colored illustrations. Warne issued it in 1870, new edition, 18mo, o/6 limp cloth sewed, given by the *Eng Cat.*

256 AUGUSTA BETHELL, later PARKER *Maude Latimer.* 18mo. Illustrated. 1/6 cloth 1868 (*Eng Cat*)

Eighteenpenny Juveniles. The first edition was issued by Smith, Elder & Co., London, 1863, Fcp 8vo, 202 pp., 4 illustrations, 3/6, listed in the *Reader* on Nov. 14, 1863, as "Just ready." Warne issued it in their *Birthday Series* in 1879, 18mo, illustrated, 1/6 cloth, given by the *Eng Cat.*

257 COUNT DE BUFFON *Buffon's Natural History Modernized.* 18mo. Colored illustrations. o/6 wrappers, 1/o, 1/6 cloth 1868 (*Eng Cat*)

National Books. This has the joint imprint of Scribner, Welford & Co., New York, 1869, 13 cm., 252 pp. It was reissued in this series, 2 plates, o/6 stiff wrappers, 1/o, 1/6 cloth with colored illustrations, advertised in the *Ath* on Nov. 15, 1879. The first edition was in 44 vols., Paris, 1749–1804, by Buffon and others. In England it was issued by T. Bell, London, 6 vols., 1775, *The Natural History of Animals, Vegetables, and Minerals.* It was also issued by William Creech, Edinburgh, 5 vols., 1780, *Natural History General and Particular*; and it was issued in London with the same title, 8 vols., 1781. There was a second edition issued by A. Strahan & T. Cadell, London, 9 vols., 1785, with the same title.

258 JOHN FOXE *The Book of Martyrs. Condensed.* 18mo. Colored illustrations. o/6 sewed, 1/o cloth 1868 (*Eng Cat*)

National Books. This has the joint imprint of Scribner, Welford & Co., New York, 1869, 13 cm., 252 pp. It was reissued in 1879, o/6 stiff wrappers with 2 plates and at 1/o, 1/6 cloth with colored plates, *National Books*, advertised in the *Ath* on Nov. 15. It was first issued in Latin in the 16th century. In English it was first issued by John Day, London, 1563, *Actes and Monuments*, complete. An abridgement of *The Book of Martyrs* was issued by Samuel Wood, New York, 1810, 21.5 cm., 603 pp., and had previously been issued in New York, 1794, 939 pp., illustrated. It was issued by Robert Carter & Brothers, New York, 1855, *The Acts and Monuments of the Church*, 26.5 cm., 1082 pp., illustrated.

259 MRS. HENRY H.B. PAULL *Tom Watson.* 32mo. o/6 cloth, colored frontispiece, o/4 sewed, plain 1868 (*Eng Cat*)

Sixpenny 32mo Books. This has no date and is the first edition. It was also issued in the *Home Library*, 32mo, colored frontispiece, 1/o cloth, in 1878, given by the *Eng Cat.* The *BM* gives this latter series as from the Christian Knowledge Society, London, 19 vols., 1878–84. The *U Cat* gives it the same, jointly with J. B. Young, New York, 1879–, 19 cm.

260 HOLME LEE (HARRIET PARR) *Tuflongbo and Little Content.* Fcp 8vo. Illustrated. 2/6 cloth 1868?

2/6 Gift Books. This is 1868, 17 cm., in grass-green morocco cloth (Wolff's copy). The first edition was *The Wonderful Adventures of Tuflongbo and His Elfin Company, in Their Journey with Little Content*, issued by Smith, Elder & Co., London, 1861, 18.5 cm., 245 pp., 8 illustrations by W. Sharpe, listed in the *British Quarterly Review* for Jan. 1862. It was issued in the *Illustrated*

Fairy Library No. 6, 244 pp., in 1877, listed by the *Bks* on Jan. 4, 1878, 1/o sewed, 1/6 cloth, and reissued in the *Fairy Library* in 1897, 12mo, 1/6 cloth, listed in *PC* on Sept. 11.

261 ANONYMOUS *Sabbath Talks About Jesus.* 18mo. Colored illustrations. 1/o cloth   1868?

Shilling Juveniles. The *Eng Cat* gives this as published in 1868, but it was listed in this series in an ad in the *Ath* on Dec. 9, 1865. The first edition was *Sabbath Talks with the Little Children About Jesus*, issued by J. P. Jewett, Boston, etc., 1856, 16 cm., anonymous, 139 pp., illustrated. The first English edition was issued by Knight & Son, London, (1860), 18mo, anonymous, illustrated, 1/o. Knight reissued it, a new edition, anonymous, 1/o, 1/4, illustrated, listed in the *Reader* on May 20, 1865.

262 ANONYMOUS *Sabbath Talks with Little Children.* 18mo. Colored illustrations. 1/o cloth   1868?

Shilling Juveniles. The remarks about the *Eng Cat* and the *Ath* in the preceding item also apply here. The first edition was probably *Sabbath Talks with Children on the Psalms of David*, Boston, 1860, probably issued by Jewett. The *BM* gives the title as I've given it, London (1861), anonymous, illustrated, probably issued by Knight & Son, London. The latter reissued it, a new edition, in 1865, 18mo, anonymous, illustrated, 1/o, 1/4, listed in the *Reader* on May 20.

263 ANNA L. BARBAULD *Hymns in Prose.* 18mo. Illustrated. o/9 cloth   1868?

Ninepenny Juveniles. This has 20 illustrations. The first edition was issued by J.

Johnson, London, 1781, 12mo, 1/o, *Hymns in Prose for Children*, noticed in the *Critical Review* (monthly) for Aug. 1781. It was issued in the United States by John Trumbull, Norwich, 1786. Warne reissued it, new edition, 18mo, illustrated, o/6 limp cloth sewed, in 1870, given by the *Eng Cat*.

264 DR. ISAAC WATTS *Divine and Moral Songs for Children.* 18mo. Illustrated. o/9 cloth   1868?

Ninepenny Juveniles. This has 50 illustrations and is probably undated. Warne reissued it in 1869, 16mo, illustrated, 1/o cloth, listed in the *Ath* on Mar. 6; they reissued it in 1870, 18mo, 50 illustrations, o/6 limp cloth sewed, given by the *Eng Cat*. The first edition was issued by M. Lawrence, London, 1715, *Divine Songs, Attempted in Easy Language; for the Use of Children*, 15.5 cm., 49 pp. *Select Poems and Short Essays in Prose from Dr. Watts* was issued by Blamire, London, in 1783, 12mo, 3/o, listed in the *Critical Review* (monthly) for Sept. *Dr. Watts' Hymns and Moral Songs for the Use of Children* was issued by J. Marshall & Co., London, in 1785, revised and altered, small 12mo, o/6, noticed in the *Critical Review* for Jan. 1786. It was issued in the United States with the original title, sold by B. Franklin & D. Hall, Philadelphia, 1750, 13.9 cm., 41 pp., the 12th edition, printed in London and reprinted in Philadelphia.

265 ANONYMOUS *Home Duties.* 18mo. Colored frontispiece. o/9 cloth   1868?

Ninepenny Juveniles. This is the first edition, with the joint imprint of Scribner, Welford & Co., New York, 1869, 15 cm., 103 pp.

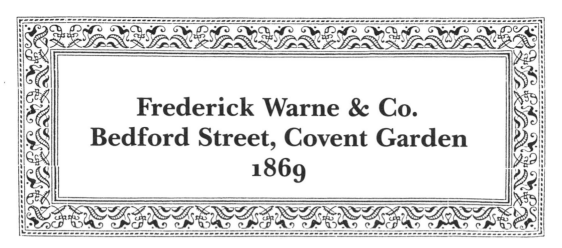

Frederick Warne & Co.
Bedford Street, Covent Garden
1869

266 ANONYMOUS *The Arabian Nights'
Entertainments.* New Edition. Cr 8vo.
1/0 sewed, 1/6 cloth   Feb. 27 (*Ath*)

Chandos Classics No. 5. This is 1869, 632
pp., a reissue of the Warne new edition of
1865, Cr 8vo, illustrated, 5/0 cloth, the
present issue without the illustrations. It is
edited by G. F. Townsend, revised for family reading, listed in the *Reader* on Sept.
30, 1865. F. J. Harvey Darton gives the
first translation as Galland, 1704–17, and
the *U Cat* gives A. Bell, London, 4 vols.-in-
2, 1706, 17 cm., illustrated. Longmans,
London, issued a new edition, corrected,
4 vols., 1798, the Galland translation,
amended and greatly enlarged from the
Paris edition in 4 vols. of 1786, noticed in
the *Critical Review* (monthly) for Nov.
1799. A translation by Edward Forster in 5
vols. was issued by Miller, London, 1802,
8vo, illustrated, 60/0 boards, reviewed in
the *Critical Review* for Feb. 1803; this edition was issued, revised and corrected
with additions, notes by G. M. Bussey, by
Thomas, London, 10 parts, 8vo, 24 illustrations, in 1839. It was issued by Knight &
Co., London, in parts in 1838, 39, translated and arranged for family reading by
E. W. Lane, from the second London edition, illustrated by Harvey; this edition
was issued by Harpers, New York, in 12
parts in 1848, 49 and also in 2 vols. The
U Cat gives the first American edition as issued by H. & P. Rice, etc., Baltimore, 2
vols., 1794, 17.5 cm., C. S. Francis & Co.,

New York, issued it in 3 vols., 18mo, vol. 1
noticed in the *Merchants' Magazine* for
Aug. 1847 and 3 vols. noticed in Jan.
1848. Warne issued a new edition, p 8vo,
0/6 sewed, as *Notable Novels* No. 145, the
Townsend issue, 224 pp., listed in the *Bks*
for Dec. 1890.

267 (ANNA B. WARNER) *The Howards of
Glen Luna.* Cr 8vo. 0/6 sewed, 1/0 cloth
June (*Bks*)

Notable Novels No. 8. This is 1869. The first
edition was *Dollars and Cents* by Amy
Lothrop (Anna Warner), issued by G. P.
Putnam, New York, 1852, 2 vols., 19 cm.,
in brown, blue, or purple cloth with either
plain yellow endpapers or buff with ads. It
was deposited May 3 and advertised in the
New York Daily Times on Apr. 21 as "At
once" and advertised in *Lit W* on May 8 as
"Next week." They issued the fourth edition, 2 vols., $1.50, advertised in the *New
York Daily Times* on July 12, 1852. The first
English edition was issued by James Nisbet, etc., London, 1852, *Glen Luna* by
Lothrop, Cr 8vo, 464 pp., 6/0 cloth, advertised as "This day" and listed in the *Ath* on
July 10. It was also issued by Thomas Nelson & Sons, London and Edinburgh,
1852, 17 cm., anonymous, 521 pp., 3/6
cloth, listed in the *Ath* on Dec. 11, 1852,
Grace Howard and the Family at Glen Luna.
It was also issued by George Routledge
& Co., London, 1853, illustrated, 1/6
boards, 2/0 cloth, as *Speculation* by Amy

Lothrop, deposited Feb. 18 and listed in the *Ath* on Feb. 12. It was issued by Clarke, Beeton & Co., London, in 1853, with the original title, 1/6 boards, 2/0 cloth, advertised on Feb. 12, the ad stating that they were paying the authoress for it.

268 ALEXANDER C. EWALD *The Civil Service Text-Book of Précis.* 12mo.
1/0 limp cloth   June 19 (*Spect*)

I suspect that this is an abridgment of *A Guide to the Civil Service*, by Henry White, revised by Ewald, issued by Warne, 1867, 8th edition. They issued the ninth edition, Cr 8vo, 2/6 cloth, advertised in the *Ath* on May 16, 1868; they issued the 10th edition, 1869, Fcp 8vo, 2/6 cloth, advertised in the *Spect* on Feb. 6; and they issued the 13th edition, completely rewritten by Ewald, in 1881, 209 pp., 1/0 boards, 1/6 cloth, "On our table" in the *Ath* on Oct. 29, 1881. I think the first edition may have been issued by P. S. King, London. The second edition was *Guide to the Civil Service Examinations*, London, 1858; King issued *Guide to Civil Service as to Appointments*, new edition, 1859, p 8vo, 2/6 by Henry White.

269 REUBEN & SHOLTO PERCY (THOMAS BYERLEY & JOSEPH ROBERTSON) *The Percy Anecdotes.*
Vol. 1 [New edition.] Fcp 8vo.
1/0 boards   Aug. (*Bks*)

Chandos Library. Vol. 2 was issued in Sept. 1869. This is a cheaper edition of the 2 vols. issued in this library in Oct. 1868. 2 vols., 3/6 cloth each, preface by John Timbs, vol. 1 in Sept. and vol. 2 in Nov. 1868. I have a copy of vol. 2 of the present edition, no date, with the joint imprint of Scribner, Welford & Co., New York, 17.5 cm., pp. (391)–587, in double columns, printed verbatim from the original. It is in buff boards, printed in red and black with 4 portraits on the front and with "Chandos Library" on the front. There are publisher's ads on the endpapers and

on 2 leaves at the back. I think the first edition was in 41 monthly parts and 20 vols., issued by T. Boys, London, 1820–23, given by the *U Cat*, 14 cm., portraits. Part 14, 2/6, was listed in the London *Times* on Jan. 3, 1821, as "On Jan. 1"; and part 35 at 2/6 was listed by the *Edinburgh Review* as published June–Sept., 1822. The issue is confusing because both the *Eng Cat* and the *U Cat* give 20 vols. as published by J. Cumberland, London, 1821–23, in the *Eng Cat* and 1820–26 in the *U Cat.*, 13.5 cm., frontispieces (portraits). The *U Cat* says Cumberland issued it in 41 monthly parts and that vols. 5–7 of the 20 vols. had the imprint of T. Boys, 1820–21. It was issued in 1887 by Warne, *Chandos Classics* Nos. 123–126, 4 vols., Cr 8vo, 1/6 sewed, 2/0 cloth each, with the introduction by Timbs, advertised in the *Ath* on Apr. 2. It was issued in the United States by William B. Gilley, New York, 20 vols., 1821–22, 13.5 cm., illustrated. J. & J. Harper, New York, issued a revised edition, to which was added a collection of American anecdotes, 8vo, 240 pp., listed in the *North American Review* for Oct. 1832.

270 ANONYMOUS *Handbook of Besique.*
32mo. Illustrated. 0/6 cloth   Aug.?

Illustrated Bijou Books No. 24. This is the first edition, reviewed in the *Ath* on Sept. 11, 1869.

271 FLORENCE MARRYAT (MRS. ROSS CHURCH, later LEAN) *Nelly Brooke.*
New edition. 12mo. 2/0 boards,
2/6 half red roan   Oct. 16 (*Ath*)

Companion Library No. 41. This is 1869. I have a copy, a reissue in the *Companion Library*, no date, with the Warne imprint on the front cover and the joint imprint with Scribner, Welford & Armstrong, New York, 17.5 cm., 444 pp., in yellow pictorial boards, printed in red, green, and black, with the series title at the foot of the spine. There are publisher's ads on the endpapers and a commercial ad on the back cover. I date it as 1874 from the lists on the endpapers. The first edition was issued by A. K. Loring, Boston, 1868, 255 pp., $.75 paper, listed in *ALG&PC* (fortnightly) on July 15. The first English edition was issued by Bentley, London, 3 vols., 1868, 20 cm., 31/6, listed in the *Ath* on Sept. 26. Wolff's copy of the Loring issue is in pinkish brown wrappers, lettered in black, with ads on the inside and back covers.

272 ELIZA COOK *The Poetical Works of Eliza Cook.* Complete edition. Cr 8vo. 1/6 sewed, 2/o cloth   Oct. 30 (*Spect*)

Chandos Classics No. 6. This has the joint imprint with Scribner, Welford & Co., New York (preface 1869), 19 cm., 624 pp. Warne issued *Poems* in the *Chandos Poets*, Cr 8vo, portrait, 7/6 cloth, listed in the *Spect* on Oct. 30, 1869; and they issued it at 3/6, with the preface, listed in the *Spect* on Nov. 13, 1869; the 3/6 was reissued, listed in the *Spect* on Sept. 24, 1870. The *BM* gives *Poems*, second series, as issued by Simpkin, Marshall, London, 1845, 275 pp. The *Eng Cat* gives *Poems*, vol. 1, 7/6; vols. 2–4, 12mo, 5/o each, Simpkin, Marshall, 1846–53. In the United States the complete poems was issued by U. Hunt, Philadelphia, 1845, 288 pp., illustrated, and there was a second edition, 1848, New York.

273 (SUSAN WARNER & ANNA WARNER) *Say and Seal.* [New edition.] 12mo. 2/o boards, 2/6 half red roan Nov. 6 (*Ath*)

Companion Library No. 42. Warne issued this in the *Star Series* No. 13, 1/6 sewed, 2/o cloth, in 1875 for the sewed edition, advertised in the *Ath* on Apr. 17 as "Now ready," and in Apr. and May 1876 for the cloth issues. It was issued by arrangement with James Nisbet, London, who issued them in their *Golden Ladder Series*. The Warne sewed issue was 16.2 cm., in gray wrappers cut flush, decorated in red,

green, and black and printed in blue, with gray endpapers, and had the series title on the title page, front cover, and spine. The publishing history of this work is bewildering, and I certainly do not have the definitive record. This is in large part due to Bentley's advertising department being in complete disarray. *BAL* gives the first edition as issued by Bentley, London, 1860, 17 cm., anonymous, 746 pp., frontispiece, in lavender cloth, with green endpapers, published Mar. 6 according to Bentley's records and listed in the *Ath* on Mar. 10. *BAL* also gives a library edition with 6 illustrations, published Mar. 15, 1860, listed in the Ath on Mar. 10. *BAL* states that Bentley printed a third edition of 2,500 copies but did not issue it; they sold the copies and plates to C. H. Clarke, London, on Apr. 3, 1860. Clarke issued it in the *Parlour Library* No. 211, Fcp 8vo, 1/6 boards, listed in the *Ath* on Apr. 28, 1860. Warne editions were listed in *PC* on Nov. 15, 1860; Dec. 30, 1871; Dec. 8, 1874; May 1, 1875; and Nov. 3, 1879. I now give the Bentley ads as they appeared in the periodicals. He advertised in the *Ath* on Dec. 10, 1859, Fcp 8vo, illustrated, 2/6 boards; Cr 8vo, illustrated, 5/o, as "Just ready" and listed Dec. 17. He advertised it as *Bentley's Standard Novels* in the *Saturday Review* on Mar. 31, 1860, 3/o, and listed it as such in *PC* as published Mar. 1–15, 3/o boards, 7/6, illustrated; he listed it as such in the *Bks* as published Apr. 26–May 16, 2/6 boards, 3/6. Sadleir does not give this as ever issued in this series! It was advertised in the *Ath* on Mar. 3, 1860, Cr 8vo, illustrated, 7/6; 3/o boards, as "On Mar. 5," and advertised on Mar. 10 as "Just published," and listed on Mar. 10. It was advertised on Mar. 17, 20th thousand, illustrated, 3/o, and on Mar. 24 as the 4th thousand, library edition, 7/6. It was advertised on May 5 as the 17th thousand, 2/6, 7/6, as "This day." The first American edition was issued by J. B. Lippincott & Co., Philadelphia, 2 vols., 1860, 19 cm., $2.00 in purple or brown cloth, with pale buff endpapers with ads. It is anonymous, but the preface is signed by Elizabeth Wetherell (Susan Warner) and Amy Lothrop (Anna Warner). It was deposited on Mar. 15 and listed in *APC&LG* on Mar. 31. A *Harper's Weekly* ad of Apr. 21 stated the 30,000 copies of the English edition had already been sold.

274 CATHERINE D. BELL *Sydney Stuart.* Fcp 8vo. Illustrated. 2/6 cloth Nov. 13 (*Ath*)

2/6 Gift Books. This has no date, 248 pp. The first edition was issued by Edmonston & Douglas, Edinburgh, etc., 1856, 309 pp., at 4/6. The first American edition was issued by A.D.F. Randolph, New York, 1857, 15.5 cm., 333 pp., frontispiece. Warne issued it in their *Star Series* No. 16, 16mo, 1/0 sewed, listed in the *Spect* on Apr. 22, 1876.

275 MRS. JEROME MERCIER *Christabel Hope.* Fcp 8vo. Illustrated. 2/6 cloth Nov. 27 (*Ath*)

2/6 Gift Books. This is the first edition (1869).

276 ANONYMOUS *Tales for Boys and Girls.* Fcp 8vo. Illustrated. 2/6 cloth Nov. 27 (*Ath*)

2/6 Gift Books. This is also given by the *Eng Cat*, but otherwise I cannot trace it. It was placed in the *Golden Links Series* in the 1870s, illustrated, 2/6 cloth.

277 HANNAH R. GELDART *Mary Leigh.* 12mo. Illustrated. 2/0 cloth Nov. 27 (*Ath* ad)

2/0 Gift Books. This is the first edition, no date. Warne issued it in their *Home Circle Gift Books* in 1882, 12mo, illustrated, 2/0 cloth, given by the *Eng Cat*. They issued it in the *Star Series* No. 120, in 1891, 16mo, 1/6 sewed, 2/0 cloth, listed in *PC* on Apr. 25.

278 HOLME LEE (HARRIET PARR) *Poor Match.* Fcp 8vo. Illustrated. 2/6 cloth Nov. 27 (*Ath* ad)

2/6 Gift Books. The first edition was issued by Smith, Elder & Co., London, 1863, *The True History of Poor Match*, 18.3 cm., 219 pp., illustrated by Walter Crane, 3/6 cloth, listed in the *Spect* on Dec. 5, 1863. Warne issued a duplicate of the Smith, Elder edition, no date, with a new title page and frontispiece, *Poor Match*. Warne issued it in 1868, 12mo. 2/0, listed in the *Spect* on Feb. 1, and issued it in the *Incident and Adventure Library* as *My Dog Match*, in the 1870s, 17 cm., 219 pp., illustrated, 2/0 cloth. Smith, Elder issued the second edition, 1864, frontispiece and 4 plates by Walter Crane, purple cloth, 4 pp. of ads. This was the first book illustrated by Crane.

279 AUNT LOUISA (LAURA VALENTINE) *The Child's Finger-Post.* 18mo. Illustrated. 1/6 cloth Nov. 27 (*Ath* ad)

Eighteenpenny Juveniles. This is also given by the *Eng Cat*, but otherwise I cannot trace it. Warne placed it in *Little Books for Little People* before 1879, square Cr 8vo, illustrated, 2/0 cloth.

280 ANONYMOUS *Birthday Stories for the Young.* 18mo. Illustrated. 1/6 cloth Nov. 27 (*Ath* ad)

Eighteenpenny Juveniles. This is also given by the *Eng Cat*, but otherwise I cannot trace it.

281 ANONYMOUS *Birthday Tales for the Young.* 18mo. Illustrated. 1/6 cloth Nov. 27 (*Ath* ad)

Eighteenpenny Juveniles. I cannot trace this.

282 CAROLINE HADLEY *Children's Sayings.* 16mo. Illustrated. 2/0 cloth Nov. 27 (*Ath* ad)

2/0 Large Type Books. Warne issued it in 1868, fourth edition, 2/0, listed in the *Spect* on Jan. 18, 1868. They issued it in the

Birthday Series in 1873, new edition, 18mo, illustrated, 1/6 cloth; and in 1885, 12mo, 1/6, given by the *Eng Cat*. The first edition was issued by Smith, Elder & Co., London, 1862, 16mo, 2/6, noticed in the *Spect* on Dec. 27, 1862. The first American edition was issued by Sheldon & Co., New York, 1863, 18 cm., 160 pp., illustrated, $.90, advertised in the *New-York Times* on Nov. 19 as "Nearly ready."

283 (ELIZABETH S. SHEPPARD)
Old Gingerbread and the Schoolboys.
16mo. Illustrated. 2/0 cloth   Nov. 27
(*Ath* ad)

2/0 Large Type Books. This was probably issued with the joint imprint of Scribner, Welford & Co., New York, no date. Warne also issued it in the *Round the Globe Library* in 1873, 12mo, colored frontispiece, 1/0 cloth, listed in the *Ath* on Oct. 18. The first edition was issued by Smith, Elder & Co., London, 1858, 17 cm., anonymous, 120 pp., 4 colored illustrations, 3/0, listed in the *Spect* on Oct. 2. The first American edition was issued by the General Protestant Episcopal Sunday School Union, and Church Book Society, New York, 1861, 15.5 cm., anonymous, 108 pp., illustrated.

284 LADY B.C.G.   ***Mrs. Gordon's Household.***   18mo. Colored illustrations. 1/0 cloth   Nov. 27 (*Ath* ad)

Shilling Juveniles. This is the first edition, no date, 128 pp.

285 TOM HOOD, THE ELDER   ***Tom Hood's Comic Readings in Prose and Verse.***
2 vols. Fcp 8vo. 1/0 boards each
Dec. 4 (*Ath*)

This is a first edition, thus, no date, 17 cm., with *Warne's Useful Books* on the cover. *The Comic Poems of Thomas Hood* was issued by Edward Moxon, London, in 1867, edited by Samuel Lucas with a preface by Thomas Hood the younger, listed in *Notes & Queries* on May 4.

286 ANONYMOUS   ***The Earth We Live On.***
12mo. Colored frontispiece. 1/0 cloth
1869 (*Eng Cat*)

Round the Globe Library No. 2. I cannot trace this.

287 ANONYMOUS   ***The Italian Boy and Industrial Men of Note.***   12mo. Colored frontispiece. 1/0 cloth   1869 (*Eng Cat*)

Round the Globe Library No. 3. I cannot trace this.

288 PROFESSOR COWPER, ET AL.
Home Teachings in Science.   12mo.
Colored frontispiece. 1/0 cloth
1869 (*Eng Cat*)

Round the Globe Library No. 4. This has no date and 158 pp., with diagrams, and has the series title on the cover. It is the first edition. There was a reissue in the 1890s with the series title on the spine.

289 ANONYMOUS   ***Chat in the Playroom, and Life at a Farmhouse.***   12mo. Colored frontispiece. 1/0 cloth   1869 (*Eng Cat*)

Round the Globe Library No. 5. I cannot trace this.

290 ANONYMOUS   ***Our Ponds and Our Fields.***   12mo. Colored frontispiece. 1/0 cloth   1869 (*Eng Cat*)

Round the Globe Library No. 6. I cannot trace this.

291 ANONYMOUS   ***Brave Bobby, Peter and His Pony, etc.***   12mo. Colored frontispiece. 1/0 cloth   1869 (*Eng Cat*)

Round the Globe Library No. 7. I cannot trace this.

292 ANONYMOUS   ***The Peasants of the Alps; Passe-Tout, or The New Fishing Smack.***   12mo. Colored frontispiece. 1/0 cloth   1869 (*Eng Cat*)

Round the Globe Library No. 8. I cannot trace this. *The New Fishing-Smack* was in the

Crofton Series of o/9 Juveniles, Demy 18mo, colored frontispiece, o/9 cloth, before 1880.

293 ANONYMOUS *Frances Meadows, Traits of Character, etc.* 12mo. Colored frontispiece. 1/o cloth 1869 (*Eng Cat*)
Round the Globe Library No. 9. I cannot trace this.

294 ANONYMOUS *Uncle John's Adventures and Travels.* 12mo. Colored frontispiece. 1/o cloth 1869 (*Eng Cat*)
Round the Globe Library No. 10. I cannot trace this.

295 (ELIZABETH S. SHEPPARD) *Unica.* 16mo. Illustrated. 1/6 cloth 1869 (*U Cat*)
Large Type Book for Children. This is 1869, with 121 pp. The first edition was issued by Smith, Elder & Co., London, 1858. It was issued in the United States by Robert Carter & Brothers, New York, 1865, 15.5 cm., 106 pp., illustrated. It was issued by Warne in *Round the Globe Library*, 12mo, colored frontispiece, 1/o cloth, in 1871, given by the *Eng Cat.*

296 CLARA REEVE & HORACE WALPOLE *The Old English Baron and the Castle of Otranto.* Cr 8vo. o/6 sewed, 1/o cloth 1869?
Notable Novels No. 9. This is 21.5 cm., with 107 pp. The first edition of the first title was printed for the author by W. Keymer, Colchester, 1777, as *The Champion of Virtue*, 190 pp., frontispiece; and the second edition was issued by E. & C. Dilly, London, 1778, 232 pp., frontispiece. The first American edition was probably issued by Stewart A. Cochran, Philadelphia, 1797, 17 cm., 213 pp. The first edition of the second title was issued by T. Lownds, London, 1765, translated by William Marshall from the original Italian of Onuphrio Muralto, 200 pp. The second edition was by Walpole and was issued by William Bathoe & T. Lownds, London, 1765, 200 pp. It was also issued by J. Hoey, etc., Dublin, 1765, 17 cm., 146 pp., by Muralto. The first American edition was probably issued by the Shakespeare-Gallery, New York, 1801 (with *Lothaire* by Harriet Lee), 18 cm., 216 pp. Warne reissued it in *Notable Novels* at o/6 sewed, 107 pp., in 1871, listed by *PC* as published Jan. 1–15; and reissued it again in the series at o/6 sewed, listed by the *Bks* as published in Oct. 1887. See 1874, *The Children of the Abbey, etc.*

297 ANNA M. PORTER *The Hungarian Brothers.* Cr 8vo. o/6 sewed, 1/o cloth 1869?
Notable Novels No. 10. This has 126 pp. in double columns. I've put this title and the preceding title here because of their nos. in the series. The first edition was issued by Longmans, London, 1807, 3 vols., 12mo, 13/6, in May. They issued the third edition, 3 vols., 12mo, 16/6, listed in the *Critical Review* (London) for Aug. 1814. The first American edition was issued by Bradford & Inskeep, Philadelphia, etc., 2 vols., 1809, 17.5 cm. Warne reissued it in the series in Jan. 1872, o/6 sewed. See 1874, *The Scottish Chiefs, etc.*

Frederick Warne & Co.
Bedford Street, Covent Garden
1870

298 CHARLES SPENCER *The Bicycle...*
Fcp 8vo. Illustrated. 1/o boards Mar. 5
(*Ath*)

Useful Books. This is the first edition, with the joint imprint of Scribner, Welford & Co., New York, 17 cm., 54 pp. It was reissued as *The Modern Bicycle*, the same, no date, 17 cm., 132 pp., listed in the *Spect* on July 8, 1876; it was reissued again in 1878, 12mo, 1/o, with the latter title, given by the *Eng Cat.*

299 LOUISA L. GREENE *The Burtons of Burton Hall.* 12mo. Illustrated. 2/o cloth
Mar. 5 (*Spect*)

2/o Gift Books. The *Eng Cat* gives this as a new edition, and it is possible that the first edition was *Winter and Summer at Burton Hall*, which the *Eng Cat* gives as issued by Hogg, London, in 1861, Fcp 8vo, 2/6. The 8th edition was advertised by Warne in the *Ath* on Dec. 4, 1875, Fcp 8vo, 2/o cloth. Warne issued it in their *Birthday Series* in 1877, no date, 18mo, frontispiece and illustrations, 1/6 green decorated cloth, given by the *Eng Cat.*

300 CHARLES BOX *The Theory and Practice of Cricket.* [New Edition.]
Fcp 8vo. 1/o boards Mar. (*Bks*)

Useful Books. The first edition was issued by Warne, 1868, 17 cm., 165 pp., 2/6 half-bound, listed in the *Spect* on May 16.

301 JOHN S. ROBERTS, ed.
The Legendary Ballads of England and Scotland. Cr 8vo. 1/6 sewed, 2/o cloth July (*Bks*)

Chandos Classics No. 7. This has the joint imprint of Scribner, Welford & Co., New York, no date, 19 cm., 628 pp., and it was reissued by Warne in the series, 1890. The first edition was issued by Warne in *Chandos Poets*, no date, 628 pp., illustrated, 7/6, listed in *Notes & Queries* on Feb. 1, 1868.

302 P.O.P. *The Nabob's Cookery Book.*
12mo. 1/o boards Sept. 10 (*Ath*)
This is the first edition, no date.

303 X. B. SAINTINE (JOSEPH X. BONIFACE)
Picciola. Fcp 8vo. Illustrated. 2/6 cloth
Sept. 10 (*Ath*)

2/6 Gift Books. This has no date, 258 pp. The first edition was issued in Paris, 1836, 22.5 cm., 419 pp., frontispiece (portrait). The first edition in English was issued by Henry Colburn, London, 2 vols., 1837, 21 cm., 16/o, advertised in the *Spect* on Feb. 18 as "On Feb. 21." The first American edition was issued by Carey, Lea & Blanchard, Philadelphia, 1838, 19.5 cm., 204 pp., advertised in the Washington, D.C., *Globe* (daily) by a bookstore, on Oct. 29, anonymous, and this is an accurate date for the first American edition. It had reviews in the *New York Review*, a quarterly, and in the Boston *Christian Examiner* (bimonthly), in Jan. 1839. Warne issued it in their *Star Series* No. 17, 16mo, 1/o sewed, listed in the *Spect* on Apr. 15, 1876, and at 1/6 cloth, listed there on May 13.

304 ELESNORA MONTAGU, later HERVEY *The Rock Light.* 12mo. Illustrated. 2/o cloth　Nov. 12 (*Ath*)

2/o Gift Books. This is the first edition, no date. It was placed in the *Home Circle Gift Books*, shortly thereafter, 12mo, illustrated, 2/o cloth; it was reissued in this latter series in 1883, given by the *Eng Cat.* Warne issued it in the 1890s in the *Bedford Library*, illustrated, 1/6 cloth.

305 ISABEL PLUNKETT (ISABELLA PLUNKET) *Hester's Fortune.* Fcp 8vo. Illustrated. 2/6 cloth　Nov. 12 (*Ath*)

2/6 Gift Books. This is the first edition, 1870. The first American edition was issued by E. P. Dutton, New York, 1871, 16mo, 247 pp., illustrated. Warne issued it in the *Golden Links Series*, 12mo, illustrated, 2/6 cloth, in 1882, given by the *Eng Cat.*

306 MRS. JEROME MERCIER *Campanella.* Fcp 8vo. Illustrated. 2/6 cloth　Nov. 12 (*Ath*)

2/6 Gift Books. This is the first edition, no date. It was issued in the *Golden Links Series*, 12mo, illustrated, 2/6 cloth, in 1882, given by the *Eng Cat.*

307 ANONYMOUS *Willie Herbert and His Six Little Friends.* 16mo. Illustrated. 2/o cloth　Nov. 12 (*Spect*)

2/o Large Type Books. This is the first edition, with the joint imprint of Scribner, Welford & Co., New York, no date, 147 pp.

308 F. HARDY & J. R. WARE *The Modern Hoyle.* 16mo, 1/o boards, 2/o cloth Nov. 12 (*Spect*)

Modern Manuals No. 2. This is the first edition, with the joint imprint of Scribner,

Welford & Co., New York, no date, 16 cm., 182 pp. Warne issued an enlarged edition, edited by Professor Hoffmann (Angelo Lewis), 24mo, 1/o boards, 1/6 cloth, advertised in the *Ath* on Oct. 1, 1887. Warne, New York, advertised it in the *Nation* on Oct. 6, 1887, square 18mo, diagrams, $.50 boards. Warne advertised it in the *Times Weekly Edition* (London) on Sept. 11, 1891, square Fcp 8vo, 1/o boards, 1/6 cloth.

309 LOUISA L. GREENE *The Little Castle Maiden and Other Tales.* 12mo. Illustrated. 2/o cloth　Nov. 19 (*Ath*)

2/o Gift Books. This is the first edition, no date. It was issued by E. P. Dutton & Co., New York, at $1.00, listed in the *Nation* on Feb. 23, 1871. Warne issued the 4th edition at 2/o cloth, advertised in the *Ath* on Dec. 4, 1875. Warne issued it in their *Illustrated Fairy Library* No. 1 in 1877, 12mo, 1/o sewed, 1/6 cloth, listed in the *Spect* on Oct. 27.

310 ANONYMOUS *Modern Etiquette in Private and Public.* 16mo. 1/o boards, 2/o cloth　Nov. 26 (*Ath*)

Modern Manuals No. 1. This is the first edition, no date, 16 cm., 192 pp. Warne reissued it in 1887, a new and revised edition, no date, 15 cm., 184 pp., given by the *Eng Cat.* They issued it in New York, square 18mo, illustrated, $.50 boards, listed in the *Nation* on Mar. 10, 1887. They reissued it in England in 1891, 1/o boards, 1/6 cloth, advertised in the *TWEd* on Sept. 18, 1/o boards, 1/6 cloth.

311 ANONYMOUS *Modern Out-Door Amusements.* 16mo. 1/o boards, 2/o cloth　Dec. 10 (*Ath*)

Modern Manuals No. 3. This is the first edition, with the joint imprint of Scribner, Welford & Co., New York, no date, 16 cm., 179 pp., containing pieces on swimming, archery, pedestrianism, cricket, etc.

312 ANONYMOUS **Modern Pastime; or, In-Door Amusements.** 16mo. 1/o boards, 2/o cloth   Dec. 10

Modern Manuals No. 4. This is the first edition, with the joint imprint of Scribner, Welford & Co., New York, no date, 16 cm., 179 pp.

313 MARY E. BROMFIELD **Daddy Dick.** 18mo. Colored frontispiece. o/9 cloth 1870 (*Eng Cat*)

Ninepenny Juveniles. This is the first edition, no date, 106 pp.

314 ANONYMOUS **Naughty Nix.** 18mo. Colored frontispiece. o/9 cloth 1870 (*Eng Cat*)

Ninepenny Juveniles. This is the first edition, no date.

315 ALEXANDER H. THOMPSON **Stenography etc.** [New edition.] 12mo. 1/o   1870 (*Eng Cat*)

The first edition was issued by Warne, 1868, 12mo, 30 pp., illustrated, 1/o, listed in the *Spect* on July 25.

316 ANONYMOUS **Home Recreations and Foreign Travel.** Fcp 8vo. Illustrated. 2/6 cloth   1870?

2/6 Gift Books. This is the first edition, but I am not certain of the date as it is not in the *Eng Cat* and the *BM* gives a joint imprint with Scribner, Welford & Armstrong (circa 1870), 315 pp. It fits in this series as either 1869 or 1870. It was placed in the *Golden Links Series*, colored illustrations, 2/6 cloth, after 1871.

317 JOHN J. MECHI **Vines.** 1/0 sewed Feb. (*Bks*)

I have not found this in any other listing.

318 MRS. ABBY M. DIAZ **The William Henry Letters from Crooked Pond School.** Fcp 8vo. Illustrated. 1/0 sewed   Apr. 1 (*Ath*)

This is the first English edition, no date, 16.5 cm., 251 pp. The first edition was issued by Fields, Osgood & Co., Boston, 1870, 17.5 cm., 257 pp., illustrated, $1.50, advertised in the *New-York Times* on Dec. 15, 1870, as "This day." The American title was *The William Henry Letters*. They appeared in *Our Young Folks* (Fields, Osgood) *passim*, Mar. to Oct. 1869, and a third new packet appeared in the Nov. 1870 issue. Presumably the packets started earlier, as the Mar. 1869 issue contained the ninth packet.

319 SAMUEL JOHNSON **Lives of the Most Eminent English Poets.** New edition. Cr 8vo. 1/6 sewed, 2/0 cloth   Apr. 15 (*Spect*)

Chandos Classics No. 9. This has no date, 19 cm., 588 pp., and includes the "Preface to Shakespeare" and the review of "The Origin of Evil" and probably had a joint imprint with Scribner, Welford & Armstrong, New York. Warne issued it in the *Chandos Library,* Cr 8vo, 3/6, listed in the *Spect* on Nov. 3, 1877. The first English edition was in 4 vols., 1779, 8vo, issued by C. Bathurst, J. Buckland, W. Stra-

han, London, etc. The second edition was noticed in the *Gentleman's Magazine* (monthly) for Sept. 1781. The first Dublin edition (unauthorized), 3 vols., 1779, was issued by Whitestone, Williams, etc., etc., Dublin. The second and third vols. were issued in 1781. Tinker states that this is the only set traced in which vols. 2 and 3 are dated 1779. Vols. 5–10 of the *Lives* were issued as for vols. 1–4, 1781, reviewed in the *Gentleman's Magazine* for May 1781. These lives were the prefaces, biographical and critical, of the poets in Johnson's *Works of the English Poets.* This latter work was issued in 68 vols., 1779–81, by J. Nichols, London. It was also issued in 68-vols.-in-58, 1779–81, by C. Bathurst, J. Buckland, W. Strahan, London, 16 cm., portraits. In the United States it was issued with the present title by Benjamin Johnson, Philadelphia, 2 vols., 1803, new edition, 22 cm.

320 MRS. JEROME MERCIER **Only a Girl's Life.** 12mo. Illustrated. 2/0 cloth Apr. 29 (*Ath*)

Home Circle Gift Books. This is the first edition, no date. Warne issued it in the *Star Series* No. 70, 16mo, 1/0 sewed, 1/6 cloth, listed in the *Spect* on Mar. 5, 1881.

321 ROBERT BURNS **Poetical Works.** Cr 8vo. 1/0 sewed, 1/6 cloth Apr. 29 (*Spect*)

Chandos Classics No. 8. The first edition was *Poems, Chiefly in the Scottish Dialect,* printed at Kilmarnock by John Wilson, 1786, 8vo, 240 pp., 3/0 sewed, 612 copies, on July 31. The second and third editions were printed for the author, Edinburgh, 1787, 20.7 cm., 368 pp., frontispiece (portrait). The third edition was also issued by A. Strahan, T. Cadell, London; W. Creech, Edinburgh, 1787, 21 cm., 372 pp., frontispiece (portrait), the first London edition. The first Irish edition was issued by James Magee, Belfast, 1787, 16.6 cm., 274 pp., frontispiece (portrait). Appleton & Co., New York, issued *The Complete Works of Robert Burns*, edited by James Currie, abridged, 1842, 12mo, 575 pp., called the first complete American edition. It was listed in the *United States Magazine* (monthly) for Dec. 1842. Warne issued *Robert Burns' Poetical Works, the National Edition*, 1896, 20 cm., 614 pp., 1/0, reviewed in *PC* on May 2, 1896.

322 ANONYMOUS *Young England's Nursery Book.* 16mo. Colored illustrations. 2/0 cloth June 17 (*Ath*)

This is also given by the *Eng Cat*, but otherwise I cannot trace it.

323 ANONYMOUS *Young England's Picture Book.* 16mo. Colored illustrations, 2/0 cloth June 17 (*Ath*)

I cannot trace this.

324 ANONYMOUS *The Ladies' and Gentlemen's Model Letter-Writer.* Fcp 8vo. 1/0 boards June 24 (*Ath*)

Useful Books. This is probably the first edition, no date, 178 pp., although I cannot explain the *Eng Cat* entry that gives it also in 2 vols., 0/6 each, issued in 1871. Warne reissued it in *Useful Books*, 12mo, 1/0, in 1880, given by the *Eng Cat*.

325 THE DRUID (HENRY H. DIXON) *Saddle and Sirloin.* Revised and re-edited. 12mo. Illustrated. 2/6 boards Aug. 12 (*Ath*)

"The Druid" Sporting Series No. 1. This has no date, 471 pp., frontispiece (portrait)

and an engraved extra title page, with a preface (1870). The first edition was issued by Rogerson & Tuxford, London, 1870, 18 cm., 486 pp., frontispiece (portrait) and an extra engraved title page, reviewed in the *Spect* on Apr. 30. Warne reissued it in 1878, 12mo, 2/0 boards, given by the *Eng Cat*; Warne advertised it in the *TWEd* on Jan. 19, 1877, 2/6 boards. It was also reissued in 1880, no date, 471 pp., 2/0 boards, with the engraved title page and pictorial yellow boards printed in red, blue, and black, with the series title on the front cover and spine, plain endpapers, and a publisher's ad on the back cover. A new and cheaper library edition was advertised in the *TWEd* on May 24, 1888, Cr 8vo, 2/0; a library edition was advertised there on Sept. 5, 1890, Cr 8vo, 3/6 cloth.

326 THE DRUID (HENRY H. DIXON) *The Post and the Paddock.* Revised and re-edited. 12mo. Illustrated. 2/6 boards Aug. 12 (*Ath*)

"The Druid" Sporting Series No. 2. This has no date, 367 pp., frontispiece (portrait), with a preface (1857), and with an added engraved title page. The first edition was issued by Piper, Stephenson & Co., London (1856), 17.5 cm., 232 pp. They issued a new edition, 12mo, 360 pp., 3/6, listed in the *PC* as published Dec. 14–31, 1859. A new edition was issued by Rogerson & Tuxford, London, 1862, 5/0. All the reissues given in the preceding entry also apply here. In addition, the present title was reissued in 1885, p 8vo, 2/0 boards, given by the *Eng Cat*.

327 MRS. HENRY KEARY *Sam; or, A Good Name.* 12mo. Colored frontispiece. 1/0 cloth Aug. 26 (*Ath*)

Round the Globe Library. This is the first edition, no date.

328 (AMY LOTHROP) (ANNA WARNER)
Edith and Mary at Holly Farm. 12mo.
Colored frontispiece. 1/0 cloth
Aug. 26 (*Ath*)

Round the Globe Library. This has no date
and was deposited at the *BM* on Oct. 18.
The first edition was *Hard Maple*, issued by
Shepard, Clark & Brown, Boston, 1859,
18 cm., anonymous, 255 pp., illustrated,
in blue or red cloth, with yellow endpapers, deposited Oct. 29 and listed in
APC&LG on Nov. 12. Routledge, London,
issued it as *The Birth-Day Visit to Holly Farm*,
deposited Mar. 9 and listed in *PC* on Apr.
2, 1860. Nisbet, London, issued it, listed in
the *Ath* on Dec. 5, 1868.

329 R.C.W., ed.   ***The Modern Joe Miller.***
16mo. Illustrated. 1/0 boards, 2/0 cloth
Sept. 9 (*Ath*)

Modern Manuals No. 5. This is the first edition, no date, 182 pp. Warne reissued it in
1875 at 2/6 cloth with Scribner, Welford,
New York, in the imprint.

330 HENRY J. LOARING, ed.   ***A Selection
of Common Sayings, Words, and Customs.***
[New edition.] 12mo. 1/0   Sept. 30 (*Spect*)
The first edition was issued by Warne
(1870), 12mo, 3/6. Sheets were apparently
sent to the United States, as the *U Cat* gives
Porter & Coates, Philadelphia (1873), 17.5
cm., 230 pp., printed in England.

331 ANNIE WEBB (MRS. J. B. WEBB, later
WEBB-PEPLOE) ***Benaiah.*** [New edition.]
12mo. Illustrated. 2/0 cloth   Nov. 11
(*Ath* ad)

Home Circle Gift Books. The first edition was
issued by Jackson, Walford & Hodder,
London, in 1865, square Cr 8vo, 121 pp.,
illustrated, 3/6 cloth, listed in the *Reader*
on Nov. 4. It was issued by Hodder &
Stoughton, London, at 2/6, in 1869. It
was issued in the United States by Claxton, Remsen & Haffelfinger, Philadelphia, 16mo, illustrated, listed in *Putnam's*

Monthly for Dec. 1869. Warne reissued it in
the present series in 1882, given by the
Eng Cat, and issued it in the *Bedford Library*,
12mo, illustrated, 1/6 cloth, in 1889, given
by the *Eng Cat*.

332 R.C.W., ed.   ***Modern Humour,
Anecdote, and Wit.*** 16mo. Illustrated.
1/0 boards, 2/0 cloth   Nov. 11 (*Ath* ad)
Modern Manuals No. 6. This is the first edition, no date, 15.5 cm., 184 pp., probably
with the joint imprint of Scribner & Co.,
New York.

333 W.H.G. KINGSTON   ***Washed Ashore.***
Fcp 8vo. Illustrated. 2/0 cloth   Nov. 11
(*Ath* ad)

Incident and Adventure Library. The first
edition was issued by Jackson, Walford &
Hodder, London, 1866, square 16mo, illustrated, 3/6 cloth, listed in the *Ath* on
Oct. 6. Hodder & Stoughton, London, issued a new edition in Dec. 1868, 16mo,
2/6. It was issued in the United States by
Claxton, Remsen & Haffelfinger, Philadelphia, in 1868, $1.50, listed in the *Nation*
on Nov. 12. Warne issued it and the following title in 1 vol., 1871, 399 pp., illustrated, 5/0, and sheets were used by
R. Worthington, New York, for an issue,
no date. Warne reissued the present title
in the present series in 1881, given by the
Eng Cat; and in the *Bedford Library*, new
edition, no date, 12mo, 213 pp., illustrated, 1/6 cloth, listed by *PC* on Nov. 24,
1894. Kingston issued over 100 titles for
young people.

334 W.H.G. KINGSTON   ***Adrift in a Boat.***
Fcp 8vo. Illustrated. 2/0 cloth   Nov. 11
(*Ath* ad)

Incident and Adventure Library. The first
edition was issued by Hodder & Stoughton, London, 1869, 16mo, 2/6, noticed in
the *British Quarterly Review* for Jan. 1870.
Warne issued it with the preceding title in
1 vol., 1871, 399 pp., illustrated, 5/0.

Warne reissued the present title in the present series in 1881, given by the *Eng Cat*; and in the *Bedford Library* in 1889, 12mo, illustrated, 1/6 cloth, given by the *Eng Cat*.

335 ROBERT M. BALLANTYNE
Silver Lake. Fcp 8vo. Illustrated.
2/0 cloth   Nov. 11 (*Ath* ad)
Incident and Adventure Library. The first edition was issued by Jackson, Walford & Hodder, London, 1867, 12mo, 110 pp., illustrated, 3/6. Sheets were used by J. B. Lippincott & Co., Philadelphia, who issued it, 1868, 18 cm., 110 pp., illustrated.

336 HELENA PEAKE **The Boy's Book of Heroes.** 12mo. Illustrated. 2/6 cloth
Nov. 11 (*Ath* ad)
Golden Links Series. This is the first edition, no date, 17 cm., 264 pp., and probably has Scribner, Welford, New York, in the imprint. Warne issued it in the *Daring Deeds Library* in 1880, no date, 12mo, 265 pp., illustrated, 2/6 cloth, given by the *Eng Cat*; in 1896 they issued a new edition, Cr 8vo, illustrated, 2/0 cloth, listed in *PC* on Feb. 15.

337 JACOB B. DE LIEFDE **Walter's Escape.**
[New edition.] 12mo. Illustrated. 2/6 cloth   Nov. 18 (*Ath*)
Golden Links Series. This has no date, 17.5 cm., 197 pp. The first edition was issued by Hodder & Stoughton, London, 1870, 12mo, 3/6 cloth, listed in the *Ath* on Nov. 5. By 1880 this was in the *Daring Deeds Library*, illustrated, 2/6 cloth; and in the 1890s it was in the *Daring and Doing Library*, illustrated, 1/6 cloth.

338 MADAME EDMOND DE PRESSENSÉ
Madeleine's Trial, and Other Stories.
[New edition.] 12mo. Illustrated.
2/6 cloth   Nov. 18 (*Ath*)
Golden Links Series. This was issued in France as *Scènes d'Enfance et de Jeunesse*,

1870. The first English edition was issued by Hodder & Stoughton, London, 1870, 12mo, 232 pp., 3/6, listed in the *Ath* on Nov. 5.

339 SIDNEY DARYL (SIR DOUGLAS STRAIGHT) *A Life's Voyage.* 12mo. Illustrated. 2/6 cloth   Nov. 18 (*Ath*)
Golden Links Series. The first edition was issued by Hodder & Stoughton, London, 1868, 167 pp., illustrated, with the title *With the Tide; or, A Life's Voyage.* It was issued in the United States with the same title by Claxton, Remsen & Haffelfinger, Philadelphia, 1869. By 1880 this was in the *Daring Deeds Library*, illustrated, 2/6 cloth.

340 LAURA VALENTINE **The Victoria Picture Reading Book.** 8vo. Illustrated.
1/0 cloth   Dec. 16 (*Ath*)
This is the first edition, no date, 21 cm., 152 pp. The *U Cat* gives also Scribner, Welford & Armstrong, New York (1871), 21 cm., 152 pp., illustrated.

341 WILLIAM COMBE **Doctor Syntax: His Three Tours.** Cr 8vo. Colored illustrations. 1/6 sewed, 2/0 cloth
Dec. (*Bks*)
Chandos Classics No. 12. These are poems, no date, 19 cm., 376 pp. The first edition was in 3 vols., R. Ackermann's Repository of Arts, London, 23 cm., anonymous, 276, 277, and 279 pp., colored illustrations, 21/0 boards each. Vol. 1 was *The Tour of Doctor Syntax in Search of the Picturesque*, 1812; a second edition was reviewed in the *Critical Review* (London) for May 1813. Vol. 2 was *Doctor Syntax's Second Tour in Search of Consolation*, 1820, listed by the *Edinburgh Review* as published Aug.–Nov. 1820. *The Third Tour of Doctor Syntax in Search of a Wife* was 1821, listed in the same as published Mar.–July 1821. The first American edition of vol. 1 was issued by William Charles, Philadelphia (circa

1817), 280 pp., from the second London edition. The first American edition of vol. 2 was issued by H. C. Carey & I. Lea, Philadelphia, 1822, 22.5 cm., 277 pp. Part 1 of the second tour, with 6 plates, was listed in the *North American Review* (quarterly) for Apr. 1822. The first American edition of the third tour was issued by J. Clarke, Philadelphia, 1829, 24mo, 213 pp., frontispiece. Carey, Lea & Carey, Philadelphia, issued 3 vols., 18mo, 78 colored plates, $6.00, advertised in the *American Quarterly Review* (Philadelphia) for June 1827, "Recently received from London." Warne also issued it in *Chandos Classics* with the joint imprint of Scribner, Welford, New York, no date, possibly the present edition; they reissued it in 1892, 20 cm., 376 pp., colored plates.

342 SAMUEL BUTLER *Hudibras.* Cr 8vo. 1/6 sewed, 2/0 cloth   Dec. (*Bks*)

Chandos Classics No. 13. This has no date, 331 pp. The *U Cat* gives also Scribner, Welford & Armstrong, New York, no date, 18 cm., 331 pp. This is a poem, first issued in 3 parts, anonymous. Part 1 was issued by Richard Marriot, London, 1663 (1662), 17.5 cm., 268 pp.; and also 1863, 15 cm., 128 pp. Part 2 was issued by John Martyn & James Allestry, London, 1664 (1663), 20.5 cm., 216 pp. Part 3 was issued by Simon Miller, London, 1678, 18.5 cm., 285 pp. The first American edition was in 1 vol., Wright, Goodenow & Stockwell, Troy, New York, 1806, 18 cm., 286 pp.

343 EDWARD HOPPUS *Hoppus's Measurer.* Enlarged and revised. Oblong 8vo. 2/0 red roan   1871 (*Eng Cat*)

This has no date, 228 pp., edited by William Richardson. It was reissued in 1895 at 2/0. The second edition, *Practical Measuring Made Easy,* was issued by E. Wicksteed, London, 1738, oblong 8vo, 176 pp.

344 ANONYMOUS *The Modern English Letter-Writer.* p 8vo. 1/0, 1/6   1871 (*Eng Cat*)

I cannot trace this. *The Letter-Writer of Modern Society* was issued in 1883, Cr 8vo, 2/6, by Warne, listed in the *Spect* on June 30.

345 (SAMUEL COPELAND) *Wheat.* 12mo. Illustrated. 1/0   1871 (*Eng Cat*)

Useful Books. This has no date, 17.5 cm., 172 pp., by the Old Norfolk Farmer, with a preface signed S. C. The first edition was issued by Houlston & Wright, London, 1865, 172 pp., the same.

346 THE DRUID (HENRY H. DIXON) *Scott and Sebright.* Revised and re-edited. 12mo. Illustrated. 2/6 boards   1871 (*Eng Cat*)

"The Druid" Sporting Series No. 3. This has no date, my copy, 17.7 cm., frontispiece and an added engraved title page and 2 portraits, with a preface (June 10, 1862). It is in yellow pictorial boards, printed in red, black, and blue, with the series title on the front and spine, and with the joint imprint of Scribner, Welford & Co., New York. There are publisher's ads on the endpapers and on a leaf at the back, and a commercial ad on the back cover. The first edition was issued by Rogerson & Tuxford, London, 1862, Fcp 8vo, 426 pp., 5/0 cloth. It was reissued at 2/6 boards, advertised in the *TWEd* on Jan. 19, 1877; it was reissued at 2/0 boards in 1878, given by the *Eng Cat*. It was again reissued in 1880, 17.6 cm., identical to the present edition, at 2/0 boards, but with plain endpapers and no publisher's ad. It was reissued in 1888, Cr 8vo, a library edition at 2/0, advertised in the *TWEd* on May 24, and issued in the library edition at 3/6 cloth, advertised in the same on Sept. 5, 1890.

347 THE DRUID (HENRY H. DIXON)
Silk and Scarlet. Revised and re-edited.
12mo. Illustrated. 2/6 boards
1871 (*Eng Cat*)

"The Druid" Sporting Series No. 4. This is my copy, no date, 17.4 cm., 369 pp., frontispiece and an added engraved title page, with the joint imprint of Scribner, Welford & Co., New York. It is in yellow pictorial boards, printed in red, blue, and black, with the series title on the front and spine, and with a preface (1859). There are publisher's ads on the endpapers and on 32 pp. at the back, and a commercial ad on the back cover. There are 3 portraits and a folding illustration in addition to the frontispiece. The first edition was issued by Rogerson & Tuxford, London, 1859, 398 pp., with folding plates and full-page portraits, 5/0, listed by *PC* as published July 15–30, with 380 pp. [*sic*]. Warne reissued it as for the preceding item and in addition reissued it in 1885, p 8vo, 2/0, given by the *Eng Cat*.

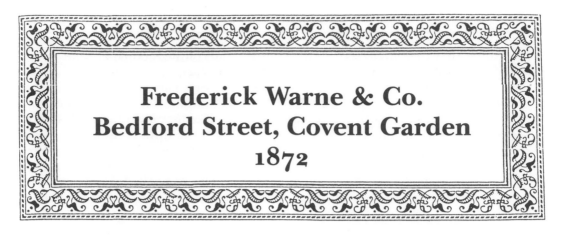

Frederick Warne & Co.
Bedford Street, Covent Garden
1872

348 THOMAS MOORE *The Poetical Works of Thomas Moore.* Cr 8vo. 1/0 sewed, 1/6 cloth Jan. 16–31 (*PC*)

Chandos Classics No. 11. This has no date, 636 pp. It was reissued in this series in 1879, listed in the *Bks* for June. The first edition was issued by J. & T. Carpenter, London, 1801, *The Poetical Works of the Late Thomas Little, Esq.*, 17 cm., 175 pp., 7/6, issued in June. There was a new edition in Apr. 1871, listed in the *Critical Review* (London). They issued it at 7/0 boards, 1801, reviewed in the same for Feb. 1802. Longmans, London, issued the *Poetical Works*, 10 vols., from Oct. 1840 to July 1841, 18 cm., frontispieces, 5/0 each. *The Poetical Works* was issued by E. & J.B. Young & Co., New York, 1800, 18 cm., 670 pp.; and *The Poetical Works of the Late Thomas Little* was issued by Hugh Maxwell, Philadelphia, 1804, 19 cm., 193 pp. Carey, Lea, and Carey, Philadelphia, issued *The Poetical Works*, complete, in 1827, 8vo, $5.25, advertised in the *American Quarterly Review* as recently received from London, June 1827. Warne issued this in the *Chandos Poets* in 1872, p 8vo, 646 pp., portrait, illustrations, 7/6 cloth, listed in the *Spect* on Feb. 10; they issued it also in 1872, 12mo, portrait, illustrations, 3/6 cloth, listed by *PC* as published May 1–15.

349 ABBY M. DIAZ *William Henry and His Friends.* 12mo. Illustrated. 1/0 sewed Feb. 24 (*Ath*)

The first edition was issued by James R. Osgood & Co., Boston, in 1871, 18 cm., 265 pp., illustrated, $1.50, listed in the *Nation* on Nov. 16. The present edition is the first English edition, no date, 263 pp.

350 AGNES & MARIA CATLOW *The Children's Garden.* [New edition.] 12mo. Illustrated. 1/0 boards Apr. 13 (*Ath*)

The first edition was issued by Cassell, Petter & Galpin, London, 1865, 18.5 cm., 126 pp., illustrated.

351 (MIRIAM C. HARRIS) (MRS. SIDNEY S. HARRIS) *The Two Cousins.* 12mo. 2/0 boards, 2/0 cloth May 18 (*Ath*)

Companion Library No. 4. Apparently this was put in this series as No. 4 when the original No. 4 was no longer in print. This is also given by the *Eng Cat*, but otherwise I cannot trace it.

352 (THOMAS C. HALIBURTON) *The Season-Ticket, by Sam Slick.* New edition. 12mo. 2/0 boards, 2/6 cloth June 29 (*Ath*)

Companion Library No. 52. This has no date, 330 pp. The first appearance was in the *Dublin University Magazine* where it ran Apr. 1859–Mar. 1860. The first book edition was issued by Bentley, London, 1860, 20.5 cm., anonymous, 376 pp., listed in the *Ath* on Mar. 3. They issued it as *Standard Novels* No. 8, third series, 1861, new edition, Fcp 8vo, 330 pp., 2/6 white cloth, 3/0 claret cloth; they reissued it in 1866, new edition, 12mo, anonymous, 330 pp., 2/o boards in their *Globe Novels*, listed in the *Reader* on Jan. 13, 1866.

353 FLORENCE MARRYAT (MRS. ROSS CHURCH, later LEAN) *Petronel.* [New edition.] 12mo. 2/o boards, 2/6 cloth   June 29 (*Ath*)
Companion Library No. 47. The first edition was issued by Bentley, London, 3 vols., 1870, p 8vo, 31/6, listed in the *Ath* on July 2. The first American edition was issued by A. K. Loring, Boston, 1870, listed in *Lit W* on Aug. 1 as "Recently published" and listed in *ALG&PC* (fortnightly) on Aug. 15.

354 FLORENCE MARRYAT (MRS. ROSS CHURCH, later LEAN) *The Prey of the Gods.* [New edition.] 12mo. 2/o boards, 2/6 cloth   June 29 (*Ath*)
Companion Library No. 50. This is my copy, no date, 17.5 cm., 313 pp., with the Warne imprint on the front and in the ads and the joint imprint of Scribner, Welford & Armstrong, New York, on the title page. It is in yellow pictorial boards, printed in red and black, with the series title at the foot of the spine and publisher's ads on the end-papers and on a leaf at the back, and a commercial ad on the back. The first edition was issued by Bentley, London, 3 vols., 1871, 31/6, listed in the *Ath* on Sept. 9. In the United States it was issued by James R. Osgood & Co., Boston, 1871, $1.25, listed in the *Ind* on Nov. 2, in the *Nation* on Nov. 16, and in *ALG&PC* (fortnightly) on Nov. 15; and by Harper & Brothers, New York, 1871, 8vo, $.30 paper, advertised in the *New-York Times* on Nov. 11, listed in the *Nation* on Nov. 16 and in *ALG&PC* (fortnightly) on Nov. 15.

355 FLORENCE MARRYAT (MRS. ROSS CHURCH, later LEAN) *The Girls of Feversham.* [New edition.] 12mo. 2/6 boards, 2/6 cloth   June 29 (*Ath*)
Companion Library No. 51. The first edition was issued by Bentley, London, 1869, 2

vols., 21/o, listed in the *Spect* on Mar. 13. The first American edition was issued by A. K. Loring, Boston, 1869, 131 pp., $.75 paper, advertised in the *New-York Times* on May 3 and listed in the *Nation* on May 6. Sadleir and Wolff had copies of the first edition, in chocolate fine-morocco cloth, with a dedication to the author's mother.

356 FLORENCE MARRYAT (MRS. ROSS CHURCH, later LEAN) *Veronique.* [New edition.] 12mo. 2/o boards, 2/6 cloth   July 20 (*Ath*)
Companion Library No. 48. This has 400 pp. The first edition was issued by Bentley, London, 3 vols., 1869, Cr 8vo, 31/6 in apple-green cloth with a dedication to Charles Dickens, listed in the *Ath* on Aug. 28. The first American edition was issued by A. K. Loring, Boston (1869), 8vo, 200 pp., $.75 paper, listed in the *Nation* on Sept. 30 and in *ALG&PC* (fortnightly) on Oct. 1.

357 FLORENCE MARRYAT (MRS. ROSS CHURCH, later LEAN) *Her Lord and Master.* [New edition.] 12mo. 2/o boards, 2/6 cloth   July 20 (*Ath*)
Companion Library No. 49. This has no date, 310 pp. The first edition was issued by Bentley, London, 3 vols., 1871, Cr 8vo, 31/6 in grass-green cloth with chocolate endpapers (Wolff's copy), listed in the *Ath* on Mar. 4. The first American edition was issued by Harper & Brothers, New York, 1871, 8vo, 117 pp., $.50 paper, in the *Library of Select Novels*, advertised in the *New-York Times* on June 17 as "This day" and noticed in the *Ind* on June 22.

358 WILLIAM COWPER *The Poetical Works of William Cowper.* Complete edition. Cr 8vo. 1/o sewed, 1/6 cloth   July (*Bks*)
Chandos Classics No. 14. This has no date, 19 cm., 611 pp., and probably has the joint imprint with Scriber, Welford & Co., New York. Warne issued it in *Chandos Poets*, Cr

8vo, 7/6, listed in the *Spect* on Nov. 9, 1872; they also issued it in 1872 in *Landsdown Poets*, Cr 8vo, 3/6 cloth, listed in the *Spect* on Nov. 23. The first edition of *Poems* was in 2 vols., issued by J. Johnson, London, 8vo, 5/0 each; vol. 1, 1782, reviewed in *Critical Review* (London) for Apr. 1872, and vol. 2, 1785, reviewed in the *Gentleman's Magazine* for Dec. 1785 and Mar. 1876. *Poems* in 2 vols., third edition, p 8vo, was issued by J. Johnson, 1787. *The Life and Posthumous Writings of William Cowper, Esq.*, vol. 3, edited by William Hayley, was issued by J. Johnson, 1804, 4to, 21/0 boards, reviewed in the *Critical Review* for Jan. 1805. In the United States *Poems* was issued by Benjamin Johnson, Philadelphia, 2 vols., 1803; that publisher also issued the *Poetical Works of William Cowper*, 1806, 15 cm., illustrated.

359 JANE WEBB, later LOUDON
The Mummy. [New edition.] 12mo.
2/0 boards, 2/6 cloth   Aug. 24
(*Ath*)
Companion Library No. 53. This has no date. It was also issued by Warne in 1872 in brown decorated cloth. The first edition was issued by Henry Colburn, London, 3 vols., 1827, 19.5 cm., anonymous.

360 HUGH M. WALMSLEY **The Life Guardsman.** [New edition.] 12mo.
2/0 boards   Sept. 28 (*Ath*)
Companion Library No. 55. The first edition was issued by Bentley, London, 3 vols., 1871, Cr 8vo, 31/6, listed in the *Ath* on Feb. 4. The present edition had 440 pp.

361 HENRY C. ADAMS **Stories of the Kings. Stories of the Prophets.** 2 vols. 12mo.
Illustrated. 2/0 cloth each   Oct. 19 (*Spect*)
Home Circle Gift Books. These were also given by the *Eng Cat*, but otherwise I cannot trace them.

362 (HELEN C. KNIGHT) **Jane Hudson.**
12mo. Colored frontispiece. 1/0 cloth
Oct. 19 (*Ath*)
Round the Globe Library. Warne issued this in 1871 as *Sixpenny 32mo Books*, colored frontispiece, 0/6 cloth, and plain, 0/4 sewed; they issued it also in *Dawn of Day Books*, 32mo, frontispiece, 0/4 cloth, before 1879. The first edition was probably issued by the American Sunday-School Union, Philadelphia, 16 cm., 247 (that is, 243) pp., illustrated, which the *U Cat* gives as (1847), anonymous. It was issued in London by the Religious Tract Society, 18mo, 1/0, 1/6, which the *BM* gives as (1848), anonymous.

363 ANONYMOUS **The Leonards.** 18mo.
Illustrated. 1/6 cloth   Oct. 19 (*Ath*)
Birthday Series. This is probably the first edition. It is in the *Eng Cat*, but otherwise I cannot trace it.

364 AUNT FRIENDLY (SARAH S. BAKER)
Little Josey. 12mo. Colored frontispiece.
1/0 cloth   Oct. 19 (*Ath*)
Round the Globe Library. This has no date and 91 pp. It was issued in 1871 or before as *Sixpenny 32mo Books*, 0/6 cloth, colored frontispiece, 0/4 sewed, plain frontispiece. Also 1866

365 AUNT LOUISA (LAURA VALENTINE)
Aunt Louisa's Sunday Books. 3 vols., 4to, 1/0 sewed, 2/0 cloth each   Oct. 16–31
(*PC*)
These titles were "The Childhood of Jesus," "Children of the Old Testament," and "Parables of Our Lord." The *BM* gives 8 nos., London (1866–72), 4to, and the *U Cat* gives 1 vol., 188–?, 27 cm., unpaged, colored plates.

366 (HELEN C. KNIGHT) **Robert Dawson.**
12mo. Colored frontispiece. 1/0 cloth
Nov. 9 (*Ath* ad)
Round the Globe Library. This was also issued in *Dawn of Day Books*, 32mo, frontis-

piece, o/4 cloth, before 1879. The first edition was probably issued by the American Sunday-School Union of Philadelphia, 24mo, which the *U Cat* gives as (copyright 1846), anonymous. The first English edition was probably issued by the Religious Tract Society, London, which the *BM* gives as (1847), anonymous.

367 LAURA VALENTINE, ed. *The Victoria Geography.* Demy 8vo. 16 maps, partly colored, 2/o cloth   Nov. 9 (*Ath* ad)

This is the first edition with the joint imprint of Scribner, Welford & Armstrong, New York, no date, 21 cm., 184 pp. It has "Victoria Educational Books" on the cover and was possibly issued in early 1873.

368 LEGH RICHMOND *The Dairyman's Daughter.* 12mo. Colored frontispiece. 1/o cloth   Nov. 9 (*Ath* ad)

Round the Globe Library. This was issued in *Sixpenny 32mo Books* in 1866. This was one of the stories in *Annals of the Poor* as was the following title. Warne issued *Annals of the Poor* in 1877, 16mo, 1/o sewed, 1/6 cloth, which, I suspect, is in the *Star Series* No. 40, although No. 40 is missing in all Warne lists of the series. Warne also issued it in their *National Books*, imperial 32mo, o/6 stiff wrappers, 2 plates, and 1/o, 1/6 cloth with colored plates, no date, new edition, 13 cm., 247 pp., given in a Nov. 15, 1879, ad in the *Ath*. A dealer offered it, no date, new edition, 13.7 cm., in colored pictorial yellow boards, with colored illustrations and a memoir of the author. The present title appeared in the *Christian Guardian* by "Simplex" in 1809, and both the *BM* and the *U Cat* give it as issued by W. Kent & Co., London (1810?), 15 cm., 106 pp., illustrated. It was printed by Ephraim Whitman, Goshen (1812), 18 cm., 23 pp., and was issued by Davidson & Bourne, Harrisburg, Virginia, 1813, 13 cm., 108 pp. The first edition of *Annals of the Poor* was issued by Hatchard, London, in 1814, 12mo, 7/o,

listed in the London *Critical Review* (monthly) for May. It was issued by Whiting & Tiffany, New Haven, Conn., 1815, 14.5 cm., 288 pp.; and by Sheldon & Goodwin, Hartford, Conn., 1815, 14.5 cm., 216 pp.

369 LEGH RICHMOND *The Young Cottager.* 12mo. Colored frontispiece. 1/o cloth   Nov. 9 (*Ath* ad)

Round the Globe Library. This is one of the stories in *Annals of the Poor* (see the preceding item). Warne issued it in *Sixpenny 32mo Books*, circa 1868, 95 pp. The present title was printed for the author, London, 1815, anonymous, 75 pp.; the 26th edition was issued in 1817, 17 cm., illustrated, 47 pp. It was issued at New Haven, Conn., 1815, 15 cm.

370 LITCHFIELD MOSELEY *Penny Readings in Prose and Verse.* Fcp 8vo. 1/o   Nov. 9 (*Spect*)

This is the first edition, no date, 16.5 cm., 240 pp., with an illustrated cover.

371 LAURA VALENTINE *Aunt Louisa's Sunday Books.* 4to. 1/o sewed   Nov. 1–15 (*PC*)

This was *Children of the New Testament*. See No. 365 above.

372 JOHN MILTON *The Poetical Works of John Milton.* Cr 8vo. 1/o sewed, 1/6 cloth Nov. 23 (*Spect*)

Chandos Classics No. 15. This has no date, 19 cm., 581 pp. The Nov. 23 listing was for the 1/o, and the 1/6 was listed Nov. 30. It probably had the joint imprint of Scribner, Welford & Armstrong, New York, because the *Chandos Poets* issue, of the same year, at 7/6, had the joint imprint, listed in the *Spect* on Dec. 21. Warne reissued it in the present series, 1888, the same; and it was issued in 1889, Cr 8vo, illustrated, 8/6, listed in the *Spect* on July 13. *Poems of Mr. John Milton* was printed for Humphrey

Moseley, London, 1645, portrait, the first edition of the collected minor poems, in English and Latin. It was reprinted by Thomas Dring, London, 1673, 290 pp., portrait, *Poems, etc., upon Several Occasions. . . .* Nine sonnets, some translations, and juvenile poems were added. The Latin poems follow the English ones with a separate title page and pagination.

373 ANONYMOUS *Warne's National Nursery Library: Little Red Riding Hood; Cinderella.* Fcp 8vo. 1/0 boards each Nov. 23 (*Ath*)

The *Eng Cat* gives a new and improved edition, 6 vols., 1/0 each, issued by Warne, 1872–80. These had colored plates and probably had the joint imprint with Scribner, Welford & Armstrong, New York.

374 WILLIAM WORDSWORTH *The Poetical Works of Wordsworth.* Cr 8vo. 1/0 sewed, 1/6 cloth Nov. 30 (*Spect*)

Chandos Classics No. 16. This has the joint imprint of Scribner, Welford & Armstrong, New York, no date, 19 cm., 530 pp. It is a reprint of the Longmans edition of 1827, which was in 5 vols. Warne reissued it in the present series, 1889, 628 pp.; they issued it in 1889 also, Cr 8vo, illustrated, 8/6, listed in the *Spect* on July 13. Warne issued it in *Chandos Poets*, at 7/6, listed in the *Spect* on Dec. 21, 1872. *Lyrical Ballads, with Other Poems* was issued by Longmans, London, 2 vols., 1800, and the fourth edition was issued in 1805. They issued *Poems*, 2 vols., 1807, Cr 8vo, 11/0, listed in the *Edinburgh Review* as published Apr.–July. I have seen 7 different original bindings given for this issue, all in various shades of boards, or boards with a contrasting back strip, all with paper labels. Longmans issued it, 2 vols., 1815, 8vo, frontispieces, 28/0, in blue boards with a drab backstrip. They issued vol. 3, 1820, 8vo, frontispiece. They issued *Poems* in 5 vols., 1827, Cr 8vo, 45/0; and issued *The Miscellaneous Poems of*

William Wordsworth, 4 vols., 1820, Cr 8vo, frontispieces, in gray-blue boards with paper labels, untrimmed. In the United States *The Poetical Works of William Wordsworth* was issued by Cummings, Hilliard & Co., Boston, 4 vols., 1824, 18.5 cm., in drab boards, uncut, carefully following the latest English edition, listed in the *North American Review* (quarterly) for Apr. 1825.

375 ANNIE KEARY *Philis Phil.* 12mo. Illustrated. 2/0 cloth Dec. 7 (*Ath*)

Home Circle Gift Books. This is the first edition, no date. Warne issued it in the *Bedford Library,* 12mo, illustrated, 1/6 cloth, listed in *PC* on Oct. 5, 1895.

376 HENRY BOYLE LEE *Napoleon Buonaparte.* 12mo. Illustrated. 2/6 cloth Dec. 21 (*Spect*)

This is the first edition, no date. The *Eng Cat* gives it as issued in 1873. I have never found this in any Warne list, although it fits the specifications for the *Daring Deeds Library.* It was issued in the *Incident and Adventure Library* in 1889, Fcp 8vo, illustrated, 2/0 cloth, given by the *Eng Cat.* It was placed in the *Daring & Doing Library,* Cr 8vo, illustrated, 1/6 cloth, in the 1890s.

377 JACOB ABBOTT *Stuyvesant.* [New edition.] 18mo. 1/0 1872 (*Eng Cat*)

I am doubtful of this item as I cannot place it in any Warne series. The first English edition was issued by Ward & Co., London (1853), 138 pp., and the first American edition was issued by Harper & Brothers, New York (copyright 1853), 17 cm., anonymous, 203 pp., illustrated.

378 (HORACE E. SCUDDER) *Dreamland; or, Children's Fairy Stories.* 12mo. 1/0, 1/6 1872 (*Eng Cat*)

I doubt this *Eng Cat* entry. It also gives an issue in the *Illustrated Fairy Library* No. 7 in

1877, illustrated, 1/0 sewed, 1/6 cloth. It is also given by the *BM* and the *U Cat* as 1877, no date, 183 pp.

379 ANONYMOUS ***Henry Burton.*** 18mo. Illustrated. 1/6 cloth   1872 (*Eng Cat*) *Birthday Series.* This is the first edition. It was reissued in this series in 1879, no date, 188 pp., given by the *Eng Cat.*

380 HARRIET MYRTLE (LYDIA F. MILLER) ***Twilight Stories at Overbury Farm.*** 18mo. Frontispiece. 1/0   1872 (*Eng Cat*)

This is probably the first edition, no date, 143 pp.

Frederick Warne & Co.
Bedford Street, Covent Garden
1873

381 HUGH M. WALMSLEY *The Chasseur d'Afrique and the Brig and the Lugger.* 12mo. 2/0 boards Apr. 5 (*Spect*)

Companion Library No. 54. The first edition was issued by Chapman & Hall, London, 1864, p 8vo, 293 pp., 10/6, *The Chasseur d'Afrique and Other Tales* (just one other tale), listed in the *Ath* on Nov. 26.

382 A LADY (MILLICENT W. COOK) *How to Dress on £15 a Year, as a Lady.* Fcp 8vo. 1/0 boards Apr. 19 (*Ath*)

Useful Books. This is the first edition, no date, 122 pp. Warne issued the sixth edition, 1/0 boards, advertised in the *Spect* on June 28, 1873, as "Now ready." The authoress fell out with Warne when they advertised a book on beauty as though it were by her, and she transferred her book to Routledge, who issued it at 1/0 boards in June 1874, a new edition thoroughly revised.

383 JOHN G. LOCKHART & ROBERT SOUTHEY *The Spanish Ballads. The Chronicle of the Cid.* Cr 8vo. 1/6 sewed, 2/0 cloth May 17 (*Spect*)

Chandos Classics No. 20. This has no date, 466 pp., the second title occupying pp. 175–466. Warne reissued it in 1875, Cr 8vo, 3/6, listed in the *Spect* on Apr. 10. The first edition of the first title was *Ancient Spanish Ballads . . .* , translated by Lockhart, Blackwood, Edinburgh, 1823, 25 cm., 209 pp. The first American edition

was issued by Wiley & Putnam, New York, 1842, a new edition revised, 21 cm., 272 pp., noticed in the *Merchants' Magazine*, a New York monthly, for Jan. 1842. The first edition of the second title was issued by Longmans, London, 1808, translated by Southey from the Spanish of R. Diaz De Bivar called El Cid, 27 cm., 468 pp., 35/0 boards, reviewed in the *Critical Review*, a London monthly, for Jan. 1809. The first American edition was issued by Daniel Bixby, Lowell, Mass., 1846, 24 cm., 486 pp., listed in the *Merchants' Magazine* for Feb. 1847.

384 ANONYMOUS *The Sheep: Its Varieties and Management in Health and Disease.* Fcp 8vo. Illustrated. 1/0 boards May 31 (*Ath*)

Country Library. This is the first edition, no date, 16.7 cm., 119 pp., yellow pictorial boards. I have a copy, no date, probably 1875 judging from the ads, with the joint imprint of Scribner, Welford & Armstrong, New York, 16.7 cm., 119 pp., frontispiece and textual illustrations, in yellow pictorial boards, printed in red, blue, and black, with the series title on the front cover and the publisher's ads on the endpapers and back cover. It was issued in 1882, revised and considerably enlarged by George Armatage, new edition, no date, 211 pp., 1/6, given by the *Eng Cat*. This latter edition was reissued in 1892 at

1/o, listed in *PC* on Mar. 19. It was issued, 1893, 220 pp., illustrated, 2/6, listed in *PC* on Apr. 1.

385 STONEHENGE (JOHN H. WALSH)
The Dog. Its Varieties and Management in Health and Disease. Fcp 8vo. Illustrated. 1/o boards   June 7 (*Ath*)
Country Library. The *BM* gives this as anonymous, no date. Longmans issued *The Dog in Health and Disease*, 1859, by Stonehenge, and they issued the second edition in 1872 and the fourth edition in 1887. I suspect this Warne edition is condensed from *British Rural Sports*, by Stonehenge, the sixth edition of which, entirely new, was issued by Warne, 1865, the first five editions having been issued by George Routledge & Co., London, starting in 1856. Warne reissued it in the present series, 1890, 180 pp., illustrated, 1/o, given by the *Eng Cat*. It was issued, 1896, revised and brought up to date by George Armatage, Cr 8vo, 267 pp., illustrated, 1/o sewed, 2/6, listed in *PC* on Dec. 12, 1896; this latter edition was issued by Warne in New York, at $1.00, listed in the *New-York Times* on Dec. 23, 1896, 16 plates and textual illustrations.

386 GEORGE ARMATAGE **Cattle.** Fcp 8vo.
Illustrated. 1/o boards   June 7 (*Ath*)
Country Library. This is the first edition, no date, 120 pp., with the joint imprint of Scribner, Welford & Armstrong, New York. It was reissued at 1/6 in 1882, given by the *Eng Cat*.

387 HENRY HALLAM & J. L. DE LOLME
The Constitutional History of England. Edward I to Henry VII. By Henry Hallam. The Constitution of England. By J. L. De Lolme. Cr 8vo. 1/6 sewed, 2/o cloth June 7 (*Ath* ad)
Chandos Classics No. 18. This has no date, 362 pp., with the joint imprint of Scribner, Welford & Armstrong, New York. The first title formed chapter VIII of *View of*

the *State of Europe During the Middle Ages*, which was issued in 2 vols. by John Murray, London, 1818, 28 cm.; and in 2 vols., 1827, 4to, 80/o, listed in the *Monthly Review* (London) for Aug. 1827; Murray issued the second edition of the same in 3 vols., 8vo, 36/o, advertised in the *Spect* on Dec. 19, 1829. *The State of Europe. . .* was issued by T. Dobson & Son, Philadelphia, 4 vols., 1821, 2 cm. Chapter VIII was issued by Wells & Lilly, Boston, 3 vols., 8vo, from the second London edition, listed in the *North American Review* (quarterly) for Oct. 1829. The first edition of the second title was *Constitution de l'Angleterre*, Amsterdam, 1771. It was issued in London by G. Kearly, 1775. Robinson, London, issued the third edition, 1781, 8vo, 6/o boards, reviewed in the *Critical Review*, a London monthly, for Oct. 1781; Robinson issued the fourth edition, corrected and enlarged, 8vo, 6/6 boards, reviewed there for Nov. 1784. Both titles as in the present edition were issued in 1 vol. by A. Murray, London, 1870. Warne reissued it in the *Chandos Classics*, noticed in *Notes & Queries* of Feb. 28, 1874.

388 EDWARD GIBBON & SIMON OCKLEY
The Saracens: Their History and the Rise and Fall of Their Empire. Cr 8vo. 1/6 sewed, 2/o cloth   June 7 (*Spect*)
Chandos Classics No. 19. This has the joint imprint of Scribner, Welford & Armstrong, New York, no date, 450 pp. This is another edition of *History of the Saracen Empire* by Gibbon and *History of the Saracens* by Ockley, in 1 vol., issued by A. Murray, London, 1870, which consists of chapters 50–52 of *The Decline and Fall* of Gibbon and the third edition of Ockley's work, which was issued in Cambridge, 1755. The second edition of the Ockley work was issued in London, 2 vols., 1718. Warne reissued this in the present series in the 1880s.

389 ANONYMOUS *Our Favourite Nursery Rhymes.* 16mo. Illustrated. 1/o sewed, 2/o June 21 (*Ath*)

This has no date, 149 pp. The first edition was issued by Warne (1865), small 4to, 168 pp., illustrated, 3/6, listed in the *Ath* on Sept. 23. It was reissued at the end of 1868 at 3/6 and with colored illustrations at 5/o.

390 NATHANIEL HAWTHORNE *Twice-Told Tales.* Cr 8vo. 1/6 sewed, 2/o cloth July 19 (*Ath*)

Chandos Classics No. 17. This has no date, 374 pp., and contains the second series. Warne reissued it, 1893, as *Chandos Classics* No. 148, Cr 8vo, 1/6 sewed, 2/o cloth, 2/6 imitation Roxburghe, listed in the *PC* for Aug. 19. The first edition of the second series was in a 2-vol. issue by James Monroe & Co., Boston, 1842, with vol. 1 being the first series, 18 cm., in black or brown cloth with cream or yellow endpapers, top edges untrimmed, $2.25. It was listed in the *Boston Quarterly Review* for Apr. 1842. The first English edition of the second series was pirated by Kent & Richards, London (1849), 18 cm., 312 pp., frontispiece, in rose cloth with white endpapers, edges untrimmed, listed in the *Spect* on Feb. 3 and received at the *BM* on Feb. 13. The sheets were used by William Tegg & Co., London, for a reissue, 1850, with a cancel title page. Henry G. Bohn, London, issued it in 2 vols., 1/o green boards, printed in blue, in Nov. and Dec. 1851, and issued it in 1 vol. also in 1851, 18.5 cm., 358 pp. George Routledge, London, also issued it in 2 vols. in 1851, dated 1852, 1/o boards, 1/6 cloth each, listed by *PC* as published Nov. 29–Dec. 13, 1851. The first Irish edition was issued by James McGlashan, Dublin, 1850, a piracy. Warne also issued this with no date, one such issue being a new edition with the colophon dated June 4, 1883.

391 HUGH M. WALMSLEY *Branksome Dene.* 12mo. 2/o boards, 2/6 cloth Aug. 2 (*Ath*)

Companion Library No. 56. The first edition was issued by Bentley, London, 3 vols., 1872, advertised in the *Ath* on Apr. 6 as "Now ready." Wolff's copy is in blue cloth with cream endpapers, dedicated to the memory of Richard Bentley. Wolff states that the Bentley private catalog gives the publication date as Aug. 5, 1872, but this must be a misprint for Apr. 5 as it was advertised as stated above and also reviewed in the *Ath* on Apr. 20. Hutchinson, London, issued it in 1892, Cr 8vo, 2/6, listed in the *Spect* on May 28.

392 JOHN H. PEPPER *Science Simplified.* 7 vols. Cr 8vo. Illustrated Aug. 30 (*Spect*)

These titles were extracted from *Cyclopaedic Science Simplified*, first issued by Warne in 1869, 19.5 cm., illustrated. They also issued it in a revised edition, no date, 19.5 cm., 685 pp., illustrated, and the *Eng Cat* gives such, 9/o, issued in 1873. All seven of the present vols. have the joint imprint of Scribner, Welford & Armstrong, New York, no date, 19 cm., illustrated. The first three, *Chemistry*, 144 pp.; *Electricity*, 146 pp.; and *Light*, 126 pp., were issued at 2/o cloth each, and were issued in 1 vol. in 1876, Cr 8vo, 5/o, listed in the *Spect* on Mar. 4. The last four titles were *Heat*, 88 pp.; *Magnetism*, 87 pp.; *Pneumatics*, 98 pp.; and *Acoustics*, pages unknown, issued at 1/6 cloth each.

393 ROBERT M. BALLANTYNE *Jarwin and Cuffy.* Fcp 8vo. Illustrated. 2/o cloth Oct. 18 (*Ath*)

Incident and Adventure Library. This is the first edition, no date, 179 pp. It was issued in the United States by James Pott, New York, 1882.

394 FRANCES F. BRODERIP **The Daisy and Her Friends.** 18mo. Illustrated. 1/6 cloth Oct. 18 (*Ath*)

Birthday Series. The first edition was issued by Warne, 1869, Cr 8vo, illustrated, 3/6, advertised in the *Ath* on Apr. 24.

395 HENRY C. ADAMS **Gannet Island; or, Willie's Birthday.** 12mo. Illustrated. 2/0 cloth Oct. 18 (*Ath*)

Home Circle Gift Books. This was also given by the *Eng Cat*, but otherwise I cannot trace it.

396 GRACE GREENWOOD (SARA J. CLARKE, later LIPPINCOTT) **Stories from Famous Ballads. For Children.** 18mo. Illustrated. 1/6 cloth Oct. 18 (*Ath*)

This has no date, 141 pp., with additions by Aunt Louisa (Laura Valentine). This was placed in the *Illustrated Fairy Library* probably in 1878, 12mo, 1/0 sewed, 1/6 cloth. The first edition was issued by Ticknor & Fields, Boston, 1860, 16.5 cm., 141 pp., illustrated. It was later issued by James R. Osgood & Co., Boston, 1871, 16.5 cm., 178 pp., illustrated, with four more stories.

397 ANNIE KEARY **Tilly Trickett; or, Try.** 12mo. Colored frontispiece. 1/0 cloth Oct. 18 (*Ath*)

Round the Globe Library. This is the first edition, no date.

398 OLD MERRY, ed.(EDWIN HODDER) **On Earth, Above and Below.** Fcp 8vo. Illustrated. 2/0 cloth Oct. 18 (*Ath*)

I suspect this is in the *Incident and Adventure Library*, but I have not found it in any Warne list. It is also given by the *Eng Cat*, but otherwise I cannot trace it.

399 FELICIA HEMANS **Poetical Works of Mrs. Hemans.** Cr 8vo. 1/6 sewed, 2/0 cloth Oct. 18 (*Spect*)

Chandos Classics No. 23. This has no date, 552 pp. *Poems* was issued by T. Cadell & W.

Davies, London, 1808, 28 cm., 111 pp., illustrated, by Felicia O. Browne, her first published work, supposedly written between the ages of 8 and 13. *Poetical Remains of the Late Mrs. Hemans* was issued by William Blackwood & Sons, Edinburgh, etc., 1836, 16.5 cm., 321 pp., 8/6, advertised in the *Spect* on Mar. 19 as "Just published." *The Works of Mrs. Hemans* was issued in 7 vols., monthly at 5/0, illustrated each, by Blackwood, Edinburgh, etc., 17.5 cm., vol. 1 reviewed in the *Spect* on June 1; vol. 2 listed June 29; vol. 3 on Aug. 3; and vol. 7 on Dec. 21, 1839. In the United States *Poems* was issued by Hilliard, Gray, Little & Wilkins, Boston, 2 vols., 1826–27, 18mo, reviewed in the *American Quarterly Review* (Philadelphia) for Mar. 1827. *The Poetical Works of Mrs. Felicia Hemans* was issued by Evert Duyckinck, New York, 2 vols., 1828, the fourth American edition, containing many new poems not in any previous edition, listed in the *North American Review* (quarterly) for Jan. 1829.

400 A LADY **Beauty.** Fcp 8vo. 1/0 boards Oct. 18 (*Spect*)

Useful Books. This is the first edition. Warne also issued it in *Illustrated Bijou Books* No. 25, 32mo, illustrated, 0/6 cloth, probably in 1873.

401 ELEANORA L. HERVEY (E. L. MONTAGU, later HERVEY) **The Children of the Pear Garden, and Their Stories.** 12mo. Illustrated. 2/0 cloth Oct. 25 (*Ath*)

Home Circle Gift Books. This is the first edition, no date.

402 SKIMBLE SKAMBLE **Original Fairy Tales.** [New edition.] 18mo. 1/0 Dec. 27 (*Ath*)

The first edition was *Fairy Tales by Skimble Skamble* issued by Whittaker, London, in 1868, p 8vo, 3/6. Warne issued it in *Illustrated Books for Children* after 1920.

403 SUSAN COOLIDGE (SARAH C. WOOLSEY) *What Katy Did.* 12mo. Illustrated. 2/o cloth. Dec.?

I place this here as it was reviewed in the *Ath* on Jan. 31, 1874. Warne issued it in the *Home Circle Gift Books* series, probably in 1877. The first edition was issued by Roberts Brothers, Boston, 1873, 18 cm., 274 pp., illustrated, $1.50 cloth, advertised in the *New-York Times* on Dec. 21, 1872, and deposited on Jan. 7, 1873, and listed in *PW* on Nov. 28, 1872. The first English edition was issued by Ward, Lock & Tyler, London, no date, 238 pp., 1/o sewed, 1/6, 2/o, listed in the *Ath* on Sept. 27, 1873. Warne issued this in the *Star Series* No. 32 in 1876, 16mo, 1/o sewed, 1/6 cloth.

404 F. J. PAUL *The Children of Elfland.* 18mo. Illustrated. 1/6 cloth   Dec.?

Birthday Series. I place this here as it was "On our table" in the *Ath* for Jan. 31, 1874. I cannot trace it.

405 ANONYMOUS *Ten Little Niggers.* 4to. Colored illustrations. Music. 1/o sewed, 2/o linen   1878

Juvenile Drolleries. This is the first edition, no date, with the joint imprint of Scribner, Welford & Armstrong, New York, 27 cm., 12 leaves, cover title. It was listed in the *Ath* on Aug. 23. It was reissued in 1875, o/6 sewed, 1/o, listed in the *Bks* for Sept. See *Nine Niggers More*, 1874

406 (EDWIN HODDER) *Ole Merry's Travels on the Continent.* [New edition.] Fcp 8vo. Illustrated. 2/o cloth   1873 (*Eng Cat*)

Incident and Adventure Library. This has no date, the joint imprint of Scribner, Welford & Armstrong, New York, 198 pp., with the series title on the cover. The first edition was issued by Hodder & Stoughton, London, no date, 17 cm., anonymous, 198 pp., illustrated, noticed in the *British Quarterly Review* for Jan. 1870 and thus

probably issued in Oct. 1869. They reissued it at 2/6, new edition, in 1871. It was issued in the United States by J. B. Lippincott & Co., Philadelphia, 1873, anonymous, 198 pp., illustrated, listed in *Godey's Lady's Book* for Nov. 1873 and thus probably issued in Aug. or Sept.

407 SUSAN COOLIDGE (SARAH C. WOOLSEY) *The New-Year's Bargain.* Cr 8vo. Illustrated. 1/o sewed, 1/6 cloth 1873 (*Eng Cat*)

This has no date, 182 pp. Warne also issued it in the *Illustrated Fairy Library*, 12mo, illustrated, 1/o sewed, 1/6 cloth, probably in 1878. The present edition is possibly the first English edition. It was also issued by Seeley, Jackson & Halliday, London, 1873, 222 pp., illustrated, 3/6, with the illustrations of the American edition, listed in the *British Quarterly Review* for Jan. 1873, and thus probably issued in Oct. 1872. It was issued by Ward, Lock & Tyler, London, in 1875, *Beeton's Good-Aim Series* No. 16, 18mo, o/9 sewed, 1/o, 1/6 cloth, listed in the *Spect* on June 26. The first edition was issued by Roberts Brothers, Boston, 1872, 19 cm., 231 pp., illustrated, listed in *ALG&PC* (fortnightly) on Jan. 1, 1872 and in the *Nation* on Jan. 11 and listed in *Scribner's Monthly* for Dec. 1871 and thus probably issued in Nov.

408 ABBY M. DIAZ *William Henry's School Days.* 18mo. Illustrated. 1/6 cloth   1873 (*Eng Cat*)

Birthday Series. This has no date, 251 pp.

409 CAROLINE M. GEMMER *Children of the Sun, etc. Poems for the Young.* [New edition.] 18mo. Illustrated, 1/6 cloth   1873 (*Eng Cat*)

Birthday Series. The first edition was Warne, London; Scribner, Welford & Armstrong, New York, 1869, 19 cm., 144 pp., illustrated, 3/6, "On our table" in the *Ath* for Jan. 23, 1869.

410 H. D. RICHARDSON *Domestic Pigs.*
New edition. 12mo. Illustrated. 1/0
1873 (*Eng Cat*)

Country Library. This has no date, 18 cm.,
152 pp., illustrated by W. Oldham and
Harrison Weir, with "The Country Library and Family Circle Books" on the
front cover. *Pigs* was issued by J. McGla-
shan, Dublin, 1847, 106 pp., illustrated by
Oldham. A new edition, much enlarged,
was issued by W. S. Orr, London, *Domestic
Pigs*, probably in 1852, 148 pp., illustrated, 1/0. There was an edition of *Domestic Pigs* issued by Rogerson, London, in the
1850s, 152 pp., illustrated. One or both of
the latter two had illustrations by Oldham
and Weir.

411 JOHN T. TROWBRIDGE *Jack Hazard
and His Fortunes.* Fcp 8vo. Illustrated.
2/0 cloth 1873 (*Eng Cat*)

Incident and Adventure Library. The first En-
glish edition was issued by Sampson Low,
London, 1871, 3/6, listed in the *Ath* on
Nov. 11. In the United States it ran in *Our
Young Folks* (Fields, Osgood & Co.), Jan.–

Dec. 1871, and was issued by James R. Osgood & Co., Boston, 1871, 18 cm., 254
pp., illustrated, $1.50, advertised in the
New-York Times on Nov. 15, 1871, as "This
day." It was also issued by Porter & Coates,
Philadelphia, 1871, 18 cm., 254 pp., illustrated. Warne reissued it in the present series in 1881, the same, given by the *Eng
Cat.*

412 (FRANZ HOFFMANN) *Fritz; or,
Experience Teacheth Wisdom.* 18mo.
Illustrated. 1/6 cloth 1873?

Birthday Series. This has the joint imprint
of Scribner, Welford & Armstrong, New
York, no date, 15.5 cm., 182 pp., translated from the German, with "Warne's
Birthday Library" on the spine. *Fritz; or,
Filial Obedience* was issued by the Lutheran
Board of Publication, Philadelphia, 1870,
17.5 cm., 125 pp., illustrated. *Fritz, or The
Struggle of a Young Life* was issued by Nisbet, London, in 1872, 18mo, anonymous,
1/6, listed in the *Ath* on Nov. 30, 1872.
Warne also issued it in the *Bedford Library*,
12mo, illustrated, 1/6 cloth, in the 1890s.

Frederick Warne & Co.
Bedford Street, Covent Garden
1874

413 FREDERICK MARRYAT **The King's Own.** Cr 8vo. o/6 sewed   Apr. 11 (*Ath* ad)

Notable Novels No. 14. This has no date, 160 pp. The first edition was issued by Colburn & Bentley, London, 3 vols., 1830, 20 cm., anonymous, 31/6 boards, advertised in the *Spect* on Mar. 27 as "Just published" and given by the Bentley private catalog as published on Apr. 15. Saunders & Otley, London, issued a second edition, revised, in 1836, 3 vols., p 8vo, anonymous, advertised in the *Spect* on May 21. Bentley issued it as *Standard Novels* No. 65, 1838, 427 pp. The first American edition was issued by Carey & Hart, Philadelphia, 2 vols., 1834, anonymous, reviewed in the *Knickerbocker* for Oct.

414 FREDERICK MARRYAT **The Naval Officer; or, Scenes and Adventures in the Life of Frank Mildmay.** Cr 8vo. o/6 sewed   Apr. 11 (*Ath* ad)

Notable Novels No. 15. This has the joint imprint of Scribner, Welford & Armstrong, New York, no date, 150 pp. The first edition was issued by Henry Colburn, London, 3 vols., 1829, anonymous, 28/6 boards, listed in the *Spect* on Mar. 21, his first novel. Colburn issued it, 1834, 3 vols., *Naval and Military Library* Nos. 1–3, using the original sheets. He issued it as *Colburn's Modern Standard Novelists* No. 10 in Dec. 1835, as *Frank Mildmay*. Colburn & Bentley advertised it in the *Spect* on Jan. 28, 1832,

3 vols., p 8vo, anonymous, 28/6 boards. This title and the preceding and following titles were issued in 1 vol. by Warne as *Novelist's Library* No. 1, Cr 8vo., printed in double columns with separate pagination and with the series title on the front, spine, and title page, listed in the *Spect* on May 9, 1874, 1/6 boards, 2/o cloth. The first American edition was issued by Carey, Lea & Blanchard, Philadelphia, 2 vols., 1833, 21 cm., anonymous, $1.25, advertised in the Washington, D.C., *Globe*, (daily) on Dec. 15, 1833, and I've found this to be very accurate in giving the date of issue.

415 FREDERICK MARRYAT **Newton Forster.** Cr 8vo. o/6 sewed   Apr. 11 (*Ath* ad)

Notable Novels No. 16. This has no date, 147 pp. The first edition was issued by James Cochrane & Co., London, 3 vols., 1832 (1831), 22 cm., 24/o boards, listed in the *Spect* on Dec. 17, 1831. The first American edition was issued by Carey, Lea, and Blanchard, Philadelphia, 2 vols., 1833, 20 cm., anonymous, $1.25, 1,000 copies finished in Dec. 1833 according to the cost book of Carey & Lea. It was advertised by a Washington, D.C., bookstore in the *Globe* (daily), on Dec. 20, 1833, and advertised in the *National Gazette and Literary Record* on Dec. 24. It was also issued by Wallis & Newell, New York, 1836, 12mo, anonymous, 217 pp, in their *Franklin Library Edi-*

tion. Warne issued it in the *Novelist's Library* (see the preceding item).
Also 1887

416 ANNE PRATT **The Flowering Plants of Great Britain. Part 1.** [New edition.] Colored illustrations. 5/0 sewed   Apr. 25 (*Spect* ad)

This was issued in 12 monthly parts. Part 2 was ready in a June 2 ad, and part 3 was ready in a June 27 ad. *The Flowering Plants and Ferns of Great Britain* was issued by the Society for Promotion of Christian Knowledge, London, (1855), 5 vols., colored plates; and they issued The *British Grasses, Sedges, etc.* (1859). Both titles were issued by Warne in 6 vols. in 1873, Roy 8vo, 75/0. Warne reissued the latter, 1891, 4 vols., reissued 1899–1900 and 1905. *The Flowering Plants of Great Britain* was issued by Warne in 1886, new edition, 3 vols., 8vo, colored plates, 42/0.

417 MARIA CUMMINS & ANNA B. WARNER **The Lamplighter. Mabel Vaughan. The Howards of Glen Luna.** Cr 8vo 1/6 boards, 2/0 cloth   July 11 (*Spect*)

Novelist's Library No. 4. This combines *Notable Novels* Nos. 5, 6, and 8 in 1 vol.
See 1867 for the first title; 1868 for the second; 1869 for the third

418 ANONYMOUS **The English Girl in a Convent School.** Fcp 8vo. 1/0 sewed July 18 (*Ath*)

Readable Books No. 1. This is the first edition, no date.

419 THE BROTHERS GRIMM **Grimm's Fairy Tales.** Cr 8vo. 1/6 sewed, 2/0 cloth Aug. 15 (*Ath*)

Chandos Classics No. 24. This has no date, translated by Mrs. Paull. It was listed in the *Spect* for Aug. 1, 1874, at 3/6, arranged for young people by Mrs. Paull. Warne issued it in 1872, Cr 8vo, illustrated, 5/0, about

Dec. 7, 1872. They issued it in 1887, reviewed in the *Spect* for Nov. 26, and in 1889, Demy 8vo, colored illustrations, 7/6, advertised in the *Spect* on Oct. 19. It was issued by Warne, New York, in the *Chandos Classics*, listed in the *Nation* on Aug. 23, 1894. They issued it in the *Fairy Library*, 12mo, illustrated, 1/6 cloth, translated by Mrs. Paull and L. A. Wheatley, listed in *PC* on May 13, 1893; they reissued it in that series in 1897, listed in *PC* on Sept. 11. The first edition was *Kinder- und Haus-Märchen*, Berlin, 3 vols., 18 cm: vol. 1, 1812; vol. 2, 1815; vol. 3, 1818. The fist English edition was *German Popular Stories*, translated by Edgar Taylor, 2 vols., 17.5 cm., illustrated by Cruikshank, 7/0 each: vol. 1, C. Baldwyn, London, 1823, listed by the *Quarterly Review* as published July–Sept. 1822; vol. 2, James Robins & Co., London, etc., 1826. I think Robins reissued vol. 1, 1825, 18 cm., 240 pp. *German Popular Stories* was issued in Boston, 2 vols., 18mo: vol. 1 Boston, listed in the *North American Review*, a quarterly, for July 1826; and vol. 2, Munroe & Francis, Boston, listed Oct. 1828. John Murray, London, issued *The Fairy Ring*, 1846, translated by John Taylor, with 12 illustrations by Richard Doyle, noticed in the *Westminster Review*, a quarterly, for Mar.; and it was issued by E. Kearny, New York, 1849, 18 cm., 376 pp., illustrated.

420 HANS C. ANDERSEN **Hans Andersen's Fairy Tales.** Cr 8vo. 1/6 sewed, 2/0 cloth Aug. 15 (*Spect*)

Chandos Classics No. 25. This is a translation by Mrs. Paull, arranged for young people, probably with the joint imprint of Scribner, Welford & Armstrong, New York, 664 pp. Warne issued it, 1867, Cr 8vo, 671 pp., illustrated, 5/0, 6/0, listed in the *Ath* on Nov. 17, 1866. They issued it with joint Scribner imprint, 1868, 19.5 cm., 671 pp., illustrated, 5/0, a reissue of the previous issue, listed in the *Spect* on

Feb. 8. They issued it also in 1874, 3/6, listed in the *Spect* on Sept. 19, and in 1882, Cr 8vo, 7/6, listed in the *Spect* on Sept. 9. The first edition was issued by C. A. Reitzel, Copenhagen, in three series. The first series was 1835, 4 tales, 61 pp., issued May 8; the second series was 1835, 3 tales; and the third series was 1837, 2 tales. These were reissued ca. 1843, 13 cm. The three series in 1 vol. was issued, 1837, and again ca. 1843. Four English editions were issued in 1846. The first English edition was *Wonderful Stories for Children* (ten tales), issued by Chapman & Hall, London, 1846, 16.6 cm., 127 pp., four colored plates, 4/6 in dark green cloth, listed in the *Spect* on Feb. 7. This was translated by Mary Howitt, who supposedly learned Danish for the purpose and was horrified to find the author's name spelled with an "o" on the title page. *A Danish Story Book and the Nightingale and Other Tales* was issued by Joseph Cundall, London, 2 vols., translated by Charles Boner from a German translation, 17 cm., illustrated, 3/6, listed in the *Spect* on May 9 as "Just published" but given as issued in Feb. by *Early Children's Books. . .* , issued by the Pierpont Morgan Library. *Danish Fairy Legends and Tales* was issued by William Pickering, London, 1846, 16.5 cm., 197 pp., 14 stories, translated by Caroline Peachy, issued in May according to the Osborne Collection. *A Poet's Bazaar* was issued by H. G. Bohn, London, in 1846, translated by Beckwith. The first American edition was issued by Wiley & Putnam, New York, in 2 series, 1846, square 16mo, illustrated, the first series listed in the *Merchant's Magazine* (monthly), 10 stories, for May, 142 pp. It was *Wonderful Stories for Children* in the Howitt translation. *Andersen's Story Book* with a memoir by Howitt was issued by C. S. Francis, Boston, 3 series in one, in 1848, 176, 186, 165 pp., illustrated, $.75, listed by *Lit W* as published Nov. 11–18, 1848. I think Francis issued the series sep-

arately also, as one of them was listed by *Lit W* as published July 10–17, 1848, at $.37. Also 1883, 97. See 1865, 77

421 JAMES HALLIWELL-PHILLIPPS, ed. *The Nursery Rhymes of England.* [New edition.] Fcp 8vo. Illustrated. 1/o picture cover, 2/o cloth   Sept. 5 (*Ath*)
This has the joint imprint of Scribner, Welford & Armstrong, New York, 16.5 cm., 333 pp., and it has an added engraved title page with the imprint of J. R. Smith, London, fifth edition. Warne issued it also, small Cr 8vo, at 3/6, listed in the *Spect* on Nov. 21, 1874. They issued it in 1886, 250 copies for England and America, illustrated, listed in *Notes & Queries* for Oct. 30. The first edition was as vol. 4 of *Early English Poetry*, ed. by Halliwell, issued by the Percy Society, London, 1842, 19.5 cm., 192 pp. The *BM* gives the third edition as 1844; the *U Cat* gives the third edition, printed in London, as reprinted by Munroe & Francis, Boston, 1843 (*sic*), 15 cm., 264 pp.

422 ANONYMOUS *Nine Niggers More.* 4to. Music. 1/o sewed   Sept. 12 (*Ath*)
Juvenile Drolleries. This was included in *Ten Little Niggers, and Other Nursery Rhymes,* issued by Warne in the *Day-Dawn Library* in 1890, illustrated. Warne issued *A Book of Drolleries,* ca. 1875, small 4to, (12), (12), 12 pp., colored illustrations, ed. by Aunt Louisa (Laura Valentine), containing *Ten Little Niggers, Nine Niggers More,* and *A Frog He Would A-wooing Go.*

423 AESOP *The Fables of Aesop.* 80 illustrations. 1/o picture boards   Sept. 19 (*Spect*)
Warne issued *Aesop's Fables with Applications,* Cr 8vo, 1/6 sewed, 2/o cloth, *Chandos Classics* No. 100, ed. by G. F. Townsend and Laura Valentine, listed in the *Spect* on Jan. 7, 1882. They issued *Aesop's Fables,* ed. by Townsend, 1887, 12mo, 364 pp., illus-

trated, 1/0, given by the *Eng Cat*. Warne first issued *The Fables of Aesop* in the Croxall translation with additions by Townsend, p 8vo, 264 pp., illustrated, 5/0, listed in the *Spect* on Jan. 13, 1866. *Vita and Fabula* was issued in Milan, 1476, in Latin, and in Naples, 1485, with an Italian translation. Caxton, Westmyster, issued it in his translation from the French, 1484. It was issued by Francis Barlow, London, 1666, 29.5 cm., illustrated, in English, French, and Latin. It was issued by R. Sare, etc., London, 1692, translated by Sir Roger L'Estrange. It was issued by A. & J. Churchill, London, 1703, 18.5 cm., illustrated, in English and Latin. The first edition of the Croxton translation, *Fables of Aesop and Others*, was issued by J. Tonson & J. Watts, London, 1722, 20.5 cm., 344 pp., illustrated. In the United States it was issued by Robert Bell, Philadelphia, 1777, translated by Robert Dodsley, *Select Fables of Aesop and Other Fabulists*, 371 pp.

424 CHARLES BEACH *Too Good for Anything.* Fcp 8vo. Illustrated. 2/0 cloth Oct. 17 (*Ath*)

Incident and Adventure Library. This is also given by the *Eng Cat*, but otherwise I cannot trace it. Charles Beach actually existed and was not a pseudonym for Mayne Reid as some references state. This was reissued in this series in 1881 and was placed in the *Daring and Doing Library* later, Cr 8vo, illustrated, 1/6 cloth.

425 LAURA VALENTINE, ed. *The Brave Days of Old.* Fcp 8vo. Illustrated. 2/0 cloth Oct. 17 (*Ath*)

Incident and Adventure Library. This is the first edition, no date, 208 pp. It was reissued in this series, the same, in 1881, given by the *Eng Cat*; it was issued in the *Daring and Doing Library* in 1895, Cr 8vo, illustrated, 1/6 cloth, listed in *PC* on July 20.

426 LAURA VALENTINE, ed. *Daring and Doing.* Fcp 8vo. Illustrated. 2/0 cloth Oct. 17 (*Ath*)

Incident and Adventure Library. This is the first edition, no date, 208 pp. It was reissued in this series in 1881, the same, and placed in the *Daring and Doing Library*, probably about 1895.

427 ANONYMOUS *Alice's New Book, and Other Tales.* Square 16mo. Illustrated. 1/0 cloth Oct. 17 (*Ath*)

Now and Then Juvenile Series. This is the first edition, with large type and a colored illustration on every alternate page. It is also given by the *Eng Cat*, but otherwise I cannot trace it.

428 ANONYMOUS *Harry's Horses, and Other Tales.* Square 16mo. Illustrated. 1/0 cloth Oct. 17 (*Ath*)

Now and Then Juvenile Series. This is probably the first edition, with the joint imprint of Scribner, Welford & Armstong, New York, no date. The *U Cat* gives the pages as (193)–286, which I cannot explain. It apparently indicates that this title was part of a larger work. It has large type and colored plates on every alternate page.

429 ANONYMOUS *Honeycombe House, and Other Tales.* Square 16mo. Illustrated. 1/0 cloth Oct. 17 (*Ath*)

Now and Then Juvenile Series. This is the first edition, with large type and colored plates on every alternate page. It is also given by the *Eng Cat*, but otherwise I cannot trace it.

430 ANONYMOUS *Mina's Pets, and Other Tales.* Square 16mo. Illustrated. 1/0 cloth Oct. 17 (*Ath*)

Now and Then Juvenile Series. This is the first edition with large type and colored illustrations on every alternate page. It is also given by the *Eng Cat*, but otherwise I cannot trace it.

431 ANONYMOUS *The Children and the Robin, etc.* 18mo. Illustrated. 1/6 cloth Oct. 17 (*Ath*)

Birthday Series. This is also given by the *Eng Cat.* *The Children and the Robin; Harriet Gray, and Other Stories* was issued by T. Nelson & Sons, Edinburgh and London, 1853.

432 ANONYMOUS *The Orphan Girl (and Other Tales).* 18mo. Illustrated. 1/6 cloth Oct. 17 (*Ath*)

Birthday Series. This has no date and is also given by the *BM* and the *Eng Cat.*

433 ISABELLA K. PLUNKET *The Children's Band.* 12mo. Colored frontispiece. 1/o cloth Oct. 17 (*Ath*)

Round the Globe Library. This is the first edition, no date

434 ANNIE KEARY *Hetty.* 12mo. Colored frontispiece. 1/o cloth Oct. 17 (*Ath*)

Round the Globe Library. This is the first edition, no date.

435 ANNA M. HALL (MRS. S. C. HALL) *Grace Huntley, and Other Stories.* 12mo. Illustrated. 2/6 cloth Oct. 17 (*Ath*)

Golden Links Series. This is also given by the *Eng Cat,* but otherwise I cannot trace it. I suspect this and the following two titles originally appeared in *Chambers's Edinburgh Journal.* Warne issued the present title in the *Star Series* No. 33, 16mo, 1/o sewed, 1/6 cloth, probably toward the end of 1876.

436 ANNA M. HALL (MRS. S. C. HALL) *The Merchant's Daughter.* 12mo. Illustrated. 2/6 cloth Oct. 17 (*Ath*)

Golden Links Series. I cannot trace this. It was issued in the *Star Series* No. 34, 16mo, 1/o sewed, 1/6 cloth, probably at the end of 1876.

437 ANNA M. HALL (MRS. S. C. HALL) *The Daily Governess, and Other Stories.* 12mo. Illustrated. 2/6 cloth Oct. 17 (*Ath*)

Golden Links Series. The *U Cat* gives *Stories of the Governess* by Mrs. Hall, issued by J. Nisbet, London (1852), 22 cm., 128 pp., illustrated; and *The Governess* by her, issued by W. & R. Chambers, 1858, 99 pp., in the *Miniature Library of Fiction,* from *Chambers's Edinburgh Journal.* Warne issued it in the *Star Series* No. 35, 16mo, 1/o sewed, 1/6 cloth, probably at the end of 1876.

438 SAMUEL T. COLERIDGE *The Poetical Works of S. T. Coleridge.* Cr 8vo. 1/6 sewed, 2/o cloth Oct. 24 (*Spect*)

Chandos Classics No. 31. This has no date, 680 pp. Warne issued it in the *Lansdowne Edition* in 1875, 3/6, listed in the *Spect* on Mar. 27. *Poems on Various Subjects* was issued by G. G. & J. Robinson, London, etc., 1796, 17.5 cm., 188 pp., 5/o in drab paper boards with white paper labels, issued Apr. 16. *Poems* was issued by J. Cottle, Bristol, & Messrs. Robinson, London, 1797, second edition, 18 cm., 278 pp., 6/o in dull green paper boards, with a white spine and paper labels, advertised in the *Morning Post* on Oct. 28. It included poems by Charles Lamb and Charles Lloyd. *Poems* was issued by Longmans, London, 1803, third edition, 18 cm., 202 pp., in paper boards. *The Poetical Works* was issued by William Pickering, London, 3 vols., 1828, 15/o, in Aug; and the *Poetical and Dramatic Works* was issued by him, 3 vols., Cr 8vo, 36/o cloth boards, with many added poems now first collected and revised by the author. It was advertised in the *Spect* on Apr. 25 as "This day." In the United States *Poetical Works* was issued by Hilliard, Gray & Co., Boston, in 1835, 3 vols., 287 pp. Vol. 1 listed in the *North American Review* (quarterly) for July. *The Poetical Works* was issued by Herman Hooker, Philadelphia, 1842, 256 pp., edited by Herman Hooker.

439 THOMAS HOOD, THE ELDER *The Poetical Works of Thomas Hood.* Cr 8vo. 1/6 sewed, 2/0 cloth   Oct. 24 (*Spect*)
Chandos Classics No. 34. This has no date, 615 pp. Warne reissued it in this series in the 1880s, and there is a known copy in the original dark blue cloth, with an inscribed date (1894). The first collected edition of the poems in England was issued by Edward Moxon, London. He issued *Poems*, 2 vols., 1846, 12/0, listed in the *Spect* on Jan. 10, 1846; and *Poem of Wit and Humour*, 1 vol., 1847. He issued the third edition of *Poems* in 1848, 2 vols., 12/0, advertised in the *Spect* on June 17. In the United States *Poems* was issued by Little Brown, Boston, 2 vols., 1844. *Prose and Verse* was issued by Wiley & Putnam, New York, 2 vols., in 1845, *Library of Choice Reading*, listed in the *Knickerbocker* and in *Godey's Lady's Book* for Sept. They issued *Poems* in 1 vol., in 1846, 12mo, 229 pp., listed in *North American Review* (quarterly) for July. Porter & Coates, Philadelphia, issued *The Poetical Works of Thomas Hood*, 2 vols., given by the *U Cat* as (1845).

440 PERCY B. SHELLEY *The Poetical Works of Percy Bysshe Shelley.* Cr 8vo. 1/6 sewed, 2/0 cloth   Oct. 24 (*Spect*)
Chandos Classics No. 28. This has no date and 613 pp. *Poems* was issued in the *Albion Edition*, Cr 8vo, 3/6, in 1888, listed in the *Spect* on Sept. 15. *The Poetical Works of Percy Bysshe Shelley . . .* , vol. 1, part 1, was issued by William Benbow, London, 1826; he issued *Miscellaneous and Posthumous Poems* in 1 vol., 1826. *The Works of Percy Bysshe Shelley* in 2 vols., 12mo, 12/0 boards, was listed in the *Westminster Review* (quarterly) for Jan. 1835, no publisher given. The first authorized collection, *The Poetical Works of Percy Bysshe Shelley*, was issued by Edward Moxon, London, 4 vols., 1839, 8vo, portrait, 5/0 each, edited by Mrs. Shelley. Vol. 1 was listed in the *Spect* on Jan. 26, and the vols. appeared monthly; an edition was listed in the *Spect* on Nov. 23, 1839, complete. In the United States *The Poetical Works of Percy Bysshe Shelley* was issued by Porter & Coates, Philadelphia, 1839, 25 cm., 391 pp. The first complete American edition was issued by J. S. Redfield, New York, 1845, 17.5 cm., 750 pp, reviewed in the *Knickerbocker* for Jan. 1846.

441 THOMAS CAMPBELL *The Poetical Works of Thomas Campbell.* Cr 8vo. 1/6 sewed, 2/0 cloth   Oct. 24 (*Spect*)
Chandos Classics No. 29. This has no date, 296 pp. *Poems* was issued 2 vols.-in-1 by Longmans, London, 1810, 17 cm. *The Poetical Works of Thomas Campbell* was issued by Henry Colburn, London, 2 vols., 1828, 20.5 cm., portrait, 18/0 boards, said to be now first collected. It was listed in the *Edinburgh Review* as published Apr.–Nov. 1828 and given as published in June by the *Eng Cat*. In the United States *The Poetical Works of Thomas Campbell* was issued by D. W. Farrand & Green, Albany, etc., 2 vols., 1810, 19.5 cm., with a sketch by (W. Irving). It was issued in 1 vol., 1810, by Philip H. Nicklin & Co., Baltimore, etc., 18 cm., 296 pp. with the sketch. It was issued in New York, 1821, 18mo, said to contain pieces not in any former edition, listed by the *North American Review* (quarterly) for Apr.

442 JOHN KEATS *The Poetical Works of John Keats.* Cr 8vo. 1/6 sewed, 2/0 cloth Oct. 24 (*Spect*)
Chandos Classics No. 30. This has the joint imprint of Scribner, Welford & Armstrong, New York, no date, 281 pp. Either this or a shortly reissued edition was in red cloth with 13 pp. of ads at the back. Warne issued it in the *Lansdowne Edition* in 1876, illustrated, 3/6 cloth, 8/6 leather, advertised in the *Spect* on Mar. 4. It was reissued in the present series in late 1879 or early 1880 in green cloth with 13 pp. of ads at the back and 4 leaves serving as endpapers, listing the present series through

No. 75. It was also reissued in 1889, London and New York, in dark blue cloth and in printed gray wrappers, the latter having 16 pp. of ads at the back and 4 leaves serving as endpapers, listing the series through No. 132. *Poems* was issued by C. & J. Ollier, London, 1817, 19 cm., 121 pp. *The Poetical Works of John Keats* was issued by A. & W. Galignani, Paris, 1829. The same was issued by William Smith, London, 1840, 24.5 cm., 73 pp., and also 1841, 13 cm., 240 pp., frontispiece. *The Poetical Works of Coleridge, Shelley, and Keats* was issued by Desilver, Thomas & Co., Philadelphia, 1835; and *The Poetical Works of John Keats* was issued by Wiley & Putnam, New York, 1846, 2 vols.-in-1, 18.5 cm., and also in 2 parts, 1847, 12mo.

443 HOMER **The Iliad of Homer.** Cr 8vo. Illustrated. 1/6 sewed, 2/0 cloth   Oct. (*Bks*)

Chandos Classics No. 32. This has no date, 452 pp., in Pope's translation. Warne reissued it in this series in the 1890s. They issued it and *The Odyssey* in the *Chandos Edition* in 1874, Cr 8vo, 3/6, listed in the *Spect* on Nov. 7, and issued it again in 1875, with notes by Buckley, at 7/6, listed in the *Spect* on Nov. 27. The first edition of the Pope translation was issued by Bernard Lintot, London, 6 vols., 1715–20. Both the *Iliad* and the *Odyssey* were issued by J. Johnson, etc., London, 5 vols., new edition, 1801. *The Iliad* was issued in the United States by J. Crukshank, etc., Philadelphia, 1795, 18 cm., 484 pp.

444 JULIA CHANDLER **Anybody's Bundle.** p 8vo. 1/0 boards   Oct. 31 (*Spect*)

This is the first edition, no date, 154 pp.

445 HOMER **The Odyssey of Homer.** Cr 8vo. Illustrated. 1/6 sewed, 2/0 cloth Nov. 28 (*Spect*)

Chandos Classics No. 33. This has the joint imprint of Scribner, Welford & Armstrong, New York, no date, 345 pp., in Pope's translation. The first edition in this translation was issued by Bernard Lintot, London, 5 vols., 1725–26. See *The Iliad* above. *The Odyssey* was issued in the United States by W. Durell, New York, 2 vols., 1808.

446 SIR WALTER SCOTT **Essays on Chivalry, Romance, and the Drama.** Cr 8vo. 1/6 sewed, 2/0 cloth   Nov. (*Bks*)

Chandos Classics No. 27. This has the joint imprint of Scribner, Welford & Armstrong, New York, no date, 564 pp. The first edition was issued by R. Cadell, Edinburgh, 1834, 395 pp., illustrated. Warne reissued it in the present series in the 1880s.

447 CHARLES BEACH **The Way to Win.** Fcp 8vo. Illustrated. 2/0 cloth   Dec. 5 (*Ath* ad)

Incident and Adventure Library. Warne issued this also as *Waifs of the World; or, Adventures Afloat and Ashore*, 12mo, 3/6, listed in the *Spect* on Jan. 2, 1875. It was placed in the *Daring and Doing Library* in the 1890s. The first edition was *The Way to Win: A Story of Adventures Afloat and Ashore*, issued by Lockwood & Co., London, 1869, 278 pp., 3/6, listed in the *Ath* on Nov. 20.

448 ANONYMOUS **Military Enterprises.** 16mo. Colored illustrations. 0/6 sewed, 1/0, 1/6 cloth   Dec. 5 (*Ath* ad)

National Books. The 0/6 had two plates, the 1/0 had 12 plates, and the 1/6 had 16 plates. This has the joint imprint of Scribner, Welford & Armstrong, New York, no date, 13 cm., 248 pp. This was advertised in the *Ath* on Nov. 15, 1879, in this series, as No. 9, all three prices.

449 ANONYMOUS *Naval Enterprises.* 16mo. Colored illustrations. o/6 sewed, 1/0, 1/6 cloth   Dec. 5 (*Ath* ad)

National Books. This has no date, and the plates are as for the preceding item. It was advertised in the *Ath* on Nov. 15, 1879, as No. 10 in this series, all three prices.

450 SUSAN COOLIDGE (SARAH C. WOOLSEY) *What Katy Did at School.* 12mo. Illustrated. 2/0 cloth   Dec. 12 (*Ath* ad)

Home Circle Gift Books. This was also listed in the *Spect* on Jan. 2, 1875. There was an edition listed in the *Ath* on Oct. 17, 1874, 12mo, 2/0 cloth, with no publisher given. Warne issued it in the *Star Series* No. 26, 16mo, 1/0 sewed, no date, 223 pp., listed in the *Spect* on July 15, 1876. The first edition was issued by Roberts Brothers, Boston, 1874, 17 cm., 278 pp., illustrated, listed by *PW* on Nov. 1 and by the *Ind* on Nov. 27. The first English edition was issued by Ward, Lock & Tyler, London, in 1874, no date, 236 pp., 1/0 sewed, 1/6, 2/0 cloth, *Lily Series* No. 33, listed in the *Ath* and in the *Spect* on Feb. 28. It was issued by Goubaud & Son, London, in 1876, Cr 8vo, 1/6, listed in the *Spect* on Aug. 12.

451 SIR WALTER SCOTT *Lives of Eminent Novelists and Dramatists.* New edition, revised. Cr 8vo. 1/6 sewed, 2/0 cloth   Dec. (*Bks*)

Chandos Classics No. 26. This has the joint imprint of Scribner, Welford & Armstrong, New York, no date, 617 pp. This consists of the prefaces in *Ballantyne's Novelists Library* plus the lives of Dryden and Swift. Warne, London and New York, reis-

sued it in the present series, 1887, 19 cm., 617 pp. It was issued by A. & W. Galignani, Paris, 2 vols.-in-1, 1825, 16.5 cm.; and by A. M. Schlesinger, Berlin, 2 vols. 1825, 18 cm. In the United States it was issued by Carey & Lea, Philadelphia, 1825, 2 vols., 16mo.

452 JANE PORTER, ELIZABETH HELME & ANNA M. PORTER *The Scottish Chiefs. St. Clair of the Isles. The Hungarian Brothers.* Cr 8vo. 1/6 boards, 2/0 cloth   1874

Novelist's Library No. 2. This is my copy, no date, 19.5 cm., 256, 138, 126 pp., in double columns, orange pictorial boards, with the series title on the front, spine, and title page. The imprint on the title page is joint with Scribner, Welford & Armstrong, New York. There are publisher's ads on the endpapers and 3 pp. of Chapman & Hall ads on small paper inserted at the front, and a commercial ad on the back cover. It consists of *Notable Novels* Nos. 1, 3, and 10. The author of *The Hungarian Brothers* is given as Jane Porter! I date this from its no. in the series and from the Chapman & Hall list. For the first title see 1866; for the second title see 1867; for the third title see 1869.

453 REGINA M. ROCHE, JANE PORTER & CLARA REEVE *The Children of the Abbey. Thaddeus of Warsaw. The Old English Baron.* Cr 8vo. 1/6 boards, 2/0 cloth 1874

Novelist's Library No. 3. This contains *Notable Novels* Nos. 4, 7, and 9. I date it from its no. in the series.

For the first title see also 1867; 1868 for the second title; 1869 for the third title.

454 WILLIAM C. RUSSELL *Representative Actors.* [New edition.] Cr 8vo. 1/6 sewed, 2/o cloth   Feb. 13 (*Ath*)

Chandos Classics No. 35. This has the joint imprint of Scribner, Welford & Armstrong, New York, no date, 496 pp. Warne issued it in 1872 in the *Chandos Library*, Cr 8vo, portraits, 3/6, advertised in the *Spect* on Feb. 3; they reissued it in the present series in 1888. The first edition was *Representative Actors, 1500–1850*, issued in London, 1865.

455 SAMUEL T. COLERIDGE *The Poetical Works of S. T. Coleridge.* Cr 8vo. 1/6 sewed, 2/o cloth   Mar. 27 (*Spect*)

Chandos Classics No. 31. This has no date and 680 pp. Warne also issued this in the *Lansdowne Edition* at 3/6, listed in the *Spect* on Mar. 27, 1875. *Poems on Various Subjects* was issued by G. G. & J. Robinson, London, etc., 1796, 17 cm., 188 pp. and (4) pp. of errata and ads, 6/o in drab paper boards, white paper labels, on Apr. 16. The second edition was issued by J. Cottle, Bristol; Messrs. Robinsons, London, 1797, 17.5 cm., 278 pp., 6/o in dull green paper boards, backed in white, with white paper labels, advertised in the *Morning Post* as published Oct. 28. It includes poems of Charles Lamb and Charles Lloyd. T. N. Longman & O. Rees, London, issued the third edition in 1803, 17.5 cm., 202 pp., in drab paper boards or in pink boards backed in drab. There was an edi-

tion of *Poems*, listed in the *Quarterly Review*, 8vo, as published Oct.–Dec. 1811. *The Poetical Works of Samuel Taylor Coleridge* was issued by William Pickering, London, 3 vols., 1828, 15/o, in Aug.; Pickering issued *The Poetical and Dramatic Works*, 3 vols., 1829, Cr 8vo, 36/o in cloth boards, advertised in the *Spect* on Apr. 25 as "This day." It has numerous added poems now first collected and revised by the author. In the United States *Poetical Works* was issued by Hilliard, Gray & Co., Boston, 3 vols., 16mo. Vol. 1 with 284 pp. was listed in the *North American Review* (quarterly) for July 1835. *Poetical Works* was also issued by Hooker, Philadelphia, 1842, 256 pp., edited by Herman Hooker.

456 (SUSAN WARNER) *Daisy.* 16mo. 1/o sewed, 1/6 cloth   Apr. 14 (*Ath*)

Star Series No. 1. The cloth editions of this and the following 12 titles came out in Apr. and May 1876. The wrappered editions were advertised in the *Ath* on Apr. 10, 1875, to be ready on Apr. 14, and were advertised on Apr. 17 as "Now ready." Warne issued these by arrangement with James Nisbet & Co., London, who issued them in their *Golden Ladder Series*. Nisbet advertised the series in the *Ath* on Nov. 20, 1875, 24 titles including all the present 13, colored illustrations, 2/6 cloth, 3/6 cloth. The present title has 344 pp. Warne issued it in 1876, listed in *PC* on Dec. 8. The first American edition was issued by J. B. Lippincott & Co., Philadelphia, 1868, 12mo, $2.00 cloth, advertised in the *New-York Times* on June 6 as "Just published" and listed in the *Nation* on June 18. They also issued it in 1869, 12mo, $1.75 cloth, listed in the *Nation* on Aug. 5. The first English edition was issued by James Nisbet, London, 1868, 344 pp., colored illustrations, 3/6 cloth, listed in the *Ath* on June 6. Both the first editions were anonymous.

457 (SUSAN WARNER) *Daisy in the Field.* 16mo. 1/o sewed, 1/6 cloth   Apr. 14 (*Ath*)
Star Series No. 2. See No. 456 above. This has 332 pp. It have a cloth copy in rust, no date, new edition, probably in 1879, 16.7 cm., 332 pp., elaborately blocked in black and gold with a vignette on the cover. It has no author on the title page and Elizabeth Wetherell (Susan Warner) on the front cover; there are 16 pp. of publisher's ads at the back. It has gray endpapers with publisher's ads, and the series title appears on the front cover, spine, and title page. Warne issued it in 1876, listed in *PC* on Dec. 8. The first edition was issued by James Nisbet & Co., London, 1869, 18 cm., 332 pp., illustrated, in green or blue cloth, bevelled cover and brown endpapers, with 16 pp. of ads at the back. It was deposited July 16 and listed in the *Ath* on July 17. They issued a new edition, advertised in the *Ath* on Jan. 8, 1870 as "In the press," and a new edition, listed in *PC* on Nov. 3, 1879. The first American edition was issued by J. B. Lippincott & Co., Philadelphia, 1869, 19 cm., 380 pp., $1.75 purple or green cloth with pinkish white or buff endpapers and 4 pp. of publisher's ads. It was deposited Aug. 10 and listed in *ALG&PC* on Aug. 16 and advertised in the *New-York Times* on Aug. 3, anonymous, as "Just published."

458 ALICE GRAY (JULIA A. MATHEWS) *Nettie's Mission.* 16mo. 1/o sewed, 1/6 cloth   Apr. 14 (*Ath*)
Star Series No. 3. This was issued by James Nisbet & Co., London, 1866, 3/6, in the *Golden Ladder Series*, listed in the *Ath* on Oct. 6. In the United States it was issued by Robert Carter & Brothers, New York, 1869, 16 cm., 141 pp., illustrated, as *Golden Ladder Series* No. 1.
See No. 456 above.

459 ELIZABETH PRENTISS *Stepping Heavenward.* 16mo. 1/o sewed, 1/6 cloth   Apr. 14 (*Ath*)
Star Series No. 4. See No. 456 above. The first edition was issued by A.D.F. Randolph, New York (1869), 19.5 cm., 426 pp., from the *Advance*, listed in the *Nation* on Nov. 4. The first English edition was issued by James Nisbet & Co., London, 1870, small 8vo, 3/6, colored illustrations, listed in the *Ath* on Dec. 11, 1869. They issued the fourth edition in 1872, 12mo, 280 pp., 2/6 cloth, listed in *PC* as published Jan. 1–15, 1872; they issued it again in 1879, 12mo, 2/6, listed in the *Spect* on Aug. 16.

460 (SUSAN WARNER) *Willow Brook.* New edition. 16mo. 1/o sewed, 1/6 cloth   Apr. 14 (*Ath*)
Star Series No. 5. This is my copy, no date, 16.2 cm., 311 pp., in gray wrappers cut flush, decorated in red, green, and black, and printed in blue, with the series title on the front cover, spine, and title page. The author is given on the front cover as Elizabeth Wetherell (Susan Warner), but there is no name on the title page. It has gray endpapers with publisher's ads, and there are 4 pp. of publisher's ads at the back and a commercial ad in blue on the back cover. The first edition was issued by Robert Carter & Brothers, New York, 1874, 17.5 cm., anonymous, 348 pp., frontispiece and plates, 4 pp. of ads, bound in brown or green cloth, with yellow endpapers. It was advertised in the *New-York Times* on Feb. 21, $1.25, and listed in *PW* on Feb. 28. The first English edition was issued by James Nisbet & Co., London, 1874, anon-

ymous, 3/6, in the *Golden Ladder Series*, listed in the *Ath* on Mar. 14 and in *PC* on Mar. 16. Nisbet issued *Giving Honour*, containing this title and *The Little Camp on Eagle Hill*, 12mo, anonymous, 3/6, listed in the *Spect* on Sept. 30, 1876; reissued in 1879, listed in *PC* on Dec. 31, 1879. Warne reissued it in 1876, listed in the *Bks* on Dec. 2. See No. 456 above.

461 (SUSAN WARNER) *Sceptres and Crowns and The Flag of Truce*. 16mo. 1/0 sewed, 1/6 cloth   Apr. 14 (*Ath*)
Star Series No. 6. See No. 456 above. Warne reissued this, 12mo, 3/6, listed in the *Spect* on Jan. 9, 1875; they issued it in 1876, listed in the *Bks* for Dec. 2, and reissued it in the *Star Series* No. 75, listed in *PC* on Oct. 15, 1881. The first edition of the first title was issued by Robert Carter & Brothers, New York, 1875, 17.5 cm., anonymous, 427 pp., illustrated, $1.25, in green, orange, or brown cloth, with yellow, pink, or cream endpapers. It was listed in *PW* on Sept. 26, 1874, and in the *Ind* on Oct. 1. It had a long, scathing review in *Scribner's Monthly* for July 1875. The first English edition was probably issued by George Routledge & Sons, London (1874), Fcp 8vo, anonymous, 1/0 sewed, 1/6, 2/0 cloth, listed in the *Spect* on Dec. 5, 1874, and in the *Ath* on Nov. 7. James Nisbet & Co., London, issued *Sceptres and Crowns, and The Flag of Truce* in 1874, 12mo, anonymous, 3/6 cloth, listed in the *Spect* on Dec. 12, 1874, and in *PC* on Dec. 18. *Sceptres and Crowns* was issued by Ward, Lock & Tyler, London, in 1875, 12mo, anonymous, 1/0 sewed, 1/6, 2/0 cloth, listed in the *Spect* on June 26 and in *PC* on July 16. The first edition of the second title was issued by Robert Carter & Brothers, New York, 1875 (copyright 1874), 17.5 cm., anonymous, 397 pp., illustrated, in lavender or brown cloth, with pink endpapers. It has 2 pp. of ads and was listed in *PW* on Nov. 21, 1874, and in the *Ind* on Nov. 26. The first separate English edition was is-

sued by George Routledge & Sons, London, (1875), Fcp 8vo, anonymous, 1/0 sewed, 1/6, 2/0 cloth, listed in the *Spect* and *Ath* on Jan. 16, 1875. Ward, Lock & Tyler, London, issued it in 1875, 0/6 sewed, deposited on Aug. 11 and listed in the *Ath* on Oct. 9.

462 GRACE KENNEDY *Dunallan*. 16mo. 1/0 sewed, 1/6 cloth   Apr. 14 (*Ath*)
Star Series No. 7. See No. 456 above. This has 344 pp. and was also issued by Warne at 3/6 cloth in 1875, 12mo, listed in the *Spect* on May 22. The first edition was issued by William Oliphant, Edinburgh; Hamilton, Adams, London, 3 vols., 1825, 19 cm., anonymous, 18/0, listed by the *Edinburgh Review* as published Oct. 1824–Jan. 1825. They issued a second edition, 3 vols., 12mo, 1825; and third and fourth editions in 2 vols., 1826 and 1829 respectively, the latter at 15/0, still anonymous. There was a sixth edition in 1841, 12mo, 7/0, listed by the *Edinburgh Review* as published May–July 1841. The first American edition was issued by Charles Ewer, etc., Boston; Jonathan Leavitt, New York, 2 vols., 1827, 19 cm., anonymous, noticed in the *Christian Examiner*, Boston, a bimonthly, as published in Sept.–Oct. 1827.

463 GRACE KENNEDY *Father Clement*. 16mo. 1/0 sewed, 1/6 cloth   Apr. 14 (*Ath*)
Star Series No. 8. See No. 456 above. Warne also issued this in the *Golden Links Series*, 12mo, illustrated, 2/0 cloth, advertised in the *Ath* on Dec. 11, 1875. The first edition was issued by William Oliphant, Edinburgh, 1823, 15.5 cm., anonymous, 370 pp., frontispiece. In the United States it was issued by three firms, all 1827: Crocker & Brewster, Boston, etc., 15.5 cm., anonymous, 252 pp.; Bliss & White, New York, anonymous, 246 pp., from the fourth Edinburgh edition; and E. Duyckinck, New York, 15 cm., anonymous, 246 pp., from the sixth Edinburgh edi-

tion. The *U Cat* gives also T. B. Peterson, Philadelphia, (1825), 19 cm., anonymous, 155 pp.

464 ELIZABETH WETHERELL (SUSAN WARNER) *The Wide, Wide World.* 16mo. 1/6 sewed, 2/0 cloth   Apr. 14 (*Ath*)

Star Series No. 9. See No. 456 above. Warne also issued this as *Notable Novels* No. 124, p 8vo, o/6 sewed, listed by the *Bks* for July 1888. The first edition was issued by G. P. Putnam, New York, 2 vols., 1851, 19 cm., $1.50, in purple, blue, brown, or green cloth, with pink endpapers with ads or plain yellow. It was deposited Dec. 14, 1850, and advertised in *Lit W* on Dec. 14 as "Now ready"; there is a known copy inscribed Dec. 14. The 13th edition, 2 vol., $1.50, was advertised in the *Lit W* on Apr. 17, 1852, as "Recent." The first English edition was issued by Sampson Low, London, 2 vols., 1851, Fcp 8vo, 12/0, edited by a clergyman of the Church of England, listed in the *Ath* on Dec. 20, 1851, and in *PC* on Jan. 15, 1852. It was imported by John Chapman, London, and issued in 2 vols., Cr 8vo, 7/0, advertised in the *Ath* on Feb. 14, 1852. It was issued by James Nisbet, Low, etc., London, 1852, Cr 8vo, 657 pp., 5/0, called an author's edition, with a preface by Anna Warner (Dec. 20, 1851). It was listed in the *Ath* on Aug. 7 and in *PC* on Aug. 15. James Nisbet, London, issued it, 2 vols., 1853, author's edition, frontispiece and engraved title page, 6/0, with the preface by Anna Warner, advertised in the *Spect* on Feb. 19, 1853, as "This day." The Nisbet, Low, etc., London, edition was issued as a second edition, 2 vols., 1852, listed in the *Ath* on Aug. 7, 1852, and in *PC* on Aug. 15. This brief discussion does not elucidate the whole complexity of this title's publishing history. Later in 1852 and early 1853 it was also issued by George Routledge, Clarke, Beeton, Nelson, Bohn, Eginton, and Farrington, all in London.

465 ELIZABETH WETHERELL (SUSAN WARNER) *Queechy.* 16mo. 1/6 sewed, 2/0 cloth   Apr. 14 (*Ath*)

Star Series No. 10. See No. 456 above. Warne also issued it as *Notable Novels* No. 125, p 8vo, o/6 sewed, given by the *Eng Cat* as issued in 1888. The first American edition was issued by G. P. Putnam, New York, 2 vols., 1852, 19 cm., $1.75 cloth, purple, brown, black, or blue, with yellow or buff endpapers, with ads or plain. There are 10 or 8 pp. of ads in vol. 1. There were 7,000 copies, deposited Apr. 23, advertised in *Lit W* on Apr. 17 as "On Apr. 24," delayed to secure copyright in England. It was listed by *Lit W* as published Apr. 10–May 15, and there is a known copy inscribed Apr. 27. There was a new edition listed in *Lit W* on May 15, 1852. The first English edition was issued by James Nisbet, etc., London, 2 vols., 1852, 18 cm., 12/0 in decorated blue cloth, with a preface (Mar. 24, 1852), listed in the *Ath* and *Literary Gazette* on Apr. 24 and in *PC* on May 1. Nisbet issued a new edition, 2 vols., 1853, 19.5 cm., frontispiece and title vignette by Birket Foster, 12/0, with the preface, listed in the *Ath* on Apr. 16. There were new editions also, listed on Nov. 27, 1852, and Mar. 12, 1853. George Routledge, London, issued it in 1853, 544 pp., 2/0 boards, 2/6 cloth, with a pictorial title page and a frontispiece, the first illustrated edition, listed in the *Ath* on Apr. 16. Mumby in *The House of Routledge* states that Routledge made an arrangement with Nisbet to issue a 2/0 boards edition and to pay Nisbet o/2 per copy, but then the House of Lords ruled that there was no copyright in American works and the money was never paid.

466 ELIZABETH WETHERELL (SUSAN WARNER) *Melbourne House.* 16mo. 1/6 sewed, 2/0 cloth   Apr. 14 (*Ath*)

Star Series No. 11. This has no date, a new edition, 551 pp., with Susan Warner on the cover. The first edition was issued by Robert Carter & Brothers, New York, 2 vols., 1864, 20 cm., anonymous, illustrated, $3.50 pink or brown cloth with yellow or cream endpapers. It was deposited on Oct. 26 and listed in the *Ind* on Nov. 24 and in *ALG&PC* (fortnightly) on Nov. 15. They issued a new edition in 1 vol., at $2.00, advertised in the *New-York Times* on Dec. 20, 1865, as "Just published." The first English edition was issued by James Nisbet, London, 1865, 17 cm., anonymous, 553 pp., colored illustrations, 3/6, in the *Golden Ladder Series*. It was listed in the *Ath* on Nov. 26, 1864, and advertised then as "This day." Nisbet issued the second edition, the same, listed in the *Reader* on Feb. 11, 1865; and the third edition, Fcp 8vo, 2/0 boards, listed there on May 27, 1865. It was also issued by Routledge, Warne & Routledge, London and New York, 1865, Fcp 8vo, 2/0 boards, 2/6 cloth, listed in the *Ath* on Dec. 10, 1864, and in *PC* on Dec. 15 and 31.

467 ALICE GRAY (JULIA A. MATHEWS) ***Drayton Hall and Other Tales.*** 16mo. 1/6 sewed, 2/0 cloth   Apr. 14 (*Ath*)

Star Series No. 12. This has no date, 567 pp., with the author's name on the cover. The first English edition was issued by James Nisbet, London, 1871, anonymous, 567 pp., illustrated, 3/6, entitled *Drayton Hall; or, Lawrence Bronson's Victory, and Other Tales*, listed in the *Ath* on Apr. 22. The correct title should have had "Laurence." The first American edition was issued by Robert Carter & Brothers, New York, 6 vols., 1871–72, in the *Drayton Hall Series*, consisting of the six tales in the above, No. 1 being *Laurence Bronson's Victory*, 1872, 17.5 cm., 191 pp., illustrated. The six vols. were also issued by D. D. Merrill, St. Paul (copyright 1871). I cannot explain the inconsistency in the dates for the Carter issue but have given the *U Cat* entries.

468 THE OLD BUSHMAN (HORACE WHEELWRIGHT) ***Sporting Sketches. Home and Abroad.*** [New edition.] 12mo. 2/0 boards. Apr. 17 (*Ath*)

The first edition was issued by Warne, 1866, 19.5 cm., 434 pp., portrait, 7/6, listed in the *Ath* on Apr. 28. An issue at 2/6 was listed in the *Spect* on May 1, 1875.

469 CHARLOTTE RIDDELL (MRS. J. H. RIDDELL) ***Pheemie Keller.*** [New edition.] 12mo. 2/0 boards   Apr. 17 (*Ath*)

Companion Library No. 66. This has no date, 451 pp. Sadleir had a copy in the *Companion Library*, with the imprint of Gall & Inglis, London, no date, a yellowback. This ran in the *Shilling Magazine* (London), May 1865–May 1866. The first book edition was issued by Tinsley Brothers, London, 3 vols., 1866, 31/6 in red-brown cloth and cream endpapers, by F. G. Trafford, listed in the *Ath* on Mar. 24. They issued it in 1 vol., 1867, 452 pp., 6/0 in brown cloth, Wolff's copy being by Mrs. J. H. Riddell, a presentation copy with an inscribed date (Christmas 1866). However, it was advertised in the *Spect* on Dec. 8, 1866, as anonymous, "On Dec. 11," and advertised on Jan. 5, 1867, as "This day." This is the first 1-vol. edition and not the Arnold edition below as Sadleir states. Sadleir had an edition issued by F. Enos Arnold, London, 1870, anonymous, frontispiece, 2/0 salmon-pink cloth with pale chocolate endpapers, which he called the first illustrated and first 1-vol. edition. It was listed in the *Ath* on Dec. 18, 1869. The first American edition was issued by Harper & Brothers, New York, 1866, 8vo, 142 pp., $.50 paper, by Trafford, *Library of Select Novels* No. 272, advertised in the *New-York Times* on July 3 as "Recent" and listed in the *Nation* on July 12. It was also issued by the American News Col., New York, 1866, by Trafford, listed in *ALG&PC* (fortnightly) on July 16.

470 CHARLOTTE RIDDELL (MRS. J. H. RIDDELL) *Austin Friars.* [New edition.] 12mo. 2/o boards   Apr. 24 (*Ath*)

Companion Library No. 58. This has the joint imprint of Scribner, Welford & Armstrong, New York, no date, 386 pp, in blue boards decorated in red and black. It is from the sheets of an issue by Gall & Inglis, London, no date, in their *Companion Library*, in pink boards decorated in black and red, Wolff's copy. This ran in *Tinsley's Magazine* beginning in Apr. 1869, anonymous. The first edition was issued by Tinsley Brothers, London, 3 vols., 1870, 20 cm., anonymous, 31/6 in smooth blue cloth with cream endpapers, with a 16-page catalog at the back of vol. 3 (Feb. 1870). It was advertised as "This day" and listed in the *Ath* on May 14.

471 CHARLOTTE RIDDELL (MRS. J. H. RIDDELL) *Maxwell Drewitt.* [New edition.] 12mo. 2/o boards   Apr. 24 (*Ath*)

Companion Library No. 61. The first edition was issued by Tinsley Brothers, London, 3 vols., 1865, 19 cm., 31/6 in brown cloth, by F. G. Trafford, with a 16-page catalog at the back of vol. 3, undated. It was advertised in the *Ath* on Oct. 21 as "Next week" and listed on Oct. 28. Wolff had two bindings, 3 vols., 1865, which he termed secondary, with no publisher on the spine: one in rose-madder cloth and yellow endpapers, and the other in dark green cloth with a different blocking. Tinsley Brothers issued it in 1 vol., 1866, new edition, p 8vo, 452 pp., 6/o, listed in the *Reader* on June 16, the first 1-vol. edition. Sadleir had a copy issued by F. Enos Arnold, London, 1869, new edition, frontispiece, vignette title, and plates, 2/o boards, 2/6 cloth, his copy being in rose-madder cloth with pale chocolate endpapers. The 2/o boards was listed in the *Ath* in Dec. 1869. Sadleir thought this was the first 1-vol. edition. The first American edition was issued by Harper & Brothers, New York,

1866, 8vo, 167 pp., $.75 paper, *Library of Select Novels* No. 266, by Trafford. It was advertised in the *New-York Times* on Mar. 17 as "This day" and listed in the *Nation* on Mar. 29.

472 HENRY NEELE *The Romance of History. England.* Cr 8vo. Illustrated. 1/6 sewed, 2/o cloth   May 8 (*Ath*)

Chandos Classics No. 36. This has no date, 598 pp., and probably has the joint Scribner, Welford & Armstrong, New York, imprint. Warne issued it in 1872, p 8vo, 598 pp., illustrated, at 5/o cloth, listed by *PC* as published July 16–Aug. 1. The first edition was issued by Edward Bull, London, 3 vols., 1828, Cr 8vo, 31/6, reviewed in the *Gentleman's Magazine* (monthly) for Dec. 1827. Bull issued a new edition in 3 vols., 31/6, advertised in the *Spect* on Oct. 18, 1828; they reissued it again, 12mo, illustrated, vol. 1 at 6/o cloth being listed in the *Edinburgh Review* as published Oct. 1833–Jan. 1834. Edward Churton, London, issued it in 15 illustrated parts, 1/o, No. 12 advertised in the *Spect* on May 14, 1836. The first American edition was issued by Carey, Lea & Carey, Philadelphia, 2 vols., 1828, 19 cm., listed in the *North American Review* (quarterly) for Jan. 1829.

473 LEITCH RITCHIE *The Romance of History. France.* Cr 8vo. Illustrated. 1/6 sewed, 2/o cloth   May 8 (*Ath*)

Chandos Classics No. 37. This has no date, 560 pp., probably with the joint imprint of Scribner, Welford & Armstrong, New York. Warne issued it in 1872, Cr 8vo, 560 pp., illustrated, 5/o cloth, listed in the *Spect* on July 27. The first edition was issued by Edward Bull, London, 3 vols., 1831, 19 cm., 31/6, listed in the *Spect* on Dec. 18, 1830. The first American edition was issued by J. & J. Harper, New York, 2 vols., 1831, 12mo, listed in the *North American Review* (quarterly) for July 1831.

474 CHARLES MACFARLANE *The Romance of History. Italy.* Cr 8vo. Illustrated. 1/6 sewed, 2/o cloth   May 22 (*Spect*)

Chandos Classics No. 38. This has no date, 568 pp., probably with the joint Scribner imprint. Warne issued it in 1872, p 8vo, 568 pp., illustrated, 5/o cloth, listed by *PC* as publisher Oct. 16–31. The first edition was issued by Edward Bull, London, 3 vols., 1832, advertised in the *Spect* on Oct. 22, 1831, as "Just ready." It was reissued in 1834, vol. 1 at 6/o published in July. The first American edition was issued by J. & J. Harper, New York, 2 vols., 1832, 19.5 cm., $1.25, advertised by a Washington, D.C., bookstore in the *Globe*, a daily, on Mar. 6 as "Published this day."

475 JOAQUIN T. DE TRUEBA Y COSIO *The Romance of History. Spain.* Cr 8vo. Illustrated. 1/6 sewed, 1/o cloth   May 22 (*Spect*)

Chandos Classics No. 39. This has no date, 579 pp., and probably has the joint Scribner imprint. Warne issued it in 1872, Cr 8vo, 579 pp., illustrated, 5/o cloth, listed in the *Spect* on Aug. 31. The first edition was issued by Edward Bull, London, 3 vols., 1830, p 8vo, 31/6 boards, listed in the *Spect* on Oct. 31, 1829, anonymous, and listed by the *Edinburgh Review* (quarterly) as published June–Sept. 1829. The first American edition was issued by J. & J. Harper, New York, 2 vols., 1830, 19 cm., listed in the *North American Review* (quarterly) for Apr. 1830.

476 JOHN H. CAUNTER *The Romance of History. India.* Cr 8vo. Illustrated. 1/6 sewed, 2/o cloth   May 22 (*Spect*)

Chandos Classics No. 40. This has no date, 514 pp., and probably has the joint Scribner imprint. Warne issued it in 1872, p 8vo, 514 pp., illustrated, 5/o cloth, listed by *PC* as published Aug. 2–15. The first edition was issued by Edward Churton,

London, etc., 3 vols., 1836, p 8vo, 31/6 boards, advertised in the *Spect* on Dec. 19, 1835, as "This day."

477 FLORENCE MARRYAT (MRS. ROSSI CHURCH, later LEAN) *Mad Dumeresq.* 12mo. 2/o boards   May 22 (*Ath*)

Companion Library No. 68. This has no date, pink boards, with 2 pp. of ads and a commercial ad on the back cover. The first edition was issued by Bentley, London, 3 vols., 1873, advertised in the *Ath* on Nov. 22 as "Now ready." The only American edition I've found is that issued by John W. Lovell, New York (1887), 12mo, paper, *Lovell's Library* No. 991.

478 MARIA M. GRANT *Artiste.* 12mo. 2/o boards   May 22 (*Ath*)

Companion Library No. 72. The first edition was issued by Hurst & Blackett, London, 3 vols., 1871, listed in the *Ath* on July 1. It was issued in the United States by A. K. Loring, Boston, no date, 24 cm., 144 pp., in paper wrappers at $.50, listed in the *Nation* on May 8, 1873. It was also issued by George Munro, New York (1878), 4to, 36 pp., illustrated, paper *Seaside Library* No. 312, probably in Apr.

479 CHARLOTTE RIDDELL (MRS. J. H. RIDDELL) *Far Above Rubies.* New edition. 12mo. 2/o boards   June 12 (*Ath*)

Companion Library No. 62. The first edition was issued by Tinsley Brothers, London, 3 vols., 1867, 18.5 cm., 31/6 in claret cloth, listed in the *Ath* on May 18. They issued the second edition, 3 vols., in 1867, advertised in the *Spect* on July 20 as "This day"; they issued it in 1 vol. in 1867, 6/o, advertised in the *Spect* on Dec. 21 as "next week." The first American edition was issued by J. B. Lippincott & Co., Philadelphia, 1867, 12mo, $1.75 cloth, listed in the *Nation* on June 13 and in *ALG&PC* (fortnightly) on June 15.

480 CHARLOTTE RIDDELL (MRS. J. H. RIDDELL) *A Life's Assize.* [New edition.] 12mo. 2/o boards   June 12 (*Ath*)

Companion Library No. 63. This has no date and 393 pp. Wolff had two copies of the boards edition, both with no date and in the *Companion Library*: one in pale yellow boards, decorated in red, blue, and brown, and the other in bright blue boards decorated in violet, black, and shades of indigo. The present edition had the joint imprint of Scribner, Welford & Armstrong, New York. The first edition was issued by Tinsley Brothers, London, 3 vols., 1871, 31/6 in chocolate cloth, listed in the *Ath* on Dec. 17, 1870. Sadleir's copy was a presentation copy, dated Christmas 1870 in vol. 1 and with a 16-page catalog (Nov. 1870) at the back of vol. 3. They issued it in 1 vol., new edition, in 1871, at 6/o, listed in the *Spect* on Nov. 11. The first American edition was issued by Harper & Brothers, New York, 1871, 8vo, 157 pp., $.50 paper, *Library of Select Novels* No. 360, advertised in the *New-York Times* on Apr. 29 as "This day" and listed in the *Nation* on May 4. It ran in *St. James's Magazine* (Skeet), beginning in Mar. 1868.

481 FLORENCE MARRYAT (later CHURCH, later LEAN) *No Intentions.* [New edition.] 12mo. 2/o boards   June 12 (*Ath*)

Companion Library No. 69. This ran in *London Society* (Bentley), Jan. 1873–Feb. 1874, and the first English book edition was issued by Bentley, 3 vols., 1874, p 8vo, 31/6 in red-brown cloth, listed in the *Ath* on Mar. 21. The Bentley private catalog states that it was published Mar. 14 and that at that time Mrs. Church had eight children. The first American edition was issued by D. Appleton & Co., New York, 1874, 8vo, $.75 paper, advertised in the *New-York Times* on Mar. 21 as "This day" and listed in *PW* on Mar. 21.

482 CHARLOTTE RIDDELL (MRS. J. H. RIDDELL) *City and Suburb.* [New edition.] 12mo. 2/o boards   June 19 (*Spect*)

Companion Library No. 65. The first edition was issued by Charles J. Skeet, London, 3 vols., 1861, Cr 8vo, 31/6, by F. G. Trafford, listed in the *Ath* on Apr. 13. Skeet issued a second edition in 3 vols., advertised in the *Spect* on May 4, 1861, as "On May 6"; they issued a new edition in 1 vol., 1862, Cr 8vo, 482 pp. 5/o, advertised in the *Spect* on Oct. 19, 1861 as "In Dec."; and a new edition in 1864, p 8vo, 6/o, by Trafford, listed in the *Reader* on Dec. 24, 1864. Tinsley Brothers issued a new edition, 1866, p 8vo, 482 pp, 6/o in crimson cloth, by Trafford, listed in the *Reader* on Jan. 26, 1866. This latter edition was stated by Sadleir to be the first 1-vol. edition! It was issued by F. Enos Arnold, London, in 1869 at 2/o, listed in the *Bks* for June. Sadleir had a copy in boards, no date, issued by Gall & Inglis, Edinburgh and London, with *Companion Library* on the front cover.

483 MARIA M. GRANT *Victor Lescar.* 12mo. 2/o boards   June 19 (*Spect*)

Companion Library No. 71. The first edition was *Lescar the Universalist*, issued by Chapman & Hall, London, 3 vols., 1874, 19 cm., anonymous, 31/6 in purple cloth with dark cream endpapers printed with publisher's ads. The first American edition was issued by George Munro, New York (1878), 4to, 84 pp., $.20 paper, *Seaside Library* No. 398, *Victor Lescar*, advertised in the *New-York Times* on Sept. 20, anonymous, "Out today." It was also issued by G. W. Carleton, New York, 1879, 17.5 cm., 352 pp., *Sorry Her Lot Who Loves too Well*; reissued, 1884, *So True a Love*.

484 MARIA M. GRANT *Bright Morning.* 12mo. 2/o boards   June 26 (*Spect*)

Companion Library No. 70. This has the joint imprint of Scribner, Welford & Armstrong, New York, no date, 409 pp. The first edition was issued by Chapman & Hall, London, 3 vols., 1873, Cr 8vo, 31/6, listed in the *Ath* on Jan. 26. In the United States it was issued by G. W. Carleton & Co., New York, 1878, 384 pp., $1.00 paper, $1.50 cloth, *Once and Forever*, advertised in the *New-York Times* on June 11 as "This week" and on July 28 as ready. It was issued with the present title by George Munro, New York (1878), 4to, 53 pp., illustrated, $.20 paper, *Seaside Library* No. 378, advertised in the *New-York Times* on June 27 as "Tomorrow" and on June 28 as "Today."

485 CHARLOTTE RIDDELL (MRS. J. H. RIDDELL) *The Rich Husband.* [New edition.] 12mo. 2/o boards   June 26 (*Spect*)

Companion Library No. 60. This has 442 pp. The first edition was issued by Charles J. Skeet, London, 3 vols., 1858, anonymous, 31/6, listed in the *Ath* on Apr. 24. The *Eng Cat* gives it as by Rainey Hawthorne, the first pseudonym used by Riddell. Tinsley Brothers, London, issued it in 1 vol., 1867, new edition, 442 pp., by Riddell, 6/o in bright brown cloth with white endpapers and with a preface (Nov. 1, 1866). It was listed in the *Reader* on Nov. 24, 1866. In the preface the authoress states that there is a slight shortening and the correction of errors. It was issued by F. Enos Arnold, London, in 1870, 2/o, by F. G. Trafford, issued about Apr. 2. The first American edition was issued by T. B. Peterson & Brothers, Philadelphia (1867), 12mo, $1.50 paper, $2.00 cloth, advertised in the *New-York Times* on Mar. 21 as "On Mar. 23" and on Mar. 23 as "This day."

486 CHARLOTTE RIDDELL (MRS. J. H. RIDDELL) *The World in the Church.* New edition. 12mo. 2/o boards   July 10 (*Spect*)
Companion Library No. 64. This has no date, 444 pp., in pale yellow pictorial

boards. The first edition was issued by Charles J. Skeet, London, 3 vols., 1863, p 8vo, 31/6, by F. G. Trafford, listed in the *Ath* on Nov. 1, 1862. Skeet issued a second edition, 3 vols., 1863 (1862), p 8vo, 31/6, listed in the *Reader* on Jan. 24, 1863. Tinsley Brothers, London, issued it in 1 vol., 1865, new edition, 596 pp., by Trafford, advertised in the *Spect* on Mar. 18 as "This day."

487 CAROLINE PICHLER *The Signal Rocket.* 12mo. 1/o   July 10 (*Spect*)
Warne issued this in *Readable Books* in 1876 or 77, Fcp 8vo, 1/o sewed. The first edition was *Die Schweden in Prag*, Wien, 3 vols., 1827, 19 cm., illustrated. The first English edition was *Waldstein; or The Swedes in Prague*, Rodwell, London, 2 vols., 1828, translated by J. D. Rosenthal (Haas?). *The Swedes in Prague* was issued by James Burns, London, 1845, 192 pp., translated by James D. Haas. Wolff had a copy issued by Edward Lumley, no date, *The Swedes in Prague*, 192 pp., frontispiece, translated by James D. Haas.

488 ANONYMOUS *Warne's Shilling Atlas.* [New edition.] 4to. 26 maps. 1/o   July?
This was "On our table" in the *Ath* on Sept. 4. The *U Cat* gives *Warne's One Shilling Atlas*, no date, 25 cm., 12 colored maps. *Warne's Sixpenny Atlas*, square imperial, o/6 sewed, 16 maps in color, was advertised in the *Spect* on Jan. 8, 1876.

489 CERVANTES *Adventures of Don Quixote de La Mancha.* New and revised edition. Cr 8vo. 1/6 sewed, 2/o cloth Aug. 7 (*Spect*)
Chandos Classics No. 42. This has no date, 567 pp., omitting some chapters, and is in the Motteux translation. Warne issued it, 1866, 22.7 cm., 710 pp., illustrated by A. B. Houghton, 12/6, in the Charles Jarvis translation, listed in the *Reader* on Nov. 25, 1865. They issued it in the *Boy's Own*

Library in 1865, 8vo, 766 pp., illustrated by Tony Johannot, 5/o, listed in the *Reader* on Dec. 9, 1865. They issued it in the Jarvis translation in 1876, 8vo, illustrated, 7/6, listed in the *Spect* on Aug. 12; and they issued it in 1875, Cr 8vo, 3/6, listed in the *Spect* on Aug. 28. The first edition was *El Ingenioso Hidalgo Don Quixote de la Mancha*, Madrid, 2 parts, 1605, 1615. The first English edition was issued by Ed Blounte & W. Barret, London, 1612, 1620, part 1 translated by Thomas Skelton and part 2 not by him. The first edition of the Motteux translation was issued by Samuel Buckley, London, 4 vols., 1700–03, translated by several hands and published by Peter Motteux. The first edition of the Jarvis translation was issued by J. & R. Tonson, London, 2 vols., 1742, 4to, illustrated. The Smollett translation was issued by Rivington, London, 2 vols., in 1755, 4to, 50/o, listed by the *Gentleman's Magazine* as published in Mar. In the United States it was issued by Conrad, Philadelphia, etc., 4 vols., 1803.

490 ANONYMOUS **Beauties of German Literature.** Cr 8vo. 1/6 sewed, 2/o cloth Aug. 14 (*Spect*)
Chandos Classics No. 41. The *Eng Cat* gives Burns, 1847, 12mo, 5/o, reduced to 3/o, but otherwise I cannot trace it.

491 G.P.R. JAMES **Richelieu.** Cr 8vo. o/6 sewed Aug. 21 (*Spect*)
Notable Novels No. 17. This has no date, 177 pp., and probably has the joint imprint of Scribner, Welford & Armstrong, New York. I have a copy (1880), 19.4 cm., 177 pp. in double columns, o/6, yellow pictorial wrappers, printed in red, blue, and brown, with the series title on the front cover and spine, without the joint imprint. There are 5 pp. of publisher's ads at the back and publisher's ads on the endpapers, with a commercial ad on the back cover. The first edition was issued by Henry Colburn, London, 3 vols., 1829, 20 cm., anonymous, 31/6, dedicated to (Sir Walter Scott). Colburn & Bentley, London, issued a second edition, revised, 3 vols., 1831, p 8vo, anonymous, with a new preface in which Sir Walter Scott is named. It was advertised in the *Spect* on Mar. 12. It was issued in *Colburn's Modern Standard Novelists* No. 17, 1839, in Mar.; it was issued in the *Parlour Library* No. 146, by Thomas Hodgson, London, 1856, on Aug. 1. The first American edition was issued by J. & J. Harper, New York, 2 vols., 1829, 20.5 cm., anonymous, *Library of Select Novels*, listed in the *North American Review* (quarterly) for Oct. They issued a second edition, 1833.

492 G.P.R. JAMES **Darnley.** Cr 8vo. o/6 sewed Aug. 21 (*Spect*)
Notable Novels No. 18. The first edition was issued by Colburn & Bentley, London, 3 vols., 1830, 19.5 cm., anonymous, 31/6, in boards with labels and white endpapers, advertised in the *Spect* on Jan. 23 as "Just published." Bentley issued it, 1836, *Standard Novels* No. 53; and Simms & M'Intyre, London and Belfast, issued it in the *Parlour Library* No. 46 in 1850. Smith, Elder & Co., London, issued it in 1846 as No. 9 in a reissue of James's works, medium 8vo, frontispiece, 8/o cloth, with some corrections and a new preface, listed in the *Spect* on July 4. The first American edition was issued by J. & J. Harper, New York, 2 vols., 21 cm., anonymous, listed in the *North American Review* (quarterly) for July.

493 G.P.R. JAMES **Philip Augustus.** Cr 8vo. o/6 sewed Aug. 21 (*Spect*)
Companion Library No. 19. This has no date. The first edition was issued by Colburn & Bentley, London, 3 vols., 1831, 19.5 cm., anonymous, 31/6 boards, published June 8 according to the Bentley private catalog, advertised in the *Spect* on Apr. 16 as "Just ready" and listed there on

July 2. Bentley issued it as *Standard Novels* No. 59, 1837, 463 pp., with a new advertisement by James. Smith, Elder & Co., London, issued it as No. 5 of a reissue of James's works, revised and corrected, medium 8vo, 8/o, listed in the *Spect* on July 5, 1845. It was issued in the *Parlour Library* No. 56, 1851, 448 pp., 1/6 boards, 2/o cloth, on Apr. 1, Sims & M'Intyre, London and Belfast. The first American edition was issued by J. & J. Harper, New York, 2 vols., 8vo, anonymous, *Library of Select Novels* Nos. 9 and 10, listed in the *New-England Magazine* (Boston) for Nov. 1831.

494 (MARGARET ROBERTS) *Sydonie's Dowry.* 12mo. Illustrated. 2/6 cloth Aug. 21 (*Ath*)

Golden Links Series. The first edition was issued by Bell & Daldy, London (1865), Cr 8vo, anonymous, 6/o, advertised in the *Spect* on May 27 as "Now ready." Warne issued it in the *Star Series* No. 29, 16mo, 1/o sewed, 1/6 cloth, in late 1876 or early 1877. Wolff had a copy issued by Warne, no date, anonymous, 220 pp., frontispiece and 3 plates, in red-brown cloth with buff endpapers and a multi-colored picture pasted on the front and a 32-page catalog at the back. It was a presentation copy (Easter 1881).

495 ANONYMOUS *Warne's Picture Natural History.* 3 vols. 12mo. Colored illustrations. 1/o picture boards, 1/6 cloth each Sept. 11 (*Spect*)

The 3 vols. were: 1, *Animals*; 2, *Birds and Animals*; and 3, *Fish, Insects, and Reptiles.* These were also given by the *Eng Cat*, but otherwise I cannot trace them.

496 ANONYMOUS *Acquarium Conicum.* 4to. 1/o sewed Oct. 2 (*Ath*)

Juvenile Drolleries. I cannot trace this.

497 EDWARD P. ROE *From Jest to Earnest.* 16mo. 1/o sewed Oct. 16 (*Ath* ad)

Star Series No. 14. This has no date, 312 pp., the first English edition. The 1/6 cloth in the series was issued in 1876, listed in the *Spect* on May 13. The Oct. 16 *Ath* ad said this was copyright in Great Britain and issued at the same time in England and America. Warne issued it in 1878, Cr 8vo, illustrated, 2/6, listed in the *Spect* on Mar. 2. The first American edition was issued by Dodd & Mead, New York, (1875), 19 cm., 548 pp., in terra-cotta cloth with yellow endpapers, listed in *PW* on Sept. 25 and in the *Ind* on Oct. 7. It was reprinted with a revised preface, using the same title page, but Roe was listed as the author of 4 books instead of 3.

498 FREDERIC MACCABE *The Art of Ventriloquism.* 12mo. 1/o boards Oct. 23 (*Ath*)

Useful Books. This is the first edition, no date, 16.5 cm., 110 pp., with the series title on the cover. It was issued by Robert M. DeWitt, New York, copyright 1875, 16.5 cm., 56 pp. I have a copy, no date, probably (1895), 17 cm., 110 pp. in white boards, with the front cover in red and black with a portrait and with the series title. There are publisher's ads on the endpapers and on 1 page at the back and a commercial ad on the back cover. The author's first name is "Frederic" on the cover and "Frederick" on the title page and in the ads.

499 ANONYMOUS *Lucy and Arthur and the Little Cousins.* 18mo. Illustrated. 1/6 cloth Oct. 23 (*Ath*)

Birthday Series. This has no date. It was issued in 1842, square, 3/o, listed in the *Edinburgh Review* as published Apr.–June.

500 CHRISTOPHER SCHMID *The Boy Adventurers.* 18mo. Illustrated. 1/6 cloth Oct. 23 (*Ath* ad)

Birthday Series. This was also given by the *Eng Cat*, but otherwise I cannot trace it.

501 ANONYMOUS *Wedding Chimes.*
32mo. 1/6 Oct. 23 (*Ath*)

This has no date, 11 cm., 128 pp., with an added illustrated title page in color. It is for noting marriages of relatives and friends and contains blank pages.

502 ANONYMOUS *Immortelles.* 32mo.
1/6 Oct. 23 (*Spect*)

This has no date. It is given by the *Eng Cat*, but otherwise I cannot trace it.

503 JONATHAN SWIFT *Gulliver's Travels.*
New and revised edition. 18mo.
Illustrated. 1/6 cloth Oct. 23 (*Ath*)

Birthday Series. This has no date and 188 pp. Warne issued it in 1887, 4to, 27.4 cm., paper on boards with a chromolithograph on the front of Gulliver and other smaller scenes, blue cloth spine. There is a picture of it in *Victorian Publishers' Book-Bindings in Paper* by Ruari McLean, Berkeley and Los Angeles, 1983. The first edition was issued by Benjamin Motte, London, 2 vols., 1726, in 4 parts, portrait, 4 maps, *Travels in Several Remote Regions of the World* by Lemuel Gulliver. Vol. 1 was issued on Oct. 28. Motte also issued it in 1 vol. in 1738, 8vo, anonymous, 4/0, listed by the *Gentleman's Magazine* as published in Mar. J. Stone & R. King, London, issued it in 1727, an unauthorized abridged edition for children. In the United States it was issued by Young & M'Culloch, Philadelphia, 1787, 64 leaves, abridged; and by W. Young, Philadelphia, 1794, 159 pp., illustrated, abridged. W. Durell & Co., New York, issued it in 1812, 19.5 cm., 338 pp., frontispiece, containing all 4 parts.

504 ANONYMOUS *The Romans and the Danes.* 12mo. Colored frontispiece. 1/0 cloth Oct. 23 (*Ath*)

Round the Globe Library. This is the first edition, no date.

505 ANONYMOUS *The Island Hermitage.*
12mo. Colored frontispiece. 1/0 cloth
Oct. 23 (*Ath*)

Round the Globe Library. This is the first edition, no date.

506 GRACE KENNEDY *Anna Ross.* 12mo.
Colored frontispiece. 1/0 cloth Oct. 23
(*Ath*)

Round the Globe Library. This has no date. The first English edition was probably W. Oliphant, Edinburgh, as this firm issued the fourth edition, 1829, 15 cm., 175 pp., anonymous, illustrated. In the United States it was issued by the American Sunday-School Union, Philadelphia (1823), 16 cm., anonymous, 164 pp., illustrated. It was also issued by William Burgess, Jr., New York, 1826, anonymous, 156 pp., illustrated.

507 ANTONIO S. MASKELYNE *True and False Riches.* 12mo. Illustrated. 2/6 cloth Oct. 23 (*Ath*)

Golden Links Series. The first edition was issued by Warne in 1873, 7/6. Warne issued it in *Home Circle Gift Books*, 12mo, illustrated, 2/0 cloth, in 1877, given by the *Eng Cat*.

508 SARAH TRIMMER *The Story of the Robins.* 12mo. Colored illustrations. 2/0 cloth Oct. 23 (*Ath*)

Home Circle Gift Books. Warne issued it with the joint imprint of Scribner, Welford & Co.., New York, 1870, 160 pp., colored illustrations, 3/6. They issued it in the *Golden Links Series*, 12mo, colored illustrations, 2/6 cloth, in 1883, given by the *Eng Cat*. The first edition was *Fabulous Histories Designed for the Instruction of Children, Respecting Their Treatment of Animals*, T. Longman, R. G. & J. Robinson, etc., London, 1786, 17.5 cm., 227 pp., with a dedication (Nov. 3, 1785). They issued the second edition, 1786, 17.5 cm., 203 pp. The first American edition was issued by Wil-

liam Gibbons, Philadelphia, 1794, 16 cm.,
214 pp.
See No. 525 below.

509 JOHN T. TROWBRIDGE *Doing His Best.* Fcp 8vo. Illustrated. 2/o cloth
Oct. 23 (*Ath*)
Incident and Adventure Library. This has no
date. Warne issued it in the *Daring and Doing Library,* Cr 8vo, illustrated, 1/6 cloth, in
the 1890s. The first edition was issued by
James R. Osgood & Co., Boston, 1873, 18
cm., 279 pp., illustrated.

510 MRS. HENRY H. B. PAULL *Dick the Sailor.* 16mo. 1/6 cloth   Nov. 6 (*Ath*)
This is the first edition, 1875. It was later
placed in the *Round the Globe Library,*
12mo, colored frontispiece, 1/o cloth.

511 E. WYNNE *The Old Bible.* 12mo.
Illustrated. 2/o cloth   Dec. 11 (*Ath* ad)
Home Circle Gift Books. This is the first edition, no date. It was issued in the *Beford Library* by Warne, small Cr 8vo, illustrated,
1/6 cloth, in the 1890s. Warne reissued it
in 1882, 12mo, illustrated, 2/o cloth, given
by the *Eng Cat.*

512 ANONYMOUS *The Home Riddle Book.*
12mo. 1/o   Dec. 25 (*Spect*)
The *BM* gives this as no date, Warne's
Modern Manuals.

513 ANONYMOUS *Cock Robin.* Square
16mo. Colored illustrations. 1/o cloth
1875 (*Eng Cat*)
Now and Then Juvenile Series. This is a large-
type book with 24 pp. of colored plates,
and probably is the first edition.

514 ANONYMOUS *Little Totty, and Other Nursery Tales.* Square 16mo. Colored
illustrations. 1/o cloth   1875 (*Eng Cat*)
Now and Then Juvenile Series. This has no
date, a large-type book with 24 pp. of colored plates, containing the title story and

"Red Riding Hood," "Cinderella," and
"Dame Trot and Her Cat." *Little Totty* was
issued by McLoughlin Brothers, New
York, in the 1870s, 14 cm., 12 pp., colored
illustrations. This Warne edition probably
contains 4 vols.-in-1, as three of the titles
included were given separately in Warne
lists.

515 ANONYMOUS *Nursery Alphabet.*
Square 16mo. Colored illustrations. 1/o
cloth   1875 (*Eng. Cat*)
Now and Then Juvenile Series. This is a large-
type book with 24 pp. of colored plates.

516 MARY SHERWOOD (MARY M. BUTT)
Little Woodman and the May-Bee. 32mo.
Colored frontispiece. o/6   1875 (*Eng Cat*)
This was later given in Warne lists as *Dawn
of Day Books,* 32mo, plain frontispiece, o/4
sewed. *The May-Bee* was issued by F. Houlston & Son, Wellington, Salop, 1821, second edition, 29 pp., illustrated; it was issued in the United States by the American
Tract Society, New York, 11 cm., 16 pp., illustrated, which the *U Cat* gives as (183-?)
and the *BM* gives as (1820?). Houlston &
Son issued the sixth edition, 1825, 12mo,
29 pp., illustrated.

517 ANONYMOUS *The Three Bears.*
Square 16mo. Colored illustrations. 1/o
cloth   1875 (*Eng Cat*)
Now and Then Juvenile Series. This is a large-
type book with 24 pp. of colored plates.

518 LAURA VALENTINE *Eastern Tales by Many Story Tellers.* Cr 8vo. Illustrated.
1/6 cloth, 2/o cloth   1875 (*Eng Cat*)
Chandos Classics No. 43. This has no date
and 540 pp. It was first issued in 1875,
about Oct. 23, at 3/6, by Warne. They reissued it in the 1880s with the series title and
no. on the spine.

519 CHARLOTTE RIDDELL (MRS. J. H. RIDDELL) *Home, Sweet Home.* New edition. 12mo. 2/0 boards 1875 (*Eng Cat*)

Companion Library No. 74. This has no date and 413 pp. The first edition was issued by Tinsley Brothers, London, 3 vols., 1873, 19 cm., 31/6, listed in the *Ath* on Mar. 22. Wolff's copy is in red-brown cloth, but he thinks it might possibly be a secondary binding. W. M. Ellis in *Wilkie Collins, Le Fanu, and Others* gives it as brown. Tinsley Brothers issued it, 1873, Cr 8vo, 413 pp., 2/0 boards, 2/6 cloth, listed in the *Spect* on Nov. 1.

520 CHARLOTTE RIDDELL (MRS. J. H. RIDDELL) *Joy After Sorrow.* 12mo. 2/0 boards 1875

Companion Library No. 75. I put this in here because of its no. in the series. Tinsley Brothers, London, issued it, 1873, Cr 8vo, 2/0 boards, 2/6 cloth, listed in the *Spect* on June 28. The *Eng Cat* calls this Tinsley issue a new edition, but I have been unable to find an earlier one.

521 CHARLOTTE RIDDELL (MRS. J. H. RIDDELL) *The Earl's Promise.* 12mo. 2/0 boards 1875 (*Eng Cat*)

Companion Library No. 76. This has no date and 399 pp. The first edition was issued by Tinsley Brothers, London, 3 vols., 1873, 19.5 cm., 31/6 in grass-green cloth, listed in the *Ath* on July 19. Wolff also had a copy in bright blue cloth. It ran in *People's Magazine* (Society for the Promotion of Christian Knowledge) beginning in July 1872. Tinsley Brothers issued it in 1874, p 8vo, 2/0 boards, 2/6 cloth, listed in the *Ath* on Mar. 21, 1874.

Also 1878

522 CHARLOTTE RIDDELL (MRS. J. H. RIDDELL) *Mortomley's Estate.* 12mo. 2/0 boards 1875

Companion Library No. 77. I place this here because of its no. in the series. Warne is-

sued it in 1877, 3/6, given by the *Eng Cat*. The first edition was issued by Tinsley Brothers, London, 3 vols., 1874, 19 cm., 31/6 in red-brown cloth with cream endpapers (Wolff and Sadleir). Sadleir also had a copy in red cloth, and both had a copy in gray-black morocco cloth. Tinsley issued it in 1875, 2/0 boards, 2/6 cloth, listed in the *Spect* on Mar. 6.

523 CHARLOTTE RIDDELL (MRS. J. H. RIDDELL) *Frank Sinclair's Wife, and Other Stories.* 12mo. 2/0 boards 1875

Companion Library No. 78. I place this here because its no. in the series. Warne issued it in 1877, new edition, 3/6, given by the *Eng Cat*. The first edition was issued by Tinsley Brothers, London, 3 vols., 1874, in dark purple-brown cloth with pale yellow endpapers. The title story takes up vol. 1 and pp. (1)–(68) in vol. 2; "My First Love" takes up (69) to the end of vol. 2; "My Last Love" occupies (1)–(202) in vol. 3; and two other stories finish vol. 3. Tinsley advertised this first edition Dec. 6, 1873–Feb. 28, 1874, as "Just ready." Tinsley issued it, p 8vo, 2/0 boards, 2/6 cloth, listed in the *Ath* on Sept. 19, 1874.

See *My First Love* and *My Last Love* (item 543), 1876

524 AUNT FRIENDLY (SARAH S. BAKER) *Apple Pie.* Square 16mo. Colored illustrations. 1/0 cloth 1875 (*Eng Cat*)

Now and Then Juvenile Series. This is a large type book with 24 pp. of colored plates. The Osborne Collection has a copy issued by Warne (1869), 18.3 cm., 8 pp., 0/3 cover title, with 6 illustrations in color, *Aunt Friendly's Colored Picture Books.*

525 SARAH TRIMMER *The Robin Redbreasts.* 16mo. Colored illustrations. 0/6 sewed, 1/0 cloth, 1/6 cloth 1875 (*Eng Cat*)

National Books. This has no date, 14 cm., 238 pp. I suspect that it is *The Story of the*

Robins (see No. 508 above). Warne reissued it in this series, imperial 32mo, o/6 stiff wrappers with 2 plates and 1/o, 1/6 cloth with colored plates, advertised in the *Ath* on Nov. 15, 1879.

526 ANONYMOUS ***London in Miniature.***
32mo. Map. o/6 cloth   1875 (*BM*)
Illustrated Bijou Books No. 26. The *BM* gives this a (1875), 86 pp., and also as a new edition (1878), 83 pp.

Frederick Warne & Co.
Bedford Street, Covent Garden
1876

527 BLANCHARD JERROLD **Black Eye Susan's Boys.** Fcp 8vo. 1/0 boards
Feb. 5 (*Spect*)

This is the first edition, no date.

528 WILLIAM C. RUSSELL, ed. **The Book of Authors.** Cr 8vo. 1/6 sewed, 2/0 cloth
Feb. 19 (*Spect*)

Chandos Classics No. 44. This has no date, 516 pp. The first edition was issued by Warne with the joint imprint of Scribner, Welford & Co., New York (1871), 516 pp., frontispiece (7 portraits), 3/6, listed in the *Ath* on Aug. 5.

529 P. A. NUTTALL **Spelling Bee Guide.** Fcp 8vo. 1/0 Feb. 26 (*Spect*)

This is (1876), Warne's edition, condensed from *The Standard Pronouncing Dictionary of the English Language*, ed. by Nuttall, this latter issued by Routledge, Warne & Routledge, London and New York, 1863, 896 pp., reissued 1864 and 1869.

530 (SUSAN WARNER) **The Little Camp on Eagle Hill.** 12mo. 1/6 Mar. 18 (*Spect*)

Warne also issued this in the *Star Series* No. 42, 16mo, 1/0 sewed, 1/6 cloth, listed in the *Spect* on Sept. 8, 1877. The first English edition was issued by James Nisbet, London, 1873, 16mo, colored illustrations, 3/6, in the *Golden Ladder Series*, listed in the *Ath* on Sept. 27. Nisbet also issued it with *Willow Brook* (see No. 60 above). The first American edition was issued by Robert Carter & Brothers, New York, 1874, 17.5 cm., 429 pp., illustrated, in green, brown, terra-cotta, or orange cloth, with yellow endpapers, listed in *PW* on Sept. 22, 1873, and advertised there on Sept. 15 as "Ready." Goubaud & Son, London, issued it, listed in *PC* on Dec. 18, 1876.

531 CATHERINE D. BELL **Horace and May.** 16mo. 1/0 sewed Mar. 25 (*Spect*)

Star Series No. 19. This has no date and 363 pp. Warne issued it in 1866, new edition, Fcp 8vo, 363 pp., illustrated, 3/6, listed in the *Reader* on June 23. The first edition was *Unconscious Influence*, issued by W. P. Kennedy, Edinburgh, probably with Hamilton, London, 1855, 368 pp. The first American edition was issued by A.D.F. Randolph, New York, 1856, 413 pp.

532 CATHERINE D. BELL **Margaret Cecil.** 16mo. 1/0 sewed Mar. 25 (*Spect*)

Star Series No. 23. Warne issued this, 1866, Fcp 8vo, 404 pp., illustrated, *3/6 Gift Books*, listed in the *Reader* on Aug. 11. The first edition was issued by W. P. Kennedy, Edinburgh, probably with Hamilton, London, 1851, by Cousin Kate. The first American edition was issued by D. Appleton & Co., New York, 1852, 17.5 cm., 316 pp., $.50 paper, $.75 cloth, by Cousin Kate, advertised in *Lit W* on Mar. 13 as "Now ready."

533 CATHERINE D. BELL *Home Sunshine.*
16mo. 1/o sewed　Mar. 25 (*Spect*)

Star Series No. 25. Warne also issued this, 1866, 375 pp., 3/6, listed in the *Spect* on Oct. 6. The first edition was issued by W. P. Kennedy, Edinburgh; Hamilton, London, 1859, 371 pp., 4/6.

534 ELIZABETH WATTS *Modern Practical Gardening. Vegetables, Flowers, and Fruit.*
12mo. 2/o　Apr. 8 (*Spect*)

This was issued by Warne, 1867, 3 parts in 1 vol., separate pagination, colored illustrations. It was issued in 1871, Fcp 8vo, 564 pp., colored illustrations, 3/6 cloth, advertised in the *Spect* on Apr. 22. It was advertised there on Mar. 14, 1874, the same, and listed there on May 15, 1875, Cr 8vo, 3/6; it was reissued about Mar. 4, 1876, the same. The three separate books, Fcp 8vo, illustrated, 1/o picture boards or cloth each, were advertised in the *TWEd* on Mar. 7, 1890; all three in 1 vol., Cr 8vo, 564 pp., 3/6, was listed there on Apr. 19. For *Vegetables* see No. 69; for *Flowers and the Flower Garden* see No. 22; for *The Orchard and Fruit Garden* see No. 152.

535 CHARLOTTE RIDDELL (MRS. J. H. RIDDELL) *The Race for Wealth.* [New edition.] 12mo. 2/o boards　Apr. 8 (*Spect*)

Companion Library No. 67. This ran in *Once a Week* (Bradbury & Evans), Jan. 6–Sept. 18, 1866. The first book edition was issued by Tinsley Brothers, London, 3 vols., 1866, 31/6 in bright brown cloth. Wolff also had a set in claret cloth with pale yellow endpapers, with no publisher's name on the spine, which he thought might have been a secondary issue. Tinsley Brothers issued it, 1867, 502 pp., 6/o. The first American edition was issued by Harper & Brothers, New York, 1866, 8vo, 168 pp., $.75 paper, *Library of Select Novels* No. 278, advertised in the *New-York Times* on Nov. 15 as "This day." The first English edition was listed in the *Ath* on Aug. 18.

536 MICHAEL SCOTT *Tom Cringle's Log.*
Cr 8vo. o/6 sewed　Apr. 15 (*Ath* ad)

Notable Novels No. 20. I have a copy of this, no date, 21.3 cm., 232 pp. in double columns, yellow pictorial wrappers, printed in red and black with the series title on the front and spine and No. 20 at the foot of the spine. It has a printer's date (Dec. 2, 1884), a list of the series on the inside front cover ending with No. 84, 6 pp. of publisher's ads at the back, and commercial ads on both sides of the back cover. There are no endpapers. It was listed by *PC* for May 1885. The first edition was issued by Blackwood, Edinburgh; Cadell, London, 2 vols., 1833, 18 cm., anonymous, 12/o, from *Blackwood's Magazine*. Sadleir had a copy in dark-green morocco cloth, with white endpapers, unblocked, and a copy in dark-green fine-ribbed cloth, with yellow endpapers, blocked in blind. He also had a set, second edition, 1834, in dark green cloth with white endpapers overlaid with a brown mesh; and he cites a known copy of the second edition bound as for the second binding given above. The first edition was listed in the *Ath* on Nov. 2, 1833, and the second edition was advertised in the *Spect* on Nov. 1, 1833. George Routledge & Sons, London and New York, issued it in 1876, 232 pp., yellow pictorial boards, 2/o, listed in the *Spect* on Jan. 29; and Ward, Lock & Tyler, London, issued it in 1875, 436 pp., 2/o boards, listed in the *Spect* on Oct. 9. It ran in *Blackwood's Magazine*, June 1831–Aug. 1833. I am not happy with my discussion of the American editions, but I've gathered the following information: The *U Cat* gives E. L. Carey & A. Hart, Philadelphia, etc., 3 vols., 1833, first and second series, the joint imprint being with Carey, Hart & Co., Baltimore; and also the same, jointly with Lilly, Wait & Co., Boston, 2 vols., 1833, 20.5 cm.; and also the same jointly with Allen & Ticknor, Boston, 2 vols., 1833, second series, 20.5 cm. The

North American Review (quarterly) listed it as issued by Carey, Lea & Blanchard, Philadelphia, 2 vols., the listing in the July 1833 issue; it lists in the Apr. 1834 issue vol. 3, 173 pp. It lists for Jan. 1834, Carey & Hart, Philadelphia, 2 vols., second series. A Washington, D.C., bookstore advertised in the *Globe*, a Washington daily, on May 1, 1833, 2 vols., anonymous, "Published this morning," no publisher given; the store advertised on Nov. 27, 1833, a second series, 2 vols., $1.25, anonymous. These latter ads are very reliable indicators of American issues. Neither Sadleir or Wolff speaks of series.

537 CHARLOTTE RIDDELL (MRS. J. H. RIDDELL) *Too Much Alone.* [New edition.] 12mo. 2/o boards Apr. 15 (*Spect*)
Companion Library No. 59. The first edition was issued by Charles J. Skeet, London, 3 vols., 1860, p 8vo, by F. G. Trafford, 31/6, listed in the *Ath* on Feb. 18. Skeet issued a new edition, Cr 8vo, 5/o, advertised in the *Spect* on Oct. 19, 1861, and a new edition in 1864, p 8vo, 5/o, listed in the *Reader* on Dec. 24, 1864; both of these issues were by F. G. Trafford. Tinsley Brothers, London, issued a new edition in 1865, p 8vo, 6/o, by Trafford, listed in the *Reader* on Oct. 14. An edition at 2/o boards was listed in the *Ath* on Aug. 14, 1869, no publisher given. In the United States it was issued by T.O.H.P. Burnham, Boston, 1866, listed in *ALG&PC* (fortnightly) on Nov. 15.

538 CATHERINE D. BELL *Ella and Marian.* 16mo. 1/o sewed Apr. 15 (*Spect*)
Star Series No. 20. Warne issued this also as 3/6 *Gift Books*, new edition, Fcp 8vo, 402 pp., illustrated, 3/6, listed in the *Reader* on June 2, 1866. The first edition was issued by W. P. Kennedy, Edinburgh; Hamilton, London, 1858, 436 pp., 5/o, *Rest and Unrest*. The first American edition was issued

by A. D. F. Randolph, New York (1858), 16mo, 410 pp., *Rest and Unrest* by Cousin Kate.

539 CATHERINE D. BELL *Rosa's Wish.* 16mo. 1/o sewed Apr. 15 (*Spect*)
Star Series No. 22. Warne also issued this as 3/6 *Gift Books*, new edition, illustrated, advertised in the *Ath* on Dec. 9, 1865, and in the *Spect* on Dec. 8, 1866. Warne also issued it at 3/6, new edition, 12mo, listed in the *Spect* on Feb. 15, 1868. The first edition was issued by W. P. Kennedy, Edinburgh; Hamilton, London, 1861, 385 pp., 4/6.

540 CATHERINE D. BELL *The Grahams.* 16mo. 1/o sewed Apr. 15 (*Spect*)
Star Series No. 24. The first edition was issued by Warne, 1866, 12mo, 398 pp., illustrated, 3/6, listed in the *Ath* on Apr. 28. It was reissued in 1866, listed in the *Spect* on Oct. 6.

541 ANONYMOUS *The Gentleman's Art of Dressing with Economy.* Fcp 8vo. Illustrated. 1/o boards May 13 (*Spect*)
Useful Books. This is by a lounger at the clubs, no date, the first edition.

542 JOHN N. MASKELYNE *Modern Spiritualism . . .* Fcp 8vo. Illustrated. 1/o boards June 3 (*Spect*)
Useful Books. This has the joint imprint of Scribner, Welford & Armstrong, New York, no date, 17 cm., 182 pp., the first edition.

543 CHARLOTTE RIDDEL (MRS. J. H. RIDDELL) *My First Love* and *My Last Love.* 12mo. 2/o boards June 3 (*Ath*)
Companion Library No. 80. The first edition of the first title was issued by F. Enos Arnold, London, 1869, 8vo, anonymous, 80 pp., frontispiece and 9 full-page illustrations, *St. James' Magazine Christmas Box for 1869*. It is in white wrappers cut flush, ar-

morially printed in gold, red, blue, and black. The back and inside covers have ads, and there are 40 pp. of ads (Dec. 1869) preceding the frontispiece and single leaves of ads on colored paper inserted in the text at four places. The first edition of the second title was issued by F. Enos Arnold, London, 1870, 8vo, anonymous, 1/o. Both of these stories appeared in *Frank Sinclair's Wife, and Other Stories* (see No. 523 above). In the United States both stories were issued by John W. Lovell, New York (1891), authorized edition, $.50, *International Series* No. 164, listed in the *Nation* on July 23. See the next two items.

544 CHARLOTTE RIDDELL (MRS. J. H. RIDDELL) *My First Love.* Fcp 8vo.
1/o sewed   June 10 (*Acad*)
Readable Books No. 3. See the preceding item.

545 CHARLOTTE RIDDELL (MRS. J. H. RIDDELL) *My Last Love.* Fcp 8vo.
1/o sewed   June 10 (*Acad*)
Readable Books No. 4. See No. 543 above.

546 CHARLOTTE RIDDELL (MRS. J. H. RIDDELL) *The Ruling Passion.* 12mo.
2/o boards   June 24 (*Ath*)
Companion Library No. 79. This has no date and 465 pp. The first edition was issued by Bentley, London, 3 vols., 1857, 20.5 cm., by Rainey Hawthorne, 31/6 in half-cloth boards with labels or dark olive-gray cloth, listed in the *Ath* on Oct. 31.

547 BRET HARTE *Gabriel Conroy.* 12mo.
2/o boards   Oct. 14 (*Ath*)
Companion Library No. 81. This ran in *Scribner's Monthly Magazine*, Nov. 1875–Aug. 1876, and the first book edition was issued by Warne (1876), 3 vols., 19.5 cm., listed in the *Ath* on May 27. It has a publisher's preface stating that it has been partly issued in *Scribner's Magazine* and is now published in advance of that series in

order that the copyright may be fully maintained. Warne issued parts 1 and 2, 1/o each, 74 and 152 pp. respectively, with the joint imprint of Scribner, Welford & Armstrong, New York, in light sage-green wrappers, with Oct. and Nov. 1875 respectively on the front cover with the words "To be completed in thirty parts"—but no other parts are known. Warne stated that they bought the copyright from Harte and later sold it to Chatto & Windus, London, and that they reissued the 2/o edition in Feb. 1877. Chatto & Windus issued it at 6/o in 1880 and issued a new edition in 1880, 12mo, 2/o boards, listed in the *Spect* on Apr. 17. The first American edition was issued by the American Publishing Co., Hartford, 1876, 8vo, 466 pp., illustrated, in mauve cloth, sold by subscription. It was deposited Sept. 20. The first Canadian edition was issued by Belford Brothers, Toronto, 1876, 18.5 cm., 423 pp.

548 CHARLES MACKAY *The Poetical Works of Charles Mackay.* Cr 8vo.
1/6 cloth, 2/o cloth   Oct. 28 (*Spect*)
Chandos Classics No. 46. This has the joint imprint of Scribner, Welford & Armstrong, New York, no date, 626 pp., now for the first time collected. *Songs and Poems* was issued in London, 1834. *The Hope of the World, and Other Poems* was issued by Bentley, London, noticed in the *Westminster Review* (quarterly) for Jan. 1841. *Legends of the Isles, and Other Poems* was issued by William Blackwood & Sons, Edinburgh, listed in the same for Sept. 1845. *Ballads and Lyrical Poems* was issued by George Routledge & Co., London and New York, 1856, second edition; and it was reissued in 1860, at 5/o, advertised in the Spect on Apr. 14 as recent. Routledge & Co., London and New York, issued the *Poetical Works*, 1857, Fcp 8vo, illustrated by Gilbert, 5/o, listed in the *Ath* on Sept. 26.

549 ALEXANDER POPE *The Poetical Works of Alexander Pope.* Cr 8vo. 1/6 sewed, 2/o cloth   Oct. 28 (*Spect*)

Chandos Classics No. 45. This has no date, 607 pp. Warne reissued it, 1894, 607 pp. *The Works* was issued by B. Lintot, London, 1717, vol. 1, 30.5 cm., 468 pp.; and vol. 2, L. Gilliver, London, 1735, 30 cm., illustrated. *The Poetical Works* was issued by R. & A. Foulis, Glasgow, 3 vols., 1768, 13 cm., illustrated. *The Poetical Works* was issued by B. Johnson, etc., Philadelphia, 5 vols., 1804, 14.2 cm.; and 3 vols. were issued at Philadelphia, listed in the *North American Review* (quarterly) for June 1819, no publisher given.

550 JOHN HABBERTON *Helen's Babies.* 2/o boards   Dec. 30 (*Ath*)

Warne also issued this at 2/6, 12mo, anonymous, illustrated, listed in the *Spect* on Mar. 10, 1877. They issued it as *Notable Books* No. 3, Cr 8vo, o/6 sewed, listed in the *Bks* for Feb. 1883, and placed it in *Notable Novels* No. 103, o/6 sewed, probably in 1888. They issued it as *Popular Library* No. 4, no date, 12mo, anonymous, 185 pp., 1/o sewed, before Apr. 19, 1889. The first edition was issued by A. K. Loring, Boston (1876), 17.5 cm., anonymous, 206 pp., listed in both the *Ind* and the *Nation* on July 27. In England it was also issued by Sampson Low, London, in 1876, 16mo, anonymous, 1/o sewed, 2/6 cloth, advertised as "Now ready" in the *Ath* on Dec. 9 and in the *Spect* on Dec. 16, claiming it to be the only edition issued in England with the sanction of the author and in which he participated financially. David Bryce & Son, Glasgow, issued it, 1877, square 8vo, with a pictorial title page, in Dec. 1876. Ward, Lock & Tyler, London, issued it at 1/o sewed, advertised in the *Ath* on Jan. 6, 1877, as "Just ready"; and George Routledge & Sons, London, issued it, 160 pp., 1/o boards, my copy, advertised in the *Ath* on Feb. 3, 1877. At least 12 English houses issued it in 1876–77.

551 ELIZABETH PRENTISS *Urbane and His Friends.* 16mo. 1/o sewed, 1/6 cloth 1876

Star Series No. 27. The first American edition was issued by A. D. F. Randolph, New York (copyright 1874), 19.5 cm., 287 pp., noticed in *Harper's New Monthly Magazine* for Apr. 1875 and hence probably issued in Jan. or Feb. The first English edition was issued by James Nisbet, London, 1875, 12mo, 2/6, listed in the *Ath* on Dec. 26, 1874. This title and the following two titles are placed here because of their nos. in the series, but they could have been issued in early 1877.

552 ELIZABETH PRENTISS *Aunt Jane's Hero.* 16mo. 1/o sewed, 1/6 cloth   1876

Star Series No. 30. The first edition was issued by A. D. F. Randolph, New York (1871), 19.5 cm., 292 pp., advertised in the *Nation* and in the *Ind* as "On Oct. 20" and listed in *ALG&PC* (fortnightly) on Nov. 1. The first English edition was by Warne, issued in 1872, 12mo, 288 pp., colored illustrations, 2/6 cloth, listed in the *Spect* on July 20 and by *PC* as published July 16–Aug. 1. Ward, Lock & Tyler, London, issued it in 1872, 230 pp., 1/o sewed, 1/6, 2/o cloth, listed in the *Ath* on Oct. 12.

553 CATHERINE D. BELL *Aunt Ailie.* 16mo. 1/o sewed, 1/6 cloth   1876

Star Series No. 31. Warne also issued this in 1866, Fcp 8vo, 412 pp., illustrated, 3/6 and 4/o cloth, listed in the *Reader* on Sept. 22. The first edition was issued by Edmonston & Douglas, Edinburgh; Hamilton, London, 1861, Fcp 8vo, 412 pp., 5/o.

554 AUNT LOUISA, ed. (LAURA VALENTINE) *The Excelsior Poetry Book for the Young.* 18mo. Illustrated. 1/6 cloth 1876 (*Eng Cat*)

Birthday Series. This is the first edition, no date.

555 MRS. HAWTREY *Village Songs*. 16mo. Illustrated. 1/0 sewed, 2/0 cloth 1876 (*Eng Cat*)

This is the first edition, no date, 100 illustrations.

556 CATHERINE D. BELL *Allen and Harry*. [New edition.] Square 16mo. 1/0, 1/6 1876–1879 (*Eng Cat*)

Warne also issued this as an *Eighteenpenny Juvenile* in 1866, 18mo, 184 pp., illustrated, 1/6 cloth, listed in the *Reader* on June 9. The first edition was issued in Edinburgh jointly with Hamilton, London, *Set About It at Once*, 1847, 18mo, 2/6. Hamilton issued a new edition with the same title, 18mo, 2/6, in 1863. See No. 54 in 1866.

557 J. E. CARPENTER *Penny Readings in Prose and Verse*. Vols. 11 and 12. Fcp 8vo. 1/0 boards each 1876 (*Eng Cat*)

For earlier vols. see No. 16 in 1865 and No. 109 in 1866.

558 FREDERICK MARRYAT *Peter Simple*. Cr 8vo. 0/6 sewed 1876

Notable Novels No. 21. I place this and the following 3 titles here because of their nos. in the series, but they could have been issued in the first quarter of 1877. This title has no date, 187 pp. Warne reissued it in this series, 0/6 sewed, listed by the *Bks* for May, 1885. It was again reissued in this series, probably in 1887, my copy, 21.2 cm., 187 pp. in double columns, yellow wrappers, pictorial printed in red and black, with the series title on the front and spine with the no. at the base of the spine. There are commercial ads on both sides of the back cover and a publisher's ad on the inside front cover (listing the series through No. 100), and there is a leaf of publisher's ads at the back. The first English edition was issued by Saunders & Otley, London, 3 vols., 1834, 19 cm., anonymous, 31/6, boards and labels. They issued the second edition, reset, 3 vols., 1834, half-cloth

boards and labels. They issued the third edition, revised, advertised in the *Spect* on May 9, 1835, as "Just ready"; and they issued the illustrated edition, 3 vols., 1837, in dark blue cloth. The first edition was listed in the *Ath* on Nov. 16, 1833, and advertised on Nov. 9 as "Just out." Bentley, London, issued it as *Standard Novels* No. 62, 1838, 462 pp. The first American edition was issued by Carey & Hart, Philadelphia, etc., 3 vols., 19 cm., anonymous, vols. 1 and 2, 1833, and vol. 3, 1834, each vol. with an 18-page catalog (Sept. 1833) at the back. Vol. 1 has no vol. no. and has a publisher's ad stating that it was issued alone, as there was no probability of its early completion. This referred to its run, passim, in the *Metropolitan Magazine*, Jan. 1832–Dec. 1833. A Washington, D.C., bookstore advertised vol. 1 in the *Globe*, a Washington daily, on Nov. 5, 1833, $.75, and it was listed in the *North American Review* (quarterly) for Jan. 1834. Vol. 2 was advertised in the *Globe* on Dec. 10, 1833, $.62½, "Just received," and listed in the *North American Review* for Apr. 1834. Vol. 3 was advertised in the *Globe* on Feb. 19, 1834, and listed in the *North American Review* for Apr. 1834. The *Globe* ads give very accurate dates for American issues. It was also issued by Merklein, Chambersburg, 1834, 2-vols.-in-1, 14 cm., 487 pp.

559 G.P.R. JAMES *Mary of Burgundy*. Cr 8vo. 0/6 sewed 1876

Notable Novels No. 22. This has the joint imprint of Scribner, Welford & Armstrong, New York, no date, 194 pp. The first English edition was issued by Longmans, London, 3 vols., 1833, 20 cm., anonymous, 31/6 boards, listed in the *Ath* on Apr. 27. Smith, Elder & Co., London, issued it as No. 2 of a new and illustrated edition, in 1844, medium 8vo, 8/0, listed in the *Spect* on Sept. 28. Simms & M'Intyre issued it in the *Parlour Library* No. 38, 1850, 304 pp., listed in the *Spect* on Mar. 9. In the United States it was issued by J. & J.

Harper, New York, 2 vols., 1833, 12mo, *Library of Select Novels* Nos. 31, 32, $1.25, advertised in the *Globe*, a Washington, D.C., daily, on Aug. 25; this is a very accurate indication of the date of issue. It was also issued in the *Novelist's Library*, Philadelphia (1833), 23 cm., anonymous.

560 FREDERICK MARRYAT *Jacob Faithful.*
Cr 8vo. o/6 sewed 1876

Notable Novels No. 23. This has the joint imprint of Scribner, Welford & Armstrong, New York, no date, 155 pp. This ran in the *Metropolitan Magazine*, Sept. 1833–Dec. 1834. The first English edition was issued by Saunders & Otley, London, 3 vols., 1834, 22 cm., anonymous, 31/6 boards, listed in the *Ath* and in the *Spect* on Sept. 20. They issued a second edition, revised, in 1834, advertised in the *Spect* on May 9 as "Just ready." Bentley issued it as *Standard Novels* No. 63, 1838, 407 pp. The first American edition was issued by Carey & Hart, Philadelphia, etc., 3 vols., 1834, 19 cm., anonymous. Vols. 2 and 3 each have two 12-page catalogs (Mar. 1834 and Oct. 1833) at the back. It was advertised in the *Globe*, a Washington, D.C., daily, on Dec. 4, 1834, as complete. Vol. 2 was listed in the *North American Review* (quarterly) for Oct. 1834, and vol. 3 was listed in Jan. 1835, the latter being given as Allen & Ticknor, Boston.

561 G.P.R. JAMES *The Gipsy.*
Cr 8vo. o/6 sewed 1876

Notable Novels No. 24. This has no date. The first edition was issued by Longmans, London, 3 vols., 1835, 18.5 cm., anonymous, 31/6 boards, listed in the *Ath* and in the *Spect* on Apr. 25. Smith, Elder & Co., London, issued it as No. 1 of a new and revised edition of James' works, issued quarterly, medium 8vo, 8/o, No. 1 listed in the *Spect* on July 8, 1844. Simms & M'Intyre, London & Belfast, issued it in the *Parlour Library* No. 34, 1/o boards, 1/6 cloth, on Dec. 1, 1849. The first American edition was issued by Harper & Brothers, New York, 2 vols., 1835, 18 cm., anonymous, $1.25, advertised in the *Globe*, a Washington, D.C., daily, on Aug. 1, 1835, as "Published this morning," and noticed in the *American Quarterly Review* (Philadelphia) for Sept. 1835. Harpers issued it in 1 vol., in 1836, listed in the latter for Apr.

562 ANONYMOUS *The Natural History Album.* Fcp 8vo. Illustrated. 2/6 picture boards 1876

This has colored illustrations and was reviewed in the *Ath* on Dec. 30, 1876. The only title close to this that I've found is *Warne's Picture Natural History*, 3 vols., 12mo, 1/o each, 1875, given by the *Eng Cat* (See No. 495).

Frederick Warne & Co.
Bedford Street, Covent Garden
1877

563 OLIVER GOLDSMITH *The Poems and Plays of Oliver Goldsmith. With the Addition of The Vicar of Wakefield.*
Cr 8vo. 1/6 sewed, 2/0 cloth   Jan.?

Chandos Classics No. 47. This has the joint imprint of Scribner, Welford & Armstrong, New York, no date, 482 pp. It was issued either in late 1876 or early 1877. The first collected edition of the poems was *Poems*, issued by James Magee, Belfast, 1775, 64 pp. The first collected edition of the poems and plays was *Poems and Plays*, issued by Price, etc., Dublin, 1777, 18.5 cm., 328 pp. *The Poetical and Dramatic Works of Oliver Goldsmith* was issued by Rivington, T. Carnan & F. Newbery, London; etc., 2 vols., 1780, portrait, now first collected, the first edition edited by Thomas Evans. The first authorized edition of *The Vicar of Wakefield* was issued by F. Newbery, London, 2 vols., 1776, 17.4 cm., anonymous, 5/0 sewed, 6/0 bound, advertised in the *Public Advertiser* on Mar. 27, 1766, as "This day." Newbery issued the second and third editions, 1766, about May 31 and Aug. 27 respectively. The first Dublin edition was issued by W. & W. Smith, etc., Dublin, 2 vols., 1766, 16.3 cm., anonymous. The first edition may have been pirated by Eugene Swiney, Corke (i.e., London), 2 vols., 1766, 17 cm., anonymous. The first American edition was issued by William Mentz, Philadelphia, 2-vols.-in-1, 1772, 16.6 cm., anonymous, 180 pp.

564 GEORGE SALE, ed. *The Koran.*
Cr 8vo. 1/6 sewed, 2/0 cloth
Feb. 3 (*Spect*)

Chandos Classics No. 48. This has no date, a preliminary discourse of 145 pp. and the text of 470 pp. The first English edition was *The Alcoran of Mahomet*, London, 1649, 18.5 and 15.5 cm., 407 pp. The first George Sale edition was issued by J. Wilcox, London, 1734, 4to, 187, 508 pp., with a folding map and tables, *The Koran*. It was listed by the *Gentleman's Magazine* (London), at £1, as published in Nov. 1733. In the United States it was issued as *The Koran* by Isaiah Thomas, Jr., Springfield, Mass., 1806, 20.5 cm., 524 pp. Warne issued this also at 3/6, listed in the *Spect* on Mar. 3, 1877; they issued it at 7/6 in 1881, a new edition, listed in the *Spect* on Feb. 26; and they issued it in 1891, medium 8vo, maps, 7/6, advertised in *Notes & Queries* on Nov. 14.

565 MARIA EDGEWORTH *Helen.* 16mo.
1/6 sewed, 2/0 cloth   Feb. 24 (*Spect*)

Star Series No. 37. Warne issued this in 1879, Cr 8vo, illustrated, 2/6, listed in the *Spect* on July 12. The first English edition was issued by Bentley, London, 3 vols., 1834, 19.5 cm., 31/6, listed in the *Ath* and in the *Spect* on Mar. 1 and published Feb. 22 according to the Bentley private catalog. Bentley issued it as *Standard Novels* No. 71, 1838, 455 pp., and issued it in 1875, advertised in the *Spect* on July 4 as "Just

published." The first American edition
was issued by Carey, Lea, and Blanchard,
Philadelphia; Allen & Ticknor, Boston, 2
vols., 1834, 21.5 cm., 1,500 copies, finished on Apr. 4 and advertised in the *National Gazette and Literary Record* on Apr.
15. *The Cost Book of Carey & Lea* states that
Harpers printed *Helen* on them 10 days after their issue was out, but that Carey, Lea,
and Blanchard sold all that they printed.
The Harper edition was 2 vols., 1834,
given by the *U Cat.*

566 CHARLOTTE RIDDELL (MRS. J. H.
RIDDELL) *Above Suspicion.* [New
edition.] 12mo. 2/o boards   Mar. 10
(*Ath*)

Companion Library No. 82. This ran in *London Society* (Low), Aug. 1874–Jan. 1876,
and the first book edition was issued by
Tinsley Brothers, London, 3 vols., 1876,
probably issued the latter part of 1875 for
it was advertised as either ready or forthcoming from Oct. 9 to Nov. 13, 1875. The
first American edition was issued by Estes
& Lauriat, Boston, 1876, listed in *PW* on
July 10 and in the *Ind* on July 27.

567 SAMUEL WOOD *The British
Bird-Preserver.* Fcp 8vo. Illustrated.
1/o boards   Mar. 24 (*Ath* ad)

Useful Books. This has no date, 126 pp. The
U Cat gives this as a new edition, which
probably refers to a later reissue.

568 MARIA M. GRANT *The Sun-Maid.*
12mo. 2/o boards   Mar. 31 (*Ath*)

Companion Library No. 83. This has no
date. The first edition was issued by Bentley, London, 3 vols., 1876, anonymous,
advertised in the *Ath* on Aug. 26 as
"Ready" and reviewed on Sept. 2. The first
American edition was issued by Harper &
Brothers, New York, 1877, 8vo, anonymous, 145 pp., $.50 paper, advertised in
the *New-York Times* on Feb. 1 and noticed in
Godey's Lady's Book for Apr. 1877.

569 JOSEPH HATTON *Clytie.* 12mo.
2/o boards   Apr. 14 (*Spect*)

Companion Library No. 85. This has no date
and 365 pp. The first edition was issued by
Chapman & Hall, London, 3 vols., 1874,
18.5 cm., 31/6, listed in the *Ath* on June 6.
Lindley & Co., London, issued it at 2/o
about July 22, 1876. It ran in the *Gentleman's Magazine*, Mar. 1873–June 1874.
The first American edition was issued by
Lovell, Adam, Wesson & Co., New York,
12mo, 373 pp., $1.25 linen boards, $1.50
cloth, advertised in the *New-York Times*
on Nov. 17, 1876, and listed by *PW* on
Oct. 14.

570 JOSEPH HATTON *The Valley of
Poppies.* 12mo. 2/o boards   Apr. 14 (*Ath*)
Companion Library No. 90. This has no date
and 367 pp. It ran in the *Gentleman's Magazine* (Grant & Co.), Jan.–Dec. 1871, anonymously. The first book edition was issued
by Chapman & Hall, London, 2 vols.,
1872, Cr 8vo, anonymous, 21/o in grass-
green cloth with cream endpapers, Wolff's
copy with a presentation (Christmas
1871). It was listed in the *Ath* on Dec. 16,
1871.

571 JOSEPH HATTON *Christopher
Kenrick.* 12mo. 2/o boards   Apr. 14 (*Ath*)
Companion Library No. 91. This has no
date. This ran in the *Gentleman's Magazine*,
anonymously, Oct. 1868–June 1869, *The
Life and Adventures of Christopher Kenrick.*
The first book edition was issued by Bradbury, Evans & Co., London, 2 vols., 1869,
21/o in brown cloth, bevelled boards, with
café-au-lait endpapers and with ads at the
back of vol. 2. It was listed in the *Ath* on
June 5. The first American edition was issued by G. P. Putnam & Son, New York,
1869, 18.5 cm., 408 pp., $1.75, 2-vols.-in-
1, listed in the *Nation* on Oct. 14.

572 FRANCES H. BURNETT *That Lass o'
Lowrie's.* Fcp 8vo. 1/0 sewed Apr. 14
(*Ath* ad)

Readable Books No. 5. This is the first English book edition, no date, 206 pp., listed by *PC* as published Apr. 15–30. It ran in *Scribner's Monthly*, Aug. 1876–May 1877, and the first American book issue was issued by Scribner, Armstrong & Co., New York, 1877, 12mo, 4 illustrations by Alfred Fredericks, $1.50 in gilt and red decorated cloth. It was advertised in the *New-York Times* on Apr. 7 as "This day" and listed in *PW* on Apr. 7. They issued the third edition, the same, advertised in the same on Apr. 14 as "Just published"; they advertised a paper issue, 12mo, $.90, on Aug. 2, 1877, as "Now ready." A review in *Scribner's Monthly* for Dec. 1877 disclosed that the issue has an author's note stating that it and *Surly Tim, and Other Stories* were the only works under her name that had been prepared and corrected for book issue under her supervision. Ward, Lock & Tyler, London, issued it, no date, 18 cm., 181 pp., 1/0 sewed, 1/6, 2/0 cloth, about July 10, 1877. Warne issued it in the *Star Series* No. 51, 16mo, 1/0 sewed, 1/6 cloth, listed in the *Spect* on Aug. 10, 1878; they reissued it in that series, the same, listed in the *Bks* for Mar. 1881. They issued it in the *London Library* No. 21, 12mo, 1/0 sewed, listed by the *Bks* in June 1888; and they issued it in the *Library of Fiction* No. 13, Cr 8vo, 2/0 boards, listed in *PC* on June 20, 1891.
See also the *Zephyr Library* in 1900

573 JOSEPH HATTON *Bitter Sweets.*
12mo. 2/0 boards Apr. 28 (*Ath*)

Companion Library No. 86. This has no date. The first edition was issued by Tinsley Brothers, London, 3 vols., 1865, 20 cm., 31/6, listed in the *Ath* on Mar. 18.

574 HENRY STANNARD *Outdoor Common
Birds.* Fcp 8vo. Illustrated. 1/6 boards
Apr. 28 (*Ath*)

Useful Books. This has no date and 215 pp. The first edition was issued by Warne, no

date, Cr 8vo, illustrated, 5/0 cloth, advertised in the *Ath* on Apr. 26, 1873. They issued it in 1890, Fcp 8vo, illustrated, 1/0 pictorial boards, advertised in the *TWEd* on May 2.

575 JOSEPH HATTON *The Tallants
of Barton.* [New edition.] 12mo.
2/0 boards Apr. 28 (*Spect*)

Companion Library No. 88. This has no date and 374 pp. The first edition was issued by Tinsley Brothers, London, 3 vols., 1867, 19.5 cm., 31/6, listed in the *Ath* on May 4. It was issued by Bradbury, Evans & Co., London, in 1868, 12mo, 2/6, listed in the *Spect* on Oct. 24. The first American edition was issued by Roberts Brothers, Boston, in 1868, square 16mo, $1.25 cloth, *Handy-Vol. Series*, advertised in the *New-York Times* on Nov. 25 as "Just ready" and listed in the *Nation* on Dec. 3.

576 JOSEPH HATTON *Not in Society,
and Other Tales.* 12mo. 2/0 boards
May 5 (*Ath*)

Companion Library No. 87. This has no date. The first edition of *Not in Society* was issued by Bradbury, Evans & Co., London, 1868, by Vaughan Morgan, ed. by Joseph Hatton, Cr 8vo, 10/6, listed in the *Ath* and in the *Spect* on Nov. 21. It ran in the *Gentleman's Magazine* (Bradbury, Evans), June–Nov. 1868.

577 JOSEPH HATTON *In the Lap of
Fortune.* 12mo. 2/0 boards May 5 (*Ath*)

Companion Library No. 89. This has no date, 367 pp. The first edition was issued by Chapman & Hall, London, 3 vols., 1873, 19 cm., 31/6, listed in the *Ath* on Apr. 12.

578 (CATHERINE S. WYNNE) *A Horrid
Girl.* 12mo. 2/0 boards May 12 (*Ath*)

Companion Library No. 84. This has no date and 364 pp. The first edition was issued by Bentley, London, 3 vols., 1876, anonymous, advertised in the *Ath* on Oct. 7 as "On Oct. 9."

579 ANONYMOUS *Selections from the Talmud. Translated from the Original by Hymen Polano.* Cr 8vo. 1/6 sewed, 2/0 cloth   May 26 (*Spect*)

Chandos Classics No. 51. This has no date and 359 pp. It is the first English edition thus. Warne issued it at 2/0, Cr 8vo, blue cloth, uncut, advertised in *Notes & Queries* on Nov. 14, 1891. The same was issued in Philadelphia, 1876, 382 pp. I think it was issued *passim* by Warne in the 1880s and 1890s.

580 ROBERT JOHNSTON *The Arctic Expedition of 1875–76.* Demy 8vo. Folding map. Illustrated, 1/0 picture cover   June 2 (*Ath* ad)

This is the first edition, no date, 21.5 cm., 104 pp.

581 JOHN L. CHERRY, ed. *Life and Remains of John Clare.* Cr 8vo. 1/6 sewed, 2/0 cloth   June 16 (*Spect*)

Chandos Classics No. 53. This has the joint imprint of Scribner, Welford & Armstrong, New York, no date, 349 pp. It was replaced in the series as No. 53 by Bunyan's *Holy War* in 1882 or 1883. The first edition was issued by Warne, London; J. Taylor & Son, Northampton, 1873, Cr 8vo, 349 pp., illustrated, 5/0, advertised by Warne in the *Ath* on Feb. 15.

582 WILLIAM DODD *The Beauties of Shakespeare.* Cr 8vo. 1/6 sewed, 2/0 cloth   July 21 (*Spect*)

Chandos Classics No. 54. This has no date and 351 pp. Warne issued it in 1873, 10/6, listed in the *Spect* on Dec. 6. The first edition was issued by T. Waller, London, 2 vols., 1752, 22 cm. It was issued in the United States by R. M'Dermut & D. Arden, New York, 1814, 12 cm., 347 pp.

583 JOHN OXENFORD, ed. *The Book of French Songs. To which is added Miss Costello's early French poetry.* Cr 8vo.

Illustrated. 1/6 sewed, 2/0 cloth   Aug. 18 (*Spect*)

Chandos Classics No. 49. This has 475 pp. and was a joint imprint with Scribner, Welford & Armstrong, New York. The first edition was by H. Ingrame & Co., London, 1855, 18 cm., 253 pp., illustrated, *The Illustrated Book of French Songs from the Sixteenth to the Nineteenth Century.*

584 VIRGIL *The Works of Virgil.* Cr 8vo. 1/6 sewed, 2/0 cloth   Aug. 18 (*Acad*)

Chandos Classics No. 52. This has the joint imprint of Scribner, Welford & Armstrong, New York, no date, 492 pp. It is the Dryden translation. The first edition of this translation was issued by Jacob Tonson, London, 1697, 36 cm., 630 pp., illustrated. In the United States it was issued by T. & J. Swords, New York, 2 vols., 1803, the first American edition. It was also issued in Baltimore, 1814, 2-vols.-in-1; and in Philadelphia, 2 vols., 1814, 13 cm.

585 MATILDA BETHAM EDWARDS *The Sylvestres.* New edition. 12mo. 2/0 boards   Aug. 18 (*Spect*)

Companion Library No. 93. This has no date. This ran in *Good Words* (Strahan), beginning in Jan. 1871. The first book edition was issued by Hurst & Blackett, London, 3 vols., 1871, Cr 8vo, 31/6, listed in the *Ath* on Oct. 14. The first American edition was issued by J. B. Lippincott & Co., Philadelphia, 1872, illustrated, listed in the *Ind* and in *PW* on Jan. 25. I have a copy of the present title, a reissue in the *Companion Library*, probably in 1880, a new edition, 17.6 cm., 376 pp., in pale blue pictorial boards, printed in red and black, with the series title on the spine. Publisher's ads are on the front endpapers, giving the series through No. 107, and on the back endpapers, giving the *Chandos Classics* through No. 82; a publisher's ad is on the back cover.

586 MATILDA M. POLLARD *When We Were Young; or, Seventy Years Ago.*
Fcp 8vo. 1/0 sewed   Aug. 18 (*Ath* ad)
Readable Books No. 6. This is the first edition, no date.

587 JOHN TIMBS *The Romance of London.* 2 vols.: 1. "Historic Sketches, Remarkable Duels, etc."; 2. "Supernatural Stories, Sights and Show, etc."
Cr 8vo. 1/6 sewed, 2/0 cloth each
Aug. 25 (*Ath*)
Chandos Classics Nos. 55, 56. These have the joint imprint of Scribner, Welford & Armstrong, New York, no date, 509, 473 pp. The first edition was *Romance of London: Strange Stories, Scenes, etc.*, Bentley, London, 3 vols., 1865, 19.5 cm., 31/6, noticed in *Notes & Queries* on June 17. Warne issued it with the joint imprint, 2 vols., frontispieces, 3/6 cloth each, with the Bentley title, in the *Chandos Library* (1872).

588 MATILDA BETHAM EDWARDS *Now or Never.* New edition. 12mo. 2/0 boards
Aug. 25 (*Acad*)
Companion Library No. 92. This has no date, 423 pp. The first edition was issued by Edmonston & Douglas, Edinburgh, 1859, anonymous, in red-brown cloth with bright orange-rust endpapers, dedicated to the authoress's cousin, Amelia B. Edwards. There is a 12-page catalog at the back.

589 ALAIN R. LE SAGE *Adventures of Gil Blas of Santillane.* Cr 8vo. Illustrated.
1/6 sewed, 2/0 cloth   Sept. 1 (*Ath*)
Chandos Classics No. 50. This has no date and 505 pp. The first edition was *L'Histoire de Gil Blas de Santillane*, the third edition of which was issued at Rouen, 3 vols., 1721–24. The first English edition was issued by Jacob Tonson, London, 2 vols., 1716, 15 cm., and the second edition, 3 vols., 1725, illustrated, *The History and Adventures of Gil Blas of Santillane*. It was issued in the

United States by William Spotswood, Philadelphia, 1790, 16.3 cm., 166 pp. It was also issued in 4 vols. in the Smollett translation, by both Fielding Lucas, Jr., etc., Baltimore, and Richard Scott, New York, both 1814.

590 (SUSAN WARNER) *The Old Helmet.*
16mo. 1/6 sewed, 2/0 cloth   Sept. 8 (*Spect*)
Star Series No. 44. This has no date and 608 pp. The first American edition was issued by Robert Carter & Brothers, New York, 2 vols., 1864, 19.5 cm., anonymous, deposited Dec. 1, 1863, and advertised in the *New-York Times* on Dec. 4, 1863, 12mo, $2.50, as "This morning." There was an issue with green, brown, or black cloth and cream endpapers; another issue with different stamping in purple or black cloth; and still a third stamping in black or green cloth with the joint imprint of J. B. Lippincott & Co., Philadelphia, with the latter company at the foot of the spine. The book received a long, scathing review in the *Knickerbocker* for Mar. 1864. The first English edition was issued by James Nisbet, London, 2 vols., 1864 (1863), 21 cm., anonymous, 12/0, in smooth green cloth, listed in the *Ath* on Dec. 12, 1863. Nisbet issued a new edition, at 2/0 boards, 608 pp., listed in the *Ath* on Jan. 30, 1864; and they issued it in 1 vol. in 1864, Fcp 8vo, colored plates, 3/6 cloth, listed in the *Ath* on Feb. 6, 1864. It was also issued by Routledge, Warne & Routledge, London, 1864, Fcp 8vo, anonymous, 437 pp., 2/0 boards, listed in the *Ath* on Jan. 16; and issued by them at 2/6 cloth, listed Jan. 30, 1864; and issued by them, 440 pp., illustrated, 3/6 cloth, listed on Feb. 20, 1864.

591 ELIZABETH PRENTISS *The Flower of the Family.* 16mo. 1/0 sewed, 1/6 cloth
Sept. 15 (*Spect*)
Star Series No. 38. This has no date and 250 pp. The first American edition was issued by A.D.F. Randolph, New York, 1854,

16mo, anonymous, 385 pp., $.75, advertised in the *New York Daily Times* on Nov. 23, 1853, as "On Nov. 25" and reviewed in the *Ind* on Dec. 15, 1853. Randolph reissued it in 1883, a new edition, $1.50, listed in the *Nation* on Dec. 13. It was issued in England in 1854 by T. Nelson & Sons, London and Edinburgh; W. Collins, London; and Low, London, all anonymous. There was a listing in the *Ath* on June 17, 1854, Fcp 8vo, anonymous, 2/0 cloth; the Nelson issue was listed in the *Spect* on Sept. 23, 1854, Fcp 8vo, anonymous, 1/0 fancy boards.

592 (MARGARET ROBERTS) *Madame Fontenoy.* 16mo. 1/0 sewed, 1/6 cloth Sept. 15 (*Ath* ad)

Star Series No. 39. The first edition was issued by John & Charles Mozley, London, 1864, 18 cm., anonymous, 224 pp., 4/6. They issued it in 1872, 224 pp., in redbrown cloth with yellow endpapers, Wolff's copy. In the United States it was issued by Leypoldt & Holt, New York, in 1866, the Tauchnitz edition, anonymous, $.75, listed in the *Nation* on June 1. George Munro, New York, issued it (1878), quarto paper, 24 pp., *Seaside Library* No. 195.

593 (MARY DENISON) *That Husband of Mine.* Square Fcp 8vo. Illustrated. 1/0 picture cover Sept. 15 (*Spect*)

American Humour. Helen's Babies Series. This has no date, 175 pp. The first American edition was issued by Lee & Shepard, Boston; etc., 1877, 17.5 cm., anonymous, 227 pp., $.50 paper, $1.00 cloth, advertised in the *New-York Times* on Aug. 10 as "On Aug. 11" and on Aug. 11 as "Today." It was listed in both the *Nation* and the *Ind* on Aug. 9. Lee & Shepard reissued it in 1885, a new edition, anonymous, $.50 paper and $1.00 cloth, advertised in the *Nation* on May 7. In England it was issued by George Routledge & Sons, London and New York, in 1877, Fcp 8vo, anonymous, advertised in the *Ath* on Sept. 15. My copy has no date, 16.6 cm., 153 pp. It was also issued by Ward, Lock & Co., London (1877), anonymous, 183 pp., 1/0 sewed; and by Houlston, London, in 1877.

594 ELIZABETH PRENTISS *Toward Heaven.* 16mo. 1/0 sewed, 1/6 cloth Sept. 15 (*Spect*)

Star Series No. 41. This has no date and 246 pp. The first edition was issued by A.D.F. Randolph, New York, *The Percys* (1870), 341 pp., frontispiece, $1.25, listed in the *Nation* on Dec. 22, 1870, and in *Christian Union* (weekly) on Jan. 4, 1871. The first English edition was issued by Ward, Lock & Tyler, London, with the New York title, 1/0 sewed, 1/6, 2/0 cloth, the 1/0 listed in the *Spect* on Apr. 4, 1874, and the 1/6 listed there on Aug. 1.

595 JOHN TIMBS *A Century of Anecdote from 1760 to 1860.* Cr 8vo. 1/6 sewed, 2/0 cloth Sept. 15 (*Ath* ad)

Chandos Classics No. 57. This has no date and 597 pp. The 1/6 issue was listed in the *Spect* on Nov. 3. The first Warne edition was in the *Chandos Library* in 1872, p 8vo, 597 pp., frontispiece (portraits), 3/6 cloth, listed by *PC* as published Oct. 1–15. Warne reissued it at 2/0, listed by the *Bks* for June 1894. The first edition was issued by Bentley, London, 2 vols., 1864, 19 cm., frontispieces, portraits.

596 (CARRIE M. COE) *Me!* Second edition. Square Fcp 8vo. Illustrated. 1/0 picture cover Sept. 15 (*Ath* ad)

American Humour. Helen's Babies Series. This has no date and is probably the first English edition. The first American edition was issued by G. W. Carleton & Co., New York, 1877, 17.5 × 14.5 cm., 176 pp., entitled *Me! July and August.*

597 ABBY M. DIAZ *Brother Billy, Dorry Baker, and Bubby Short.* Square Fcp 8vo. Illustrated. 1/o picture cover   Sept. 15 (*Ath* ad)

American Humour. Helen's Babies Series. This has no date and 251 pp. and is probably the first English edition, if not the only edition, as I cannot locate an American edition!

598 SUSAN COOLIDGE (SARAH C. WOOLSEY) *Queen Blossom.* Square Cr 8vo. Illustrated. 2/o cloth   Sept. 29 (*Ath* ad)

Little Books for Little People. This ad in the *Ath* was for books for the 1877–78 season. The story was in *A Round Dozen*, issued by Roberts Brothers, Boston, 1883.

599 MRS. CLIFFORD BUTLER *Little Elsie's Summer at Malvern.* Square Cr 8vo. Illustrated. 2/o cloth   Sept. 29 (*Ath* ad)

Little Books for Little People. Warne lists give this as *Little Elsie's Country Visit.* The *Eng Cat* gives the title I've given, issued by James Nisbet, London, 1870, p 8vo, 2/6, but otherwise I cannot trace it.

600 JOSEPH A. COLLIER *Pleasant Paths for Little Feet.* Square Cr 8vo. Illustrated. 2/o cloth   Sept. 29 (*Ath* ad)

Little Books for Little People. The *U Cat* gives an issue by the American Tract Society, New York (1864), 16 cm., 234 pp. The first English edition was issued by James Nisbet, London, 1869 (1868), 18.5 cm., 159 pp., illustrated, 2/6. Warne issued it in the *Round the Globe Library*, 12mo, colored frontispiece, 1/o cloth, advertised in the *Ath* on Oct. 28, 1882.

601 ELIZABETH PRENTISS *Little Threads.* Square Cr 8vo. Illustrated. 2/o cloth Sept. 29 (*Ath* ad)

Little Books for Little People. The first edition was issued by A.D.F. Randolph, New York, 1863, 17.5 cm., 191 pp., illustrated. Ran-

dolph reissued it in 1870, listed in *Harper's New Monthly Magazine* for Jan. 1871. In England it was issued by James Nisbet, London, 1864, anonymous, illustrated, 2/6; and by Nimmo, Edinburgh; W. Simpkin & R. Marshall, London, in 1864, Fcp 8vo, anonymous, 124 pp., 1/o, listed in the *Reader* on Dec. 31, 1864. It contains three stories. Warne issued it in their *Round the Globe Library*, 12mo, colored frontispiece, 1/o cloth, listed in an *Ath* ad for Oct. 28, 1882, as books for the 1882–83 season.

602 RICHARD H. DANA, JR. *Two Years Before the Mast.* Cr 8vo. o/6 sewed Oct. 6 (*Ath* ad)

Notable Novels No. 26. This has no date, 149 pp., in illustrated yellow wrappers, with ads on the inside and back covers and on 4 pp. at the back, giving the series as ending with No. 25. Warne reissued it in this series at o/6 sewed, listed in the *Bks* for Apr. 1887. The first edition was issued by Harper & Brothers, New York, 1840, 16 cm., anonymous, 483 pp., *Harper's Family Series* No. 106, advertised in the *Globe*, a Washington, D.C., daily newspaper on Sept. 25 as "Received this day," and reviewed in the *Knickerbocker* for Oct. The first English edition was issued by Edward Moxon, London, 1841, 24 cm., anonymous, 124 pp., 3/6 in yellow pictorial wrappers, printed in double columns. It was listed in the *Spect* on Feb. 6 and advertised in the *Ath* on Feb. 6. Moxon issued a second edition, 1841, the same, in printed wrappers. It was also issued by J. Cunningham, London, 1841, 156 pp., as part of the *Novel Newspaper*.

603 (MARGARET ROBERTS) *Margaret Woodward.* 12mo. Illustrated. 2/6 cloth Oct. 27 (*Ath* ad)

Golden Links Series. This has no date and 269 pp. Warne issued it in the *Star Series* No. 121, 16mo, 1/o sewed, 1/6 cloth, probably in 1891. The first edition was issued in London, 1857, 309 pp., *Summerleigh Manor* by Joseph Masters.

604 JANIE BROCKMAN *Seven O'Clock.* Square Cr 8vo. Illustrated. 2/0 cloth Nov. 3 (*Spect*)

Little Books for Little People. This is the first edition, no date, 145 pp. Warne issued it in their *Home Circle Gift Books*, 12mo, illustrated, 2/0 cloth, advertised in the *Ath* on Oct. 28, 1882.

605 FREDERIC E. WEATHERLY *Elsie in Dreamland.* Square 16mo. Illustrated. 1/0 sewed, 2/0 cloth   Nov. 10 (*Ath*)

This is given also by the *Eng Cat*, but the closest entries in *BM* and *U Cat* are for *Elsie's Expedition* (1874), Royal 16mo, illustrated, 3/6, listed in the *Spect* on Nov. 14, 1874.

606 (MARGARET ROBERTS) *Osé.* 12mo. Illustrated. 2/0 cloth   Nov. 10 (*Ath*)

Home Circle Gift Books. This is the first edition, no date.

607 MORTIMER & FRANCES COLLINS *Sweet and Twenty.* 12mo. 2/0 boards Nov. 17 (*Ath*)

Companion Library No. 94. This has no date and 363 pp. The first edition was issued by Hurst & Blackett, London, 3 vols., 1875, Cr 8vo, 31/6, by Mortimer Collins, in green cloth with rose-pink endpapers. It was listed in the *Ath* on Apr. 17.

608 JULIA B. GODDARD *The Boy and the Constellations.* 12mo. Illustrated. 1/0 sewed, 1/6 cloth   1877 (*Eng Cat*)

Illustrated Fairy Library No. 2. This has no date and 137 pp. The first edition was issued by Warne, 1866, large square 8vo, 137 pp., illustrated, 5/0 cloth, listed in the *Spect* on Oct. 5. It was imported by Scribner, Welford & Co., New York, in 1866, Cr 8vo, illustrated, $2.50 cloth, advertised in the *Nation* on Dec. 6, 1866.

609 HANS C. ANDERSEN *Tales for the Young.* [New edition.] 12mo. Illustrated. 1/0 sewed, 1/6 cloth   1877 (*Eng Cat*)

Illustrated Fairy Library No. 8. This was issued late in 1877, as it was listed in the *Bks* for Jan. 4, 1878.

Also 1865, 97. See 1874, 83

610 (ELIZABETH PRENTISS) *Six Little Princesses.* 12mo. Illustrated. 1/0 sewed, 1/6 cloth   1877 (*Eng Cat*)

Illustrated Fairy Library No. 9. This has no date and 243 pp. This probably contains also *The Story Lizzie Told.* The first edition of the title story was issued by A.D.F. Randolph, New York (1871), 18.5 cm., anonymous, 75 pp., illustrated. The first edition of the second story was issued by Randolph (1870), 18.5 cm., anonymous, 48 pp., illustrated. Warne issued it in the *Fairy Library*, 12mo, 1/6 cloth, listed in *PC* on Sept. 11, 1897.

611 ELIZABETH PRENTISS *The Three Magic Wands.* 12mo. Illustrated. 1/0 sewed, 1/6 cloth   1877 (*Eng Cat*)

Illustrated Fairy Library No. 10. This has 214 pp. Warne issued it as *Nidworth's Choice* in their *Star Series* No. 111, 16mo, 1/0 sewed, 1/6 cloth, listed in the *Spect* on July 28, 1888. This title was given in Warne lists, but I think it probably was *Nidworth and His Three Magic Wands.* The first edition had this latter title, issued by Roberts Brothers, Boston, 1870, 17 cm., 279 pp., frontispiece, $1.25 cloth, advertised in the *New-York Times* on Oct. 11 as "On Oct. 15" and on Oct. 15 as "This day" and listed in the *Nation* on Oct. 21. The first English edition was issued by James Nisbet, London, in 1873, 18mo, 2/0, 2/6, listed in the *Spect* on Dec. 6, 1873. It was also issued by Ward, Lock & Tyler, London, 1/0 sewed, 1/6, 2/0, listed in the *Ath* on June 19, 1875. The present edition was probably issued late in 1877, as it was listed in the *Bks* for Jan. 4, 1878.

612 LOUIS HOFFMANN (ANGELO LEWIS)
*Card Tricks Without Sleight-of-Hand;
or Magic Made Easy.* 32 mo. Illustrated.
o/6 cloth   1877 (*Eng Cat*)

Illustrated Bijou Books No. 27. This has no
date and 96 pp. This came out at the end
of 1877, as it was listed in the *Bks* on Jan. 4,
1878. George Routledge & Sons, London,
issued it in 1865, new edition, 32mo, o/6,
according to the *Eng Cat*.

613 ANONYMOUS *Pleasant Hours with
Foreign Authors.* 12mo. Illustrated.
2/o cloth   1877 (*Eng Cat*)

Home Circle Gift Books. This was issued by
Warne in 1875, 12mo, 2/6, listed in the
Spect on May 21.

614 ANONYMOUS *History of the
Reformation for Children.* 3 vols.
[New edition.] 18mo. Illustrated.
1/6 cloth each   1877 (*Eng Cat*)

Birthday Series. The 3 vols. were Great Britain, Germany, and Switzerland, etc. Other
than the *Eng Cat*, I cannot trace this.

615 S. STACKHOUSE *Hardy Plants for
Little Front Gardens.* 12mo. Illustrated.
1/o boards   1877 (*Eng Cat*)

Useful Books. This is the first edition, with
the joint imprint of Scribner, Welford &
Armstrong, New York, no date, 17 cm.,
120 pp., colored frontispiece, in pink pictorial boards, printed in red, green, and
black, with publisher's ads on the back
cover and endpapers. It was advertised in
the *Ath* on Feb. 23, 1878, as No. 54 in this
series. I have a copy, no date, as described
above, with the publisher's ads on the back
paste-down dated Apr. 17, 1886, and with
a printer's date (May 25, 1886). It was advertised by Warne in the *TWEd* on Mar. 7,
1890, Fcp 8vo, illustrated, 1/o picture
boards or cloth.

616 MARIA EDGEWORTH *Early Lessons.*
p 8vo. Illustrated. 2/6 cloth
1877 (*Eng Cat*)

This was revised and re-edited by Laura
Valentine, reviewed in the *Ath* on Aug.
12, 1876. The first edition was in 10 vols.,
J. Johnson, London, 1801, 4¼ × 3 in.,
anonymous but with the author's name on
the covers, o/6 each. Vols. 1 & 2 contained
Harry and Lucy, 112 and (120) pp. respectively, probably in marbled boards or
wrappers, a second issue of which was
1801, in marbled boards. Vols. 3–5 contained *Rosamond,* 127, (68), and (96) pp.
respectively, parts 2 and 3 in marbled
wrappers. Vols. 6–9 contained *Frank,*
(112), (112), (92), and (96) pp. respectively
in marbled wrappers except for vol. 8 in
marbled boards. Vol. 10 contained *Little
Dog Trusty, etc.,* (108) pp., in marbled
boards. There was a 10-vol. edition, 1809,
with the author's name on the title pages
except for *Harry and Lucy,* and with revised
pagination in some cases. In the United
States it was issued by J. Maxwell, Philadelphia, 4 vols., 1821, 15 cm., colored illustrations. Jacob Johnson, Philadelphia, issued *Rosamond,* 2 vols., 1808, 13.5 cm.
See 1889

617 MARIA EDGEWORTH *The Parent's
Assistant.* p 8vo. Illustrated. 2/6 cloth
1877 (*Eng Cat*)

Warne issued *The Parent's Assistant and
Tales* in 1875, 12mo, 5/o, listed in the *Spect*
on June 26. The first edition was in 3 vols.,
issued by J. Johnson, London, 1795, anonymous. The second edition was issued by
Johnson, 3 vols., 1796, part 1, 14 cm.,
anonymous, 226 pp.; and part 2, 2 vols.,
14.3 cm., anonymous. The third edition
was issued by Johnson, 6 vols., 1800, with
the author's name; Sadleir had an illustrated edition, 6 vols., 1800, small 8vo,
by Edgeworth, and he had a sixth edition,
6 vols., issued by Johnson, 1813, small
12mo. The first American edition was is-

sued by Joseph Milligan, Georgetown, 3 vols., 1809, 14.5 cm.
See 1889

618 MARIA EDGEWORTH **Moral Tales.** p 8vo. Illustrated, 2/6 cloth   1877 (*Eng Cat*)

Warne issued this at 2/6, Cr 8vo, listed in the *Spect* on Mar. 2, 1878, and issued it with the following title in 1 vol., in 1874, edited by Laura Valentine, 5/0, listed in the *Spect* on June 20. The first edition was *Moral Tales for Young People*, issued by J. Johnson, London, 5 vols., 1801, 18 cm., frontispieces, 3/0 each. In the United States it was issued by Johnson & Warner, Philadelphia, 3 vols., 1810, 14 cm.; it was also issued in New York, 3 vols., 1818.
See 1889

619 MARIA EDGEWORTH **Popular Tales.** p 8vo. Illustrated. 2/6 cloth   1877 (*Eng Cat*)

This was listed in the *Spect* on Mar. 2, 1878. Warne issued it with the preceding title in 1 vol. (see above); and issued the two titles in 1 vol. (1874), new edition, re-edited and revised by Laura Valentine, 18.3 cm., 632 pp., illustrated, with a prcfacc (July 1874), containing 17 stories, in their *Victoria Gift Book Series*. The first edition was issued by J. Johnson, London, 3 vols., 1804, 12mo, 15/0 boards, in Apr. 1804. The first American edition was issued by James Humphreys, Philadelphia, 2 vols., 1804, 18 cm.
See 1889

620 ROBERT ST. JOHN CORBET **Ralph Luttrel's Fortunes.** 12mo. Illustrated. 2/6 cloth   1877 (*Eng Cat*)

Daring Deeds Library. The first edition was issued by Warne, 1867, 12mo, 374 pp., illustrated, 3/6. They issued it, 1869, the same, listed in the *Spect* on Dec. 5, 1868; they reissued it in the present series, Cr 8vo, illustrated, 2/6 cloth, listed by *PC* on Nov. 16, 1895.

621 MICHAEL SCOTT **The Cruise of the Midge.** Cr 8vo. 0/6 sewed   1877

Notable Novels No. 25. I put this title here because of its no. in the series. The first edition was issued in two series, 19 cm., anonymous. The first series was issued by Carey & Hart, Philadelphia; Allen & Ticknor, Boston, 2 vols., 1834, $.75 each, vol. 1 advertised in the *Globe*, a Washington, D.C., daily, on Nov. 1, and vol. 2 on Dec. 19, 1834. The second series was issued in 2 vols. by Carey & Hart, Philadelphia; W. D. Ticknor, Boston, 1835, advertised in the *Globe* on Aug. 29, $1.25. The *U Cat* also gives Wallis & Newell, New York, 1835, 18.5 cm., anonymous, 318 pp. The first English edition was issued by William Blackwood, Edinburgh; Cadell, London, 2 vols., 1836, Fcp 8vo, anonymous, 12/0 in dark green cloth with white endpapers with a mesh design in brown. Sadleir gives also a second issue in dark green cloth of a different grain and blocking, with yellow endpapers. In Paris it was issued by Baudry's European Library, 1836, anonymous, 448 pp.

622 AUNT FANNY (FRANCES E. BARROW) **Big Night Caps.** 16mo. Illustrated. 1/0 picture boards, 1/6 cloth   1877

Large Type Book. This was in an ad in the *Ath* for Sept. 29 and was listed as "On our table" on Dec. 15. The first edition was issued by D. Appleton & Co., New York, *The Big Nightcap Letters*, 1861, 15.5 cm., 182 pp., illustrated, $.50, No. 5 in the series, listed in the *Atlantic Monthly* for Jan. 1861 as "Recent" and advertised in the *New-York Times* on Dec. 5, 1860, by Aunt Fanny, as "This day." The first English edition of this title and the other five titles in the series was issued by Edmonston & Douglas, Edinburgh; Hamilton, London, by Aunt Fanny, 2/0 each, reviewed in the *Spect* on Dec. 26, 1868.

623 AUNT FANNY (FRANCES E. BARROW)
Baby Night Caps. 16mo. Illustrated.
1/0 picture boards, 1/6 cloth   1877
Large Type Books. This was in the *Ath* as for the preceding title. The first edition was issued by D. Appleton & Co., New York and London, 1860, 15.5 cm., 140 pp., $.50, advertised in the *New-York Times* on Dec. 6, 1859, as "This week" and listed in the *Atlantic Monthly* for Feb. 1860 as "Recent." The first English edition was as given in the preceding title.

624 AUNT FANNY (FRANCES E. BARROW)
Old Night Caps. 16mo. Illustrated.
1/0 picture boards, 1/6 cloth   1877
Large Type Books. This was reviewed in the *Ath* on Mar. 2, 1878. The first edition was issued by D. Appleton & Co., New York, 1859, as *Nightcaps*, 15.5 cm., by Aunt Fanny, 171 pp., illustrated, $.50, advertised in the *New-York Times* on Dec. 10, 1858, as "On Dec. 9" and listed in *Godey's Lady's Book* for Feb. 1859. The first English edition was as given for the preceding two titles.

625 AUNT FANNY (FRANCES E. BARROW)
New Night Caps. 16mo. Illustrated.
1/0 picture boards, 1/6 cloth   1877
Large Type Books. This title was reviewed in the *Ath* on Mar. 2, 1878. The first edition was issued by D. Appleton & Co., New York and London, 1860, 15.5 cm., 207 pp., illustrated, $.50, *The New Nightcaps Told to Charley,* listed in the *Atlantic Monthly* for Feb. 1860, but issued for Christmas 1859. The first English edition was as for the above titles.

626 AUNT FANNY (FRANCES E. BARROW)
Little Night Caps. 16mo. Illustrated.
1/0 picture boards, 1/6 cloth   1877
Large Type Books. This title was reviewed in the *Ath* on Mar. 2, 1878. The first edition was issued by D. Appleton & Co., New York, 1861, 15.5 cm., by Aunt Fanny, 178 pp., illustrated, $.50, *The Little Night-Cap Letters,* advertised in the *New-York Times* on Dec. 5, 1860, as "This day" and listed in the *Atlantic Monthly* for Dec. 1860 as "Recent." The first English edition was as given for the preceding title in the series.

627 AUNT FANNY (FRANCES E. BARROW)
Fairy Night Caps. 16mo. Illustrated.
1/0 picture boards, 1/6 cloth   1877
Large Type Books. This title was reviewed in the *Ath* on Mar. 2, 1878. The first edition was issued by D. Appleton & Co., New York, 1861, 15.5 cm., 215 pp., illustrated, $.50, advertised in the *New-York Times* on Dec. 5, 1860, as "This day" and listed in the *Atlantic Monthly* for Dec. 1860 as "Recent," by Aunt Fanny. The first English edition was as for the above titles in the series, 16 cm., 211 pp., illustrated.

628 G.P.R. JAMES *Henry Masterton.*
Cr 8vo. o/6 sewed   Feb. 23 (*Ath* ad)
Notable Novels No. 28. The first English edition was issued by Colburn & Bentley, London, 3 vols., 1832, 19 cm., anonymous, 31/6 boards, advertised in the *Spect* on May 12 as "Just ready" and given by the *Eng Cat* as issued in June. Bentley issued it as *Standard Novels* No. 61, 1837, 494 pp., in Nov., my copy with No. 60 on the title page. Simms & M'Intyre, London and Belfast, issued it in the *Parlour Library* No. 61, 1851, 464 pp., on July 1. There was an edition listed in *PC* as published June 17–29, 1847, medium 8vo, frontispiece, no publisher given. The first American edition was issued by J. & J. Harper, New York, 2 vols., 1832, 12mo, anonymous, in green printed cloth, *Library of Select Novels* Nos. 29, 30, listed in *North American Review* (quarterly) for Jan. 1833.

629 G.P.R. JAMES *John Marston Hall.*
Cr 8vo. o/6 sewed   Feb. 23 (*Ath* ad)
Notable Novels No. 29. The first edition was *The Life and Adventures of John Marston Hall*, issued by Longmans, London, 3 vols., 1834, 19 cm., anonymous, 31/6 boards, listed in the *Ath* on Apr. 26. It has a 12-page catalog (Feb. 1834) at the front of vol. 1. There was an edition in 1847, *The Little Ball o' Fire*, 8vo, 1 illustration, cloth, listed by *PC* as published Dec. 14–29, no publisher given. It was issued by Simms & M'Intyre, London and Belfast, in the *Parlour Library* No. 63, 1851, 448 pp. The first American edition was issued by Harper & Brothers, New York, 2 vols., 1834, 17.5 cm., anonymous, $1.25, in green printed cloth, advertised in the *Globe*, a Washington, D.C., daily on July 7. It had a dedication signed by James, and was *Library of Select Novels* Nos. 37, 38.

630 FREDERICK MARRYAT *Japhet in Search of a Father.* Cr 8vo. o/6 sewed Feb. 23 (*Ath* ad)
Notable Novels No. 30. This is my copy, no date, 19.3 cm., 150 pp. in double columns, pictorially printed in red, blue, and black, with the series title on the front and the title and No. (28, *sic*) on the spine. There are publisher's ads on the inside covers, with the series ending with No. 33, and 6 pp. at the back, and a 4-page Chapman & Hall insert on small paper at the back; a commercial ad is on the back cover. The first edition was issued by Saunders & Otley, London, 3 vols., 1836, 21 cm., anonymous, 31/6 boards with paper labels, listed in the *Ath* on Dec. 19, 1835. They issued a second edition in 3 vols., 1836, in dark blue cloth, from first edition sheets. It ran in the *Metropolitan Magazine*, Oct. 1834–Jan. 1836. I give here an outline of the American issues, but reference should be made to Sadleir I, page 233, for all the complications. Wallis & Newell, New York, issued it in 4 parts in light blue wrappers, $.12½ for part 1 and $.06¼ for each of

the last three. Parts 1 and 2 were 1835, and parts 3 and 4 were 1836. The parts were issued, Apr. 1835–Feb. 1836. They issued it in 1 vol., anonymous, 223 pp. Carey & Hart, Philadelphia, etc., issued it, 2 vols., 1835, 1836, 19 cm., anonymous, vol. 1 in half cloth boards with labels and with a 24-page catalog (Jan. 1835) at the back. This was advertised in the *Globe*, a Washington, D.C., daily, on Feb. 24, 1836, 2 vols., concluded, $.75, "This day." It was also issued by H. C. Boswell, Trenton, New Jersey, 1835, 22 cm., 167 pp.; and by Harper & Brothers, New York, in 1836, by Marryat, listed in the *North American Review* (quarterly) for Apr.

631 CHARLOTTE RIDDELL
(MRS. J. H. RIDDELL) *The Earl's Promise.*
[New edition.] 12mo. 2/0 boards
Mar. 2 (*Bks*)
This is a reissue in the *Companion Library*.
Also 1875

632 FREDERICK MARRYAT *The Pirate, and the Three Cutters.* Cr 8vo. o/6 sewed
Mar. 2 (*Bks*)
Notable Novels No. 27. This has no date and 111 pp. The first edition was issued by Longmans, London, 1836, 15.2 × 23.5 cm. sheet size, 315 pp., frontispiece (portrait) and illustrations, the latter all dated 1835, 31/6 cream glazed paper boards with yellow endpapers, listed in the *Ath* on Dec. 19, 1835. An engraved title precedes the printed title. There was a later issue in dull plum cloth, with yellow endpapers. Longmans issued it also in a large paper edition, at the same time, 1836, 18.3 × 27 cm. sheet size, with India proofs of the plates, 52/6, in half dark green cloth, with green board sides and white endpapers. Both stories appeared in the *Naval Annual*, issued by Longmans, London; Desilver, Thomas & Co., Philadelphia, 1836, 315 pp., illustrated. A Fullerton & Co., London, etc., issued it in parts, 1845, in cream

paper wrappers, printed in brown, with the text reset. They issued it in 1 vol., bound from the parts, 1845, frontispiece (portrait) and illustrations, with an engraved title, bound in dark olive green cloth with no imprint on the spine. Henry G. Bohn issued it in 1861, new edition, p 8vo, illustrated, 5/0, reissued by Bell & Daldy, London, 1867. In America there were three editions in 1836, all with the two stories plus *Moonshine*, the latter having appeared in the *Keepsake* for 1836 but hadn't appeared in book form in England until *Olla Podrida* in 1840. Carey & Hart, Philadelphia, issued it, 2 vols., 1836, narrow 8vo, in half cloth boards with labels, listed in the *North American Review* (quarterly) for Apr. 1836, and advertised by a Washington, D.C., bookstore in the *Globe*, a Washington daily, on Jan. 19, 1836, 2 vols., $.62½, and on Feb. 9, 2 vols., $.37 each. *The Three Cutters: and Other Tales* was issued by John L. Piper, New York, 1836, reviewed in the *Knickerbocker* for Feb. 1836. *Stories of the Sea* was issued by Harper & Brothers, New York, 1836, 232 pp., in dark green cloth, reviewed in the *Knickerbocker* for Feb. 1836.

633 MRS. J. W. LOUDON (JANE WEBB, later LOUDON) *The Amateur Gardener's Calendar.* [New edition.] 12mo.
Illustrated. 2/0 boards   Mar. 9 (*Spect*)
Useful Books. The first edition was issued by Longmans, London, 1847, 12mo, 372 pp., illustrated, 7/6, noticed in the *Gentleman's Magazine* (monthly) for Aug. 1847. This Warne edition is revised and edited by William Robinson. Warne first issued it, 1870, 20 cm., 376 pp., illustrated, 7/6, listed in the *Spect* on Dec. 11, 1869. They issued it in 1873, large Cr 8vo, illustrated, 7/6, advertised in the *Spect* on Feb. 8. They reissued it in the *Useful Books* series, no date, 12mo, 192 pp., 1/0, in 1880, given by the *Eng Cat*; and reissued it in 1890, Fcp

8vo, illustrated, 1/0 picture boards or cloth, advertised in the *Times Weekly Edition* (London) on Mar. 7, 1890.

634 STEPHEN T. AVELING *Carpentry and Joinery.* 12mo. Illustrated. 1/0 boards, 1/6 cloth   Mar. 9 (*Spect*)

Useful Books. This listing in the *Spect* was for the 1/0, and the 1/6 was listed on Apr. 27. The first edition was Warne, London; Scribner, Welford & Co., New York (1871), 18.5 cm., 120 pp., illustrated, 2/6, listed in the *Spect* on July 8. They reissued it in 1875, royal 16mo, 2/0, listed in the *Spect* on Mar. 13.

635 IZAAK WALTON & CHARLES COTTON *The Complete Angler.* [A new illustrated edition.] Cr 8vo. 1/6 sewed, 2/0 cloth Mar. 9 (*Ath*)

Chandos Classics No. 58. This has no date and 467 pp. edited by George C. Davies. Warne reissued it in 1888. *The Compleat Angler* was issued by Richard Marriot, London, 1653, 14.5 cm., 246 pp., illustrated, signed Iz. Wa. The first edition with the Cotton contribution was the fifth of 1676. *The Compleat Angler* by Walton and Cotton was issued by H. Kent, London, 1750, 312 pp., illustrated. It was issued by C. Tilt, London; T. Wardle, Philadelphia, etc., 2 vols., 1837, 11 cm. Warne also issued it at 3/6, listed in the *Spect* on Mar. 16, 1878.

636 J. H. INGRAHAM *The Prince of the House of David.* New edition. 16mo. Illustrated. 1/0 sewed, 1/6 cloth   Apr. 3 (*Bks*)

Star Series No. 45. This has no date and 269 pp. It was also issued at 2/6, p 8vo, illustrated, listed in the *Bks* for Apr. 3, 1878. Warne issued it as *Notable Novels* No. 115, p 8vo, 0/6 sewed, probably in 1888. The first edition was issued by Pudney & Russell, New York, 1855, 19.5 cm., 456 pp., frontispiece, $1.25, listed in *APC&LG* (weekly)

on Nov. 24. The first English edition was issued by Arthur Hall, Virtue, London, 1859, Fcp 8vo, illustrated, 5/0, listed in the *Ath* on Mar. 12. Alexander Strahan, London, issued it in June 1869.

637 J. H. INGRAHAM *The Pillar of Fire.* New edition. 16mo. Illustrated. 1/0 sewed, 1/6 cloth   Apr. 3 (*Bks*)

Star Series No. 46. This has no date and 348 pp. It was also issued at 2/6, listed in the *Bks* on Apr. 3. I have a copy, no date but probably 1889, new edition, 16.5 cm., 348 pp., in red silk grained cloth, elaborately blocked in gold and black, with the series title on the front, spine, and title page, pale green figured endpapers. It has the no. in the series in blind at the bottom of the front cover. The first edition was issued by Pudney & Russell, New York, etc., 1859, 20 cm., 600 pp., frontispiece, $1.25, advertised in the *New-York Times* on Apr. 11 as "Just published" and advertised in *Harper's Weekly* on Mar. 26 as "On Apr. 11." It was also issued by George G. Evans, Philadelphia, 1859, reviewed in *De Bow's Review* (monthly) for Mar. 1860 and thus issued Dec. 1859 or earlier. The first English edition was issued by Virtue Brothers & Co., London, 1865, Fvp 8vo, 8 illustrations, 5/0 cloth, listed in the *Ath* on Oct. 7.

638 J. H. INGRAHAM *The Throne of David.* New edition. 16mo. Illustrated. 1/0 sewed, 1/6 cloth   Apr. 3 (*Bks*)

Star Series No. 47. This has no date and 352 pp. It was also listed in the *Bks* on Apr. 3 at 2/6. The first edition was issued by George G. Evans, Philadelphia, 1860, 19 cm., 603 pp., illustrated, $1.25, listed in *APC&LG* (weekly) on May 5 and advertised in the *Ind* on May 10 as "Now ready." The first English edition was issued by Virtue Brothers & Co., London, 1866, Fcp 8vo, 8 full-page illustrations, 5/0 cloth, listed in the *Ath* on Sept. 22, 1866, and in the *Spect* on Sept. 29. It was issued by Alexander Strahan, London, in 1869.

639 ANONYMOUS *Little Tales for Tiny Tots.* [New edition.] 16mo. Illustrated. 1/o boards, 1/6 cloth   Apr. 3 (*Bks*)
Large Type Books. This was issued by Whittaker, London, in 1870, 1/o. It was reviewed in the *Ath* on Mar. 2, 1878.

640 FREDERICK MARRYAT *The Pacha of Many Tales.* Cr 8vo. o/6 sewed   Apr. 3 (*Bks*)
Notable Novels No. 33. I have a copy, no date, 19.4 cm., 154 pp. in double columns, yellow pictorial wrappers, printed in red, blue, and black with the series title on the front and spine and No. 33 at the base of the spine. There are publisher's ads on the back cover, of date 1880, and 4 pp. at the back, with the series ending with No. 47 of 1880. The first English edition was issued by Saunders & Otley, London, 3 vols., 1835, 20.5 cm., anonymous, 31/6 boards with labels, listed in the *Ath* on May 13 and advertised in the *Spect* on May 9 as "Just ready." Wolff's copy had an 8-page catalog (Dec. 1834) at the back of vol. 1. Sadleir also had a copy in olive-brown glazed linen, with paper labels. There was a second edition, 3 vols., 1835, in dark blue cloth, the first edition sheets with new prelims. Bentley, London, issued it in *Standard Novels* No. 68, 1838, 378 pp. The first edition was issued by Carey & Hart, Philadelphia, etc., 2 vols., 1834, 19.5 cm., anonymous, advertised by a Washington, D.C., book store in the *Globe*, a Washington daily, on Dec. 4, 1834, and listed in the *North American Review* (quarterly) for Jan. 1835, but this latter listing was for Allen & Ticknor, Boston. This firm possibly issued it jointly with Cary & Hart.

641 LADY MARY ANNE BARKER, later BROOME *Spring Comedies.* 12mo. 2/o boards   Apr. 6 (*Spect*)
Companion Library No. 97. The first edition was issued by Macmillan & Co., London and New York, 1871, 20 cm., 340 pp., 7/6, listed in the *Ath* on Apr. 29.

642 LADY MARY ANNE BARKER, later BROOME *Station Life in New Zealand.* 12mo. 2/o   Apr. 6 (*Spect*)
This was reissued in Sept., listed in the *Spect* and *Acad* on Sept. 7. The first edition was issued by Macmillan, London, 1870, Cr 8vo, 238 pp., 7/6, listed in the *Ath* on Dec. 18, 1869. They reissued it in 1871 and 1874, at 3/6. It was issued in the United States by D. C. Lent, New York, 1872, 17.5 cm., 238 pp. colored frontispiece.

643 MORTIMER COLLINS (EDWARD J.M. COLLINS) *A Fight with Fortune.* 12mo. 2/o boards   Apr. 6 (*Ath*)
Companion Library No. 96. This has no date and 367 pp. The first edition was issued by Hurst & Blackett, London, 3 vols., 1876, Cr 8vo, 31/6, listed in the *Ath* on Apr. 15.

644 J.J. *Jones's Journey to Paris.* 12mo. 1/o picture cover   May 25 (*Ath* ad)
This was issued by Scribner, Welford & Co., New York (1878), 16mo, 190 pp., illustrated, $.50 in stiff boards, advertised in the *New York Times* on July 23 as "On July 24." The *BM* gives the second edition, London (1878), illustrated. Warne issued it as *Popular Library* No. 7, 12mo, illustrated, 1/o sewed, advertised in the *Times Weekly Edition* (London) on July 19, 1889.

645 JOSEPH HATTON *The Queen of Bohemia.* 12mo. 2/o boards   June 29 (*Ath*)
Companion Library No. 98. This has no date and 376 pp. The first edition was issued by Chapman & Hall, London, 2 vols., 1877,

Cr 8vo, 21/o in gray cloth and yellow end-papers, listed in the *Ath* on Oct. 27. There is a dedication to William Black (Oct. 1876). The first American edition was issued by Harper & Brothers, New York, 1882, 51 pp., *Franklin Square Library* No. 247, $.15 paper, advertised in the *New-York Times* on Apr. 28 as "This day" and listed in the *Nation* on May 25.

646 MRS. ABBY M. DIAZ *Silas Y. Fry.*
12mo. Illustrated. 1/o picture cover
July 13 (*Ath* ad)

This is also given by the *Eng Cat*, but otherwise I cannot trace it.

647 BERTHE VADIER (CÉLESTE V. BENOIT) *My Star.* Fcp 8vo. 1/o sewed   July 13 (*Ath* ad)

Readable Books No. 8. This is the first English edition, 1878, translated from the French. Warne later mistakenly listed this as No. 14 in the series.

648 FRANCES H. BURNETT *That Lass o' Lowrie's.* Fcp 8vo. 1/o sewed   July 13 (*Ath* ad)

This is a reissue in *Readable Books*.
See 1877, 1900

649 REGINALD HEBER *The Poetical Works of Reginald Heber.* New edition. Cr 8vo.
1/6 sewed, 2/o cloth   July 27 (*Spect* ad)

Chandos Classics No. 60. This has no date and 433 pp. It wasn't listed in the *Acad* and the *Spect* until Dec. 7, at 2/o. *Poems and Translations of Reginald Heber* was issued by Longmans, London, 1812, 18 cm., 180 pp.; it was issued by J. Murray, London, 1829, new edition, 22 cm., 143 pp. The present title was issued by J. Murray, 1841, 17 cm., 454 pp., frontispiece; and by Lea & Blanchard, Philadelphia, 1841, 17.5 cm., 309 pp.

650 GEORGE HERBERT *The Works of George Herbert in Prose and Verse.*
Cr 8vo. 1/6 sewed, 2/o cloth
Aug. 17 (*Spect*)

Chandos Classics No. 59. This has no date and 488 pp. It was reissued in the 1880s. The first edition was issued by William Pickering, London, 2 vols., 1836, 1838, with frontispieces, with the present title. *The Works of the Reverend George Herbert* was issued by George Routledge & Co., London, 1853, 16.5 cm., 392 pp., frontispiece (portrait), ed. by W. Jerdan; Routledge issued the present title, 1854, 17 cm., 466 pp., illustrated, 5/o cloth, ed. by R. A. Willmott. This latter edition was issued by D. Appleton & Co., New York and London, 1854, 17 cm., 466 pp., illustrated, with an added title page with the Routledge imprint. Routledge issued it *passim* until at least 1893.

651 CHARLES KNIGHT *Half-Hours with the Best Authors.* 4 vols. New edition, remodeled and revised. Illustrated.
1/6 sewed, 2/o cloth each   Aug. 17 (*Ath*)

Chandos Classics Nos. 61–64. These have no dates and were reissued in the series in the 1880s. Warne issued it in 2 vols. in 1865, portraits, illustrations, Cr 8vo, 12/o cloth, or in 4 vols. at 14/o cloth, advertised in the *Spect* on Aug. 26. They issued the present edition in 1866, 21/o in cloth, listed in the *Spect* on Dec. 1, 1866; they issued it in 2 vols. at 10/o cloth, listed in the *Reader* on Sept. 8, 1866, and advertised in the *Spect* on May 16, 1868. They issued it in the *Cavendish Library* in 4 vols., Cr 8vo, frontispieces, 3/6 cloth each, advertised in *Notes & Queries* for June 1889; and they issued it in the *Chandos Edition* in New York, 4 vols., frontispieces, in maroon cloth, boxed at $6.00, advertised in the *Nation* on Dec. 9, 1886. The first edition was issued by Charles Knight, London, 4 vols. (1847–48), 18 cm., portraits, 5/o cloth each, having issued it in 1/6 parts, 3 parts to the vol.

Vol. 1 was listed in the *Ath* on June 5, 1847; vol. 2 on Oct. 30; and vol. 3 on Mar. 18, 1848. Knight reissued it in 1850 in 1½ penny weekly numbers, o/6 monthly parts, and 2/6 quarterly vols., all with the portraits. The first weekly number was advertised in the *Ath* on Apr. 6, 1850, as "This day." It was issued by George Routledge & Co., London, in 1853, new edition, 2 vols., 8vo, portraits, 10/0, advertised in the *Ath* on Feb. 19 as "Ready"; they issued the third edition in 1854, 4 vols., 19.5 cm., 14/0, or in 2 vols. at 12/0. Routledge reissued the third edition in 1855, 2 vols., p 8vo, illustrated, at 12/0, listed by *PC* as published Jan. 31–Feb. 14, 1855. They reissued it in 2 vols. in May 1856, and in 4 vols. in July 1856. They issued the fourth edition (1859) in 4 vols. at 14/0 cloth, listed in *PC* as published Mar. 31–Apr. 14, 1859, having issued it in 22 fortnightly o/6 parts, beginning Mar. 1, 1859. They issued it in 2 vols. in 1860 and in 11 monthly 1/0 parts in 1863. George Routledge & Co., New York, issued it in 4 vols. in 1854, Cr 8vo, illustrated, $3.50, advertised in the *New York Daily Times* on Nov. 3 as "Just published." The first American edition was issued by Wiley & Putnam, New York, 4 vols., 1847–49, 19 cm., $1.50 cloth each, in their *Library of Choice Reading*. Vol. 1 was listed in the *Knickerbocker* for Oct. 1847. Vols. 2–4 were issued by John Wiley, New York, as Wiley & Putnam had dissolved before May 1848. Vol. 2 was listed by *Lit W* as published May 13–20, 1848, in the cloth edition or in paper in 2 parts at $.62½ each. Vols. 3 and 4 were listed as published Sept. 1–15, 1849. The *U Cat* gives a 6-vol. edition, illustrated (1848?), issued by both the Argyle Press, New York, and by Porter & Coates, Philadelphia.

652 M. M. BELL (MARY L. MARTIN) *The Admiral's Will.* 16mo. 1/0 sewed, 1/6 cloth   Aug. 24 (*Spect*)
Star Series No. 48. This is the first edition, no date, 284 pp.

653 A.C.D. *Sylvia and Janet.* 16mo. 1/0 sewed, 1/6 cloth   Sept. 21 (*Spect*)
Star Series No. 49. The first edition was issued by Warne (1870), small Cr 8vo, illustrated, 3/6, listed in the *Spect* on Nov. 7. Warne also issued it in their *Golden Links Series*, 12mo, illustrated, 2/6 cloth, probably in 1879.

654 MARY R. HIGHAM *Cloverly.* 16mo. 1/0 sewed, 1/6 cloth   Oct. 5 (*Ath* ad)
Star Series No. 53. This is the first English edition, no date, 252 pp. The first edition was issued by A.D.F. Randolph, New York (copyright 1875), 18 cm., 256 pp.

655 MRS. HENRY H. B. PAULL *Straight Paths and Crooked Ways.* 16mo. 1/6 sewed, 2/0 cloth   Oct. 12 (*Spect*)
Star Series No. 50. This is the first edition, no date, 345 pp.

656 MRS. HENRY H. B. PAULL *Englefield Grange.* 16mo. 1/6 sewed, 2/0 cloth Oct. 12 (*Spect*)
Star Series No. 52. This is the first edition, no date, 380 pp.

657 ALFRED H. ENGELBACH *The Danes in England.* 12mo. Illustrated. 2/6 cloth Oct. 12 (*Spect* ad)
Daring Deeds Library. This is the first edition, no date. It was reissued in this series in 1882, given by the *Eng Cat*; Warne issued it in the *Incident and Adventure Library*, Fcp 8vo, illustrated, 2/0 cloth in 1889, given by the *Eng Cat*; it was placed in the *Daring and Doing Library* at 1/6 cloth in the 1890s.

658 CHARLES & MARY LAMB *Tales from Shakespeare.* 12mo. Illustrated. 2/0 cloth   Oct. 12 (*Ath* ad)
Home Circle Gift Books. Warne issued this in the *Chandos Classics* No. 83, new edition, Cr 8vo, illustrated, 1/6 sewed, 2/0 cloth, no date, 312 pp., about Apr. 16, 1881, and re-

issued it in that series, 1888. The first edition was issued by T. Hodgkins, London, 2 vols., 1807, 17.5 cm., by Charles Lamb, plates, 8/o, reviewed in the *Critical Review*, London (monthly), for May. Mary's name did not appear on the title page for the first 6 editions. The 14 comedies were by Mary, and the 6 tragedies by Charles. Eight of the tales were issued as single nos. by William Godwin, London, prior to the 2-vols. issue. These tales were commissioned by William Godwin for his juvenile library. Godwin issued the second edition, 2 vols. 1809, 12mo. The first American edition was issued by Bradford & Inskeep, Philadelphia, etc., 2 vols., 1813, 20 cm., by Charles and Mary. It was issued by Munroe & Francis, Boston, in 1832, 18mo, by Charles Lamb, 414 pp., listed in the *North American Review* (quarterly) for Jan. 1833. It was advertised by a Washington, D.C., bookstore in the *Globe*, a Washington daily, on May 4, 1837, by Charles Lamb, 366 pp., $.62, from the first reprint from the fifth London edition, no publisher given.

659 JANIE BROCKMAN **Worth Doing.** Square Cr 8vo. Illustrated. 2/o cloth Nov. 9 (*Ath*)

Little Books for Little People. This is the first edition, no date, 145 pp. It was issued in *Home Circle Gift Books* in 1882, 12mo, illustrated, 2/o cloth, advertised in the *Ath* on Oct. 28.

660 WILLIAM I. CHADWICK **The Magic Lantern Manual.** 12mo. Illustrated. 1/o picture cover, 1/6 cloth Nov. 30 (*Ath* ad)

This is the first edition, with 100 illustrations and 138 pp., by W. J. Chadwick (*sic*). It was issued in the United States by the Scovill Manufacturing Co., New York, 1886, second edition, 12mo, illustrated. Warne issued the second edition, Cr 8vo,

illustrated, 1/o cloth boards, 1/6 cloth, no date, with 154 pp., in 1885, given by the *Eng Cat*.

661 CHARLES GIBBON **Robin Gray.** 12mo. 2/o boards Dec. 7 (*Ath*)

Companion Library No. 99. The first edition was issued by Blackie & Son, London, 3 vols., 1869, 19.5 cm., 31/6 in green cloth, with yellow endpapers, listed in the *Ath* on Feb. 27. The first American edition was issued by Harper & Brothers, New York, 1873, 22.5 cm., 144 pp. in double columns, listed in *PW* on Feb. 22 and in the *Ind* on Feb. 20. Henry S. King & Co., London, issued it in May 1877, 2/o boards; they issued it, 1872, Cr 8vo, 3/6, frontispiece, *Cornhill Library of Fiction*, list *Spect* Apr. 27.

662 CHARLES GIBBON **For Lack of Gold.** 12mo. 2/o boards Dec. 7 (*Ath*)

Companion Library No. 100. The first edition was issued by Blackie & Son, London, 3 vols., 1871, Cr 8vo, 31/6, listed in the *Ath* on Apr. 15. Henry S. King & Co., London, issued it, 1872, Cr 8vo, frontispiece, 3/6, in the *Cornhill Library of Fiction*, listed in the *Spect* on Apr. 27. King issued it, 1877, 12mo, 2/o boards, listed in the *Spect* on May 12. The first American edition was issued by Harper & Brothers, New York, 1871, 8vo, $.50 paper, advertised in the *New-York Times* on Aug. 3 as "This day" and listed in the *Nation* on Aug. 3.

663 JOHN SAUNDERS **Hirell.** 12mo. 2/o boards Dec. 7 (*Ath*)

Companion Library No. 101. This has no date and 421 pp. The first edition was issued by Bentley, London, 3 vols., 1869, 19 cm., anonymous, in brown cloth with cream endpapers, advertised in the *Ath* on July 10 as "On July 12." It ran in *St. James's Magazine* (Skeet) beginning in Apr. 1868. The first yellowback issue was by Henry S. King & Co., London, in 1876, anonymous, 2/o boards, in Nov. The first American edition was issued by Harper & Brothers, New York, 1870, 22 cm., anonymous, 157 pp., $.50 paper, *Library of Select Novels*, noticed in the *Ind* on Feb. 12 and listed in *ALG&PC* (fortnightly) on Feb. 15.

664 J. C. HUTCHINSON, ed. *Fugitive Poetry, 1600–1878.* Cr 8vo. 1/6 sewed, 2/o cloth   Dec. 7 (*Spect*)

Chandos Classics No. 66. This is probably the first edition. It is given by the *Eng Cat* also, but otherwise I cannot trace it.

665 JOHN SAUNDERS *Abel Drake's Wife.* Fcp 8vo. 1/o sewed   Dec. (*Bks*)

Readable Novels No. 9. The first edition was issued by Lockwood & Co., London, 1862, p 8vo, 338 pp., 10/6, listed in the *Ath* on Mar. 29. They issued the second edition, 1862, 19.5 cm., 338 pp., 10/6, advertised in the *Spect* on June 14 as "Now ready"; they issued the third edition in 1863, p 8vo, 6/o, advertised in the *Spect* on Mar. 28 as "Just ready." Sampson Low, London, issued the fourth edition in 1863, Cr 8vo, 312 pp., 5/o, listed in the *Reader* on Nov. 14 as "Just ready"; Low issued the fifth edition in 1866, 12mo, 312 pp., 2/6 boards, listed in the *Reader* on Apr. 21. Henry S. King & Co., London, issued it in 1872, Cr 8vo, frontispiece, 3/6, in the *Cornhill Library of Fiction*, listed in the *Spect* on Oct. 18; King issued it in 1876, frontispiece, 2/o boards, advertised in the *Spect* on Nov. 25. The first American edition was issued by Harper & Brothers, New York, 1862, 8vo, 162 pp., $.25 paper, advertised in the *New-York Times* on June 28 as "This day," *Library of Select Novels* No. 221.

666 SIR THOMAS D. LAUDER *The Wolfe of Badenoch.* Cr 8vo. o/6 sewed   1878 (*Eng Cat*)

Notable Novels No. 31. The first edition was issued by Cadell & Co., Edinburgh; Simpkin, Marshall, London, 3 vols., 1827, 18 cm., anonymous, 24/o, in blue paper boards, labels, white endpapers, listed by the *Quarterly Review* (London) as published Jan.–Mar. 1827. They issued a second edition in 3 vols., 1827. George Routledge & Sons, London, issued it in 1868, Cr 8vo, 1/o sewed, listed in the *Ath* on June 20.

667 WILLIAM GODWIN *Caleb Williams.* Cr 8vo. o/6 sewed   1878 (*Eng Cat*)

Readable Novels No. 32. This has no date and 144 pp. The first edition was issued by B. Crosby, London, 3 vols., 1794, 18 cm., 10/6 sewed, *Things as They Are; or, The Adventures of Caleb Williams*. It was reviewed in the *Critical Review*, London (monthly) for July. G. G. & J. Robinson, London, issued the third edition, corrected, 3 vols., 1797, with the preface suppressed in the first edition. There was a fourth edition in 1815, 3 vols., listed in the *Critical Review* for Jan. 1816. It was issued in *Colburn and Bentley's Standard Novels* No. 2, 1831, 6/o, advertised in the *Spect* on Mar. 26 as "On Apr. 1." The first American edition was issued by H. & P. Rice, Philadelphia, 2 vols., 1795, 17 cm. It was issued by J. & J. Harper, New York, 2 vols., 12mo, *Library of Select Novels* Nos. 11 and 12, in Nov. 1831, *The Adventures of Caleb Williams*.

668 MORTIMER & FRANCES COLLINS *Frances.* 12mo. 2/o boards   1878

Companion Library No. 95. This has no date and 397 pp. I put it here because of its no. in the series. The first edition was issued by Hurst & Blackett, London, 3 vols., 1874, Cr 8vo, by Mortimer Collins, 31/6, listed in the *Ath* on Aug. 1.

669 FRANCES H. BURNETT *Theo.* Fcp 8vo. 1/o sewed   1878

Readable Books No. 7. I place this here because of the no. in the series. The first American edition was issued by T. B. Peterson & Brothers, Philadelphia (1877),

17.5 cm., 232 pp., $.50 paper and $1.00 cloth, listed in *PW* on Sept. 22, 1877. It was issued by Charles Scribner's Sons, New York, in 1879, authorized edition, 16mo, 183 pp., $.30 paper, advertised in the *New-York Times* on May 17 as "This day" and listed in the *Nation* on June 5. The *Eng Cat* and *BM* both give both Warne and Ward, Lock & Co. (1877), 177 pp. Warne certainly issued it in 1877, and it was "On our table" in the *Ath* for Dec. 8, 1877. The first Canadian edition was issued by J. R. Robertson, Toronto, 1877, 21.5 cm., 41 pp. in double columns.

670 MATILDA BETHAM EDWARDS *Charlie and Ernest.* 18mo. Illustrated. 1/6 cloth
1878 (*Eng Cat*)

Birthday Series. The first edition was Charles and Ernest, issued by Edmondston & Douglas, Edinburgh, 1859, 17 cm., 180 pp., illustrated. Warne placed it in the *Oakleaf Library* at 1/0 in the 1890s.

671 (HELEN C. WRIGHT) *Taking a Stand.* 32mo. Colored frontispiece. 1/0 cloth
1878 (*Eng Cat*)

Home Library. This was issued by H. Hoyt, Boston (1860), 16mo, 94 pp., illustrated. This and the following six titles were given by the *BM* as from the Christian Knowledge Society, London, 19 vols., 1878–84. The *U Cat* gives it as issued by the Society for Promoting Christian Knowledge, London; E. & J. B. Young, New York, 1879–, 19 cm.

672 (SUSAN & ANNA WARNER) *The Rose in the Desert.* 32mo. Colored frontispiece. 1/0 cloth
1878 (*Eng Cat*)

Home Library. The first American edition was issued by Carlton & Porter, Sunday-School Union, New York (1862, i.e., 1863), anonymous, deposited Mar. 9, 1863, one of the eight beatitude stories. *BAL* had not seen nor could locate a copy.

Routledge, Warne & Routledge, London, issued it in 1864, listed in the *Bks* on May 31 and in *PC* on June 1. The *Golden Ladder Stories*, illustrative of the eight beatitudes, by (Susan & Anna Warner) were issued by James Nisbet & Co., London, 1863, 17.5 cm., 479 pp., frontispiece and 7 plates, 7 pp. of ads, in green cloth with red-brown endpapers, listed in the *Ath* on Nov. 29, 1862; and a new edition was listed Jan. 31, 1863. Routledge, Warne & Routledge, London, issued it as *Two School Girls and Other Tales*, listed in the *Ath* on Oct. 28 and Nov. 25, 1865. For the Warne edition see *The Golden Ladder*, 1885. The *BM* gives the present edition as London, 1864, 16mo. See the preceding title for the *Home Library* titles.

673 ANONYMOUS *Gertrude, Annie, and Lucy.* 32mo. Colored frontispiece. 1/0 cloth 1878 (*Eng Cat*)

Home Library. I cannot trace this.

674 ANONYMOUS *Little Crosses.* 32mo. Colored frontispiece. 1/0 cloth 1878 (*Eng Cat*)

Home Library. There was an issue with this title issued by Nelson & Sons, London, 1881 (1880), 18mo, 121 pp., 1/0, but whether the present title or not, I don't know.

675 ANONYMOUS *Daph and Her Charge.* 32mo. Colored frontispiece. 1/0 cloth
1878 (*Eng Cat*)

Home Library. I cannot trace this.

676 ANONYMOUS *Robbie, the Herd Boy.* 32mo. Colored frontispiece. 1/0 cloth
1878 (*Eng Cat*)

Home Library. This was also issued in Warne's *Daw of Day Books*, 32mo, frontispiece, 0/4 cloth.

677 ANONYMOUS *Home Sunshine.* 32mo. Colored frontispiece. 1/0 cloth 1878 (*Eng Cat*)

Home Library. Home Sunshine; or, Bear and Forbear was issued by the Society for Promoting Christian Knowledge, London, in 1873, 18mo, 1/0. This was possibly the present title; another possibility was *Home Sunshine: Tales of Interest and Delight, for Young Readers*, issued by Dean, London (1865), 18mo, 1/6. For other issues of the title in the *Home Library* see No. 671 above.

678 OLIVER GOLDSMITH *The Vicar of Wakefield.* Cr 8vo. 0/6 sewed 1878 (*Eng Cat*)

Notable Novels No. 34. This has no date and 107 pp. I have a copy, no date, 19.5 cm., 107 pp., in pictorial yellow wrappers, printed in red, blue, and black, with a memoir of the author and printer's date (Jan. 30, 1884). The series title is on the front and spine and there are 2 pp. of publisher's ads at the front and 15 pp. at the back and a commercial ad on the back cover. The ads give the nos. of all series through 1883. The first authorized edition was issued by F. Newbery, London, 2 vols., 1766, 17.4 cm., anonymous, 5/0 sewed, 6/0 bound, advertised in the *Public Advertiser* on Mar. 27 as "This day." Newbery issued the second edition, 1766 (May 31), and the third edition, 1776 (Aug. 29). The first Irish edition was issued by W. & W. Smith, etc., Dublin, 2 vols., 1766, 16.3 cm., anonymous. A pirated edition, possibly the first edition, was issued by Eugene Swiney, Corke (i.e., London), 2 vols., 1766, 17 cm., anonymous. The first American edition was issued by William Mentz, Philadelphia, 1772, 2 vols.-in-1, 16.6 cm., anonymous, 180 pp. Warne issued it in 1866, pott 4to, colored illustrations, at 7/6, listed in the *Spect* on Jan. 5, 1867.

Frederick Warne & Co.
Bedford Street, Covent Garden
1879

679 SAMUEL PEPYS *The Diary of Samuel Pepys, from 1659 to 1669.* Cr 8vo. 1/6 sewed, 2/0 cloth   Feb. (*Bks*)

Chandos Classics No. 67. This is edited by Richard Lord Braybrooke and has 639 pp. Warne reissued it in the series, 1887 and 1889, and issued it in New York in 1892, 12mo, 4.75, etc., in smooth dark blue linen boards, advertised in the *Nation* on Sept. 1. It was issued in the *Chandos Library*, Cr 8vo, 768 pp., 3/6, listed in the *Spect* on Feb. 5, 1870, and reissued in 1874, the same. The first edition was issued by Colburn, London, 2 vols., 1825, 4to, 7 portraits and 6 plates, 126/0, reviewed in the *Westminster Review* (quarterly) for Oct. Colburn continued to issue new editions, the fifth in 1854 in 4 vols., and issued the *Diary and Correspondence of Samuel Pepys* in 5 vols., a new and revised edition, 10/6 each, vol. 1 advertised in the *Illustrated London News* on May 27, 1848, and vol. 5 on Aug. 4, 1849. At a Southgate and Barrett auction of May 26, 1857, 344 copies, Demy 8vo, and copyright, and 402 copies, p 8vo, of the fifth edition of 1854 were for sale, purchased by Bohn for £310 for the copyrights and £560 for the stock. The first American edition was the *Diary and Correspondence of Samuel Pepys*, edited by Braybrooke, issued by J. B. Lippincott & Co., Philadelphia, 4 vols., 1855, 22 cm., portraits, from the fifth London edition. The *U Cat* also gives the same title issued by Bigelow Brown & Co., New York (1854?), 4 vols. (fourth edition), 22 cm., illustrated.

680 JOHN EVELYN *The Diary of John Evelyn, Esq., F.R.S., from 1641 to 1705–06.* Cr 8vo. 1/6 sewed, 2/0 cloth   Mar. 1 (*Spect*)

Chandos Classics No. 68. This has no date and 619 pp., edited by William Bray. Warne reissued it in this series, 1889, 1891; and they issued it in the *Chandos Library* in 1871, Cr 8vo, 784 pp., frontispiece, 3/6 cloth, listed in the *Spect* on Dec. 2, 1871. They issued it in the *Cavendish Library*, large Cr 8vo, frontispiece, 3/6 cloth, advertised in *Notes & Queries* for June 1889. Warne, New York, issued it in 1892, 12mo, $.75 in smooth dark blue linen boards, etc., advertised in the *Nation* on Sept. 1, 1892. The first edition was *Memoirs Illustrative of the Life and Writings of John Evelyn, Comprising His Diary, from . . . 1641 to 1705–06, etc.*, edited by William Bray, issued by Henry Colburn, London, 2 vols., 1818, 31 cm., illustrated. Colburn issued the third edition in 5 vols., 1827–28; and issued a new edition, revised and enlarged, 4 vols., in 1850, vols. 1 and 2 reviewed in the *Gentleman's Magazine* (monthly) for July. In the United States it was issued by G. P. Purnam & Sons, New York, 1870, with the same title, 18.5 cm., 783 pp.

681 GEORGE H. TOWNSEND, ED. *The Every-Day Book of Modern Literature.* 2 vols., Cr 8vo. 1/6 sewed, 2/0 cloth each Mar. 29 (*Ath*)

Chandos Classics No. 69, 70. These have no dates and 463, 472 pp. The first edition was issued by Warne, London; Scribner, Welford & Armstrong, New York (1870), 19 cm., 936 pp., 7/6. Warne issued a new edition in 1875, 5/0.

682 HUGH M. WALMSLEY *Zulu Land: Its Wild Sports and Savage Life.* Second edition. 2/0 boards Apr. 5 (*Spect*)
This is 1879, 374 pp., and is mostly from *The Ruined Cities of Zulu Land*, issued by Chapman & Hall, London, 2 vols., 1869, 19 cm., illustrated, 18/0. Warne issued an illustrated edition in 1872, 374 pp., 3/6, listed in the *Spect* on Jan. 18, 1873; they re-issued it, listed in the *Spect* on Mar. 15, 1879. In the United States it was issued with the present title by R. Worthington, New York, in the 1870s, a special edition, 18 cm., 374 pp., illustrated.

683 ANTHONY F. THOMSON *The Milestones of Life.* 12mo. 1/0 sewed, 1/6 cloth Apr. 19 (*Spect*)
Star Series No. 56. The first edition was issued by Warne, 1866, small 8vo, 282 pp., frontispiece, 5/0.

684 SILAS K. HOCKING *Alec Green.* 16mo. 1/0 sewed, 1/6 cloth May 3 (*Spect*)
Star Series No. 54. This has no date and 227 pp., the first edition. Warne issued it also in 1884, 19 cm., 227 pp., illustrated, 2/6, with an added title page, given by the *Eng Cat.*

685 SARAH TYTLER (HENRIETTA KEDDIE) *Sweet Counsel.* 16mo. 1/0 sewed, 1/6 cloth May 10 (*Ath* ad)
Star Series No. 55. Warne also issued this in 1877, 12mo, 2/6, listed in the *Spect* on Sept. 29. The first edition was issued by Warne, 1866, square 12mo, 308 pp., frontispiece, 5/0, advertised in the *Ath* on Feb. 3 and listed in the *Reader* on Feb. 10. The author's name appeared only on the binding. It was issued in Boston, 1866, a reprint of the English edition.

686 FLORENCE MARRYAT (MRS. ROSS CHURCH, later LEAN) *Fighting the Air.* 12mo. 2/0 boards May 10 (*Ath* ad)
Companion Library No. 102. This was first issued by Tinsley Brothers, London, 3 vols., 1875, p 8vo, 31/6 in royal blue cloth with cream endpapers, reviewed in the *Ath* on Sept. 18. They issued it at 2/0 boards in 1878, listed in the *Ath* on June 1. The only American edition I've found was issued by John W. Lovell, New York (1887), 18.5 cm., 302 pp., in paper, *Lovell's Library* No. 999.

687 FLORENCE MARRYAT (MRS. ROSS CHURCH, later LEAN) *A Harvest of Wild Oats.* New edition. 12mo. 2/0 boards May 10 (*Ath* ad)
Companion Library No. 103. This has no date and 380 pp. The first English edition was issued by Tinsley Brothers, London, 3 vols., 1877, Cr 8vo, 31/6, advertised in the *Ath* on May 12 as "Now ready"; but due to the unreliability of Tinsley ads, this probably meant it was in press. It was advertised in the *TWEd* on July 6. They issued it at 2/0 boards, listed in the *Ath* on June 1, 1878. The first American edition was issued by G. W. Carleton, New York, 1877, $1.00 paper, $1.50 cloth, from advanced sheets, advertised in the *New-York Times* on June 20 as "Just published" and listed in *PW* on June 23.

688 W. G. WILLS *The Love That Kills.* 12mo. 2/0 boards May 10 (*Ath* ad)
Companion Library No. 105. The first edition was issued by Tinsley Brothers, London, 3 vols., 1867, p 8vo, 31/6, listed in the *Ath* on Jan. 26. They issued it at 2/0 boards, a yellowback, in 1878, listed in the *Spect* on Apr. 13.

689 SAMUEL LOVER *Rory O'More.* New edition. Cr 8vo. 0/6 sewed May 10 (*Ath* ad)
Notable Novels No. 37. This has no date and 184 pp. Warne issued it in their *Library of*

Fiction No. 18, Cr 8vo, 2/0 boards, in 1892. It was issued by Bentley, London, 3 vols., 1837, 19.5 cm., illustrated, 31/6 in boards with labels, with an 8-page catalog of James Duncan (Mar. 1837) at the back of vol. 1. Each vol. had a frontispiece and 4 plates. It was advertised in the *Spect* on Apr. 29. Bentley issued the second edition, 3 vols., advertised in the *Spect* on Sept. 9, 1837, as "Just published"; and a new edition in 3 vols., p 8vo, 15/0, listed by the *Edinburgh Review* as published May–July 1838. It was issued as *Standard Novel* No. 76, 1839, 419 pp., my copy, containing new material. It was issued by David Bryce, London, new edition, revised and corrected, a reprint of the *Standard Novel*, 2/0, beige printed cloth, listed in the *Ath* on May 24, 1856. The first American edition was issued by Carey, Lea & Blanchard, Philadelphia, 2 vols., 1837, 19 cm., 1,000 copies finished Nov. 1837 and advertised in the *National Gazette and Literary Record* on Nov. 4. Lea & Blanchard, Philadelphia, issued it, 1846, 275 pp., illustrated.

690 JAMES T. CHILD *Into Thin Air.*
Fcp 8vo. 1/0 sewed   May (*Bks*)
Readable Books No. 10. This is the first edition, no date, 188 pp.

691 FRANCES H. BURNETT *Natalie, and Other Stories.* Fcp 8vo. 1/0 sewed
May (*Bks*)
Readable Books No. 12. This is the first edition, no date, 17.7 cm., in stiff yellow wrappers, with a preface (May 1879). Warne also issued it in the *London Library* No. 14, 12mo, 1/0 sewed, advertised in the *Ath* in Apr. 2, 1887.

692 JAMES MONTGOMERY *The Poetical Works of James Montgomery.* Cr 8vo.
1/6 sewed, 2/0 cloth   June 14 (*Spect*)
Chandos Classics No. 71. This has no date, 535 pp., with the series title at the head of

the title page. Warne issued a new edition in 1877, Cr 8vo, in cloth, listed in the *Spect* on Oct. 27. Longmans, London, issued it in 3 vols., 1820, 17 cm.; and they issued it in 4 vols., 1826–27. In the United States it was issued by T. Bedlington, Boston, 1825, 15 cm., 216 pp.

693 LOUISA M. ALCOTT *Little Women.*
16mo. 1/0 sewed, 1/6 cloth   June 21
(*Spect*)
Star Series No. 57. This has no date, 193 pp. I have a copy (1888), 16.5 cm., 193 pp., in greek silk grain cloth elaborately decorated on the front and spine in gold and black, with the series title on the front, spine, and title page, and with the no. in the series in blind at the bottom of the front cover. It has figured endpapers, white on pale green, and a 21-page catalog at the back. Warne issued this title and the next in 1 vol. in 1879, 16mo, 1/6 sewed, 2/0 cloth, as *Star Series* No. 162. The first edition was as part 1 of *Little Women*, issued by Roberts Brothers, Boston, 1868, 17.5 cm., 341 pp., illustrated, $1.50 in purple or green cloth, deposited Oct. 3 and advertised in the *New-York Times* on Sept. 30 as "Just published." Parts 1 and 2 were advertised there on Aug. 7, 1869, as the 22nd thousand "Now selling." The first English edition was issued by Sampson Low, London, 1869, part 1, 17 cm., 341 pp., illustrated, 3/6 in brown cloth, listed in the *Ath* on Dec. 12, 1868. Low issued it about Oct. 26, 1872, at 1/6 boards, 2/0 cloth.

694 LOUISA M. ALCOTT *Little Wives.*
16mo. 1/0 sewed, 1/6 cloth   June 21
(*Spect*)
Star Series No. 58. This has no date and 213 pp. It was also issued in 1879 with the preceding title, in 1 vol. (see previous item). The first edition was issued as part 2 of *Little Women* by Roberts Brothers, Boston, 1869, 17.5 cm., 358 pp., illustrated, $1.50

in brown, green, or purple cloth. It was advertised in the *New-York Times* on Apr. 16 as "Just ready" and listed in the *Nation* on Apr. 8. They issued both parts in 1 vol., 1869, 12mo, illustrated, 350 pp., 3/6 cloth, listed in the *New Englander* (New Haven), a quarterly, for Oct. The first English edition was issued by Sampson Low, London, 1869, as *Little Women Wedded*, 16mo, illustrated, 3/6 cloth, listed in the *Ath* on June 12. Low issued it in 1872, new edition, 16mo, 242 pp., 1/6 limp boards, 2/0 flexible cloth, listed in the *Ath* on Oct. 26. Low issued both parts in 1 vol., 1871, 12mo, 3/6 cloth, listed in the *Spect* on Sept. 17; and issued the second edition of the latter, 1871, 464 pp.; and issued the fourth edition of it, 1871, 464 pp. Ward, Lock & Tyler, London, issued it in 2 vols., part 1 as *Little Women* and part 2 as *Good Wives*, in 1871, 1/0 sewed, 1/6, 2/0 cloth, listed in the *Ath* on Feb. 4 and Mar. 11 respectively.

695 JOSEPH HATTON *Cruel London.* 12mo. 2/0 boards June 28 (*Spect*)

Companion Library No. 106. This has no date, 390 pp., with 4 pp. of ads and a commercial ad on the back cover. The first edition was issued by Chapman & Hall, London, 3 vols., 1878, 19 cm., 31/6 in cherry-red cloth with yellow endpapers, listed in the *Ath* on June 22. In the United States it was issued by John W. Lovell, New York (1883), 378 pp., in paper, *Lovell's Library* No. 137.

696 EDWARD P. ROE *Barriers Burned Away.* 16mo. 1/0 sewed, 1/6 cloth July 12 (*Spect*)

Star Series No. 59. This has no date and 341 pp. It was also listed in the *Spect* on July 19, Cr 8vo, 2/6. The first edition was issued by Dodd & Mead, New York, 1872, 19 cm., 488 pp., illustrated, $1.75 in orange or green cloth, yellow endpapers, listed in *PW* on Nov. 28 and in the *Ind* on Dec. 5. A

new edition, the 3rd thousand, was advertised in the *New-York Times* as on Dec. 10, 1872; the 5th thousand was advertised as on Dec. 19; and 100,000 copies sold, advertised on May 19, 1882. It ran serially in the *Evangelist*, New York. The first English edition was issued by George Routledge & Sons, London and New York, in 1874, Cr 8vo, 3/6, listed in the *Ath* on Oct. 17.

697 EDWARD P. ROE *Opening a Chestnut Burr.* 16mo. 1/0 sewed, 1/6 cloth July 12 (*Spect*)

Star Series No. 60. This has no date and 294 pp. It was also listed in the *Spect* on July 19, Cr 8vo, 2/6. The first edition was issued by Dodd & Mead, New York (1874), 19.5 cm., 561 pp., $1.75. There were three printings: No. 1 in blue or green cloth; No. 2 in blue cloth; and No. 3 in red cloth, all with yellow endpapers. It was advertised in the *New-York Times* on Sept. 28 as "This day" and listed in *PW* on Oct. 3. The first English edition was issued by George Routledge & Sons, London and New York (1874), 3/6 cloth, listed in the *Ath* and *Spect* on Nov. 7.

698 CHARLES E. BAKER *Landlords, Tenants, and Lodgers. Forty Forms.* 12mo. 2/0 cloth Aug. 23 (*Spect*)

Warne's Legal Hand-Books. This has no date and 181 pp., the first edition. A new edition was issued in 1884, 1/0 cloth, advertised in the *Ath* on Feb. 16; the fourth edition, 1884, 1/0 cloth, advertised in the *Ath* on Feb. 16; and the fourth edition, 1889, Cr 8vo, 183 pp., was issued in 1889, probably in Dec.; and it was issued as *Useful Books* in 1892, 12mo, 1/0, probably the fifth edition, revised, listed in *PC* on Jan. 7, 1893.

699 ELIEZER EDWARDS *Sir Rowland Hill, D.C.B. A Biographical and Historical Sketch.* 12mo. 1/0 picture cover Sept. 6 (*Spect*)

This is the first edition, 1879, 119 pp.

700 DARLEY DALE (FRANCESCA M. STEELE) *Helen Leslie.* 12mo. Illustrated. 2/0 cloth Oct. 25 (*Ath*)
Home Circle Gift Books. This is the first edition, no date, 192 pp. Warne also issued this as *Star Series* No. 68, 16mo, 192 pp., 1/0 sewed, 1/6 cloth, listed in the *Spect* on Feb. 26, 1881. They issued it as *Helen's Secret,* a reissue of the *Star Series,* listed in the *Bks* for Mar. 1882.

701 EDMUND SPENSER *The Faery Queen.* Cr 8vo. 1/6 sewed, 2/0 cloth Oct. (*Bks*)
Chandos Classics No. 72. This has no date and 413 pp. The first edition of part 1 (books 1–3) was issued by William Ponsonbie, London, 1590, 4to, 606 pp., with a printer's device of J. Wolfe on the title page. The *U Cat* also gives J. Wolfe, London, 1850, 4to, the first issue of part 1. The first edition of part 2 (books 4–6) was issued by William Ponsonbie, London, 1596, 4to, 518 (i.e., 520) pp. In the United States it was issued by D. Appleton & Co., New York, 1854, illustrated, 820 pp.

702 JOHN KEBLE *The Christian Year.* Cr 8vo. 1/6 sewed, 2/0 cloth Oct. (*Bks*)
Chandos Classics No. 74. This has no date and 405 pp. The first edition was issued by J. Parker, Oxford; C. & J. Rivington, London, 2 vols., 1827, 17.5 cm., 10/6, in July according to the *Eng Cat.* The first American edition was issued by Carey, Lea & Blanchard, Philadelphia, 1834, 19 cm., anonymous, 415 pp., 1,500 copies, finished July 22.

703 GILBERT WHITE *The Natural History of Selborne and the Naturalist's Calendar.* New edition. Cr 8vo. Illustrated. 1/6 sewed, 2/0 cloth Nov. 1 (*Ath* ad)
Chandos Classics No. 73. This has no date and 470 pp., edited by G. C. Davies. The first edition was *The Natural History and Antiquities of Selborne,* issued by B. White & Son, London, 1789, 4to, 468 pp., illustrated with 7 plates including a folding frontispiece, 21/0, reviewed in the *Gentleman's Magazine* in Jan. and Feb. 1789. Fifty copies were issued on large paper with 1 of the plates colored. It was issued in 2 vols. with the *Naturalist's Calendar* added by White, by Cochrane & Co., London, 1813, 21 cm., illustrated. *The Natural History of Selborne with Additions* was issued in 1830, 6/6, listed in the *Westminster Review* (quarterly) for Oct., no publisher given; and *The Natural History of Selborne . . . with Notes by Thomas Brown* was issued by Chambers, Edinburgh, in 1833 as *British Library* No. 1, reviewed in the *Westminster Review* (quarterly) for July. The first American edition was issued by Carey & Lea, Philadelphia, 1832, 16mo, 342 pp., $.75, *The Natural History of Selborne,* 1,000 copies finished Jan. 26, 1832. It was advertised in the *National Gazette and Literary Record* on Apr. 23 and advertised by a Washington, D.C., bookstore in the *Globe,* a Washington daily, on May 2, 1832, as "This day."

704 CHARLES LAMB *Poems and Essays.* Cr 8vo. 1/6 sewed, 2/0 cloth Nov. 1 (*Ath* ad)
Chandos Classics No. 75. This has no date and 639 pp. I don't know the contents of this title, but the title has no previous record so far as I can determine. Lamb contributed 4 sonnets to Coleridge's first vol. in 1796, and he wrote *Blank Verse* with Charles Lloyd in 1798; his *Collected Prose and Verse* was issued in 1818.

705 JOHN BUNYAN *The Holy War.* Imperial 32mo, 2 plates. 0/6 stiff wrappers; 1/0, 1/6 cloth with colored plates Nov. 15 (*Ath* ad)
National Books No. 5. This was issued as *Chandos Classics* No. 53 in 1882 or 1883, replacing the former No. 53, *Life and Remains of John Clare.* The first edition was

issued by Dorman Newman & Benjamin Alsop, London, 1682, 16.5 cm., 397 pp. The first American edition was issued by T. Fleet, Boston, 1736, 14.5 cm., 301 pp., frontispiece.

706 RICHARD JEFFERIES (JOHN R. JEFFERIES) *The Scarlet Shawl.* Fcp 8vo. 1/o sewed 1879

Readable Books No. 11. I put this here because of its no. in the series. The first edition was issued by Tinsley Brothers, London, 1874, 19 cm., 309 pp., 10/6, listed in the *Ath* on July 18. They issued it, no date, new edition, p 8vo, 1/o, listed in the *Spect* on Aug. 25, 1877.

707 FREDERICK MARRYAT *Mr. Midshipman Easy.* Cr 8vo. o/6 sewed 1879 (*Eng Cat*)

Notable Novels No. 35. This has no date and 160 pp. The first edition was issued by Saunders & Otley, London, 3 vols., 1836, 19 cm., anonymous, 31/6, half-cloth, boards and labels, listed in the *Ath* on Sept. 3. They issued a second edition, 3 vols., 1836, boards and labels, with "Second edition" on the labels. It used first-edition sheets, and the title page was overprinted. Bentley issued it as *Standard Novels* No. 66, 1838, anonymous, 387 pp. In the United States it was issued by Carey & Hart, Philadelphia, 1836, 21 cm., anonymous, 274 pp., listed in the *North American Review* (quarterly) for Jan. 1837 and advertised by a Washington, D.C. bookstore in the *Globe*, a Washington daily, on Oct. 19, 1836, "Just published and this day received," no publisher given. It was also issued by Marsh, Capen & Lyon, Boston, 2 vols., 12mo, listed in the *North American Review* as for the Carey & Hart issue.

708 G.P.R. JAMES *Attila.* Cr 8vo. o/6 sewed 1879

Notable Novels No. 36. This has no date, but the *BM* gives it as (1879), and I place it here because of its no. in the series. The first edition was issued by Longman, London, 3 vols., 1837, 20 cm., anonymous, 31/6, listed in the *Ath* and *Spect* on Mar. 11. Thomas Hodgson, London, issued it, 1854, 367 pp., as *Parlour Library* No. 111. The first American edition was issued by Harper & Brothers, New York, 2 vols., 1837, 19 cm., anonymous, in purple figured cloth with printed paper labels, mentioned in the *Knickerbocker* for May as "Nearly ready" and advertised by a Washington, D.C., bookstore in the *Globe*, a Washington daily, on June 23.

709 (RUDOLPH E. RASPE) *The Adventures of Baron Munchausen.* Fcp 8vo. Illustrated. 2/o cloth 1879 (*Eng Cat*)

Incident and Adventure Library. This has no date. Warne issued it in 1878, 32.5 cm., 103 pp., illustrated, 10/6, listed in the *Spect* on Dec. 7, 1878. The first edition was issued by Smith, Oxford, 1786, 17.5 cm., a 49-page pamphlet, *Baron Munchausen's Narrative of His Marvellous Travels and Campaigns in Russia etc.*, edited by R. E. Raspe, 1/o, noticed in the *Critical Review* (monthly) for Dec. 1785. G. Kearsley, London, bought the rights from Smith and added 15 chapters to Raspe's 5 (the latter being chapters 4–6). He issued it as *Gulliver Revived*, 1786, third edition, 12mo, illustrated, 2/o, noticed in the *Critical Review* for July. He issued the fourth edition, 1786, 172 pp., illustrated. It was issued in New York, 1787. *The Surprising Travels and Adventures of Baron Munchausen* was issued by Trübner & Co., London, in 1858, Cr 8vo, illustrated by Crowquill, 7/6, advertised in the *Spect* on Nov. 20 as "This day." The same was issued by D. Appleton & Co., New York, new edition, $2.50, advertised in the *New-York Times* on Nov. 10, 1858, as "In Nov." Warne issued the present title as *Chandos Classics* No. 114, in 1884, Cr 8vo, 268 pp., illustrated,

1/6 sewed, 2/0 cloth, listed in the *Ath* on Nov. 22; and they issued it in the *Daring Deeds Library* also in 1884, 12mo, illustrated, 2/6 cloth, listed in the *Ath* on Nov. 22.

710 CHARLES E. BAKER *Wills. Nearly 150 Forms.* 12mo. 1/0 cloth   1879 (*Eng Cat*) *Warne's Legal Hand-Books.* This is the first edition, no date, 214 pp. Warne issued the third edition, 12mo, 1/0, in 1881, given by the *Eng Cat*.

Frederick Warne & Co.
Bedford Street, Covent Garden
1880

711 EDWARD BULWER LYTTON **Pelham.**
Cr 8vo. 0/6 sewed   Jan. 24 (*Ath* ad)
Notable Novels No. 38. The *Ath* ad for this and the following 7 titles said "Immediate publication." The first edition was issued by Henry Colburn, London, 3 vols., 1828, 19.5 cm., anonymous, 31/6 in boards with labels, listed by the *Edinburgh Review* (quarterly) as published Nov. 1827–Apr. 1828. Colburn issued the second edition, 3 vols., 1828, with a preface to the second edition (Oct. 1828), listed in the *Ath* on Oct. 29. *Colburn's Modern Novelists* No. 1, published by Bentley for Colburn, was issued in 1835, 2 vols., new edition, revised, portrait, 5/0, with a new introduction. Vol. 1 was advertised in the *Spect* on Jan. 17, 1835, and vol. 2 advertised Feb. 14 as "Now ready." Chapman & Hall, London, issued it in 0/7 parts and in 1 vol., the latter, 1849, 19.5 cm., 304 pp., frontispiece, 3/6, advertised in the *Spect* on Dec. 16, 1848, as "This day." The first American edition was printed by J. & J. Harper for Collins & Hannay, etc., New York, 2 vols., 1828, 20 cm., anonymous, listed in the *North American Review* (quarterly) for Jan. 1829. The second edition, the same, was listed there in Apr.

712 EDWARD BULWER LYTTON
The Disowned. Cr 8vo. 0/6 sewed
Jan. 24 (*Ath* ad)
Notable Novels No. 39. The first edition was issued by Henry Colburn, London, 4 vols., 1829, 20 cm., anonymous, 42/0, listed in the *Ath* on Dec. 3, 1828, and in the *Spect* on Nov. 29. Wolff states that Lytton was paid £800 for it. He issued the second edition, 3 vols., 1829, listed in the *Ath* on Dec. 24, 1828. Chapman & Hall issued it, 1852, Cr 8vo, 313 pp., frontispiece, 3/6, listed in the *Spect* on May 29. The first American edition was issued by J. & J. Harper, New York, 2 vols., 19 cm., anonymous, in boards with a pink muslin spine and yellow printed paper labels. It was listed in the *North American Review* (quarterly) for Apr. 1829. There was a second edition, listed in July.

713 EDWARD BULWER LYTTON **Devereux.**
Cr 8vo. 0/6 sewed   Jan. 24 (*Ath* ad)
Notable Novels No. 40. The first English edition was issued by Henry Colburn, London, 3 vols., 1829, 10 cm., anonymous, 31/6 boards with labels, listed in the *Spect* on July 11 and listed by the *Eng Cat* as published in July. Wolff states that Lytton received £1,500 for this. It was issued by Chapman & Hall, London, 1852, 19 cm., 303 pp., frontispiece, 3/6, with a new preface, listed in the *Spect* on Oct. 6. The first American edition was issued by J. & J. Harper, New York, 2 vols., 1829, 20 cm., anonymous, in boards with a pink muslin spine, yellow labels and white endpapers. It was listed in the *North American Review* (quarterly) for Oct. 1829.

714 EDWARD BULWER LYTTON
Paul Clifford. Cr 8vo. o/6 sewed
Jan. 24 (*Ath* ad)

Notable Novels No. 41. The first edition was issued by Colburn & Bentley, London, 3 vols., 20 cm., anonymous, 31/6 in boards with labels. It has a dedication signed E.L.B. and was advertised in the *Spect* on May 8 as "Just published" and given by the Bentley private catalog as published May 4. This is the novel with the often quoted opening line: "It was a dark and stormy night." There was a second edition, with a new preface, some additions and a few deletions, reviewed in the *Spect* on Sept. 25, 1830. It was issued as *Standard Novels* No. 47, 1835, 469 pp., illustrated by "Phiz," in July. Chapman & Hall issued it in weekly 1½ penny nos. and monthly o/7 parts and then in 1 vol., 1848, 20 cm., 308 pp., frontispiece by "Phiz," with a story by another author on pp. (289)–308. It was a new and revised edition, listed in the *Spect* on Aug. 19. The first American edition was issued by J. & J. Harper, New York, 2 vols., 1830, 20 cm., anonymous, with the signed dedication. It was in boards with a pink muslin spine and yellow labels, noticed in the *American Quarterly Review* (Philadelphia) on Sept. 1 and listed in the *North American Review* (quarterly) for Oct.

715 EDWARD BULWER LYTTON *Eugene Aram.* Cr 8vo. o/6 sewed   Jan. 24 (*Ath* ad)
Notable Novels No. 42. The first edition was issued by Colburn & Bentley, London, 3 vols., 1832, 20 cm., anonymous, 24/0 in boards, half-cloth, with labels, listed in the *Spect* on Jan. 6, 1832, and given as published Jan. 1, 1832, by the Bentley private catalog. Bentley issued it as *Standard Novels* No. 34, 1833, 453 pp., in Nov., my copy. It was issued by Chapman & Hall, London, 1849, Cr 8vo, 296 pp., frontispiece by "Phiz" and with a new preface, said to be corrected and revised throughout, 3/6, listed in the *Spect* on May 17. The first

American edition was issued by J. & J. Harper, New York, 2 vols., 1832, 18.5 cm., anonymous, *Library of Select Novels* Nos. 19 and 20. It was advertised by a Washington, D.C., bookstore in the *Globe*, a Washington daily, on Apr. 3, and listed in the *North American Review* (quarterly) for Apr.

716 EDWARD BULWER LYTTON *The Last Days of Pompeii.* Cr 8vo. o/6 sewed
Jan. 24 (*Ath* ad)

Notable Novels No. 43. The first English edition was issued by Bentley, London, 3 vols., 1834, 20.5 cm., anonymous, 31/6 in half-cloth boards with labels or in smooth dark gray cloth with labels. It was published Sept. 20 according to the Bentley private catalog and was listed in the *Ath* on Sept. 27. Bentley issued the second edition, 1835, 3 vols., revised, with a new preface, anonymous, advertised in the *Spect* on Apr. 4 as "Just published." Bentley issued it as *Standard Novels* No. 72, 1839, 419 pp., in Dec., my copy. There was an edition in 1848, Fcp 8vo, 448 pp., 6/o cloth, listed by *PC* as published June 28–July 14, no publisher given. It was issued by Chapman & Hall, London, 1850, a new edition, corrected and revised, Cr 8vo, frontispiece by "Phiz," 3/6. It has a new preface and was listed in the *Spect* on Apr. 27. The first American edition was issued by Harper & Brothers, New York, 2 vols., 1834, 19.5 cm., anonymous, in pink muslin with labels and white endpapers, reviewed in the *Knickerbocker* for Nov. It has 28 numbered pp. of ads and 8 unnumbered pp. at the back of vol. 2.

717 EDWARD BULWER LYTTON *Rienzi.*
Cr 8vo. o/6 sewed   Jan. 24 (*Ath* ad)
Notable Novels No. 44. Warne also issued this as *National Novels* No. 6, Cr 8vo, 1/o sewed, 1/6, in 1893, probably in Mar. The first edition was issued by Saunders & Otley, London, 3 vols., 1835, 20 cm., anonymous, 31/6 in boards with a half-cloth

spine and labels or in gray moiré cloth with labels, the latter being a later printing in the view of Sadleir. Wolff had a copy in boards without the cloth spine. There is a dedication (Dec. 1, 1835). It was listed in the *Ath* on Dec. 19, 1835, and in the *Spect* on Dec. 26. Chapman & Hall issued it, 1851, corrected and revised edition, with a new preface by the author, Cr 8vo, frontispiece, 3/6, or 4/6 with illustrations, listed in the *Spect* on Mar. 18. They based this issue on a serial issue in 1½ penny nos. and 0/7 monthly parts, beginning on Oct. 30, 1847. In the United States it was issued by Harper & Brothers, New York, 2 vols., 1836, 20 cm., anonymous, reviewed in the *Knickerbocker* for Feb. 1836; it was also issued by Carey & Hart, Philadelphia, 2 vols., 1836, anonymous, reviewed in the *Southern Literary Messenger* for Feb. 1836. It was advertised in the *Globe*, a Washington, D.C., daily, by a Washington bookstore on Jan. 25, 1836, $.62½, "Just published," and on Apr. 1, $.75, "Just published," no publishers being given.

718 EDWARD BULWER LYTTON *Ernest Maltravers.* Cr 8vo. 0/6 sewed   Jan. 24 (*Ath* ad)

Notable Novels No. 45. Warne also issued this as *National Novels* No. 4, Cr 8vo, 1/0 sewed, 1/6 cloth, in 1892. The first edition was issued by Saunders & Otley, London, 3 vols., 1837, 21 cm., anonymous, 31/6 in boards, half-cloth with labels and white endpapers, listed in the *Ath* on Sept. 30. They issued the second edition in 1838, advertised in the *Spect* on Feb. 10 as "Just ready." Chapman & Hall, London, issued it in 2 parts with *Alice*, 1851, new edition, corrected and revised, Cr 8vo, frontispiece, 3/6 cloth, listed in the *Ath* on July 26 (part 1) and list *Literary Gazette* on Dec. 27, 3/6 (part 2). The first American edition was issued by Harper & Brothers, New York, 2 vols., 1837, 20 cm., anonymous, reviewed in the *Knickerbocker* for Dec. 1837 and in the *Southern Literary Messenger* for

Jan. 1838. It is in green embossed cloth with labels and with ads at the back of vol. 2 with various pagings. They issued a second edition, listed in *Lit W* as published Mar. 18–25, 1848. The first American edition was advertised in the *Globe*, a Washington, D.C., daily, by a Washington bookstore on Dec. 5, 1837, 2 vols., "Added during the last two weeks."

719 WILLIAM H. MAXWELL *Stories of Waterloo.* Cr 8vo. 0/6 sewed   Feb. (*Bks*)

Notable Novels No. 45. This has no date and 163 pp. The first edition was issued by Colburn & Bentley, London, 3 vols., 1829, p 8vo, anonymous, 28/6 in boards with labels, *Stories of Waterloo and Other Tales.* It was listed in the *Spect* on Oct. 17. Bentley issued it as *Standard Novels* No. 31, 1833, anonymous, 384 pp., in Aug., my copy. The first American edition was with the English title, issued by J. & J. Harper, New York, 2 vols., 1830, 21 cm., anonymous, listed in the *North American Review* (quarterly) for July.

720 WILLIAM H. MAXWELL *The Bivouac; or, Stories of the Peninsular War.* Cr 8vo. 0/6 sewed   Feb. (*Bks*)

Notable Novels No. 47. This has no date and 184 pp. The first edition was issued by Bentley, London, 3 vols., 1837, p 8vo, 31/6 in boards with labels, published July 27 according to the Bentley private catalog, but advertised in the *Spect* on Mar. 11 as "Just ready." Bentley ads at this time are to be taken with a grain of salt. It was listed by the *Edinburgh Review* (quarterly) as published Aug.–Nov. 1837. Bentley issued it as *Standard Novels* No. 73, 1839, in Mar., my copy. The first American edition was issued by Carey & Hart, Philadelphia, 2 vols., 1837, 12mo, anonymous, listed by the *American Monthly Magazine* as published Mar. 15–May 26, 1838, and advertised in the *Globe*, a Washington, D.C., daily, by a Washington bookstore on Mar. 24, anonymous, "Just received."

721 THOMAS ROSCOE *The Italian Novelists.* Cr 8vo. 1/6 sewed, 2/o cloth Mar. 13 (*Spect*)

Chandos Classics No. 76. This has no date and 619 pp. Warne reissued it in this series, 1892. The first edition was issued by Septimus Prowett, London, 4 vols., 1825, 20 cm., 42/o, listed in the *Edinburgh Review* as published Jan.–Apr. 1825 and by the *Quarterly Review* as published Apr.–June.

722 THOMAS ROSCOE *The German Novelists.* Cr 8vo. 1/6 sewed, 2/o cloth Mar. 13 (*Spect*)

Chandos Classics No. 77. This has no date and 623 pp. The first edition was issued by Henry Colburn, London, 4 vols., 1826, 20.5 cm., 38/o, listed in the *Quarterly Review* as published Apr.–June 1826.

723 THOMAS ROSCOE *The Spanish Novelists.* Cr 8vo. 1/6 sewed, 2/o cloth Mar. 13 (*Spect*)

Chandos Classics No. 78. This has no date and 515 pp. The first edition was issued by Bentley, London, 3 vols., 1832, 18.5 cm., 27/o cloth, listed in the *Spect* on Nov. 3.

724 JOSIAH G. HOLLAND *Paul Benedict.* 12mo. 2/o boards Mar. 13 (*Spect*)

Companion Library No. 107. This has no date and 441 pp. The first American edition was issued by Scribner, Armstrong & Co., New York, 1875, 19.5 cm., 441 pp., illustrated, $1.75, advertised in the *New-York Times* on Oct. 9 as "On Oct. 16" and listed in *Lit W* (monthly) on Nov. 1, *Sevenoaks*. Charles Scribner's Sons, New York, issued it in 1882, listed in the *Nation* on Mar. 16; they issued it in 1892, 12mo, $.50, in their *Yellow Paper Series*, advertised in the *New-York Times* on May 7 as "Today." The first English edition was *The Story of Sevenoaks*, issued by Warne, 1875, Cr 8vo, illustrated, 6/o, advertised in the *Ath* on Oct. 23 as "Ready." It was copyright in Great Britain, and Warne changed the ti-

tle for the present edition because there was a town in England called Sevenoaks and the story had no connection with the town. It ran serially in *Scribner's Monthly Magazine*, Jan.–Dec. 1875. Warne also issued it in 1876, Cr 8vo, 3/6, listed in the *Spect* on July 15. I have a copy of the present title, a reissue in the series (1884), 18 cm., 441 pp., in pale blue pictorial boards, printed in red and black, with the series title on the spine and with a printer's date of Feb. 7, 1884. It has plain white endpapers and a commercial ad on the back cover.

725 EDWARD BULWER LYTTON *Alice.* Cr 8vo. o/6 sewed Mar.?

Notable Novels No. 48. I place this here because of its no. in the series. The first edition was issued by Saunders & Otley, London, 3 vols., 1838, 20 cm., anonymous, 31/6, half-cloth and boards, with labels, with a leaf of ads in the front of each vol., listed in the *Ath* and *Spect* on Mar. 17. The Chapman & Hall issue of *Alice* in 1851 is given above in No. 718. The first American edition was issued by Harper & Brothers, New York, 2 vols., 1838, anonymous, with a leaf of ads in vol. 1 (May 1838) and 8 leaves of ads at the back of vol. 2. It was in pink cloth with labels and white endpapers. It was reviewed in the *Knickerbocker* for May, listed in the *American Monthly Magazine* for June, and advertised by a Washington, D.C., bookstore in the *Globe*, a Washington daily, on Apr. 23, 1838, as "Expected."

726 G.P.R. JAMES *The Robber.* Cr 8vo. o/6 sewed Apr.?

Notable Novels No. 49. This is my copy, no date, 19.3 cm., 176 pp. in double columns, in yellow pictorial wrappers, printed in red, blue, and black, with the series title on the front and spine and with the no. at the base of the spine. There are publisher's ads on the inside front cover and on 1 page at the front and on 6 pp. at the back.

The ads give the series as ending with No. 47. The first edition was issued by Longman, London, 3 vols., 1838, 19.5 cm., 31/6, listed in the *Ath* on Mar. 31 and in the *Spect* on Apr. 21. They issued the second edition, the same, advertised in the *Spect* on Nov. 10, 1838, as "This day." It was issued by Smith, Elder & Co., London, in 1846, No. 8 in a reissue of James's works, revised and corrected, medium 8vo, 8/o, listed in the *Spect* on Apr. 4. Simms & M'Intyre, London and Belfast, issued it in the *Parlour Library* No. 37, in 1850, 1/o boards, 1/6 cloth, listed in the *Spect* on Mar. 9. The first American edition was issued by Harper & Brothers, New York, 2 vols., 1838, listed by the *American Monthly Magazine* as published Mar. 15–May 26 and advertised by a Washington, D.C., bookstore in the *Globe*, a Washington daily, on May 25, 1838.

727 MRS. HENRY H.B. PAULL *Evelyn Howard.* p. 8vo. 2/6 boards   May 15 (*Spect*)

The first edition was issued by Warne, no date, Cr 8vo, illustrated, 6/o, listed in the *Spect* on Oct. 16. It was issued in the *Companion Library* No. 137, 12mo, 2/o boards, listed in the *Ath* on Apr. 21, 1883; they issued it in the *Star Series* No. 89, 16mo, 1/6 sewed, 2/o cloth, in 1884.

728 MRS. JEROME MERCIER *Arum Field.* Cr 8vo. 2/6 boards   May 15 (*Spect*)

The first edition was issued by Warne in 1877, Cr 8vo, 3/6, listed in the *Ath* on Mar. 17. They issued it in the *Companion Library* No. 138, 12mo, 2/o boards, listed in the *Ath* on Apr. 21, 1883. The only edition given by the *U Cat* and the *BM* is Wells Gardner, Darton, 1891, 20 cm., 407 pp., illustrated.

729 JULIA LUARD *Clare Savile.* Cr 8vo. 2/6 boards   May 15 (*Spect*)

The first edition was issued by Warne in 1869, Cr 8vo, 474 pp., 5/o, listed in the

Spect on Dec. 18, 1869. It was advanced to 6/o, listed in *PC* for Nov. 1–15, 1872. Warne issued it in the *Companion Library* No. 133, 12mo, 2/o boards, probably in 1882.

730 MRS. HENRY H.B. PAULL *Leyton Auberry's Daughters.* 16mo. 1/6 sewed, 2/o cloth   June 19 (*Spect*)

Star Series No. 64. This is the first edition, no date, 380 pp.

731 JANE A. NUTT *Dorothy. An Autobiography.* 16mo. 1/o sewed, 1/6 cloth
June 26 (*Spect*)

Star Series No. 63. This is the first edition, no date, 233 pp. Warne issued it in the *Zephyr Library* at 1/6, probably in 1900 (see 1900).

732 EDWARD GIBBON *The Life and Letters of Edward Gibbon, with the History of the Crusades.* Cr 8vo. 1/6 sewed, 2/o cloth   Aug. 21 (*Spect*)

Chandos Classics No. 79. This has no date and 508 pp., with the *History* occupying pp. 357–486. Warne reissued it in this series, 1889, 508 pp. The first edition of the *Life* was as *Autobiography*, issued in London, 2 vols., 1829–30. It was issued as *The Autobiography of Edward Gibbon, Esq.* by Buckland & Sumner, New York, 1846, 23 cm., 381 pp. *The Crusades. A.D. 1095–1261*, from *The Decline and Fall*, consisting of the end of chapter 57 and chapters 58–61 from that work, was issued in London, 1869, edited by A. Murray.

733 ANONYMOUS *Hedington Manor.* New edition. 16mo. 1/6 sewed, 2/o cloth   Aug. 28 (*Spect*)

Star Series No. 65. This has no date and 374 pp. Warne reissued it in this series in 1881, listed in the *Bks* in Nov. The first edition was as *Baptista*, issued by Bell & Daldy,

London, in 1863, p 8vo, anonymous, 5/0. Warne issued it with the same title in 1872, 12mo, anonymous, 3/6.

734 THOMAS GRAY, JAMES BEATTIE & WILLIAM COLLINS *The Poetical Works of Gray, Beattie, and Collins.* Cr 8vo. 1/6 sewed, 2/0 cloth   Sept. 11 (*Ath* ad)

Chandos Classics No. 80. This has no date and 483 pp. The first London edition of *Poems by Mr. Gray* was issued by J. Dodsley, London, 1768, 18 cm., 119 pp., and a new edition was issued by J. Murray, London, 1778, 17.6 cm., 158 pp., with 3 plates. *The Poems of Mr. Gray* was issued by Dodsley in 1775, 4to, 15/0, edited by William Mason, listed in the *Gentleman's Magazine* for May.

735 THOMAS PERCY *Reliques of Ancient English Poetry.* New edition. Cr 8vo. 1/6 sewed, 2/0 cloth   Sept. 11 (*Ath* ad)

Chandos Classics No. 81. This has no date, 438 pp., and a preface dated 1880. The first edition was issued by J. Dodsley, London, 3 vols., 1765, 17.3 cm., anonymous, frontispieces in vols. 1 and 2. The dedication is signed by Percy but was written by Samuel Johnson, to whom Percy gives credit in the preface for much practical advice and help in the selection and editing of early material. Warne issued it in Cr 8vo, 2/0 blue cloth, uncut, edited by Edward Walford, advertised in *Notes & Queries* on Nov. 14, 1891, but I cannot say when it was issued. In the United States it was issued in 3 vols., 1823, 21 cm., the first American edition from the fifth London edition, by J. E. Moore, Philadelphia, and Cummings, Hilliard & Co., Boston, and J. V. Seaman, New York. These three may have been a joint imprint.

736 THOMAS HAMILTON *Cyril Thornton.* Cr 8vo. 0/6 sewed   Oct.?

Notable Novels No. 50. This has no date and 216 pp. The first edition was issued by William Blackwood & Sons, Edinburgh; etc., 3 vols., 1827, 19.5 cm., anonymous, 31/6 in boards and labels, given by the *Eng Cat* as published in May and listed by the *Quarterly Review* as published Apr.–June. They issued a second edition, 3 vols., anonymous, 21/0, advertised in the *Spect* on Mar. 14, 1829, as "This day." Blackwood issued it as *Standard Novels* No. 5 in 1842, small 8vo, frontispiece, 6/0 cloth, listed in the *Spect* on Mar. 5, and issued it in 1845 at 3/6 and 4/0 cloth, advertised in the *Spect* on Nov. 1 as "This day." They issued it, 1868, new edition, 17.5 cm., 460 pp., 2/0 boards, 2/6 cloth, advertised in the *Ath* on Nov. 2, 1867, as "In press." All these editions had the title *The Youth and Manhood of Cyril Thornton.* The American editions were issued by Wells & Lilly, Boston, 3 vols.-in-1, 1827, 17 cm., anonymous, listed in the *North American Review* (quarterly) for Apr. 1828; and J. & J. Harper, New York, 2 vols., 1827, 18 cm., anonymous, 6/0 dark green linen printed in black each, *Library of Select Novels* Nos. 1 and 2, with the English title.

737 LAURA VALENTINE, ed. *Gems of National Poetry.* Cr 8vo. 1/6 sewed, 2/0 cloth   Nov. (*Bks*)

Chandos Classics No. 82. This has no date and 540 pp. It was issued by Warne in 1866 at 5/0; they issued it in 1887, Cr 8vo, 3/6, listed in the *Spect* on May 7.

738 WILLIAM PAUL *Villa Gardening.* Third edition, revised and re-edited. Cr 8vo. Illustrated. 2/0 boards Nov. (*Bks*)

This has no date and 280 pp. Warne issued *Villa Gardening*, no date, third edition, revised and re-edited, illustrated, 3/6, advertised in the *Ath* on Apr. 8, 1876; they issued the same in 1879, 2/6, listed in the *Spect* on Apr. 5. The first edition was *The Hand-Book of Villa Gardening*, issued by Piper, Stephenson & Spence, London, 1855, 18 cm., 138 pp., 2/6.

739 JOHN G. LOCKHART *Reginald Dalton.*
Cr 8vo. o/6 sewed   Dec. (*Bks*)
Notable Novels No. 51. This has no date and
195 pp. The first edition was issued by
William Blackwood & Sons, Edinburgh,
etc., 3 vols., 1823, 19.5 cm., anonymous,
31/6 in June. It was issued by William
Blackwood & Sons, Edinburgh, 1842, Fcp
8vo, anonymous, 505 pp., 1 plate, 6/o,
Standard Novels No. 10, in cloth, listed in
the *Spect* on Oct. 29. They issued it in 1845
at 3/6 and 4/o, advertised in the *Spect* on
Dec. 6, 1845. The first yellowback edition
was issued by William Blackwood & Sons,
Edinburgh & London, 1868, new edition,
18 cm., anonymous, 505 pp., 2/o boards,
2/6 cloth, *Standard Novels*, listed in the *Ath*
on Jan. 16, 1869. The first American edition was issued by E. Duyckinck, etc., New
York, 2-vols.-in-1, 1823, 19.5 cm., anonymous, listed in the *North American Review*
(quarterly) in Oct. 1823.

740 A SINGER (FREDERICK J. CROWEST)
Advice to Singers. New and enlarged
edition. 12mo. 1/o   1880 (*Eng Cat*)
This has 124 pp. The first edition was issued by William Reeves, London, in 1878,
18mo, 1/o, 1/6. Warne issued the fourth
edition in 1889, 128 pp., by Crowest, and
the tenth edition (1914), 128 pp.

741 CHARLES E. BAKER *The Law of
Husband and Wife.* 12mo. 1/o cloth
1880 (*Eng Cat*)
Warne's Legal Hand-Books. This is the first
edition, no date, 164 pp., with the series title on the cover. They issued *Husband and
Wife, and the Married Women's Property Act,
(1882)*, new edition, no date, 12mo, 184
and 10 pp., given by the *Eng Cat* as issued
in 1882.

Frederick Warne & Co.
Bedford Street, Covent Garden
1881

742 FRANCES H. BURNETT *A Fair Barbarian.* 12mo. 1/o boards, 3/6 cloth Feb. 26 (*Ath*)

The listing in the *Ath* and in the *Spect* on Feb. 26 was for the 3/6. The 1/o was listed by the *Bks* as published in Feb. This is the first edition. My copy of the 1/o has no date, 17.6 cm., 184 pp., in pictorial boards of pale blue, printed in darker blue, red, and black. It has been recased, and there is a page of publisher's ads at the front and 3 leaves at the back. The list of the *Companion Library* in the ads ends with No. 107. This was very shortly placed in *Readable Books* No. 14. Warne issued it in the *London Library* No. 2, new edition, 12mo, 1/o sewed, in 1885, probably in Apr. The 4th edition, 20th thousand, 1/o sewed, was advertised in the *Ath* on July 25, 1885. I have a copy, no date, 17.5 cm., 184 pp., in white wrappers cut flush, with a vignette and decoration on the front in red and brown. There are commercial ads on the inside front and both sides of the back cover, in brown, and 2 pp. of publisher's ads at the back, from which I date it as issued in 1893. The *Tavisstock Library* titles end with (No. 6), and the *London Library* title ends with (No. 43). There is no indication of the series in which it is issued. The first American edition was issued by James R. Osgood, Boston, 1881, 17.5 cm., 258 pp., $1.00, advertised in the *New-York Times* on Mar. 23 as "On Mar. 26" and on Mar. 26 as if ready. It was listed in *PW* on Apr. 7, and

the 7th thousand, $1.00, was advertised in the former on Apr. 7 as "Now ready." It ran in *Scribner's Monthly*, Feb.–Apr. 1881, and Charles Scribner's Sons, New York, issued it in 1888, new edition, 12mo, $.50 in yellow paper covers, advertised in the *New-York Times* on June 7 as "Today."

743 MRS. W.M.L. JAY (JULIA L.M. WOODRUFF) *Without and Within.* 16mo. 1/6 sewed, 2/o cloth Feb. 26 (*Spect*)

Star Series No. 66. The first edition was issued by E. P. Dutton & Co., New York, etc., 1870, 18.5 cm., 488 pp., $2.00, *Shiloh; or, Without and Within*, advertised in the *New-York Times* on Dec. 15, 1870, and listed in the *Nation* on Dec. 1, 1870. Dutton issued the third edition in 1871, the same, advertised in the *Nation* on Apr. 13. Ward, Lock & Tyler, London, issued it in 1874 as *Shiloh*, 12mo, 1/o sewed, 1/6, 2/o cloth, listed in the *Ath* on Apr. 25; they issued it at 3/6, Cr 8vo, listed in the *Spect* on Jan. 9, 1875. The first English edition was issued by James Nesbet, London, 1871, 12mo, 3/6, listed in the *Ath* on Apr. 29, *Without and Within*.

744 (SUSAN WARNER) *Pine Needles.* 16mo. 1/o sewed, 1/6 cloth Mar. (*Bks*)

Star Series No. 67. The first American edition was *Pine Needles and Old Yarns*, issued by Robert Carter & Brothers, New York, 1877, 19.5 cm., anonymous, 346 pp., frontispiece, $1.50, advertised in the *New-*

York Times on Mar. 17 as "This morning" and listed in *PW* on Mar. 24. It has a 12-page catalogue and was bound in green, blue, or terra-cotta cloth with pale yellow endpapers. The first English edition was issued by James Nisbet & Co., London, 1877, 17.5 cm., anonymous, 248 pp., illustrated, with a 16-page catalog at the back, in the *Golden Ladder Series*. It is bound in blue cloth with a bevelled cover and brown endpapers. It was listed in the *Ath* and *Spect* on Mar. 10, 2/6, and advertised in the *Times Weekly Edition* on Mar. 16 as "Now ready." It was also issued by Nicholson, Wakefield, etc., London, in 1878, listed in the *Ath* on Aug. 24.

745 FRANCES TROLLOPE ***The Widow Barnaby.*** Cr 8vo. o/6 sewed   Mar. (*Bks*)

Notable Novels No. 52. This has no date, 204 pp., and 8 pp. of ads. The first edition was issued by Bentley, London, 3 vols., 1839, 20.5 cm., 24/o, listed in the *Spect* on Dec. 22, 1838, and in the *Ath* on Dec. 29. He issued it as *Standard Novels* No. 81, 1840, 494 pp., in Oct., my copy with the no. given as 80 on the title page. The copyright was sold to Ward & Lock, London, in Feb. 1856, and they issued it, 1856, new edition, small format, 494 pp., 2/o pictorial boards (Sadleir's copy) and 2/6 cloth, listed by *PC* as published Apr. 14–30. It was purchased by C. H. Clarke, London, at a Southgate & Barrett auction in May 1859, and issued by them in the *Parlour Library* No. 215 (1860), new edition. Warne reissued it in *Notable Novels*, (1883), my copy, 19.5 cm., 204 pp., in yellow pictorial wrappers, printed in red, blue, and black, with the series title on the front and spine. There are publisher's ads on the inside covers, and a page at the front and 5 leaves at the back, with a commercial ad on the back cover. The list of the series in the ads ends with No. 69, and the *Star Series* ends with No. 84.

746 MATTHEW H. BARKER ***Top Sail-Sheet Blocks.*** Cr 8vo. o/6 sewed   Mar.?

Notable Novels No. 53. This has no date and 192 pp. The first edition was issued by Bentley, London, 3 vols., 1838, 21 cm., by the Old Sailor, illustrated by Cruikshank, 31/6, listed in the *Ath* on Apr. 7. It was issued by Routledge, Warne & Routledge, London and New York, 1859, Fcp 8vo, 444 pp., 2/o, yellow pictorial boards, by the Old Sailor, listed in the *Ath* on Jan. 29.

747 G.P.R. JAMES ***The Huguenot.*** Cr 8vo. o/6 sewed   Apr. (*Bks*)

Notable Novels No. 54. This is my copy (1881), 19.2 cm., 190 pp. in double columns, reprinted from the original edition, in yellow pictorial wrappers, printed in red, blue, and black with the series title on the front and spine. There are publisher's ads on the inside and back covers, a page of publisher's ads at the front and a leaf at the back, and a 4-page catalog of W. H. Smith & Son and Chapman & Hall, on small paper, inserted at the back. The list of the series in the ads ends with No. 47. The first edition was issued by Longmans, London, 3 vols., 1839, 19 cm., anonymous, 31/6, listed in the *Ath* and *Spect* on Dec. 15, 1838. Smith, Elder & Co., London issued it as No. 3 in a new issue of James's works, 1845, medium 8vo, 407 pp., illustrated, 8/o cloth, listed in the *Spect* on Jan. 4. Routledge, Warne & Routledge, London & New York, issued it in 1864, Fcp 8vo, 448 pp. 1/o sewed. The first American edition was issued by Harper & Brothers, New York, 2 vols., 1839, 19 cm., anonymous, but with a dedication signed by James. It was advertised by a Washington, D.C., bookstore in the *Globe*, a Washington daily, on Jan. 28, 1839, as "Just published" and reviewed in the *Knickerbocker* for Feb. 1839.

748 EDWARD WALFORD **The Life and Political Career of the Earl of Beaconsfield.** Fcp 8vo. 1/0 sewed   Apr. 30 (*Spect*)

This is the first edition. The *Spect* listing was for a Cr 8vo issue at 1/6. Warne issued a second edition, no date, 192 pp., listed by the *Bks* as published in July, the only edition given by both the *BM* and the *U Cat*.

749 FLORENCE WILFORD **Vivia.** p 8vo. 2/6 boards   May (*Bks*)

The first edition was issued by Warne, 1870, Cr 8vo, 5/0, listed in the *Ath* on Dec. 25, 1869. They advanced the price to 6/0 in 1872, noted in the *PC* on Nov. 15. The first American edition was issued by D. Appleton & Co., New York, 1871, 24 cm., 173 pp., $.50 paper, advertised in the *New-York Times* on June 17 as "This day."

750 SILAS K. HOCKING **Chips.** Square 16mo. Illustrated. 1/0 cloth June 4 (*Ath* ad)

This is the first edition, no date, 87 pp. It was advertised in the *Ath* also on Nov. 5 as the "21st thousand." Warne issued it in their *Welcome Library* No. 1, Cr 8vo, illustrated, 1/0 cloth in 1893, listed in *PC* for Sept. 9.

751 JOHN G. LOCKHART **Memoirs of the Life of Sir Walter Scott, Bart.** New edition, condensed and revised. Cr 8vo. 1/6 sewed, 2/0 cloth   July (*Bks*)

Chandos Classics No. 84. This has 749 pp. Warne reissued it in this series in 1888. They also reissued it in the series in 2 vols. in 1891, a new edition condensed and revised, 4/0 cloth, listed by *PC* on Mar. 7. Warne issued it at 3/6, listed in the *Spect* on Oct. 22, 1881. I'm not happy with the publishing history of this work that I've found. The first English edition was issued in Edinburgh, 7 vols., 1837–1838, 20 cm. There was an issue reviewed in the *Westminster Review*, a quarterly, for Jan. 1849, Robert Cadell, Edinburgh; Houlston & Stoneman, London, 1848. In the United States it was issued by Otis Broader & Co., Boston, 7 vols., 12mo, which a review in the *Christian Examiner*, Boston, a bimonthly, for Jan. 1839 gave as 1837, but I conjecture that it should be 1837–1838. Carey, Lea, and Blanchard, Philadelphia, issued it in 2 vols. 1837, 24 cm., frontispieces, and it was advertised in the *Globe* by a Washington, D.C., book dealer on June 8, 1837, as part 2, "Just received," no publisher given. There was a review in the *American Quarterly Review*, Philadelphia, for Sept. 1837, parts 1–4, Philadelphia, 1837. T. B. Peterson, Philadelphia, issued it, 1836, 590 pp., frontispiece (portrait). Both the Carey, Lea & Blanchard and the Peterson editions are taken from the *U Cat*.

752 WILLIAM J. GORDON **The Bijou Biography of the World.** 48mo. 1/6 cloth, 2/6 roan   Aug. 6 (*Spect*)

This is the first edition, no date, 9 cm., 640 pp. It was advertised in *Notes & Queries* on Sept. 3, and the same ad had *The Bijou Gazetteer of the World* by W. H. Rosser, all the same. The first edition of the latter was issued by Warne (1871), 48mo, 636 pp. Warne reissued it at 1/6 in 1873 and 1876; they issued a new and revised edition, 1883, edited by W. J. Gordon, 9 cm., 640 pp.

753 THEODORE E. HOOK **Jack Brag.** Cr 8vo. 0/6 sewed   Sept. (*Bks*)

Notable Novels No. 56. The first edition was issued by Bentley, London, 3 vols., 1837, p 8vo, anonymous, 31/6 in half cloth boards, with labels, in an edition of 2,000 copies, advertised in the *Spect* on Mar. 11 as "Just published" and listed Mar. 25. The second edition, the same, was advertised on Sept. 2 as "Just published." The first edition had an errata slip tipped on to the first page of text. Bentley issued it as *Standard Novels* No. 75, 1839, revised by the author, 441 pp., in Aug. David Bryce, London, purchased 6 Hook titles at Hodgson's Rooms about Feb. 26, 1856, for £478; they issued *Jack Brag* in July 1856, 2/o cloth boards, reissued in May, 1859, 2/o boards, 441 pp. *Jack Brag* was sold at Hodgson's Rooms on June 8, 1858, for £46, probably to Darton & Hodge, London, as they issued it in the *Parlour Library* No. 275, in 1863. Chapman & Hall issued it, 1867, as *Select Library of Fiction* No. 99, tenth edition, 441 pp., 2/o boards, in Mar. The first American edition was issued by Carey, Lea & Blanchard, Philadelphia, 2 vols., 1837, 18 cm., anonymous, advertised by a Washington, D.C., book dealer in the *Globe*, a Washington daily, on May 6 as "just added."

754 FREDERICK MARRYAT *The Phantom Ship.* Cr 8vo. o/6 sewed　Sept. (*Bks*)

Notable Novels No. 57. The first English edition was issued by Henry Colburn, London, 3 vols., 1839, 19 cm., 31/6, in half smooth dark violet cloth, listed in the *Ath* on Apr. 13. It ran in *Colburn's New Monthly Magazine*, Mar. 1837–Aug. 1839. It was issued by Bentley as *Standard Novels* No. 106, 1847, 385 pp., in Mar., my copy. In the United States there were four editions, all dated 1839. Carey & Hart, Philadelphia, 2 vols., 20 cm., was reviewed in the *Knickerbocker* for June. Wolff's copy was in boards with a muslin spine and labels, white endpapers, with the verso of the title page having "Entered . . . in the year 1838 by F. Marryat in the clerk's office of the district court of the eastern district of Pennsylvania." Wolff conjectured that since Marryat was in the United States in 1838, the American edition was possibly issued in 1838, though dated 1839. This seems hardly possible since it didn't finish its run in Colburn's magazine until Aug. 1839. It was also issued by Weeks, Jordah & Co., Boston, 21 cm., 133 pp.; by William H.

Colyer, New York, 19 cm., 229 pp.; and by Charles Lane, Sandbornton, N. H., 2 vols., 13 cm.

755 ANONYMOUS *Nursery Gems. Little Red Riding Hood. Puss in Boots.* 32mo. Illustrated. 2/o each　Sept. 24 (*Spect*)

These have no dates and 24 pp.

756 ISAAC D'ISRAELI *Curiosities of Literature.* New edition. 3 Vols. Cr 8vo. 1/6 sewed, 2/o cloth each　Oct. 15 (*Ath*)

Chandos Classics Nos. 93–95. These have no dates and were edited by the Earl of Beaconsfield. Warne issued it in 3 vols. in 1866, with portraits, edited by the Earl of Beaconsfield. Vol. 1 was listed in the *Reader* on June 16, Cr 8vo, 471 pp., 3/6; vol. 2 on Aug. 25, 3/6; and vol. 3 on Sept. 22, 546 pp., 4/o. They issued it in 1 vol. in 1866, p 8vo, 672 pp., 5/o, listed in the *Reader* on Oct. 27. The first edition of vol. 1 of the first series was issued by John Murray, London, 1791, 8vo, anonymous, 531 pp., at 6/o boards, reviewed in the *Critical Review* (monthly) for Dec. 1791. Murray issued a second vol. of the first series, 1793, 8vo, 575 pp., at 7/o boards; and a third vol., 1817, 8vo, 490 pp., 12/o boards, listed by the *Quarterly Review* as published Oct.–Dec. 1816. Murray issued a second series, 3 vols., 1823, 8vo, anonymous, 36/o, in Dec. 1822. Edward Moxon, London, issued the ninth edition, probably containing both series, in 6 monthly vols., 5/o cloth each, vol. 1 listed in the *Spect* on Feb. 22, 1834, and vol. 6 in July. In the United States the first series was issued by W. Gibbons, Philadelphia, 1791, 531 pp., just vol. 1.

757 ISAAC D'ISRAELI *Calamities and Quarrels of Authors.* New edition. Cr 8vo. 1/6 sewed, 2/o cloth　Oct. 15 (*Ath*)

Chandos Classics No. 97. This has no date and 552 pp., edited by the Earl of Beaconsfield. Warne issued it in 1866, new edition, edited by the Earl of Beaconsfield, p 8vo., 552 pp., portraits, 4/0, listed in the *Reader* on Oct. 27, 1866. The first edition of the first title was issued by John Murray, London, *The Calamities of Authors*, 2 vols., 1812, 19 cm., anonymous, 16/0 boards, in June. The first edition of *Quarrels of Authors* was issued by John Murray, London, 3 vols., 1814, 20 cm., anonymous, 24/0, in Apr. Edward Moxon, London, issued the *Miscellanies of Literature*, 1840, new edition, revised and corrected, 24 cm., 484 pp., listed by the *Edinburgh Review* as published Apr.–July 1840. It contained both of the present titles and others. It was issued in the United States as *Miscellanies of Literature*, 3 vols., by J. & H. G. Langley, New York, 1841, new edition, revised and corrected, anonymous, 1,170 pp., vol. 1 containing *Calamities of Authors* and vol. 3 consisting of *Quarrels of Authors*, noticed in the *Merchant's Magazine*, New York (monthly) for June. The first American edition of the first title of the present work was issued by James Eastburn, New York, etc., 2 vols., 1812, 18.5 cm.; and the first edition of the second title was issued by Eastburn, Kirk & Co., New York, etc., 2 vols., 1814, 18.5 cm.

758 ISAAC D'ISRAELI *Amenities of Literature.* New edition. 2 vols. Cr 8vo. 1/6 sewed, 2/0 cloth each   Oct. 15 (*Ath*)

Chandos Classics Nos. 98, 99. This has no dates, edited by the Earl of Beaconsfield. Warne issued it in 1866, copyright edition, large Cr 8vo, portraits, 5/0, edited by the Earl of Beaconsfield, advertised in the *Spect* on Sept. 29. The first edition was issued by Edward Moxon, London, 3 vols., 1841, 8vo, 36/0, listed in the *Spect* on Aug. 14. Moxon issued the second edition, 1842, the same, 24/0, listed by the *Edinburgh Review* as published Apr.–June. In the United States it was issued by J. & H. G. Langley, New York, 2 vols., 1841, 19 cm., listed by the *United States Magazine* (monthly) for Oct. 1841.

759 JOHN T. LUCAS *Prince Ubbely Bubble's New Story Book.* p 8vo. Illustrated. 2/6   Oct. 15 (*Ath*)

The first edition was issued by John Camden Hotten, London, no date, 16mo, 4/6 in 1860. Hotten issued the second series in 1869, illustrated, 4/6, listed in the *Spect* on Dec. 18, 1869.

760 JAMES A. MAITLAND *Captain Jack.* 12mo. 2/0 boards   Oct.?

Companion Library No. 108. This was bought at a sale of the *Select Library of Fiction* by W. H. Smith in July 1881. The first English edition was issued by Tinsley Brothers, London, 2 vols., 1867, p 8vo, 21/0 in smooth dark blue cloth with white endpapers. It was listed in the *Ath* on Apr. 20. Chapman & Hall, London, issued it as *Select Library of Fiction* No. 130 in 1868, 12mo, 2/0 boards, listed in the *Ath* on June 27. Wright gives an American edition issued by T. B. Peterson & Brothers, Philadelphia (1866?), 19 cm., 392 pp., as *The Old Patroon*.

761 FREDERICK W. ROBINSON *Carry's Confession.* 12mo. 2/0 boards   Oct.?

Companion Library No. 109. This and the following Robinson titles were all purchased at a sale of the *Select Library of Fiction* by W. H. Smith in July 1881. The first edition was issued by Hurst & Blackett, London, 3 vols., 1865, p 8vo, anonymous, 31/6 in grass-green cloth with chocolate endpapers, with an 8-page catalog at the back of vol. 3, listed in the *Ath* on Mar. 4. It was issued by Chapman & Hall, London, 1868, 12mo, anonymous, 410 pp., 2/0 boards, as *Select Library of Fiction* No. 123, listed in the *Ath* on Apr. 25 and reissued (1870), third edition, 12mo, anonymous, 410 pp., 2/0 boards, given by the *BM*. The first American edition was issued by Harper & Brothers, New York, 1865, 8vo, anonymous, 190 pp. in double columns, $.75 paper, advertised in the *New-York*

Times on July 19 as "This day" and listed in *ALG&PC* (fortnightly) on Aug. 1. I place this title and the following Robinson titles here because No. 125 below (item 777) was listed by the *Bookseller* as published in Oct.

762　FREDERICK W. ROBINSON *Christie's Faith.* New edition. 12mo. 2/0 boards Oct.?

Companion Library No. 110. This has no date and 431 pp. The first edition was issued by Hurst & Blackett, London, 3 vols., 1867, p 8vo, anonymous, 31/6 in maroon cloth with gray chocolate endpapers and with a 16-page catalog at the back of vol. 3, listed in the *Ath* on Nov. 24, 1866. Chapman & Hall, London, issued it, 1868, new edition, 12mo, anonymous, 431 pp., 2/0 boards, in the *Select Library of Fiction* No. 131, listed in the *Ath* on Sept. 26. The first American edition was issued by Harper & Brothers, New York, 1867, 18 cm., anonymous, 519 pp., $1.75 cloth with bevelled edges, advertised in the *New-York Times* on Apr. 16 as "This day" and listed in *ALG&PC* (fortnightly) on Apr. 15.

763　FREDERICK W. ROBINSON *One and Twenty.* 12mo. 2/0 boards Oct.?

Companion Library No. 111. The first edition was issued by Hurst & Blackett, London, 3 vols., 1858, p 8vo, anonymous, 31/6 in brown morocco cloth with pale yellow endpapers and a 24-page catalog at the back of vol. 2. It was listed in the *Spect* on May 8. Chapman & Hall, London, issued it, 1867, 12mo, 2/0 boards, as *Select Library of Fiction* No. 111, listed in the *Ath* on Aug. 17. In the United States it was issued by Robert M. DeWitt, New York, in 1860, anonymous, $.50 paper, noticed in *Godey's Lady's Book* (monthly) for Oct. The *U Cat* gives this DeWitt edition as (1874), which was possibly a reissue or perhaps just plain wrong.

764　FREDERICK W. ROBINSON *Slaves of the Ring.* 12mo. 2/0 boards Oct.?

Companion Library No. 112. The first edition was issued by Hurst & Blackett, London, 3 vols., 1862, p 8vo, anonymous, 31/6, listed in the *Ath* on Nov. 1. It was issued by Chapman & Hall, London, 1867, second edition, 12mo, 2/0 boards, *Select Library of Fiction* No. 106, listed in the *Spect* on June 8; and reissued, 1870, third edition, the same, given by the *BM*. The first American edition was issued by T.O.H.P. Burnham, Boston, etc., 1863, 24 cm., anonymous, 171 pp., $.50 paper in double columns, listed by the *Knickerbocker* as published Mar. 12–Apr. 11 and advertised in the *Ind* on Apr. 16 as "Now ready."

765　FREDERICK W. ROBINSON *Under the Spell.* New edition. 12mo. 2/0 boards Oct.?

Companion Library No. 113. This has no date and 408 pp. The first edition was issued by Hurst & Blackett, London, 3 vols., 1861, p 8vo, anonymous, 31/6, listed in the *Spect* on June 22. Chapman & Hall, London, issued it, 1867, 12mo, 2/0 boards, *Select Library of Fiction* No. 104, listed in the *Spect* on May 18; and reissued it (1870), third edition, the same, given by the *BM*. The first American edition was issued by Ballou, Boston, 1862, 22.5 cm., anonymous, 191 pp., illustrated, in double columns, with "The Actress" on the cover but "Under the Spell" on the title page. It was issued by Robert M. DeWitt, New York, in 1869, 8vo, 136 pp., $.50 paper, listed in *Putnam's Monthly*, New York, for Nov.

766　FREDERICK W. ROBINSON *A Woman's Ransom.* 12mo. 2/0 boards Oct.?

Companion Library No. 114. The first edition was issued by Hurst & Blackett, London, 3 vols., 1864, p 8vo, by Robinson, 31/6, listed in the *Spect* on Dec. 26, 1863. Chapman & Hall, London, issued it, 1866,

12mo, 372 pp., 2/0 boards, *Select Library of Fiction* No. 77, listed in the *Spect* on Feb. 10; and they reissued it (1870), fourth edition, the same, given by the *BM*. The first American edition was issued by T.O.H.P. Burnham, Boston, 1864, 12mo, by Robinson, 412 pp., $1.50, advertised in the *Ind* on Mar. 10, from advanced sheets, "This day."

767 FREDERICK W. ROBINSON *Mattie: A Stray.* 12mo. 2/0 boards Oct.?

Companion Library No. 115. The first edition was issued by Hurst & Blackett, London, 3 vols., 1864, p 8vo, anonymous, 31/6, listed in the *Ath* on June 4. Chapman & Hall, London, issued it, 1866, 12mo, anonymous, 2/0 boards, *Select Library of Fiction* No. 84, listed in the *Spect* on July 14; reissued, probably in 1868, fourth edition, 18.1 cm., anonymous, 371 pp., 2/0 pictorial boards, my copy, with printer's date (Dec. 1, 1868) and with ads of Apr. 1869; reissued in 1870, fifth edition, 12mo, anonymous, 2/0 boards, given by the *BM*; probably reissued in late 1876 or early 1877, with a new no. in the series, No. 339, the same. The first American edition was issued by Harper & Brothers, New York, 1865, anonymous, 157 pp., double columns, $.75 paper, advertised in the *New-York Times* on Jan. 31 as "Just published."

768 FREDERICK W. ROBINSON *Owen: A Waif.* 12mo. 2/0 boards Oct.?

Companion Library No. 116. The first edition was issued by Hurst & Blackett, London, 3 vols., 20 cm., anonymous, 31/6, listed in the *Ath* on May 3. It was issued by Chapman & Hall, London, (1870), new edition, 12mo, anonymous, *Select Library of Fiction* No. 170, listed in the *Spect* on Sept. 10.

769 FREDERICK W. ROBINSON *The House of Elmore.* 12mo. 2/0 boards Oct.?

Companion Library No. 117. The first edition was issued by Hurst & Blackett, Lon-

don, 3 vols., 1855, anonymous. It was issued by Chapman & Hall, London, 1865, 12mo, anonymous, 2/0 boards, *Select Library of Fiction* No. 68, listed in the *Spect* on Sept. 16. They reissued or renumbered it or both at the end of 1876 or early 1877, as No. 341. It was issued by Robert M. DeWitt, New York, which the *U Cat* gives as (1873).

770 FREDERICK W. ROBINSON *Milly's Hero.* 12mo. 2/0 boards Oct.?

Companion Library No. 118. The first edition was issued by Hurst & Blackett, London, 3 vols., 1866, anonymous, 31/6, listed in the *Ath* on Dec. 23, 1865. It was issued by Chapman & Hall, London, no date, fourth edition, 461 pp.; and (1869), fifth edition, 12mo, by Robinson, 461 pp., 2/0 boards, listed in the *Ath* on Feb. 6.

771 FREDERICK W. ROBINSON *Mr. Stewart's Intentions.* 12mo. 2/0 boards Oct.?

Companion Library No. 119. The first edition was issued by Hurst & Blackett, London, 1865, 3 vols., p 8vo, by Robinson, 31/6, listed in the *Ath* on Nov. 26, 1865. It was issued by Chapman & Hall, London, 1866, 12mo, by Robinson, 384 pp., 2/0 boards, *Select Library of Fiction* No. 83, listed in the *Spect* on June 16. The first American edition was issued by T.O.H.P. Burnham, Boston, etc., 8vo, $.75 paper, listed in *ALG&PC* (fortnightly) on Nov. 15, 1865.

772 FREDERICK W. ROBINSON *Wildflower.* 12mo. 2/0 boards Oct.?

Companion Library No. 120. The first edition was issued by Hurst & Blackett, London, 3 vols., 1857, anonymous, listed in the *Spect* on Jan. 17, 1857. It was issued by Chapman & Hall, London, 1866, 12mo, by Robinson, 2/0 boards, listed in the *Spect* on Nov. 10, *Select Library of Fiction* No. 91. The first American edition was issued by

Robert M. DeWitt, New York (1858), 22 cm., anonymous, 206 pp., $1.00, listed in *Godey's Lady's Book* for Sept. 1858.

773 FREDERICK W. ROBINSON *Woodleigh.* New edition. 12mo. 2/0 boards Oct.?

Companion Library No. 121. This has no date and 414 pp. The first edition was issued by Hurst & Blackett, London, 3 vols., 1859, anonymous, 31/6, listed in the *Ath* on Apr. 23. It was issued by Chapman & Hall, London, 1867, new edition, 17.7 cm., author's name on the title page only, 414 pp., 2/0 pictorial boards, my copy, *Select Library of Fiction* No. 113, listed in the *Ath* on Sept. 28.

774 JOSEPH S. LEFANU *Checkmate.* 12mo. 2/0 boards Oct.?

Companion Library No. 122. This and the following LeFanu titles were purchased at the sale of the *Select Library of Fiction* by W. H. Smith in July 1881. I place them here because No. 125 below (see item 777) was listed by the *Bks* as published in Oct. The first edition of the present title was issued by Hurst & Blackett, London, 3 vols., 1871, 19.5 cm., 31/6 in apple-green cloth with old-rose endpapers and with a 16-page catalog (Jan. 1871) at the back of vol. 3. It was listed in the *Ath* on Jan. 28. Chapman & Hall, London, issued it, 1876, third edition, 12mo, 2/0 boards, *Select Library of Fiction* No. 331, listed in the *Ath* on Sept. 2. It began a run in the *Sunday Mercury,* New York, on Jan. 8, 1871. The first American book edition was issued by Evans, Stoddart & Co., Philadelphia, 1871, 24 cm., 182 pp., illustrated, listed in *ALG&PC* (fortnightly) on Mar. 15.

775 JOSEPH S. LEFANU *All in the Dark.* New edition. 12mo. 2/0 boards Oct.?

Companion Library No. 123. This has no date and 374 pp. It ran in the *Dublin University Magazine*, Feb.–June 1866, and the

first book edition was issued by Bentley, London, 2 vols., 1866, 20 cm., 21/0, listed in the *Ath* on June 2. Bentley issued the second edition, 1866, the same, advertised in the *Spect* on Aug. 4. Chapman & Hall, London, issued it (1870), 12mo, 2/0 boards, *Select Library of Fiction* No. 162, listed in the *Spect* on Apr. 16. The first American edition was issued by Harper & Brothers, New York, 1866, 22 cm., 107 pp., *Library of Select Novels*, listed in *ALG&PC* (fortnightly) on Nov. 15.

776 JOSEPH S. LEFANU *Guy Deverell.* New edition. 12mo. 2/0 boards Oct.?

Companion Library No. 124. This has no date and 372 pp. It ran in the *Dublin University Magazine*, Jan.–July 1865, and the first book edition was issued by Bentley, London, 3 vols., 1865, p 8vo, 31/6 in carmine cloth with cream endpapers. It was listed in the *Ath* on Sept. 30. Bentley issued the second edition, the same, advertised in the *Spect* on Oct. 14, 1865; and the third edition, the same, advertised on Nov. 18, 1865. Bentley issued a new edition, 1866, 19 cm., 414 pp., frontispiece, 6/0, listed in the *Reader* on Apr. 7, 1866. Chapman & Hall, London, issued it (1869), new edition, 12mo, 2/0 boards, *Select Library of Fiction* No. 160, listed in the *Ath* on Nov. 20. The first American edition was issued by Harper & Brothers, New York, 1866, 23.5 cm., 149 pp., $.50 paper, advertised in the *New-York Times* on Jan. 25 as "This day."

777 JOSEPH S. LEFANU *The House by the Churchyard.* New edition. 12mo. 2/0 boards Oct. (*Bks*)

Companion Library No. 125. This has no date and 456 pp. This ran in the *Dublin University Magazine*, Oct. 1861–Feb. 1863, and the first book edition was issued by Tinsley Brothers, London, 3 vols., 1863, 21 cm., 31/6 in blue cloth, listed in the *Ath* on Jan. 10. They issued a second edition in 3 vols., advertised in the *Spect* on Apr. 11,

1863, as "This day." Bentley, London, issued it, 1866, new edition, 20 cm., 476 pp., 6/o cloth, listed in the *Reader* on Aug. 18. Chapman & Hall, London, issued it (1870), new edition, 18.2 cm., 456 pp., 2/o boards, *Select Library of Fiction* No. 169, listed in the *Ath* on July 2. In the United States it was issued by G. W. Carleton, New York, 3-vols.-in-1, 1866, 18 cm., 528 pp., probably with the joint imprint of Tinsley Brothers.

778 JOSEPH S. LEFANU *The Tenants of Malory.* New edition. 12mo. 2/o boards Oct.?

Companion Library No. 126. This has no date and 405 pp. It ran in the *Dublin University Magazine*, Feb.–Oct. 1867, and the first book edition was issued by Tinsley Brothers, London, 3 vols., 1867, 19 cm., 31/6 in scarlet cloth, with cream endpapers, listed in the *Ath* on Sept. 7. Chapman & Hall, London, issued it in 1871, new edition, 12mo, 2/o boards, *Select Library of Fiction* No. 177, listed in the *Spect* on Feb. 18. In the United States it ran in *Littell's Living Age* and was issued in book form by Harper & Brothers, New York, 1867, 23 cm., 176 pp. in double columns, $.50 paper, *Library of Select Novels* No. 300. It was advertised in the *New-York Times* on Oct. 26 as "This day" and in the *Nation* on Oct. 17 as "Just ready." The *U Cat* also gives a Harper edition, 1867, 23 cm., 107 pp. in double columns, which is possibly an error. It was also issued by Littell & Gay, Boston, 1867, $.50, advertised in the *New-York Times* on Nov. 5 as "Now ready" and in the *Nation* on Nov. 7 as "Now ready."

779 JOSEPH S. LEFANU *Uncle Silas.* 12mo. 2/o boards Oct.?

Companion Library No. 127. Warne reissued this (1883), new edition, 18 cm., 462 pp., 2/o, white pictorial boards, printed in red, green, and black, my copy, with publisher's ads on the endpapers and on 1 leaf

at the back and with a commercial ad on the back cover. The series ends with No. 143 in the ads, and the *Star Series* ends with No. 84. In a preliminary word the author states that a leading situation in the story is repeated with slight variation from a short magazine tale of some 15 pp., anonymous, by him, published long ago as "A Passage in the Secret History of an Irish Countess" and afterward issued anonymously in a small vol. under an altered title. The present tale ran in the *Dublin University Magazine* ending in Dec. 1864, and the first book edition was issued by Bentley, London, 3 vols., 1864, 21 cm., 31/6 in claret cloth with cream endpapers. It was listed in the *Ath* on Dec. 17, 1864. Bentley issued a second edition, 1865, 3 vols. same binding, same collation, 500 copies, in Apr.; and a third edition in 1865, 3 vols., advertised in the *Spect* on Apr. 29. Bentley issued a new edition, 1865, p 8vo, 462 pp., frontispiece and vignette title page, 6/o in green cloth, *Bentley's Favourite Novels* No. 11, with a new preface (Dec. 1864), listed in the *Spect* on Aug. 12. Chapman & Hall, London, issued it (1869), third edition, 18.2 cm., 462 pp., 2/o boards, *Select Library of Fiction* No. 144, listed in the *Ath* on Apr. 17; reissued, 1879, new edition, 12mo, 2/o boards (Sadleir's copy). I cannot reconcile the various editions. Wolff had a copy of the second edition in 3 vols., which was published in Apr. 1865 according to the Bentley private catalog. However, the *Reader* lists a third edition in 3 vols. on Mar. 25, 1865! The third edition was advertised in the *Spect* on Apr. 29 as if ready. The designation of the Chapman & Hall edition as the third is, thus, completely mystifying, especially as Bentley issued a new edition after the third edition. The first American edition was issued by Harper & Brothers, New York, 1865, 8vo, 159 pp. in double columns, $.75 paper, *Library of Select Novels* No. 251. It was advertised in the *New-York Times* on Apr. 1 as "This day" and listed in *ALG&PC* (fortnightly) on Apr. 15.

780 JOSEPH S. LEFANU *Willing to Die.*
New edition. 12mo. 2/o boards Oct.?

Companion Library No. 128. This has no date. The first edition was issued by Hurst & Blackett, London, 3 vols., 1873, 20 cm., 31/6, in brown cloth with greenish-black endpapers and with a 16-page catalog at the back of vol. 3. It was listed in the *Ath* on May 17. Chapman & Hall, London, issued it in 1876, 12mo, 2/o boards, *Select Library of Fiction* No. 327, listed in the *Ath* and *Spect* on June 24.

781 JOSEPH S. LEFANU *Wylder's Hand.*
New edition. 12mo. 2/o boards Oct.?

Companion Library No. 129. This has no date and 387 pp. It ran in the *Dublin University Magazine*, June 1863–Feb. 1864, and the first book edition was issued by Bentley, London, 3 vols., 1864, p 8vo, 31/6 in gray-purple morocco cloth with cream endpapers, listed in the *Ath* on Feb. 13. Chapman & Hall, London, issued it (1871), new edition, 12mo, 2/o boards, *Select Library of Fiction* No. 178, listed in the *Spect* on Jan. 28. The first American edition was issued by G. W. Carleton, New York, 1865, 19 cm., 480 pp., $1.75, advertised in the *New-York Times* on June 6 as "This week" and on June 9 as if ready.

782 CHARLES KNIGHT & LAURA VALENTINE, ed. *Half Hours of English History.* New edition. 4 vols. Cr 8vo. 1/6 sewed, 2/o cloth each Oct. 22 (*Ath* ad)

Chandos Classics No. 85–88. Vols. 1 and 2 are edited by Knight, and vols. 3 and 4 by Valentine. parts 1–9 were issued in London (1851), selected and illustrated by Knight. George Routledge & Co., London, issued it in 2 vols., 8vo, 2/6 each, in 1851, and also in 1 vol. at 4/6; they issued a complete edition, 1853, 2-vols.-in-1. Warne issued a new edition in 1867, 8vo, 687 pp., 5/o, to the death of Queen Elizabeth.

783 MARY HOWITT *Friends and Foes. Hope On! Hope Ever! My Own Story.*
3 vols. Cr 8vo. Illustrated. 1/o cloth each Nov. 5 (*Ath* ad)

The *Ath* ad was for books in the 1881–82 season. The first title is given by the *Eng Cat*, but otherwise I cannot trace it. The second title was first issued by Thomas Tegg, London, in 1840, 18mo pocket vol., 2 illustrations, 2/6, *Tales for People and Their Children* No. 2, listed in the *Spect* on May 23. Warne placed it in their *Welcome Library*, Cr 8vo, illustrated, 1/o cloth, in the 1890s. The first American edition of the second title was issued by James Monroe & Co., Boston, 1840, 15.5 cm., 225 pp., listed in the *New York Review* (quarterly) for Jan. 1841 and in the *Merchants' Magazine* (monthly) for Feb. The third title was issued in London, 1845; and by D. Appleton & Co., New York, 1845, 15.5 cm., 176 pp., frontispiece.

784 MARY HOWITT *Alice Franklin. All Is not Gold that Glitters.* Cr 8vo. Illustrated. 1/o cloth each Nov. 5 (*Ath* ad)

The *Ath* ad gave books for 1881–82 season. The first title was first issued in London, 1843, and in the United States by D. Appleton & Co., New York, etc., 1843, 15.5 cm., 174 pp., 2 frontispieces. I can find the second title only in the *Eng Cat*. Both titles were issued in the *Welcome Library* by Warne in the 1890s, Cr 8vo, illustrated, 1/o cloth each.

785 MARY HOWITT *The Ford Family. The Durant Family.* 12mo. Illustrated. 2/o cloth each Nov. 5 (*Ath* ad)

Home Circle Gift Books. The ad in the *Ath* gave books for the 1881–82 season. I cannot trace these.

786 EDWARD GIBBON *The Decline and Fall of the Roman empire.* 4 vols. Cr 8vo. 1/6 sewed, 2/o cloth each Nov. (*Bks*)

Chandos Classics Nos. 89–92. Warne reissued these in this series, 1887 and 1894.

Warne issued this also in the *Chandos Library*, Cr 8vo, 3/6, earlier; and in 3 vols. in 1881, Cr 8vo, 15/0, listed in the *Spect* on Oct. 22. The first edition was *The History of the Decline and Fall of the Roman Empire*, issued by W. Strahan; T. Cadell, London, 6 vols., 1776–88, 4to, frontispiece, maps. Vol. 1 was issued Feb. 17, 1776; there was a second edition of vol. 1 in 1776 and a third edition in 1882. Vols. 2 and 3 were issued in 1781, 42/0 boards, reprinted almost unabridged in the *Critical Review*, London (monthly), Mar.–June 1781. Vols. 4–6 were issued in Apr. 1788, 63/0 boards, reprinted almost unabridged in the *Critical Review* for July, Aug., Oct., Dec. 1788 and Feb. and Mar. 1889. A new edition in 8 vols., 4to, was reviewed in the *Gentleman's Magazine* (monthly) for Aug. 1782, no publisher given, and it certainly could not have been the whole work. In the United States it was issued by William Y. Birch & Abraham Small, Philadelphia, 8 vols., 1804–05, 22 cm., frontispiece, folding maps. The fourth American edition, from the last London edition, was issued in New York, 1826, 6 vols., 8vo, complete, listed in the *North American Review* (quarterly) for Oct.

787 ISAAC D'ISRAELI **The Literary Character of Men of Genius.** New edition. Cr 8vo. 1/6 sewed, 2/0 cloth Nov. (*Bks*)
Chandos Classics No. 96. This has no date and 462 pp., edited by the Earl of Beaconsfield. The first edition was *The Literary Character, Illustrated by the History of Men of Genius*, issued by John Murray, London, 1818, 22 cm., anonymous, 366 pp., 9/6 boards, listed by the *Quarterly Review* as published Jan.–Mar. 1818. There was a third edition in 1822, 2 vols., enlarged, reviewed in the *Gentleman's Magazine* (monthly) for Mar., no publisher given. The first American edition was issued by James Eastburn & Co., New York, 1818,

20.5 cm., anonymous, 302 pp., $1.25, listed in the *North American Review* (bimonthly) for Sept.

788 J. DAZLEY THEOBALD **Magic and Its Mysteries.** 12mo. Illustrated. 1/0 boards Nov. (*Bks*)
Useful Books. This is the first edition, no date, 144 pp. I have a copy, no date, 16.8 cm., 144 pp., a reissue in *Useful Books*, with the series title on the cover, probably issued in 1895. It is in pictorial cream boards, printed in red, blue, and black, with textual illustrations. There are publisher's ads on the endpapers and back cover.

789 BESSIE TREMAINE **Washing and Cleaning.** 12mo. 1/0 1881 (*Eng Cat*)
Useful Books. This is the first edition, no date, 116 pp. Warne reissued it in 1890, Cr 8vo, 1/0 boards, advertised in the *TWEd*, London, on May 2.

790 ANONYMOUS **Eildon Manor.** 12mo. Illustrated. 2/6 cloth 1881 (*Eng Cat*)
Golden Links Series.
Also 1865

791 ELIZABETH EILOART **The Boy with an Idea.** 12mo. Illustrated. 2/6 cloth 1881 (*Eng Cat*)
Daring Deeds Library. The first edition was issued by Warne in 1873, 12mo, 3/6 cloth, listed in the *Ath* on Sept. 13 and reviewed on Nov. 8. Warne reissued it in this series in 1895, new edition, Cr 8vo, illustrated, 2/6 cloth, listed in *PC* on Dec. 7. The first American edition was issued by G. P. Putnam's Sons, New York, 1874, small 8vo, 295 pp., illustrated, $1.75 cloth, listed in the *Nation* on Oct. 2, 1873.

792 GEORGE W. CABLE **Madame Delphine: a Novelette, and Other Tales.** Fcp 8vo. 1/0 sewed 1881 (*Eng Cat*)
Readable Books No. 16. The first American edition was issued by Charles Scribner's

Sons, New York; Warne, London, in 1881, square 12mo, 125 pp., $.75 cloth, advertised in the *New-York Times* on July 1 as "This day" and listed in the *Nation* on July 7. It ran in *Scribner's Monthly* from May to July 1881. The first English edition was issued by Warne in 1881, Cr 8vo, 3/6, listed in the *Spect* on June 18.

793 CHARLES E. BAKER **The Law of Master and Servant.** 12mo. 1/0 1881 (*Eng Cat*)

Warne's Legal Hand-Books. This is the first edition, no date, 176 pp.

794 MAYNE REID **The Queen of the Lakes.** Fcp 8vo. 1/0 sewed 1881?

Readable Books No. 17. The first edition was issued by Beadle & Adams, New York, as *El Capitan*, which ran in the *Saturday Journal*, No. 466 of Feb. 15 to No. 473 of Apr. 5, 1879. They issued it as *Beadle's Dime Library* No. 74, *The Captain of the Rifles*, on Aug. 13, 1879. The first English edition was issued by William Mullen & Son, London and Belfast, 1879, Cr 8vo, 2/6 cloth, listed in the *Ath* on Dec. 20, 1879, with the present title.

Frederick Warne & Co.
Bedford Street, Covent Garden
1882

795 EDWARD P. ROE *Without a Home.*
16mo. 1/0 sewed, 1/6 cloth Jan. (*Bks*)

Star Series No. 76. This has no date and 387 pp. The first edition was issued by Dodd, Mead & Co., New York (1881), 19 cm., 560 pp., $1.50, in green, maroon, or purple-brown cloth and yellow endpapers, with 6 pp. of ads, advertised in the *New-York Times* on Oct. 15 as "Next week" and as "Now published" on Oct. 21, and listed in *PW* on Oct. 22. They issued the second edition, the 23rd thousand, advertised in the *New-York Times* on Dec. 3 as "This week," and issued the third edition, the 26th thousand, advertised on Dec. 17. They issued it in 1885, illustrated, in quarto paper at $.25, listed in the *Nation* on May 28. The first English edition was issued by Ward, Lock & Co., London, 2 vols. (1881), Cr 8vo, 10/6, listed in the *Ath* on Dec. 17, 1881. They issued it with no date, 478 pp., at 2/0 boards, listed in the *Spect* on Jan. 28, 1882; and issued it, 12mo, 2/0 boards, 2/6 cloth, listed in the *Spect* on Sept. 9, 1882. Although I've given this as listed by the *Bks* in Jan. 1882, it was listed in the *Spect* on Dec. 24, 1881, at 1/6.

796 JULIA A. MATHEWS *Bessie Harrington's Venture.* 16mo.
1/0 sewed, 1/6 cloth Jan. (*Bks*)

Star Series No. 74. The first English edition was issued by James Nisbet, London, 1878, 12mo, 3/6. The first American edition was issued by Roberts Brothers, Bos-

ton, 1878, 19 cm., 368 pp. I cannot find that Warne ever issued titles for Nos. 71–73 in this series! Warne reissued it in this series, the same in 1883, listed in the *Bks* in Feb.

797 CHARLES DICKENS *The Pickwick Papers.* Cr 8vo. 0/6 sewed Feb. 25 (*Ath* ad)

Notable Novels No. 59. I have a copy of a re-issue in this series, probably in 1895, 21.3 cm., 247 pp. in double columns, in a new binding in white pictorial wrappers, printed in blue, red, and black, with the series title on the cover. There are commercial ads on the inside and back covers, the front cover ad having a date (Oct. 25, 1894). It was first issued by Chapman & Hall, *The Posthumous Papers of the Pickwick Club*, 20 monthly parts in 19, in 1/0 green pictorial wrappers, edited by "Boz," illustrated by Seymour, "Phiz," and Buss. No. 1 was issued on Mar. 31, 1836. The parts were bound up and issued in 1 vol., 1837, 21 cm., by Dickens, 609 pp., illustrated by "Phiz" and Seymour, listed in the *Ath* on Nov. 11, 1837. Chapman & Hall, London, issued it in 32 1½d weekly nos. of 16 pp. each and in 8 monthly parts at 0/7 sewed each, carefully revised and corrected by the author, small 8vo, double columns. No. 1 was issued on Mar. 27, 1847, and part 1 about Apr. 7. The parts were bound up and issued in 1 vol., new preface, frontispiece, 4/6 sewed, 5/0 cloth, and 7/6 half-morocco, about Oct. 9, 1847. In the United States it was issued in 5 parts by Carey, Lea, and Blanchard, Philadelphia, 1836, 37, 20 cm., edited by "Boz," probably with the joint imprint of Wiley & Putnam, New York. Part 1 was noticed in the *Southern Literary Messenger* for Nov. 1836, part 2 was reviewed in the *Knickerbocker* for Mar. 1837, and 5 parts were listed by the *New York Review* as published Jan. 1–Mar. 15, 1838. It was issued complete, 1 vol., 8vo, illustrated, reviewed in the *Knickerbocker* for Mar. 1838, as issued by Wiley & Putnam, New York. Part 1 was advertised in the *Globe*, a Washington, D.C., daily, by a Washington book dealer on Nov. 9, 1836, "Just received"; part 2 on Jan. 30, 1837, "Just received"; part 3 on May 22, 1837, "Just published and received"; part 4 on Sept. 27, 1837, "Received"; and 4 parts were advertised on Dec. 14, 1837, $1.75. It was also issued by James Turney, Jr., New York, 1836–38 in 26 parts, 25.5 cm., illustrated, in picture wrappers in varying shades of blue-green and apple-green; Turney issued it in 1 vol., 1838, 23 cm., 609 pp., frontispiece, added engraved title page, and plates by Seymour, "Phiz," and Crowquill, in green cloth, listed by the *New York Review* as published Jan. 1–Mar. 15, 1838. It was also issued by W. H. Colyer, New York, 2 vols., 1838, 12mo, illustrated by Seymour, "Phiz," and Crowquill, with an engraved title page and frontispiece in each vol., bound in green boards.

798 (MARGARET ROBERTS) *Denise.*
12mo. 2/6 boards Feb.?

Warne issued this in 1875, 12mo, 3/6, listed in the *Spect* on Nov. 13; and issued it in 1883, 12mo, 2/0 boards, *Companion Library* No. 136, listed by the *Bks* for May. The first edition was issued by Bell & Daldy, London, 2 vols., 1863, 17 cm., anonymous, 10/0. They issued the second edition, 1864, 311 pp., 6/0. The first American edition was issued by J. G. Gregory, New York, 2 vols., 1864, 18.5 cm.,

anonymous, $.75 cloth each, advertised in the *New-York Times* on June 11 as "On June 11."

799 ROSS GORDON *The Doctor of the Rungapore.* Fcp 8vo. 1/0 sewed
Mar. 18 (*Ath* ad)

Readable Books No. 18. This is the first edition, no date, 171 pp., said in the ad to be "Now ready."

800 F.M.P. (FRANCES M. PEARD)
One Year, or a Story of Three Homes.
12mo. 2/0 boards Mar.

Companion Library No. 130. The first edition was issued by Warne, London; Scribner, Welford & Co., New York, 1869, 20 cm., 456 pp., illustrated, 5/0 and 6/0, listed in the *Ath* on Nov. 28, 1868. The first American edition was issued by H. H. & T. W. Carter, Boston, 1871, 20.5 cm., 418 pp.

801 CHARLES DICKENS *Nicholas Nickleby.* Cr 8vo. 0/6 sewed Mar.?

Notable Novels No. 62. This first appeared in 20 monthly parts in 19, in 1/0 green wrappers, edited by "Boz," issued by Chapman & Hall, London, and illustrated by "Phiz." No. 1 was issued on Mar. 31, 1838, and parts 19 & 20 listed in the *Spect* on Oct. 5, 1839. They issued it in 1 vol., 1839, 22.5 cm., 624 pp., illustrated by "Phiz" and with a frontispiece (portrait) by Maclise, bound in green cloth at 21/0 and listed in the *Ath* on Oct. 26. They again issued it in parts at 0/7 sewed each, (part 1) in Nov. 1847, ending with (part 8 and a portion of part 9) on May 27, 1848. The parts were bound up and issued in 1 vol., 1848, Cr 8vo, 499 pp., frontispiece, 5/0, listed in the *Spect* on June 3. In the United States it was issued by James Turney, Jr., New York, 1839, 8vo, 624 pp., illustrated, after being issued in parts in 1838 and 1839, in green wrappers, with the same design as on the English parts. It was also issued by Carey, Lea & Blanchard, Philadelphia, in 20 parts, monthly, in yellow wrappers. No. 4 was advertised in the *Globe*, a Washington, D.C., daily, by a Washington bookstore, on Sept. 3, 1838, as "Just published"; part 5 on Sept. 26 as "Just received"; No. 8 on Feb. 1, 1839; and No. 18 on Oct. 3, 1839. The parts were bound up in 1 vol. and issued by Lea & Blanchard, Philadelphia, 1839, 24 cm., 404 pp., 2 illustrations by "Phiz." It was also issued by W. H. Colyer, New York, 2 vols., 1839, 19 cm., 4 illustrations by "Phiz."

802 RICHARD H. STODDARD *Henry W. Longfellow. A Memoir.* 12mo. Illustrated. 1/o, 1/6 Apr. 15 (*Spect*)

This is the first edition thus, no date, 63 pp. Stoddard also wrote *Henry Wadsworth Longfellow: A Medley in Prose and Verse*, issued by G. W. Harlan & Co., New York, 1882, 22.5 cm., 251 pp. frontispiece (portrait).

803 LOUISA M. ALCOTT *Moods.* 16mo. 1/o sewed, 1/6 cloth Apr. 15 (*Spect*)

Star Series No. 77. This has no date and 256 pp. The first edition was issued by A. K. Loring, Boston (copyright 1864), 17 cm., 297 pp., illustrated, $1.50, advertised in the *Ind* on Jan. 5, 1865, and listed in *ALG&PC* (fortnightly) on Jan. 16. The first English edition was issued by George Routledge & Sons, London and New York (1866), Fcp 8vo, 230 pp., 1/o boards, listed in the *Ath* on Aug. 25; reissued in 1871, the same, listed in the *Spect* on June 24. See also 1900

804 EDWARD EGGLESTON *The Hoosier School-Boy.* Square 16mo. Illustrated. 1/o picture cover, 1/6 cloth Apr. 29 (*Ath* ad)

The ad in the *Ath* gave this as *Columbia Library* No. 1, a new series of copyrighted American literature. I have been unable to locate this series, and I think the series was aborted. It is the first edition, 143 pp., issued Apr. 15 according to *BAL*. The first American edition was issued by Charles Scribner's Sons, New York, 1883, 19 cm., 181 pp., illustrated, $1.00, advertised in the *New-York Times* on Sept. 22 as "This day" and listed in the *Nation* and the *Ind* on Sept. 27. They issued the 11th thousand, the same, advertised in the *New-York Times* on Oct. 11 as "This day." It ran in *St. Nicholas* beginning in Dec. 1881 and appearing *passim* and still in the Oct. 1882 issue. In Canada it was issued by J. Ross Robertson, Toronto, 1883, 8vo, (46) pp. in double columns, terra-cotta wrappers, $.15, a piracy. Scribner supplied Orange Judd, New York, with 105 copies, and it was issued with the Orange Judd imprint, 1883, according to *BAL*.

805 CHARLES LEVER *Harry Lorrequer.* Cr 8vo. o/6 sewed Apr.?

Notable Novels No. 60. Warne also issued this in their *Library of Fiction* No. 23, Cr 8vo, 2/o boards, probably in 1893. There is a known copy, no date, 19.2 cm., pink pictorial boards, printed in red, blue, and black with the series title on the spine. I have a copy as just described, no date, 19.2 cm., 404 pp., with publisher's ads on the endpapers, giving the *London Library* through (No. 43) and the *Tavistock Library* through (No. 6). It has a commercial ad on the back cover. It ran in the *Dublin University Magazine*, Feb. 1837–June 1844 and was issued by William Curry, Jr., Dublin, etc., in 11 monthly 1/o parts in pink illustrated wrappers, 22 cm., illustrated by "Phiz." Part 1 was listed in the *Spect* on Mar. 9, 1839, and part 10 was listed Dec. 21, 1839. It was issued in 1 vol. by the same, 1839, 22 cm., anonymous, 344 pp., 20 illustrations by "Phiz," at 12/o, listed in the *Ath* on Jan. 25, 1840. Wolff had a copy in dark green cloth, and Sadleir had a copy in rose-madder cloth with primrose endpapers, probably of a later binding. See

Sadleir for a discussion of five possible bindings. In the *PC* list of publications for July 14–29, 1850, a Chapman & Hall, London, issue was given, 8vo, reduced to 7/0. They issued it in 1857, 22 cm., 344 pp., illustrated by "Phiz"; and issued it in 1862, 12mo, frontispiece, 2/0 boards, listed in the *Ath* on June 28. The first American edition was issued by Carey & Hart, Philadelphia, 1840, 23.5 cm., anonymous, 402 pp., illustrated by "Phiz," noticed in the *Knickerbocker* for Nov.

806 FREDERICK MARRYAT **The Dog Fiend.** Cr 8vo. 0/6 sewed   Apr.?

Notable Novels No. 61. This has no date and 153 pp. Warne reissued it in this series in 1893, no date, 153 pp., in the new format in white wrappers in a larger size, given by the *BM*. The first book edition was issued by Henry Colburn, London, 3 vols., 1837, 22 cm., anonymous, 31/6 in cloth-backed boards, listed in the *Ath* on June 17. An editorial note in the *Spect* for July 15 said some parts of the story had appeared in the *Metropolitan* at least 18 months earlier and that large extracts had appeared in American newspapers. In fact, an installment appeared in the *Metropolitan* for Aug. 1837. It was also issued by W. Rushton, Calcutta, 1837, anonymous, 256 pp. Bentley issued it as *Standard Novels* No. 107, 1847, 400 pp., in May, *The Dog Fiend*, my copy. It was issued by George Routledge & Co., London and New York, in 1856, new edition, 12mo, 396 pp., 2/6 cloth, listed by *PC* as published June 14–30; Routledge issued it, 1856, Fcp 8vo, 309 pp., 1/6 boards, listed in the *Ath* on Nov. 15, *The Dog Field*. In the United States it was issued by Carey & Hart, Philadelphia, 2 vols., 1837, 18.5 cm., by Marryat. Sadleir's copy of vol. 1 had an inscribed date (Apr. 1837), thus causing him to believe that vol. 1 preceded the first English edition. It was also issued by W. H. Colyer,

New York, 1837, 18.5 cm., by Marryat, 246 pp.; and by C. Lane, Sandbornton, N.H., 2 vols., 1837, 18 cm.

807 (MARGARET ROBERTS) **On the Edge of the Storm.** 12mo. 2/0 boards   Apr.?

Companion Library No. 131. I have a copy (1893), new edition, 18.9 cm., anonymous, 367 pp., in cream pictorial boards, printed in red, blue, green, and black, with the series title on the spine, *Library of Fiction* No. 28. It has publisher's ads on the endpapers and on 8 pp. at the back and a commercial ad on the back cover. The adds give the *Library of Continental Authors* ending with (No. 9) and *Notable Novels* ending with No. 152. The first edition was issued by Warne, London; Scribner, Welford & Co., New York, 1869, 18.5 cm., anonymous, 367 pp., illustrated, 5/0, 6/0, listed in the *Ath* on Dec. 19, 1868. Scribner, Welford imported it and issued it in 1869, Cr 8vo, anonymous, illustrated, $2.50 cloth, advertised in the *Nation* on Feb. 4 as "Just imported." Warne advanced the price to 6/0, given in *PC* with the publications of Nov. 1–15, 1872. The first truly American edition was issued by G. P. Putnam & Son, New York, 1869, 18.5 cm., anonymous, 405 pp., frontispiece, $1.75 cloth, listed in *ALG&PC* (fortnightly) on Sept. 15.

808 SILAS K. HOCKING **Poor Mike.** Square 16mo. Illustrated. 1/0 cloth Oct. 25 (*Ath* ad)

The *Ath* ad was listed No. 1 for the 1882–83 season. This has no date and 88 pp., a first edition. Warne issued it in 1893, Cr 8vo, illustrated, 1/0 cloth, in the *Welcome Library* No. 2.

809 (MARGARET ROBERTS) **Tales Old and New.** 12mo. Illustrated. 2/0 cloth Oct. 28 (*Ath* ad)

Home Circle Gift Books. Warne also issued this about Oct. 23, 1875, 12mo, anonymous, illustrated, 3/6. The first edition was issued by Bell & Daldy, London, 1872, Cr 8vo, anonymous, 5/0.

810 RICHARD ANDRE *Oakleaf Library.*
6 vols., 4to. Colored illustrations.
1/0 picture boards, 1/6 cloth each
Oct. 28 (*Ath* ad)

These have no dates and 32 pp. each. I have no other information on them: *Animated Tea Service: Pictures and Story*; *Ada's Birthday: Pictures and Story*; *Dottie's Big Bath*; *Georgie's Money Box*; *Grandmother's Thimble*; and *Jack's Slate: Scribbles and Scratches.*

811 NATHANIEL HAWTHORNE
Tanglewood Tales, (and) A Wonder-Book.
Cr 8vo. 1/6 sewed, 2/0 cloth
Nov. 11 (*Ath* ad)

Chandos Classics No. 107. This has no date and 379 pp. Warne reissued it in this series in 1883, listed by the *Bks* for Apr.; and reissued it in 1884 and 1885. The first edition of the first title was issued by Chapman & Hall, London, 1853, 18 cm., 251 pp., illustrated and with an engraved title page, in green cloth with white endpapers coated pale yellow on one side, *Tanglewood Tales for Girls and Boys*. It was advertised in the *Ath* on Aug. 13 as "This day" and listed on Aug. 20 and listed in the *Literary Gazette* also on Aug. 20. They paid £64 to the American publishers for this, and the American issue was held up so that Chapman & Hall could publish first. The first American edition was issued by Ticknor, Reed & Fields, Boston, 1853, 17 cm., 336 pp., illustrated, $.87½, in an issue of 3,000 copies, in red, green, purplish blue, or reddish brown cloth with pale yellow endpapers. There is an 8-page catalog with various dates found in most copies (Aug. 1853 in one known copy). It was deposited Aug. 25 and advertised in *Lit W* on Aug. 27 as "On Sept. 3," and published Sept. 20 according to the publisher's records.

There was a second printing, 1853, the same, 800 copies, printed Sept. 16, to sell at $.88. The first edition of the second title was issued by Ticknor, Reed & Fields, Boston, 1852, 17.5 cm., 256 pp., illustrated, $.75 cloth, in an edition of 3,067 copies, in various colored cloths, with pale yellow endpapers. It was deposited Dec. 22, 1851, and published Nov. 8 according to the publisher's records; it was advertised in *Lit W* on Nov. 15 as "This day," *A Wonder-Book for Girls and Boys*. There was a second printing, 1852, the same, 1,600 copies, printed Dec. 4, 1851. The first English edition was issued by Henry G. Bohn, London, 1852, 17.5 cm., 213 pp., illustrated with a new plate added, 2/6 in green cloth with white endpapers, coated in cream on one side. It was from sheets supplied by the American publisher, for which Bohn paid £40 or less. It was listed in the *Ath* on Dec. 27, 1851, and also in the *Literary Gazette*.

812 DAVID HUME *The History of England from the Invasion of Julius Caesar to the Abdication of James the Second, 1688.*
6 vols. New edition. Cr 8vo. 1/6 sewed, 2/0 cloth each 1882

Chandos Classics No. 101–106. These have no dates. The first edition was issued by A. Millar, London, 6 vols., 1754–62, 25.5 cm. It was issued in the United States by Coale & Thomas, Baltimore, 7 vols., 1810, 22 cm., with frontispieces; and by Levis & Weaver, Philadelphia, new edition, illustrated.

813 C.R.C. (CHRISTABEL COLERIDGE)
Lady Betty. 12mo. 2/0 boards
1882 (*Eng Cat*)

Companion Library No. 132. The first edition was issued by Warne (1869), 19.5 cm., 379 pp., illustrated, 5/0, advertised in the *Ath* on Nov. 27.

814 (MARGARET ROBERTS) *Blind Thyrza, Zabdiel, etc..* 12mo. Illustrated. 2/o cloth 1882 (*Eng Cat*)

Home Circle Gift Books. Except for the *Eng Cat* I cannot trace this.

815 (MARGARET ROBERTS) *Duke Ulrich.* 12mo. Illustrated. 2/o cloth 1882 (*Eng Cat*)

Home Circle Gift Books. Fair Else and Duke Ulrich was issued by Warne (1877), 12mo, anonymous, illustrated, 3/6, listed in the *Ath* on Oct. 27.

816 (MARGARET ROBERTS) *Fair Else.* 12mo. Illustrated. 2/o cloth 1882 (*Eng Cat*)

Home Circle Gift Books. See the preceding item.

817 CHARLES R. LOW *Tales of Old Ocean.* 12mo. Illustrated. 2/6 cloth 1882 (*Eng Cat*)

Daring Deeds Library. The first edition was issued by Hodder & Stoughton, London, 1869, 12mo, 302 pp., 5/o, listed in the *Ath* on Oct. 2. Warne issued it at 3/6 in 1871.

818 ERNEST FOSTER *Men of Note.* 12mo. Illustrated. 2/6 cloth 1882 (*Eng Cat*)

Daring Deeds Library. This is the first edition, no date, 250 pp., reviewed in the *Ath* on Dec. 9, 1882, and listed in the *British Quarterly Review* for Jan. 1883. Warne reissued this in this series in 1895, Cr 8vo, illustrated, 2/6 cloth, listed in *PC* on Nov. 16.

819 L.S.F. WINSLOW *The Lawn-Tennis Annual.* 12mo. 1/o 1882 (*Eng Cat*)

This is the first edition, and probably no more were issued.

820 WILLIAM FLOYD *Hints on Dog Breaking.* 12mo. Illustrated. 1/o 1882 (*Eng Cat*)

Useful Books. This is 1882, 44 pp., with a prefatory note signed J. K. It has an added chapter by F. R. Bevan. The first edition was *Observations on Dog Breaking*, printed for the author by J. Harding, London, 1821, 22.5 cm., 23 pp. Warne reissued the present title in 1887, 12mo, illustrated, 1/o cloth, given by the *Eng Cat*.

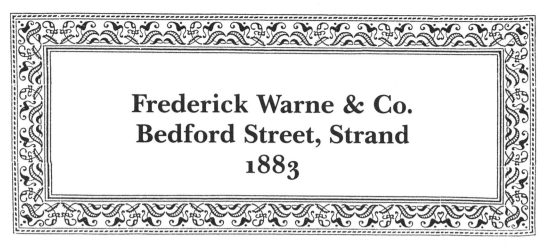

Frederick Warne & Co.
Bedford Street, Strand
1883

821 (METTA VICTOR) *A Bad Boy's Diary.* Unabridged edition. Cr 8vo. o/6 sewed Jan. (*Bks*)

Notable Books No. 1. This is my copy, no date, 19.3 cm., 126 pp. in double columns, yellow pictorial wrappers, printed in red, blue, and black, with publisher's ads on the inside covers and 1 page at the front and 4 pp. at the back, with a commercial ad on the back cover. There is no mention of the series anywhere, and the clothing is identical to that of the *Notable Novels*. The *Notable Novels* ends with No. 63 and the *Companion Library* with No. 139 in the ads. Warne reissued it (1885), my copy, identical to the preceding issue but there is a printer's date (Apr. 18, 1885), different publisher's ads and those on the inside covers only, and a different commercial ad on the back cover. *Notable Books* ends with No. 9 and *Notable Novels* with No. 84 in the ads. Warne advertised in the *Ath* on Feb. 3, 1883, that the first and second editions of 10,000 each were sold out and that a third edition of 10,000 was now ready. This was placed in the *Notable Novels* as No. 101, probably in 1888, but whether reissued or not I don't know. The present title and *More Leaves from a Bad Boy's Diary* were issued in 2 vols. by J. S. Ogilvie & Co., New York (copyright 1880), 17 cm., anonymous, illustrated. Vol. 1 was listed in *PW* on Mar. 27, 1880, and the complete edition in 1 vol., 17 cm., anonymous, 276 pp., illustrated, was listed on Dec. 18. In En-

gland both parts were issued by Alfred Hayes, London (1882), anonymous, 276 pp., 1/o, advertised in the *Times Weekly Edition* on Jan. 26, 1883, as "Just published." *A Bad Boy's Diary* was issued by W. Simpkin & R. Marshall, London, in 1882, unabridged edition, 4to, anonymous, 31 pp., o/6, given by the *Eng Cat*. George Routledge & Sons, London, issued both parts (1883), Demy 8vo, anonymous, 160 pp., o/6, in Feb. 1883.

822 (METTA VICTOR) *The Blunders of a Bashful Man.* Cr 8vo. Illustrated. o/6 sewed Feb. (*Bks*)

Notable Books No. 2. This has no date and 125 pp. Warne placed this in *Readable Novels* No. 102, probably in 1888, but whether reissued at that time or not I don't know. I have a copy (1895), 19.4 cm., anonymous, 125 pp., textual illustrations, in pink pictorial wrappers, printed in red, blue, and black, with publisher's ads on the inside covers and a commercial ad on the back cover. There is no indication of series anywhere, and *Standard Novels* ends with (No. 16) and the *London Library* ends with (No. 49). The first edition was issued by J. S. Ogilvie & Co., New York, in 1881, $.10, *People's Library* No. 41, advertised in the *New-York Times* on June 23, 1881, as "Just issued." They also issued it (copyright 1881), 17 cm., anonymous, 160 pp., illustrated, $.25, listed in *PW* on Oct. 29, 1881. In England it was issued by George Routledge & Sons, London and New York (1883), Demy 8vo, anonymous, 93 pp., o/6 sewed, listed in the *Bks* for Feb. and advertised in the *Ath* on Mar. 3. It was also issued by Ward, Lock & Co., London and New York (1883), 8vo, anonymous, 84 pp., o/6 sewed, advertised in the *Bks* for Mar. 1883.

823 EDWARD BULWER LYTTON *Night and Morning*. Cr 8vo. o/6 sewed   Feb. (*Bks*)

Notable Novels No. 66. Warne also issued it in 1892, Cr 8vo, 1/o sewed, *National Novels* No. 2. The first edition was issued by Saunders & Otley, London, 3 vols., 1841, 20.5 cm., anonymous, 31/6 half-cloth boards with labels, listed in the *Ath* on Jan. 16, 1841. They issued a second edition in 1841, the same, advertised in the *Spect* on June 5 as "Just published." Chapman & Hall, London, issued it in o/7 monthly parts as part of a new issue of the works; part No. 43 (No. 4 of *Night and Morning*) was listed in the *Spect* on Feb. 1, 1851. They bound up the parts and issued it in 1 vol., 1851, 19 cm., 367 pp., frontispiece by "Phiz," 4/o cloth, listed in the *Spect* on Mar. 22. The first American edition was issued by Harper & Brothers, New York, 2 vols., 1841, 19.5 cm., anonymous, in smooth blue cloth, with ads in vol. 2 dated 1840 and Feb. 1841. It was reviewed in the *Knickerbocker* for Mar. and advertised in the *Globe*, a Washington, D.C., daily, by a Washington book dealer on Mar. 1 as "Just published." Harpers also issued it in 1850, $.25 paper, as *Library of Select Novels* No. 139, advertised in *Lit W* on Apr. 6 as "This week."

824 FREDERICK MARRYAT *Poor Jack*. Cr 8vo. o/6 sewed   Feb. (*Bks*)

Notable Novels No. 67. I have a copy in this series, no date, 21.5 cm., 158 pp. in double columns, yellow pictorial wrappers, printed in red and black with the series title on the front and spine. There are commercial ads on both sides of the back cover and a publisher's ad on the inside of the front cover, giving *Notable Novels* ending with No. 84 and *Notable Books* ending with No. 9, thus dating this issue as 1885. Warne issued it in the *Daring Deeds Library* in 1891, 12mo, illustrated, 2/6 cloth, listed in *PC* for Nov. 7, 1891. It was first issued in 12 monthly 1/o parts, Longmans, London, illustrated, in cream wrappers printed in black, Jan.–Dec. 1840. Part 1 was listed in the *Spect* on Dec. 28, 1839, and part 12 on Dec. 5, 1840. They issued it in 1 vol., 1840, 23.5 cm., 384 pp., illustrated, 14/o, dark navy blue cloth with pale yellow endpapers, listed in the *Spect* on Jan. 2, 1841. Reference should be made to Sadleir for the first issue, although he concludes that it would be foolish to describe a first issue! It was issued in French, *Le Pauvre Jack*, Paris, 2 vols., 1841; and in English by Baudry, Paris, 1841, in his *Collection of British Authors*, in plain wrappers. It was issued by Henry G. Bohn, London, in 1859, Cr 8vo, 390 pp., illustrated, reduced to 6/o, with a frontispiece and uncut in green pictorial cloth, listed in *PC* as published Jan. 1–15, 1859. In the United States it was issued by N. C. Nafis, New York, 1840, 221 pp.; and by Carey & Hart, Philadelphia, 2-vols.-in-1, 1840 (probably also in 2 vols.). It was advertised by a Washington, D.C., bookstore in the *Globe*, a Washington daily, on Mar. 18, 1840, as No. 1, 3 illustrations, $.12, "This day," a pamphlet; also listed in the *New York Review* (quarterly) for Apr. 1840. I have not ascertained the publisher of this part issue.

825 WILLIAM T. HICKMAN *From Poverty to Wealth*. 12mo. 2/o boards   Mar. 10 (*Ath*)

Companion Library No. 140. This has no date and 380 pp. The first edition was issued by Chapman & Hall, London, 3 vols., 1881, 19 cm., 31/6, advertised in the *Ath* on Feb. 12 as "Next week" and reviewed on Feb. 26.

826 ROBERT S. BURN **Hints for Farmers.**
12mo. 1/0 boards Mar. (*Bks*)

Books for the Country. The first edition was issued by Routledge, Warne & Routledge, London, 1861, 16.5 cm., 171 pp.

827 (METTA VICTOR) **Miss Slimmens in Search of a Husband. Embracing Miss Slimmens' Window and Miss Slimmens' Boarding House.** Cr 8vo. o/6 sewed Mar. (*Bks*)

Notable Books No. 4. This has no date and 128 pp. The first appearance of *Miss Slimmens' Window* was in *Godey's Lady's Book,* where it ran Jan.–June 1859. It was then issued as *Miss Slimmens' Window and Other Papers* by Derby & Jackson, New York, 1859, 18.5 cm., 312 pp., illustrated, $1.00, by Mrs. Mark Peabody. It contained the title story and 3 other pieces not concerning Miss Slimmens, listed in the *Ind* on Sept. 15. They issued a second edition in 1859, $1.00, advertised in the *New-York Times* on Sept. 30. *Miss Slimmens' Window* was also issued by J. S. Ogilvie & Co., New York, in 1881, anonymous, illustrated, $.10, advertised in the *New-York Times* on May 10 as "This morning"; and they issued it with 147 pp., illustrated, $.25, listed in the *Nation* on Apr. 27, 1882. *Miss Slimmens' Boarding House* first appeared in *Godey's Lady's Book,* where it ran Jan.–Sept. 1860; and it was issued by J. S. Ogilvie & Co., New York (copyright 1882), 17.5 cm., anonymous, 188 pp., listed in *PW* on June 19, 1882. *Miss Slimmens' Boarding House and Miss Slimmens' Window* was issued by George Routledge & Sons, London and New York (1883), complete edition, 21.6 cm., anonymous, 191 pp., o/6 sewed, my copy, advertised in the *Ath* on Mar. 3 and listed in the *Bks* for Mar. *Catching a Husband* was issued by Ward, Lock & Co., London and New York (1883), 8vo, anonymous, 95 pp., o/6 sewed. It contains both stories and was listed in the *Bks* for Mar.

828 CHARLES DICKENS **Oliver Twist.**
Cr 8vo. o/6 sewed Mar.

Notable Novels No. 63. This ran in *Bentley's Miscellany,* Feb. 1837–Apr. 1839, and was issued in 3 vols. by Bentley, London, 1838, by "Boz," illustrated by Cruikshank, 25/0 in maroon cloth, listed in the *Ath* on Nov. 10. Bentley issued the second edition, the same, advertised in the *Spect* on Dec. 22, 1838. Chapman & Hall issued the third edition, 1841, 3 vols., 21 cm., illustrated by Cruikshank, with an author's introduction to the third edition, with a plate in vol. 3 replaced. Sadleir lists three bindings—gray-purple cloth, sage-green cloth, and grass-green cloth. Bradbury & Evans, London, issued the first 1-vol. edition, 1846, a new edition, revised and corrected, tall 8vo, 312 pp., frontispiece and 23 plates by Cruikshank, in slate-gray cloth, with the author's preface to the third edition. They previously issued it in 10 monthly 1/0 parts, part 1 on Jan. 1 and part 8 on July 31, 1846, etc. The parts had the illustrations. Chapman & Hall issued it in 1850, Cr 8vo, frontispiece by Cruikshank, 3/6, listed in the *Spect* on Apr. 20. In the United States it was issued by Lea & Blanchard, Philadelphia, 2 vols., 1839, in tan boards with a pink cloth spine and with paper labels, advertised in the *Globe,* a Washington, D.C., daily, by a Washington bookstore on Dec. 27, 1838, as "Just received" and listed in the *New York Review* (quarterly) for Apr. 1839. They also issued it 2-vols.-in-1, 1839, 23 cm., 212 pp. in double columns, illustrated by Cruikshank, advertised in the *Globe* on Apr. 13, 1839, $.37. It was also issued by U. P. James, Cincinnati, 2 vols., 1839, 19 cm., using the Lea & Blanchard text, bound in tan boards with a floral patterned pink cloth spine, with paper labels. It was also issued by William H. Colyer, New York, 1839, 20 cm., 296 pp., 4 illustrations by Cruikshank. Carey, Lea & Blanchard, Philadelphia, issued *Oliver Twist by "Boz"* with *Other Tales and Sketches from Bentley's Miscellany*, 1837, 18.5 cm., 186 pp. This contained the first 2 chapters of *Oliver Twist* and was issued in 2,000 copies, finished Apr. 1837. Carey, Lea & Blanchard issued it in wrappered parts, 26 cm., with a cover title. In 1838 the parts contained all the chapters from *Bentley's Miscellany* through chapter fifth, book second, illustrated. The remaining nos., containing text up to chapter fifth, book third, were reprinted weekly from *Bentley's Miscellany*. The balance of the novel was printed from the 3-vol. English edition, the last part appearing early in 1839. I take this and the following from the bibliography by W. G. Wilkins. William & Jemima Welker, New York, issued it in numbers, No. 1 in Jan. 1838, beginning with chapter 20 of book first. Previous chapters were issued in June 1838 as a supplement to vol. 1 (which was vol. 3 of the English edition). The final chapters were in the no. for Apr. 1839. I trust this made sense to Mr. Wilkins!

829 FREDERICK CHAMIER **Ben Brace.**
Cr 8vo. o/6 sewed   Mar. (*Bks*)
Notable Novels No. 64. This has no date and 188 pp. The first edition was issued by Bentley, London, 3 vols., 1836, 20 cm., 31/6 in half-cloth boards with paper labels, listed in the *Ath* on Feb. 20 and published on Feb. 16 according to the Bentley private catalog, the latter describing three frontispieces by Cruikshank that apparently did not come off. About one third of the work consists of Southey's Nelson, expanded and dramatized. Bentley issued it as *Standard Novels* No. 77, 1840, my copy, third edition revised, 419 pp., with a new preface by the author, issued in Dec. 1839. He issued a second edition revised, in 3 vols., with additions, advertised in the *Spect* on July 30 as "Just published." It was issued by C. H. Clarke, London, in 1860, new edition, 419 pp., *Parlour Library* No. 210. The first American edition was is-

sued by Carey, Lea & Blanchard, Philadelphia, 2 vols., 1836, 20.5 cm., in an edition of 1,250 copies, finished on Apr. 12.

830 FREDERICK CHAMIER **Tom Bowling.**
Cr 8vo. o/6 sewed   Mar. (*Bks*)
Notable Novels No. 65. This is my copy, no date, 19.3 cm., 191 pp. in double columns, yellow pictorial wrappers, printed in red, blue, and black, with the series title on the front and spine. There are publisher's ads on the inside covers and a commercial ad on the back cover. The series ends with No. 69 in the ads. The first edition was issued by Henry Colburn, London, 3 vols., 1841, 17 cm., 31/6 in boards, with paper labels, and 4 pp. of publisher's ads in vol. 1, listed in the *Ath* on July 24. Henry Lea, London, purchased it at an auction in May 1857 and issued it in 1857, small format, 2/0, about July 18; Lea reissued it at 2/0 pictorial boards in Sept. 1860, no date, with the front picture also on the back, with a pictorial spine. *The Life and Adventures of Tom Bowling* was issued by T. B. Peterson & Brothers, Philadelphia, in Jan. or Feb. 1865.

831 JAMES GREENWOOD **Tag, Rag, and Co.** Cr 8vo. 3/6; Fcp 8vo, 1/0 sewed Mar. (*Bks*)
Readable Books No. 22? This has no date and 244 pp., a first edition. The cloth edition was also listed in the *Ath* on Mar. 17, and both prices were advertised in the *Ath* on Apr. 14. Warne also issued it as *Notable Books* No. 7, Cr 8vo, o/6 sewed, probably in 1884.

832 JAMES GREENWOOD **Odd People in Odd Places.** Cr 8vo. 3/6; Fcp 8vo, 1/0 sewed   Mar. (*Bks*)
Readable Books No. 23? This is the first edition, no date and 244 pp. The cloth edition was also listed in the *Ath* and *Spect* on Mar. 24, and both prices were advertised

in the former on Apr. 14. Warne also issued it as *Notable Books* No. 8, Cr 8vo, o/6 sewed, in 1884, according to the *Eng Cat*.

833 ANONYMOUS *The Shilling Cookery Book.* Colored illustrations. 1/o Apr. 14 (*Ath* ad)

Warne's Popular Cookery Book, 250th thousand, colored plates, 1/o was advertised in the *Times Weekly Edition* on Dec. 13, 1889.

834 FRANCES M. WHITCHER *The Widow Bedott Papers.* Cr 8vo. o/6 sewed Apr. (*Bks*)

Notable Books No. 5. This has no date and 127 pp. The first appearance was in *Neal's Saturday Gazette* in 1845 or 46. The first book edition was issued by J. C. Derby, New York, 1856, 19 cm., 403 pp., illustrated, edited and with an introduction by Alice B. Neal, listed in the *Ind* on Nov. 15, 1855, and noticed in the *New York Daily Times* for Nov. 23. Oakley & Mason, New York, issued it, new edition, 12mo, 403 pp., 8 illustrations, $1.75, advertised in the *Nation* on Jan. 30, 1868. The first English edition was issued by Sampson Low, London, 12mo, 403 pp., 7/6, with the Neal introduction, listed in the *Spect* on Jan. 19, 1856, and by *PC* as published Jan. 1–14.

835 MARY H. FOOTE *The Led-Horse Claim.* Cr 8vo. Illustrated, 3/6; 12mo, 2/o boards May 5 (*Ath*)

This is the first English edition, no date, 248 pp. The 3/6 edition was advertised in the *Ath* on Apr. 14, and the 2/o issue was listed there on May 5 and in the *Spect* on Apr. 28. The first American edition was issued by James R. Osgood & Co., Boston, 1883, 17.5 cm., 279 pp., illustrated, $1.25, advertised in the *New York Daily Times* on Apr. 21 as "This day" and listed in the *Christian Union* on Apr. 26 and in the *Nation* on May 3. It ran in the *Century*, the Century Co., New York, illustrated, Nov. 1882–Mar. 1883.

836 MARY ADAMS (E. S. PHELPS WARD) *An Honourable Surrender.* Fcp 8vo. 1/o sewed May (*Bks*)

Readable Books No. 20? This is the first English edition, no date, 190 pp. The first American edition was issued by Charles Scribner's Sons, New York, 1883, 17.5 cm., 323 pp. Warne also issued this in their *London Library*, 12mo, 1/o sewed, probably in 1898.
See also 1900

837 ROBERT SOUTHEY *The Life of Nelson.* Cr 8vo. 1/6 sewed, 2/o cloth June (*Bks*)

Chandos Classics No. 108. This has no date and 351 pp. Warne also issued it in the *Daring Deeds Library*, 12mo, illustrated, 2/6 cloth, in 1883, given by the *Eng Cat*; and in their *Popular Library* No. 11, 12mo, 360 pp., illustrated, 1/o sewed, 1/6 cloth, listed by *PC* on May 23, 1891, and advertised in the *Times Weekly Edition* on June 5. Warne issued it at 3/6, Cr 8vo, listed in the *Spect* on Dec. 22, 1888. The first edition was issued by John Murray, London, 2 vols., 1813, 16.5 cm., portrait, 10/o boards (a few copies, p 8vo, 15/o, 1 vol.). It was listed by the *Quarterly Review* as published Jan.–Mar., and in 1 vol. at 15/o, Apr.–June. In the United States it was issued by Eastburn, Kirk & Co., New York, etc., 2 vols., 1813, 15 cm., portrait.

838 FREDERICK MARRYAT *The Poacher.* Cr 8vo. o/6 sewed June (*Bks*)

Notable Novels No. 68. This has no date and was reissued by Warne about 1895, 146 pp. The first edition was *Joseph Rushbrook* issued by Longmans, London, 3 vols., 1841, 20.5 cm., anonymous, in half-cloth boards with labels and with a 16-page catalog (Feb. or July 1841) at the front of vol. 1. The first American edition was issued by Carey & Hart, Philadelphia, 2 vols., 1841, by Marryat, in boards with a purple cloth spine, labels, and white endpapers. There are 2 leaves of ads at the front of vol. 2.

839 ARTHUR S. HARDY *But Yet a Woman.* Cr 8vo. o/6 sewed   July 17 (*PC*)

Notable Novels No. 69. This was also issued as *Readable Books* No. 21?, Fcp 8vo, 1/o sewed, listed in *PC* on July 17, no date, 248 pp.; and issued in the *London Library,* 12mo, 1/o sewed, probably in 1899. The first edition was issued by Houghton, Mifflin & Co., Boston and New York, 1883, 18.5 cm., 348 pp., $1.26, advertised in the *Christian Union* on Apr. 19, the first edition sold out before publication, the second edition immediately, and listed in *PW* on Apr. 28. They issued it in 1885 at $.50, listed in the *Nation* on July 16. The first English edition was issued by Macmillan & Co., London, 1883, Cr 8vo, 275 pp., 4/6 and 1/o sewed. Both prices were advertised in the *Ath* on June 23; the 4/6 was listed in the *Ath* and *Spect* on June 23, and the 1/o was advertised in the *Spect* on June 30. It was also issued by Ward, Lock & Co., London (1883), 183 pp., o/6 sewed, 1/o cloth, listed in *PC* on July 17.
See 1900

840 EDWARD P. ROE *A Knight of the Nineteenth Century.* 16mo. 1/o sewed, 1/6 cloth   July (*Bks*)

Star Series No. 83. The first American edition was issued by Dodd, Mead & Co., New York, 1877, 19 cm., 582 pp., $1.50, in maroon or green cloth with cream endpapers, advertised in the *New-York Times* on Sept. 29 as "Now ready" and listed in *PW* on Oct. 20. The first English edition was issued by Ward, Lock & Co., London (1877), 18 cm., 520 pp., colored illustrations, 10/6, listed in the *Ath* and *Spect* on Oct. 13. They also issued it in their *Home Treasure Library* (1877), the same, 3/6 cloth; and they issued it in 1878, 12mo, 1/o sewed, 1/6, 2/o, listed in the *Bks* for Apr. 3.

841 EDWARD P. ROE *Near to Nature's Heart.* 16mo. 1/o sewed, 1/6 cloth July (*Bks*)

Star Series No. 84. The first American edition was issued by Dodd, Mead & Co., New York (copyright 1876), 19 cm., 556 pp., $1.75, with 3 pp. of ads, bound in red, blue, maroon, or terra-cotta cloth with pale yellow endpapers, advertised in the *New-York Times* on Sept. 27 as "Next week" and on Sept. 30 as "Now ready," and listed in *PW* on Sept. 30, 1876. It was advertised in *PW* on Sept. 16 as first edition exhausted, second edition now printing. *BAL* gives another printing with different stamping from the first printing of 12,000 copies, the later printing being in terra-cotta cloth with pale yellow endpapers. Actually, the 15th thousand was advertised in the *New-York Times* on Nov. 30, 1876. The first English edition was issued by Ward, Lock & Tyler, London, in 1876, 2 vols, Cr 8vo, 10/6, listed in the *Ath* on Oct. 7 and in *PC* on Oct. 17. They issued it (1878), 1/o sewed, 1/6, 2/o cloth, listed in the *Spect* on June 15; and an edition, 12mo, 3/6, was listed in the *Spect* on July 6, 1878.

842 GEORGE A. SALA *Quite Alone.* 12mo. 2/o boards   Aug. 18 (*Ath*)

Companion Library No. 143. The first edition was issued by Chapman & Hall, London, 3 vols., 1864, p 8vo, 31/6 in dark purple cloth with pale yellow endpapers, listed in the *Ath* on Nov. 26, 1864. There is an advertisement at the front of vol. 1 relating how the book was finished from page 185 on in vol. 3, by somebody else (Andrew Halliday). Wolff had a Warne edition, no date, in white pictorial boards. The first American edition was issued by Harper & Brothers, New York, 1865, 8vo, 195 pp. in double columns, frontispiece (portrait), $.75 paper, advertised in the *New-York Times* on Jan. 6, 1865, as "This day."

843 JOSEPH S. LEFANU *The Rose and the Key.* 12mo. 2/o boards   Aug. 25 (*Spect*)
Companion Library No. 142. The first edition was issued by Chapman & Hall, London, 3 vols., 1871, Cr 8vo, 31/6 in brown cloth, listed in the *Ath* on Oct. 14.

844 ALEXANDRE DUMAS, PÈRE
The Three Musketeers. Cr 8vo.
o/6 sewed   Sept. (*Bks*)

Notable Novels No. 70. Warne also issued a new edition, 1896, 8vo, 384 pp., illustrated, in Nov., given by the *Eng Cat*, 2/o. The first edition was *Les Trois Mouquetaires*, Paris, 8 vols., 1844, 20.5 cm. It was issued in French in New York by P. Gaillardet, 1846, 28 cm., 268 pp. The first edition in English, according to Sadleir, was issued by Bruce & Wylde, London, 1846, 687 pp., 4/6 cloth, *Library of Foreign Romance* No. 1, translated by William Barrow. It was also issued by George Vickers, London, 1846, 25.5 cm., 132 pp., illustrated, in an incomplete edition. In the United States it was issued as *The Three Guardsmen* by Taylor Wilde & Co., Baltimore, 1846, 22.5 cm., 257 pp., in paper, translated by Park Godwin and listed in the *Merchants' Magazine* (monthly) for May. A second edition was issued by W. Taylor & Co., New York and Baltimore, 1846, revised and corrected, 24 cm., 257 pp. It was also issued with the same title by T. B. Peterson, Philadelphia, in 1847, translated by Park Benjamin, listed in *Godey's Lady's Book* for Sept.

845 ELIZABETH PRENTISS **Our Ruth.**
16mo. 1/o sewed, 1/6 cloth   Oct. 13 (*Ath* ad)

Star Series No. 87. The first edition was issued by James Nisbet, London, 1877, p 8vo, 2/6.

846 EDWARD P. ROE **His Sombre Rivals.**
16mo. 1/o sewed, 1/6 cloth   Oct. 15 (*PC*)

Star Series No. 85. This has no date and 282 pp., the first English edition. The 1/6 issue was advertised in the *Ath* on Sept. 22 as a new copyright work. It was also issued by Ward, Lock & Co., London, in 1884, 282 pp., 2/o boards, 2/6 cloth, probably in June. The first edition was issued by Dodd, Mead & Co., New York (copyright 1883), 19 cm., 487 pp., $1.50 in terracotta, green, or maroon cloth, in an edition of 25,000 copies, deposited on Sept. 19, advertised in the *New-York Times* on Sept. 29 as "This day" and advertised in *Christian Union* on Sept. 27 as "On Sept. 27," and listed in the *Nation* on Oct. 11. They issued a second edition of 5,000 copies, $1.50, advertised in the *Nation* on Dec. 13 as "In press."

847 JOHN T. TROWBRIDGE **Philip Farlow and His Friends.** Fcp 8vo. Illustrated. 2/o cloth   Oct. 20 (*Ath*)

Incident and Adventure Library. This has no date and 180 pp., the first English edition. Warne also issued it in 1894, new edition, 12mo, illustrated, 1/6 cloth, listed in *PC* on Nov. 24. The first American edition was issued by Lee & Shepard, Boston, copyright 1883, 19 cm., 235 pp., illustrated, *Phil and His Friends.*

848 DIGBY D. DAWSON **Mr. Maudle's Red-Room Lectures.** Cr 8vo. o/6 sewed   Oct. (*Bks*)

Notable Books No. 6. This is the first edition, no date, 118 pp.

849 M. A. ELLIS **Only a Child.** 12mo. Illustrated. 2/o cloth   Nov. 10 (*Spect*)

Home Circle Gift Books. This is the first edition, no date, 145 pp.

850 (ANNIE KEARY) **Blind Man's Holiday.** 12mo. Illustrated. 2/o cloth   Nov. 10 (*Spect*)

Home Circle Gift Books. This has no date, 153 pp. The first edition was issued by Griffith & Farran, London, 1860 (1859), anonymous, 182 pp., illustrated.

851 ANONYMOUS **Our Favourite Nursery Songs.** Imp 16mo. Illustrated. 1/o picture wrappers   Nov. 10 (*Ath* ad)

This is the first edition, no date, 157 pp.

852 ANONYMOUS *Our Favourite Nursery Tales.* Imp 16mo. Illustrated. 1/0 picture wrappers   Nov. 10 (*Ath* ad)

This is the first edition, no date, 157 pp.

853 PLUTARCH *Plutarch's Lives.*
4 vols., Cr 8vo. 1/6 sewed, 2/0 cloth each Nov. 10 (*Ath* ad)

Chandos Classics Nos. 110–113. These have no dates, translation by J. and W. Langhorne, the first 2 vols. on Grecian lives and last 2 on Roman lives. This translation was first issued by E. & C. Dilly, London, 6 vols., 1770, 21 cm., frontispieces. The first edition was *Vitae Romanorum et Graecorum*, Philip Giunta, 1517.

854 ELIZABETH PRENTISS *The Home at Greylock.* 16mo. 1/0 sewed, 1/6 cloth Nov. (*Bks*)

Star Series No. 86. The first edition was issued by James Nisbet, London, 1876, Cr 8vo, 2/6, listed in the *Ath* on Sept. 30. Nisbet reissued it in 1879, new edition, Cr 8vo, 2/6, listed in the *Spect* on Dec. 13. The first American edition was issued by A.D.F. Randolph, New York, 1876, 19.5 cm., 338 pp., $1.50, listed in the *Nation* in three issues, Dec. 21, 1876–Jan. 4, 1877.

855 FRANCIS BACON *The Essays of Lord Bacon, Including His Moral and Philosophical Works.* Cr 8vo. 1/6 sewed, 2/0 cloth   Nov. (*Bks*)

Chandos Classics No. 109. This has no date, 530 pp. Warne also issued the essays in 1891, Cr 8vo, 2/0 in blue cloth, uncut edges, advertised in *Notes & Queries* on Nov. 14. The *Essays* were first issued in 1597. *The Essays or Councils, Civil and Moral . . . and a Discourse of the Wisdom of the Ancients . . .* was issued by Samuel Smith & Benjamin Watford, London, 1701, one of 4 simultaneous issues. The *Works*, with some added pieces never before collected in any edition, with a life by Mallet, was is-

sued by A. Millar, London, 4 vols., in 1740, folio, 90/0, advertised in the *Gentleman's Magazine* for Apr. as "This day" (May 1).

856 CHRISTABEL COLERIDGE *Hanbury Mills.* 12mo. 2/0 boards   1883

Companion Library No. 135. The first edition was issued by Warne (1872), large Cr 8vo, anonymous, 464 pp., illustrated, 6/0, *Household Novels*, listed in the *Spect* on Jan. 11, 1873.

857 ANONYMOUS *Queen's Gift Stories.*
8 vols. 0/6 each   1883 (*Eng Cat*)

I cannot trace these.

858 JOANNA H. MATHEWS *Little Sunbeams.* 16mo. 1/6 sewed, 2/0 cloth   1883 (*Eng Cat*)

Star Series No. 88. The first edition was issued by James Nisbet, London, 1872 (1871), 12mo, colored illustrations, 3/6, listed in the *Ath* on Dec. 9, 1871.

859 HANS C. ANDERSEN *Fairy Tales.*
5 vols. 12mo. 1/6 each   1883 (*Eng Cat*)

These were issued in 1 vol. in 1889, Demy 8vo, colored plates, 7/6, a complete edition edited by Mrs. Paull, advertised in the *Spect* on Oct. 19.

Also 1874. See 1865, 77, 97

860 JOHN G. EDGAR *Sea Kings and Naval Heroes.* 12mo. Illustrated. 2/6 cloth 1883?

Daring Deeds Library. The first edition was issued by Bell & Daldy, London, 1861 (1860), Fcp 8vo, illustrated, 5/0, listed in the *Spect* on Nov. 3, 1860. It was issued by George Routledge & Sons, London, in 1865, Fcp 8vo, illustrated, 2/6, advertised in the *Spect* on Dec. 2. It was issued by Warne (1875), 18 cm., 344 pp., illustrated, 3/6. In the United States it was issued by Harper & Brothers, New York, 1863, 18 cm., 421 pp., illustrated, $.50 paper, listed in the *Knickerbocker* as published Mar. 12–Apr. 11.

861 ALEXANDRE DUMAS, PÈRE *Twenty Years After.* Cr 8vo. o/6 sewed 1883?

Notable Novels No. 71. Warne also issued this and item No. 844 above, in 1 vol., 1/0 sewed. I have a copy (1893) in *Notable Novels* in the later larger size, 22 cm., 254 pp. in double columns, a new translation from the original French edition. It is in light gray wrappers, printed in red, blue, and black, with the series title on the cover and the series no. at the foot of the spine. There is a publisher's ad on the inside back cover giving the *Tavistock Library* ending with No. 4 and the *Library of Continental Authors* with No. 9. There are commercial ads on the back cover and inside front cover. Warne also issued it in 1897, 8vo, 574 pp., frontispiece, given by the *Eng Cat* as issued in Feb. The *BM* gives an edition, 1896, 573 pp., frontispiece, by Warne. The first edition was Paris, 10 vols., 1845, *Vingt Ans Aprés*, 21 cm. The first edition in English, according to Sadleir, was issued by Bruce & Wylde, London, 2 vols., 1846, 19 cm., 3/6 cloth each, the *Library of Foreign Romance* Nos. 3 and 4, translated by William Barrow. They first issued it in fortnightly penny nos. of 16 pp. each and sixpenny parts of 96 pp. Thomas Hodgson, London, issued it as *Parlour Library* No. 148, as *Cardinal Mazarin* (1856), 179 pp., on Aug. 18. In the United States it was issued by Taylor, Wilde & Co., Baltimore, 1846, 23 cm., 319 pp. in double columns. It was also issued by Williams & Brothers, New York, 1848, $.75, listed by *Lit W* as published Jan. 29–Feb. 5.

Frederick Warne & Co.
Bedford Street, Covent Garden
1884

862 WILLIAM M. THAYER *From Log-Cabin to White House.* Cr 8vo. o/6 sewed, 1/o cloth   Apr. 5 (*Ath* ad)

This is the life of James Garfield. Warne also issued it as *Popular Library* No. 5, 12mo, 1/o sewed, in 1889, and as *Popular Books* No. 4, 12mo, o/6 sewed, probably in 1891; and they issued it in 1894, Cr 8vo, illustrated, 2/o, listed by the *PC* on Nov. 24. The first edition was issued by James H. Earle, Boston (copyright 1880), 19 cm., 478 pp., illustrated, listed in the *Ind* on Feb. 24, 1881. The *U Cat* also gives it as 1881, 19 cm., 416 pp., frontispiece. The first English edition was issued by Hodder & Stoughton, London, 1881, 20 cm., 344 pp., portrait, 5/o, advertised in the *Ath* on Sept. 24 as "Now ready." They issued the third edition, the same, advertised in the *TWEd* on Oct. 14, with a supplementary chapter, "This day"; the fifth edition was advertised there on Nov. 25; and an edition at 1/o with the portrait, and at o/6 sewed and 3/6 cloth, was advertised there on Feb. 1, 1884 as "Now ready." They issued the 40th edition, 1893, 348 pp., illustrated. Ward, Lock & Co., London, issued it in 1884, no date, 327 pp., illustrated, o/6 sewed, advertised in the *Ath* on Apr. 5; they also issued it in 1884 at 2/o boards, 2/6, 3/6, illustrated.

863 MARIAN JAMES *Anne Dynevor.* 16mo. 1/6 sewed, 2/o cloth   Apr. 12 (*Ath*)

Star Series No. 90. This is my copy, no date, 16.5 cm., 376 pp., in stiff yellow wrappers, printed in red, blue, and black, with the series title on the title page. It is rather an unusual binding in that it is cut flush. There is a printer's date (Feb. 23, 1884) and publisher's ads on the gray endpapers and on the back cover, with the series ending with No. 88. The first edition was issued by Warne in 1875, 12mo, illustrated, 3/6, listed in the *Spect* on May 29 and again on Nov. 13.

864 FREDERICK W. ROBINSON *No Man's Friend.* 12mo. 2/o boards   May 10 (*Ath*)

Companion Library No. 144. This has no date and 398 pp. The first edition was issued by Chapman & Hall, London, 3 vols., 1867, 20 cm., 31/6 in grass-green cloth with cream endpapers, listed in the *Ath* on May 11. The first American edition was issued by Harper & Brothers, New York, 1867, 8vo, 180 pp., $.75 paper, *Library of Select Novels* No. 295, advertised in the *New-York Times* on Aug. 10 as "Just published" and advertised in the *Nation* on Aug. 8 as "Just published."

865 FREDERICK W. ROBINSON *Poor Humanity.* 12mo. 2/o boards May 24 (*Ath*)

Companion Library No. 145. This has no date and 403 pp. This first appeared in *Cassell's Magazine*, chapters 35–44 appearing in Feb. 1868, anonymous. The first book edition was issued by Chapman & Hall, London, 3 vols., 1868, 20 cm., anonymous, 31/6 in royal blue cloth with yellow endpapers, listed in the *Ath* on Mar. 21. The first American edition was issued by Harper & Brothers, New York, 1868, 8vo, 178 pp., $.50 paper, *Library of Select Novels* No. 313, advertised in *Harper's Weekly* on May 9 as "Just ready" and listed in *ALG&PC* (fortnightly) on May 15.

866 CHARLES DICKENS *Barnaby Rudge.* Cr 8vo. o/6 sewed   May?

Notable Novels No. 75. Warne reissued it in this series, probably in 1895, my copy, in the new larger format, no date, 21.2 cm., 264 pp. in double columns, white pictorial wrappers, printed in red, blue, and black, with the series title on the front and the no. at the foot of the spine. There are commercial ads on the back and inside covers, the inside front cover containing a date (Oct. 25, 1894). This was first issued as part of *Master Humphrey's Clock,* which was issued by Chapman & Hall, London, in 88 weekly nos. at o/3 in white wrappers, and 20 monthly shilling parts in green wrappers, No. 1 on Apr. 4, 1840, and part 1 on May 1. They were 26.6 cm., illustrated by Cattermole and "Phiz." *Barnaby Rudge* began with No. 46 on Feb. 13, 1841. Chapman & Hall bound up the parts and issued *Master Humphrey's Clock* in 3 vols.; vol. 1, 1840, and vols. 2 and 3, 1841, *Barnaby Rudge* occupying pp. 229–306 of vol. 2 and all of vol. 3, with the illustrations. Vol. 1 was listed in the *Ath* on Oct. 17, 8/0; vol. 2 on Apr. 10, 1841, 8/0; and vol. 3 on Dec. 18, 10/6. The first separate issue of *Barnaby Rudge* was in 1 vol., 1841, using the plates from the first edition, 25 cm., illustrated, 13/0 in purple brown cloth, listed in the *Ath* on Dec. 18, 1841. Chapman & Hall issued a new edition, revised and corrected, in 1849, small 8vo, frontispiece by "Phiz," new preface, 4/0 cloth, listed in the *Spect* on Apr. 28; and they issued it in 1863, new edition, p 8vo, 416 pp., 5/0, listed in the *Spect* on Oct. 10. They issued it in the People's Edition, 1866, 2 vols. in green boards with a vignette in black on the front, my copy, with frontispieces and with vol. 2 containing also *Reprinted Pieces.* Both Baudry and A. & W. Galignani in Paris issued it in 2 vols., *Barnaby Rudge,* 1842. In the United States it was issued in 19 parts in white wrappers, double columns, by Lea & Blanchard, Philadelphia, all dated 1841, No. 19 with a postscript (Nov. 1841). A listing in the *Knickerbocker* for Apr. 1841 stated that both Lea & Blanchard and E. Littell, Boston, were issuing it in parts by arrangement with Chapman & Hall. Lea & Blanchard issued it, 1842, 25.5 cm., 323 pp., illustrated by "Phiz," Cattermole, and Sibson, noticed in the *Southern Literary Messenger* for Feb. and advertised in the *Globe,* a Washington, D.C., daily, by a Washington bookstore on Dec. 23, 1841, as complete, 1 vol., "Received this day." It was issued by E. Littell, 1842, royal 8vo, 241 pp. in double columns, without the illustrations. I suspect Littell was issuing the parts of *Master Humphrey's Clock* as they came out in England, as the *Globe* advertisement on Apr. 25, 1840, stated that No. 1, $.12, portrait and illustrations, "Will be received the morning of Apr. 29." William H. Colyer, New York, issued *Master Humphrey's Clock,* 2 vols., 1841, in blue boards with a gray cloth spine.

867 CHARLES DICKENS *The Old Curiosity Shop.* p 8vo. o/6 sewed   June?

Notable Novels No. 76. About this time this series was issued in a new and larger format, 21.3 cm. instead of 19.5 cm. Warne reissued this in 1887, p 8vo, o/6 sewed, listed by the *Bks* for Apr. This was first issued as vol. 1 and part of vol. 2 of *Master Humphrey's Clock* (see *Barnaby Rudge* above). Pages (1)–36, (49)–79, (97)–103, and 128–132 were taken up with the clock material, and the *Old Curiosity Shop* ends on page 223 of vol. 2. Chapman & Hall, London, issued the first separate edition of the *Old Curiosity Shop,* 1841, 27 cm., illustrated by "Phiz" and Cattermole, omitting the clock matter and thus causing confusion in the pagination, some pages having two numbers. It was issued at 13/0 and listed in the *Ath* on Dec. 18, 1841. Chapman & Hall reissued the works in parts at 0/7 each, part 17 beginning the present title, in June 1848. These parts were bound up in 1 vol. and issued in 1848, Cr 8vo, frontispiece, 4/0 in double columns, with a new preface, listed in the *Spect* on Oct. 28, 1848. They issued it in 2 vols., 1866, People's Edition, with frontispieces, in green boards with a vignette in black on the covers. The first American edition was issued as *The Old Curiosity Shop and Other Tales*, by Lea & Blanchard, Philadelphia, 1841, 24.1 cm., 362 pp. in double columns, $.75, illustrated by "Phiz" and Cattermole, advertised in the *Globe*, a Washington, D.C., daily, by a Washington bookstore on Nov. 10, 1841, and reviewed in the *Christian Examiner* (bi-monthly) for Mar. 1842. It contains the clock material on pp. 9–32 and 359–362. For the possibility that Lea & Blanchard issued the English parts see *Barnaby Rudge* above. The present title was also issued by William H. Colyer, New York, 2 vols., 1843, 12mo, containing everything except *Barnaby Rudge*.

868 SOPHIA L. CLIFFORD *Marie May.*
16mo. 1/0 sewed, 1/6 cloth   July 19 (*Spect*)

Star Series No. 92. This has no date and 239 pp., probably the first edition. Warne reissued it in 1892, Cr 8vo, 2/0 boards, 2/6 cloth, as *Library of Fiction* No. 27, no date, 239 pp., in cream pictorial boards, listed in the *Ath* on Dec. 17, 1892.
Also 1900

869 FRANCES H. BURNETT *Through One Administration.* 12mo. 2/0 boards
Aug. 23 (*Ath*)

Companion Library No. 146. This has no date and 445 pp. This was the last title is-

sued in this series, and it was also issued as *Library of Fiction* No. 1. The first edition was issued by Warne, 3 vols., 1883, Cr 8vo, 31/6, listed in the *Spect* on Apr. 21 and in the *Ath* on Apr. 28. Warne reissued it in the *Library of Fiction* series in 1885, my copy, no date, 18.2 cm., 445 pp., 2/0 boards, in white pictorial boards, printed in red, blue, green, and black, with the series title on the spine. It has a printer's date (Aug. 19, 1885), publisher's ads on the endpapers and on a leaf at the back, and a commercial ad on the back cover. In the ads the *Library of Fiction* ends with No. 4 and the *Star Series* with No. 99. It was again reissued in this series in 1887, 12mo, 2/0 boards, advertised in the *Ath* on Apr. 2. I think it was also reissued, the same, in 1893. Warne issued it in 1905, probably in the spring, p 8vo, 0/6 sewed, probably as a *Standard Novel*. This ran in the *Century* (the Century Co., N.Y.), Nov. 1881–Apr. 1883. The first American edition was issued by James R. Osgood & Co., Boston, 1883, 12mo, 564 pp., $1.50, advertised in the *New-York Times* on May 12 as "Just published" and listed in the *Nation* on May 17 and in *PW* on May 19.

870 SAMUEL WARREN *Ten Thousand a Year.* 2 vols., p 8vo. 0/6 sewed each; 1 vol., 1/0 sewed   Sept.?

Notable Novels Nos. 77 and 78. Warne reissued the 1-vol. edition in 1891, my copy, no date, complete edition, 21.4 cm., 244 and 235 pp. in double columns, yellow pictorial wrappers, printed in red, blue, green, and black. There are publisher's ads on the inside front cover and on 7 pp. at the back, and commercial ads on both sides of the back cover. In the ads the *Notable Novels* ends with No. 146 and the *Star Series* ends with No. 118. It was reissued in 1896, 8vo, 1/0 sewed, listed in *PC* for June 20. The first edition was issued by Carey & Hart, Philadelphia, 6 vols., 19.5 cm., anonymous, vol. 1–4, 1840, and vols. 5 and 6, 1841, in buff boards with half-cloth claret spines and paper labels. Vol. 5 was listed in the *United States Magazine* (monthly) for July 1841. They issued it also, 1848, new edition, $.25, listed in *Lit W* as published Jan. 29–Feb. 5. It ran in *Blackwood's Magazine*, Oct. 1839–Aug. 1841. The first English edition was issued by William Blackwood & Sons, Edinburgh and London, 3 vols., 1841, 19.5 cm., anonymous, 31/6 in gray-purple cloth, listed in the *Spect* on Nov. 13. Wolff's copy was a presentation copy inscribed (Nov. 15, 1841). They issued it in 2 vols., 1854, new edition, revised 19.5 cm., 9/0, advertised in *Notes & Queries* on Aug. 5 as "This day," previously having been issued in weekly 1½ penny nos. and in 8 monthly 1/0 parts. The American edition was advertised in the *Globe*, a Washington, D.C., daily, by a Washington bookstore on June 23, 1841, $.25 paper per vol.

871 (JOHN HAY) *The Bread-Winners.* 12mo. 2/0 boards Oct.?

Library of Fiction No. 2. This is my copy, 1884, 18 cm., anonymous, 310 pp., in yellow pictorial boards, printed in red, blue, and black, with the series title on the spine. It has "Entered at Stationers' Hall, copyright 1883" on the verso of the title page and has a printer's date (Sept. 3, 1884). There are publisher's ads on the inside covers and on 4 pp. at the back and a page at the front, with a commercial ad on the back cover. In the ads the *Companion Library* ends with No. 146 and the *Star Series* with No. 87. This ran in the *Century* (the Century Co., N.Y.), Aug. 1883–Jan. 1884, and the first American book edition was issued by Harper & Brothers, New York, 1884, 17.5 cm., anonymous, 319 pp., $1.00 in decorated green cloth, advertised in the *New-York Times* on Dec. 28, 1883, as "Tomorrow" and on Dec. 29 as "This day" and listed in the *Nation* on Jan. 24 and in the *Christian Union* on Jan. 3, 1884. They issued a new edition in 1892, 16mo, $1.00 cloth, advertised in the *New-York Times* on

June 28; and they issued it in 1894 at $.50, advertised in the same on Nov. 28 as "Recent." The first English edition was issued by Warne in 1883, Cr 8vo, anonymous, 310 pp., 6/0, advertised in the *Ath* on Dec. 15, 1883, as if ready, and listed in the *Spect* on Jan. 5, 1884.

872 FREDERICK MARRYAT *Percival Keene.* p 8vo. 0/6 sewed Oct.?

Notable Novels No. 79. The first English edition was issued by Henry Colburn, London, 3 vols., 1842, 19 cm., 31/6 in half-cloth boards with labels or in brown cloth with yellow endpapers, listed in the *Ath* on Sept. 3 and advertised in the *Spect* on Aug. 27 as "On Sept. 1." In the United States it was issued by Wilson & Co., New York, 1842, 31.5 cm., 63 pp. in double columns, my copy. It has a caption title and is extra No. 10 of *Brother Jonathan*, dated Sept. 21, claiming to be the first American edition. It was also issued by J. Winchester, New York, 1842, 40 cm., 26 pp., with a caption title, extra Nos. 23 and 24 of *The New World*, dated Sept. 20, claiming to be the first American edition. It was also issued by Harper & Brothers, New York, 1842, noticed in the *Southern Literary Messenger* and in the *Southern Quarterly Review* for Jan. 1843.

873 M. BIRD *Una.* 16mo. 1/0 sewed, 1/6 cloth Oct.?

Star Series No. 93. This is the first edition, no date, 231 pp. It was reviewed in the *Ath* on Nov. 8.

874 CHARLES H. BARSTOW *Old Ransom.* Square 16mo. 1/0 Oct.?

This is the first edition, no date, 85 pp. It was reviewed in the *Ath* on Dec. 13.

875 NATHANIEL HAWTHORNE *Mosses from an Old Manse.* Cr 8vo. 1/6 sewed, 2/0 cloth Nov. 8 (*Ath* ad)

Chandos Classics No. 115. This has no date and 445 pp., deposited at the *BM* on Dec.

17. The first edition was issued by Wiley & Putnam, New York, 2 vols., 1846, 19.3 cm., $.50 each in printed pale buff wrappers, or in 1 vol., $1.25 in purple, blue, or green cloth, *Library of Choice Reading*, deposited June 5, and reviewed in the *Harbinger* (weekly) on June 27. It was also issued by them in 1850, 12mo, cloth, advertised in *Lit W* on Aug. 3 as "This week." Wiley & Putnam, London, issued it, 1846, 2 vols., 7/0 in green cloth with buff endpapers, yellow-coated on one side, *Library of American Books* Nos. 17 and 18. It used American sheets and had cancel titles, listed in *PC* on July 15 and in the *Ath* on July 18. The first edition set up in England was issued by George Routledge & Co., London, 1851, 17.6 cm., 256 pp., 1/0 boards, 1/6 cloth, listed in the *Ath* on Sept. 13. It had the same contents as the first American edition but with 1 piece omitted. There was a second printing, 1852, and a third printing, 1853.

876 SAMUEL WARREN *Passages from the Diary of a Late Physician.* 2 vols. p 8vo. 0/6 sewed each; 1 vol., 1/0 sewed Dec.?
Notable Novels Nos. 80 and 81. These have no dates. This ran in *Blackwood's Magazine*, Aug. 1830–Aug. 1837, off and on, and was eventually issued in 3 vols. by Blackwood, vol. 3 coming out more than 5 years after the first 2 vols. The first edition of the first 2 vols. was issued by J. & J. Harper, New York, 2 vols., 1831, 16 cm., anonymous, Harper's Stereotyped Edition, advertised in the *Globe*, a Washington, D.C., daily, by a Washington bookstore on Dec. 26, 1831, as "Just received." The first English edition in book form of the first 2 vols. was issued by William Blackwood, Edinburgh, etc., 2 vols., 1832, 17 cm., anonymous, illustrated, 12/0, advertised in the *Spect* on Mar. 17 as "This day." Wolff had a copy of the second edition, 2 vols., 1833, anonymous, illustrated, a presentation copy inscribed (May 9, 1833). William Blackwood & Sons, Edin-

burgh, issued the fourth edition, 2 vols., Fcp 8vo, anonymous, 12/0, advertised in the *Spect* on Jan. 14, 1837. The first edition of vol. 3 was issued by Blackwood, 1838, 17 cm., by Warren, illustrated, 6/0, advertised in the *Spect* on Dec. 16, 1837, and they advertised a new edition in 3 vols., 18/0 on Dec. 9. Blackwood issued the fifth (the sixth?) edition in 2 vols., 12/0, listed in the *Spect* on Feb. 26, 1842. There was a new edition, probably the seventh, in 2 vols., 12/0 cloth, advertised in the *Spect* on June 1, 1844, as "This day"; and they issued it in 1 vol., 1854, 19.5 cm., 500 pp. in double columns, after a serial issue in weekly 1½ penny nos. or in 4 monthly 1/0 parts, the latter beginning in Sept. 1853. The earliest edition of vol. 3 in the United States was probably issued by Harper & Brothers, New York, 3 vols., 1845, from the fifth London edition, the complete work.

877 THOMAS C. HALIBURTON *The Clockmaker.* Reprinted from the original editions. Cr 8vo. 0/6 sewed 1884
Notable Novels No. 74. This is my copy, no date, 19.2 cm., by Haliburton, 188 pp. in double columns, yellow wrappers, printed in red, blue, and black, with the series title on the front and the title and no. on the spine. There are publisher's ads on the inside covers and on a page at the front and on 2 pp. at the back, with a commercial ad on the back cover. In the ads the series ends with No. 73 and the *Companion Library* ends with No. 143. It contains all three series of the *Clockmaker*. The first edition of the first series was issued by Joseph Howe, Halifax, 1836, 19.7 cm., anonymous, 221 pp., the first 21 sketches having appeared in the *Novascotian*. *The Clockmaker*, series 1, was issued by Bentley, London, 1837, 19.5 cm., anonymous, illustrated, 10/6, listed in the *Ath* on Apr. 1. *The Sayings and Doings of Sam Slick of Slickville* was issued by Carey, Lea, & Blanchard, Philadelphia, 1837, first series,

19.5 cm., anonymous, 218 pp., 1,000 copies finished in Nov. 1837. They issued a second edition, 1839, of 2,000 copies, 179 pp., finished Dec. 1837. Benjamin B. Mussey, Boston, issued the first series, 1838, and the *Globe*, a Washington, D.C., daily, had an ad by a Washington bookstore on May 4, 1838, "Just received," with no publisher given. Bentley issued the second series, 1838, 19.5 cm., anonymous, illustrated, 10/6, listed in the *Ath* on July 14. Bentley issued *Sam Slick's Sayings and Doings* in 1838, the first and second series, a new and illustrated edition, 2 vols., 21/0, advertised in the *Spect* on Nov. 3, 1838; and issued the fourth edition, the same, advertised in the *Spect* on Feb. 23, 1839. Lea & Blanchard, Philadelphia, issued the second series, 1838, *The Clockmaker*, 19 cm., anonymous, 220 pp., listed in the *New York Review* (quarterly) for Oct. 1838. William H. Colyer, New York, issued an edition of 240 pp., probably the second series, listed in the *North American Review* (quarterly) for July 1840; the *Globe* advertised the second series on Sept. 3, 1838, as "This day," no publisher given. Bentley issued the third series, 1840, anonymous, illustrated, 10/6, by Sam Slick, listed in the *Ath* on Nov. 7. *The Clockmaker's Journey* was issued by Lea & Blanchard, 1840, the third series, 19.5 cm., anonymous, 215 pp., reviewed in the *Knickerbocker* for Dec. 1840.

878 LEW WALLACE **Ben-Hur.** 16mo. 1/6 sewed, 2/0 cloth 1884
Star Series No. 91. This has no date and 458 pp., in blue cloth blocked in gold and black. Warne reissued this in the *Star Series* in 1887, 16mo, 2/0 cloth, 458 pp., in blue pictorial cloth with sprinkled edges, given by the *Eng Cat*; they issued it in 1888, Cr 8vo, 3/6, listed in the *Spect* on Sept. 22; and they issued it in the *Popular Library* No. 6 in 1889, 12mo, 1/0 sewed. I have a copy, 1902, 21.6 cm., 207 pp., 1/0 in buff wrappers, pictorially printed in brown, printed in double columns and with ads on the endpapers, back cover, and a leaf at the back. The first edition was issued by Harper & Brothers, New York, 1880, 17.5 cm., 552 pp., $1.50, in powder-blue cloth with gray endpapers, in an edition of 2,500 copies, deposited Oct. 22 and published Nov. 12 according to the publisher's records. It was listed in the *Ind* on Nov. 18 and advertised in the *New-York Times* on Nov. 12 as "This day." The 110th thousand was advertised in the *New-York Times* on Aug. 27, 1886, 16mo, 552 pp., $1.50 cloth, as "Now ready"; a new edition from new plates, the same, was advertised on Oct. 3, 1887. In editorial matter in the *New York Times Book Review* for Jan. 13, 1900, it was stated that the book was in the 92nd edition from Harpers and that 680,000 copies had been sold! By agreement with Sampson Low, London, on Nov. 9, 1880, plates were sent to Low, who issued it, 1881, 17.5 cm., 552 pp., 6/0 in red cloth, with 32 pp. of ads at the back. It was listed in the *Ath* on Feb. 26 and in *PC* on Mar. 1. They issued a new edition in 1881, 12mo, 6/0, advertised in the *Spect* on Mar. 12.

879 JAMES GREENWOOD **Dining with Duke Humphrey.** Cr 8vo. 0/7 sewed 1884 (*Eng Cat*)
Notable Books No. 9. The first edition was *Curiosities of Savage Life*, issued by S. O. Beeton, London, 2 vols., 1863, 64, series 1 and 2, colored plates, 7/6 each. Warne issued it with the same title in 2 vols. in 1865, 6/0 each.

880 WILLIAM J. GORDON **The Bijou Calculator and Mercantile Treasury.** 32mo. 1/6 1884 (*Eng Cat*)
This is the first edition, no date, 640 pp. It has been variously given as 32mo, 64mo, and 48mo. I've given the 32mo from the *BM*.

881 HENRY J. NICOLL *Great Orators. Burke, Fox, Sheridan, Pitt.* Cr 8vo. 1/6 1884 (*Eng Cat*)

The first edition was issued by Macniven & Wallace, Edinburgh, etc., 1880, 18 cm., 254 pp., 2/6 and 3/0 cloth, advertised in the *Spect* on Nov. 6 as "Just published." It was issued as *Brilliant Speakers* by Ward, Lock & Co., London and New York, in 1888, Cr 8vo, illustrated, 1/0 sewed, 1/6, advertised in the *Ath* on Sept. 29.

882 HENRY J. NICOLL *Great Scholars. Buchanan, Bentley, Porson, Parr and Others.* Cr 8vo. 1/6 1884 (*Eng Cat*)

This has no date and 251 pp. The first edition was issued by Macniven & Wallace, Edinburgh, etc., 1880, 18 cm., 251 pp., 2/6 and 3/0 cloth, advertised in the *Spect* on Nov. 6. Ward, Lock & Co., London and New York, issued it in 1888, Cr 8vo, illustrated, 1/0 sewed, 1/6, advertised in the *Ath* on Sept. 29. They also issued it with the preceding title in 1 vol. in Sept., 3/6.

883 HENRY J. NICOLL *Thomas Carlyle.* Cr 8vo. 1/6 1884 (*Eng Cat*)

This has no date and 255 pp. The first edition was issued by Macniven & Wallace, Edinburgh, etc., 1881, 18 cm., 248 pp., frontispiece (portrait), 2/6. They issued a revised edition in 1881, 255 pp. Ward, Lock & Co., London and New York, issued it, 255 pp., 1/0 cloth, probably in 1885, and reissued it in 1888, illustrated, 1/0 sewed, 1/6, advertised in the *Ath* on Sept. 29.

884 JAMES C. WATT *Great Novelists. Scott, Thackeray, Dickens, Lytton.* Cr 8vo. 1/6 1884 (*Eng Cat*)

This has no date and 260 pp. The first edition was issued by Macniven & Wallace, Edinburgh, etc. 1880, 18 cm., 260 pp., 2/6 and 3/0 cloth, advertised in the *Spect* on

Nov. 6. Ward, Lock & Co., London and New York, issued it, illustrated, 1/0 cloth, in 1885 or 1886, and reissued it in 1888, illustrated, 1/0 sewed, 1/6, advertised in the *Ath* on Sept. 29.

885 PETER ANTON *England's Essayists. Addison, Bacon, DeQuincey, Lamb.* Cr 8vo. 1/6 1884 (*Eng Cat*)

The first edition was issued by Macniven & Wallace, Edinburgh, etc., 1883, 18 cm., 252 pp., 2/6 cloth. Ward, Lock & Co., London and New York, issued it in 1888, Cr 8vo, illustrated, 1/0 sewed, 1/6, advertised in the *Ath* on Sept. 29; they issued it with the preceding title in 1 vol., 3/6 cloth, probably in 1888 also.

886 PETER ANTON *Masters in History. Gibbon, Grote, Macaulay, Motley.* Cr 8vo. 1/6 1884 (*Eng Cat*)

The first edition was issued by Macniven & Wallace, Edinburgh, etc., 1880, 18 cm., 252 pp., 2/6 and 3/0 cloth, advertised in the *Spect* on Nov. 6. It was issued by Ward, Lock & Co., London and New York, probably about 1885, at 1/0 cloth, and they reissued it in 1888, illustrated, 1/0 sewed, 1/6, advertised in the *Ath* on Sept. 29.

887 JOHN R. SEAGER *The Municipal Elections Act, 1884.* 12mo. 1/0 cloth 1884 (*Eng Cat*)

This is the first edition, no date, 91 pp.

888 LAURA VALENTINE *The Knight's Ransom.* 12mo. Illustrated. 2/6 cloth 1884 (*Eng Cat*)

Daring Deeds Library. The first edition was *The Ransom*, issued in London, 3 vols., 1846. Warne issued it, 1870, Cr 8vo, illustrated, 5/0, listed in the *Spect* on Nov. 6, 1869, and in the *Ath* on Nov. 16. It was a thorough revision of the original edition. I have a copy issued by Warne in 1891, no date, 18.4 cm., 471 pp., frontispiece, *Library of Fiction* No. 12, in pink pictorial boards, printed in very dark green and black, with the series title on the spine in a circular device at the base of the spine. It has the original plain white endpapers, and the only ad appearing is a publisher's ad on the back cover giving as new, works first issued in 1880! Thus this is an unusual yellowback.

889 WILLIAM J. GORDON ***Warne's Discount and Commission Tables.***
18mo. 1/0 cloth   1884 (*Eng Cat*)

This is probably the first edition. It was advertised in *PC* on May 11, 1895, at 1/0 cloth and is given by *BM* as Warne (1939).

890 (R. K. PHILP) ***The Best of Everything.***
12mo. 2/0 boards, 2/6 cloth   1884
(*Eng Cat*)

Warne issued a new edition in 1873, Cr 8vo, 2/6 cloth, listed in the *Ath* on Dec. 20, 1873. The first edition was *Best of Everything*, issued by W. Kent & Co., London, 1870, Cr 8vo, 402 pp., 2/6, listed in the *Ath* on Oct. 15. The first American edition was issued by J. B. Lippincott, Philadelphia, 1870, 19.5 cm., 408 pp.

891 SMALMAN SMITH (SIR JOHN SMALMAN SMITH) ***A Guide to the Modern County Court.*** 1/0, 1/6   1884, 85 (*Eng Cat*)

The first edition was issued by Warne, 1882, Cr 8vo, 168 pp., at 2/6 cloth, advertised in the *Ath* on Oct. 28.

Frederick Warne & Co.
Bedford Street, Covent Garden
1885

892 SAMUEL LOVER *Handy Andy.* p 8vo.
0/6 sewed Jan.?

Notable Novels No. 82. This has no date,
21.6 cm., yellow pictorial wrappers,
printed in red, blue, and black, with the
series title on the spine and with publisher's ads on the back and inside covers.
Warne issued it in the *Library of Fiction* No.
16, Cr 8vo, 2/0 boards, listed in *PC* for July
11, 1891. It ran in *Bentley's Miscellany*, Jan.
1837–May 1839, and was issued by Frederick Lover and Richard Groombridge,
London, in 12 monthly 1/0, illustrated
parts, Demy 8vo, from Jan. 1 to Dec. 1,
1842. They issued it in 1 vol., 1842, 21.5
cm., 380 pp., illustrated, 13/0, in dark
green cloth, with yellow endpapers, listed
in the *Ath* on Dec. 10 and advertised in
the *Spect* on Dec. 3 as "Now ready." It
was issued by Henry G. Bohn, London,
1845, 23 cm., 380 pp., illustrated; and reissued, 1846, illustrated, in red cloth. David Bryce, London, issued it in 1854, Fcp
8vo, 2/0 boards, listed by *PC* as published
Aug. 1–15. Bryce's entire stock was sold at
a Hodgson auction in June 1858, and a
few days later the copyright of *Handy Andy*
was sold for £390. Henry Lea was probably the purchaser, as he issued it in 1858,
2/0 boards, listed by *PC* as published Dec.
1–14, and reissued it about July 9, 1864,
new edition, 2/0 boards. Darton & Co.,
London, issued it in 1859 as *Parlour Library*
No. 197. In the United States it was issued in parts by D. Appleton & Co., New

York (probably the 12 English parts), Nos.
1–6 noticed in the *Merchants' Magazine*
(monthly) for Aug. 1842. D. Appleton &
Co., New York, etc., issued it, 1843, illustrated, noticed in the *Knickerbocker* for Jan.
in 2 forms.

893 HELEN MATHERS, later REEVES
Found Out. 12mo. 1/0 sewed, 2/6 cloth
Jan. 24 (*Ath* ad)

London Library No. 1. This is the first edition, no date, 188 pp. The ad said "Just
published," and the 2/6 edition was listed
in the *Spect* on Feb. 7. The 50th thousand
was advertised in the *Ath* on Feb. 28, 1/0,
"Now ready," and the 70th thousand, 1/0,
2/6, seventh edition, was advertised there
on July 25. The first American edition was
issued by George Munro, New York
(1885), 12mo, 93 pp., in paper, *Seaside Library Pocket Edition* No. 438, listed in *PW* on
May 2.

894 G.P.R. JAMES *Forest Days.* p 8vo. 0/6
sewed Mar.?

Notable Novels No. 83. The first edition was
issued by Saunders & Otley, London, 3
vols., 1843, 19 cm., anonymous, 31/6 in
boards with a gray-purple cloth spine, labels, and white endpapers. It has a Longmans 32-page catalog at the front of vol. 1
(Jan. 1843) and was listed in the *Ath* on
Jan. 14 and in the *Spect* on Jan. 21. In the
United States it was issued by Harper &
Brothers, New York, 1843, 24.5 cm., in

double columns, *Library of Select Novels* No. 14. It was also issued by J. Winchester, New York, 1843, 31.5 cm., 70 pp., extra Nos. 59–61 of *The New World*.

895 CHARLES MARVIN *The Russians at the Gates of Herat.* 12mo. Maps, portraits. 1/o sewed, 2/6 cloth
Apr. 11 (*Ath*)
This is the first edition, no date, 176 pp. It was advertised in the *Ath* on Mar. 21 as "On Mar. 23," and the 2/6 was listed, Cr 8vo, in the *Spect* on Apr. 4. A second edition of 20,000 was advertised in the *Ath* on Mar. 28 as "Now ready." Warne issued it as *Popular Library* No. 9, with maps and portraits, 12mo, 1/o sewed, probably in 1889. In the United States an authorized edition was issued by Charles Scribner's Sons, New York, 1885, 19 cm., 185 pp., portraits and maps, advertised in the *New-York Times* on Apr. 14 as "Immediately, the first edition being exhausted by advance orders, the second edition in press." The second edition was advertised on Apr. 16 as "This morning," and a new edition with an American preface was advertised on May 14 as "Ready today." These were $.50 in the *Yellow Paper Series* and $1.00 cloth. It was also issued by Harper & Brothers, New York (1885), 29.5 cm., 46 pp., illustrations, portraits and 3 maps, *Franklin Square Library* No. 463, $.20 paper, advertised in the *New-York Times* on Apr. 24 as "This day" and listed in the *Christian Union* on May 7. It was also issued by George Munro, New York (1885), 12mo, 106 pp., maps and portraits, in paper, *Seaside Library Pocket Edition* No. 457, advertised in the *New-York Times* on May 2 as "Out today" and listed in *PW* on May 23.

896 EDWARD BULWER LYTTON *The Last of the Barons.* p 8vo. o/6 sewed   Apr.?
Notable Novels No. 84. The first edition was issued by Saunders & Otley, London, 3 vols,. 1843, 20.5 cm., anonymous, with the preface signed E.L.B., 31/6 in boards, half-cloth and labels, listed in the *Ath* on Feb. 25. Chapman and Hall, London, issued it in weekly nos. and monthly parts, and bound it up in 1 vol., 1850, 18.5 cm., 464 pp., frontispiece by "Phiz," with a new preface, listed in the *Spect* on Dec. 1, 1849. In the United States it was issued by Wilson & Co., New York, 1843, 28 cm., 106 pp., caption title, the extra No. 19 of *Brother Jonathan*, dated Feb. It was also issued by J. Winchester, New York, 1843, 28.5 cm., 107 pp., caption title, extra Nos. 56–58 of *The New World*, dated Feb. It was also issued by Harper & Brothers, New York, etc., 1843, 23 cm., 227 pp., reviewed in *Graham's Magazine* (monthly) for Apr. and noticed in *Dial* (quarterly) for Apr.

897 (SUSAN WARNER) *The House in Town.* 16mo. 1/o sewed, 1/6 cloth
May 1 (*PC*)
Star Series No. 98. The first English edition was issued by James Nisbet, London, 1871, 12mo, anonymous, colored illustrations, 3/6 in the *Golden Ladder Series*, listed in the *Ath* on Sept. 23 and in *PC* on Nov. 1. It and the following title were issued in 1 vol., 1872, 12mo, 414 pp., at 3/6, listed in the *Ath* on Oct. 12. The first American edition was issued by Robert Carter & Brothers, New York, 1872, 17.5 cm., anonymous, 424 pp., illustrated, $1.25, advertised in the *New-York Times* on Sept. 20 as "This morning" and listed in *ALG&PC* (fortnightly) on Sept. 15. It was in green cloth with pink endpapers, and some copies have an 8-page catalog. For some reason the date is 1872, without doubt.

898 (SUSAN WARNER) *Trading.* 16mo. 1/o sewed, 1/6 cloth   May 1 (*PC*)
Star Series No. 99. The first English edition was issued by James Nisbet, London, 1872, Fcp 8vo, anonymous, 214 pp. 2/6 cloth, listed in the *Ath* on Oct. 12 and in *PC*

on Nov. 1. It was issued along with the preceding title in 1 vol. The first American edition was issued by Robert Carter & Brothers, New York, 1873, 17.5 cm., anonymous, 437 pp., illustrated, with 10 pp. of ads (Apr. 1872 or Oct. 1872), received at the Boston Athenaeum on Nov. 7, 1872, and listed in the *Publishers' and Stationers' Weekly Trade Circular* on Oct. 17.

899 (ANNA WARNER) *Stories of Vinegar Hill.* 16mo. 1/6 sewed, 2/0 cloth
May 15 (*PC*)

Star Series No. 96. The first English edition was issued by James Nisbet, London, 1871, 17.2 cm., anonymous, 361 pp., colored illustrations, 3/6 in orange-red cloth, bevelled covers, with *Golden Ladder Series* on the spine, deposited on Sept. 16 and listed in the *Ath* on Sept. 23 and in *PC* on Oct. 2. The first American edition was issued by Robert Carter & Brothers, New York, 6 vols., 1872, 17.5 cm., anonymous, illustrated, in a box, $3.00, advertised in the *New-York Times* on Sept. 20, 1871, as "This morning" and listed in *Godey's Lady's Book* for Dec. 1871 and thus probably issued in Sept. Story No. 1 had 153 pp., No. 3 had 149 pp., No. 5 had 185 pp., and No. 6 had 178 pp.

900 (SUSAN WARNER) *What She Could; and Opportunities.* 16mo. 1/6 sewed, 2/0 cloth   May 15 (*PC*)

Star Series No. 97. The first English edition of the first title was issued by James Nisbet, London, 1871, 12mo, anonymous, colored illustrations, 3/6, in the *Golden Ladder Series*, listed in the *Ath* on Oct. 15 and in *PC* on Nov. 15, 1870. The first American edition was issued by Robert Carter & Brothers, New York, 1871, 17.5 cm., anonymous, 339 pp., illustrated, $1.25, listed in *ALG&PC* on Nov. 1, 1870, and advertised in the *Nation* on Oct. 20 as "Just published." It is in black, terra-cotta, or purple cloth, with yellow or pink endpapers and

12 pp of ads. *Opportunities* was issued by Robert Carter & Brothers, New York, 1871, 17.5 cm., anonymous, 382 pp., illustrated, in purple or terra-cotta cloth, with yellow or pink endpapers, listed in *ALG&PC* on Mar. 1, 1871. Nisbet issue both titles in 1 vol., advertised in *PC* on Mar. 16, 1871, as "New and recent," and a later edition was listed in the *Ath* on Jan. 10, 1880.

901 JAMES M. COBBAN *Tinted Vapours.* A Nemesis. 12mo. 1/0 sewed   May (*Bks*)

London Library No. 3. This is the first edition, probably with no date, 176 pp. The third edition, 15th thousand, was advertised in the *Ath* on July 25, 1/0 sewed, 2/6 cloth. Warne reissued it as *The Missing Partner*, p 8vo, 0/6 sewed, in 1889, as *Notable Novels* No. 132. In the United States it was issued by D. Appleton & Co., New York, 1885, $.25 paper, listed in the *Ind* on July 16, *A Nemesis.* It was also issued as *Tinted Vapours* by George Munro, New York (1885), 12mo, paper, 152 pp., *Seaside Library Pocket Edition* No. 485, listed in *PW* on July 4.

902 WILLIAM H. MAXWELL *The Fortunes of Hector O'Halloran and His Man Mark Antony O'Toole.* p 8vo. 0/6 sewed
May (*Bks*)

Notable Novels No. 85. This was first issued in 13 monthly, illustrated 1/0 parts in pale tan wrappers, printed in black, issued by Bentley, London, etc., part 1 at the end of Mar. 1842, part 3 on Apr. 30, and part 13 with an ad dated May 1, 1843. The parts were bound up in 1 vol. and issued by Bentley, London, etc. (1843), 23 cm., 412 pp., illustrated by Leech, 14/0 in sage-green cloth with yellow endpapers, issued May 16 according to the Bentley private catalog. It was remaindered to William Tegg & Co., London, who issued it, new edition, 8vo, illustrated, 9/0, advertised in the *Spect* on Aug. 2, 1845. Tegg reissued it in 1850 and 1853, 20 cm., 412 pp., illustrated. Bentley issued it as *Standard Novels* No. 121, 1851, 432 pp., later renumbered as 109. The first American edition was issued by D. Appleton & Co., New York, etc., 1843, 22 cm., 412 pp., illustrated, listed in the *United States Magazine* for July. They also issued it in parts, one of which was noticed in *Godey's Lady's Book* for Jan. 1843, and 3 parts were ready by Sept. 1842.

903 FREDERICK MARRYAT **Masterman Ready.** p 8vo. o/6 sewed   May (*Bks*)
Notable Novels No. 86. Warne also issued this in the *Daring Deeds* Library in 1891, 12mo, illustrated, 2/6 cloth, listed in *PC* on Nov. 7. Warne issued it in New York in 1885, Cr 8vo, illustrated, $2.00, advertised in the *Christian Union* on Dec. 3, 1885. The first English edition was issued by Longmans, London, 3 vols; vol. 1, 1841; vols. 2 and 3, 1842, Fcp 8vo, illustrated, 22/6, with a catalog at the end of vol. 1 (Feb. 1, 1841), or in some copies no ads, or, as in Wolff's copy, a 32-page catalog (Oct. 1842) at the back of vol. 2. Vol. 1 is in navy-blue cloth, and vol. 2 and 3 in dark slate cloth; vol. 1 had yellow endpapers, and vols. 2 and 3 had cream endpapers (Sadleir's copy). Vol. 1 was listed in the *Ath* on May 1, 1841; vol. 2 on Apr. 23, 1842; and vol. 3 on Dec. 24, 1842, each at 7/6. Longmans reissued it in 3 vols., 1845 and 1850, and issued it in 2 vols., new edition, 1851, Fcp 8vo, illustrated, 12/0, listed in the *Spect* on Sept. 20. Henry G. Bohn, London, issued it in 2 vols. in 1853, Fcp 8vo, illustrated, 10/0, about Dec. 12, 1853, and reissued it, new edition, 1 vol., 1857, p8vo, 476 pp., illustrated, 5/0, 6/0, listed in the *Spect* on Nov. 15, 1856. The first edition in America was issued by D. Appleton & Co., New York; etc., 1841–1843, 3 vols., 15 cm., frontispieces. Vol. 1 was listed in the *New York Review* for July 1841, and vol. 2 was listed in *Godey's Lady's Book* for July 1842.

904 JOHN S. WINTER (HENRIETTA STANNARD) **Bootles' Baby.** 12mo. Illustrated. 1/o sewed   Early June
London Library No. 4. This is the first English edition, no date, 118 pp. Warne issued the third edition, 30th thousand, at 1/o sewed, 2/6 cloth, advertised in the *Ath* on July 25. This was reissued in the series, 1891, my copy, 17.6 cm., 118 pp., frontispiece, full-page and textual illustrations, in white pictorial wrappers, printed in red, blue, and black, with the series title on the cover. There are 10 pp. of publisher's ads at the back, giving *Notable Novels* through No. 145 and the *Star Series* through No. 118, and commercial ads on the back and inside covers. I have a cloth copy, no date, probably 1892, 17.2 cm., with the same contents as the preceding copy, in light grayish-purple smooth cloth, both covers plain except for a decorated title and author in red and black on the front. There are 12 pp. of publisher's ads at the back giving *Notable Novels* through No. 152 and the *Star Series* through No. 124. The endpapers are figured. I have another copy, no date, probably 1895, 17.2 cm., with the same contents as the preceding issue, in white pictorial wrappers, printed in red, blue, yellow, and black, a different cover from the 1891 wrappered edition above. There are 12 pp. of publisher's ads at the back with the *Star Series* ending with No. 130 and the *Detective Stories* with (No. 3), and there are commercial ads on the back and inside covers. Warne issued this title along with *Houp-La* in 1 vol. in 1901, p 8vo, o/6 sewed, *Standard Novels*, given by the *Eng Cat* as issued in May. Editorial matter in the *New York Times Book Review* on Oct. 7, 1899, gave it as illustrated, $.25 paper, issued by Warne, New York. In the United States it was issued as *Mignon* by Harper & Brothers, New York, 1885, 17.5 cm., 119 pp., illustrated, *Handy Series* No. 3, $.25 paper, advertised in the *New-York Times* on May

16 and listed in the *Nation* on June 4 and in the *Christian Union* on June 4. It was also issued by George Munro, New York, with the same title (1885), 12mo, 83 pp., illustrated, in paper, *Seaside Library Pocket Edition* No. 492, listed in *PW* on Aug. 29.

905 HAWLEY SMART **Struck Down.** 12mo. 1/0 sewed, 2/6 cloth   June 27 (*Ath* ad) *London Library* No. 5. This is the first edition, no date, 175 pp., in cream wrappers printed in red. The *Ath* ad said "Just published," and the 2/6 was listed in the *Spect* on June 27. The 1/0 is in pale gray wrappers, printed in red on the front and spine with title, etc. (Sadleir's copy). The third edition, 30th thousand, the same, was advertised in the *Ath* on July 25, and Warne issued a fourth edition (1886), with 175 pp. Warne issued it, 1893, Cr 8vo, 2/0 boards, 2/6 cloth in their *Library of Fiction* No. 26, 238 pp., listed in *PC* on Feb. 25. In the United States it was issued by D. Appleton & Co., New York, 1885, $.25 paper, advertised in the *New-York Times* on July 23 as "This day" and listed in *PW* on Aug. 15 and in the *Nation* on Aug. 20. It was also issued by George Munro, New York (1885), 113 pp., paper, *Seaside Library Pocket Edition* No. 550, probably issued in Sept. or Oct.

906 JOHN S. WINTER (HENRIETTA STANNARD) **Houp-La.** 12mo. Illustrated. 1/0 sewed, 2/6 cloth   July 27 (*Ath* ad) *London Library* No. 6. This is the first edition, no date, 116 pp. This was advertised in the *Ath* on July 25 as "On July 27." The 2/6 is in smooth gray cloth, lettered in red and black on the front, with tan and white patterned endpapers. There are a frontispiece and 5 illustrations by W. Ralston, and a 16-page catalog at the back. The 1/0 is in white wrappers cut flush, pictorially printed in red and blue. Warne issued a fourth edition (1886), a reissue in this series. I have a reissue in this series, 1889,

17.5 cm., 116 pp., white pictorial wrappers, printed in blue and red, with the series title on the front. Commercial ads are on the inside front and outside back covers and on 1 page in front and back. There are publisher's ads on a page at the front, on the inside back cover, and on 9 pp. at the back, giving the *London Library* as ending with No. 30 and the *Star Series* as ending with No. 114. The illustrations are present. I have another copy, no date, probably 1897, 17.5 cm., 116 pp., contents as for the preceding copy, in white wrappers, pictorially printed in red and brown, with a different cover from the preceding copy and no series title. Commercial ads are on the back and inside covers, and publisher's ads are on 16 pp. at the back, giving the *Welcome Library* as ending with *The Ruler of the House* and the *Bedford Library* ending with *Natty's Violin*. Warne issued this with *Bootles' Baby* (see item 904) in 1 vol., in 1901, p 8vo, 0/6 sewed, *Standard Novels*, given by the *Eng Cat* as issued in May. In the United States it was issued by Harper & Brothers, New York, 1885, 17.5 cm., 117 pp., illustrated, $.25 paper, *Handy Series* No. 26, advertised in the *New-York Times* on Oct. 3 as "This day" and listed in the *Nation* on Oct. 22. It was also issued by George Munro, New York (1885), 12mo, paper, *Seaside Library Pocket Edition* No. 600, in Nov.

907 A.J.B. BERESFORD HOPE **Strictly Tied Up.** 12mo. 2/0 boards   Aug. 15 (*Ath*) *Library of Fiction* No. 4. This is my copy, no date, 18.2 cm., 369 pp., yellow pictorial boards, printed in red, green, and black, with the series title on the spine. This has a commercial ad on the back cover, plain white endpapers, and 6 pp. of publisher's ads at the back. The first edition was issued by Hurst & Blackett, London, 3 vols., 1880, Cr 8vo, anonymous, 31/6, listed in the *Ath* on Oct. 16. They issued the third edition, 1881, 19.5 cm., 360 pp., 6/0, listed in the *Spect* on July 23. In the United States

it was issued by George Munro, New York, 1883, 32.5 cm., 46 pp., $.20 paper, *Seaside Library* No. 1521, listed in *PW* on Feb. 17.

908 MRS. ALEXANDER (ANNIE HECTOR) *At Bay.* 12mo. 1/0 sewed Aug. (*Bks*)
London Library No. 7. This is the first edition, no date, 178 pp. It was also issued at 2/6, listed in the *Spect* on Aug. 8. Warne issued the 40th thousand, 1/0 sewed, 1/6 cloth, advertised in the *Ath* on May 29, 1886; and issued it in the *Library of Fiction* No. 30, no date, Cr 8vo, 2/0 boards, 256 pp., listed in the *Ath* on Aug. 26, 1893. The first American edition was issued by Henry Holt, New York, 1885, 17 cm., 308 pp., containing also *Valerie's Fate*. It was issued in the *Leisure Hour Series* at $1.00 and in the *Leisure Moment Series* at $.30 paper, advertised in the *New-York Times* on Aug. 29 as "This day" and listed in *Lit W* and *PW* on Sept. 5. It was also issued by J. S. Ogilvie, New York (1885), 187 pp., listed in *PW* on Sept. 12.

909 MAY CROMMELIN (MARIA DE LA CHEROIS CROMMELIN) *Goblin Gold.* 12mo. 1/0 sewed, 2/6 cloth Oct. 3 (*Ath* ad)
London Library No. 8. This is the first edition, no date, 153 pp. In the United States it was issued by Harper & Brothers, New York, 1885, 162 pp., *Handy Series* No. 36, $.25 paper, advertised in the *New-York Times* on Nov. 21 as "Today" and listed in the *Nation* on Nov. 26. It was also issued by George Munro, New York (1885), $.10 paper, *Seaside Library Pocket Edition* No. 647, advertised in the *New-York Times* on Dec. 5 as a late issue and listed in *PW* on Jan. 16, 1886.

910 FLORENCE SCANNELL *Sylvia's Daughters.* Small 4to. Illustrated. 2/6 boards Oct. 17 (*Ath*)
This is the first edition, 112 pp., advertised in the *Christian Union* on Dec. 3, illus-

trated, by Warne, New York. The *BM* gives it as dated 1886, for the English edition.

911 LAURA VALENTINE *Peril and Adventure on Land and Sea.* Fcp 8vo. Illustrated. 2/0 cloth Nov. 7 (*Ath*)
Incident and Adventure Library. This was placed in the *Daring Deeds Library* in the 1890s. It is given by the *Eng Cat*, but otherwise I cannot trace it.

912 LAURA VALENTINE *Valour and Enterprise.* Fcp 8vo. Illustrated. 2/0 cloth Nov. 7 (*Ath*)
Incident and Adventure Library. This was issued in the *Daring and Doing Library*, Cr 8vo, illustrated, 1/6 cloth, listed in *PC* on Jan. 12, 1895. The present edition is also given by the *Eng Cat*, but otherwise I cannot trace it.

913 CECILIA S. LOWNDES *New Honours.* 12mo. Illustrated. 2/0 cloth Nov. 14 (*Ath* ad)
Home Circle Gift Books. This is the first edition, no date, 194 pp. It was issued in the *Bedford Library*, 12mo, illustrated, 1/6 cloth, listed in *PC* on Nov. 2, 1895. The present edition was listed in the *Spect* on Sept. 26, 1885.

914 CECILIA S. LOWNDES *Lena Graham.* 12mo. Illustrated. 1/0 cloth Nov. 14 (*Ath* ad)
Home Circle Gift Books. This is probably a first edition, as it was reviewed in the *Ath* on Dec. 12. It was listed in the *Spect* on Sept. 26. It was issued in the *Bedford Library*, 12mo, illustrated, 1/6 cloth, listed in *PC* on Nov. 2, 1895.

915 STUART C. CUMBERLAND (CHARLES GARNER) *The Rabbi's Spell.* 12mo. 1/0 sewed Nov. 14
Warne's Christmas Annual. This is the first English edition, no date, 183 pp. It was

listed in the *Spect* on Oct. 24, Cr 8vo, 2/6. Warne advertised the 10th thousand in the *Ath* on May 29, 1886, 1/o sewed, 1/6 cloth. It was issued in the *Popular Library* No. 8, 12mo, 1/o sewed, advertised in July 1889 in the *TWEd*. In the United States it was issued by D. Appleton & Co., New York, 1885, 12mo, 193 pp., in the *New 25¢ Series*, in paper, advertised in the *New-York Times* on Nov. 14 as "This day." It was also issued by George Munro, New York (1885), $.10 paper, *Seaside Library Pocket Edition*. No. 641, advertised in the *New-York Times* on Dec. 5 as a late issue.

916　ROBERT E. A. WILLMOTT, ed. *The Poets of the Nineteenth Century.* New edition. Cr 8vo. Illustrated. 1/6 sewed, 1/o cloth　1885 *Chandos Classics* No. 116. This has no date and 620 pp. Warne issued it, 1866, new edition, 383 pp., illustrated, 12/6; and issued it in the *Chandos Library* in 1868, new edition, illustrated, noticed in *Notes & Queries* on Dec. 12, 1868; and issued it in 1878, new edition, Cr 8vo, 2/6, listed in the *Spect* on Aug. 31. The first English edition was issued by George Routledge & Co., London and New York, 1857, 23 cm., 397 pp., illustrated. In the United States it was issued by Harper & Brothers, New York (copyright 1857), 23 cm., 616 pp., illustrated, with English and American additions.

917　ANONYMOUS *The Albion Temperance Reciter.* p 8vo. 1/o cloth　1885 (*Eng Cat*) This is the first edition, no date, 176 pp. It was issued by Warne, 1890, 176 pp., and issued in 1895 as *Albion Reciter* No. 1, 1/o, advertised in *PC* on May 11.

918　JOHN R. SEAGER *The Franchise Act.* Fcp 8vo. 1/o　1885 (*Eng Cat*) I cannot trace this.

919　JOHN R. SEAGER *The Representation of the People Act, 1884.* Fcp 8vo. 1/o cloth　1885 (*Eng Cat*) The *BM* gives only the second edition, 1885, 96 pp.

920　ANONYMOUS *Three Kittens.* 8vo. Colored illustrations. 1/o picture boards 1885 (*Eng Cat*) This has no date, 36 pp., and 20 full-page illustrations in color.

921　ANONYMOUS *Billiards Simplified; or, How to Make Breaks.* 8vo. Diagrams. 1/o 1885 (*Eng Cat*) This has no date and 181 pp. The first edition was probably issued by Burroughes & Watts, London, which the *BM* gives as (1884?), 181 pp.

922　WILLIAM C. DAY *Behind the Footlights.* 12mo. Illustrated. 1/o, 2/6　1885 (*Eng Cat*) This is 1885, 191 pp.

923　SILAS K. HOCKING *Our Joe.* Square 16mo. Illustrated. 1/o cloth 1885 (*Eng Cat*) This is the first edition, no date, 90 pp. It was placed in the *Welcome Library* about 1893.

924　ANONYMOUS *The Housekeeper's Guide.* p 8vo. 1/o　1885 (*Eng Cat*) I cannot trace this.

925　ANNIE KEARY *Tinker Dick.* 18mo. 1/o　1885 (*Eng Cat*) This is the first edition, no date, 128 pp.

926　MABEL *Our Dog Laddie.* 8vo. Illustrated. 1/o　1885 (*Eng Cat*) This is the first edition, no date, 36 pp.

927 JOHN L. MOTLEY **The Rise of the Dutch Republic.** New edition. 3 vols., Cr 8vo. 1/6 sewed, 2/0 cloth each   1885? *Chandos Classics* Nos. 117–119. These have no dates. The first edition was issued by John Chapman; Chapman & Hall, London, 3 vols., 1856, 22 cm., 42/0, listed in the *Spect* on Feb. 23 and by *PC* as published Feb. 14–29. George Routledge & Co., London, issued it in 3 vols. in 1858, revised by the author, p 8vo, 18/0, listed in the *Spect* on Feb. 27. The first American edition was issued by Harper & Brothers, New York, 3 vols., 1856, 23 cm., $6.00 muslin, etc., advertised in the *New York Daily Times* on Apr. 12 and noticed by *Putnam's Monthly* as published in May. Warne issued it in 1891, 3 vols., Cr 8vo, 10/6, advertised in *Notes & Queries* on Nov. 19, but it could have been issued much earlier.

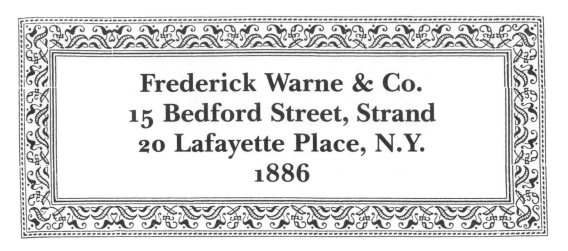

928 JOHANN VON GOETHE *Faust*.
Cr 8vo. 1/6 sewed, 2/0 cloth   Jan. 23
(*Ath* ad)

Chandos Classics No. 120. This has no date and 424 pp., the translation by Bayard Taylor. The *Ath* ad said "Next week." Warne advertised it in *Notes & Queries* on Nov. 14, 1891, Cr 8vo, 2/0, in blue cloth, uncut, probably a reissue at some time before this ad of the *Chandos Classics* edition. The first edition of the Bayard Taylor translation was issued by Alexander Strahan, London, 2 vols., 1871, 19 cm., 28/0. The poem was begun by Goethe with a fragment, 1790, continued with part 1, 1808, and part 2, 1832. The first edition of the complete work was issued in Stuttgart and Tübingen, Germany, 1834 (*Printing and the Mind of Man*). The *U Cat*, however, gives Heidelberg, 2 parts, 1 vol., 1832, 19 cm., 223 pp. The first English edition was issued by Moxon, London, 1833, 8vo, 12/0 boards, translated by A. Hayward, issued in Apr. according to the *Eng Cat* and listed in the *Edinburgh Review* as published Jan.–July 1833. The first American edition was issued by Daniel Bixby, Lowell, Mass., etc., 1840, in the Hayward translation, 18mo, 317 pp., the first American from the third London edition. It was listed in the *New York Review* (quarterly) for Oct.

929 EDWARD P. ROE *A Young Girl's Wooing*. 16mo. 1/0 sewed, 1/6 cloth Jan. (*Bks*)

Star Series No. 94. The first English edition was issued by Warne (1884), Cr 8vo, 408 pp., 6/0, listed in the *Spect* on Oct. 18 and in the *Ath* on Oct. 25. The first American edition was issued by Dodd, Mead & Co., New York (copyright 1884), 19 cm., 340 pp., frontispiece, $1.50, in green, terracotta, or gray cloth, with yellow endpapers. It was issued in an edition of 25,000 copies, advertised in the *New-York Times* on Oct. 11 as "This day" and advertised in *PW* on Oct. 11 as "On Oct. 11" and listed in the *Ind* on Oct. 16.
Also 1900

930 EDWARD P. ROE *Taken Alive*. 12mo. 0/6 sewed   Feb. 15 (*PC*)

This is the first edition, not seen and not located by *BAL*. Its first American appearance was in *Taken Alive and Other Stories, with an Autobiography*, issued by Dodd, Mead & Co., New York (1889), 19.5 cm., 375 pp., frontispiece (portrait), $1.50, in blue-green cloth with cream endpapers and with a 63-page catalog at the back. This contains also *Found Yet Lost*, *The Queen of Spades*, and *An Unexpected Result*, the first issued by Dodd, Mead & Co. in Apr. 1888, the third issued by them in Apr. 1883, and for the second see 1888 below.

931 SUSAN & ANNA WARNER *The Gold of Chickaree.* 16mo. 1/6 sewed, 2/0 cloth Mar. 15 (*PC*)

Star Series No. 101. The first English edition was issued by James Nisbet, London, 1877 (1876), 352 pp., 3/6, deposited Nov. 24, 1876, listed in the *Ath* on Oct. 21 (*sic*) and in the *Spect* on Oct. 28 (*sic*) and in *PC* on Dec. 18. They reissued it in 1879, new edition, 12mo, 3/6, listed in the *Spect* on Aug. 16. The first American edition was issued by G. P. Putnam's Sons, New York, 1876, 19 cm., 426 pp., $1.75, in green, blue, brown, or terra-cotta cloth, with pink or yellow endpapers and 4 pp. of ads. It was received at the Boston Athenaeum on Nov. 25 and advertised in the *New-York Times* on Nov. 23 as "Now ready" and listed in the *Ind* on Nov. 30. Putnam's Sons reissued it in 1877, new edition, 12mo, $1.75, advertised in the *New-York Times* on Oct. 13.

932 SUSAN WARNER *Diana.* 16mo. 1/6 sewed, 2/0 cloth Mar. 15 (*PC*)

Star Series No. 102. The first American edition was issued by G. P. Putnam's Sons, New York, 1877, 19 cm., 460 pp., $1.75, in green or terra-cotta cloth, with green or cream endpapers, advertised in the *New-York Times* on Oct. 27 as "Now ready" and listed in *PW* on Oct. 20 and in the *Nation* on Oct. 25. The first English edition was issued by James Nisbet & Co., London, 1877, Cr 8vo, illustrated, 3/6, advertised in the *TWEd* on Oct. 26 as "Just published" and listed in the *Ath* on Nov. 3 and in *PC* on Nov. 2. Nisbet reissued it, 1878, frontispiece, with 4 pp. of ads, in blue cloth; and reissued it in 1879, new edition, Cr 8vo, 3/6, listed in the *Spect* on Nov. 22.

933 SUSAN & ANNA WARNER *Wych Hazel.* 16mo. 1/6 sewed, 2/0 cloth Mar. (*Bks*)

Star Series No. 100. This has no date and 422 pp. The first edition was issued by James Nisbet & Co., London, 1876, copyright, 19.5 cm., anonymous, 422 pp., frontispiece, 3/6 in red or green cloth with brown endpapers, listed in the *Ath* on Feb. 26 and in *PC* on Mar. 16. The first American edition was issued by G. P. Putnam's Sons, New York, 1876, 19 cm., by Susan and Anna Warner, 528 pp., $2.00 in terra-cotta or green cloth with yellow endpapers, 2 pp. of ads, advertised in the *New-York Times* on Apr. 25 as "Now ready" and listed in *PW* on Apr. 29 and in the *Nation* and *Ind* on May 4. The second edition was advertised in the *New-York Times* on Apr. 26 as "On Apr. 28"; the third edition was advertised on May 13, $2.00, "Just published"; and a new edition was advertised on Oct. 13, 1877, $2.00, as "Ready."

934 NATHANIEL HAWTHORNE *The Scarlet Letter.* p 8vo. 0/6 sewed Mar. (*Bks*)

Notable Novels No. 88. The first edition was issued by Ticknor, Reed & Fields, Boston, 1850, 18.5 cm., 322 pp., $.75, in brown cloth with cream endpapers, with 4 pp. of ads at the front with various dates, in an edition of 2,500 copies, advertised in *Lit W* on Mar. 9 as "On Mar. 16" and listed as published Mar. 16–23. Hawthorne received $270 in royalties. They issued a second edition of 2,500 copies, 1850, with a preface, $.75, on Apr. 22, from which Hawthorne received $281. James Fields states that he sent Richard Bentley (London) sheets of the first part on Feb. 28, 1850, and the remainder on Mar. 18, but Bentley refused to publish it as there were already two pirates at work. It was imported by Delf, London, who issued it in 1850, Fcp 8vo, 326 pp., at 5/0, listed by *PC* as published Mar. 29–Apr. 13 and Oct. 30–Nov. 19. It was also imported by John Chapman, London, who issued it in 1851, 12mo, 4/0, advertised in the *Ath* on June 28. A truly English edition was issued by J. Walker; David Bogue, London, etc., 1851, 17.5 cm., 320 pp., 4/0, in rose cloth with white endpapers coated on one side in cream. It was listed in the *Ath* and the *Literary Gazette* on May 17 and in *PC* on June 2. It was also issued by George Routledge & Co., London, 1851, 17.3 cm., 252 pp., 1/o, in green boards printed in blue, and at 1/6 cloth, listed in the *Ath* on May 24. Routledge reissued it, 1852, 53, 54 (35th thousand), and 56 (37th thousand). It was also issued by Henry G. Bohn, London, 1852, with the same collation and contents as the Bogue edition, 1/o in green boards and 1/6 cloth, *Bohn's Cheap Series* No. 38.

935 MRS. W.M.L. JAY (JULIA L.M. WOODRUFF) **Holden with the Cords.** 16mo. 1/6 sewed, 2/o cloth Mar. (*Bks*)
Star Series No. 103. The first edition was issued by E. P. Dutton & Co., New York, 1874, 19 cm., 517 pp., $2.00, listed in the *Nation* on Sept. 17 and in *PW* on Sept. 19. Dutton issued the 3rd thousand in 1874, 517 pp., $2.00, advertised in the *Nation* on Nov. 12. The first English edition was issued by James Nisbet & Co., London, 1874, Cr 8vo, 7/6, listed in the *Ath* and *Spect* on Oct. 31. Nisbet also issued it in 1875, 12mo, 3/6, listed in the *Spect* on Oct. 9.

936 CHARLES LEVER **Jack Hinton, the Guardsman.** p 8vo. o/6 sewed Mar. (*Bks*)
Notable Novels No. 89. Warne issued it in the *Library of Fiction* No. 21, Cr 8vo, 416 pp., 2/o boards, probably in 1892. This formed vol. 1 of "*Our Mess*," issued in 3 vols., 1843, 44 by William Curry Jr. & Co., Dublin, etc., edited by Charles Lever and illustrated by "Phiz," in rose-madder cloth with pale yellow endpapers. Vol. 1 ran in the *Dublin University Magazine*, Mar.–Dec. 1842. Curry issued "*Our Mess*" in 35 monthly 1/o parts in 34, No. 1 on Jan. 1, 1842, and Nos. 12 and 13 (the end of Jack Hinton) on Dec. 3, 1842. Vol. 1, 1843, had 396 pp., a frontispiece (portrait) and illus-

trations by "Phiz," listed in the *Spect* on Dec. 3, 1842, 14/o. Chapman & Hall, London, listed it in the *PC* for Aug. 1, 1850, 8vo, reduced to 7/o; and they issued it in 1857, Cr 8vo, 8 illustrations by "Phiz," 4/o, listed in the *Spect* on May 2—and it was still being advertised in Feb. 1859. The first American edition was issued by Carey & Hart, Philadelphia, 1843, 24 cm., 400 pp., illustrated by "Phiz," advertised in the *Globe*, a Washington, D.C., daily, by a Washington bookstore on Dec. 17, 1842, $.50, "Received this day."

937 MRS. ALEXANDER (ANNIE HECTOR) **Beaton's Bargain.** 12mo. 1/o sewed, 1/6 cloth Apr. 10 (*Spect*)
London Library No. 9. This is the first edition, no date, 188 pp. The first American edition was issued by Henry Holt, New York, 1886, 17 cm., 253 pp., *Leisure Hour Series* No. 187, $1.00, and *Leisure Moment Series*, $.25 paper, listed in *PW* on May 15 and in the *Nation* and *Ind* on May 20. Holt issued the 5th thousand, advertised on May 20. It was also issued by George Munro, New York (1886), 12mo, 205 pp., paper, *Seaside Library Pocket Edition* No. 794, listed in *PW* on May 29; and by J. S. Ogilvie, New York (1886), listed in *PW* on May 29; and by Norman Munro, New York (1886), 12mo, paper, *Munro's Library* No. 567, listed in *PW* on June 5.
Also 1900

938 G.P.R. JAMES **Morley Ernstein.** p 8vo. o/6 sewed Apr. (*Bks*)
Notable Novels No. 90. This has no date and 184 pp. The first edition was issued by Saunders & Otley, London, 3 vols., 1842, p 8vo, 31/6, in dark green cloth with labels, listed in the *Ath* on May 14. It was issued by Smith, Elder & Co., London, as No. 7 of their reprints of James's novels, 8/o, listed in the *Spect* on Jan. 3, 1846. In the United States it was issued by J. Winchester, New York, 1842, $.19, extra Nos.

3–5 of *The New World*, called the first edition. It was advertised in the *Globe*, a Washington, D.C., daily, by a Washington bookstore on June 18, 1842, as "Received this day." It was also issued by Harper & Brothers, New York, 1842, 18 cm., reviewed in the *Southern Quarterly Review* for Oct.

939 FREDERICK MARRYAT
The Privateersman. [New edition.]
p 8vo. o/6 sewed   Apr. (*Bks*)
Notable Novels No. 91. This has no date. It ran in *Colburn's New Monthly Magazine*, Aug. 1845–June 1846, and was issued by Longmans, London, 2 vols., 1846, 17.5 cm., 12/0, in dark purple-gray cloth with cream endpapers, some copies with ads. There is a 32-page catalog (May 1846) at the back of vol. 1. The title was *The Privateer's-Man, One Hundred Years Ago*, and it was listed in the *Ath* and the *Spect* on July 4. Henry G. Bohn, London, issued it in 2 vols. in 1853; issued a new edition in 1856, 12mo, 412 pp., 5/0, listed by *PC* as published Feb. 29–Mar. 14; and issued it in 1860, new edition, p 8vo, 8 illustrations, 5/0, advertised in *Notes and Queries* on Apr. 28. It was issued in the United States by Carey & Hart, Philadelphia, in 2 sections. Sadleir had a copy of the first section, *Log of a Privateersman, a Hundred Years Ago*, in brownish-salmon wrappers, 8vo, 48 pp., with 1846 on the cover and an ad on the back cover (Apr. 1, 1846). This first section covered about 300 pp. of the 750 in the London edition. Thus it is possible that the American edition was first.

940 BĪDPĀĪ **The Fables of Pilpay.**
Revised edition. Cr 8vo. Illustrated.
1/6 sewed, 2/0 cloth   May 22 (*Spect*)
Chandos Classics No. 121. This has no date and 274 pp. and is the same as the Baldwin, Cradock & Joy, etc., London, 1818, edition. It originated in India and was translated into Persian in the sixth century and into Arabic in the eighth century. *The*

Morall Philosophie of Doni was issued by Denham, London (1570), 19 cm., 111 leaves, illustrated; and *Kalila and Dimna* was issued by J. Parker, Oxford; Longmans, London, 1819, 8vo, translated by Wyndham Knatchbull, in light blue boards with a paper spine. *The Instructive and Entertaining Fables of Pilpay* was listed by the *Gentleman's Magazine* as published in Nov. 1746, 12mo, illustrated, 2/6; and it was issued with the same title in Newport, R.I., 1784, fourth edition, 119 pp., illustrated.

941 MARY H. FOOTE *John Bodewin's Testimony.* 12mo. 1/0 sewed, 1/6 cloth May 29 (*Ath* ad)
London Library No. 10. This is the first English edition, no date, 180 pp. The ad in the *Ath* is for the 10th thousand. The first American edition was issued by Ticknor & Co., Boston, 1886, 19 cm., 344 pp., $1.50, advertised in the *New-York Times* on Apr. 24 and listed in the *Nation* on May 6. They reissued it in 1888, $.50 paper, listed in the *Nation* on Oct. 25.
Also 1900

942 OCTAVE FEUILLET *Aliette.* Cr 8vo.
1/0 sewed, 2/6 cloth   June 26 (*Ath* ad)
Library of Continental Authors No. 1. This is the first English edition, a translation of *La Morte*, which was first issued in Paris, 1886, 19 cm., 306 pp. Warne reissued it in this series in 1891, Cr 8vo, 1/0 sewed, listed by *PC* on Oct. 24. The first American edition was issued by D. Appleton & Co., New York, 1886, 18.5 cm., 250 pp., translated by J. H. Hager, $.50 paper, $.75 half-bound, listed in the *Nation* on May 20 and in *Christian Union* on May 6.

943 EVELYN EVERETT-GREEN **The Last of the Dacres.** 12mo. 1/0 sewed, 1/6 cloth June (*Bks*)
London Library No. 11. This is the first edition, no date, 179 pp.
Also 1900

944 SAMUEL LOVER *Treasure Trove.*
p 8vo. o/6 sewed June (*Bks*)

Notable Novels No. 92. Warne also issued
this as *He Would Be a Gentleman*, 1892, my
copy, 18.2 cm., 450 pp., yellow pictorial
boards, printed in red, blue, and black,
with the *Library of Fiction* on the spine, this
being No. 21 of that series. It has publisher's ads on the endpapers and on 2
leaves at the back, and there is a commercial ad on the back cover. The dedication is
dated Jan. 1, 1844. In the ads the *Chandos
Classics* end with No. 132. This was first issued in England as £ *S. D.: Treasure Trove*,
in parts, 1/o monthly, part 1 listed in the
Spect on Jan. 6, 1844, and part 10 on Oct.
14 1843, etc. The parts were bound up in
1 vol. and issued as *Treasure Trove* by Frederick Lover, London, 1844, 8vo, 411 pp.,
with frontispiece and 25 plates by Lover,
listed in the *Ath* on Jan. 4, 1844. Sadleir's
copy is in light claret cloth with pale yellow
endpapers, and Wolff's copy is in scarlet
cloth. Henry G. Bohn, London, issued it,
1845, the same, 9/o; and David Bryce,
London, issued it (1854), Fcp 8vo, 2/o
boards, bright green, printed in black;
and Darton & Hodge, London, issued it
(1862) as *Parlour Library* No. 275. The first
American edition was issued by D. Appleton & Co., New York, etc., 1844, 23.5 cm.,
173 pp., illustrated, with the parts title,
listed in *Godey's Lady's Book* for Mar. It was
also issued by J. Winchester, New York,
1844, 29 cm., 80 pp., extra no. of *The New
World*, dated Jan. 1844, with the parts title
as a caption title.

945 FIRDAUSI *The Sháh Námeh.* Cr 8vo.
1/6 sewed, 2/o cloth July 17 (*Spect*)

Chandos Classics No. 122. This has no date
and 412 pp., translated and abridged by
James Atkinson and edited by J. A. Atkinson. Warne advertised it in the *Times
Weekly Edition*, on July 19, 1889, Cr 8vo,
1/6 stiff wrappers, 2/o cloth, 2/6 half Rox-

burghe; and reissued it in the present series, 1892, new edition, 412 pp. They issued it in New York in smooth dark blue
cloth with paper labels in red and black,
uncut edges, $2.00, listed in the *Nation* on
Oct. 14, 1886. The first edition was in
Persian (A.D. 1010), 6,000 rhyming coup-
lets. It was issued in London by S. Wes-
ton, 1815, 8vo, 125 pp., *Episodes from the
Shah Nemeh*, listed in the *Critical Review*
(monthly) for Aug. It was issued in London in 4 vols. in 1831, 8vo, 210/o in
boards, listed in the *Westminster Review*
(quarterly) for Oct. The first edition from
which the present edition was taken was issued by the Oriental Translation Fund
and sold by John Murray, etc., London,
1832, 8vo, 608 pp., illustrated, 16/o, reviewed in the *Monthly Review* (London)
for Oct.

946 GEORGE OHNET *Edmée.* Cr 8vo. 1/o
sewed Aug. (*Bks*)

Library of Continental Authors No. 2. This is
the first English edition, no date, 189 pp.
Warne issued the second edition in this series, 1887. The first edition was issued in
Paris, 1886, *Les Dames de Croix-Mort*, 18
cm., 327 pp., and the present edition is a
translation of the 80th French edition.

**947 WILLIAM G. WATERS *My Friend
Bellamy.* 12mo. Illustrated. 1/o sewed**
Aug. (*Bks*)

London Library No. 12. This is the first edition, no date, 124 pp.

**948 PRINCESS OLGA CANTACUZÈNE-
ALTIERI *Irène.* Cr 8vo. 1/o sewed Sept.?**

Library of Continental Authors No. 3. This is
the first English edition, no date, 192 pp.,
reviewed in the *Ath* on Oct. 2. The first edition was issued in Paris, 1886, 319 pp.

949 LEON DE TINSEAU *Hélène.* Cr 8vo.
1/o sewed Oct. (*Bks*)

Library of Continental Authors No. 4. This is
the first English edition, no date, 208 pp.,

from the 24th French edition. Warne issued it in the United States, 1887, $.35 paper, listed in *PW* on Jan. 15, 1887, and in the *Ind* on Feb. 3. The first edition was issued in Paris, *Madame Villeferon Jeune*, 18.5 cm., 391 pp.

950 ANNE MARSH, later MARSH-CALDWELL *Two Old Men's Tales.* p 8vo. o/6 sewed Oct. (*Bks*)

Notable Novels No. 93. The first edition was issued by Saunders & Otley, London, 2 vols., 1834, p 8vo, anonymous, 21/0 boards with labels, listed in the *Ath* on May 3. Bentley issued this as *Standard Novels* No. 94, 1844, my copy, 364 pp., in May; and Simms & M'Intyre, London and Belfast, issued it in the *Parlour Library* No. 43, 1850, 287 pp., also in May. The first American edition was issued by Harper & Brothers, New York, 2 vols., 1834, 20 cm., anonymous, $1.25, in claret colored linen cloth with white endpapers, advertised in the *Globe*, a Washington, D.C., daily, by a Washington bookstore on Sept. 3 and reviewed in the *Knickerbocker* for Sept.

951 BEATRICE MARSHALL *Nancy's Nephew.* 12mo. Illustrated. 2/0 cloth Nov. 6 (*Spect*)

Home Circle Gift Books. This was reviewed in the *Ath* on Dec. 18 and is also given by the *Eng Cat*, but otherwise I cannot trace it. Warne also issued this in the *Bedford Library* in 1889, 12mo, illustrated, 1/6 cloth, given by the *Eng Cat*.

952 CECILIA S. LOWNDES *Linford Green.* 12mo. Illustrated. 2/0 cloth Nov. 6 (*Ath*)

Home Circle Gift Books. This is the first edition. It is also given by the *Eng Cat*. Warne also issued it in 1895 in the *Bedford Library*, 12mo, illustrated, 1/6 cloth, listed in *PC* on Nov. 2.

953 HENRY FRITH *The Wrecking of the "Samphire."* 12mo. Illustrated 1/0 cloth Nov. 13 (*Ath* ad)

Gordon Library No. 1. This has 128 pp. and is also in the *Eng Cat*, but otherwise I cannot trace it.

954 R. ANDRE *The Outpost.* 12mo. Illustrated. 1/0 cloth Nov. 13 (*Ath* ad)

Gordon Library No. 2. This has 128 pp. and is also given by the *Eng Cat*.

955 WILLIAM J. GORDON *Under the Avalanche.* 12mo. Illustrated. 1/0 cloth Nov. 13 (*Ath* ad)

Gordon Library No. 3. This is 1886, 126 pp. It was reviewed in the *Ath* on Dec. 11.

956 ARTHUR L. KNIGHT *The Gun-Room Heroes.* 12mo. Illustrated. 1/0 cloth Nov. 13 (*Ath* ad)

Gordon Library No. 4. This is also given by the *Eng Cat*, but otherwise I cannot trace it.

957 WILLIAM J. GORDON *The King's Thrope.* 12mo. Illustrated. 1/0 cloth Nov. 13 (*Ath* ad)

Gordon Library No. 5. This was "On our table" in the *Ath* for Dec. 25 and is also given by the *Eng Cat*.

958 THOMAS KEYWORTH *Granny's Boy.* p 8vo. Illustrated. 2/6 cloth Nov.?

This is probably the first edition, as it was reviewed in the *Ath* on Dec. 11 and is also given by the *Eng Cat*.

959 LEOPOLD WAGNER, ed. *Modern Readings and Recitations in Prose and Verse.* p 8vo. 1/0 cloth Nov.?

Albion Reciter. This is the first edition, no date, 144 pp. It was "On our table" in the

Ath for Dec. 18 and was reissued in this series in 1895, 1/0, advertised in *PC* on May 11.

960 FRANCES H. BURNETT *A Woman's Will.* 12mo. 1/0 sewed Dec. 7 (*Bks*)
London Library No. 13. This is the first edition, no date, 119 pp. This was reissued in the series in 1889, my copy, no date, 17.4 cm., 119 pp., in light gray wrappers printed in blue with the series title on the cover, and a printer's date (Apr. 30, 1889). It has commercial ads on the back and inside covers and a page of publisher's ads at the front and back, the ads giving the series through No. 30.

961 ELIOT WARBURTON *The Crescent and the Cross.* Cr 8vo. 2/0 boards, 2/6 cloth 1886 (*Eng Cat*)
This is my copy, 1886, 18.7 cm., 380 pp. including an appendix and index, in white boards, pictorially printed in dark blue and with a vignette in blue on the back cover. It has a printer's date (Oct. 15, 1886) and plain white endpapers. It may have been reissued in 1887, as it was noticed in the *Spect* on July 16, 1887, no details given. Warne issued it in New York in 1887, 12mo, $1.00 cloth, advertised in the *Nation* on Oct. 6. The first edition was issued by Henry Colburn, London, 2 vols., 1845, 20 cm., illustrated, 25/0, listed in the *Ath* on Nov. 16, 1844. Colburn issued the second edition, revised and corrected, 2 vols., in 1845, illustrated, 21/0, advertised in the *Spect* on May 17 as "Now ready"; and issued the third edition, the same, advertised on Sept. 27; the fourth edition, the same, advertised on Feb. 14, 1846, "Now ready"; and the eighth edition in 1850, revised with a new preface, illustrated, 10/6, advertised in the *Spect* on Dec. 7, 1850, as "Now ready." Hurst & Blackett, London, the successors of Colburn, issued it, 1855, 11th edition, 20 cm., illustrated, 380 pp.,

and purchased the copyright for 420 g. and the Colburn stock for 58/10. They issued the 12th edition in 1856, illustrated, 6/0, advertised in *Notes & Queries* on Nov. 12 as "Just published"; and issued the 15th edition in 1859, illustrated, 5/0, advertised in *Notes & Queries* on Mar. 5. The first American edition was issued by Wiley & Putnam, New York, 2 vols, 1845, 18 cm., *Library of Choice Reading*, noticed in the *Knickerbocker* for July and also in *Godey's Lady's Book* for July. G. P. Putnam, New York, issued a new edition, 12mo, $1.00 in green cloth, listed in *Lit W* as published Aug. 19–26, 1848; and issued it in 1849, 12mo, illustrated, $2.00 cloth, advertised in *Lit W* on Aug. 25.

962 THE OLD SAILOR (MATTHEW H. BARKER) *Tough Yarns.* p 8vo. 0/6 sewed 1886 (*Eng Cat*)
Notable Novels No. 87. The first edition was issued by Effingham Wilson, London, 1835, 17.5 cm., anonymous, 351 pp., illustrated, 10/6, in green or blue cloth, by the old sailor, frontispiece, vignette title page, 7 full-page and textual illustrations by Cruikshank. It was listed in the *Spect* on Nov. 29, 1834, and in the *Ath* on Dec. 13. It contains 11 tales. The first American edition was issued by Carey & Hart, Philadelphia, 2 vols., 1835, 12mo, anonymous, $1.25, advertised in the *Globe*, a Washington, D.C., daily, by a Washington bookstore on May 7, 1835, "Just received" and listed in the *North American Review* (quarterly) for July.

963 FRANKLIN FOX *How to Send a Boy to Sea.* 12mo. 1/0 1886 (*Eng Cat*)
Useful Books. This is the first edition, 1886, 112 pp. Warne reissued it in 1890, Fcp 8vo, 1/0 cloth, advertised in the *Times Weekly Edition* on May 2.

964 ANONYMOUS ***The Boys of Holy Writ and Bible Narratives.*** 12mo. Illustrated. 2/6 cloth 1886 (*Eng Cat*)

Golden Links Series. This has no date and 296 pp., with 6 plates. The first edition was issued by Warne, 1865, square 12mo, 296 pp., colored illustrations, 3/6, listed in the *Ath* on Sept. 23.

965 ANONYMOUS ***Female Characters of Holy Writ.*** 12mo. Illustrated. 2/6 cloth 1886 (*Eng Cat*)

Golden Links Series. The first edition was issued by Warne in 1866, 3/6, advertised in the *Ath* on May 26.

Frederick Warne & Co.
London and New York
1887

966 RICHARD COBBOLD *The History of Margaret Catchpole.* p 8vo. o/6 sewed Feb. (*Bks*)

Notable Novels No. 94. The first edition was issued by Henry Colburn, London, 3 vols., 1845, 20.5 cm., anonymous, illustrated by the author, 31/6, in plum cloth with a 24-page catalog at the back of vol. 3 dated 1845. It was listed in the *Ath* on Mar. 1. Colburn issued a second edition, 2 vols., 1845, Fcp 8vo, illustrated, 12/o, advertised in the *Spect* on Apr 19; and a third edition, 1845, 19.5 cm., 393 pp., illustrated, 10/6, advertised in the *Spect* on Jan. 10, 1846. It was issued by Longmans, London, new edition, in 1848, Fcp 8vo, 2 illustrations, 7/6, advertised in the *Spect* on Jan. 29. It was issued by Simms & M'Intyre, London and Belfast, 1852, 368 pp., as *Parlour Library* No. 74, on Mar. 1. The first American edition was *The History and Extraordinary Adventures of Margaret Catchpole* issued by D. Appleton & Co., New York, 1846, 167 pp., illustrated, paper, the first American from the third English edition, by Cobbold. It was listed in the *Merchants' Magazine* (monthly) for May and noticed in the *Southern Quarterly Review* for Apr.

967 BLANCHE WILLIS HOWARD, later VON TEUFFEL *Guenn: A Wave on the Breton Coast.* 12mo. Illustrated. 2/o boards Mar. 26 (*Ath*)

Library of Fiction No. 5. This has no date, in salmon pink boards with 2 pp. of ads and

ads on the endpapers giving the series through No. 4, and there is a commercial ad on the back cover. It was reissued in 1891, Cr 8vo, 2/o, which was either an issue in boards in the series or in the *Crown Library* at 2/o cloth. It was listed in the *Spect* on Oct. 10. I have a copy, no date, issued in 1893, 19 cm., 439 pp., cream pictorial boards, printed in red, blue, and black with the series title on the spine. It has publisher's ads on the endpapers and a commercial ad on the back cover. The *London Library* in the ads ends with No. (43), and the *Library of Continental Authors* ends with No. (9). The first English edition was issued by Trübner & Co., London (1883), Cr 8vo, 439 pp. illustrated, 6/o, listed in the *Spect* on Nov. 10, 1883, and in the *Ath* on Nov. 24. It was also issued by Warne, 1884, 439 pp., illustrated, 6/o, listed in the *Ath* on Feb. 23. The first American edition was *A Wave on the Breton Coast*, issued by J. R. Osgood & Co., Boston, 1884, 12mo, illustrated, $1.75, a duplicate of the Warne edition with a different title page. It was listed in *PW* on Dec. 8 and in *Lit W* on Dec. 1, 1883, and the 10th thousand was advertised in the *New-York Times* on Dec. 11, 1883, $1.75, as "Now ready."

968 LAURA VALENTINE *The Queen, Her Early Life and Reign.* Cr 8vo. Illustrated 1/o stiff picture wrappers, 1/6 cloth, 2/6 cloth Apr. 2 (*Ath* ad)

This is the first edition, 1887, 376 pp. Warne issued the third edition, the 30th thousand, advertised in the *Ath* on Apr. 23. They issued it in New York, Cr 8vo, illustrated, $.50 in a fancy cover, $.75 cloth, etc., advertised in the *Nation* on June 16, 1887. They reissued it in 1892, in England, Cr 8vo, illustrated, 2/6 boards, listed in *PC* on Oct. 15; and reissued it, revised and brought down to date, in 1896, no date, Cr 8vo, 384 pp., 1/0 wrappers with portrait; 2/6 cloth and 1/6 cloth, both illustrated. The wrapper cover had a portrait of Queen Victoria. It was listed in *PC* on Sept. 12.

969 FRANCES H. BURNETT *Theo.* 12mo. 1/0 sewed   Apr. 2 (*Ath* ad)
London Library No. 15.
Also 1878

970 BLANCHE WILLIS HOWARD, later VON TEUFFEL *Aulnay Tower.* 12mo. 2/0 boards   Apr. 23 (*Ath* ad)
Library of Fiction No. 6. This has 343 pp. I have a copy, no date, 18.4 cm., 343 pp., in pale yellow pictorial boards, printed in red, blue, and black with the series title on the spine. It has publisher's ads on the endpapers and on 3 leaves at the back and a commercial ad on the back cover. In the ads the *London Library* ends with No. (43); I place this copy as issued in 1893. The first edition was issued by Ticknor & Co., Boston, 1885, 19.5 cm., 343 pp., $1.50, advertised in the *New-York Times* on July 20 as "This day" and listed in *Lit W* on Aug. 8. They reissued it in 1888, $.50, listed in the *Nation* on Aug. 30. The *Christian Union* reported James R. Osgood & Co. as going out of business in the issue for May 14, 1885, and that it was to be succeeded by Ticknor and Co. The present title was the first publication of Ticknor & Co. Th first English edition was issued by Warne in 1885, Cr 8vo, 343 pp., 6/0, listed in the *Ath* on Sept. 12.

971 LEW WALLACE *The Fair God.* Cr 8vo. 2/0 cloth   Apr. 30 (*Spect*)
Crown Library No. 16. This is probably the first English edition, although it might have been imported by Sampson Low, London, as he advertised it in *PC* on Dec. 31, 1873. This Warne issue is 1887, 18.5 cm., 411 pp. The first edition was issued by James R. Osgood & Co., Boston, 1873, 19.5 cm., 586 pp., $2.00, in green, purple, or terra-cotta cloth with beveled boards and brown endpapers, listed in *PW* on Sept. 13 and in the *Nation* on Sept. 18. It was bound, Aug. 28–Sept. 10, from an edition of 2,500 copies. A second printing of 2,020 copies, in green or purple cloth, without the beveled covers, was bound Sept. 24–Oct. 4. Houghton, Mifflin & Co., Boston and New York, issued it in 1887, 600 pp., $1.50, advertised in the *Christian Union* on Feb. 17.

972 (SUSAN WARNER) *The End of a Coil.* 16mo. 1/6 sewed, 2/0 cloth   May 1 (*PC*)
Star Series No. 106. This has no date and 514 pp. The first American edition was issued by Robert Carter & Brothers, New York, 1880, 19 cm., anonymous, 718 pp., $1.75, in blue, brown, or terra-cotta cloth with pale yellow endpapers. It was advertised in the *New-York Times* on Oct. 2 as "On Oct. 4," listed in *PW* on Oct. 9, and deposited at the Boston Athenaeum on Oct. 11. The first English edition was issued by James Nisbet & Co., London, 1880, 19 cm., anonymous, illustrated, 3/6 cloth, in the *Golden Ladder Series.* It was listed in the *Ath* on Oct. 9 and in *PC* on Oct. 15.

973 JOHANN VON SCHILLER *The Poems and Ballads of Schiller.* Cr 8vo. 1/6 sewed, 2/0 cloth   May 28 (*Spect*)
Chandos Classics No. 127. This has 384 pp. and is a translation by Edward Bulwer Lytton. It ran in *Blackwood's Magazine* ending in Aug. 1843 and was issued by William Blackwood & Sons, Edinburgh and Lon-

don, 2 vols., 1844, 20.5 cm., 21/0, listed in the *Spect* on Mar. 30. They issued a second edition, corrected and improved, in 1852, Cr 8vo, 10/6, listed in the *Spect* on Jan. 3, 1852. It was issued in the United States by Harper & Brothers, New York, 1844, 19 cm., 424 pp., noticed in *Graham's Magazine* (monthly) for Aug. Warne issued it in New York in 1887, *Chandos Classics*, $1.00, in smooth blue cloth, listed in the *Nation* on Aug. 18. It was also issued by George Routledge & Sons, London, 1887, 19 cm., 276 pp., with an introduction by Henry Morley, *Morley's Universal Library* No. 51. A collection of Schiller's poems, *Gedichte*, was issued in Leipzig, 2 vols., 1800–03, 18 cm.

974 FREDERICK MARRYAT *Newton Forster.* p 8vo. 0/6 sewed   May (*Bks*)

This is a reissue in *Notable Novels*. Also 1874

975 ANNE WARNER *The Blue Flag and Cloth of Gold.* 16mo. 1/0 sewed, 1/6 cloth   June 1 (*PC*)

Star Series No. 107. The first edition was issued by Robert Carter & Brothers, New York, 1880, 18 cm., 359 pp., frontispiece, with 6 pp. of ads, in blue, terra-cotta, maroon, or brown cloth, with buff endpapers, listed in *PW* on Sept. 27, 1879 (*sic*). The first English edition was issued by James Nisbet & Co., London, 1880, Cr 8vo, 275 pp., 2/6 cloth, listed in the *Ath* on Nov. 22, 1879, and in *PC* on Dec. 6.

976 (SUSAN WARNER) *The Letter of Credit.* 16mo. 1/6 sewed, 2/0 cloth June 15 (*PC*)

Star Series No. 105. The first American edition was issued by Robert Carter & Brothers, New York, 1882, 19 cm., anonymous, 733 pp., $1.75, in blue, light brown, mustard, green, or terra-cotta cloth with cream endpapers. Some copies have 10 pp. of ads (Oct. 1880). It was deposited Oct. 8, 1881, advertised in the *New-York*

Times on Oct. 15, and listed in *PW* on Oct. 15. The first English edition was issued by James Nisbet & Co., London, 1881, Cr 8vo, anonymous, 3/6, in the *Golden Ladder Series*, deposited Oct. 10 and listed in the *Ath* on Oct. 15, 1881.

977 CHARLES LEVER *Tom Burke of "Ours."* p 8vo. 0/6 sewed   June (*Bks*)

Notable Novels No. 95. Warne reissued this in this series, no date, probably 1895, my copy, 21.2 cm., 216 pp. in double columns, white pictorial wrappers, printed in red, blue, and black with the series title on the front and the no. at the base of the spine. There is a dedication (Nov. 25, 1843). Commercial ads are on the back cover and the inside front cover, and publisher's ads are on the inside back cover and on 4 leaves at the back. The ad on the front cover bears a date (Oct. 25, 1894), and the ad on the back cover lists the *Library of Fiction* through No. 32. The first edition was as vols. 2 and 3 of *"Our Mess,"* edited by Charles Lever, 3 vols., 1843–44, 8vo, illustrated with frontispieces and plates by "Phiz," in rose-madder cloth with pale yellow endpapers. It was issued by William Curry Jr. & Co., Dublin, etc., vol. 2 listed in the *Ath* on Dec. 9, 1843, 13/0; and vol. 3 listed Sept. 21, 1844, 11/0. Curry had issued it in 35 monthly 1/0 parts; Nos. 24 and 25 as well as Nos. 34 and 35 were double nos. Part 1 was advertised in the *Ath* on Jan. 28, 1843, as "This day," and part No. 14 began vol. 2, listed in the *Spect* on Feb. 4. Part No. 26 began vol. 3. In the *PC* listing for July 14–29, 1850, 2 vols., 8vo, reduced to 7/0 each were given as by Chapman & Hall, London. The latter issued it, 1857, illustrated by "Phiz"; and issued it in 2 vols. in 1859, Cr 8vo, 8 illustrations by "Phiz" in each vol., 4/0 each, advertised in *Notes & Queries* on Feb. 5. The first American edition was issued by Carey & Hart, Philadelphia, 1844, 23 cm., 310 pp., illustrated by "Phiz," in dark blue cloth with 12 pp. of ads at the back.

978 CHARLES DICKENS *The Life and Adventures of Martin Chuzzlewit.*
p 8vo. 0/6 sewed   June (*Bks*)

Notable Novels No. 96. This was first issued by Chapman & Hall, London, 20 parts, monthly at 1/0, in 19, green wrappers with a cover design by "Phiz." The parts appeared Jan. 1, 1843–July 1844, 22.5 cm., 624 pp., edited by "Boz," illustrated by "Phiz." They issued it in 1 vol., 1844, 22 cm., 624 pp., illustrated by "Phiz," 21/0, in blue cloth, with a preface (June 25, 1844), listed in the *Ath* on July 13. A. & W. Galignani, Paris, issued it in 2 vols., 1844, 12mo, edited by "Boz." Chapman & Hall issued it in 1½ penny weekly nos. and 0/7 monthly parts, then bound up in 1 vol., Cr 8vo, 5/0, with a new preface, listed in the *Spect* on Dec. 1, 1849. In the United States it was issued by J. Winchester, New York, in the supplement to *The New World*, vol. 1, Nos. 1–12, and probably also continuing in vol. 2. Vol. 1, Jan.–Dec. 1843, took the story to chapter 32, the latter being issued in London in Dec. 1843. In the listing in the *Knickerbocker* for May 1843 it was stated that *The New World* issued the parts with 4 other serials at 1/0. It was issued as 1 vol., no date, 29 cm., 250 pp., reviewed in the *Knickerbocker* for Sept. 1844. It was also issued by Harper & Brothers, New York, 1844, 8vo, 312 pp., illustrated by "Phiz," having been issued in 7 parts, in blue wrappers at $.06½ each, part 1 noticed in the *Southern Literary Messenger* for May 1843 and part 3 in Nov. The *Knickerbocker* for Mar. 1843 reported that the first 2 chapters have appeared. It was edited by "Boz." It was also issued by Lea & Blanchard, Philadelphia, 1844, 8vo, 320 pp., illustrated by "Phiz" with a frontispiece and 12 plates, noticed in the *Southern Literary Messenger* for Sept. 1844. It was issued without authorization, as Dickens refused to send them advanced sheets. I think it was also issued by them in parts.

979 ANNE MARSH, later MARSH-CALDWELL *Mount Sorel.* p 8vo.
0/6 sewed   June (*Bks*)

Notable Novels No. 97. This is my copy, no date, probably 1887, 21 cm., 182 pp. in double columns, yellow pictorial wrappers, printed in red, green, and black with the series title on the front and the title and no. on the spine. There are commercial ads on both sides of the back cover and publisher's ads on the inside front cover and on 7 pp. at the back. The series in the ads ends with No. 93. The first appearance was in 4 monthly vols., 3/0 sewed each, Jan. 1–Apr. 1, 1845, in a new experiment by Chapman & Hall, London. Sadleir has the dates incorrect. They issued it in 2 vols., 1845, 19.5 cm., anonymous, 14/0 in rose-madder cloth, with a 4-page prospectus at the front of vol. 1 (Nov. 1844), listed in the *Spect* on Apr. 5. There was a second issue, 2 vols., 1845, in rose-madder cloth, with a catalog at the end of vol. 2 (Sept. 1846) and with the prospectus of 1 leaf only. Thomas Hodgson, London, issued it (1856), 365 pp., in the *Parlour Library* No. 134; it was reissued by C. H. Clarke, London, in 1860 at 1/6 boards. The first American edition was issued by Harper & Brothers, New York, 1845, anonymous, 156 pp., listed in *Godey's Lady's Book* for June.

980 G.P.R. JAMES *The Brigand.* p 8vo.
0/6 sewed   June (*Bks*)

Notable Novels No. 98. The first edition was *Corse de Léon*, issued by Longmans, London, 3 vols., 1841, 19 cm., 31/6, listed in the *Ath* and *Spect* on Feb. 20. It was issued by Smith, Elder & Co., London, in 1846, medium 8vo, frontispiece, 8/0 cloth, No. 10 in a reissue of James's novels, listed in the *Spect* on Oct. 10. The first American edition was issued by Harper & Brothers, New York, 2 vols., 1841, with the English title, given a short review in the *Knickerbocker* for May and listed in the *New York Review* (quarterly) for July.

981 JEAN MIDDLEMASS **A Girl in a Thousand.** 12mo. 1/0 sewed June (*Bks*)

London Library No. 16. The first edition was issued by Chapman & Hall, London, 2 vols., 1885, Cr 8vo, 21/0, listed in the *Ath* on Oct. 17.

Also 1900

982 ALICE PRICE (ADELINE SERGEANT) **A Wilful Young Woman.** 12mo. 1/0 sewed June (*Bks*)

London Library No. 17. This is 1887, 190 pp. The first edition was issued by Hurst & Blackett, London, 3 vols., 1886, Cr 8vo, 31/6, listed in the *Ath* on Oct. 30. In the United States it was issued by Harper & Brothers, New York, in 1886, anonymous, 60 pp., $.20 paper, *Franklin Square Library* No. 556, listed in the *Nation* on Dec. 16 and *PW* on Dec. 18, 1886. It was also issued by George Munro, New York (1886), 283 pp., *Seaside Library Pocket Edition* No. 908, in Dec. 1886. It was also issued by John W. Lovell, New York (1887), 12mo, anonymous, 272 pp., paper, *Lovell's Library* No. 857, in Jan. 1887.

Also 1900

983 COUNTESS OF ——— (COUNTESS MARIE DE MIRABEAU) **Harlette.** Cr 8vo. 1/0 sewed Aug. (*Bks*)

Library of Continental Authors No. 5. This is the first edition in English, 208 pp. The first edition was in Paris, 1886, anonymous, 355 pp.

984 ALEXANDER C. EWALD, ed. **The Spectator. Selected Essays.** Cr 8vo. 1/6 sewed, 2/0 cloth Oct. 1 (*Ath* ad)

Chandos Classics No. 128. This is the first edition thus. This was listed in the *Spect* on Nov. 19. It was still advertised in Nov. 1891, Cr 8vo, 2/0, blue cloth, uncut edges. Warne issued it in New York, *Chandos Classics* No. 128, noticed in the *Christian Union* on Nov. 3, 1887.

985 SUSAN COOLIDGE (SARAH WOOLSEY) **What Katy Did Next.** 16mo. 1/0 sewed, 1/6 cloth Oct. 1 (*Ath* ad)

Star Series No. 104. The first English edition was issued by Warne in 1886, Cr 8vo, illustrated, 3/6 cloth, advertised in the *Ath* on Oct. 23. The first American edition was issued by Roberts Brothers, Boston, 1886, 17.5 cm., 323 pp., frontispiece, listed in the *Nation* on Oct. 28 and in *PW* on Oct. 30.

986 LOUIS HOFFMANN (ANGELO LOUIS) **Tips for Tricyclists.** 24mo. Illustrated 1/0 boards, 1/6 cloth Oct. 1 (*Ath* ad)

This Oct. 1 ad was for the second edition, "Now ready." The first edition was Warne, 1887, 115 pp., illustrated. They issued the fourth edition, 1890, 142 pp., illustrated, still advertised in Sept. 1891, 1/0 boards, 1/6 cloth. Warne issued it in New York in 1888, small square, illustrated, $.50, advertised in the *New-York Times* on May 20.

987 HARRY PARKES **The Man Who Would Like to Marry.** Oblong p 8vo. Illustrated. 1/0 limp printed wrapper Oct. 29 (*Ath* ad)

The *Ath* ad said second edition, "Now ready." The first edition was issued by Warne (1887), oblong p 8vo, with 12 plates. Warne also issued the fourth edition in 1887, advertised in the *Ath* on Nov. 26; and the fifth edition in 1887, the same, 1/0 sewed, advertised in the *Spect* on Dec. 10. The 12th edition was advertised in the *Times Weekly Edition* on May 24, 1889; it was issued oblong 4to, 0/6, listed in the *Bks* for July 1890.

988 HARRY PARKES **The Girl Who Wouldn't Mind Getting Married.** Oblong 8vo., Illustrated. 1/0 limp printed wrapper. Nov. 26 (*Ath* ad)

This is the first edition, no date, 24½ × 29½ cm., 12 plates. The *Ath* ad said "Just ready." Warne issued the third edition, the same, advertised in the *Spect* on Dec. 10, 1887, and the tenth edition, advertised in the *TWEd* on May 24, 1889; and they issued it in oblong 4to, o/6, listed in the *Bks* for July 1890.

989 WILLIAM T. ADEY, ed. *Sunday School Readings, Recitations, and Dialogues, in Prose and Verse.* p 8vo. 1/o cloth 1887 (*Eng Cat*)

Albion Reciter. Warne reissued this, 1891, 142 pp., and it was advertised in *PC* on May 11, 1895, at 1/o.

990 LEOPOLD WAGNER, ed. *New Readings from American Authors, in Prose and Verse.* p 8vo. 1/o cloth 1887 (*Eng Cat*)

Albion Reciter. Warne reissued this, 1889, 144 pp., and advertised it in *PC* on May 11, 1895, 1/o.

991 WILLIAM J. GORDON *Pursued.* 12mo. 1/o 1887 (*Eng Cat*)

I cannot trace this.

992 HOMER GREENE *The Blind Brother.* Square 16mo. 1/o 1887 (*Eng Cat*)

I am doubtful of this *Eng Cat* entry. The *BM* gives only T. Nelson & Sons, London, 1888, 144 pp.; the *U Cat* gives T. Y. Crowell & Co., New York (copyright 1887), 20 cm., 229 pp., illustrated, and gives also with the same imprint and date, 166 pp., illustrated.

993 JOHN P. GROVES *The Major's Complaint.* 12mo. 1/o 1887 (*Eng Cat*)

I cannot trace this.

994 D. RICHMOND *Katie.* 12mo. Illustrated. 2/o cloth 1887 (*Eng Cat*)

Home Circle Gift Books. The first edition was issued by Bell & Daldy, London, 1862, 305 pp., illustrated. A second edition was listed in the *Ath* on Sept. 25, 1875, 3/6 cloth, issued by Bell & Daldy, no date, 305 pp., illustrated.

995 ANONYMOUS *Young England's Nursery Rhymes.* Cr 8vo. Colored illustrations. 1/6 picture boards, 2/6 cloth 1887 (*Eng Cat*)

This is the first edition, no date, the 1/6 in colored, glazed, pictorial yellow boards with a colored pictorial title page, a frontispiece, and colored illustrations, listed in the *Spect* on Oct. 8. Warne issued a second edition, the 40th thousand, advertised in the *Ath* on Nov. 26, 1887.

996 HENRY COCKTON *The Life and Adventures of Valentine Box.* p 8vo. o/6 sewed 1887?

Notable Novels No. 99. Warne issued this in their *Crown Library,* 1889, 19 cm., 602 pp., 2/o cloth; and in their *Library of Fiction* No. 15, Cr 8vo, 2/o boards, listed in *PC* on July 11, 1891. It was first issued in 20 monthly parts in 19, by Robert Tyas, London, No. 1 listed in the *Spect* on Apr. 6, 1839, and Nos. 19–20 listed Oct. 10, 1840. Tyas issued it in 1 vol., 1840, 22 cm., 620 pp., illustrated, 21/o, listed in the *Ath* on Oct. 17. George Routledge & Co., London, issued it in 1844, 8vo, reduced to 1/6 cloth, advertised in the *Illustrated London News* on Nov. 16. Henry Lea, London, issued it, 2/o boards, in 1859. The first American edition was issued by Carey & Hart, Philadelphia, 1841, 24 cm., 395 pp., illustrated by "Phiz," reviewed in the *Southern Literary Messenger* for Oct. They reissued it in 1848, new edition, $.50, listed by *Lit W* as published Feb. 26–Mar. 4.

997 G.P.R. JAMES *The Smuggler.* p 8vo. o/6 sewed 1887?

Notable Novels No. 100. The first English edition was issued by Smith, Elder & Co., London, 3 vols., 20 cm., 31/6 in boards, half brown-purple cloth with labels, listed in the *Ath* on May 10 and in the *Spect* on May 17. It has a 24-page catalog at the back of vol. 1 (Dec. 1844). Simms & M'Intyre, London and Belfast, issued it, 1851, 447 pp., *Parlour Library* No. 49, on Nov. 1, 1850. The first American edition was issued by Harper & Brothers, New York, 1845, in the *Library of Select Novels*, noticed in the *Southern Quarterly Review* for July and in the *Southern Literary Messenger* for Aug.

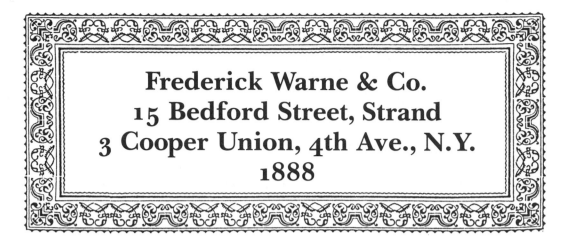

Frederick Warne & Co.
15 Bedford Street, Strand
3 Cooper Union, 4th Ave., N.Y.
1888

This New York address was given in the Nation *on July 5, 1888, in a Warne ad and in the* New-York Times *on May 20.*

998 AMELIA E. BARR *A Daughter of Fife.* 16mo. 1/6 sewed, 2/0 cloth   Feb.?

Star Series No. 108. The first English edition was issued by J. Clarke & Co., London, 1886, Cr 8vo, 335 pp., 3/6 cloth. The second edition was advertised in the *Times Weekly Edition* on Nov. 26, Cr 8vo, 3/6. The first American edition was issued by Dodd, Mead & Co., New York, 1886, 17 cm., 335 pp., $1.00, advertised in the *New-York Times* on Apr. 3 as "Now ready" and listed in the *Nation* on Apr. 22.

999 AMELIA E. BARR *The Bow of Orange Ribbon.* 16mo. 1/6 sewed, 2/0 cloth Mar. 3 (*Spect*)

Star Series No. 109. This is 1888 with 309 pp., a reissue of the Clarke first edition. The first edition was issued by Dodd, Mead & Co., New York, 1886, 18 cm., 445 pp., $1.00 cloth, deposited Oct. 20 and listed in the *Lit W* on Oct. 30 and in the *Nation* and *Ind* on Nov. 4. They reissued it in 1893, 8vo, 372 pp., with illustrations, 4 in color, $2.50 cloth and $3.50 silk, advertised in the *New-York Times* on Nov. 4. The first English edition was issued by J. Clarke & Co., London, 1886, Cr 8vo, 309 pp., 3/6, listed in the *Ath* on Dec. 25, 1886.

1000 AMELIA E. BARR *Between Two Loves.* 16mo. 1/6 sewed, 2/0 cloth Mar. 17 (*Ath*)

Star Series No. 110. This is a reissue of the Clarke edition, and Warne reissued it in this series, 1894, 311 pp. The first American edition was issued by Harper & Brothers, New York, 1886, 17.5 cm., 176 pp., *Handy Series* No. 102, $.25 paper, advertised in the *New-York Times* on Nov. 13 as "Latest issues" and probably issued on Nov. 13. It was listed in the *Nation* on Nov. 25. It was issued by Dodd, Mead & Co., New York, in 1889, $1.25, listed in the *Nation* on Apr. 25. The first English edition was issued by J. Clarke & Co., London, 1886, Cr 8vo, 311 pp., 3/6 cloth, advertised in the *TWEd* on Nov. 26.

1001 ARCHIBALD C. GUNTER *Mr. Barnes of New York.* p 8vo. 0/6 sewed   Mar. (*Bks*)

Notable Novels No. 110. Warne reissued this in this series, my copy, no date, probably 1896, 21.2 cm., 128 pp. in double columns, white pictorial wrappers, printed in red, blue, and black with the series title on the front and the title and no. on the spine. There are commercial ads on the back and inside covers, one of which contains a date (Feb. 6, 1896). The first edition was issued by Deshler Welch & Co., New York, 1887, 20 cm., 250 pp., $.50 paper, my copy, listed in the *Nation* on Apr. 14 and in *PW* on Apr. 30, but not received by the latter. It was also issued by the Home Publishing Co., New York, 1887, 21 cm., 250 pp., in green cloth. This latter company was founded and operated by Gunter. In England it was issued by Henry Vizetelly & Co., London, 1887, 250 pp.; and by George Routledge & Sons, London, 1887, my copy, 192 pp., at 1/0, in pale blue wrappers, and in cloth at 1/6, reissued in 1888, Demy 8vo, o/6 sewed. Both of these English editions were "On our table" in the *Ath* on Oct. 29. It was also issued by Ward, Lock & Co., London, in 1888, o/6 sewed, probably in May.

1002 HECTOR H. MALOT *Zyte.* Cr 8vo. 1/0 sewed   Mar. (*Bks*)

Library of Continental Authors No. 6. This is the first edition in English, 1888, 256 pp. Warne also issued it in New York, $.35 paper, translated by J. E. Simpson, advertised in the *New-York Times* on May 20, 1888, and in the *Nation* on Apr. 26, in the English series. The first edition was issued in Paris, 1887, 18.5 cm., 431 pp. B. Westermann & Co., New York, issued it, probably in French, listed in the *Nation* on Nov. 18, 1886 (*sic*).

1003 EVELYN EVERETT-GREEN *Ruthven of Ruthven; or, All or Nothing.* 12mo. 1/0 sewed   Apr. (*Bks*)

London Library No. 18. This is also given by the *Eng Cat*. Warne issued it in New York in 1888, *London Library*, 12mo, $.25 paper, advertised in the *Nation* on July 5. Also 1900

1004 G.P.R. JAMES *Arrah Neil.* p 8vo. o/6 sewed   Apr. (*Bks*)

Notable Novels No. 111. This is my copy, 1888, author's copyright edition, 21.4 cm.,

159 pp. in double columns, yellow pictorial wrappers, printed in red, blue, and black with the series title on the front and the title and no. on the spine. A commercial ad is on the inside front cover, and the back cover is missing. There is a printer's date (Feb. 1888). The first edition was in the United States. It was issued by J. Winchester, New York (1844), 24 cm., 160 pp., probably as an extra no. of *The New World*, noticed in the *Merchants' Magazine* for Sept. 1844 as already issued. It was also issued by Harper & Brothers, New York, 1844, 8vo, 139 pp., *Library of Select Novels* No. 40, noticed in the *Southern Literary Messenger* for Sept. The first English edition was issued by Smith, Elder & Co., London, 3 vols., 1845, 19.5 cm., 31/6 in half-cloth boards, listed in the *Ath* on Nov. 1. It was issued by Simms & M'Intyre, London and Belfast, 1853, 384 pp., *Parlour Library* No. 94, on Apr. 1. This ran in the *Dublin University Magazine* July 1843–Aug. 1844.

1005 ANNE MARSH, later MARSH-CALDWELL *Emilia Wyndham.* p 8vo. o/6 sewed   Apr. (*Bks*)

Notable Novels No. 112. The first English edition was issued by Henry Colburn, London, 3 vols., 1846, 19.5 cm., anonymous, 31/6, half gray-purple cloth, boards, labels, listed in the *Ath* on Mar. 28. Colburn issued it in his *Standard Novels*, 1848, 18 cm., anonymous, 504 pp., frontispiece, 6/0, listed by *PC* as published Dec. 29, 1847–Jan. 15, 1848. Simms & M'Intyre, London and Belfast, issued it, 1848, anonymous, 350 pp., 1/0 boards, *Parlour Library* No. 14, listed by *PC* as published Mar. 11–25. It was reissued in the *Parlour Library* by C. H. Clarke, London, in 1860 at 2/0 boards. The first American edition was issued by Harper & Brothers, New York, 1846, 8vo, anonymous, 165 pp., *Library of Select Novels* No. 81, noticed in the *Southern Literary Messenger* for July.

1006 CHARLES LEVER *The O'Donoghue.*
p 8vo. o/6 sewed   Apr. (*Bks*)
Notable Novels No. 114. This first appeared
in 13 monthly 1/0 parts in 11, parts 10–11
as well as 12–13 being double nos. No. 1
was issued on Dec. 30, 1844, and Nos. 12–
13 in Nov. 1845. These were issued by William Curry Jr. & Co., Dublin, etc., and he
issued it in 1 vol., 1845, 22 cm., 410 pp., illustrated by "Phiz" with a frontispiece and
25 plates. It was 14/0 in scarlet cloth, listed
in the *Ath* on Nov. 22. There was a later
binding, 1845, in rose-madder cloth. It
passed to Chapman & Hall, London, who
issued it in 1850, 8vo, reduced to 7/0.
They issued it, 1858, Cr 8vo, 8 illustrations by "Phiz," 4/0; and issued the 8th edition, 1866, 17 cm., 369 pp., 6/0. In the
United States it was issued by Carey &
Hart, Philadelphia, 1845, reviewed in the
Harbinger (weekly) for Dec. 20, 1845. It
was also issued by William H. Colyer, New
York, probably in 1845, 144 pp.

1007 JOHN BANIM (i.e., MICHAEL BANIM)
The Ghost-Hunter and His Family. p 8vo.
o/6 sewed   Apr.?
Notable Novels No. 113. The first edition
was issued by Smith, Elder & Co., London,
1833, 17 cm., 330 pp., 6/0, in dark green
cloth, uncut, with watered endpapers, No.
1 of the *Library of Romance* by the O'Hara
Family, with the series title on the spine.
It was advertised in the *Ath* on Jan. 5,
1833, as "Just published" and listed in the
Spect on Jan. 12. It was issued by Simms &
M'Intyre, London and Belfast, 1852, 284
pp., as *Parlour Library* No. 70, by John
Banim. In the United States it was in the
Novelist's Magazine, Philadelphia (1833)
and was issued by Carey, Lea & Blanchard,
Philadelphia, 1833, 18 cm., 269 pp., by the
O'Hara Family, in an edition of 2,000 copies. It was advertised in the *Globe*, a Washington, D.C., daily, by a Washington bookstore on Mar. 19, 1833, $.75, and listed in
the *North American Review*, Boston (quarterly), for July.

1008 FRANCES H. BURNETT *The Fortunes
of Philippa Fairfax.* 12mo. 1/0 sewed,
1/6 cloth   May 1 (*PC*)
London Library No. 20. This is the first edition, 1888, 124 pp., reviewed in the *Ath* on
June 23.

1009 ALICE PRICE *A Rustic Maid.* 12mo.
1/0 sewed   May (*Bks*)
London Library No. 19. This is 1888, 224
pp. Warne issued it in New York, 12mo,
$.25 paper, advertised in the *Nation* on
July 5, 1888. The first edition was issued
by Sampson Low, London, 3 vols., 1885,
31/6, advertised in *Notes & Queries* on Jan.
10, 1885, as "Nearly ready" and in the
TWEd on Jan. 30 as ready.
Also 1900

1010 GAY PARKER *Mr. Perkins of New
Jersey; or, The Stolen Bonds.* p 8vo. o/6
sewed   May (*Bks*)
Notable Novels No. 126. The first American
edition was issued by J. S. Ogilvie, New
York, 1888, listed in *PW* on Apr. 7 and in
Public Opinion (weekly) on Apr. 21. The
first English edition was probably George
Routledge & Sons, New York, 1888, Demy
8vo, 157 pp., o/6 sewed, probably issued
in Apr.

1011 ALEXANDER C. EWALD, ed.
The Tatler. Selected Essays. Cr 8vo.
1/6 sewed, 2/0 cloth, 2/6 imitation
Roxburghe   June 16 (*Ath*)
Chandos Classics No. 129. This is the first
edition thus, 1888, 478 pp. It was advertised in *Notes & Queries* on Nov. 14, 1891,
Cr 8vo, 2/0, in blue cloth, uncut. Warne
issued it in New York, 12mo, $1.00, in
smooth dark blue cloth, with white paper
labels printed in red and black, *Chandos
Classics* No. 129, listed in the *Nation* on Oct.
4, 1888.

1012 EDWIN L. ARNOLD *England as She Seems.* 12mo. 1/o sewed June 16 (*Ath* ad)

Popular Library No. 2. This is the first edition, 1888, 128 pp. The *Ath* ad said "Just published." Warne issued it in New York, $.30 paper, listed in the *Nation* on Aug. 16, 1888.

1013 LÉON GOZLAN *Monkey Island.* 12mo. 1/o sewed, picture cover June 16 (*Ath* ad)

Popular Library No. 3. This is 1888, 156 pp. The first edition was *Les Émotions de Polydore Marasquin*, Paris, 1857, 18 cm., 291 pp. The first English edition was issued by Ward, Lock & Tyler, London, 1873, *The Man Among the Monkeys* (with other stories), anonymous, 312 pp., illustrated. Henry Vizetelly & Co., London, issued it, 1888, as *The Emotions of Polydore Marasquin*, 19 cm., 257 pp., illustrated, advertised in the *Ath* on Nov. 19, 1887, 3/6, and in the *TWEd* on Feb. 17, 1888. They reissued it, 1890, second edition, p 8vo, 1/o sewed, Sadleir's copy.

1014 MARGARET DELAND *John Ward, Preacher.* 12mo. 1/o sewed June?

Popular Library No. 1. This has no date and 288 pp. I may be wrong in placing this in June, as *Popular Library* No. 2 was advertised in the *Ath* on June 16 as "Just published" and No. 3 was advertised then also. To add to the complications, Warne advertised it in a display ad in the *Ath* on Feb. 23, 1889. Warne issued the eighth edition, 1890, 288 pp., and issued it in the *Star Series* No. 124, 16mo, 1/o sewed, 1/6 cloth, listed in *PC* on Sept. 24, 1892. The first English edition was issued by Longmans, London, 1888, Cr 8vo, 473 pp., 6/o, listed in the *Ath* on June 23. It was a reprint of the American edition, and Longmans claimed that it was the only authorized edition in England and that they paid royalties to the authoress. They issued the

third edition, the same, advertised in the *Spect* on Oct. 6; and they issued it, 1889, Cr 8vo, 2/o boards, 2/6 cloth, listed in the *Ath* on Mar. 2. It was issued by Ward, Lock & Co., London, 1889, 288 pp., o/6 sewed, 1/o cloth, probably in Mar. The first edition was issued by Houghton, Mifflin & Co., Boston and New York, 1888, 20 cm., 473 pp., $1.50, listed in *Lit W* and *PW* on Apr. 28 and in the *Ind* on May 3. They issued the third edition, $1.50, advertised in the *Nation* on June 23, and the sixth edition, $1.50, advertised in the *New-York Times* on Sept. 23; and they issued it in the *Riverside Paper Series* No. 1, 37th thousand, $.50, advertised in the *New-York Times* on June 2, 1889.

Also 1900

1015 HONORÉ DE BALZAC *Cousin Pons.* Cr 8vo. 1/o sewed July (*Bks*)

Library of Continental Authors No. 7. I think this was reissued in this series in Mar. 1889; it was reissued in the series in 1894, Cr 8vo, 1/o sewed, given by the *BM*. It is a reprint of the first English edition by W. Simpkin & R. Marshall, London. Warne issued it in New York, 12mo, $.35 paper, listed in the *Nation* on Mar. 28, 1889. This was in *Le Siècle*, Paris, in 1847 and was issued there in 2 vols., 1847, 15.5 cm., *Histoire des Parens Pauvre—Le Cousin Pons—La Cousine Bette*. The first English edition was issued by Simpkin & Marshall, 1880 (1879), 19 cm., 314 pp., 2/o cloth, *Poor Relations—Cousin Pons*, translated by Philip Kent. It was listed in the *Ath* on Nov. 29, 1879. The first American edition was issued by Roberts Brothers, Boston, 1886, 19.5 cm., 426 pp., $1.50 half-morocco, translated by Katharine Wormeley. It was advertised in the *New-York Times* on Oct. 22 as in the French style, and listed in *Lit W* (fortnightly) on Oct. 30 and in *PW* on Nov. 6. They issued the third edition, advertised in the *Nation* on Nov. 18. This Roberts Brothers edition was issued by George Routledge & Sons, London, at 3/6, in Nov. 1886.

1016 EDGAR A. POE *The Complete Poetical Works and Essays on Poetry of Edgar A. Poe, Together with His Narrative of Arthur Gordon Pym.* Cr 8vo. 1/6 sewed, 2/0 cloth, 2/6 imitation Roxburghe   Sept. 15 (*Ath* ad)

Chandos Classics No. 130. This is 1888, 384 pp., series title at the head of the title page. The 1/6 issue was in stiff wrappers; the cloth, at 2/0, had printed paper labels. These were all reprints save for three poems, probably not by Poe. *Poems* was issued by Elam Bliss, New York, 1831, second edition, 16 cm., 124 pp., in olive-green cloth or tan linen, with orange, yellow, or white endpapers. *Poems* was also issued by H. M. Caldwell, New York and Boston (1850), 16.5 cm., 276 pp., frontispiece. In England *The Poetical Works of Edgar Allen Poe* was issued by Addey & Co., London, 1853, 18 cm., 144 pp., illustrated. *The Narrative of Arthur Gordon Pym* was issued by Harper & Brothers, New York, 1838, 19.5 cm., anonymous, 201 pp., with 14 pp. of ads, in black muslin or blue cloth with printed labels on the spine. It was reviewed in the *Knickerbocker* for Aug. and in the *New Yorker* for Aug. 4 as "Just published" and listed in the *North American Review* (quarterly) for Oct. In England it was issued by Wiley & Putnam, etc., London, 1838, anonymous, 252 pp., listed in the *Literary Gazette* on Oct. 20 and in *PC* on Nov. 1.

1017 EDWARD P. ROE *The Queen of Spades and Other Stories, with an Autobiography.* 16mo. 1/0 sewed, 1/6 cloth   Sept. 22 (*Spect*)

Star Series No. 112. This was listed in *PC* on Oct. 15 and Dec. 15. The autobiography and the title story appeared in *Lippincott's Monthly Magazine* for Oct. 1888 with a frontispiece (portrait). The title story was in *Taken Alive, and Other Stories—With an Autobiography,* issued by Dodd, Mead & Co., New York (1889). The present title was not located and not seen by *BAL*.

1018 RICHARD COBBOLD *Mary Anne Wellington.* p 8vo. 0/6 sewed   Sept. (*Bks*)

Notable Novels No. 127. This is my copy, no date, 21.4 cm., 184 pp. in double columns, yellow pictorial wrappers, printed in red, blue, and black, with the series title on the front and the title and no. on the spine. There are commercial ads on the back and inside covers and a page of publisher's ads at the front and 8 pp. at the back, giving the series ending with No. 126 and the *Star Series* with No. 110. The first edition was issued by Henry Colburn, London, 3 vols., 1846, 20 cm., 8 illustrations, 31/6, in claret cloth, with a 24-page catalog at the back of vol. 3. It was listed in the *Ath* on Sept. 16. Colburn issued it in 1 vol. in 1847, illustrated, at 10/6, advertised in the *Illustrated London News* on June 19. It was issued by Clarke, Beeton & Co., London, etc., 1853, new and improved edition, my copy, 17.4 cm., 332 pp., frontispiece and added pictorial title page, 1/6 glazed boards in green, printed in black with a vignette on the front, with figured endpapers with publisher's ads, 1/6. Sadleir's copy was in royal blue glazed boards. It was also issued at 2/0 cloth and was listed in the *Ath* on Apr. 9. They issued it in the *Run and Read Library* No. 6, 1854, 1/6 boards, 2/0 cloth, in June and again in Dec., the latter listed in the *Ath* on Dec. 23, 1854.

1019 LEOPOLD WAGNER, ed. *Humorous Readings and Recitations. In Prose and Verse.* p 8vo 1/0 cloth   Oct.?

Albion Reciter. This is the first edition, 144 pp. It was "On our table" in the *Ath* for Dec. 8. It was reissued in 1895, advertised in *PC* on May 11, 1/0. Warne issued it in New York in 1889, 12mo, $.50 cloth, advertised in the *Nation* on Mar. 28.

1020 RICHARD ANDRE **The King's Bell Tower.** Cr 8vo. Illustrated. 2/0 cloth Nov. 3 (*Ath*)
Stanley Library. This is the first edition, 1888, 190 pp. It was reviewed in the *Ath* on Nov. 24.

1021 WILLIAM G. STABLES **Jack Locke.** Cr 8vo. Illustrated. 2/0 cloth Nov. 3 (*Ath*)
Stanley Library. This is the first edition, 1888, 192 pp. It was reviewed in the *Ath* on Nov. 24. Warne issued it in the *Bedford Library*, 12mo, illustrated, 1/6 cloth, listed in *PC* on Nov. 20, 1897.

1022 ARTHUR N. MALAN **Ernest Fairfield.** Cr 8vo. Illustrated. 2/0 cloth Nov. 3 (*Ath*)
Stanley Library. This is the first edition, 1888, 190 pp.

1023 WILLIAM J. GORDON **The Treasure-Finder.** Cr 8vo. Illustrated. 2/0 cloth Nov. 3 (*Ath*)
Stanley Library. This is the first edition, 1888, 190 pp.

1024 A. J. DARYL **A Merry Go-Round.** Cr 8vo. Illustrated. 2/6 Nov.?
These are rhymes, a first edition, 1888, 96 pp. It was "On our table" in the *Ath* for Dec. 22.

1025 F.E.M. STEELE, ed. **The Encore Reciter. Humorous, Serious and Dramatic Selections.** 4to. 1/0 sewed Dec. 1 (*Ath* ad)
This is the first edition, 1889, 128 pp., a first series. The fifth edition was advertised in the *TWEd* on Nov. 7, 1890, and it was advertised in *PC* on May 11, 1895, 1/0.

1026 J. T. LUCAS **Thoughts in Rhyme.** Fcp 8vo. 1/6 1888 (*Eng Cat*)
This is the first edition, 1888, 53 pp. It was "On our table" in the *Ath* for Oct. 20.

1027 RICHARD D. URLIN **Hints on Business.** Cr 8vo. 1/0 1888 (*Eng Cat*)
The first edition was issued by Suttaby & Co., London, 1884 (1883), 223 pp., 3/6.

1028 CHARLES E. BAKER **The Local Government Act, 1888.** Cr 8vo. 1/0 1888 (*Eng Cat*)
This is the first edition, 1888.

1029 (VARIOUS) *Notable Novels* Nos. 101–105, 107–109. 0/6 sewed each 1888?
These were *Notable Books* Nos. 1–5 and 7–9, which were now placed in *Notable Novels* but whether reissued or not I don't know. I can't find that No. 6 was so transferred and thus there is no No. 106 for the *Notable Novels* series. See 1883 for Nos. 101–105, 107, and 108; see 1884 for No. 109; see 1895 for No. 102.

Frederick Warne & Co.
London and New York
1889

1030 W. H. AINSWORTH *The Tower of London.* p 8vo. 0/6 sewed   Jan.?

Notable Novels No. 128. This has no date and 156 pp., issued in 1889 according to the *Eng Cat.* It was first issued by Bentley, London, 13 monthly 1/0 parts in 12, Jan.– Dec. 1840. The parts were in white paper wrappers printed in black, 24 cm., illustrated by Cruikshank. Bentley issued it in 1 vol., 1840, 24 cm., 439 pp., illustrated by Cruikshank, 15/0, in brown cloth with yellow endpapers, listed in the *Spect* on Dec. 26, 1840. It was issued by Henry G. Bohn, London, 1844, fifth edition, 439 pp., illustrated; and Chapman & Hall issued it in 2 vols., 1850, Fcp 8vo, 1/0 boards, 1/6 cloth each, my copy in boards. The first American edition was issued by Lea & Blanchard, Philadelphia, 1844, 25 cm., 210 pp., illustrated. They also issued it in parts, illustrated by Cruikshank, No. 1 advertised in the *Globe*, a Washington, D.C., daily, by a Washington bookstore on Mar. 26, 1840, "This day."

1031 W. H. AINSWORTH *Windsor Castle.* p 8vo. 0/6 sewed   Jan.?

Notable Novels No. 129. The *Eng Cat* gives this as issued in 1889. This ran in *Ainsworth's Magazine*, July 1842–June 1843. It was issued in 13 monthly 1/0 parts, illustrated, by Hugh Cunningham, London. No. 1 was advertised in the *Ath* on Mar. 12, 1842, as "On Mar. 29." These 13 parts were advertised in the *Spect* on Feb. 20,

1841, Part 1 "On May 1," but apparently this did not come off. Henry Colburn, London, issued it in 3 vols., 1843, 21 cm., frontispieces by Cruikshank, 31/6 in half-cloth boards, with labels, listed in the *Ath* on May 13. Colburn issued a new edition, 1843, 8vo, 324 pp., illustrated 14/0, advertised in the *Spect* on July 8, 1843, as "Now ready." Colburn then issued it in 11 monthly 1/0 parts, illustrated, No. 2 advertised in the *Illustrated London News* on Dec. 30, 1843, as "Now ready." Chapman & Hall, London, issued it, 1850, Fcp 8vo, 1/0 in yellow glazed boards and 1/6 cloth, listed in the *Ath* on Nov. 24, 1849. The first American edition was issued by J. Winchester, New York, 1843, 54 pp., as extra Nos. 82 and 83 of *The New World*. H. Long & Brother, New York, issued it, 1850, with 8 illustrations from the London edition, $.50, advertised in *Lit W* on Apr. 27 as "Now ready."

1032 W. H. AINSWORTH *Rookwood.* p 8vo. 0/6 sewed   Jan.?

Notable Novels No. 130. The *Eng Cat* gives this as issued in 1889. The first edition was issued by Bentley, London, 3 vols., 1834, 20 cm., anonymous, 31/6 in boards and labels, published May 3 according to the Bentley private catalog and listed in the *Ath* and *Spect* on May 10. John Macrone, London, issued a new edition, revised and corrected, 3 vols., 1835, by Ainsworth, advertised in the *Spect* on Apr. 11 as "Just ready." Macrone issued the third edition, 3 vols., advertised in the *Spect* on Sept. 12, 1835, and issued the fourth edition (the first illustrated), 1836, 502 pp., 15/0 in red-brown cloth, with a frontispiece (portrait) and with illustrations by Cruikshank. It has a large new preface and 2 new chapters, advertised in the *Spect* on Apr. 30, 1836, as "Just ready. It was issued as *Bentley's Standard Novels* No. 60, 1837, 404 pp., my copy, with a new dedication and a new preface to the present edition, issued in Oct. Chapman & Hall, London, issued it, 1850, 1/0 in glazed yellow boards and 1/6 in cloth, listed in the *Ath* on Dec. 15, 1849. The first American edition was issued by Carey, Lea & Blanchard, Philadelphia, 2 vols., 1834, 21 cm., by Ainsworth, 1,200 copies, finished Dec. 10, 1834. It claimed to be from the second London edition, which must have been incorrect, as it could have come only from the first English edition. It was advertised in the *Globe*, a Washington, D.C., daily, by a Washington bookstore on Dec. 16, 1834. Lea & Blanchard, Philadelphia, issued it, 1844, as *Dick Turpin, the Highwayman*, reviewed in the *Southern Literary Messenger* for Nov. 1844.

1033 ALEXANDRE DUMAS, PÈRE *Paul Jones.* 12mo. 1/0 sewed   Feb.?
London Library No. 22. This was translated by Henry L. Williams. It was issued in *Notable Novels* No. 131, p 8vo, 0/6 sewed, probably in July 1889. Warne issued it in New York also, in 1889, 12mo, $.30 paper, translated by H. L. Williams, advertised in the *Nation* on Nov. 28 as "Now ready." The first edition was *Le Capitaine Paul*, Paris, 2 vols., 1838, 21.5 cm. The first edition in English was issued by E. P. Williams & Co., New York and Boston, 1846, 22.5 cm., 106 pp. in double columns: *Captain Paul*. It was advertised by Williams & Brothers, New York, in *Lit W* on Mar. 13, 1847, as "Now ready." The first English edition was *Captain Paul the Pirate*, issued by George

Peirce, London, 1848. Darton & Co., London, issued it (1859) as *Parlour Library* No. 188, 328 pp., as *Captain Paul*.

1034 (SUSAN WARNER) *My Desire.* 16mo. 1/6 sewed, 2/0 cloth   Mar. 2 (*Ath*)
Star Series No. 113. This has no date and 464 pp. The first American edition was issued by Robert Carter & Brothers, New York, 1879, 19.5 cm., anonymous, 629 pp., $1.75, in green, maroon, or terra-cotta cloth with white endpapers with a blue floral pattern. It has 6 pp. of ads and a note on page (6) signed S. Warner. It was received at the Boston Athenaeum on May 20, advertised in the *New-York Times* on May 10 as "On May 14," and listed in *PW* on May 17. The first English edition was issued by James Nisbet & Co., London, 1879, Cr 8vo, 3/6, deposited May 13 and listed in the *Ath* on May 17 and in *PC* on June 2.

1035 (SUSAN WARNER) *Nobody.* 16mo. 1/6 sewed, 2/0 cloth   Mar. 2 (*Ath*)
Star Series No. 114. The first American edition was issued by Robert Carter & Brothers, New York, 1883, 19 cm., anonymous, 695 pp., in red, terra-cotta, brown, or maroon cloth with pale yellow endpapers. It was deposited Sept. 16, 1882, and listed in *PW* on Oct. 7, 1882. The first English edition was issued by James Nisbet & Co., London, 1882, Cr 8vo, anonymous, 488 pp., illustrated, 3/6 cloth, listed in the *Ath* on Oct. 7 and *PC* on Oct. 16.

1036 HORACE (QUINTUS HORATIUS FLACCUS) *Horace: The Odes, Epodes, Satires, and Epistles.* Cr 8vo. 1/6 sewed, 2/0 cloth, 2/6 imitation Roxburghe   Mar. 23 (*Spect*)
Chandos Classics No. 132. This is 1889, 392 pp. Warne reissued it in this series, 1892 and 1893. Warne also issued it in New York, 12mo, $.75, in smooth blue linen boards with white paper labels, un-

trimmed edges, listed in the *Nation* on May 9, 1889; and advertised there on June 9, 1892, the same, *Chandos Classics*, translated by Ben Jonson, Milton, Dryden et al. *The Poems*, in English, were issued by Henry Brome, London, 1616, 400 pp. *The Odes, Satires, and Epistles of Horace*, in English, were issued by J. Tonson, etc., London, etc., 1684, 18 cm., illustrated. *The Works of Horace*, in English and Latin, were issued by J. Oswald, London, 1701, third edition, 405 pp. *Opera*, edited by Richard Bentley, was issued by the Cambridge University Press, 1711. In the United States the *Works of Horace*, in English, were issued by M. Carey, etc., Philadelphia, etc., 2 vols., 1808, 15 cm.

1037 CHARLES KING *Dunraven Ranch.* 12mo. 1/o sewed   Mar.?
London Library No. 23. This is 1889, 182 pp., the first edition. It appeared in *Lippincott's Monthly Magazine* in 1888. Also 1900

1038 ROBERT CROMIE *For England's Sake.* 12mo. 1/o sewed   Mar.?
London Library No. 24. This is the first edition, 1889, with 154 pp., in pictorial wrappers, printed on the front in red, dark blue, and light blue-green. The *BM* gives Warne, 1889, 8th thousand, 154 pp. Warne advertised it in the *TWEd* on June 5, 1891, Cr 8vo, 1/o.

1039 THOMAS INGOLDSBY (R. H. BARHAM) *The Ingoldsby Legends.* Cr 8vo. Illustrated. 1/6 sewed, 2/o cloth, 2/6 imitation Roxburghe   Apr. 13 (*Ath* ad)
Chandos Classics No. 131. This is 1889, with 520 pp. Warne issued it in New York, *Chandos Classics*, $.75, listed in the *Nation* on May 30, 1889. The first edition was in 3 series, 10/6 each, by Thomas Ingoldsby, issued by Bentley, London. Series 1, 1840, 21/5 cm., 338 pp., illustrated, listed in the

Spect on Feb. 8. Series 2, 1842, 21.5 cm., 288 pp., illustrated by Leech, listed in the *Spect* on Jan. 7, 1843. Series 3, 1847, 23 cm., 364 pp., illustrated by Leech and Cruikshank, advertised in the *Spect* on Dec. 19, 1846, as "Just ready." Bentley issued it in 3 vols. in 1854, p 8vo, illustrated, 21/o, advertised in the *Spect* on Oct. 7 as "This day." Selections from the first two series were issued by Carey & Hart, Philadelphia, 1844, 19.5 cm., 192 pp., illustrated, listed in the *Knickerbocker* and in *Godey's Lady's Book* for Nov. The third series was issued in Philadelphia, 1847. D. Appleton & Co., New York, issued the first series, 1852, 320 pp., reviewed in the *Southern Literary Messenger* for June, called the first American edition.

1040 FRANCES H. BURNETT *The Tide on the Moaning Bar.* 12mo. 1/o sewed Apr. 19?
London Library No. 25. This has no date, 158 pp., advertised in the *TWEd* on Apr. 19, and listed in *PC* on May 1. Warne advertised it in the *TWEd* on Dec. 2, 1892, medium 8vo, illustrated, 3/6 cloth. The first edition was issued by T. B. Peterson & Brothers, Philadelphia (1878), square 16mo, 230 pp., listed in *PW* on Sept. 28 and in *Lit W* as published in Sept., *A Quiet Life; the Tide on the Moaning Bar.* The first English edition was issued by George Routledge & Sons, London and New York (1879), Fcp 8vo, 158 pp., 1/o boards, containing also *A Quiet Life* but titled *The Tide on the Moaning Bar.* It was listed by *PC* as published Feb. 1–15.

1041 FRANCES H. BURNETT *Kathleen.* 12mo. 1/o sewed   Apr. 19?
London Library No. 26. Warne advertised this in the *TWEd* on Dec. 2, 1892, medium 8vo, illustrated, 3/6 cloth. The first American edition was issued by T. B. Peterson & Brothers, Philadelphia (1878), 17 cm., 212 pp., listed in *PW* on Jan. 26, 1878. It

had run in *Peterson's Ladies' Magazine*. The authorized edition was issued by Charles Scribner's Sons, New York (1878), 16 cm., 216 pp., $.40 paper, advertised in the *New-York Times* on Nov. 16 as "Now ready" and listed in the *Ind* on Nov. 28. This claimed to be a revised, authorized edition to replace the Peterson edition, issued without the author's permission. The Scribner title was *Kathleen Mavourneen*. The first English edition was issued by George Routledge & Sons, London and New York, 1878, Fcp 8vo, 159 pp., 1/o boards, listed by *PC* as published Feb. 1–15, *Kathleen*. Chatto & Windus, London, issued it with the Scribner title, 1879, author's revised edition, Fcp 8vo, 147 pp., 1/o sewed, listed in the *Bks* for Feb.

1042 FRANCES BURNETT *Dolly*. 12mo. 1/o sewed   Apr. 19?
London Library No. 27. This was advertised in the *TWEd* on Apr. 19. Warne advertised it in the *Spect* on Nov. 5, 1892, illustrated edition, Cr 8vo, 3/6 cloth. This ran as *Dorothea* in a periodical and was issued in book form by Porter & Coates, Philadelphia (1877), as *Dolly*, 19.5 cm., 319 pp., $1.25, listed in the *Ind* on Nov. 1 and in *PW* on Nov. 3. James R. Osgood & Co., Boston, issued it, 1884, in a revised edition, as *Vagabondia*, 19.5 cm., 392 pp., $1.50, listed in the *Nation* on Nov. 8, 1883. The first English edition was issued by George Routledge & Sons, London and New York (1878), Fcp 8vo, 219 pp., 1/o boards, listed by *PC* as published Jan. 15–31.

1043 FRANCES H. BURNETT *Lindsay's Luck*. 12mo. 1/o sewed   Apr. (*Bks*)
London Library No. 28. This ran in *Peterson's Ladies' Magazine*. The first English edition was issued by Charles Scribner's Sons, New York, 1878, 16.5 cm., 154 pp., $.30 paper, advertised in the *New-York Times* on Nov. 16 as "Now ready" and listed in the *Nation* and *Ind* on Nov. 28. This was

an authorized edition. T. B. Peterson & Brothers, Philadelphia, issued it without the author's consent (copyright 1879), 17.5 cm., 192 pp., listed in *PW* on Feb. 8, 1879, and listed in *Godey's Lady's Book* for Apr. In England it was issued by George Routledge & Sons, London and New York, 1879, 16.7 cm., 128 pp., my copy, in yellow boards, printed and decorated in red, blue, and black, listed by *PC* as published Jan. 1–17. It was also issued by Chatto & Windus, London, Fcp 8vo, 1/o sewed, advertised in the *Ath* on Jan. 25, 1879. Their ads quoted the authoress as saying it was by her own publishers and that the Peterson edition had been issued without her consent.

1044 FRANCES H. BURNETT *Pretty Polly Pemberton*. 12mo. 1/o sewed   Apr. (*Bks*)
London Library No. 29. This was advertised in the *TWEd* on Apr. 19. This ran in *Peterson's Ladies' Magazine* and was issued by T. B. Peterson & Brothers, Philadelphia (1877), 17 cm., 248 pp., listed in *PW* on Dec. 1 (no list on Nov. 24) and in the *Ind* on Dec. 6 (no list on Nov. 29). It was also issued by Charles Scribner's Sons, New York (1878), authorized edition, 16.5 cm., 213 pp., $.40 paper, revised by the author and issued with her consent. It was advertised in the *New-York Times* on Nov. 16 and listed in the *Ind* on Nov. 28, 1878. In England it was issued by George Routledge & Sons, London and New York (1878), Fcp 8vo, 192 pp., 1/o boards, listed by *PC* as published Feb. 1–15. It was also issued by Chatto & Windus, called an authorized edition; they quoted the authoress as saying it is revised for the present issue, the only one issued with her consent. It was advertised in the *Ath* on Jan. 25, 1878.

1045 FRANCES H. BURNETT *Miss Crespigny*. 12mo. 1/o sewed   Apr. (*Bks*)
London Library No. 30. This was also advertised in the *TWEd* on Apr. 19. It ran in *Pe-*

terson's Ladies' Magazine and was first issued in book form by T. B. Peterson & Brothers, Philadelphia (1878), 17.5 cm., 252 pp., listed in *PW* on May 25. All these early Burnett stories were in Peterson's magazine and were apparently not copyrighted, which gave Peterson the right to issue them without the consent of the authoress. Charles Scribner's Sons, New York issued it (1879), authorized edition, 16.5 cm., 190 pp., $.30 paper, advertised in the *New-York Times* on May 17 as "This day" and listed in *PW* on May 24. The first English edition was issued by George Routledge & Sons, London and New York (1878), Fcp 8vo, 1/o boards, listed by *PC* as published June 1–15.

1046 HARRY PARKES *That Sister-in-Law of Mine.* Oblong 8vo. Illustrated. 1/o ribbon sewed   May 24?

This was advertised in the *TWEd* on May 24. The first edition was issued by Warne, 1888, oblong 4to, illustrated, 26 pp. They issued it also in New York, 1888, 27 × 32 cm., illustrated, 27 pp., advertised in the *Nation* on July 5, $1.50 half-sateen.

1047 CHARLES KING *The Queen of Bedlam.* Cr 8vo. 2/o boards, 2/6 cloth June 29 (*Ath*)

Library of Fiction No. 7. This is the first English edition, my copy, 1889, 18.2 cm., 284 pp., yellow pictorial boards, printed in red, blue, and black with the series title on the spine. It has a printer's date (June 5, 1889), plain white endpapers, a commercial ad on the back cover, and 2 leaves of publisher's ads at the back, giving the *London Library* through No. 30. Warne reissued it in 1896, Cr 8vo, 1/o sewed, listed by *PC* for May 23. The first edition was "*Laramie*," issued by J. B. Lippincott & Co., Philadelphia, 1889, 19 cm., 277 pp., $1.00 cloth, listed in the *Ind* on June 6 and in the *Nation* on June 13.

1048 HUGH C. DAVIDSON *The Gargrave Mystery.* Cr 8vo. 2/o boards, 2/6 cloth July 13 (*Ath*)

Library of Fiction No. 8. This is the first edition, 1889, 301 pp. Warne also issued it in 1896 at o/6, advertised in *PC* on May 16.

1049 WILLIAM G. STABLES *Hints About Home and Farm Favourites for Pleasure, Prizes, and Profit.* Square Fcp 8vo, 1/o boards, 1/6 cloth   July 19?

This was advertised in the *TLS* on July 19. It is the first edition, 1889, 142 pp. It was also advertised in the *Times Weekly Edition* on May 8, 1891, the same.

1050 FRANCES H. BURNETT *Esmeralda, and Other Stories.* 12mo. 1/o sewed July?

London Library No. 31. This is my copy, no date, 17.6 cm., 187 pp., in gray wrappers, printed and decorated in plum, with a printer's date (June 22, 1889). There are commercial ads on the back and inside covers, and 1 page of publisher's ads at the front and 4 pp. at the back, giving the *London Library* through No. 32 and the *Star Series* through No. 114. The title story first appeared in *Scribner's Monthly* for May, 1877. The present edition has 4 stories that appeared in *Surly Tim, and Other Stories*, issued by Scribners in 1877 (see item 1065).

1051 HENRY COCKTON *The Sisters.* p 8vo. o/6 sewed   July?

Notable Novels No. 133. This is my copy, 1889, 21.2 cm., 155 pp. in double columns, white pictorial wrappers, printed in red, blue, and black with the series title on the front and the title and no. on the spine. It has a printer's date (May 13, 1889), commercial ads on the back and inside covers, and 4 pp. of publisher's ads at the back, the latter giving the series through No. 135 and the *London Library* through No. 33. Wolff's copy of the first edition gives G. Nodes, London, 1844, from the *Illustrated London News*, 8vo, 258 pp., illustrated by Meadows and Crowquill, 7/6, in dark green cloth with pale yellow endpapers. It has a frontispiece (portrait). It was advertised in the *Illustrated London News* on Jan. 20, 1844, as "Now ready" and listed in the *Gentleman's Magazine* (monthly) for Mar., no publisher given for either. Although Wolff's copy gives the publisher as Nodes, the *U Cat* gives the *Illustrated London News*, London, 1844, 21 cm., 258 pp., illustrated. It was issued by W. M. Clark, London, 1851, second edition, 21.5 cm., 380 pp., illustrated. The first American edition was issued by H. Long & Brother, New York (1851), 22.5 cm., 233 pp., illustrated, from the English edition. It was listed by *Lit W* as published May 3–17, 1851.

1052 ANONYMOUS **Follies, Foibles, and Fancies of Fish, Flesh and Fowl.** 4to. Illustrated. 1/0 stiff wrappers Aug. 24 (*Ath* ad)

This was also advertised in the *Spect* on Aug. 31 and is given by the *Eng Cat*.

1053 VICTOR HUGO **The Hunchback of Notre Dame.** p 8vo. o/6 sewed Aug.?

Notable Novels No. 134. The first edition was *Notre-Dame de Paris*, Paris, 2 vols., 1831, in Mar. In England it was issued by Effingham Wilson, London, 3 vols., 1833, 8vo, 24/0, translated by William Hazlitt. It was titled *Notre-Dame* and was in half-cloth boards with labels, probably issued in Aug. It was listed by the *Edinburgh Review* (quarterly) as published Aug.–Oct. 1833 and was listed in the *Spect* on Aug. 24. It was issued also by Bentley, London, 1833, 16.5 cm., 466 pp., frontispiece, translated by Frederick Shoberl, *Standard Novels* No. 32, *The Hunchback of Notre-Dame*, probably in Sept. The Bentley private catalog states that it and the Wilson edition were issued

about the same time. George Peirce, London, issued it as *Esmeralda* in parts and in 1 vol. No. 1, at o/1 with 16 pp., was advertised in the *Illustrated London News* on Nov. 16, 1844, as "On Nov. 23." It contains 3 chapters never before published in England, according to the ads. The first American edition was as *The Hunchback of Notre-Dame*, issued by Carey, Lea & Blanchard, Philadelphia, 2 vols., 1834, 19 cm., in the Shoberl translation, in an edition of 1,000 copies, finished Nov. 5. It was advertised in the *Globe*, a Washington, D.C., daily, by a Washington bookstore on Dec. 6, 1834, $1.25. Thomas Hodgson, London, issued in the *Parlour Library* No. 151, (1856), 466 pp.

1054 W. H. AINSWORTH **The Miser's Daughter.** p 8vo. o/6 sewed Aug.?

Notable Novels No. 135. The first edition was issued by Cunningham & Mortimer, London, 3 vols., 1842, 20 cm., frontispieces and illustrations by Cruikshank, 31/6, in very dark brown cloth with yellow endpapers. It was listed in the *Ath* on Oct. 15 and in the *Spect* on Oct. 29. They issued a second edition, the same, advertised in the *Spect* on Nov. 26 as "Now ready." Parry & Co., London, issued a third edition, 1848, 25 cm., 396 pp., illustrated by Cruikshank, 10/6 cloth, listed by *PC* as published Oct. 28–Nov. 13, 1847. The first American edition was issued by Wilson & Co., New York, 1842, my copy, 31.5 cm., 48 pp., extra no. of *Brother Jonathan*, dated Dec. 3, 1842, called the first complete American edition. Williams & Brothers, New York, issued it at $.50, listed by *Lit W* as published Aug. 20–27, 1847.

1055 VICTOR HUGO **Ruy Blas.** p 8vo. o/6 sewed Oct.?

Notable Novels No. 136. The first edition was issued in Paris, 1838, 23 cm., 250 pp., illustrated, based on a drama by Hugo. The novel was issued by Digby Long, London, in 1889, at 3/6, and there was an edition listed in the *Ath* on Aug. 9, 1890, Cr 8vo, 2/6, no publisher given. Warne issued it also as *London Library* No. 34. 12mo, 1/0 sewed, probably in 1889; and they issued it in New York in 1890, by H. L. Williams, based on Hugo, $.30, listed in the *Nation* on Mar. 27.

1056 CHARLOTTE BRONTË *Jane Eyre.* p 8vo. o/6 sewed Oct.?

Notable Novels No. 137. This was also listed in the *Spect* on Oct. 12, 1889, Cr 8vo, 2/0; and Warne issued it as *Standard Novels* No. 2, 8vo, o/6 sewed, listed by *PC* for Oct. 31, 1891. The first edition was issued by Smith, Elder & Co., London, 3 vols., 1847, edited by Currer Bell, 8vo, 31/6, in gray-purple cloth with dark cream endpapers. There is a 32-page catalog at the back of vol. 1 (Oct. 1847). It was listed in the *Spect* on Oct. 16 and in the *Ath* on Oct. 23. They issued a second edition, 1848, 3 vols., with the same catalog, 31/6, in plum cloth, advertised in the *Spect* on Jan. 22, 1848, as "Just published." It has a dedication to Thackeray and a preface by the authoress (Dec. 21, 1847). The third edition, 3 vols., 31/6, was advertised in the *Spect* on Apr. 15, 1848, as "Now ready"; the fourth edition, 1850, 19 cm., 460 pp., 6/0 cloth, was advertised there on Apr. 20 as "Just ready." In the United States it was issued by Harper & Brothers, New York, 1848, 24 cm., 174 pp., $.25 paper, *Library of Select Novels* No. 109, listed by *Lit W* as published Jan. 15–22, 1848, and reviewed in the *Harbinger* (weekly) on Jan. 22. It was also issued by Wilkins, Carter & Co., Boston, 1848, 19 cm., 483 pp., listed by *Lit W* as published Apr. 1–8, at $1.00. The *U Cat* gives Porter, Philadelphia, 1847, 495 pp.; an issue by William D. Ticknor & Co., Boston, 12mo, was reviewed in *Graham's American Monthly Magazine* for May 1848.

1057 F.E.M. STEELE, ed. *The Encore Reciter.* 2nd series. 4to. 1/0 sewed Nov. 1?

This was advertised in the *TWEd* on Nov. 1 as "Just ready." It is the first edition. The third edition of the second series was advertised there on Nov. 7, 1890. For the first series see 1888, and for the third series see 1890.

1058 ANONYMOUS *Old Mother Goose's Rhymes and Tales.* 8vo. Illustrated. 1/6 stiff boards, 2/6 cloth Nov. 2 (*Ath* ad)

This was also advertised in the *Spect* on Oct. 19, and both ads said imperial 16mo. It has colored plates. The *U Cat* gives Warne, New York, 1889, 8vo, 48 pp., colored plates; and the *BM* gives Warne, London, 1890, 8vo, 80 pp., illustrated. Warne issued it in 1892, imperial 16mo, illustrated, 2/6 boards, listed by *PC* for Sept. 24; and they issued it in 1896, Cr 8vo, 64 pp., colored illustrations, 1/0 picture boards, listed by *PC* on Oct. 24.

1059 AGNES STEVENS, ed. *How Men Propose.* 12mo. 1/0 sewed Nov. 10 (*Ath*)

Popular Library No. 10. The *Eng Cat* gives Warne, 1/0, 2/0, issued in 1889; the listing in the *Ath* was 2/0 cloth. The *BM* gives Warne, London, 1890. The first edition was issued by A. C. McClurg & Co., Chicago, 1888, 19 cm., 343 pp. In England it was issued by Fisher Unwin, London, 1890 (1889), 343 pp.

1060 MARIA EDGEWORTH *Forester, Angelina, The Prussian Vase, and Other Tales.* Cr 8vo. 1/0 cloth Dec. 14 (*Ath* ad)

The Village Library. This is re-edited and revised by Laura Valentine. These are from *Moral Tales.*
See 1877

1061 MARIA EDGEWORTH *Lame Jervis, The Limerick Gloves, and Other Tales.*
Cr 8vo. 1/o cloth   Dec. 14 (*Ath* ad)
The Village Library. This is re-edited and revised by Laura Valentine. The first title was issued by Cramer & Spear, Pittsburgh, 1818, 13 cm., 108 pp.

1062 MARIA EDGEWORTH *Lazy Lawrence, Garry Owen, and Other Tales and Stories.*
Cr 8vo. 1/o cloth   Dec. 14 (*Ath* ad)
The Village Library. This contains *Simple Susan*, and all are from *The Parent's Assistant*, re-edited and revised by Laura Valentine. The first title was issued by Sidney's Press, New Haven, Conn., 1809, 14.5 cm., 36 pp.; and *Simple Susan* was issued by Wells & Lilly, Boston, 1819, 14 cm., frontispiece.
See 1877

1063 MARIA EDGEWORTH *Frank, Rosamond, Harry and Lucy, and Other Tales and Stories.* Cr 8vo. 1/o cloth
Dec. 14 (*Ath* ad)
The Village Library. These are from *Early Lessons*, re-edited and revised by Laura Valentine.
See 1877

1064 NATHANIEL OGLE *Marianne.* 16mo. 1/o sewed, 1/6 cloth   Dec.?
Star Series No. 115. This had no date and 311 pp. The first edition was issued by G. B. Whittaker, London, 3 vols., 1825, 19 cm., anonymous.
Also 1900

1065 FRANCES H. BURNETT *Surly Tim, and Other Stores.* 12mo. 1/o sewed   1889
London Library No. 32. The first edition was issued by Scribner, Armstrong & Co., New York, 1877, 17 cm., 270 pp., $1.25, with an author's note stating that it and *That Lass o' Lowrie's* were the only works of hers that had been prepared and corrected for book issue under her supervision. The title story had appeared in *Scribner's Monthly* for June 1872, and the other stories except for one had also appeared there. It was listed in the *Nation* on Oct. 18 and in *PW* on Oct. 20. They issued the third edition, advertised in the *New-York Times* on Oct. 27 as "Now ready." The first edition was advertised there on Oct. 16 as "This day." In England it was issued by Chatto & Windus, 1878 (1877), 12mo, anonymous, 333 pp., 2/o boards, advertised as by special arrangement with the American publishers. It was deposited Dec. 5, 1877, and listed in the *Academy* on Nov. 24. It was also issued by Ward, Lock & Co., London (1877), 147 pp., 1/o sewed, deposited Dec. 12 and listed by the *Bks* (monthly) on Jan. 4, 1878.

1066 ROSS GORDON *Forty Thousand Pounds.* 12mo. 1/o sewed   1889 (*Eng Cat*)
London Library No. 33. I cannot find any further information about this title.

1067 WILLIAM B. KESTEVEN *Home Doctoring.* Cr 8vo. Illustrated. 1/o 1889 (*Eng Cat*)
Useful Books. This is the first edition, 1889, 156 pp.

1068 JOHN GAY *The Fables of John Gay.*
New edition. Cr 8vo. Illustrated. 1/6 sewed, 2/o cloth, 2/6 imitation Roxburghe   1889 (*Eng Cat*)
Chandos Classics No. 133. This is 1889, 313 pp., edited by W.H.K. Wright. Warne issued it in 1865, new edition, Fcp 8vo, 271 pp., illustrated, 3/6, edited by O. F. Owen, a reissue of the Routledge edition of 1854. It was listed in the *Reader* on Dec. 9, 1865. Warne also issued it in 1871, edited by Owen and illustrated by William Harvey, Cr 8vo, 5/o, advertised in the *Spect* on Nov. 18. Warne issued it in 1889, Fcp 4to, illustrated, 10/6 half-calf, 250 copies (100 to America), advertised in the *Spect* on Oct.

19. They issued it in New York in 1890, illustrated by Harvey, $.75, in smooth blue linen boards, untrimmed, advertised in the *Nation* on Feb. 20. The first edition of the first series was issued by J. Tonson, etc., London, 1727, 24.5 cm., 173 pp., illustrated. The second series was first issued by J. & P. Knapton, etc., London, 1738, 24.5 cm., 155 pp., illustrated, 5/0, frontispiece and 16 plates, listed in the *Gentleman's Magazine* as published in Dec. 1738. They issued an 8vo edition at the same time, with only a small number in the 4to edition. In the United States some form of the fables was issued by Mathew Carey, Philadelphia, 1794, 184 pp.

1069 SILAS K. HOCKING **Social Models.** 12mo. 1/0 1889 (*Eng Cat*)
I cannot discover any further information about this title.

1070 J. HOWARD **Bobbie Wilson.** Square 16mo. 1/0 1889 (*Eng Cat*)
I cannot discover any further information about this title.

Frederick Warne & Co.
London and New York
1890

1071 EDWARD BELLAMY *Looking Backward, 2000–1887.* 12mo. 0/6 sewed Feb. 15 (*PC*)

Popular Books No. 1. This has no date and 192 pp. Warne reissued this at 0/6 in 1894. The first edition was issued by Ticknor & Co., Boston, 1888, 19 cm., 470 pp., $1.50, listed in the *Ind* on Jan. 26 and in *PW* on Jan. 28. Houghton, Mifflin & Co., Boston and New York, issued it in 1889, new edition, new plates, $.50 paper, $1.00 cloth, advertised in the *New-York Times* on Sept. 22 as the 112th thousand and advertised in the *Nation* on Sept. 19 as "On Sept. 21." The first English edition was issued by William Reeves, London (1889), 256 pp., light blue wrappers, listed in *PC* on Apr. 1, 1889. George Routledge & Sons, Limited, London, etc., issued it (1890), 256 pp., 1/0 sewed, 1/6 cloth, listed in *PC* on Feb. 1. It was also issued by Ward, Lock & Co., London, etc., in 1890, 248 pp., 0/6 sewed, 1/0 cloth, listed in *PC* on Feb. 15.

1072 SAMUEL WARREN *Now and Then.* p 8vo. 0/6 sewed Feb. (*Bks*)

Notable Novels No. 138. The first edition was issued by William Blackwood & Sons, London and Edinburgh, 1848, royal 8vo, 21/0 half-bound, advertised in the *Spect* on Dec. 4, 1847, as "On Dec. 18" and in the *Ath* on Jan. 1, 1848, as "This day." The second edition, the same, was advertised in the *Spect* as "On Feb. 9, 1848." Wolff had a copy of the third edition, no date, revised

by the author, with a preface and a dedication (Dec. 18, 1847). It was 21/0 in magenta cloth with dark cream endpapers, advertised in the *Spect* on Dec. 27, 1848, as "Just published." A preface in Wolff's third edition states that this was written Nov. 21–Dec. 2, 1847, published Dec. 18, and sold out by Dec. 20, 1847. Blackwood issued a new edition in 1850, p 8vo, 10/6, advertised in the *Spect* on Dec. 28, 1850; they issued a new edition, Fcp 8vo, 6/0, advertised there on July 30, 1853; and they issued a new edition, p 8vo, 178 pp. in double columns, 2/0 cloth, listed by the *PC* as published Dec. 15–30, 1854. The first American edition was issued by Harper & Brothers, New York, 1848, 2 parts, 19 cm., 290 pp., $.50, listed by *Lit W* as published Jan. 22–29 and noticed in the *Southern Literary Messenger* for Mar. They issued a second edition in 2 parts, $.25, listed by *Lit W* as published Feb. 15–19, 1848.

1073 EDWARD BELLAMY *Dr. Heidenhoff's Process.* 12mo. 0/6 sewed Feb. (*Bks*)

Popular Books No. 2. This has no date, 126 pp. The first edition was issued by D. Appleton & Co., New York, 1880, 16.5 cm., 140 pp., *New Handy Volume Series* No. 54. $.25 paper, my copy, listed in the *Nation* on June 17 and in *PW* on June 19. The first British edition was issued by David Douglas, Edinburgh, etc., 1884, 19 cm., 234 pp., 6/0, listed in the *Ath* on Feb. 16 and in *PC* on Feb. 15. It was also issued by George

Routledge & Sons, Limited, London, etc. (1890), Demy 8vo, 96 pp., o/6 sewed, listed in *PC* on Feb. 15; and by Ward, Lock & Co., London, etc., in 1890, o/6 sewed, 1/o cloth, probably in Feb. It was also issued by William Reeves, London (1890), 139 pp., portrait, listed in *PC* on Feb. 15.

1074 SIR WILLIAM F.P. NAPIER *History of the War in the Peninsula and in the South of France.* 6 vols. Cr 8vo. 1/6 sewed, 2/o cloth, 2/6 imitation Roxburghe each Feb. (*Bks*)

Chandos Classics Nos. 134–139. These had maps and plans and were dated 1890. Warne issued it in 6 vols., 1886, and reissued it in *Chandos Classics*, 1892, and in the 1900s. The first edition was 6 vols., 23 cm., 20/o boards each, with maps and plans. Vol. 1 was issued by John Murray, London, 1828, listed by the *Edinburgh Review* (quarterly) as published Nov. 1827–Apr. 1828. Vols. 2–6 were issued by T. & W. Boone, London, 1829–1840. Vol. 2 was listed in the *Spect* on Aug. 15, 1829; a second edition, the same, was advertised there on Oct. 13, 1832. Vol. 3 was 1831, advertised in the *Spect* on Mar. 5 as "This day"; vol. 4 advertised Mar. 7, 1835, as "Just published"; vol. 5 advertised Nov. 12, 1836, as "On Nov. 15"; vol. 6 advertised on May 23, 1840. Boone issued a new and revised edition in 6 vols., issued monthly, maps and plans, 10/o cloth each, vol. 1 on Jan. 1, 1851. In the United States it was issued by D. Christy, Oxford, Ohio. He issued a vol., 1836, 504 pp., and issued 2-vols.-in-1, 1838–42, 28 cm. Carey & Hart, Philadelphia, issued it in 4 vols., 1842, 24 cm., maps and plans, from the fourth edition, reviewed in *Graham's Lady's and Gentleman's Magazine* (monthly) for Nov. 1841. J. S. Redfield, New York, issued it in 2 vols. in 1844, noticed in the *Merchants' Magazine* (monthly) for Sept.

1075 GEORGE M. FENN *The Mynns' Mystery.* Cr 8vo. 2/o boards, 2/6 cloth Mar. 15 (*Ath*)

Library of Fiction No. 9. This is the first English edition, my copy, 1890, 18.3 cm., 288 pp., yellow pictorial boards, printed in red, blue, and black with the series title on the spine. It has plain white endpapers and a commercial ad on the back cover. The first edition was issued by Frank F. Lovell, New York (1890), 205 pp., *International Series* No. 49, $.30 paper, listed in *PW* on Feb. 1 and the *Ind* on Feb. 6. Warne reissued it in this series, Cr 8vo, 2/o boards, dated 1891; and issued it in 1896, Cr 8vo, 1/o sewed, listed in *PC* on May 23.

1076 EDWARD BELLAMY *Miss Ludington's Sister.* 12mo. o/6 sewed Mar. (*Bks*)

Popular Books No. 3. This has no date and 123 pp. The first edition was issued by James R. Osgood & Co., Boston, 1884, 17.5 cm., 260 pp., $1.25, listed in the *Ind* on July 3 and in *PW* on July 5. Ticknor & Co., Boston, issued it in 1887, $.50, listed in the *Nation* on Oct. 6. The first British edition was issued by David Douglas, Edinburgh, etc., 1884, Cr 8vo, 6/o, a duplicate of the Osgood edition with a different title page. It was listed in the *Ath* and the *Spect* on Sept. 27. It was also issued by William Reeves, London, in 1890, listed in *PC* on Mar. 15. It was also issued by Ward, Lock & Co., London, etc. (1890), 19 cm., 125 pp., o/6 sewed, 1/o cloth, probably in Mar.

1077 ADA L. HARRIS *"Mine Own Familiar Friend."* p 8vo. o/6 sewed Mar. (*Bks*)

Notable Novels No. 139. This is the first edition, 1890, 125 pp., the only first edition issued in this series.

1078 E. J. CLAYDEN *"By the World Forgot."* 12mo. 1/o sewed Mar. (*Bks*)

London Library No. 35. This is the first edition, 1890, 175 pp., my copy, 1890 on the

front and title page, 17.7 cm., tan wrappers, printed and with a vignette on the front in brown. There are commercial ads on the back and inside covers.
See 1900

1079 JAMES S. BORLASE *The Police Minister.* 12mo. 1/0 sewed Mar.?
London Library No. 36. This is the first edition, 1890, 189 pp. Warne issued it as *Notable Novels* No. 146, p 8vo, o/6 sewed, listed by *PC* on Feb. 28, 1891.

1080 CAROLINE A. MASON *A Titled Maiden.* 16mo. 1/0 sewed, 1/6 cloth Apr. (*Bks*)
Star Series No. 116. This is the first English edition, no date, 312 pp. The first American edition was issued by the Congregational Sunday School & Publishing Society, Boston (copyright 1889), 19.5 cm., 447 pp., illustrated.
See 1900

1081 EMILY P. WEAVER *My Lady Nell.* 16mo. 1/0 sewed, 1/6 cloth Apr. (*Bks*)
Star Series No. 117. This is the first English edition, no date, 312 pp. The first American edition was issued by the Congregational Sunday School & Publishing Society, Boston (1889), 12mo, illustrated.
See 1900

1082 W. H. AINSWORTH *Old Saint Paul's.* p. 8vo. o/6 sewed May?
Notable Novels No. 140. I have a copy, a reissue in the series, no date, 21.1 cm., 191 pp. in double columns, white pictorial wrappers, printed in red, blue, and black with the series title on the front and the no. at the base of the spine. This is the new style of this series, which I date as about 1895. There are commercial ads on the back and inside covers. It first appeared in the *Sunday Times* in 1841 and was issued by Hugh Cunningham, London, 3 vols., 1841, 20 cm., 31/6, in dark brown cloth, with 20 illustrations by John Franklin. It was listed in the *Ath* on Dec. 4, 1841, and in the *Spect* on Dec. 11. Wolff had a copy, published for private circulation, 1842, 4to, 228 pp. in double columns, dark green cloth with white endpapers. It appeared in 2 supplements to *Ainsworth's Magazine* in June and Dec. 1846. It was issued in 12 parts, which Wolff thinks were issued by Cunningham in 1842–43 and which he thinks were bound up and issued in 1 vol. by Parry, Blenkarn & Co., London, 1847, new edition, 8vo, 434 pp., frontispiece and vignette title page by "Phiz" and the 20 illustrations by Franklin, his copy, in brown cloth with yellow endpapers. In the United States it was issued by Roberts Brothers, Boston, 1844, 29.5 cm., 75 pp. as an extra series of *Quarto Boston Notion.* An abridged edition was issued by E. P. Williams, Boston, 1844, 24.5 cm., 100 pp. in double columns, with cover title. Chapman & Hall, London, issued it in 2 vols., 1850, my copies in boards, Fcp 8vo, 1/0 boards, 1/6 cloth each, vol. 1 listed in the *Ath* on May 25 and vol. 2 on June 8.

1083 CHARLES LEVER *Arthur O'Leary.* p 8vo. o/6 sewed May?
Notable Novels No. 141. The first edition was issued by Henry Colburn, London, 3 vols., 1844, edited by Harry Lorrequer, frontispiece in each vol. and 7 plates by Cruikshank, 31/6 in green cloth with primrose-yellow endpapers. It was listed in the *Ath* on Apr. 6. He issued it in 1 vol., 1845, new edition, 23 cm., 364 pp., illustrated by Cruikshank, 12/0, advertised in the *Spect* on Dec. 7, 1844, as "Just ready." It first appeared in the *Dublin University Magazine,* Jan.–Dec. 1843, as *The Loiterings of Arthur O'Leary.* The *U Cat* gives an issue in Philadelphia, 1844.

1084 OCTAVE THANET (ALICE FRENCH) *Expiration.* Cr 8vo. Illustrated. 2/0 boards, 2/6 cloth June 7 (*Spect*)
Library of Fiction No. 10. This is the first English edition, 1890, 215 pp. The first

edition was issued by Charles Scribner's Sons, New York, 1890, 19 cm., 215 pp., illustrated, $.50 paper, $1.00 cloth, advertised in the *New-York Times* on Mar. 25 as "Today" and listed in *PW* on Mar. 29. It was also issued by Welch, Fracker & Co. (New York?), anonymous, listed in *Lippincott's Monthly Magazine* for Apr. 1890. This magazine also listed the Scribner edition in June 1890. Miss French was a midwestern American writer, and *Expiation* was an early work. I can't explain how two American publishers could have issued this title.

1085 ALEXANDRE DUMAS, PÈRE
Marguerite de Valois. p 8vo. 0/6 sewed
June (*Bks*)
Notable Novels No. 142. The first edition was *La Reine Margot*, Paris, 6 vols., 1845, 20 cm. Sadleir gives the first edition in English as issued by David Bogue, London, 1846, 18 cm., 472 pp., 3/6, *Marguerite de Valois*, in his *European Library* No. 3. It was advertised in the *Spect* on Feb. 28 and reviewed in the *Gentleman's Magazine* (monthly) for Feb. However, the *BM* gives George Peirce, London (1845), 479 pp., illustrated, *Margaret of Navarre*. The first American edition was issued by D. Appleton & Co., New York, 1846, 23 cm., 174 pp., in paper, *Library of Popular Reading* No. 3, listed in the *Knickerbocker* for May and also in the *Merchants' Magazine* (monthly) for May, *Marguerite de Valois*.

1086 ELIZABETH T. MEADE, later SMITH
Frances Kane's Fortune. 12mo. 1/0
sewed June (*Bks*)
London Library No. 37. This is the first edition, 1890, 128 pp. The first American edition was issued by John W. Lovell, New York (1890), 90 pp., *Westminster Series* No. 8, in paper, listed in *PW* on Aug. 23 and the *Literary News* for Sept.

1087 ROBERT CROMIE *A Plunge into Space.* Roy 16mo. 2/0 sewed, 3/6 cloth
July 26 (*Ath*)
This is the first edition, 1890, 240 pp. The 2/0 has colored pictorial wrappers, the front cover showing a diaphanously clad young lady in space. The endpapers list the *London Library* through No. 38.
Also 1891

1088 GEORGE ARMATAGE
The Thermometer as an Aid to Diagnosis in Veterinary Medicine. [Second edition enlarged.] Cr 8vo. Illustrated. 1/0
July (*Bks*)
This is 1890, 64 pp. The first edition was issued by A. P. Muddiman, Leighton Buzzard (1869), 46 pp. It was issued by William R. Jenkins, New York, 1891, second edition enlarged, 64 pp. Warne issued the third edition, revised and enlarged, Cr 8vo, illustrated, 1/0, dated 1894, 71 pp., listed by *PC* for Aug. 11.

1089 JAMES S. BORLASE *For True Love's Sake.* 12mo. 1/0 sewed July?
London Library No. 38. This is the first edition, 1890, 190 pp. It was advertised in the *TWEd* on July 18. Warne issued it as *Notable Novels* No. 150, p 8vo, 0/6 sewed, listed in *PC* on Mar. 5, 1892.

1090 MARY H. HOWELL *In Safe Hands.* 16mo. 1/0 sewed, 1/6 cloth Aug. (*Bks*)
Star Series No. 118. The first edition was issued by the American Sunday-School Union, Philadelphia, copyright 1888, 19.5 cm., 306 pp.

1091 ARTHUR N. MALAN *Lost on Brown Willy.* 12mo. Illustrated. 2/0 cloth
Oct. 4 (*Ath*)
This is the first edition, 1890, 192 pp. Warne issued it in their *Bedford Library*, 12mo, illustrated, 1/6 cloth, listed in *PC* on Nov. 20, 1897.

1092 EDWARD BULWER LYTTON *Harold.*
p 8vo. o/6 sewed   Oct. (*Bks*)

Notable Novels No. 143. Warne reissued this
in this series in 1894, my copy, no date, in
the new format for the series, 21.3 cm.,
192 pp. in double columns, white pictorial
wrappers, printed in red, green, brown,
and black with the series title on the front
and the no. at the foot of the spine. There
are commercial ads on the back and inside
front covers and a publisher's ad on the inside back cover giving the *Tavistock Library*
through (No. 8) and the *Library of Continental Authors* through No. 10. The first
edition was issued by Bentley, London, 3
vols., 1848, 20 cm., anonymous, 31/6 in
half-cloth boards with labels, with the dedication signed "E.B.L.," listed in the *Ath* on
June 10 and by *PC* as published May 30–
June 10. There were ads at the back of vol.
3 (June 9, 1848). Wolff had a variant binding in pale green cloth with pale yellow
endpapers, with 2 leaves of ads at the
front of vol. 1; and another copy, similar,
in light blue cloth, with the same ads. The
second edition in 3 vols. was advertised in
the *Spect* on Sept. 9 as "This day"; and the
third edition in 3 vols., 31/6, revised by the
author, with a new preface, was advertised
on Feb. 3, 1849, "In a few days." Parry &
Co., London, issued it in 3 vols., 1851,
fourth edition, revised, 19 cm. Chapman
& Hall, London, issued it in 1853, frontispiece, 4/o, listed in the *Spect* on Oct. 8.
The first American edition was issued by
Harper & Brothers, New York, preface
(1848), 24 cm., 217 pp., listed by *Lit W*
as published June 24–July 1, 1848, and
reviewed in the *Harbinger* (weekly) on
July 30.

1093 THOMAS P. WHITTAKER, ed.
Barker's Facts and Figures for 1891.
Cr 8vo. 1/o limp cloth, 2/o half-roan
Nov. 17 (*Spect*)

This has 320 pp. This and the issue for
1892 were the only two published. It was
advertised in the *Spect* on Nov. 15 as "On
Nov. 17."

1094 (HARRY PARKES) *Random Rhymes.*
Imperial 16mo. Illustrated. 1/o   Nov.
(*Bks*)

This is the first edition, no date, 24 leaves,
cover title.

1095 F.E.M. STEELE *The Encore Reciter.*
Series 3. 4to. 1/o sewed   Nov. (*Bks*)

All three series were issued in 1 vol., Cr
4to, 384 pp., 3/6, in Dec. It was still advertised in the *TWEd* on Sept. 16, 1892, the
same. For the first series see 1888; for the
second series see 1889.

1096 LAURA VALENTINE, ed. *The Old,
Old Fairy Tales.* Cr 8vo. 1/6 sewed,
2/o cloth, 2/6 imitation Roxburghe
Dec. (*Bks*)

Chandos Classics No. 141. This has no date
and 566 pp. The first edition was issued by
Warne, 1889, 8vo, 564 pp., colored illustrations, 7/6, listed in the *Ath* on Nov. 2,
1889. Warne issued it in New York, the
same, $3.00, listed in the *Nation* on Dec.
19, 1889.

1097 MRS. CLIFFORD BUTLER
Little Elsie's Country Visit. 12mo.
1/o   Dec. (*Bks*)

This was issued earlier in *Little Books for
Little People*, square Cr 8vo, illustrated, 2/o
cloth.

1098 ANNE BOWMAN *Among the Tartar
Tents.* 12mo. 2/6 cloth   1890 (*Eng Cat*)

This was also issued by Warne in 1895,
new edition, Cr 8vo, 335 pp., illustrated,
listed in *PC* on Nov. 16. The first edition
was issued by Bell & Daldy, London, 1861,
324 pp. It was issued by George Routledge
& Sons, London, Fcp 8vo, illustrated, 2/6,
Juvenile Books, advertised in the *Spect* on
Dec. 2, 1865. Warne first issued it in 1875,
12mo, 335 pp., illustrated, 3/6.

Frederick Warne & Co.
London and New York
1891

1099 G.P.R. JAMES *Agincourt.* p 8vo. o/6
sewed Jan. 17 (*PC*)

Notable Novels No. 144. The first English
edition was issued by Bentley, London, 3
vols., 1844, 20 cm., 31/6, published Nov.
12 according to the Bentley private catalog and listed in the *Ath* on Nov. 16. It was
issued by W. Simpkin & R. Marshall, London, 1848, revised and corrected, 23 cm.,
403 pp., frontispiece and preface, listed
in the *Spect* on June 2. It was also issued
by Simms & M'Intyre, London and Belfast, 1852, 384 pp., *Parlour Library* No. 76.
The first American edition was issued by
Harper & Brothers, New York, 1844, 24
cm., 157 pp., *Library of Select Novels* No. 44,
noticed in the *Southern Literary Messenger*
for Feb. 1845. Warne issued it in New
York, $.20 paper, listed in the *Literary Di-
gest* for Jan. 10, 1891.

1100 S. TURNER *Bits About Horses.*
16mo. 1/o sewed Feb. 7 (*PC*)

This was reissued in Sept. It is also given
by the *Eng Cat*, but otherwise I cannot
trace it.

1101 ROBERT CROMIE *A Plunge into
Space.* Second edition. Cr 8vo. 2/o sewed,
3/6 cloth Mar. (*PC*)

This is 1891, 240 pp., with a frontispiece
and illustrated title page, with a preface by
Jules Verne. Warne issued it in New York
in 1891, $1.25 cloth, advertised in the *Na-
tion* on Nov. 12. Warne issued it in their *Library of Fiction* No. 31, Cr 8vo, 240 pp., 2/o
boards, 2/6 cloth, a reissue of the second
edition, listed in *PC* on Nov. 16, 1895.
Also 1890

1102 MARIANNE KENT *Philip Mordant's
Ward.* 16mo. 1/6 sewed, 2/o cloth Apr.?

Star Series No. 119. The first edition was issued by Warne, 1888, Cr 8vo, 404 pp., 6/o,
listed in the *Ath* on Oct. 13. Warne also issued it as *Library of Fiction* No. 11, Cr 8vo,
2/o boards, listed in the *Spect* on May 2,
1891.

1103 WILLIAM J. GORDON *The Captain-
General.* Cr 8vo. Map. 2/o boards
June 13 (*PC*)

Library of Fiction No. 13. This has 304 pp.
The first edition was issued by Warne,
1888, 20 cm., 304 pp., frontispiece (folding map), 5/o, listed in the *Ath* on Nov. 3.
There was a third edition, 1891, 20 cm.,
304 pp., at 3/6, listed in *PC* on Dec. 5,
1891.

1104 G.P.R. JAMES *Rose D'Albret.* p 8vo.
o/6 sewed June 27 (*PC*)

Notable Novels No. 147. Warne also issued
this in New York, same series and no., $.20
paper, listed in the *Literary Digest* for July
25, 1891. The first edition was issued by
Bentley, London, 3 vols., 1844, 20 cm.,
31/6, listed in the *Ath* on May 25, and pub-

lished May 24 according to the Bentley private catalog. It is in blue-green cloth spines, boards, and labels, with white endpapers. It was issued by Thomas Hodgson, London, 1856, 336 pp., *Parlour Library* No. 138. The first American edition was issued by Harper & Brothers, New York, 1844, 8vo, 152 pp., noticed in the *Southern Literary Messenger* for Au.g

1105 WILLIAM H. MAXWELL *The Dark Lady of Doona.* p 8vo. 0/6 sewed June 27 (*PC*)

Notable Novels No. 148. Warne also issued this in New York with the same series title and no., $.20 paper, listed in the *Literary Digest* for July 25, 1891. The first edition was issued by Smith, Elder & Co., London, 1834, anonymous, 306 pp., *Library of Romance* No. 9, issued in Dec. 1833. It is in dark green cloth with the series title and no. on the spine, edges uncut, white endpapers with a design in blue and greenish gray. It was issued by Simms & M'Intyre, London and Belfast, 1846, 376 pp., *Parlour Novelist* No. 10, in stiff wrappers and cloth, containing other stories also, issued in Nov. It was issued by Thomas Hodgson, London (1854), 252 pp., *Parlour Library* No. 113. The first American edition was issued by Wallis & Newell, New York, 1835, 12mo, anonymous, 124 pp.

1106 EDMUND BOISGILBERT (IGNATIUS DONNELLY) *Caesar's Column.* 12mo. 0/6 sewed   July 4 (*PC*)

Popular Books No. 5. This is 1891, 216 pp., in gray pictorial wrappers with lettering and art on the front cover in dark blue and red. They issued it in their *Popular Library* No. 12, 12mo, 1/0 sewed, probably in 1891 also. The first edition was issued by F. J. Schulte, Chicago (1890), 20.5 cm., 367 pp., $1.25, listed in *PW* on Apr. 12 and in the *Ind* on Apr. 17. In addition to this Warne issue it was also issued in England by Ward, Lock & Co., London (1891), 242

pp., 0/6 sewed, listed in *PC* on June 27; and by Sampson Low, London, 1891, authorized edition, 367 pp., 3/6, a reissue of the American edition but by Donnelly, with a 32-page catalog (Oct. 1890), listed in the *Ath* and *PC* on July 11.

1107 ADA L. HARRIS *The Fatal Request.* Cr 8vo. 2/0 boards, 2/6 cloth   July 25 (*Ath*)

Library of Fiction No. 17. This is the first English edition, 1891, 398 pp., reviewed in *PC* on Aug. 15. The first American edition, a duplicate of this edition, was issued by the Cassell Publishing Co., New York (copyright 1891).

1108 JOHN G. WHITTIER *The Poetical Works of John Greenleaf Whittier.* Cr 8vo. 1/6 sewed, 2/0 cloth, 2/6 imitation Roxburghe   Aug. 1 (*PC*)

Chandos Classics No. 142? This is 1891 with 576 pp. Warne issued this with a life, notes, index, etc., 1891, 576 pp., in the *Albion Edition*, in July, 3/6 cloth. They also issued it in their *Lansdowne Poets*, Cr 8vo, portrait, illustrations, 3/6. There was an issue of *Poems . . .* , Boston, 1837, 16mo, 96 pp. *Poems* was issued by J. Healy, Philadelphia, etc., 1838, 19 cm., 180 pp., a second authorized collection, in brown or green cloth with white endpapers, deposited Oct. 30 and advertised in the *Penny Freeman* on Nov. 1 as "Just published." It contains 50 poems, of which 18 were in the edition of 1837. *Poems* was issued by Benjamin B. Mussey, Boston, 1849, 23.5 cm., 384 pp., frontispiece (portrait), engraved title page, and 7 plates, deposited Oct. 14, 1848, listed by *Lit W* as published Dec. 1–9, 1848. It was in decorated cloth of various colors with yellow endpapers and contained 106 poems, of which 35 were first collected. It was reprinted 1850, 54, 56, 57. *The Poetical Works of John Greenleaf Whittier* was issued by Ticknor & Fields, Boston, 2 vols., 1857, 14.5 cm., frontispiece (portrait), in blue cloth with gilt edges and chocolate endpapers, in an edition of 3,000 copies to sell at $1.50. It was deposited Aug. 29 and listed in the *American Publisher's Circular* on July 18 and reviewed in the *Knickerbocker* for Oct. It has a preface (Mar. 18, 1857), called a complete collection, with many poems first collected. There were later impressions, 1861, 62, 63, etc. The first English edition was *Ballads and Other Poems* . . . , issued by H. G. Clarke & Co., London, 1844, 14.5 cm., 216 pp., in illuminated wrappers, highly decorated, and in cloth with paper labels. It is *Clarke's Cabinet Series* No. 30 and consists of 46 poems, 29 of which were in the 1838 American edition.

1109 CHARLES KENT, ed. *Leigh Hunt as Poet and Essayist.* Cr 8vo. 1/6 sewed, 2/0 cloth, 2/6 imitation Roxburghe
Aug. 15 (*PC*)
Chandos Classics No. 143? The first edition thus was issued by Warne, 1889, 528 pp., portrait. This and the preceding title were issued in two styles of cloth at 2/0, the second style being library style, blue cloth, uncut.

1110 CHARLOTTE BRONTË *Shirley.* 8vo. 0/6 sewed   Aug. 22 (*PC*)
Standard Novels No. 1. Warne also issued this as *Notable Novels* No. 149, p 8vo, 0/6 sewed, listed in *PC* on Nov. 7, 1891. The first edition was issued by Smith, Elder & Co., London, 3 vols., 1849, 21 cm., by Currer Bell, 31/6, in claret cloth, with a 16-page catalog (Nov. 1849) at the back of vol. 1. It was advertised in the *Ath* on Oct. 20 as "On Oct. 31" and listed Nov. 3. They issued it in 1 vol., 1853, new edition, 580 pp., in gray-purple cloth, 6/0, listed in the *Spect* on Nov. 27, 1852. New editions were issued, 1858, 62, 63, 73, etc. The first American edition was issued by Harper & Brothers, New York, 1850, 8vo, 206 pp., *Library of Select Novels* No. 132, in buff

printed wrappers, $.37½, advertised in the *Lit W* on Nov. 24, 1849, as "Just published." It was also issued, 12mo, $1.00 muslin, noticed in the *Merchants' Magazine* (monthly) for Feb. 1850, 572 pp.

1111 GUSTAV VON MEYERN *A Perilous Venture.* 12mo. Illustrated. 2/6 cloth
Sept. 19 (*PC*)
Daring Deeds Library. This has no date and 312 pp. Warne reissued it in this series, no date, Cr 8vo, 312 pp., illustrated, 2/6 cloth, listed in *PC* on Dec. 14, 1895. This is a translation from the German by M. Hall. The first edition was *Teuerdank's Brautfahrt*, Leipzig, 1878, 18.5 cm., 352 pp. The first English edition was issued by Warne (1884), 312 pp., 3/6, "On our table" in the *Ath* for Nov. 22, 1884.

1112 E. L. SHUTE *Fancies Free.* 4to. Colored illustrations. 2/6 picture boards
Oct. 3 (*Ath*)
This is the first edition, in verse, no date, 36 pp., with 6 full-page illustrations and many brown-tone and colored illustrations. Warne also issued it in New York at $1.00, listed in the *Christian Union* on Dec. 5, 1891. Warne also reissued it in 1893, a new edition, Cr 4to, colored illustrations, 1/6 picture boards, cloth back, for Christmas, advertised in *PC*.

1113 A. J. DARYL *Little Merry-Makers.* Imperial 16mo. Colored illustrations. 1/6 boards   Oct. 3 (*PC*)
This is the first edition, in verse. It is also given by the *Eng Cat*. Warne reissued it in 1893, new edition, 4to, illustrated, 1/6 boards, listed in *PC* on Dec. 2, 1893.

1114 JULIA A.W. DEWITT *How He Made His Fortune.* 12mo. Illustrated. 2/6 cloth
Oct. 10 (*Ath*)
Daring Deeds Library. This is the first English edition, 1891, 317 pp. The first edition was issued by the Congregational

Sunday School and Publishing Society, Boston and Chicago (1889), 19.5 cm., 317 pp., illustrated.

1115 JAMES M. COBBAN *Sir Ralph's Secret.* 12mo. 1/o sewed Oct. 31 (*PC*)
London Library No. 40. This is also given by the *Eng Cat*, but otherwise I cannot trace it.

1116 EMILIA MARRYAT, later NORRIS *Jack Stanley.* 12mo. Illustrated. 2/6 cloth Oct. (*Bks*)
Daring Deeds Library. This is also given by the *Eng Cat*, but otherwise I cannot trace it.

1117 AUGUSTA MARRYAT *The Young Lamberts.* 12mo. Illustrated. 2/6 cloth Oct. (*Bks*)
Daring Deeds Library. This is also given by the *Eng Cat*, but otherwise I cannot trace it.

1118 EDWARD BULWER LYTTON *The Caxtons.* 8vo. o/6 sewed Nov. 7 (*PC*)
Standard Novels No. 3. The first English appearance was in *Blackwood's Magazine*, Apr. 1848–Oct. 1849. The first English book edition was issued by William Blackwood & Sons, Edinburgh and London, 3 vols., 1849, 20 cm., 31/6, in dark brown cloth, with a 32-page catalog (1849) at the back of vol. 3. It was listed in the *Spect* on Oct. 6 and in the *Ath* on Oct. 13. Blackwood issued it in 1 vol., 1853, second edition, 7/6, listed in the *Spect* on Apr. 30. It was issued by George Routledge & Co., London and New York, 1854, new edition, 20 cm., 347 pp., frontispiece, 4/o cloth, listed in the *Ath* on Sept. 30. Blackwood continued to issue it also and issued it in 2 vols., 5/o each, in 1859. The first American edition was in 2 parts, issued by Harper & Brothers, New York, 1849, 8vo, $.18¾ each. Part 1 was listed by *Lit W* as published Mar. 3–17, and part 2 was advertised there as "On Oct. 3."

1119 ANONYMOUS *The Life of Our Lord.* 4to. Illustrated. 1/o sewed Nov. 7 (*PC*)
This is the first edition, written for young children. It was also issued in Dec. at 3/6, listed in the *PC* on Dec. 12. Warne reissued it in 1894, 4to, illustrated, 1/o, listed in *PC* on Feb. 24.

1120 FREDERICK MARRYAT *The Settlers in Canada.* 12mo. Illustrated. 2/6 cloth Nov. 7 (*PC*)
Daring Deeds Library. This has 371 pp. Warne issued it in 1886, square Cr 8vo, illustrated, 6/o gilt edges, 5/o plain, advertised in the *Spect* on Dec. 4, 1886. They issued it in New York, new edition, illustrated, $2.00, advertised in the *Nation* on Nov. 25, 1886. The first English edition was issued by Longmans, London, 2 vols., 1844, 19 cm., frontispiece in each vol., 12/o, dark brown cloth with cream endpapers. This was written for young people. There is a 32-page catalog (Sept. 1844) at the back of vol. 1. It was listed in the *Ath* on Sept. 7. They issued a new edition in 1848, Fcp 8vo, 2 illustrations, 7/6, advertised in the *Illustrated London News* on Jan. 24, 1848. Henry G. Bohn, London, issued it, 1854, new edition, 18 cm., 398 pp., illustrated, 5/o, listed by *PC* as published Dec. 31, 1854–Jan. 15, 1855; reissued in 1860 in *Bohn's Illustrated Library*, p 8vo, 10 illustrations, 5/o, advertised in the *Spect* on June 30. The first American edition was issued by D. Appleton & Co., New York, etc., 2 vols., 1845, illustrated, noticed in the *Merchants' Magazine* (monthly) for Dec. 1844 and in the *Southern Literary Messenger* for Jan. 1845. They issued it, 2-vols.-in-1, in 1847, illustrated, $.75, listed by *Lit W* as published Dec. 4–11.

1121 NELLA PARKER *Home Acting for Amateurs.* 1st series. 12mo. 1/o cloth boards Dec. 5 (*Ath*)
This is the first edition, no date. It was issued in New York, 1892, 12mo, $.50 cloth,

advertised in the *Nation* on Nov. 24. The second series by Nella Parker et al., the same, both in London and New York, was listed in the *Ath* on Dec. 5 also.

1122 T. P. WHITTAKER, ed. ***Barker's Facts and Figures for 1892.*** Cr 8vo. 1/0 Dec. 12 (*PC*)

This was issued by Warne in New York, listed in the *Nation* on Feb. 25, 1892, $.50 limp cloth. See 1890 for the only other issue.

1123 JOHN B. VERITY ***Electricity Up to Date.*** 16mo. Illustrated. Folding map. 1/6 parchment Dec. 19 (*PC*)

This is the first edition, no date, 178 pp. It was issued by Warne in New York in 1892, square 18mo, $.75 cardboard covers, listed in the *Nation* on Mar. 10. Warne reissued it in 1893, third edition, Cr 8vo, illustrated, colored folding map, 1/6 sewed, 2/0 cloth, with no date and 163 pp., listed in *PC* on Apr. 1; and they issued it in New York in June 1893, 16mo, 163 pp., $.75 paper. They reissued it, 1894, new and enlarged edition, Cr 8vo, 226 pp., illustrated, colored folding map, 1/6 sewed, 2/6 cloth, advertised in the *Ath* on Mar. 3; reissued in New York in Sept., 238 pp., $.75 paper. Warne issued the fourth edition in 1895, the same, 2/0, listed in *PC* on June 22; and issued the fifth edition, 1896, 19 cm., 238 pp., the same, 2/6, listed in *PC* on Jan. 25, 1896; and issued it in New York (1896), fifth edition, 12mo, illustrated, $1.00 cloth, advertised in the *Nation* on Mar. 12.

Frederick Warne & Co.
London and New York
1892

1124 IMRE KIRALFY *Venice in London.*
Folio. Illustrated. 1/0 Jan. 23 (*PC*)
This is the first edition, a colored picture
book for children.

1125 LOUIS HOFFMANN (ANGELO LEWIS)
Card Tricks with Apparatus. 12mo.
Diagrams. 1/0 sewed Jan. 30 (*PC*)
Useful Books. This is 1892, 115 pp. It was
reissued about 1900. It is probably taken
from *Tricks with Cards*, first issued by
Warne, 1889, Cr 8vo, 250 pp., illustrated,
2/6 cloth, listed in the *Spect* on Dec. 21,
1889. This latter title has been offered by a
dealer in decorated red cloth and also
in green cloth with front and spine decorated in black, copper, silver, red, and
light green.

1126 LOUIS HOFFMANN (ANGELO LEWIS)
Card Tricks without Apparatus. 12mo.
Diagrams. 1/0 sewed Jan. 30 (*PC*)
Useful Books. This has no date and 104 pp.
It was reissued about 1900 and about
1921. It is probably from *Tricks with Cards*
(see the preceding item).

1127 GEORGE M. FENN *Lady Maude's*
Mania. Cr 8vo. 2/0 boards Mar. 26 (*Ath*)
Library of Fiction No. 19. Wolff had a copy
of this in pink pictorial boards, 1891. The
first edition was issued by Warne, London
and New York, 1890, Cr 8vo, 342 pp., 6/0,
listed in the *Ath* on Oct. 4. It was reissued
in 1891, 342 pp., 3/6, listed in *PC* on May

23. The first American edition was issued
by the United States Book Co., New York
(1890), authorized edition, 277 pp., $.50
paper and $1.00 cloth, *International Series*
No. 136, advertised in the *New-York Times*
on Nov. 29, 1890, as books of the week and
listed in *PW* on Dec. 13.

1128 G.P.R. JAMES *The Woodman.* p 8vo.
0/6 sewed   Apr. 16 (*PC*)
Notable Novels No. 151. This is 1892, 190
pp. The first edition was issued by T. C.
Newby, London, 3 vols., 1849, 31/6 in dark
gray-purple cloth with no author's name
on the binding. It was advertised in the *Ath*
on June 9 as "Just ready" and listed June
23. Newby issued the second edition, 3
vols., advertised in the *Spect* on Aug. 25,
1849. The first American edition was issued by Harper & Brothers, New York,
1849, 22 cm., 163 pp., $.25 paper, listed by
Lit W as published July 14–Aug. 4 and advertised on July 7 as "Just ready."

1129 WILLIAM M. THACKERAY *Vanity*
Fair. 8vo. Wrappers Apr. 23 (*PC*)
I conjecture that this was at 1/0 sewed,
later called *Standard Novels* No. 13 when it
was also issued in 2 vols., 0/6 sewed each.
The present *PC* listing in 0/6 sewed and
the *Eng Cat* gives 0/6, 1/0, 1892. Warne issued it as *Standard Novels* No. 13, 2 vols.,
0/6 sewed each and 1 vol., 1/0 sewed, in
8vo size, listed in *PC* on Sept. 29, 1894.
This first was issued in 20 monthly 1/0

wrappered parts in 19, Jan. 1847–July 1848. The parts had yellow wrappers, 23 cm., illustrated, and were issued by the "Punch" office, London, etc. It was issued in 1 vol. by Bradbury & Evans, London, 1848, 22.5 cm., 624 pp., frontispiece, extra vignette title page, and 38 illustrations by the author. It was bound in steel-blue cloth, 21/0, advertised in the *Ath* on July 1 as "This day" and listed July 22. They issued it 1853, 584 pp., 6/0, advertised in the *Spect* on Jan. 28, 1854, as "This day"; and issued it, 1856, new edition, p 8vo, 584 pp., 6/0, listed by *PC* as published Aug. 15–30, 1856. It was issued by Smith, Elder & Co., London, 1865, 19.5 cm., 584 pp. The first American edition was issued by Harper & Brothers, New York, 1848, 24 cm., 332 pp. in double columns, illustrated, $1.25 in purple cloth and $1.00 paper, listed in *Lit W* as published Aug. 19–26. It was also issued in 2 parts at $.50 each, part 1 listed by *Lit W* as published July 22–29, 1848, and part 2 as for the complete edition.

1130 FRANCIS E. SMEDLEY **Frank Fairlegh.** p 8vo. o/6 sewed   May 7 (*PC*)

Notable Novels No. 152. Warne reissued this in this series, 1892, 21.2 cm., 186 pp. in double columns, white pictorial wrappers, printed in red, blue, and black, with the series title on the front and the no. on the spine. There are commercial ads on the back and inside covers and a leaf of publisher's ads at the back. I think this was issued in 1895, as the front inside cover ad contains a date (Oct. 25, 1894), although the publisher's ads are still those of the 1892 issue. This ran sporadically in *Sharpe's London Magazine*, June 1846–May 1848. It was issued in 15 monthly 8vo, 1/0 parts in pale green wrappers, Jan. 1849–Mar. 1850. No. 15 was 1/6. The first 4 nos. had the imprint of Arthur Hall & Co., and the remainder with the imprint of Arthur Hall, Virtue & Co., etc. The parts had illustrations by Cruikshank. The first book

edition was issued by Arthur Hall, Virtue & Co., London, 1850, 22 cm., anonymous, 496 pp., illustrated with a frontispiece, added pictorial title page, and 28 plates by Cruikshank, 16/0 in gray-purple cloth and yellow endpapers, with no author's name on the binding. It was listed in the *Ath* on Mar. 23 and was bound up from the parts. They reissued it in 1854, 2/6 boards, 3/6 cloth, advertised in the *Spect* on Oct. 28 as "This day"; and reissued it in 1857, the same, advertised in the *Spect* on June 20. In the United States it was issued by H. Long & Brother, New York, anonymous, illustrated, advertised in *Lit W* on Mar. 22, 1851, as "New books" and reviewed in the *Southern Quarterly Review* for Apr. 1851. I cannot explain the discrepancy with the notice in the *American Whig Review* (monthly) for Aug. 1850, but I consider it reliable. Long reissued it, new edition, illustrated, advertised in *Lit W* on Mar. 5, 1853, as "Ready." It was also issued by T. B. Peterson, Philadelphia, anonymous, listed in *Godey's Lady's Book* (monthly) for Nov. 1850.

1131 SIR WALTER SCOTT **Ivanhoe.** Cr 8vo. 1/0 sewed   May 28 (*PC*)

National Novels No. 1. This was also issued by Warne in New York as No. 1 in the same series, mentioned in the *Christian Union* for July 30, 1892, in paper covers. The first edition was issued by Archibald Constable, Edinburgh, etc., 3 vols., 1820, 19.5 cm., anonymous, 30/0, with a preface signed Laurence Templeton, listed by the *Edinburgh Review* (quarterly) as published Oct. 1819–Jan. 1820. Constable issued a second edition, the same, listed by the *Quarterly Review* as published Oct.–Dec. 1819. The first American edition was issued by M. Carey & Son, Philadelphia, 2 vols., 1820, 12mo, anonymous, reviewed in the *Port Folio*, Philadelphia (quarterly) for Mar. 1820. It was also issued in Boston,

8vo, $1.50, listed in the *North American Review* (quarterly) for Oct. 1820.
See 1894

1132 ANGELICA SELBY *In the Sunlight.*
Cr 8vo. 2/o boards   May 28 (*Spect*)
Library of Fiction No. 22. This is 1892 with 276 pp. The first edition was issued by Warne, 2 vols., 1890, Cr 8vo, 12/o, advertised in the *Spect* as published in June.

1133 DOUGLAS W. JERROLD **Mrs. Caudle's Curtain Lectures.** 12mo. 1/o sewed May 28 (*PC*)
Popular Library No. 13. This ran in *Punch* during 1845, and the first book edition was issued by the *Punch* Office, London, 1846, 17.5 cm., 142 pp., illustrated. Bradbury, Evans & Co., London, issued the illustrated edition, 1866, small 4to, (202) pp., tinted frontispiece, vignette title page in red and black, and textual illustrations by Charles Keene. It is in purple cloth with very dark green endpapers and has 4 pp. of ads at the back, Wolff's copy. In the United States it was issued by Carey & Hart, Philadelphia, 1845, 18.5 cm., anonymous, 42 pp., illustrated, containing 10 "lectures," listed in the *Knickerbocker* for July. It was also issued by J. Winchester, New York, 1845, 22 cm., anonymous, 26 pp., probably with 10 "lectures," and with 48 pp. with 15 "lectures." It was also issued by W. Taylor & Co., New York, 1845, 8vo, anonymous, 26 pp., containing 15 "lectures."

1134 GEORGES OHNET (GEORGES HÉNOT) **The Ironmaster.** Cr 8vo. 1/o sewed June 11 (*PC*)
Library of Continental Authors No. 8. This has no date, 351 pp., from the 146th French edition. Warne reissued it in this series around 1908 and issued a new edition, 1899, 351 pp., frontispiece. The first edition was *Les Batailles de la Vie. Le Maître de Forges*, Paris, 1882. The 141st edition

was 1884, 486 pp. William R. Jenkins, New York, issued it at $.25, listed in the *Nation* on Oct. 2, 1884. *The Battles of Life— The Ironmaster* was issued by Wyman & Sons, London, 3 vols., 1884, authorized translation, 20 cm. Henry Vizetelly & Co., London, issued it, 1884, 19 cm., 351 pp., 6/o, *One Volume Novels* No. 1, from the 146th French edition. It was advertised in the *Ath* and *Spect* on June 7 as "This day." The second through fourth editions, all 1884, were issued in July, Oct., and Nov. respectively. The second edition was in brown cloth blocked in red and gilt, with a 16-page catalog (Apr. 1884). Vizetelly issued it, 1885, 21 cm., 351 pp., with 42 full-page illustrations, 7/6, advertised in the *Ath* on Dec. 6, 1884, as "Shortly." He issued a yellowback edition, p 8vo, 2/o boards, in June 1888, with the translator's preface (May 1884). In the United States it was issued by George Munro, New York, in 1884, *The Master of the Forges*, $.20 quarto paper, *Seaside Library* No. 1825, advertised in the *New-York Times* on May 17 as a late issue. It was issued as *The Ironmaster* by Rand McNally, Chicago and New York, 1888, my copy, 351 pp., *Rialto Series* No. 2, listed in *Lit W* on Nov. 24, 1888, in paper.

1135 GERALD GRIFFIN **The Collegians; or, The Colleen Bawn.** Cr 8vo. 2/o boards June?
Library of Fiction No. 24. This has 389 pp. The first edition was issued by Saunders & Otley, London, 3 vols., 1829, 19 cm., anonymous, 31/6, in half-cloth boards and labels, listed in the *Spect* on Feb. 28 and by the *Quarterly Review* as published Jan.– Mar. This was a second series of *Tales of the Munster Festivals*. They issued a second edition in 3 vols., 31/6, listed in the *Westminster Review* (quarterly) for Oct. 1829; and they issued a new edition in 3 vols., advertised in the *Spect* on Dec. 26, 1829. It was issued by James Duffy & Sons, Dublin, new edition, no date, Fcp 8vo, 6/o in buff cloth, by Griffin, with a frontispiece and

engraved title page, listed by the *Edinburgh Review* as published Jan.–Apr. 1842. Simms & M'Intyre, London and Belfast, issued it, 1847, 12mo, 345 pp., 1/o boards, *Parlour Library* No. 6, listed by *PC* as published July 13–29. The first American edition was issued by J. & J. Harper, New York, 2 vols., 1829, 20.5 cm., anonymous, listed in the *North American Review* (quarterly) for July.

1136 SIR WALTER SCOTT *Old Mortality.*
Cr 8vo. 1/o sewed   July 2 (*PC*)

National Novels No. 3. The first edition was as vols. 2–4 of *Tales of My Landlord*, selected and arranged by Jedediah Cleishbotham. This was issued in 4 vols. by William Blackwood, London, etc., 1816, 19.5 cm., 28/o, listed by the *Quarterly Review* as published July–Sept. Vol. 1 was *The Black Dwarf*. They issued it 4-vols.-in-2, reviewed in the *North American Review* (*sic*) for July 1817. In the United States it was issued by M. Thomas, Philadelphia, 4-vols.-in-1, 1817, 18 cm. The second American edition was issued by James Eastburn & Co., New York, 4 vols., 1817.
See 1894

1137 AMELIA E. BARR *Jan Vedder's Wife.*
Cr 8vo. 2/o boards   July 2 (*PC*)

Library of Fiction No. 25. The first English edition was issued by James Clarke & Co., London, (1885), 329 pp., 6/o. They issued a second edition, Cr 8vo, 3/6, advertised in the *Spect* on Aug. 21, 1886, as "Now ready"; they issued the third edition in 1887, Cr 8vo, 3/6, advertised in the *Spect* on Feb. 5; and they issued it in 1892 at 1/6, advertised in the *Spect* on June 4. The first American edition was issued by Dodd, Mead & Co., New York, (1885), 17.5 cm., 329 pp., $1.25 cloth, listed in *PW* and *Lit W* on Apr. 4 and in the *Nation* on Apr. 9, and advertised in the *New-York Times* on June 17, 1893, 16mo in cloth, *Pocket Edition*, "Just published." Warne also issued

this in the *Star Series* No. 123, 16mo, 1/6 sewed, 2/o cloth, dated 1892, 329 pp., listed in *PC* on July 2, 1892, also.

1138 RICHARD AVIS *Bird Preservation, Bird Mounting, and the Preservation of Bird's Eggs.* 12mo. Illustrated. 1/o
Aug. 13 (*PC*)

This has no date and 48 pp. I judge Avis to be a pseudonym. The first edition was issued by Groombridge & Sons, London, 1870, 16mo, 48 pp. The *Eng Cat* says it was also issued in 1871 at 1/o.

1139 (LAURA VALENTINE) *Aunt Louisa's Book of Nursery Rhymes.* 4to. Illustrated. 1/o   Sept. 3 (*PC*)

This is 1892, 94 pp. The Osborne Collection gives it as no date (circa 1880), 24 cm., 94 pp., illustrated, in pictorial boards.

1140 WILLIAM M. THACKERAY *The History of Pendennis.* 8vo. 2vols., o/6 sewed each; 1 vol., 1/o sewed
Sept. 10 (*PC*)

Standard Novels No. 4. Warne reissued this in this series in 1 vol., 8vo, 1/o sewed, listed in *PC* on Sept. 2, 1893. This first appeared in 24 monthly 1/o wrappered parts in 23, 23 cm., illustrated by the author. They ran Nov. 1848–Dec. 1850 with a 3-month hiatus. Part 1 was issued on Nov. 1, 1848. The parts were bound up in 2 vols. and issued by Bradbury & Evans, London, etc., 1849–50, 22.5 cm., illustrated, 26/o, in steel-blue cloth with cream endpapers, with frontispiece, extra vignette title page, and 22 illustrations in each vol. Vol. 1 was listed in the *Ath* on Jan. 12, 1850, 13/o, and vol. 2 was listed on Dec. 7, 1850, 13/o. They issued it in 1 vol., 1856 (1855), Cr 8vo, 652 pp., 7/o, listed by *PC* as published Oct. 1–13, 1855; and they reissued it, 1858, the same. It was issued in 2 vols. by Smith, Elder & Co., London, 1868–70, 21 cm., illustrated. The first American edition was issued by Harper & Brothers,

New York, 2 vols., 1850–51, 24 cm., illustrated. This contains paragraphs omitted in the English issue. Vol. 1 was listed in the *Merchants' Magazine* for June 1850, and vol. 2 was noticed there in Mar. 1851. Both vols. may have been dated 1850. Harpers also issued it in 8 parts at $.25 each, part 1 listed by *Lit W* as published Aug. 18–Sept. 1, 1849, and part 7 about Dec. 13, 1850. They reissued it, 1867, 2-vols.-in-1, small 8vo, illustrated, listed in the *North American Review* (quarterly) for July.

1141   ROSE E. MAY **Merry Moments for Merry Folk.** Imperial 16mo. Illustrated. 2/0 boards   Sept. 24 (*PC*)

This is the first edition, rhymes, no date, which the *BM* gives as 4to.
Also 1893

1142   SIR WALTER SCOTT **Waverley.** Cr 8vo. 1/0 sewed, 1/6 cloth Nov. 19 (*PC*)

National Novels No. 5. The first edition was issued by Archibald Constable, Edinburgh, etc., 3 vols., 1814, 18.9 cm., anonymous, issued in Mar. Constable issued the second edition, the same, listed by the *Edinburgh Review* (quarterly) as published May–Aug., 21/0; and issued the third edition, the same, 21/0, listed in the same as published Aug.–Nov. 1814. In the United States it was issued by Van Winkle & Wiley, New York, 2 vols., 1815, 17.5 cm., anonymous. It was also issued by Wells & Lilly, etc., Boston, 2-vols.-in-1, 1815, 17.5 cm., anonymous. There was a new edition issued in New York, 2 vols., 18mo, anonymous, listed in the *North American Review* (quarterly) for June 1819.
See 1894

1143   LAURA VALENTINE, ed. **Games for Family Parties and Children.** Cr 8vo. Illustrated. 1/0, 2/6   Nov. 26 (*Ath* ad)

This has no date and 188 pp. The first edition was issued by Warne, London; Scrib-ner, Welford & Co., New York (1868), 19 cm., 192 pp., illustrated, 2/6, listed in the *Spect* on Dec. 26, 1868.

1144   EDWARD LEAR **The Owl and the Pussy Cat, etc.** Fcp 4to, illustrated. 1/0 boards   Dec. 2

This was advertised in the *Times Weekly Edition* on Dec. 2. *Lear's Nonsense Drolleries*, containing *The Owl and the Pussy Cat*, etc., was advertised in the *Spect* on July 5, 1890, small 4to, illustrated, 1/6 boards.
See No. 32 in 1865

1145   ELIZABETH BARRETT BROWNING **The Poems of Elizabeth Barrett Browning.** Cr 8vo. 1/6 sewed, 2/0 cloth, 2/6 imitation Roxburghe   Dec. 17 (*PC*)

Chandos Classics No. 144. This is 1893, with 551 pp. Warne also issued the *Albion Poets* edition, 1892, reissued 1893–94. They also issued it in New York, $1.50 cloth, listed in the *Literary Digest* on Feb. 4, 1893. The first edition of *Poems* was issued by Edward Moxon, London, 2 vols., 1844, 18 cm., 12/0, in slate green cloth with yellow endpapers. It was published Aug. 14 in an edition of 1,500, listed in the *Spect* on Aug. 17. In some copies there is an 8-page catalog with various dates from June 1844 to July 1846. There is a variant binding with a slightly different stamping, with white or cream endpapers. Three impressions of the first edition were made. *Poems* was issued by Chapman & Hall, London, 2 vols., 1850, new edition, 16/0, in slate-blue cloth with pale yellow endpapers, published Nov. 1 and listed by *PC* as published Nov. 16–Dec. 21. They issued the third edition, 2 vols., corrected and with numerous additions, in 1853, 16/0, advertised in *Notes & Queries* on Oct. 29, 1853; and they issued the fourth edition, 3 vols., Fcp 8vo, 18/0, advertised in *Notes & Queries* on Nov. 29, 1856. In the United States *A Drama of Exile: and Other Poems* was issued by H. G. Langley, New York, 3 vols., 1845, portrait.

Poems was issued by C. S. Francis, New York, etc., 2 vols., 1850, listed by *Lit W* as published Sept. 6–21. It contains an essay by Henry Tuckerman and was several times reissued, including issues in 1857 in 3 vols. in two different forms, one in 32mo and the other in 12mo.

1146 G. A. ELLIS, ed. **The Handy Pocket Reciter.** 16mo. 1/0 limp cloth   Dec. 24 (*PC*)

This is the first edition, no date, 174 pp.

1147 JOHN S. WINTER (HENRIETTA STANNARD) **Harvest.** 12mo. 1/0 sewed 1892?

London Library No. 41. This has no date and 196 pp., a duplicate of the Trischler & Co., London, edition of 1891, issued with a new title page and with the omission of the date from the dedication. The first English edition was issued by the Hansom Cab Publishing Co., London, 1889, 2/6. In the United States it was issued by Frank F. Lovell, New York (1889), 206 pp., *International Series* No. 21, in paper, with the wrapper date (May 30, 1889), listed in the *American Bks* on July 1 and in *PW* on Oct. 12. It was also issued by George Munro, New York (1889), 169 pp., *Seaside Library Pocket Edition* No. 1202, advertised in the *New-York Times* on June 26, $.20 paper, as a late issue.

1148 REGINALD J. LUCAS **Dunwell Parva.** 12mo. 1/0 sewed   1892?

Popular Library No. 14. The first edition was issued by Warne, 1892, Cr 8vo, 190 pp., 3/6, listed in the *Ath* on Feb. 27.

Frederick Warne & Co.
London and New York
1893

1149 HENRI CAUVAIN *A Village Priest.*
Cr 8vo. 1/0 sewed Mar. 4 (*PC*)
Library of Continental Authors No. 9. This
has no date and 205 pp., a reissue of the
Trischler & Co., London, issue of 1890,
this latter listed in the *Ath* on Nov. 8, 1890,
Cr 8vo, 2/0. The first edition was *Un Cas de
Folie*, Paris, 1882. The Trischler edition
had the title, *The Original Story of a Village
Priest.*

1150 WILLIAM HAZLITT *William Hazlitt,
Essayist and Critic.* Cr 8vo. 1/6 sewed,
2/0 cloth, 2/6 imitation Roxburghe
Mar. 11 (*PC*)
Chandos Classics No. 145. This had no date
and 510 pp., with a preface (1889), a selection of Hazlitt's writings by Alexander Ireland. The first edition thus was issued by
Warne, 1889, 510 pp., portrait, in the *Cavendish Library.*

1151 B. L. FARJEON *For the Defence.*
12mo. 1/0 sewed Mar. 11 (*PC*)
London Library No. 43. This has no date
and 216 pp., a duplicate of the first edition
issued by Trischler & Co., London, 1891,
1/0 sewed, 1/6 cloth and listed by the *Bks* as
issued in June. This Warne edition has a
new title page and an index. The first
American edition was issued by John W.
Lovell, New York (1892), 301 pp., $.50 pa-
per, with *The Story of Jael* by Baring Gould

occupying pp. (219)–301. It was listed in
PW on Jan. 16, 1892, and in the *Ind* on
Feb. 4.

1152 JOHN S. WINTER (HENRIETTA
STANNARD) *Dinna Forget.* 12mo.
1/0 sewed, 1/6 cloth Mar. 25 (*PC*)
London Library No. 42. This has no date
and 214 pp., a duplicate—with a new title
page—of the first English edition issued
by Trischler & Co., London, 1890, with
214 pp. and advertised in the *TWEd* on
July 4, 1/0 sewed, 1/6 cloth as "Just out"
and listed by *Review of Reviews* (London) as
published in May. The *Times* ad claimed
that 30,000 copies had been sold in 14
days. The first American edition was issued by John W. Lovell, New York (1890),
214 pp., $.30 paper, *International Series* No.
60, listed in *Public Opinion* on May 17 and
in the *Ind* on May 22.

1153 JOHN DRYDEN *The Poetical Works
of John Dryden.* Cr 8vo. 1/6 sewed, 2/0
cloth Apr. 8 (*PC*)
Chandos Classics No. 146. This is 1893 with
575 pp. Warne issued it also in *Albion Poets*
in 1893, large Cr 8vo, 3/6 cloth, advertised
in the *Spect* on Mar. 4. Warne issued it in
New York in Apr., with a memoir, notes,
and an index, 607 pp., $1.50. *Miscellaney
Poems* was issued by Jacob Tonson, London, 1684, 18 cm., 328 pp., 1 leaf, 92 pp.
Tonson issued *The Works of Mr. John Dry-*

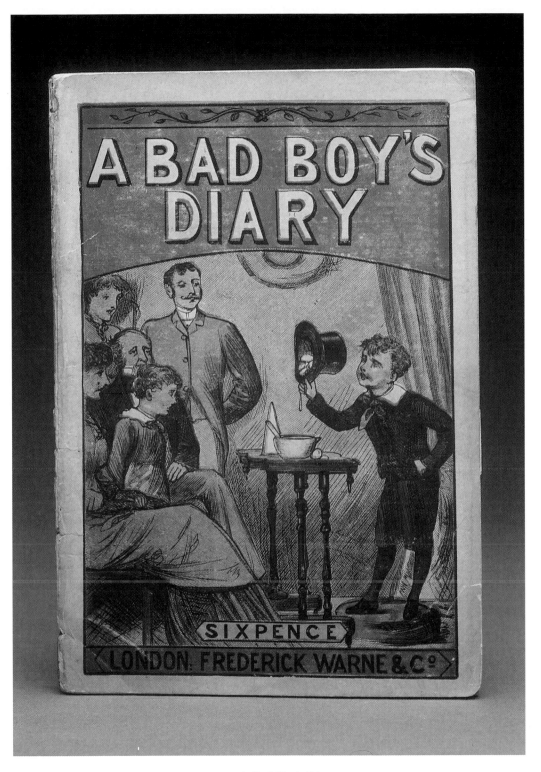

155   *A Bad Boy's Diary*

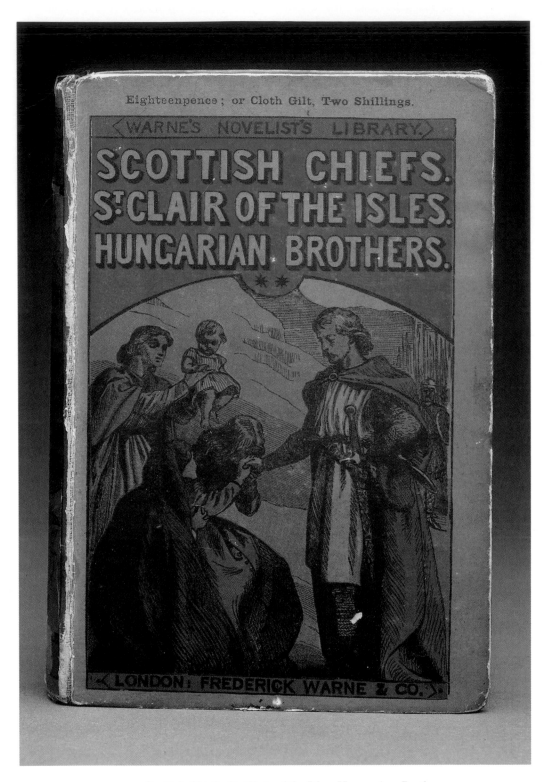

452   *Scottish Chiefs. St. Clair of the Isles. Hungarian Brothers*

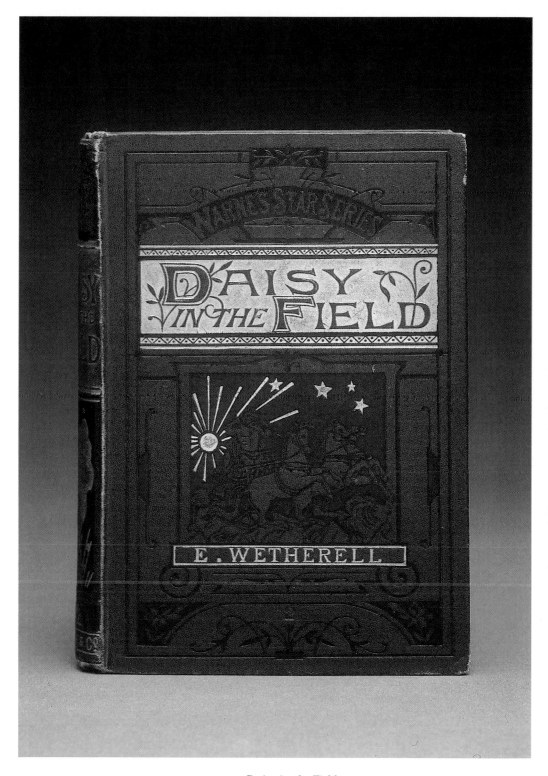

457   *Daisy in the Field*

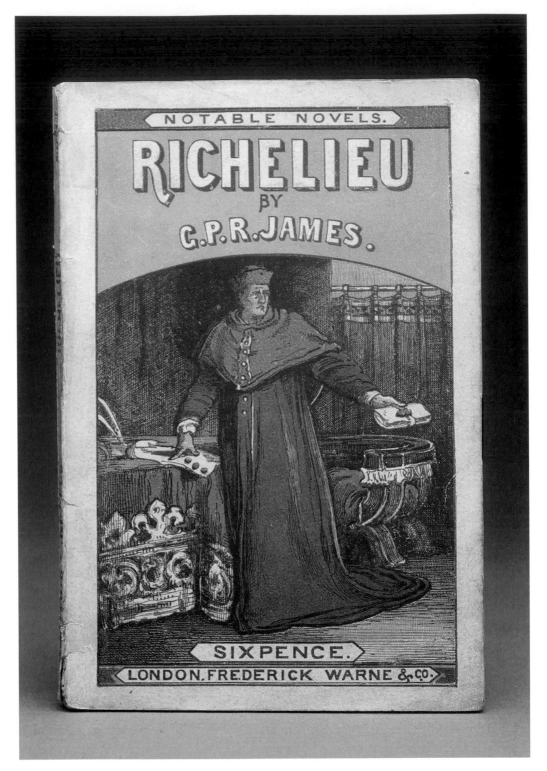

491   *Richelieu*

615   *Hardy Plants for Little Front Gardens*

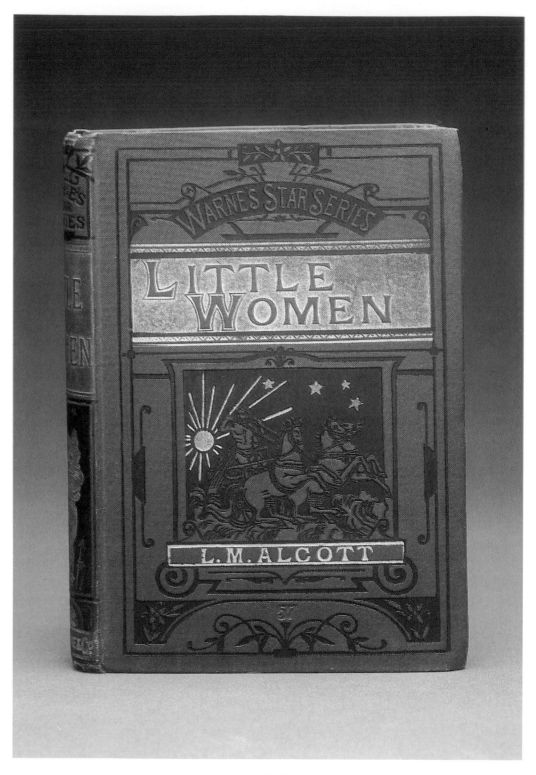

693   *Little Women*

742   *A Fair Barbarian*

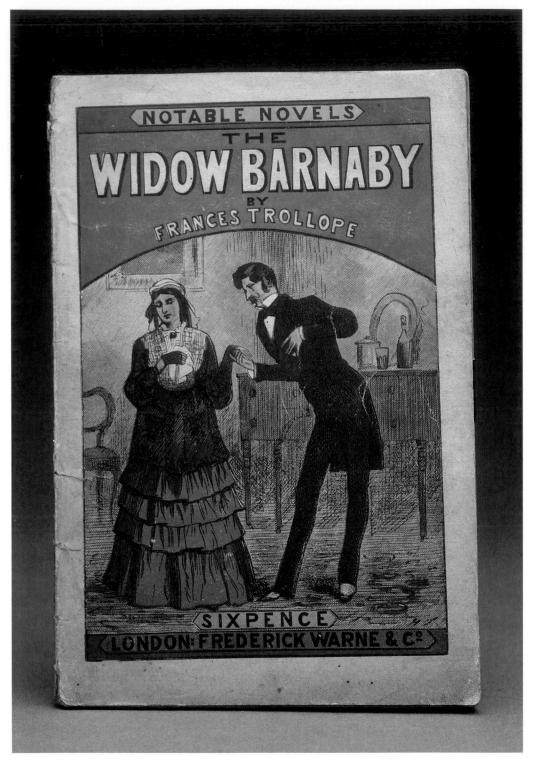

745   *The Widow Barnaby*

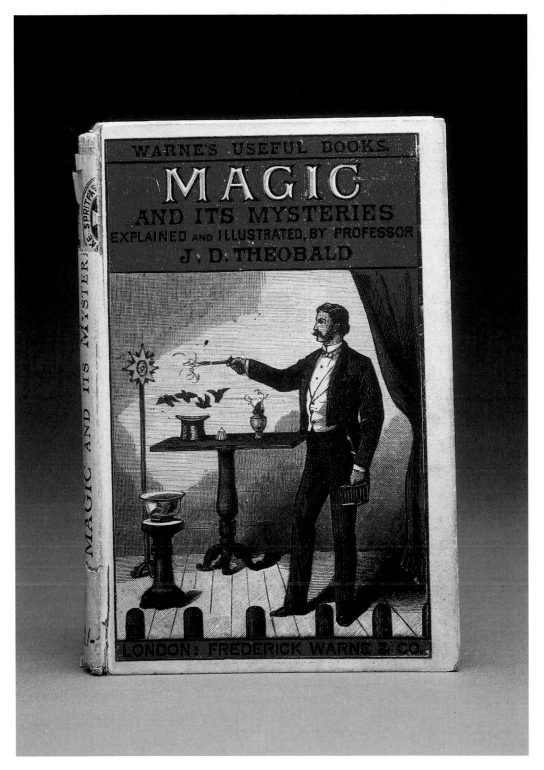

788   *Magic and Its Mysteries*

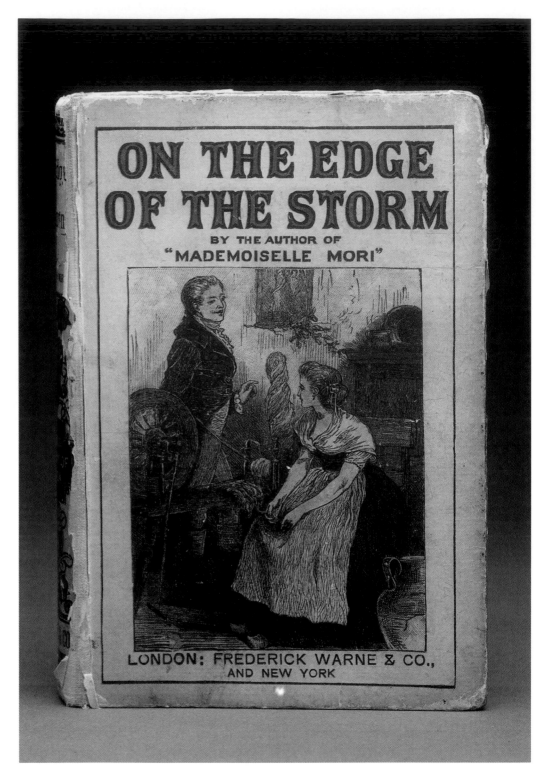

807   *On the Edge of the Storm*

906   *Houp-La*

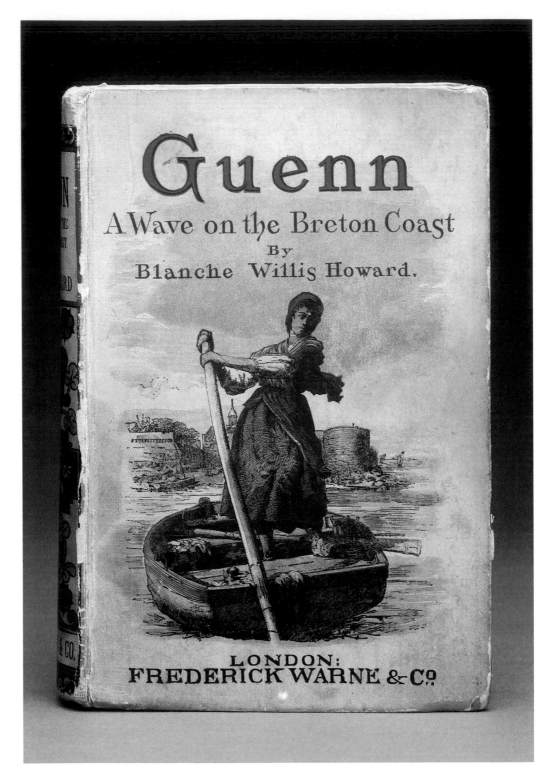

967   *Guenn, a Wave on the Breton Coast*

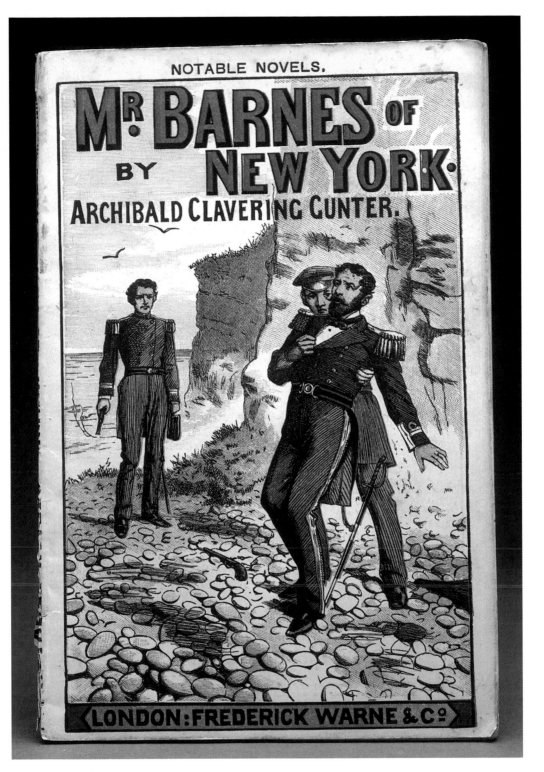

1001   *Mr. Barnes of New York*

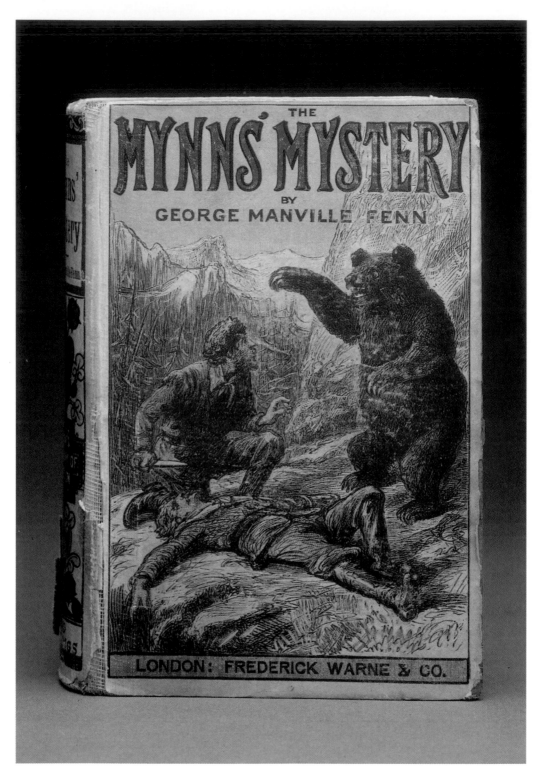

1075   *The Minn's Mystery*

NOTABLE NOVELS.

HAROLD

By

Bulwer Lytton.

LONDON:
Frederick Warne and Co.,
AND NEW YORK.

1266   *Conspiracy, A Cuban Romance*

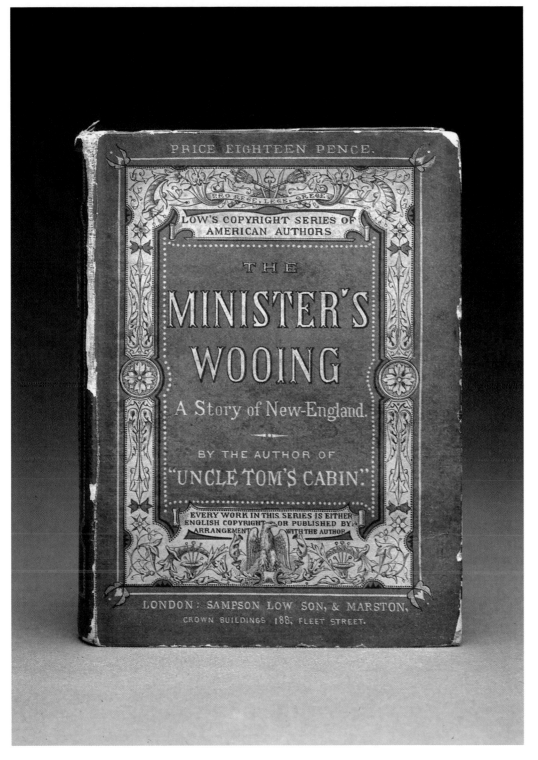

PRICE EIGHTEEN PENCE.

REG. RESE. LEGE. GRECE.

LOW'S COPYRIGHT SERIES OF
AMERICAN AUTHORS

THE
MINISTER'S
WOOING
A Story of New-England.

BY THE AUTHOR OF
"UNCLE TOM'S CABIN".

EVERY WORK IN THIS SERIES IS EITHER
ENGLISH COPYRIGHT, OR PUBLISHED BY
ARRANGEMENT WITH THE AUTHOR

LONDON : SAMPSON LOW SON, & MARSTON,
CROWN BUILDINGS 188, FLEET STREET.

47   *The Minister's Wooing*

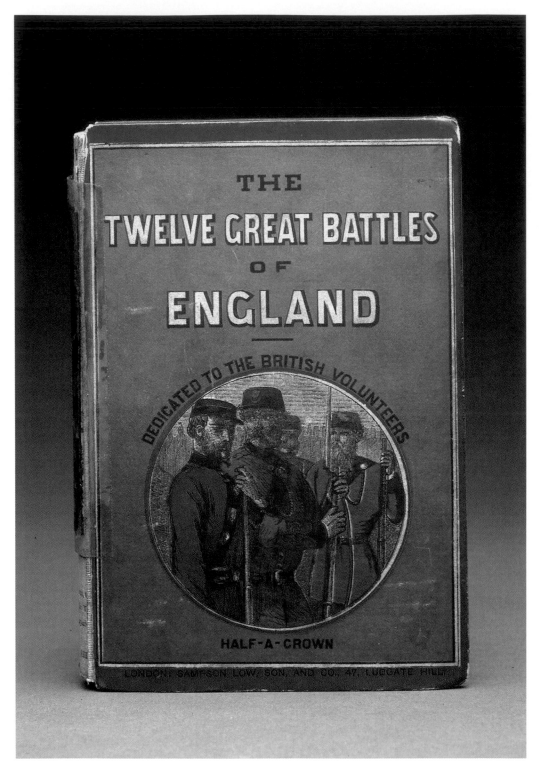

54   *The Twelve Great Battles of England*

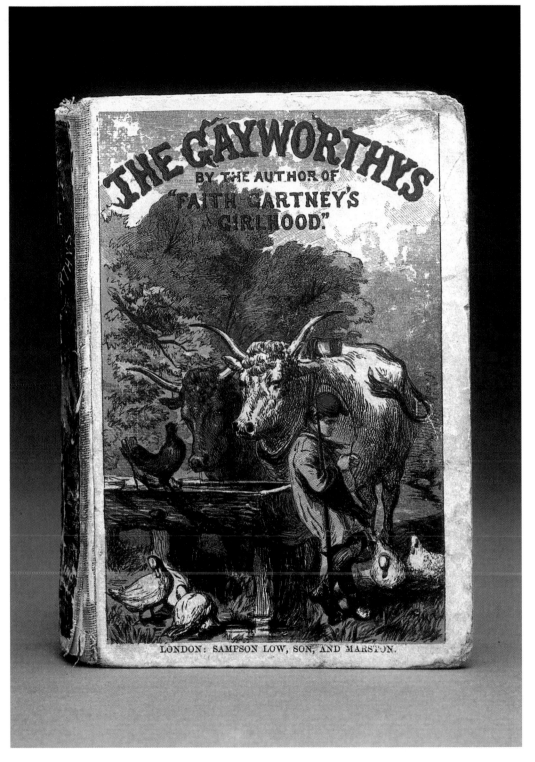

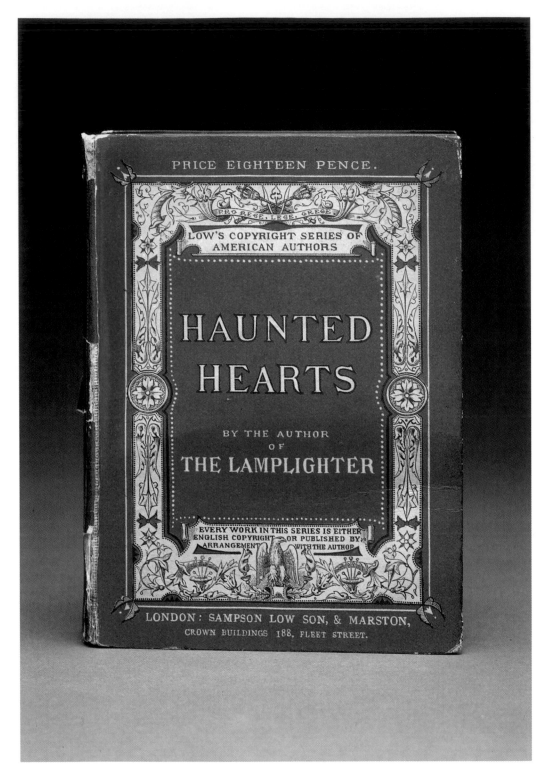

103   *Haunted Hearts*

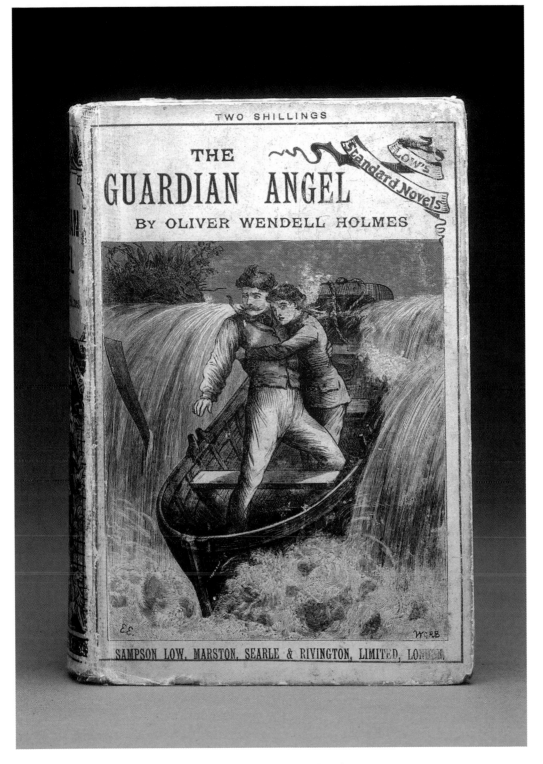

104   *The Guardian Angel*

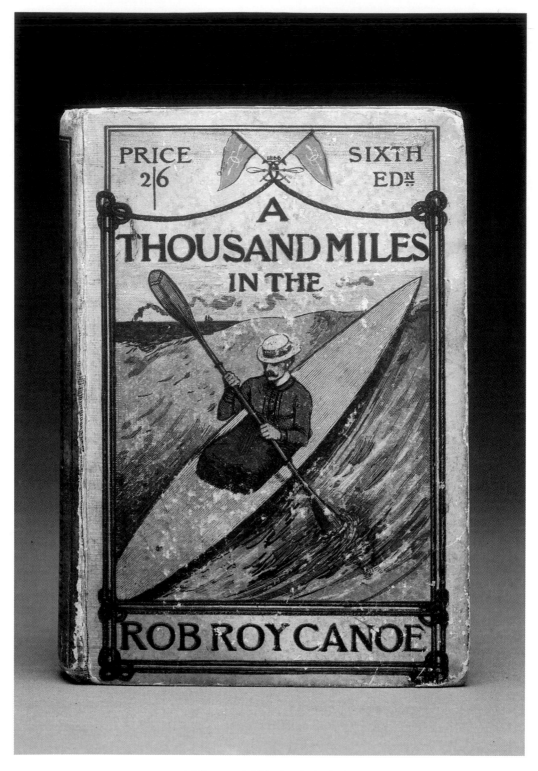

129   *A Thousand Miles in the Rob Roy Canoe*

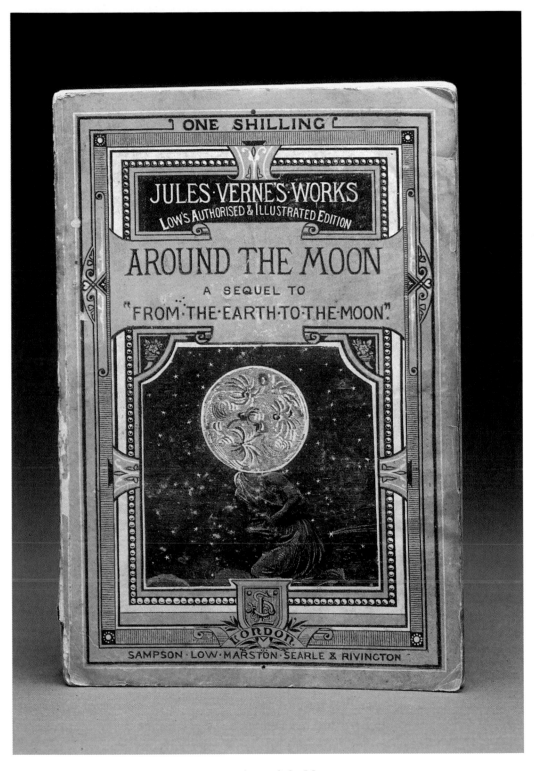

195   *Around the Moon*

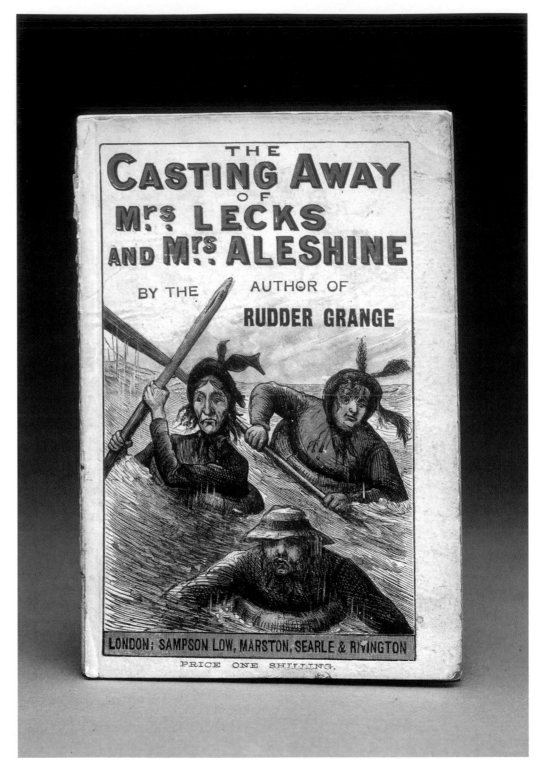

331   *The Casting Away of Mrs. Leeks and Mrs. Aleshine*

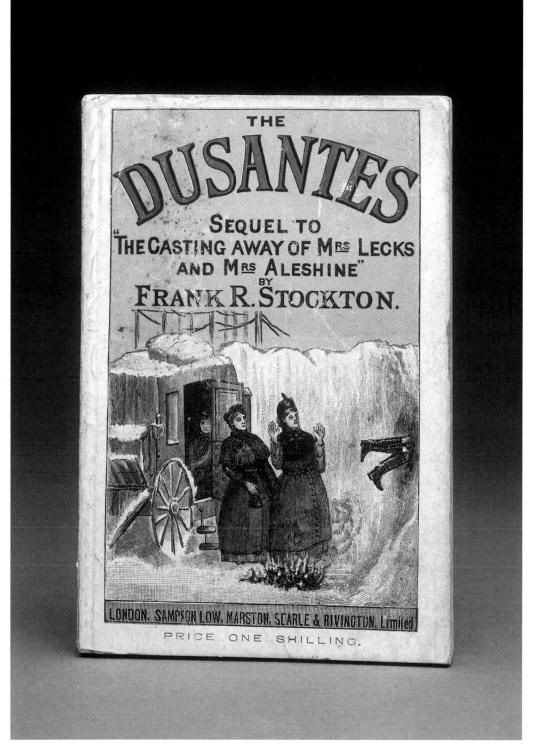

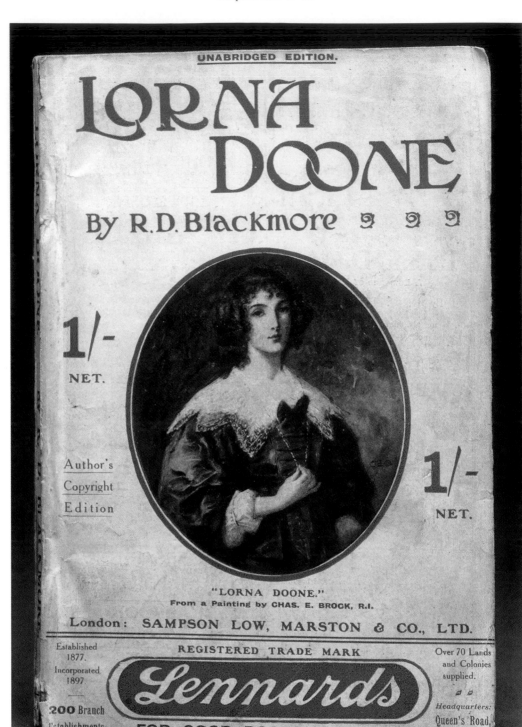

371   *Lorna Doone*

390   *Near and Far*

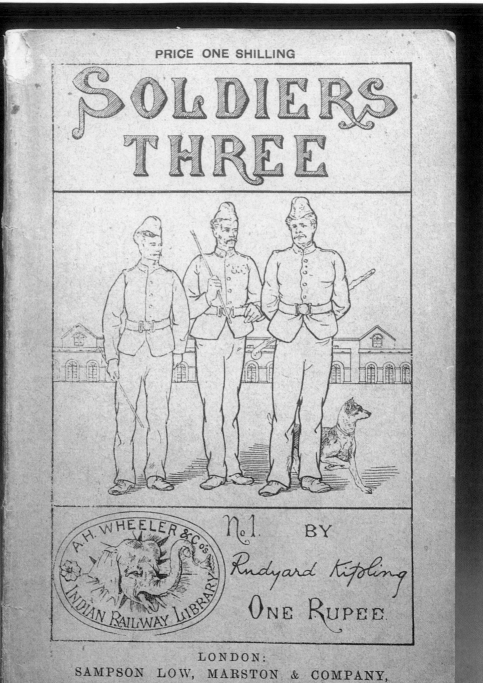

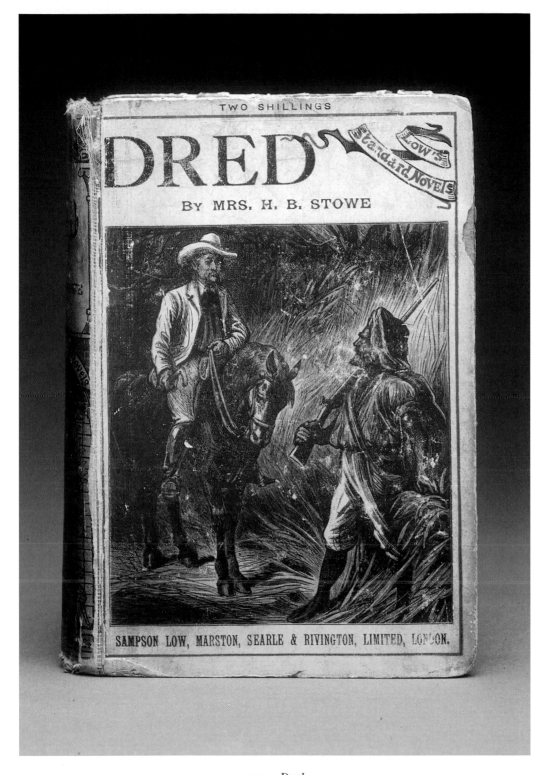

394　*Dred*

396   *The Trumpet Major*

PRICE ONE SHILLING

THE **CITY** OF DREADFUL NIGHT

A.H.WHEELER&Cᵒˢ INDIAN RAILWAY LIBRARY

ONE RUPEE

Nᵒ XIV

BY

RUDYARD KIPLING.

LONDON:
SAMPSON LOW, MARSTON & COMPANY,
Limited,
St. Dunstan's House, Fetter Lane, Fleet Street, E.C

den, 4 vols., 1693, 22.5 cm; and issued *Poems on Various Occasions,* 1701, 34 cm., 232 pp. In the United States *Poetical Works* was issued by Mitchell, Ames & White, Philadelphia, 2 vols., 1819, 12mo, illustrated.

1154 SIR WALTER SCOTT **Rob Roy.** Cr 8vo. 1/0 sewed Apr.?

National Novels No. 7. The first edition was issued by Archibald Constable & Co., Edinburgh, etc., 3 vols., 1818, 12mo, anonymous, listed by the *Edinburgh Review* as published Nov. 1817–Mar. 1818, 24/0 boards. It was reviewed in the *Gentleman's Magazine* (monthly) for Mar. Constable issued the fourth edition, 3 vols., 1818, in drab boards with green cloth spines and paper labels, uncut. The first American edition was issued by James Eastburn & Co., New York, 2 vols., 1818, 12mo, anonymous, reviewed in the *North American Review* (bi-monthly) for July. It was issued by S. H. Parker, Boston, 2 vols., in 1830, revised and corrected with notes by the author, listed in the *North American Review* for July.
Scc 1894

1155 THE BROTHERS GRIMM **Grimm's Goblins.** 12mo. Illustrated. 1/6 cloth May 13 (*PC*)

Fairy Library. This is translated by Mrs. Henry H. B. Paull. Warne reissued it in this series in 1897, 12mo, 1/6 cloth, listed in *PC* on Sept. 11. It was issued by Warne in New York along with *Wonder Tales,* in 1 vol., translated by Paull and Mrs. L. A. Heatley, 12mo, illustrated, $1.25 cloth, listed in editorial matter in the *New York Times Book Review* for Dec. 11, 1897. *Grimm's Goblins* was issued by Ticknor & Fields, Boston, 1867, 19.5 cm., 111 pp., illustrated, $1.50, listed in the *New Englander,* New Haven, Conn. (quarterly), for

June 1868, from *Household Stories.* It was issued in London by R. Meek & Co., 1876, 8vo, 296 pp., illustrated.

1156 THE BROTHERS GRIMM **Grimm's Household Stories.** 12mo. Illustrated. 1/6 cloth May 13 (*PC*)

Fairy Library. This is translated by Mrs. Henry H. B. Paull. Warne reissued it in this series in 1897, 12mo, 1/6 cloth, listed in *PC* on Sept. 11. Warne issued *Grimm's Fairy Tales,* a complete translation of *Household Stores,* by Mrs. Paull, in 1889, large 8vo, colored plates, $3.00 cloth, in New York, advertised in the *Christian Union* on Dec. 5. Addey & Co., London, issued a book, *Grimm's Household Stories,* 2 vols., 1853, illustrated, in another translation.

1157 THE BROTHERS GRIMM **Grimm's Wonder Tales for the Young.** 12mo. Illustrated. 1/6 cloth May 13 (*PC*)

Fairy Library. This is translated by Mrs. Henry H. B. Paull and Mrs. L. A. Wheatley. Warne reissued this in this series in 1897, 12mo, 1/6 cloth, listed in *PC* on Sept. 11. Warne issued it in New York with No. 1155 above in 1 vol.

1158 CHARLES KINGSLEY **Westward Ho!** 8vo. 0/6 sewed May or later?

Standard Novels No. 5. The first English edition was issued by Macmillan & Co., Cambridge, etc., 3 vols., 1855, 19 cm., 31/6, in blue cloth with a 16-page catalog at the back of vol. 1, dated Feb. or Apr. in known copies. It was advertised in the *Spect* on Feb. 24 as "On Mar. 20" and listed Mar. 17, and listed in the *Ath* on Mar. 24. They issued the second edition in 3 vols., advertised in the *Spect* on May 26; and issued the third edition, 1857, Cr 8vo, 519 pp., 7/6, advertised in the *Spect* on May 16. They issued a new edition in 1859, p 8vo, 519 pp., 6/0, listed by *PC* as published

Sept. 30–Oct. 14; this was reissued 1861, 65, 69, etc. The first American edition was issued by Ticknor & Fields, Boston, 1855, 20.5 cm., 588 pp., $1.25, in an edition of 3,000 copies, advertised in the *New York Daily Times* on Mar. 27 as "On Mar. 31," in advance of its issue in England. I think it probable that it wasn't issued in advance of the English edition!

1159 CHARLES KINGSLEY *Hereward the Wake*. 8vo. o/6 sewed May or later?
Standard Novels No. 6. This ran in *Good Words* beginning in Jan. 1865. The first English edition was issued by Macmillan & Co., London and Cambridge, 2 vols., 1866, 19.5 cm., 21/o, in crimson-lake cloth with greenish-black endpapers, with 2 pp. of ads at the back of each vol. It was listed in the *Ath* on Mar. 31 and reviewed in the *British Quarterly Review* for July. They issued the second edition, 1873, Cr 8vo, 6/o, reprinted 1874–75, Jan. and Dec. 1877, etc. They issued the third edition, 1889, 3/6. The first American edition was issued by Ticknor & Fields, Boston, 1866, 19.5 cm., 397 pp., $1.75, *Hereward the Last of the English*, listed in the *Nation* on Jan. 4, 1866, and listed in *Godey's Lady's Book* for Mar. It was also issued by Leypoldt & Holt, New York, 2 vols., the Tauchnitz edition, listed in the *Nation* on July 5, 1866, $.75 each.

1160 CHARLES KINGSLEY *Two Years Ago*. 8vo. o/6 sewed May or later?
Standard Novels No. 7. The first English edition was issued by Macmillan & Co., Cambridge, 3 vols., 1857, 19.5 cm., 31/6, in bright blue cloth with yellow endpapers, with 4 pp. of ads at the back of vol. 1 and a 24-page catalog (Jan. 1857) at the back of vols. 2 and 3. It was printed in Feb. and advertised in the *Ath* and in *Notes & Queries* on Feb. 7 as "This day" and listed in the former on Feb. 14. Macmillan issued the second edition, 3 vols., 1857, Cr 8vo, 31/6, advertised in *Notes & Queries* and in

the *Spect* on May 2 as "This day"; and they issued the third edition, Cr 8vo, 470 pp., 6/o cloth, advertised in the *Spect* on Nov. 26, 1859, as "Next week" and listed by *PC* as published Nov. 30–Dec. 12, 1859. They issued the fourth edition in Jan. 1866, reprinted 1871–77, 79, 80, etc.; and issued the fifth edition in Jan. 1889, at 3/6. The first American edition was issued by Ticknor & Fields, Boston, 19.5 cm., 540 pp., $1.25, published Mar. 25 in an edition of 3,000 copies. It was advertised in *Harper's Weekly* on Jan. 24 as "In a few days" and reviewed in *Harper's New Monthly Magazine* for May.

1161 CHARLES KINGSLEY *Hypatia*. 8vo. o/6 sewed May or later?
Standard Novels No. 8. This ran in *Fraser's Magazine*, Jan. 1852–Apr. 1853, and the first book edition was issued by John W. Parker & Son, London, 2 vols., 1853, 20.5 cm., 18/o in dark olive-brown cloth, listed in the *Spect* on Apr. 18. Sadleir and Wolff give the imprint as John W. Parker, but this does not agree with all the ads for the book. John W. Parker & Son issued the second edition, 1856, 389 pp., 6/o, advertised in the *Spect* and *Notes & Queries* on Oct. 25 as "This day"; and they issued the third edition at 6/o, advertised in the *Spect* and *Notes & Queries* on Jan. 30, 1858, as "This day." It was taken over by Macmillan & Co., Cambridge and London, who issued the fourth edition, 1863, printed in Mar., Cr 8vo, 6/o, listed in the *Reader* on Mar. 14. Macmillan issued their second edition, 1869, reprinted 1872–77, 79, 80, etc.; and they issued their third edition at 3/6 in Oct. 1888. The first American edition was issued by Crosby, Nichols & Co., Boston, 2 vols., 1854 in purple-gray cloth with yellow endpapers, with no publisher's imprint on the spine. It was noticed in the *Ind* on Dec. 1, 1853, and in the *Christian Examiner* for Jan. 1854. They issued the second edition in 1855, Cr 8vo, 487 pp., listed in *Putnam's Monthly*, New

York, for Feb. and listed in the *North American Review* (quarterly) for Apr. The *U Cat* gives New York, 2 vols., 1853 and 1854.

1162 CHARLES KINGSLEY *Alton Locke.* 8vo. 0/6 sewed   May or later?

Standard Novels No. 9. The first edition was issued by Chapman & Hall, London, 2 vols., 1850, 21 cm., anonymous, 18/0 in rose-madder cloth, with a 32-page catalog (Nov. 1849) at the back of vol. 2, listed in the *Ath* on Aug. 17 and by *PC* as published Aug. 14–29. They issued the second edition in 2 vols., p 8vo, 18/0, listed in the *Literary Gazette* on Jan. 18, 1851; issued the third edition, 1852, 19.5 cm., anonymous, 375 pp., 7/0, advertised in the *Spect* on Sept. 18 as "On Sept. 25"; and issued a cheap edition, 1856, 17 cm., 2/0, yellow pictorial boards, in the *Select Library of Fiction*, no number, listed in the *Ath* on Dec. 15, 1855. Macmillan & Co., Cambridge and London, purchased the copyright and issued a new edition, 1862, 19.5 cm., 309 pp., 4/6, with a new preface, printed in Mar. and reprinted 1874–75. Sadleir's copy is in royal-blue cloth with red-chocolate endpapers, with a 56-page catalog (Nov. 1869, *sic*) at the back. They issued their second edition, 1876, at 6/0, reprinted July and Dec. 1877, 1879, 81, etc.; and issued their third edition in Dec. 1888, reprinted 1889 at 3/6. The first American edition was issued by Harper & Brothers, New York, 1850, 19.5 cm., anonymous, 371 pp., $.75 muslin, advertised in *Lit W* on Nov. 23, 1850, as "Now ready" and listed as published Nov. 17–30.

1163 CHARLES KINGSLEY *Yeast.* 8vo. 0/6 sewed   May or later?

Standard Novels No. 10. This ran in *Fraser's Magazine*, July–Dec. 1848, and the first book edition was issued by John W. Parker, London, 1851, 19 cm., anonymous, 388 pp., 9/0 in rose-madder cloth with ads, (1)–8 at the back. It was reprinted from

the magazine with corrections and additions and listed in the *Spect* on Mar. 22 and advertised in the *Literary Gazette* on Mar. 22 as "This day." They issued the second edition, 1851, 287 pp., at 5/0, advertised in the *Spect* on Nov. 29 as "This day"; issued the third edition, 5/0, advertised in the *Spect* on Oct. 29, 1853; and issued the fourth edition, 1859, 5/0, with a new preface, advertised in *Notes & Queries* on Mar. 5 as "This day." Macmillan & Co., Cambridge and London, issued their first edition in July 1866, Cr 8vo, 5/0, reprinted 1872, 75, 77, and at 6/0, Jan. and Sept. 1878, 79, 81, etc.; and issued their second edition in Nov. 1888, at 3/6. The first American edition was issued by Harper & Brothers, New York, 1851, 20 cm., anonymous, 292 pp., listed by *Lit W* as published June 7–28 and noticed in the *Ind* on June 20.

1164 CHRISTIAN LYS (PERCY J. BREBNER) *The Doctor's Idol.* 16mo. 1/0 stiff wrappers, 1/6 cloth   June 3 (*PC*)

Tavistock Library No. 1. This is the first edition, no date, 206 pp. Warne issued it in New York in this series, in pocket size, $.50 paper, $.75 cloth, advertised in the *Nation* on Nov. 2, 1893.

1165 GEORGE F. MORANT *Poultry for Profit.* 16mo. Illustrated. 1/0 June 10 (*PC*)

Modern Manuel Series This is the first edition, 1893, 144 pp. It was reissued 1896, 144 pp., illustrated.

1166 ROBERT SOUTHEY *The Life of Wesley; and the Rise of Progress of Methodism.* Cr 8vo. 1/6 sewed, 2/0 cloth   June 10 (*PC*)

Chandos Classics No. 147. This has 607 pp. and was edited by J. A. Atkinson. Warne issued this in their *Cavendish Library*, large Cr 8vo, 3/6 cloth, uncut, advertised in the *Spect* on Jan. 12, 1889. They issued it in

New York, listed in the *Nation* on Mar. 28, 1889, and advertised there on Mar. 12, 1891, new edition, Cr 8vo, steel portrait, $1.50 cloth. The first edition was issued by Longmans, London, 2 vols., 1820, 8vo, 28/0 boards, listed by the *Edinburgh Review* (quarterly) as published Jan.–Apr. 1820 and reviewed in the *Gentleman's Magazine* for June. They issued the second edition, 2 vols., 1820, frontispieces (portraits); the third edition, 1846, 2 vols., 8vo, reviewed in the *Gentleman's Magazine* in Nov; the fourth edition, 2 vols., 1858, Cr 8vo, 12/0, edited by C. C. Southey; and a new edition, 1860, 2 vols., Cr 8vo, 12/0, advertised in the *Spect* on Mar. 10 as "Just published." In the United States it was issued by William B. Gilley, New York, 2 vols., 1820, frontispiece; and by Evert Duyckinck & George Long, New York, 2-vols.-in-1, 1820, 21.5 cm., frontispiece. An edition was listed in the *North American Review* (quarterly) for Jan. 1821, 2 vols., 8vo, $4.00, no publisher given.

1167 LUCIE H. ARMSTRONG **Etiquette for Girls.** 12mo. 1/0 boards, 1/6 cloth June 17 (*PC*)

Modern Manual Series. This has no date and 149 pp. The first edition was probably issued by Warne in the 1880s. Warne issued it in New York in 1893, 16mo, $.50, advertised in the *Nation* on Nov. 23.

1168 FREDERICK LANGBRIDGE **Miss Honoria.** 16mo. 1/0 stiff wrappers, 1/6 cloth   June 17 (*PC*)

Tavistock Library No. 2. This is the first edition, no date, 215 pp. Warne issued it in New York in this series, 1893, at $.50, listed in the *Nation* on July 27.

1169 CHARLES DICKENS **The Personal History of David Copperfield.** 8vo. 2 vols., 0/6 sewed each; 1 vols., 1/0 sewed   June?

Standard Novels No. 11. This was issued by Bradbury & Evans, London, 20 monthly

1/0 parts in 19, in green wrappers, May 1, 1849–Nov. 1, 1850, illustrated by "Phiz." They issued it in 1 vol., bound from the parts, 1850, 22.5 cm., 624 pp., illustrated by "Phiz," 21/0 cloth, listed in the *Ath* on Nov. 16. It was also issued, 1850, not bound from the parts. It was issued jointly by Bradbury & Evans and Chapman & Hall, London, 2 vols., 6/0 each, advertised in the *Spect*, vol. 1 "On Feb. 28" and vol. 2 "On Mar. 31," 1859. In the United States it was issued 20 parts in 19, from early English sheets, by John Wiley and G. P. Putnam, New York. Wiley issued parts 1–11 at $.12½ each, No. 1 about May 19, 1849, and part 2 on June 12, etc. Wiley also issued the double part 19 & 20 on Nov. 23, 1850. G. P. Putnam issued parts 12–18 in buff wrappers, $.12½ each, part 12 about Apr. 27, 1850. Putnam issued it in 2 vols., 1850, bound from the parts, frontispiece and engraved title page and plates by "Phiz," listed by *Lit W* as published Nov. 17–30, 1850. The imprint on the engraved title page was John Wiley (1850). He also issued it in 1 vol., advertised in *Lit W* on Nov. 23, 1850, as "This day." Vol. 1 of the Putnam 2-vol. issue was listed in *Lit W* as published Apr. 27–May 11, 1850, $1.00 without illustrations and $1.25 with illustrations. John Wiley also issued it in 2 vols., illustrated by "Phiz," listed by *Lit W* as published Nov. 17–30, 1850. He also issued it 2 vols.-in-1, listed the same. It was also issued by W. F. Burgess, New York (1850), 24 cm., 264 pp., illustrated by J. W. Orr, frontispiece and plates and a portrait on the title page. It is in double columns and was listed by *Lit W* as published Nov. 17–30, 1850. It was also issued by Lea & Blanchard, Philadelphia, 20 parts in 19, royal 8vo, printed in double columns, illustrated by "Phiz," in yellow wrappers at $.05 each. No. 4 was listed in *Godey's Lady's Book* for Nov. 1849. They issued it in 2 vols. at $.25 each, vol. 1 listed by *Lit W* as published Mar. 16–23, 1850, and vol. 2 advertised there on Nov. 23, 1850, as

"This day." They also issued it in 1 vol., complete, 1851, 23 cm., 327 pp. in double columns, illustrated by "Phiz," $.37½, listed by *Lit W* as published Nov. 17–30, 1850.

1170 NORMAN MACLEOD **The Old Lieutenant and His Son.** 8vo. o/6 sewed July 15 (*PC*)

Standard Novels No. 12. The first English appearance was in *Good Words*, and the first English book issue was by Alexander Strahan, London, 2 vols., 1862, Cr 8vo, anonymous, 12/0, reviewed in the *Spect* on Oct. 18. Strahan issued the 2nd thousand in 2 vols., 12/0, advertised in the *Spect* on Jan. 10, 1863; and issued it at 3/6, Cr 8vo, 401 pp., listed in the *Reader* on May 23, 1863. The first American edition was issued by T.O.H.P. Burnham, Boston, 1862, 22 cm., 130 pp. in double columns, $.30 paper, advertised in the *New-York Times* on Mar. 29 as "This day" and noticed in *Godey's Lady's Book* for June. It was issued by C. Burnet & Co., London, in 1890, o/6, advertised in the *Spect* on Aug. 23 as "Now ready."

1171 S. MOORE-CAREW (SALOME HOCKING, later FIFIELD) **A Conquered Self.** 16mo. 1/0 sewed, 1/6 cloth July 22 (*PC*)

Tavistock Library No. 3. This is the first edition, 181 pp. It was reviewed in *PC* on Aug. 5 and in the *Ath* on Sept. 2. The *BM* gives only 1894. Warne issued it in New York in 1893, in this series, pocket size, $.50 paper, $.75 cloth, listed in the *Outlook* (weekly) on Nov. 4 and advertised in the *Nation* on Nov. 2.

1172 ROBERT GRANT **The Reflections of a Married Man.** 16mo. 1/9 sewed, 1/6 cloth July 22 (*Spect*)

Tavistock Library No. 4. This has no date and 195 pp. The first edition was issued by Charles Scribner's Sons, New York, 1892,

19 cm., 165 pp., advertised in the *New-York Times* on May 27 as "Today." The 14th thousand was advertised in the *Nation* on Sept. 15, $.50 paper, $1.00 cloth. It ran in *Scribner's Magazine*, Mar.–June 1892. Scribners' Sons issued it in their Cameo edition, 16mo, portrait, advertised in the *New-York Times* on Oct. 12, 1895. In England it was issued by Gay & Bird, London, 1892, 165 pp., 4/0, from American sheets, listed by the *Bks* as published in Nov.

1173 PEN OLIVER (SIR HENRY THOMPSON) **Charley Kingston's Aunt.** Revised edition. Cr 8vo. 2/0 boards, 2/6 cloth July 29 (*PC*)

Library of Fiction No. 29. This is my copy, 1893, 18.2 cm., 272 pp., white pictorial boards, printed in red, green, and black with the series title on the spine. Publisher's ads are on 4 leaves at the back and on the endpapers, and a commercial ad is on the back cover. Warne issued it in New York in 1893, 12mo, $1.00 cloth, advertised in the *Nation* on Nov. 2. The first edition was issued by Macmillan & Co., London and New York, 1885 (1884), 12mo, 316 pp., 6/0, listed in the *Ath* on Dec. 6, 1884; and in New York, $1.00, advertised in the *New-York Times* on Jan. 3, 1885. They issued the third edition in 1885, Cr 8vo, 1/0, advertised in *Notes & Queries* on May 2.

1174 ANONYMOUS **Bible Stories in Simple Language for Little Children.** Royal 16mo. Illustrated. 1/0 boards, 2/0 cloth Aug. 16 (*PC*)

This has no date and 94 pp. The *Eng Cat* gives it as 16mo, but Warne advertised it as p 4to.

1175 AUGUSTA J. E. WILSON **Beulah.** 16mo. 1/6 sewed, 2/0 cloth Sept. 23 (*PC*)

Star Series No. 125. This has no date and 496 pp. The first edition was issued by

Derby & Jackson, New York, 1859, 19 cm., 510 pp., $1.25, listed in the *Ind* on Sept. 29 and advertised in the *New-York Times* on Sept. 27 as "Now ready." The third edition was advertised there on Sept. 30, $1.25; the 7th thousand on Oct. 17, $1.25, "Now ready"; and the 16th edition on Jan. 25, 1860, $1.25, stating that 16,000 copies had been sold in 4 months. In England it was issued by Knight & Co., London, 12mo, 2/0, in 1860.

1176 MRS. GEORGE MARTYN *A Liberal Education.* 16mo. 1/0 sewed, 1/6 cloth Oct. 7 (*PC*)

Tavistock Library No. 5. This has no date and 247 pp., the first edition. Warne issued it in New York also, in this series, pocket size, $.50 paper, $.75 cloth, advertised in the *Nation* on Nov. 2, 1893.

1177 EDMUND C. NUGENT *Charades for Acting.* [New edition.] p 8vo. Illustrated. 1/0 Oct. 14 (*PC*)

This had no date and 193 pp. The first edition was *Country-House Charades for Acting*, issued by John Canden Hotten, London (1870), 18.5 cm., 193, 38, 7 pp. This Warne issue is in their *Useful Books* series and was first issued by them in 1881, new edition, Cr 8vo, illustrated, 2/6 cloth, listed in the *Spect* on Oct. 22.

1178 AUGUSTA J. E. WILSON *At the Mercy of Tiberius.* Cr 8vo. 2/0 cloth Oct.?

Star Series No. 126. This has no date and 490 pp. At about this point this series was issued in the larger size and at 2/0 cloth only. The first edition was issued by G. W. Dillingham, New York; Sampson Low, London, 1887, 19 cm., 616 pp., listed in the *Nation* on Oct. 27 and in *PW* on Oct. 29. In England it was issued by Ward, Lock & Co., London, probably in 1889, no date, 397 pp., 1/0 sewed, 1/6 cloth; and they also issued it in their *Pansy* series at

1/0 cloth in Aug. 1891. G. W. Carleton & Co., New York, issued it the latter part of 1887, noticed in *Lippincott's Monthly Magazine* for Feb. 1888.

1179 ROBERT GRANT *The Opinions of a Philosopher.* 16mo. 1/0 stiff wrappers, 1/6 cloth Nov. 4 (*PC*)

Tavistock Library No. 6. This is the first English edition, no date, 241 pp. It ran in *Scribner's Magazine*, June–Sept. 1893, illustrated, and the first book edition was issued by Charles Scribner's Sons, New York, 1893, 18.5 cm., 224 pp., illustrated, $1.00 cloth, listed in the *Nation* on Sept. 7 and in the *Outlook*, New York (weekly), on Sept. 16. Scribner's Sons advertised the Cameo edition in the *New-York Times* on Oct. 12, 1895, 16mo, portrait, $1.25.

1180 ANNIE KEARY *Deb: A Wayside Flower.* Cr 8vo. Illustrated. 1/0 cloth Nov. 18 (*PC*)

Welcome Library No. 3. This is probably the first edition, listed in the *TWEd* on Nov. 17, illustrated, 1/0.

1181 ADELINE D. T. WHITNEY *Faith Gartney's Girlhood.* Cr 8vo. 2/0 cloth Nov.?

Star Series No. 127. This is 1893, 312 pp. The first edition was issued by A. K. Loring, Boston; F. Leypoldt, Philadelphia, 1863, 19.5 cm., anonymous, 348 pp., $1.25, in plum colored cloth, yellow endpapers, all edges trimmed, by A.D.T.W., listed in the *Ind* on July 9. The first English edition was issued by Sampson Low, London, 1865, 12mo, anonymous, 2/6 boards and 3/6 cloth, the latter with colored illustrations. It was listed in the *Ath* on Sept. 23 and in the *Reader* on Oct. 7. Low issued the third edition, 1866, Fcp 8vo, anonymous, 355 pp., colored illustrations, 1/6 boards, advertised in the *Ath* on Nov. 25, 1865, and listed in the *Reader* on Dec. 23. It was also issued by S. O. Beeton, London, in 1865, Fcp 8vo, 254 pp., 1/0 sewed, listed in the *Reader* on Dec. 9, 1865.

1182 ADELINE D. T. WHITNEY
The Gayworthys. Cr 8vo. 2/0 cloth
Dec. 16 (*PC*)
Star Series No. 128. This is 1893, 423 pp. The first American edition was issued by A. K. Loring, Boston, 1865, 19.5 cm., anonymous, 399 pp., listed in *ALG&PC* (fortnightly) on June 15. They issued the fourth edition, with the joint imprint of Sampson Low, London (copyright 1865), 19 cm., anonymous, 399 pp. The first English edition was issued by Sampson Low, London, 2 vols., 1865, p 8vo, anonymous, 16/0, listed in the *Ath* on June 24. Low issued it in 1 vol. in 1865, at 3/6; and issued it, 1866, a new edition, my copy, 17.5 cm., prefatory note and a note to the English reader, the latter signed A.D.T.W., 400 pp., 1/6, in which pictorial boards, printed in red, blue, yellow, and black, with plain white endpapers. It was advertised in the *Spect* on Dec. 9, 1865, as "This day." It was issued by S. O. Beeton, London, 1866, 17 cm., anonymous, 359 pp., 1/0 sewed, listed in the *Reader* on Nov. 18, 1865.

1183 HENRY S. CLARKE, ET AL., eds.
The Century Reciter. Three series.
Cr 4to, 1/0 sewed each Dec. (*Bks*)
The first series was listed as I've given it and was advertised in the *Ath*, *Spect*, and *PC*. The second series was edited by Leopold Wagner, listed in the *Bks* for Oct. 1894. The third series was edited by Wagner, listed in *PC* on Sept. 28, 1895. Warne issued all three series in 1 vols., 1895, 364 pp.

1184 ROSE E. MAY **Merry Moments for Merry Little Folk.** Cr 4to. Colored illustrations. Varnished pictorial covers, cloth back, 1/6 1893 (*PC*)
This was advertised in *PC* for Christmas. Also 1892

1185 WILLIAM H. AINSWORTH
The Lancashire Witches. Author's copyright edition. p 8vo.
0/6 sewed 1893?
Notable Novels No. 153. I think this was the point where this series acquired a new binding style of white wrappers cut flush, with a smaller colored illustration on the lower half of the front cover, more like a vignette. This is my copy, no date, 21.3 cm., 188 pp. in double columns, in white wrappers printed on the front pictorially in red, blue, and black, with the series title on the front and the no. at the base of the spine. There are commercial ads on the back and inside front covers and a publisher's ad on the inside back cover. The ad gives the *Library of Fiction* through No. 30 of Aug. 1893 and the *Tavistock Library* through No. (8) of June 1894. This could very well have been issued in 1894. This ran in the *Sunday Times*, and the text was bound up and issued for private circulation, 1849, 30 cm., 185 pp. in double columns. Henry Colburn, London, issued it in 3 vols., 1849, 19 cm., 31/6, listed in the *Ath* on Dec. 23, 1848. Sadleir's copy is in half-cloth boards and labels, and Wolff's copy is just boards and labels and with a 24-page catalog at the back of vol. 1. It then ran in *Ainsworth's Magazine*, July 1850–Sept. 1853; and George Routledge & Co., London, issued it, 1854, third edition, 23 cm., 492 pp., illustrated by John Gilbert, listed in the *Ath* on Mar. 4 at 6/0. The first American edition was issued by Stringer & Townsend, New York, 1849, 22 cm., 264 pp., noticed in *Godey's Lady's Book* for May and advertised in *Lit W* on May 26 as recent, thus probably issued in Mar.

1186 MAURICE JÓKAI (MÓR JÓKAI) *In Love with the Czarina, and Other Stories.* Special authorized edition. Cr 8vo. Frontispiece (portrait). 1/0 sewed Feb. 17 (*PC*)
Library of Continental Authors No. 10. This is the last title in this series. It is the first English edition, translated from the Hungarian by Louis Felbermann, no date, 156 pp. Warne issued it in New York, 1894, $.50 paper, listed in *PW* on Apr. 7 and in the *Ind* on May 3. It was issued in New York, 1898, in *Stories by Foreign Authors*, pp. 151–193, publisher unknown to me, and probably only the title story.

1187 FRANCES H. BURNETT *The Pretty Sister of Jose.* 12mo. 1/0 sewed, 1/6 cloth Feb.?
London Library No. 44. The first American edition was issued by Charles Scribner's Sons, New York, 1889, 19.5 cm., 127 pp., illustrated, $1.00, in green pictorial cloth with 8 pp. of ads. It was advertised in the *New-York Times* on Apr. 6 as "Today" and listed in *Public Opinion* on Apr. 13 and in the *Ind* on Apr. 18. The first English edition was issued by Spencer Blackett, London, 1889, my copy, 17.5 cm., 127 pp., 1/0 sewed, 1/6 cloth, advertised in the *Ath* on Apr. 20 as "Ready" and listed on Apr. 20. The 1/0 is in white wrappers cut flush, printed and decorated on the front in black with the series title, *Blackett's Select Novels*, and with ads on the endpapers and inside wrappers. The back cover has an ad with a "rainbow" effect, printed in black against a background of broad vertical stripes in blue, pale pink, yellow, dark pink, and green.

1188 HENRY HERMAN *A Dead Man's Story, and Other Tales.* 12mo. 1/0 sewed Mar. 17 (*PC*)
London Library No. 45. This is the first edition, 1894, 192 pp. Warne issued it in New York, 1894, $.50 paper, listed in *PW* on Apr. 14.

1189 HENRY HERMAN *The Postman's Daughter, and Other Tales.* 12mo. 1/0 sewed Mar. 17 (*PC*)
London Library No. 46. This is the first edition, 1894, 189 pp.

1190 SIR CLAUDE A. BRAY *Sir Joseph's Heir.* 16mo. 1/0 sewed, 1/6 cloth May 5 (*PC*)
Tavistock Library No. 7. This is the first edition, no date, 180 pp.

1191 CHARLES MEYER *The Shadows of Life.* Cr 8vo. 1/0 sewed May 19 (*PC*)
This is a series of true detective stories. It is also given by the *Bks*, but otherwise I cannot trace it. It was reissued in 1898, Cr 8vo, 1/0 sewed, listed in the *Bks* for Oct.

1192 SIR WALTER SCOTT *Novels.* 21 vols.
1/0 sewed, 1/6 cloth each   May 26 (*PC*)
National Novels Nos. 8–28. This May 26 *PC*
listing gave 25 vols. at 25/0 but identified
them only as *Waverley Novels*. Now including the previously issued 4 novels in
the *National Novels* series and the present
21, we come to 25 titles. The *Eng Cat* gives
25 Scott titles at 25/0 as issued in May
1894, but I think 4 of them were issued
previously, as I have recorded in this bibliography. Finally, the *PC* lists 28 titles in the
National Novels, 1/0 sewed, 1/6 cloth each,
on Jan. 19, 1895. It is certainly true that
there were 28 titles in the *National Novels*
series, but I think they had all been issued
by May 1894.

1193 W. SAPTE, JR. *Uncle's Ghost.* 16mo.
1/0 sewed, 1/6 cloth   June 9 (*PC*)
Tavistock Library No. 8. This is the last title
in this series. It is also given by the *Bks*, but
otherwise I cannot trace it.

1194 PATRICK H. WOODWARD *Sharretts,
the Detective.* Cr 8vo. 0/6 sewed   June 23
(*PC*)
Detective Stories No. 1. This was also given
by the *Bks*, but otherwise I cannot trace it.

1195 PATRICK H. WOODWARD *Secret
Service.* Cr 8vo. 0/6 sewed   June 23 (*PC*)
Detective Stories No. 2. This is also given by
the *Bks*. It is conceivably an abridgment of
*Guarding the Mails; or, The Secret Service of
the Post Office Department*, issued in Hartford, Conn., 1876, 23 cm., 568 pp., illustrated, but otherwise I cannot trace it.

1196 WALTER WOOD *A Pastor's
Vengeance.* 12mo. 1/0 sewed   June 23
(*PC*)
London Library No. 47. This is also given by
the *Bks*, but otherwise I cannot trace it.

1197 CHARLES H. BARSTOW *Angels
Unawares.* Cr 8vo. Illustrated. 1/0 cloth
July 21 (*PC*)
Welcome Library No. 4. This is the first edi-
tion, no date, 128 pp.

1198 ANONYMOUS *The Magic Half-
Crown.* 12mo. Illustrated. 1/6 cloth
Aug. 15 (*Spect*)
Bedford Library. It is listed in the *TWEd* on
Sept. 28, 1894, and was issued by Warne in
New York in 1894, listed in the *Outlook*,
New York (weekly), on Nov. 24.

1199 WILLIAM M. THACKERAY
The History of Henry Esmond, Esq.
8vo. 0/6 sewed   Aug. 25 (*PC*)
Standard Novels No. 14. The first edition
was issued by Smith, Elder & Co., London,
3 vols., 1852, 20 cm., written by himself,
31/6 in olive-brown cloth with labels, with
Thackeray on the spine, white endpapers,
and a 16-page catalog (Oct. 1852) at the
back of vol. 3. It was listed in the *Ath* on
Oct. 30 and in the *Spect* on Nov. 6. There
was a second edition in 3 vols., listed in the
Spect on Jan. 1, 1853. It was reduced to
15/0 in 1855. They issued it, 1858 (1857),
new edition, 20 cm., 464 pp., by Thackeray, 6/0, advertised in the *Spect* on Oct.
17, 1857. They reissued it in 1864, listed
in the *Spect* on June 18. They issued it,
1868, 8vo, 452 pp., frontispiece and 7
plates by Du Maurier, in green cloth with
beveled boards and green and white flo-
ral-patterned endpapers; reissued 1869.
The first American edition was issued by
Harper & Brothers, New York, 1852, 8vo,
193 pp. in double columns, $.50 paper, *Li-
brary of Select Novels* No. 175. It had red-
brown wrappers, decorated and printed
in black on the front. It was advertised in
the *New York Daily Times* on Nov. 20 as
"This day" and listed in *Lit W* as published
Oct. 23–Dec. 4, and advertised there on
Nov. 27 as "Just issued."

1200 WILLIAM H. AINSWORTH *Guy Fawkes.* p 8vo. o/6 sewed Sept. 29 (*PC*)

Notable Novels No. 154. This is the last title in this series. The first appearance was in *Bentley's Miscellaney,* Jan. 1840–Nov. 1841. The first edition in book form was issued by Bentley, London, 3 vols., 1841, illustrated by Cruikshank, 31/6, in claret cloth with pale yellow endpapers. It was listed in the *Ath* and in the *Spect* on July 31. It was issued by Chapman & Hall, London, 1850, Fcp 8vo, 304 pp., 1/6 boards, 2/0 cloth, listed in the *Ath* on Sept. 21; reissued 1851, listed in the *Ath* on Apr. 26. It was issued by George Routledge & Co., London, 1857, 27 cm., 359 pp., with all the Cruikshank illustrations, 6/0, in royal-blue cloth with pale yellow endpapers and also with a different grain of cloth and white endpapers (Wolff's copies). In the United States it was issued in parts by Lea & Blanchard, Philadelphia; a notice in *Godey's Lady's Book* for May 1840 stated that they were beginning, and an ad in the *Globe,* a Washington, D.C., daily, by a Washington book dealer on May 8 said "This day." They issued it in book form, 1841, 26 cm., 205 pp., illustrated, reviewed in *Graham's Lady's Magazine* for Nov. 1841. It was also issued by N.C. Nafis, New York, 1841, 267 pp.

1201 ANONYMOUS *Cecile.* 12mo. 1/0 sewed Oct. 13 (*PC*)

London Library No. 49. This is also given by the *Eng Cat* and the *Bks,* but otherwise I cannot trace it.

1202 CHARLOTTE BRONTË *Villette.* 8vo. o/6 sewed Nov. 17 (*PC*)

Standard Novels No. 15. The first edition was issued by Smith, Elder & Co., London, etc., 3 vols., p 8vo, 31/6 in olive-brown cloth with a 12-page catalog (Jan. 1853) at the back of vol. 1 (Sadleir's copy) and (Mar. 1854) (Wolff's copy). It was listed in the *Ath* on Jan. 29, by Currer Bell. It was reduced to 15/0 in 1855. They issued a new edition, 1855, 12mo, 492 pp., 6/0, listed in the *Spect* on Nov. 3; and a new edition, 1857, 12mo, 478 pp., probably in Oct., at 7/6 in limp linen. The first American edition was issued by Harper & Brothers, 1853, 20 cm., 502 pp., $.50 paper and in Cr 8vo, $1.00, advertised in the *New York Daily Times* on Mar. 5 as "This day" and advertised on Apr. 6, 22nd thousand, 8vo, $.50 paper. It was listed in *Lit W* as published Mar. 5–Apr. 4.

1203 SILAS K. HOCKING *Sweethearts Yet.* 12mo. 1/0 Nov. 24 (*PC*)

This is the first edition, 1894, with 92 pp.

1204 ANONYMOUS *The Duties of Servants.* Cr 8vo. 1/6 cloth Dec. 15 (*Spect*)

This is by a member of the aristocracy, a first edition, 1894, 119 pp. Warne reissued it 1899, 119 pp.

1205 ANONYMOUS *Waiting at Table.* Cr 8vo. 1/6 cloth Dec. 15 (*Spect*)

This is the first edition with 115 pp., by a member of the aristocracy. Warne issued it in New York in 1895, $.60, listed in the *Nation* on Feb. 1.

Frederick Warne & Co.
London and New York
1895

Frederick Warne and A. W. Duret, the partners in the firm, retired in 1895 and left the firm in the hands of Frederick Warne's three sons. Frederick Warne died on Nov. 7, 1901, at the age of 77 (editorial matter in the Ath *on the death of Warne).*

1206 W.H.G. KINGSTON **The Boatswain's Song.** Cr 8vo. Illustrated. 1/0 cloth Jan. 12 (*PC*)

Magnet Stories No. 1. This and the following 6 titles in this series were new editions, first issued by Groombridge & Sons, London, in their *Magnet Stories* series and in their *Shilling Gift Books.* Their *Magnet Stories* were issued in 8 vols., Oct. 1860–Nov. 1864, Fcp 8vo, illustrated, 2/6 cloth each. The *Shilling Gift Books* were illustrated, 1/0 cloth each, 3 stories in each vol., issued Dec. 1863–Oct. 1864 in a total of 20 vols. The present title was in vol. 8 of *Magnet Stories.*

1207 ELEANOR G. O'REILLY **When We Were Young.** Cr 8vo. Illustrated. 1/0 cloth Jan. 12 (*PC*)

Magnet Stories No. 2. This was in vol. 1 of the Groombridge *Magnet Stories* and was also issued by W. & R. Chambers, London, 1892, 275 pp., illustrated, 2/6.

1208 JULIA CORNER **The Shepherd Lord.** Cr 8vo. Illustrated. 1/0 cloth Jan. 12 (*PC*)

Magnet Stories No. 3. This was in vol. 3 of the Groombridge *Magnet Stories*, issued in Dec. 1861; it also was issued in the *Shilling Gift Books* in 1863.

1209 ANNIE WEBB, (MRS. J. B. WEBB, later WEBB-PEPLOE) **Blind Ursula and Other Stories.** Cr 8vo. Illustrated. 1/0 cloth Jan. 12 (*PC*)

Magnet Stories No. 4. This was story No. 5 in vol. 1 of the Groombridge *Magnet Stories* and was issued also in *Shilling Gift Books* (1864), 17 cm., (126) pp., illustrated, listed in the *Reader* on Nov. 12, 1864.

1210 FRANCES F. BRODERIP **Wee Maggie.** Cr 8vo. Illustrated. 1/0 cloth Jan. 12 (*PC*)

Magnet Stories No. 5. This was in vol. 8 of the Groombridge *Magnet Stories*, issued in Nov. 1864.

1211 THOMAS MILLER **Springtime and Golden Autumn.** Cr 8vo. Illustrated. 1/0 cloth Jan. 12 (*PC*)

Magnet Stories No. 6. Groombridge issued this in 2 vols., *Sweet Springtime* in vol. 6 and *Golden Autumn* in vol. 7 of their *Magnet Stories*, in Sept. 1863 and Apr. 1864 respectively.

1212 ANNA M. HALL (MRS. S. C. HALL) **Union Jack.** Cr 8vo. Illustrated. 1/0 cloth Jan. 12 (*PC*)

Magnet Stories No. 7. This was No. 1 of vol. 2 in the Groombridge *Magnet Stories*, issued in June 1861; it also was in their *Shilling Gift Books* in 1863.

1213 LYDIA CHILD *The Girl's Own Book.*
[New and revised edition.] Cr 8vo. 1/0 sewed Jan. 12 (*PC*)

This was revised and enlarged by Laura Valentine. The sixth edition was issued by T. T. & G. Tegg, London, 1833, 16mo, 272 pp. W. Tegg, London, issued the 17th edition, 1856, 15 cm., 407 pp., illustrated. New editions were issued 1861 and 1862 by Tegg, revised by Valentine. Many other editions were issued by Tegg, revised and enlarged by Valentine and others, certainly through 1876.

1214 ANNIE WEBB (MRS. J. B. WEBB, later WEBB-PEPLOE) *Naomi.* Cr 8vo. 2/0 cloth Apr. 13 (*PC*)

Star Series No. 129. The first edition was issued by Harvey & Darton, London, 1841, Fcp 8vo, 7/6, listed in the *Ath* on Dec. 19, 1840, and in the *Spect* on Dec. 26. They advertised the same in the *Spect* on Sept. 11, 1841, and Mar. 12, 1842, both as "This day." They issued the second edition, listed in the *Spect* on May 28, 1842; and the seventh edition, 1848, 12mo, 7/6 cloth, listed by *PC* as published Mar. 11–25. Arthur Hall, Virtue & Co., London, issued a new edition in 1860, Fcp 8vo, illustrated by Gilbert, 7/6, advertised in the *Spect* on Mar. 17; and Virtue Brothers & Co., London, issued it in 1863, new and revised edition, Fcp 8vo, 496 pp., illustrated, 7/6, listed in the *Reader* on Jan. 31, 1863. The first American edition was issued by Herman Hooker, Philadelphia, 1851, 422 pp., from the ninth London edition, listed by *Lit W* as published Jan. 25–Feb. 8, but noticed in the *Ind* on Jan. 9.

1215 ANNIE KEARY *Bab and Her Winkles.*
Cr 8vo. Illustrated. 1/0 cloth June 1 (*PC*)

Welcome Library No. 5. This is also given by the *Bks*, but otherwise I cannot trace it.

1216 IDA LEMON, later HILDYARD
A Divided Duty. Cr 8vo. 2/0 cloth June 15 (*Spect*)

Star Series No. 130. The first edition was issued by Warne, 1891, 6/0, advertised in the *Ath* on July 18 as "Now ready" and listed in *PC* on July 25. Warne issued the second edition in 1891, Cr 8vo, 6/0, advertised in the *Spect* on Oct. 10; they reduced it to 3/6, 384 pp., listed in *PC* on May 14, 1892. The first American edition was issued by J. B. Lippincott, Philadelphia, 1892, 12mo, 384 pp.

1217 FERGUS HUME *The White Prior.*
12mo. 1/0 sewed June 15 (*PC*)

London Library No. 48. This is the first edition, 1895, 160 pp. It was issued by Warne in New York, 1895, $.40 paper, listed in *PW* on Aug. 3. I have a copy, no date, 18.1 cm., 160 pp., front cover and spine in robin-egg–blue boards and back cover in white. The front cover is illustrated and printed in black and white, and a commercial ad is on the back cover. It has plain white endpapers and a 32-page catalog at the back. I judge this to be 1898 or later from the ads.

1218 MARY NEEDELL *Stephen Ellicott's Daughter.* Cr 8vo. 2/0 boards June 22 (*PC*)

Library of Fiction No. 32. The first edition was issued by Warne, 3 vols., 1891, Cr 8vo, 31/6, listed in the *Ath* on Feb. 21. They advertised the second edition in the *TWEd* on June 5, 3 vols.; and issued it at 6/0, Cr 8vo, 493 pp., in 1891, listed by *PC* on Oct. 3. Warne issued a new edition in 1892, Cr 8vo, 3/6, advertised in the *Spect* on Oct. 29. In the United States it was issued by J. B. Lippincott, Philadelphia, 1891, advertised in the *Ind* on Sept. 17 as "New books." It was also issued by D. Appleton & Co., New York, 1891, 19 cm., 493 pp., advertised in the *New-York Times* on Sept. 18 and listed in the *Nation* on Oct. 1, *Town & Coun-*

try Library No. 80, $.50 paper, $1.00 cloth. It was also issued by P. F. Collier, New York, 1891, 2 vols.-in-1, 18 cm.

1219 A. W. MARCHMONT *Sir Jaffray's Wife.* Cr 8vo. 2/o boards, 2/6 cloth Oct. 5 (*Ath*)

Library of Fiction. This is the first edition, 1895, 315 pp. It was issued by Rand McNally, Chicago and New York (copyright 1898), 19 cm., 305 pp., in the *Globe Library* No. 279.

1220 MADAME D'ARBLAY (FANNY BURNEY) *Diary and Letters of Madame D'Arblay.* 3 vols., Cr 8vo. 1/o cloth each Oct. 5 (*PC* ad)

Chandos Classics probably Nos. 149–151. These vols. marked the end of the wrappered editions of this series. These and later vols. were in Cr 8vo, cut edges, 2/o cloth, and in library style, blue cloth, uncut, gilt lettering, 2/o cloth. Warne issued this in 3 vols., 1892, frontispieces (portraits) in vols. 1 and 2; and issued it in New York in 1892, 3 vols., in smooth dark blue linen boards, $2.25, or in an alternate cloth binding, $3.00, listed in the *Nation* on Sept. 22. The first edition was issued by Henry Colburn, London, 7 vols., 1842–46, 19.5 cm., frontispieces (portraits), edited by the authoress's niece. There is a 16-page catalog (Feb. 1842) in vol. 1; a 24-page catalog in vol. 6; and an 8-page catalog in vol. 7., 10/6 each in brown cloth. Vol. 1 was issued Jan. 1, 1842; vol. 2 on Mar. 1; vol. 4 on July 25; vol. 5 about Nov. 19; vol. 6 about Sept. 4, 1846; and vol. 7 on Nov. 30, 1846, all given by *Spect* ads. In the United States it was issued in 2 vols. by Carey & Hart, Philadelphia, 1842; vol. 1 was noticed in *Godey's Lady's Book* for July 1842, and vols. 1 and 2 were noticed in *Graham's Magazine* (monthly) for July 1842.

1221 LAURA VALENTINE, ed. *Cameos of English Literature.* Vols. 1 & 2. 18mo. 1/6 each Oct. 5 (*PC*)

This is a modernized and revised edition of *Half Hours with the Best Authors* by Charles Knight. The present issue was in 6 vols., vols. 3 and 4 listed in *PC* on Nov. 23, 1895, and vols. 4–6 (*sic*) listed Aug. 29, 1896. Warne first issued it in 12 vols., 1894, 21/o, listed in the *TWEd* on Dec. 14, 1894. It was reissued in 12 vols., 1/6 each, in 1897, listed in *PC* on Mar. 20. Warne issued it in 12 fortnightly 1/o parts, in limp covers, or one-half white cloth at 1/6 each, or 2/o lambskin, limp, each, advertised in the *Spect* on Oct. 19, 1901.

1222 LOUISA L. GREENE *The Schoolboy Baronet.* [New edition.] Cr 8vo. Illustrated. 2/6 cloth Nov. 16 (*PC*)

The first edition was issued by Warne, 1870 (1869), 12mo, illustrated, 3/6, listed in the *Ath* on Oct. 30, 1869. It was issued in the United States by Dutton & Co., New York, 1871, 16mo, illustrated, listed in the *Nation* on Dec. 1, 1870.

1223 LAURA VALENTINE *Aunt Louisa's Book of Common Things.* 4to. Illustrated. 1/o sewed, 2/o cloth Nov. 30 (*PC*)

This is the first edition, no date, 94 pp. It was advertised in the Christmas number of *PC* as in stiff boards cut flush, 1/o, 2/o cloth.

1224 LOUISA L. GREENE *Gilbert's Shadow.* [New edition.] Cr 8vo. Illustrated. 2/6 cloth Nov. 30 (*PC*)

The first edition was issued by Warne, 1875, 12mo, illustrated, 3/6, listed in the *Spect* on June 5.

1225 ARTHUR L. KNIGHT *A Mid of the Naval Brigade, Vivian Vansittart, V. C.* Cr 8vo. Illustrated. 2/6 cloth Dec. 21 (*PC*)

This is the first edition, 1895, 268 pp.

1226 CHARLES MEYER **The Power of Gold.**
Cr 8vo. o/6 sewed   1895

Detective Series No. 3. This is the first edition, no date, 123 pp. It was given under "Season's Announcements," editorial matter in the *PC* on Mar. 9.

1227 EDWARD BULWER LYTTON
My Novel. 2 vols. 8vo. o/6 sewed each;
1 vol., 1/o sewed   1895?

Standard Novels No. 16. This is Warne, no date. This ran in *Blackwood's Magazine*, Sept. 1850–Jan. 1853, and the first English book edition was *"My Novel,"* issued by William Blackwood & Sons, Edinburgh and London, 4 vols. 1853, 20 cm., by Pisistratus Caxton on the title page and by Lytton on the spine, 42/o, in dark brown cloth, with an 8-page catalog at the back of vol. 4. It was advertised in the *Ath* on Jan. 29 as "On Feb. 4" and on Feb. 5 as "Now ready," and it listed in the *Spect* on Feb. 5. They issued the second edition, 1853, 2 vols., 21/o, advertised in the *Spect* on June 18 as "This day." It was issued by George Routledge & Co., London, 1854, 2 vols., new edition, 19.5 cm., frontispieces by Gilbert, 8/o, listed in the *Ath* on Nov. 4; reissued in 2 vols., the 26th thousand, at the end of 1855. In the United States it ran in *Harper's New Monthly Magazine*, Oct. 1850–Feb. 1853, and *Harper's* issued it in 2 parts, 1853, at o/3 ($.37½) each, part 1 listed by *Lit W* as published Dec. 4–25, 1852, advertised on Dec. 11 as "Just published"; part 2 listed by *Lit W* as published Jan. 22–Feb. 5, 1853, and advertised in the *New York Daily Times* as "On Jan. 21." Harpers issued it in 1 vol., $.50 paper, advertised in the *New York Daily Times* on Feb. 20, 1853; and they issued it in 1 vol. at $.75, advertised in the same on Mar. 12, 1853.

Frederick Warne & Co.
London and New York
1896

1228 HARVEY GOBEL *On the Shelf.*
Cr 8vo. Illustrated. 2/6   Feb. 15 (*PC*)
This is the first edition, no date, 187 pp.,
containing tales for children and young
people. Warne issued it in New York in
1896, square Cr 8vo, 14 illustrations,
$1.00 cloth, listed in the *Outlook*, New York
(weekly), on Oct. 17.

1229 (CAROLINE PEACHEY) *Kirstin's*
Adventures. [New edition.] Cr 8vo. 2/0
Feb. 15 (*PC*)
This was issued earlier in *Home Circle Gift
Books*, probably in the 1880s. The first edi-
tion was issued by Bell & Daldy, London,
1871, 271 pp., illustrated, 6/0, listed in the
Ath on Dec. 9, 1871.

1230 JOHN G. WATTS *Martin Noble.*
[New edition.] Cr 8vo. Illustrated. 2/0
Feb. 15 (*PC*)
The first edition was issued by Warne
(1877), 17 cm., 284 pp., illustrated, 3/6
cloth, listed in the *Spect* on Oct. 27.

1231 JAMES R. LOWELL *Poetical Works of*
James Russell Lowell. Including the Biglow
Papers. Cr 8vo. 2/0 cloth   May 16 (*PC*)
Chandos Classics. This has no date and 519
pp. *Poems* was issued by H. Altemus, Philadelphia, 1842, 15.5 cm., 229 pp., frontispiece (portrait); and by John Owens, Cambridge, 1844, 19 cm., 279 pp., listed in the
United States Magazine for Feb. 1844. *Poems,
second series*, was issued by George Nichols,
Cambridge, etc., 1848, 19 cm., 184 pp., reviewed in *American Review* (monthly) for
Mar. *Poems* was issued by Ticknor, Reed &
Fields, Boston, etc., 2 vols., listed by *Lit W*
as published Dec. 22, 1849–Jan. 5, 1850;
and issued as *The Poetical Works of James R.
Lowell* by Ticknor & Fields, Boston, 2 vols.,
1858, 13.5 cm., frontispiece (portrait),
listed in the *Christian Examiner* for Mar. In
England *Poems* was issued by G. E. Mudie,
London, 1844, 18 cm., 279 pp., 5/0, listed
in the *Gentleman's Magazine* for May 1844.
Poems was imported by Thomas Delf,
American Literary Agency, London, 2
vols., 12mo, 12/0, advertised in the *Ath* on
Oct. 4, 1851. *The Poetical Works of James
Russell Lowell* was issued by George Routledge & Co., London, 1852, 24mo, 334
pp., 2/0 cloth, edited and with an introduction by Andrew R. Scoble, listed in the
Literary Gazette on Dec. 27, 1851; reissued
1853, the same, at 1/0 boards, listed by *PC*
as published Nov. 14–30, 1853. The first
series of *The Biglow Papers* was issued by
George Nichols, Cambridge, etc., 1848;
imported in London by John Chapman
and issued in Dec. 1848. It was issued by
Trübner & Co., London, 1859. The second series was issued by Trübner & Co.,
London, 3 parts, in 1862, and in the
United States by Ticknor & Fields, Boston, 1867.

1232 RICHARD LYDEKKER, ed. *The Royal Natural History.* No. 1. Royal 8vo. Colored frontispiece. o/6 each   May 23 (*PC* ad)

The *PC* ad said this was to be issued in 72 weekly numbers, each with a colored frontispiece, No. 1 on May 22 and No. 2 on June 9. Later editorial matter gave No. 8 on July 21, No. 17 on Sept. 23, No. 22 on Oct. 28, No. 35 on Jan. 26, 1897, etc. I'm not sure of the accuracy of my discussion of the varied issues. The *Eng Cat* gives 8 vols., royal 8vo, illustrated, 9/0 each, 1894–97; and 16 sections, royal 8vo, 5/0 cloth, 8/0 half-morocco each, preface by P. L. Sclater, 1893–97. Warne also issued it, 12 sections in 6 vols., 1894–96, royal 8vo, 27 cm., plates partly colored, each section with a separate title page and every two sections paged continuously, 9/0 per vol. Warne also issued it in New York, in 36 monthly $.50 parts, colored illustrations, part 1 on May 1, 1894, advertised in the *Nation* on Apr. 5. Nos. 32–34 were listed in the *Outlook* (weekly) on Oct. 17, 1896; and Nos. 35 and 36 were listed on Dec. 18, 1896, $.50 each. Apparently every 3 nos. were bound up as a vol., and the 12 vols. were issued at $30 cloth, advertised in the *Outlook* on Nov. 28, 1896; and every 6 nos. were also bound up in a vol. and issued in 6 vols., $27 cloth, advertised in the same on Nov. 28, 1896.

1233 MARY H. TENNYSON (MARY H. FOLKARD) *Within Her Grasp.* Cr 8vo. 1/0 sewed   Aug. 15 (*PC*)

This is also given by the *Bks*, but otherwise I cannot trace it.

1234 THEODORA C. ELMSLIE *His Life's Magnet.* Cr 8vo. 2/0 cloth   Aug. 29 (*PC*)

Star Series. The first edition was issued by Warne, 1892, Cr 8vo, 344 pp., 6/0, listed in *PC* on Aug. 13 and in the *Spect* the same. Warne reissued it at 3/6 about Aug. 5, 1893. The first American edition was is-

sued by D. Appleton & Co., New York, 1892, 18 cm., 344 pp., noticed in the *Christian Union* on Oct. 22.

1235 CHARLES A. JONES *Little Sir Nicholas.* Cr 8vo. Illustrated. 2/6 Sept. 12 (*PC*)

The first edition was issued by Warne, 1890, 250 pp., illustrated, 3/6, in Sept.

1236 ELIZABETH T. MEADE, later SMITH *Heart of Gold.* Cr 8vo. Illustrated. 2/6 Sept. 12 (*PC*)

The first English edition was issued by Warne, 1890, 20 cm., 316 pp., illustrated, 3/6, issued in Nov. and advertised in the *Times Weekly Edition* on Dec. 19, square Cr 8vo. Warne issued it in New York at $1.50, listed in the *Nation* on Nov. 27, 1890. It was also issued by the United States Book Co., New York (copyright 1890), authorized edition, 218 pp., $.50 paper, $1.00 cloth, *International Series* No. 120, listed in *PW* on Nov. 1, 1890, the *Ind* on Nov. 20, and in *Public Opinion* on Nov. 22. The wrapper date on the paper issue was Aug. 12, 1890, but this date is largely meaningless.

1237 CHARLES H. BARSTOW *Old Bond's Atonement.* Cr 8vo. Illustrated. 1/0 cloth Sept. 26 (*PC*)

Welcome Library No. 13. This is probably the first edition. It is also listed by the *Bks*, but otherwise I cannot trace it.

1238 ANONYMOUS *Rhymes from Nursery Land.* Cr 8vo. Colored illustrations. 1/0 picture boards   Oct. 24 (*PC*)

This is the first edition, 64 pp. It is also given by the *Bks*. Warne issued *The Nursery Rhymes Book*, edited by Andrew Land, in New York, large square Cr 8vo, illustrated, $2.00, mentioned in editorial matter in the *New York Times Book Review* on Dec. 11, 1897, as recent. I don't think it could be an edition of the present title because of the difference in price.

1239 EDWARD STEP *Favourite Flowers of Garden and Greenhouse.* Parts 1–10. Colored illustrations. 1/0 sewed each Oct. 31 (*Spect* ad)

The *Spect* ad said Nos. 1–10 "Now ready." This is the first edition. Each part had 6 colored plates, and the total pages come to 636. After every 13 parts, those parts were bound up in 1 vol., 25 cm., in green cloth and issued at 15/0. Vol. 1 was listed in the *Spect* on Dec. 5, 1896, and vol. 2 was advertised on May 1, 1897, as "Now ready," although I think vol. 2 was issued in Mar. 1897.

1240 ANONYMOUS *The Dear Old Nursery Rhymes.* 4to. Colored illustrations. 2/6 picture boards, cloth back   Oct. 31 (*Spect*)

The *BM* gives only Warne, New York (1896), 48 pp. I think this is probably incorrect, as it was mentioned in editorial matter in the *New York Times Book Review* on Dec. 11, 1897, as recent, issued by Warne, New York, $1.00. The present edition is probably the first edition. It has 8 colored plates and 50 drawings. It was also listed in *PC* on Nov. 7, 1896.

1241 MARY H. DEBENHAM *My Neighbour's Garden.* 12mo. Illustrated. 1/6 cloth   Nov. 21 (*PC*)

Bedford Library. This is probably the first edition. It is also given by the *Bks*, but otherwise I cannot trace it.

1242 FERGUS HUME *Monsieur Judas.* Cr 8vo. 1/0 sewed   Nov. 21 (*PC*)

This has no date and 192 pp. The first edition was issued by Spencer Blackett, London (1891), 192 pp., 1/0 sewed, 1/6 cloth, advertised in the *Ath* and *Spect* on Mar. 28. The wrapper issue had white wrappers cut flush, pictorially decorated and lettered in black, with ads on the back cover and inside wrappers. The first American edition was issued by the Waverly Co., New York, 1891, 12mo, 192 pp., paper,

World Library No. 10 with wrapper date June 1891. It was listed in the *Ind* on June 4 and in *PW* on June 13. Warne issued it in New York, 12mo, $.35, mentioned in editorial matter, "Books for Spring," in the *New York Times Book Review* for Mar. 27, 1897.

1243 WILLIAM H. D. ADAMS *Under Many Flags.* Cr 8vo. Illustrated. 2/6 cloth Dec. 5 (*PC*)

This is a boy's book consisting of 9 sketches. It is a first edition, 1896, 236 pp.

1244 ASCOTT R. HOPE (ASCOTT R. HOPE MONCRIEFF) *The Story of the Indian Mutiny.* Cr 8vo. Maps. Illustrations. 2/6 cloth   Dec. 5 (*PC*)

This is a boy's book, 1896, 243 pp. The first edition was issued by P. Nimmo & Co., Edinburgh, 1880, 19 cm., anonymous, 224 pp., illustrated.

1245 LOUIS HOFFMANN (ANGELO LEWIS) *Arithmetical Puzzles.* Cr 8vo. Illustrated. 1/0 sewed   Dec. 5 (*PC*)

This had no date, 120 pp. It and the following two titles first appeared in *Puzzles Old and New*, issued by Warne, 1893, Cr 8vo, 394 pp., illustrated, 3/6, listed in the *Spect* on Dec. 16, 1893; reissued in 1894 and 1896. Warne issued it in New York at $1.50, listed in the *Outlook* (weekly) on June 2, 1894.

1246 LOUIS HOFFMANN (ANGELO LEWIS) *Mechanical Puzzles.* Cr 8vo. Illustrated. 1/0 sewed   Dec. 5 (*PC*)

This has no date and 144 pp. See the preceding item.

1247 LOUIS HOFFMANN (ANGELO LEWIS) *Miscellaneous Puzzles.* Cr 8vo. Illustrated. 1/0 sewed   Dec. 5 (*PC*)

This has 130 pp. and was reissued at least twice in the 1900s.
See the preceding item.

1248 EDWARD SIMS *Warne's Net Profit Tables.* 18mo. 1/0 Jan. 30 (*PC*)

This is the first edition, no date. It was re-issued about Mar. 20.

1249 MRS. ALEXANDER (ANNIE HECTOR) *Forging the Fetters, and Other Stories.* Cr 8vo. 1/0 sewed Mar. 13 (*PC*)

This has no date and 154 pp. The first edition was issued by Henry Holt, New York, 1887, *Forging the Fetters, and Other Stories*, 301 pp., *Leisure Moment Series* No. 83 at $.30 and *Leisure Hour Series* No. 203 at $1.00, listed in *PW* on June 25 and in the *Nation* on June 30. It contains 3 stories. It was advertised in the *New-York Times* on June 21 as "Today." George Munro, New York, issued it (1887), *Seaside Library Pocket Edition* No. 997, 12mo, paper, in July or Aug., containing 2 of the stories in the Holt edition. It was also issued by John W. Lovell, New York (1887), 78 pp., paper, *Lovell's Library* No. 1044, containing 4 stories, with only the title story among those in the Holt edition. In England it was issued as *Forging the Fetters* by Spencer Blackett, London, 1890, 154 pp., 1/0 sewed, 1/6 cloth, advertised in the *Spect* on June 7 as ready.

1250 CYRIL MARSH, ed. *The British Empire Portrait Gallery. South Africa.* Roy 8vo. 1/0 sewed May 1 (*Spect* ad)

The *Spect* ad said "Now ready." This is the first edition, with 56 pp., given by the *Eng Cat* as published in Apr.

1251 LAURA VALENTINE *The Life of Victoria, Our Queen and Empress. Simply Told for Children.* 4to. 1/0 sewed May 8 (*PC*)

This is the first edition, 1897, 125 pp. I'm sure it must have had illustrations, as Warne issued it in New York, p 4to, with 8 full-page illustrations and others, at $.50, listed in the *Outlook* (weekly) on July 16, 1897, and in the *Nation* on July 22.

1252 CHARLES D. FARQUHARSON *The Federation of the Powers.* 12mo. 1/0 sewed July 10 (*PC*)

This is the first edition, 1897, 125 pp. Warne issued it in New York in 1897, 16mo, $.40 paper, listed in the *New-York Times* on Oct. 23.

1253 A VAGABOND *An Original Wager.* Cr 8vo. Illustrated. 2/0 sewed, 2/6 cloth Aug. 14 & 28 (*PC*)

This has no date and 318 pp. The 2/6 was listed in *PC* on Aug. 14 and the 2/0 on

Aug. 28. The first edition was issued by Warne, 1895, 318 pp., illustrated, 3/6, listed in the *Spect* on Nov. 2.

1254 HANS C. ANDERSEN *Fairy Tales.* 12mo. 1/6 cloth   Sept. 4 (*PC*)

Fairy Library. Warne also issued this, 1892, illustrated, in beveled brown cloth, a new translation by Mrs. Paull with a special adaptation and arrangement for young people, *Hans Andersen's Fairy Tales.* They also issued it in 1897 in the *Prize Library*, Cr 8vo, 383 pp., illustrated, 2/0, listed in *PC* on Sept. 4; and they issued it in 1897 also at 3/6. They issued it in New York, *Hans Andersen's Fairy Tales*, in 1889, large 8vo, colored plates, $3.00 cloth, complete, translated by Mrs. Paull, advertised in the *Christian Union* on Dec. 5, 1889.

Also 1874, 83. See 1865, 77

1255 HANS C. ANDERSEN *Tales for the Young.* 12mo. 1/6 cloth   Sept. 11 (*PC*)

Fairy Library. This was probably in a translation by Mrs. Paull (see the preceding item).

Also 1865, 77. See 1874, 83

1256 HANS C. ANDERSEN *Dream Stories.* 12mo. 1/6 cloth   Sept. 11 (*PC*)

Fairy Library.

See 1883

1257 HANS C. ANDERSEN *Elfin Tales.* 12mo. 1/6 cloth   Sept. 11 (*PC*)

Fairy Library.

See 1883

1258 ANGELICA SELBY *On Duty.* Roy 16mo. 2/6   Oct. 2 (*PC*)

This is a story for children. The first edition was issued by Warne in 1888, square 16mo, 247 pp., 3/6, reviewed in the *Ath* on Nov. 24. The *U Cat* gives it as Warne, Lon-don and New York, 1889, 18 cm., 247 pp., illustrated.

1259 ANONYMOUS *The Dear Old Nursery Songs.* 4to. Colored plates. 2/6 boards, cloth back   Nov. 6 (*Spect*)

This is probably the first edition. It is also given by the *Bks*, but otherwise I cannot trace it.

1260 RANDOLPH CALDECOTT *Caldecott's Picture Books.* 16 vols. 0/6 each   Nov. 13 (*Spect* ad)

I think these have cover titles, partly colored illustrations, 20.5 × 23 cm. Warne issued them in 2 vols., 8 parts to the vol., same size, in 1895 or 1896. George Routledge & Sons, London, issued the 16 titles in single vols., cover titles, same size, partly colored illustrations, 1/0 each. The first 4 were issued 1878–80 and in 1 vol., 1879, *Caldecott's Picture Book*, 5/0. The first 4 titles were "The House that Jack Built," "The History of John Gilpin," "Babes in the Wood," and "Elegy on the Death of a Mad Dog." He issued the next 4 titles, 1880–81, and in 1 vol., *Caldecott's Picture Book*, vol. 2, 1881, 5/0. It contains "The Milkmaid," "Sing a Song of Sixpence," "The Queen of Hearts," and "The Farmer's Boy." He issued the next 4 titles at 1/0 each and in 1 vol., *The Hey Diddle Diddle Picture Book* (1883), 5/0. It contains "Hey Diddle Diddle and Baby Bunting," "Three Jovial Huntsmen," "A Frog He Would a-Wooing Go," and "The Fox Jumps over the Parson's Gate." He issued the last 4 in 1 vol., *The Great Panjandrum Picture Book*, (1885), 5/0. It contains "Come Lasses and Lads," "Ride a Cock Horse to Banbury and a Farmer Went Trotting upon His Grey Mare," "An Elegy on the Glory of Her Sex—Mary Blaize," and "The Great Panjandrum."

1261 MARY H. DEBENHAM **The Ruler of This House.** Cr 8vo. Illustrated. 1/0 cloth   Nov. 27 (*PC*)
Welcome Library. This is the first edition, no date, 128 pp.

1262 CHARLES H. BARSTOW **Natty's Violin.** 12mo. Illustrated. 1/6 cloth   Dec. 24 (*PC*)
Bedford Library. This is the first edition, no date, 188 pp.

1263 ANONYMOUS **Songs from Nursery Land.** Cr 8vo. Colored illustrations. 1/0 picture boards   Christmas (*PC* ad)
I cannot trace this.

1264 ANONYMOUS **Tales from Nursery Land.** Cr 8vo. Colored illustrations. 1/0 picture boards   Christmas (*PC* ad)
I cannot trace this.

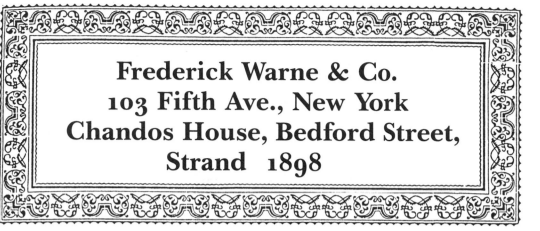

Frederick Warne & Co.
103 Fifth Ave., New York
Chandos House, Bedford Street,
Strand 1898

1265 FRANCES H. BURNETT *Louisiana.*
12mo. 1/0 sewed   Mar. (*Bks*)

London Library. The first American edition
was issued by Charles Scribner's Sons,
New York, 1880, 19 cm., 163 pp., frontispiece, $1.25 in blue-green cloth, adver-
tised in the *New-York Times* on Apr. 16 as
"This day." It ran in *Scribner's Monthly,*
Feb.–May 1880. The first English edition
was as *Louisiana and That Lass O' Lowrie's,*
issued by Macmillan & Co., London, 1880,
332 pp., illustrated, 6/0. Macmillan also issued *Louisiana,* 1883, 18.5 cm., 102 pp., illustrated, 1/0 sewed, in Mar.

1266 ADAM BADEAU *Conspiracy.* Cr 8vo.
2/0 boards, 3/6 cloth   May 21 (*Ath*)

Library of Fiction. This is my copy, no date,
319 pp., in light blue pictorial boards,
printed in red and black with the series title on the spine. There are publisher's ads
on the endpapers of date 1893 and a commercial ad on the back cover. The first edition was issued by R. Worthington, New
York, 1885, 19 cm., 324 pp., $1.25, adver-
tised in the *New-York Times* on Nov. 14 as
"Today" and listed in the *Ind* and the *Nation* on Nov. 19. In England it was issued by
Warne (1886), identical to the Worthington edition, with the joint imprint and a
new title page, 6/0, listed in the *Spect* and
Ath on Feb. 13. The first American edition
was issued by John W. Lovell, New York
(1886), *Lovell's Library* No. 756, 12mo, paper, listed in *PW* on Aug. 14.

1267 CHARLES H. BARSTOW *Through
Deep Waters.* 12mo. Illustrated. 1/6
cloth   Oct. (*Bks*)

Bedford Library. This is the first edition, no
date, 185 pp.

Frederick Warne & Co.
London and New York
1899

1268 AMELIA E. BARR *She Loved a Sailor.*
Cr 8vo. 1/6 sewed, 2/o cloth   Jan. 21
(*Spect*)

Star Series. The first edition was issued by
Dodd, Mead & Co., New York (copyright
1891), 19 cm., 459 pp., $1.25 cloth, adver-
tised in the *New-York Times* on Apr. 15,
1891, and in the *Christian Union* on May 7
as "Now published" and listed in the latter
on May 21. The first English edition was
issued by James Clarke & Co., London, no
date, Cr 8vo, 459 pp., 3/6, listed in the *Ath*
on Nov. 14, 1891.

1269 AMELIA E. BARR *Woven of Love and
Glory.* Cr 8vo. 1/6 sewed, 2/o cloth   Jan.
(*Eng Cat*)

Star Series. This ran in the *Sunday Magazine,* Isbister, London, and was in the Jan.
and Apr. issues, at least, in 1889. The
present issue has no date and 431 pp. The
first edition was issued by James Clarke &
Co., London 1890 (1889), Cr 8vo, 431 pp.,
3/6, listed in the *Ath* on Dec. 21, 1889.

1270 CHARLES M. SHELDON *In His Steps.*
Cr 8vo. 1/6 sewed, 2/o cloth   Feb.
(*Eng Cat*)

Star Series. I think the first edition was issued by the Advance Publishing Co., Chicago, 1897, 20 cm., 282 pp., $1.00, listed
in the *Outlook* (weekly) on June 18 and in
the *Ind* on June 24. Wright, however, gives
the first edition as issued by Fleming H.
Revell, New York, etc., 1897, 20 cm., 282

pp., but the earliest reference to this that
I've found was a listing in *PW* on Sept. 2,
1899, as being copyrighted in 1897. The *U
Cat* gives this Revell issue as 1897. There
were at least 10 English houses issuing it in
1898 or 1899. H. R. Allenson, London, issued it, 1898, authorized edition, 282 pp.,
issued in Apr. according to the *Eng Cat.*
George Routledge & Sons, Ltd., issued it
in Nov. 1898 at 1/o cloth, 288 pp., according to the *Eng Cat.* Ward, Lock & Co.,
Ltd., London, issued it in 1898, Cr 8vo,
307 pp., o/6 sewed, 1/o and 1/6 cloth, listed
in the *Acad* on Dec. 10, 1898. The Sunday
School Union, London, issued it (1898),
265 pp; and S. W. Partridge & Co., London, issued it, 1898, 319 pp.

1271 CHARLES M. SHELDON
The Crucifixion of Phillip Strong. Cr 8vo.
1/6 sewed, 2/o cloth   Feb. (*Eng Cat*)

Star Series. The first edition was issued by
A. C. McClurg & Co., Chicago, 1894, 18.5
cm., 267 pp., $1.00, listed in the *New-York
Times* on Nov. 18 and in the *Nation* on Nov.
22. At least 9 London houses issued it in
1898 or 1899. S. W. Partridge & Co., London, 1899, issued it in Dec. 1898, 288 pp.,
according to the *Eng Cat*; and the Sunday
School Union, London, issued it (1898),
267 pp., in Dec., according to the *Eng Cat.*
Ward, Lock & Co., Ltd., London, issued it
at o/6 sewed, 1/o and 1/6 cloth, listed in the
Bks for Jan. 1899; and George Routledge
& Sons, Ltd., London, issued it (1899),

255 pp., frontispiece, o/6 sewed, 1/o cloth, in Feb. according to the *Eng Cat*.

1272 CHARLES M. SHELDON *Robert Hardy's Seven Days*. Cr 8vo. 1/6 sewed, 2/o cloth Mar. (*Eng Cat*)

Star Series. The *Eng Cat* gives it at o/6 sewed in Mar., whereas the appendix of the same gives it as I've given it but without a date. The first edition was issued by the Congregational Sunday-School & Publishing Society, Boston and Chicago (copyright 1893), 238 pp., $.90, listed in *Public Opinion* on July 29, 1893, and in *PW* on Aug. 5. At least 6 London houses issued it in 1899. James Clarke & Co., London, issued it (1899), 201 pp., issued in Jan. 1899 according to the *Eng Cat*. It was also issued by H. R. Allenson & Co., London, 1899, 238 pp., in Jan. 1899 as given by the *Eng Cat*. It was also issued by George Routledge & Sons, Ltd., London (1899), Cr 8vo, 208 pp., o/6 sewed, 1/o cloth, given by the *Eng Cat* as Feb. 1899. It was issued by Ward, Lock & Co., Ltd., London, 1899, 305 pp., o/6 sewed, 1/o and 1/6 cloth, listed in the *Acad* for Apr. 1, 1899.

1273 CHARLES M. SHELDON *His Brother's Keeper.* Cr 8vo. 1/6 sewed, 2/o cloth Mar. (*Eng Cat*)

Star Series. The *Eng Cat* listing is o/6 sewed, 1/o, 1/6 in Mar., whereas the appendix of the same gives it as I've given it. The first edition was issued by the Congregational Sunday-School & Publishing Society, Boston and Chicago (copyright 1896), 19.5 cm., 381 pp., illustrated, $1.50, listed in the *Ind* on Oct. 8, 1896, and in *PW* on Oct. 10. In England it was issued by S. W. Partridge & Co., London, 1899, 318 pp., in June; and by the Sunday School Union, London (1899), 281 pp., in Jan. 1899. It was also issued by Ward, Lock & Co., Ltd., London (1899), 320 pp., o/6 sewed, 1/o and 1/6 cloth, advertised in the *Acad* on Feb. 18, 1899; and it was issued by George

Routledge & Sons, Ltd., London (1899), 19.5 cm., 318 pp., frontispiece, o/6 sewed, 1/o cloth, in Mar. 1899. It was also issued by H. R. Allenson & Co., London, 1899, 318 pp.

1274 CHARLES M. SHELDON *Malcolm Kirk.* Cr 8vo. 1/6 sewed, 2/o cloth Mar. (*Eng Cat*)

Star Series. The Mar. *Eng Cat* listing was o/6 sewed, whereas the appendix gives it as I've given it. The first edition was issued by the Church Press, Chicago (copyright 1898), 17 cm., 264 pp., $.50, listed in the *Nation* on Apr. 7, 1898, and in the *Ind* on Apr. 14. In England it was issued the Sunday School Union, London (1899), 255 pp., in Feb.; and by H. R. Allenson & Co., London, 1899, 255 pp., in Feb.; and by S. W. Partridge & Co., London, 1899, 224 pp. George Routledge & Sons, Ltd., London, issued it (1899), 19.5 cm., 192 pp., frontispiece, o/6 sewed, 1/o cloth, in Mar.; and Ward, Lock & Co., Ltd., London, issued it (1899), 240 pp., o/6 sewed, 1/o and 1/6 cloth, in Mar. or Apr.

1275 CHARLES M. SHELDON *Richard Bruce.* Cr 8vo. 1/6 sewed, 2/o cloth Mar. (*Eng Cat*)

Star Series. The *Eng Cat* listing for Mar. was o/6 sewed, 1/o, 1/6, whereas the appendix gives it as I've given it. The *U Cat* gives Warne, 1899, 19 cm., 288 pp., illustrated, but the *Eng Cat* gives 356 pp.! The first edition was issued by the Congregational Sunday-School & Publishing Society, Boston and Chicago (copyright 1892), 19.5 cm., 355 pp., illustrated, $1.50, listed in the *Christian Union* on Nov. 26 and in *PW* on Dec. 3, 1892 (no lists on Nov. 19 or 26). In England it was issued by H. R. Allenson & Co., London (1899), 313 pp., in Jan. 1899; and by the Sunday School Union, London (1899), 355 pp. It was issued by Ward, Lock & Co., Ltd., London (1899), 313 pp., o/6 sewed, 1/o and 1/6 cloth, listed in the *Acad* on Mar. 1. It was also issued by George Routledge & Sons, Ltd., London (1899), Cr 8vo, 326 pp., frontispiece, o/6 sewed, 1/o cloth, in Apr.

1276 CHARLES M. SHELDON
The Twentieth Door. Cr 8vo. 1/6 sewed, 2/o cloth   Mar. (*Eng Cat*)
Star Series. The *Eng Cat* entry for Mar. is o/6 sewed, 1/o, 1/6, whereas the appendix gives it as I've given it. The first edition was issued by the Congregational Sunday-School & Publishing Society, Boston and Chicago (copyright 1893), 19.5 cm., 357 pp., illustrated, $1.50, listed in *Public Opinion* and in the *Ind* on Oct. 5, 1893, and in *PW* on Oct. 14. In England it was issued by H. R. Allenson & Co., London, 1899, 320 pp., in Jan. 1899. Ward, Lock & Co., Ltd., London, issued it (1899), 19.5 cm., 320 pp., o/6 sewed, 1/o and 1/6 cloth, listed in the *Acad* on Apr. 1. It was also issued by George Routledge & Sons, Ltd., London (1899), Cr 8vo, 312 pp., frontispiece, o/6 sewed, 1/o cloth, in Apr.

1277 FRANCES H. BURNETT *A Lady of Quality.* p 8vo. o/6 sewed   Apr. (*Bks*)
Standard Novels. This is my copy, 1899, 21.5 cm., 128 pp. in double columns, in gray wrappers cut flush, printed and with a vignette in red on the front, with date 1900. There are commercial ads on the back and inside covers in red. The first American edition was issued by Charles Scribner's Sons, New York, 1896, 19 cm., 363 pp., $1.50, advertised in the *Nation* on Feb. 20 as "On Mar. 7" and listed Mar. 12, and listed in the *New-York Times* on Mar. 15 and advertised on Mar. 7 as "Today." The first English edition was issued by Warne, 1896, 19.5 cm., 368 pp., frontispiece, 6/o, in patterned olive cloth, advertised in the *Spect* on Mar. 7 as "Today" and listed Mar. 14, and listed in the *Times Weekly Edition* on Mar. 13.

1278 FRANCES H. BURNETT *His Grace of Osmonde.* p 8vo. o/6 sewed   Apr. (*Bks*)
Standard Novels. The first American edition was issued by Charles Scribner's Sons, New York, 1897, 19 cm., 465 pp., $1.50, advertised in *Public Opinion* on Nov. 18 as "Now ready" and listed Nov. 25, and listed in the *Ind* on Nov. 25. The 20th thousand was advertised in the *Nation* on Dec. 2, 1897, $1.50. The first English edition was issued by Warne in 1897, 19.5 cm., 484 pp., 6/o, in maroon cloth, with 12 pp. of ads at the back. It was advertised in the *Ath* on Oct. 30 as "On Nov. 13" and listed in *PC* on Nov. 27 and in the *Spect* on Nov. 20. Warne issued the fourth edition at 6/o, advertised in the *Spect* on Dec. 11, 1897, "In a few days."

1279 CHARLES BENNETT *Five Thousand Pounds Reward.* 12mo. 1/o sewed   Aug. (*Bks*)
London Library. This is the first edition, 1899, 128 pp., in pictorial wrappers.

1280 MAX O'RELL (LEON P. BLOUËT)
John Bull and Co. Cr 8vo. 1/o sewed   Nov. (*Eng Cat*)
The first edition was *Maison John Bull et Cie*, Paris, 1894, 12mo, 371 pp. The seventh and ninth editions were also 1894. The first English edition was issued by Warne, 1894, 20 cm., 352 pp., illustrated, 3/6, advertised in the *Ath* on Sept. 29 as "On Oct. 17" and listed Oct. 6, and listed in *PC* on Oct. 27. Warne issued the 20th thousand, the same, advertised in the *Spect* on Nov. 17, 1894. The first American edition was issued by C. L. Webster, New York, 1894, 20 cm., 319 pp., illustrated, listed in the *Nation* on Sept. 27 and in *PW* on Oct. 6. It was also issued by the Cassell Publishing Co., New York, in 1896, 16mo, $.50 paper, listed in the *New-York Times* on Sept. 13 and in the *Nation* on Sept 10.

1281 MARY KEARY *Rod's First Venture.*
Cr 8vo. Illustrated. 1/o cloth   Dec. (*Eng Cat*)
Welcome Library. I cannot trace this.

Frederick Warne & Co.
London and New York
1900

1282 J. M. MATHER *John Ruskin; His Life and Teaching.* Popular edition. Cr 8vo. Frontispiece (portrait). 1/0 sewed Apr. (*Eng Cat*)

This was listed in the *Times Weekly Edition* on May 18. The first edition was *Life and Teaching of John Ruskin*, issued by Tubbs, Brook & Chrystal, Manchester (1883), 134 pp. Warne issued the third edition, revised and enlarged, 1890, 19 cm., 174 pp., and issued editions 4–7 in 1892–1900.

1283 MRS. ALEXANDER (ANNIE HECTOR) *Beaton's Bargain.* Fcp 8vo. 1/6 1900?

Zephyr Library. This has no date, 17 cm., 188 pp. This series is given in the *Eng Cat* appendix for 1898–1900. They number 20 vols. and are not in the *Eng Cat* proper or the *U Cat* or the *BM*.
Also 1886

1284 MARY ADAMS *An Honourable Surrender.* Fcp 8vo. 1/6 1900?
Zephyr Library.
Also 1883

1285 FRANCES H. BURNETT *That Lass o' Lowrie's.* Fcp 8vo. 1/6 1900?
Zephyr Library.
Also 1877, 78

1286 ALICE PRICE *A Rustic Maid.* Fcp 8vo. 1/6 1900?
Zephyr Library.
Also 1888

1287 E. J. CLAYDEN *By the World Forgot.* Fcp 8vo. 1/6 1900?
Zephyr Library.
Also 1890

1288 LOUISA M. ALCOTT *Moods.* Fcp 8vo. 1/6 1900?
Zephyr Library.
Also 1882

1289 MARGARET DELAND *John Ward, Preacher.* Fcp 8vo. 1/6 1900?
Zephyr Library.
Also 1888

1290 JEAN MIDDLEMASS *A Girl in a Thousand.* Fcp 8vo. 1/6 1900?
Zephyr Library.
Also 1887

1291 C. A. MASON *A Titled Maiden.* Fcp 8vo. 1/6 1900?
Zephyr Library.
Also 1890

1292 JANE A. NUTT *Dorothy.* Fcp 8vo. 1/6 1900?
Zephyr Library.
Also 1880

1293 ARTHUR S. HARDY *But Yet a Woman.* Fcp 8vo. 1/6 1900?
Zephyr Library.
Also 1883

1294 NATHANIEL OGLE *Marianne.*
Fcp 8vo. 1/6   1900?

Zephyr Library.
Also 1889

1295 ALICE PRICE *A Wilful Young Woman.* Fcp 8vo. 1/6   1900?

Zephyr Library.
Also 1887

1296 EDWARD P. ROE *A Young Girl's Wooing.* Fcp 8vo. 1/6   1900?

Zephyr Library.
Also 1886

1297 EMILY P. WEAVER *My Lady Nell.*
Fcp 8vo. 1/6   1900?

Zephyr Library.
Also 1890

1298 EVELYN EVERETT-GREEN *The Last of the Dacres.* Fcp 8vo. 1/6   1900?

Zephyr Library.
Also 1886

1299 MARY H. FOOTE *John Bodewin's Testimony.* Fcp 8vo. 1/6   1900?

Zephyr Library.
Also 1886

1300 EVELYN EVERETT-GREEN *Ruthven of Ruthven.* Fcp 8vo. 1/6   1900?

Zephyr Library.
Also 1888

1301 W. K. CLIFFORD *Marie May.* Fcp 8vo. 1/6   1900?

Zephyr Library.
Also 1884

1302 CHARLES KING *Dunraven Ranch.*
Fcp 8vo. 1/6   1900?

Zephyr Library.
Also 1889

Frederick Warne & Co. London and New York 1901

1303 ISRAEL ZANGWILL *Children of the Ghetto.* p 8vo. o/6 sewed Mar. (*Eng Cat*)
Standard Novels. The first edition was issued by Heinemann, London, 3 vols., 1892, 19 cm., 31/6, listed in the *Spect* on Oct. 8. Heinemann issued the second edition, 3 vols., advertised in the *Spect* on Jan. 21, 1893, as "Just ready"; and issued it in 1 vol., 1893, third edition, 6/0, in May, reissued 1895, 99, 1901, 07. The 1901 reissue had 212 pp. In the United States it was issued by the Jewish Publication Society, Philadelphia, 1892, 2 vols., 19.5 cm., listed in *PW* on Dec. 3 and in the *Nation* on Dec. 8, 1892. It was issued by Macmillan & Co., New York, 1895, new edition, 19.5 cm., 553 pp., $1.50, listed in the *Public Opinion* for May 16 and in the *Ind* on May 23. Macmillan reissued it in 1899, listed in the *New York Times Book Review* on Sept. 30. It seems strange that Warne should have issued this but so the *Eng Cat* declares in both the text proper and in the appendix.

1304 SARAH GRAND (FRANCES E. MACFALL) *The Heavenly Twins.* p 8vo. o/6 sewed Apr. (*Eng Cat*)
Standard Novels. The first English edition was issued by Heinemann, London, 3 vols., 1893, Cr 8vo, 31/6, in Feb. Sadleir had a trial issue in smooth scarlet cloth with a 16-page catalog (Nov. 1892) at the back of vol. 3, which he states was one of three copies of advanced sheets made up for Heinemann. He also has the first pub-

lished edition in smooth dark green cloth, a presentation copy (Feb. 7, 1893). According to the authoress this work was rejected by Meredith, the reader for Chapman & Hall. Heinemann issued it in 1 vol. in 1894, at 6/0, but the *BM* gives a Heinemann edition, 1901, 244 pp., at o/6! The first American edition was issued by the Cassell Publishing Co., New York (copyright 1893), 19.5 cm., 679 pp.

1305 FLORA A. STEEL *The Potter's Thumb.* p 8vo. o/6 sewed Apr. (*Eng Cat*)
Standard Novels. The first edition was issued by Heinemann, London, 3 vols., 1894, 31/6, in dark red cloth, lettered in bronze on the front. It was advertised in the *Ath* on May 26 as "This day." Heinemann issued it in 1 vol. in Feb. 1895, 6/0; and in 1 vol. in 1898, 318 pp.; and in 1 vol. in 1901, 122 pp., o/6, the latter given by the *BM*. I cannot explain o/6 issues by both Heinemann and Warne in 1901, both for this title and the two preceding titles. The first American edition of the present title was issued by Harper & Brothers, New York, 1894, 19 cm., 351 pp., listed in the *Atlantic Monthly* for Nov. and hence probably issued between June and Aug. 1894.

1306 THOMAS S. KNOWLSON *The Art of Thinking.* Cr 8vo. 1/0 sewed Sept. (*Eng Cat*)
This is 1901, 139 pp. The first edition was issued by Warne, 1899, Cr 8vo, 139 pp.,

2/6, listed in the *Spect* on Sept. 23. Warne reissued it in 1903 and issued a revised and enlarged edition in 1906, 153 pp. Warne issued it in New York, 16mo, 139 pp., $1.00, listed in the *New York Book Review* for Jan. 13, 1900.
Also 1902

1307 WILLIAM F. MAVOR *The English Spelling-Book.* Fcp 8vo. Illustrated. 1/0 picture boards Nov. 16 (*Ath* ad)
This has 108 pp. and is illustrated by Kate Greenaway. The first edition was probably in London (1801), 168 pp., illustrated. A new edition was issued by Richard Phillips, London, 1804, revised and improved, 168 pp., illustrated. Longmans, London, issued the 396th edition, 1833, 168 pp. George Routledge and Sons, London, issued it, 1885, 18.5 cm., 108 pp., illustrated by Greenaway.

1308 KATE GREENAWAY *The Language of Flowers.* Demy 16mo. Colored illustrations. 1/0 picture boards, 1/6 white leatherette Nov. 16 (*Ath* ad)
The first edition was issued by George Routledge & Sons, London and New York (1884), 15 × 12 cm., 80 pp., colored illustrations by Kate Greenaway, 3/6 boards, 5/0, listed in the *Spect* on Aug. 23. There is a picture of it in *Victorian Publishers' Book-Bindings in Paper* by Ruari McLean, University of California Press, 1983. The first edition had a printing of 19,500 copies. The 3/6 was in green glazed pictorial boards, printed in brown, with the picture in colors on a cream ground, and a green cloth spine and bright yellow endpapers. The back cover is the same as the front. There were variations in the binding including black printing on a red background, with cream-colored endpapers; and in imitation white or tan morocco boards, with green endpapers. Routledge issued it in New York at $1.25, noticed in the *Christian Union* on Nov. 20, 1884.
See 1866

1309 GEORGE ELIOT (MARY ANN EVANS) *Adam Bede.* p 8vo. 0/6 sewed 1901?
Standard Novels. This was given in this series in the appendix of the *Eng Cat* for 1901–05. The first edition was issued by William Blackwood & Sons, Edinburgh and London, 3 vols., 1859, 21 cm., 31/6, listed in the *Ath* on Feb. 5. Sadleir describes his copy as in bright brown cloth with a 16-page catalog at the back of vol. 3; and Parrish gives his copy as in orange cloth with pale yellow endpapers. Blackwood issued the second and third editions in 3 vols., 31/6, in Apr. and May; and issued the fourth edition in 2 vols., 12/0, listed by *PC* as published June 1–14, 1859. They issued it in 1862, Cr 8vo, 6/0, advertised in the *Spect* on Jan. 25, 1862, as "On Jan. 31"; and issued it at 2/6, Cr 8vo, listed in the *Spect* on Aug. 2, 1863. The first American edition was issued by Harper & Brothers, New York, 1859, 19 cm., 496 pp. $1.00 muslin, advertised in the *New-York Times* on Mar. 18 as "This day" and listed by *APC&LG* (weekly) on Mar. 26. They reissued it, the same, advertised in the *New-York Times* on Jan. 21, 1860 as "Just issued."

Frederick Warne & Co.
London and New York
1902

1310 SIR HENRY THOMPSON *"The Unknown God?"* 16mo. 1/0 folded wrapper, 1/6 cloth. May 31 (*Ath* ad)

This is the first edition, 1902, 16 cm., 86 pp., reprinted from the *Fortnightly Review* and listed in the *TLS* on May 16. Warne issued a second and revised edition, 1903, 16mo, 86 pp., 1/0 wrappers, in Feb., given by the *Eng Cat*. Warne issued it in New York at $.60, listed in the *New York Times Book Review* on June 14, 1902, and noticed in the *Outlook* (weekly) on July 12.

1311 THOMAS S. KNOWLSON *The Art of Thinking.* Small Cr 8vo. 1/0 sewed, 2/6 cloth Nov. 28 (*Spect* ad)

This was advertised in the *TLS* on Nov. 28. It was advertised in the *Spect* on Dec. 13, 1/0 folded wrapper, 2/6 cloth, flat back, "Ready."
Also 1901

1312 HELEN BEATRIX POTTER *The Tale of Peter Rabbit.* 24mo. Illustrated. 1/0 boards, 1/6 cloth Dec. 13 (*Spect* ad)

This is the first published edition, 1902, 14.5 cm., 98 pp., 31 colored illustrations, advertised in the *TLS* on Dec. 19 and given by the *Eng Cat* as issued in Oct. The *Cambridge Bibliography of English Literature* gives a privately printed edition, 1900.

1313 EDWARD STEP *The Little Folks' Picture Natural History.* 4to. Illustrated. 4/0 picture boards, 6/0 cloth Dec. 19 (*TLS* ad)

This is probably the first edition, listed in the *TLS* on Dec. 19, 64 pp., colored illustrations. The 4/0 issue has a cloth back.

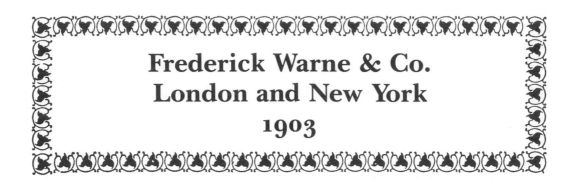

Frederick Warne & Co.
London and New York
1903

1314 HELEN BEATRIX POTTER *Tale of Squirrel Nutkin.* 16mo. 1/0 boards Sept. (*Eng Cat*)

This is the first edition, 1903, 14.6 cm., 84 pp., colored frontispiece and plates, bound in dark blue boards with a pictorial label on the front cover and with illustrated endpapers.

1315 FRANCES H. BURNETT *Editha's Burglar.* Cr 8vo. Illustrated. 1/0 Oct. (*Eng Cat*)

The first edition of *Sara Crewe and Editha's Burglar* was issued by Warne, 1888, 159 pp., illustrated. Warne reissued it, fourth edition, in 1889, small medium 8vo, illustrated, 5/0 in beveled boards, advertised in the *Spect* on Jan. 12. Warne issued the fifth edition, the same, in 1889, advertised in the *Spect* on Aug. 31 as "Just ready"; re-issued in 1890. Warne issued it in 1891, medium 8vo, illustrated, 3/6, advertised as the 20th thousand in the *Spect* on Oct. 10; and they issued it in 1899, Cr 8vo, illustrated, 2/0, as *Editha's Burglar.* In the United States it was issued with the present title by Jordan, Marsh & Co., Boston, 1889, 19 cm., 64 pp., illustrated, noticed in the *Christian Union* on Sept. 20.

1316 L. LESLIE BROOKE *Johnny Crow's Garden.* p 8vo. Illustrated. 2/6 boards Nov. (*Spect*)

This is 21.6 cm., (48) pp., 8 colored plates and illustrations by Brooke, 2/6 art boards with a cloth back. The *U Cat* gives also Warne (190-?), square 8vo, 24 leaves, 8 colored illustrations. The present edition is the first.

1317 THOMAS S. KNOWLSON *The Art of Success.* Cr 8vo. 1/0 sewed Mar. (*Eng Cat*)

The first edition was issued by Warne, 1902, p 8vo, 2/6 cloth, flat back, listed in the *Spect* on Oct. 4. Warne issued it in New York in 1902, 12mo, 163 pp., $1.00, listed in the *New York Times Book Review* on Nov. 22. Warne reissued the present edition, 1908, 163 pp., and 1909, 174 pp.

1318 L. LESLIE BROOKE *The Story of the Three Little Pigs.* Small 4to. Illustrated. 1/0 sewed Dec. 3 (*Spect* ad)

This is the first edition, no date, (23) pp., 8 colored plates and illustrations by Brooke. It is 25.5 cm. and has an art paper cover. It was advertised in the *TLS* on Dec. 9. The *U Cat* gives an edition (190-?), square 8vo, 14 leaves, partly colored. See the next item.

1319 L. LESLIE BROOKE *Tom Thumb.* Small 4to. Illustrated. 1/0 sewed Dec. 9 (*TLS* ad)

This is the first edition, no date, 23 pp., 8 colored plates and illustrations by Brooke. It is 25.5 cm. and has an art paper cover. It was advertised in the *TLS* on Dec. 9. The *U Cat* gives also (190-?), square 8vo, 14 leaves, partly colored illustrations. It was issued with *The Three Little Pigs* in 1 vol. in 1904, 4to, 2/6 art boards, listed in the *TLS* on Dec. 23 and advertised in the *Spect* on Dec. 3; reissued in Nov. 1905.

1320 JOHN W. IVIMEY *Three Blind Mice.* Small 4to. Illustrated. 1/0 sewed Dec. 9 (*TLS* ad)

This is the first edition, no date, 32 pp., 25.5 cm., limp art boards, verses by Ivimey and colored illustrations by Corbould. It was advertised in the *TLS* on Dec. 9 and in the *Spect* on Dec. 3, and given by the *Eng Cat* as issued in Nov. The *U Cat* also gives Warne (190-?), oblong 12mo (18 × 19 cm.), 32 pp., partly colored illustrations.

Frederick Warne & Co.
London and New York
1905

1321 HAROLD FREDERIC *Illumination.*
p 8vo. o/6 sewed   Spring?

Standard Novels? The first English edition was issued by Heinemann, London, 1896, 20 cm., 355 pp., 6/o, advertised in the *Ath* on Mar. 7 as "This day." Heinemann issued editions 4–6, 1896, 355 pp. The first American edition was *The Damnation of Theron Ware*, issued by Stone & Kimball, Chicago and New York, 1896, 19 cm., 512 pp., $1.50, listed in the *Nation* and *Ind* on Apr. 16 and in the *PW* on Apr. 18. There is a known copy deposited for copyright, with a receipt stamp of Mar. 6, 1896, on the front cover and title page, bound in gray wrappers. Herbert S. Stone & Co., Chicago, issued the 30th thousand in 1898, 12mo, $1.50, mentioned in editorial matter in the *New York Times* on Apr. 2 as "Books for Spring."

1322 ROBERT L. STEVENSON & LLOYD OSBOURNE *The Ebb-Tide.* p 8vo. o/6 sewed   Spring?

Standards Novels? This ran in *McClure's Magazine*, New York, beginning in Feb. 1894. The first book edition was issued by Stone & Kimball, Chicago and Cambridge, 1894, 16.6 cm., 204 pp., $1.25, in light or dark green linen or green buckram. It was listed in the *Nation* on July 26 and in *PW* on July 28. They issued the second edition on Sept. 20. The first English edition was issued by Heinemann, London, 1894, 20 cm., 237 pp., 6/o, in smooth

red cloth or in gold in 3 other cloth styles. It was listed in the *Ath* on Sept. 12 and reprinted in Oct. They issued the third impression in Sept. 1902, 19.8 cm., 6/o; and a fine paper edition in Oct. 1905, 17 cm., 237 pp., 2/o, 3/o leather. Heinemann, Warne, London, issued it, 1909, 82 pp., and Heinemann issued it 1912, 184 pp. at o/6.

1323 EDWARD STEP *Wild Flowers Month by Month.* Part 1. 8vo. Illustrated. o/8 Mar. 31 (*TLS* ad)

Part 1 was advertised in the *TLS* on Mar. 31 as "This day" and listed Apr. 7, 22.5 cm., 32 pp. It was issued in 12 fortnightly parts and issued in 2 vols., 6 parts to each. Vol. 1 was listed in the *Spect* on June 24, 22 cm., 200 pp., illustrated, 6/o; and vol. 2 was listed Aug. 26, 22 cm., 199 pp., illustrated, 6/o.

1324 ETHEL L. VOYNICH *The Gadfly.*
p 8vo. o/6 sewed   July (*Eng Cat*)

Standard Novels? The first English edition was issued by Heinemann, London, 1897, 373 pp., 6/o, in Sept. The first American edition was issued by Henry Holt, New York, 1897, 18.5 cm., identical to the English edition, with a new title page. Heinemann reissued it, 1904, 8vo, 149 pp.; and reissued it, 1912, 256 pp., o/6.

1325 HELEN BEATRIX POTTER *Tale of Mrs. Tiggy-Winkle.* 16mo. Colored illustrations. 1/0 boards   Sept. (*Eng Cat*)

This is the first edition, 1905, 14.6 cm., 84 (2) pp., frontispiece and colored illustrations, in green boards with a pictorial label on the front cover and with illustrated endpapers. The first 2 printings of the first edition are believed to be identical.

1326 L. LESLIE BROOKE *The Golden Goose Book.* 4to. Colored illustrations. 2/6 Nov. (*Eng Cat*)

This is the first edition and contains "The Golden Goose," "The Three Bears," "The Three Little Pigs," and "Tom Thumb." It has no date, and the illustrations are in color and black and white. Actually Warne issued *The Story of the Three Little Pigs* and also *Tom Thumb* and also *The Story of the Three Bears*, all (1904), 4to, 14 leaves, colored illustrations. Warne issued *The Story of the Three Little Pigs* and *Tom Thumb* in 1 vol., also, 4to, colored illustrations, 2/6, in Dec. 1904.

1327 HELEN BEATRIX POTTER *The Pie and the Patty-Pan.* Cr 8vo. Colored illustrations. 1/0 boards, 2/0 cloth   Nov. (*Eng Cat*)

This is the first edition, 1905, 18.5 cm., 51 pp., frontispiece, illustrations and colored plates, 1/0 art paper boards, flat back for the 1/0 issue.

1328 DORA W. PEARSALL *The Story of Four Little Sabots.* 16mo. Colored illustrations. 1/0 boards   Dec. (*Eng Cat*)

This is 1906, the first edition, 15.3 cm., 86 pp., verse with colored illustrations, in art paper boards, flat back.

1329 LENA & NORMAN AULT *The Rhyme Book.* 18mo. Colored plates. 1/0 boards Dec. (*Spect*)

This is the first edition 1906, 13 cm., 88 pp., written and illustrated by Lena and Norman Ault, 1/0 art paper boards, illustrated endpapers.

Victorian Yellowbacks & Paperbacks,
1849–1905

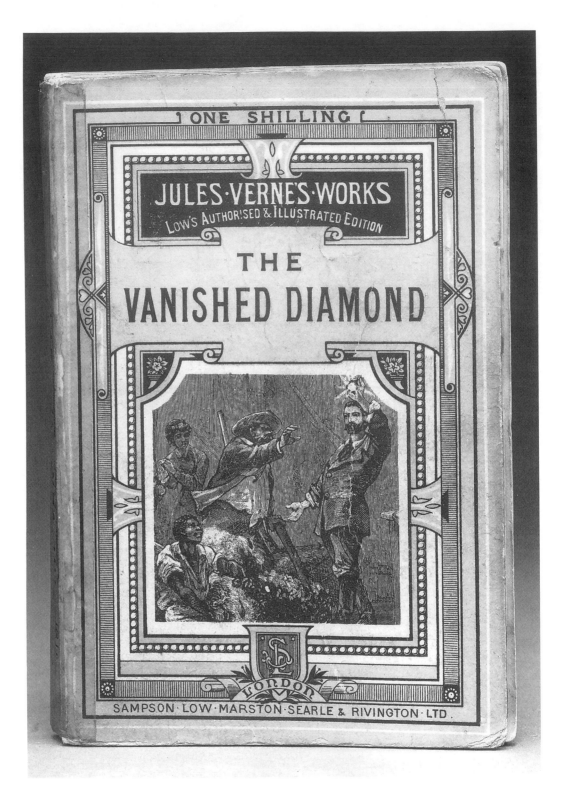

361   *The Vanished Diamond*

Victorian Yellowbacks & Paperbacks, 1849–1905

VOLUME IV

SAMPSON LOW & CO.

Short Titles and Abbreviations

Acad	*The Academy*
ALG&PC	*American Literary Gazette and Publishers' Circular*
Am Cat	*The American Catalog*
APC&LG	*American Publishers' Circular and Literary Gazette*
Ath	*The Athenaeum*
BAL	*Bibliography of American Literature*
Bks	*The Bookseller* (London)
BM	*The British Library Catalogue*
Eng Cat	*The English Catalogue*
Glover & Greene	*Victorian Detective Fiction*
Ind	*The Independent* (New York)
Lit W	*Literary World* (New York and Boston)
PC	*The Publishers' Circular and Booksellers' Record* (London)
PW	*Publishers' Weekly*
Roorbach	*Bibliotheca Americana*
Sat Rev	*The Saturday Review* (London)
Sadleir	Michael Sadleir's *Nineteenth Century Fiction*, 2 volumes
Spect	*The Spectator*
TLS	*The Times Literary Supplement* (London)
TWEd	*The Times Weekly Edition* (London)
U Cat	*The National Union Catalog*
Wolff	Robert Lee Wolff's *Nineteenth-Century Fiction*, 5 volumes
Wright	Lyle H. Wright's *American Fiction*, 3 volumes

Introduction

Sampson Low started his own business together with a reading room at Lamb's Conduit, London, in 1819 at the age of twenty-two, and he was still there in 1836. In 1837 he became the delegated publisher of *PC*. He retired from the firm in 1875 and died in 1886. His heir took over on his retirement, and on the heir's death in 1881 the firm was taken over by Edward Marston, the latter having been a partner since 1861. The firm was in its heyday from 1889 to 1893. They began issuing sixpenny pictorial paperbacks in 1902; the firm gradually declined until its finish in 1914.

Sampson Low began one of his specialities in 1854 by publishing yellowbacks and paperbacks of American authors, by issuing *Sunny Memories of Foreign Lands* by Mrs. Stowe. It was in greenish-white pictorial boards, selling at 2/o, issued in August 1854. The House of Lords on Aug. 1, 1854, defined the copyright law as offering no protection to foreign authors except they be resident in England at the time of publication of works they claimed for, thus dispersing the well-recognized protection offered them during the preceding eighteen months. Before six o'clock on the evening of Aug. 1, printers were reprinting cheap editions of American works. Low found his printers already engaged on a cheap edition of *Sunny Memories* for another house. By Sept. 9, 1954, there were seven English editions of *Sunny Memories*.

Low began a series of *English Editions of German Authors* in March 1867 by issuing *On the Heights* by Berthold Auerback, selling at 1/6 sewed and 2/o in flexible cloth. The project was made possible by arrangement with Tauchnitz of Leipzig for the exclusive issuance of the titles in Great Britain and the Colonies. The series ended with No. 33 in May 1893.

Low began the series of *Copyright Editions of American Authors*, issued in flexible boards and cloth, with *Haunted Hearts* by Maria S. Cummins, in October 1868. He issued the last title in the series, No. 25, in October 1873.

With the ending of the *American Authors* series in 1873, Low began the *Rose Library* in October 1874. Titles in the series were illustrated and sold for 1/o sewed and 2/6 cloth, and they consisted almost exclusively of American works, with an occasional French title. The numbered titles ended with No. 34 in November 1878, but unnumbered titles continued until October 1887. This series contained almost all the titles of Louisa M. Alcott and Harriet B. Stowe; in fact, most of the titles of both authors were first issued in England by Low.

Low issued the first English editions of most of Jules Verne's works, beginning in 1873. He issued the first editions of several of Richard Blackmore's works, beginning in 1869. He issued the first English editions of Rudyard Kipling's Indian tales, and he published yellowback issues of Thomas Hardy, William Black, and Richard Blakmore.

The Victorian publishing scene was enlivened by copyright squabbles, several of in which Low was a participant. *Haunted Hearts*, referred to above, was the book with which the battle was fought (for English copyright of American works), copyright being allowed by a recent judgment. In view of this new ruling, Low issued the first English edition of

The Guardian Angel by Oliver W. Holmes, in 2 volumes, at 16/o, about Nov. 2, 1867. Ward, Lock & Tyler issued it at 2/o boards in May 1868, and Low went to the Court of Chancery to get an injunction against it since the last six chapters had been published first in Montreal, thus securing copyright protection. As a result Ward, Lock & Tyler was prohibited from publishing the last six chapters!

Low published the first British edition of *An Old-Fashioned Girl* by Louisa M. Alcott, at 3/6 cloth, in April 1870. Ward, Lock & Tyler issued it at 1/o in February 1871. Low advertised in the *PC* on Feb. 15 that it had been withdrawn by Ward, Lock & Tyler, being an infringement of copyright. *BAL* states that no ads or listings of the Ward, Lock & Tyler issue have ever been found, but I've found the one here discussed, a listing in the *Spect* on Feb. 4, 1871.

Low issued the first British edition of *My Summer in a Garden* by Charles D. Warner in August 1871, at 1/6 limp boards and 2/o flexible cloth. Ward, Lock & Tyler issued it as *Pusley* in January 1873. Low complained in a letter to the *Ath* on June 7, 1873, that although the title was not protected by copyright, Low had paid the author for it, and now Ward, Lock & Tyler issued it after it had been well-promoted by Low.

Low issued the first British edition of *Backlog Studies* by Charles D. Warner at 1/6 limp boards and 2/o flexible cloth in December 1872. Ward, Lock & Tyler issued it at 1/o sewed, 1/6 cloth, in March 1873. Warner was incensed and wrote the *Ath* on May 10, 1873, stating that the work had been published simultaneously in Boston and by Low in England, the latter paying the author, and that it consisted of eleven papers. He stated that he had received a book from Ward, Lock & Tyler with the same title and with his name as author, but that it was not the same book! It contained, according to Warner, only seven of the papers (the other four being protected by copyright), and they had added a portion of his address delivered at a college anniversary, which had no connection with the volume whatsoever! He expressed his appreciation of the delicacy Ward, Lock & Tyler must have felt in preparing the volume! And so the copyright wars were fought over American books issued in England. Many English books were also issued in America, and they were simply pirated by any publisher so inclined, whether his rival had paid the author or not! It finally became the practice that one company had squatter's rights to a given English author, such, for example, as Harper & Brothers had to Anthony Trollope.

Each entry in the present volume gives the date of listing in a British periodical where known, and otherwise the date of advertisements for the title, or an approximate date obtained from ads, references, and catalogs. In almost every case the first British edition is given and, where appropriate, the first American edition. Important later editions are given as well as the first yellowback or paperback edition, if different from the Low title being noted.

Size is denoted by 32mo, 16mo, Fcp 8vo, 12mo, Cr 8vo, Demy 8vo, 8vo, and 4to as gleaned from ads, references and catalogs, or from my copies. The size is given for the tallness of bound copies, in cm., where known. A 32mo denotes a book about 12cm. tall; 16mo, about 15 cm.; Fcp 8vo indicates Sadleir's small format, or about 16.8 cm.; 12mo indicates Sadleir's large format, about 17.5 cm.; Cr 8vo, about 19 cm.; Demy 8vo, about 21 cm.; 8vo, about 23 cm.; and 4to, about 30 cm. The number of pages refers to the number of the last page of text. The words "wrappers" and "sewed" refer to paperbacks, and "boards" refers to yellowback and other boards issued as described. I have had to omit the type of binding in some cases as not known to me, and have merely stated the price. When a notation as to edition is given in brackets after the title in an entry, it means that notation describes the issue—although the words may or may not appear on the title page (as I am unable to say). When no brackets appear, the given notation appeared on the title page.

The present work makes full reference to appropriate entries in Volume 2 of Michael Sadleir's *XIX Century Fiction*; and also to entries in the five volumes of *Nineteenth Century Fiction* by Robert Wolff, issued by the Garland Publishing Co., New York and London, 1981–86.

Victorian Yellowbacks & Paperbacks,
1849–1905

Sampson Low
169 Fleet St.
1850

1 AN ENGLISHMAN *Duty of the Rich.*
12mo. 1/6 sewed   Apr. 13–29 (*PC*)

This has 26 pp. The *U Cat* gives (no publisher, 1840), 8vo, 12 pp., in four locations. The *Eng Cat* gives 12mo, 1/6, Low, issued in 1852, but the early English catalogs were unreliable.

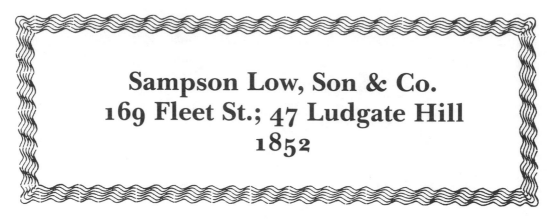

Sampson Low, Son & Co.
169 Fleet St.; 47 Ludgate Hill
1852

On Aug. 21 the company was at 169 Fleet St.; by Dec. 11, it was at 47 Ludgate Hill.

2 JODOCUS D.H. TEMME *Anna Hammer.*
8vo. 1/6 1852 (*Eng Cat*)

The first edition was issued at Eisleben, in Germany, 3 vols., 1850. The present edition is translated from the German. It was issued in the United States by Harper & Bros., New York, 1852, 24 cm., 127 pp., translated from the German by Alfred H. Guernsey.

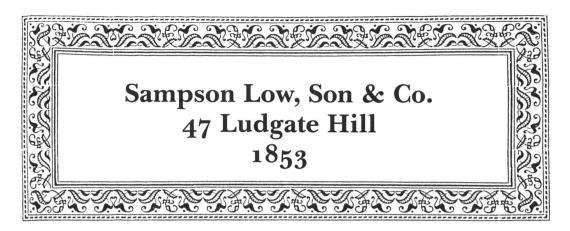

Sampson Low, Son & Co.
47 Ludgate Hill
1853

3 FANNY FORESTER (EMILY CHUBBUCK, later JUDSON) *Records of Alderbrook.* 12mo. 1/0 cloth 1853 (*Eng Cat*)

The *Eng Cat* gives 3/6 and 1/0 in 1853, but it is unreliable at this period. Low issued *Selections from Alderbrook*, 1853, 248 pp., 3/6; and issued it, 1854, 3/6, advertised in the *Ath* on June 17; and issued it at 1/0 in fancy cloth in 1857, new edition, advertised in the *Ath* on Sept. 5. The first edition of *Alderbrook* was issued by William D. Ticknor & Co., Boston, 1847, 2 vols., 20.5 cm., frontispiece (portrait), by Emily Chubbuck, in Nov. 1846. It had a printing of 480 copies, and $72 was paid for the copyright. They issued the second edition in Nov. 1846, 2 vols., in a printing of 750 copies, paying royalties of $112.50. Ticknor & Fields, Boston, 1856, issued the 11th edition, revised and enlarged, 2 vols., 20 cm.

4 CHARLES SUMNER *White Slavery in the Barbary States.* 12mo. 1/6 1853 (*Eng Cat*)

This was a lecture given before the Boston Mercantile Library Association on Feb. 17, 1847. The first edition was issued by William D. Ticknor & Co., Boston, 1847, 23.5 cm., 60 pp., a pamphlet, in Apr. Low issued it, 1853, 19 cm., 135 pp., illustrated, 4/6, a duplicate of the first American edition with a new title page.

Sampson Low, Son & Co.
47 Ludgate Hill
1854

5 HARRIET B. STOWE *Sunny Memories of Foreign Lands.* Author's edition. Fcp 8vo. Illustrated. 2/o boards   Aug. 12 (*Ath*)

This is 1854, 539 pp., in greenish-white pictorial boards, printed in black. Low issued a new edition, Fcp 8vo, illustrated, 2/o boards, advertised in the *Ath* on Sept. 16, 1854, as "This day"; and issued the author's edition at 2/o boards, advertised on Nov. 4, 1854, as "On Nov. 20." They issued the first English edition, 2 vols., 1854, 20 cm., illustrated, 12/o in red cloth with yellow endpapers, and with an 11-page catalog (July 1854) at the back of vol. 1. It was advertised in the *Ath* on July 8 as "On July 10" and was listed on July 15. Low issued the author's edition, 1854, 540 pp., illustrated, 5/o, advertised in the *Ath* on Aug. 5 as "In a few days" and listed on Aug. 19. The House of Lords on Aug. 1 defined the copyright law as offering no protection to foreign authors except they be in residence in England at the time of publication of works they claim for, thus effectively dispersing the pretty well-recognized protection offered them during the preceding 18 months. In an ad in the *Ath* on Aug. 5, Low stated that he had to take defensive action in view of this decision and hence was offering the present 2/o boards edition. Before six o'clock on Aug. 1 printers were reprinting cheap editions of American works, and Low found his printers already engaged on a cheap edition of the present work for an-

other house! By Sept. 9 there were seven English editions of *Sunny Memories*, including George Routledge & Co., London, 1854, 360 pp., 1/6 boards, 2/o cloth, listed in the *Ath* on Aug. 12; Piper, Stephenson & Spence, London and Edinburgh, 1854, Fcp 8vo, 1/o boards, advertised on Aug. 12 as "Just published"; and Thomas Nelson, London, 1854, 17 cm., 288 pp.

The first American edition was issued by Phillips, Sampson & Co., Boston; etc., 2 vols., 1854, 20 cm., illustrated in either black or purple cloth with yellow endpapers, or in blue cloth, all edges gilt with yellow endpapers. A copy was received at the Boston Athenaeum on July 17, and it was listed in *Norton's Literary Gazette and Publisher's Circular* on July 15, and in the *Ind* on July 27.

6 MARTHA S. HUBBELL *The Shady Side.* [New edition.] 1/o sewed   Aug. 26 (*Spect*)

This was also advertised as a new edition, 1/o, in the *Ath* on Sept. 15, 1857. Low issued the first English edition, 1853, 12mo., 5/6, by a pastor's wife, listed in the *Ath* on Apr. 23. They issued the second edition, 1853, Fcp 8vo, portrait, 3/6 cloth, listed in the *Ath* on May 28. The first American edition was issued by John P. Jewett, Boston; etc.; Sampson Low, London, 1853, 18.5 cm., 348 pp., anonymous, noticed in the *Ind* on Mar. 24 and listed by *Lit W* as published Apr. 9–May 7.

7 MARY LANGDON (MARY H. PIKE)
Ida May. Fcp 8vo. 1/6 boards
Sept. 9 (*Spect*)

This is the first English edition, 1854, 323 pp., edited by an English clergyman, with a first printing of 10,000 copies. It was listed by *PC* as published Sept. 1–14 and was advertised in the *Ath* on Sept. 16 as "This day." Low issued the second edition in 1855, Fcp 8vo, 323 pp., illustrated by Crowquill, 2/0 boards, 2/6 cloth, listed by *PC* as published June 14–30. Simpkin, Marshall, London; etc., issued it (1857) in the *Run and Read Library* as No. 32, at 1/6 boards, about June 6; it was reissued by Ward & Lock, London, in Nov. 1864, 2/0 boards.

The first American edition was issued by Phillips, Sampson & Co., Boston; etc., 1854, 19 cm., 478 pp., listed in the *Ind* on Nov. 16. It was advertised in the *New York Daily Times* on Nov. 4 as "On Nov. 15," but an ad on Nov. 14 said there was an unavoidable delay and publication was postponed to Nov. 22. They issued the 20th thousand at $1.25 before the end of the year.

8 MARION HARLAND (MARY V. HAWES, later TERHUNE) *Alone.* Fcp 8vo. 2/0 boards, 2/6 cloth   Oct. 28 (*Ath*)

This is the first British edition, 1854, from advanced sheets by international arrangement. Low issued the 10th thousand in 1854, illustrated by Crowquill, 2/0 boards, listed by *PC* as published Dec. 1–15; and they issued a new edition in 1856, 12mo, 374 pp., 2/6 cloth, listed in *PC* as published Feb. 29–Mar. 14. It was issued by Simpkin & Marshall, London; etc. (1857), in the *Run and Read Library* No. 33, 1/6 boards, about June 27.

The first American edition was issued by A. Morris, Richmond, 1854, 20 cm., 499 pp. Morris issued the fifth edition, 1854, 384 pp.; and the 15th edition, 1855,

384 pp. It was issued by J. C. Derby, New York; etc., in 1856, 19th thousand, 384 pp., listed in the *Ind* on Jan. 24.

9 THEODORE E. HOOK   *The Man of Many Friends.* Illustrated. 2/6 boards   Dec. 16 (*Ath*)

This was in the second series of *Sayings and Doings*, issued by Henry Colburn, London, 3 vols., 1825, anonymous. The first American edition was issued by Carey & Lea, Philadelphia, 2 vols., 1825, 18 cm., anonymous, listed in the *North American Review* for July 1825. It was issued by Wallis & Newell, New York, 1835, 75 pp., just *The Man of Many Friends*. The Colburn issue was reviewed in the *Gentleman's Magazine* (monthly) for Feb. 1825.

10 P. T. BARNUM   *The Life of P. T. Barnum. Written by Himself.* Author's edition. Cr 8vo. Illustrated. 2/6 boards, 7/6 cloth   Dec. 23 (*Ath*)

This is the first British edition, 1855, 19.5 cm., 404 pp., frontispiece (portrait), illustrations. The 7/6 issue was in red cloth, and both issues had an 11-page catalog (Jan. 1, 1855) at the back. It was listed by *PC* as published Dec. 15–30, simultaneously with the London edition, and a duplicate of it with a different title page. Low issued an author's edition, 1855, 17 cm., 372 pp., illustrated; and an author's edition, 1855, 246 pp., probably without illustrations, 1/0 sewed, listed by *PC* as published Dec. 30, 1854–Jan. 15, 1855. See 1870 for a different autobiography, *Struggles and Triumphs*. Ward & Lock, London, issued the present work, 1855, 160 pp., 1/0 sewed, *The Autobiography of P. T. Barnum*, listed by *PC* as published Jan. 1–15, 1855. It was also issued by Clarke & Beeton, London (1855), 171 pp., 1/0 boards, slightly abridged as *Barnum, the Yankee Showman, etc.*, listed in *PC* as published Jan. 15–31, 1855. It was also issued by Willoughby & Co., London (1855), 332 pp.; and by C. T. Holt, London (1855), as *Barnum, or the Life of a Humbug*.

The first American edition was issued by J. S. Redfield, New York, 1855, 19.5 cm., 409 pp., frontispiece (portrait), illus-trated, listed in the *Ind* on Dec. 21, 1854, and in the *Knickerbocker* for Dec. 1854. They issued a second edition, 1855, in boards.

Sampson, Low, Son & Co.
47 Ludgate Hill
1855

11 WASHINGTON IRVING *Wolfert's Roost.* Fcp 8vo. 1/0 sewed Feb. 28–Mar. 14 (*PC*)

Low advertised this also on Sept. 5, 1857, new edition, 1/0. This was also advertised by Thomas Constable & Co., Edinburgh, in the *Ath* on Mar. 17, 1855, author's edition, 1/0. It was probably issued jointly by Constable and Low. The first British edition was issued by Thomas Constable & Co., Edinburgh; Sampson Low, etc., London; etc., 1855, 12mo, 351 pp., 3/6, listed in the *Ath* on Jan. 20 and in the *Spect* on Jan. 27. It was *Constable's Foreign Miscellany*, vol. 4, *Chronicles of Wolfert's Roost, and Other Papers.* It was also issued by H. G. Bohm, London, 1855, *Wolfert's Roost, and Other Tales*, 280 pp., Fcp 8vo, 1/0 boards, and p 8vo, with a portrait, 1/6 boards, listed in the *Ath* on Mar. 10, and in *PC* on Mar. 15. It was also issued by George Routledge & Co., London and New York, 1855, Fcp 8vo, 251 pp., 1/0 boards, 1/6 cloth, listed in the *Spect* on Mar. 17, and by *PC* as published Feb. 28–Mar. 14, with the Bohm title.

The first American edition was issued by G. P. Putnam & Co., New York, 1855, 19 cm., 383 pp., frontispiece, $1.25, with the Constable title. It was deposited on Feb. 6 and listed in *Norton's Literary Gazette and Publisher's Circular* and in the *Ind* on Feb. 15, and advertised in the *New York Daily Times* on Feb. 5 as "On Feb. 10"; the second edition, the 10th thousand, the same, was advertised on Feb. 16 as "On Feb. 16"; and the third edition, the same, was advertised as "On Feb. 24." The first Putnam edition was in red or green cloth.

12 GEORGE FOWLER *History of the War; or, A Record of the Events . . . Between Turkey and Russia, etc.* (Second edition). Fcp 8vo. 2 folding maps. 2/0 limp cloth Mar. 31 (*Ath*)

The first edition was issued by Low, 1855, 16.5 cm., 334 pp., 2 folding maps, listed in the *Ath* on Mar. 10.

13 ANGLO-AMERICANA *To the Right Hon. Lord John Russell. . . . On Money, Morals, and Progress.* Demy 8co. 1/6 Sept. 15 (*Ath* ad)

The ad said "This day." It is the first edition, 1855, 21.5 cm., 62 pp.

14 CHARLES B. TAYLER *Truth.* Cheap edition. Fcp 8vo. 1/6 boards Sept. 20 (*Ath*)

An ad in the *Ath* on Sept. 15 said "On Sept. 20." It is 1855, with 210 pp. Low advertised it in the *Ath* on Sept. 5, 1857, new edition, 1/6; and issued it as *Persis*, 1874, new edition, 323 pp. The first British edition was issued by Low, 1853, 210 pp., a story of church history of the 17th century. The first American edition was issued by Stanford & Swords, New York, 1853, 19.5 cm., 199 pp.

15 MARION HARLAND (MARY V. HAWES, later TERHUNE) *The Hidden Path.*
Fcp 8vo. 2/o boards   Sept. 29 (*Ath*)
This is 1855. It was also listed by the *PC* as published Sept. 14–29. Low issued it in 1856, 12mo, 344 pp., 2/6 cloth, listed by *PC* as published Feb. 29–Mar. 14. It was also issued by George Routledge & Co., London and New York, 1855, 2/o boards, listed in the *Ath* on Sept. 29; and by Simpkin & Marshall, London; etc., about May 30, 1857, *Run and Read Library* No. 31, another copy of the Low issue with an added title page and a frontispiece.

The first American edition was issued by J. C. Derby, New York; etc., 1855, 19.5 cm., 434 pp., $1.25, advertised in the *New York Daily Times* on Aug. 23 as "On Aug. 25" and listed in the *Ind* on Aug. 23. The 14th thousand was advertised in the *New York Daily Times* on Oct. 3, 1855, as "Ready this day."

16 JANE EL HORNBLOWER *Nellie of Truro.*
Fcp 8vo. Illustrated. 2/o cloth   Dec. 15 (*Ath*)
This is the first British edition, 1856, from American proof sheets by arrangement with Robert Carter & Bros., New York. It was also listed by *PC* as published Dec. 15–31. Low issued a new edition in 1856, Fcp 8vo, 312 pp., 2/6 cloth, advertised in the *Ath* on Mar. 15 and listed by *PC* as published Feb. 29–Mar. 14. Simpkin & Marshall, London; etc., issued it in 1857, 19 cm., anonymous, 432 pp., 1/6 boards, as *Run and Read Library* No. 30, about May 30; and it was reissued by Ward & Lock, London, in 1864, 2/o boards, listed in the *Reader* on Dec. 3.

The first American edition was issued by Robert Carter & Bros., New York, 1856, 19 cm., anonymous, 432 pp., with an added illustrated title page, $1.00, listed in the *Ind* on Nov. 22, 1855, and in *APC&LG* on Nov. 24.

17 JOHN H. PEPPER *Popular Lectures for Young People.* Cr 8vo. 1/6   1855 (*Eng Cat*)
This is the first edition, 1855, (85) pp., illustrated, published for Addey & Co., London, by Low.

Sampson Low, Son & Co.
47 Ludgate Hill
1856

18 JOHN S. HOGAN *Canada.* 8vo. Maps.
1/6 sewed, 5/0 cloth   Jan. 12 (*Ath* ad)

The *Ath* ad said "This day." This is the first British edition, from plates or sheets from B. Dawson & Co., Montreal. Low advertised this and the next title in 1 vol., *Canada and Her Resources*, second edition, 8vo, maps, 7/0, in the *Ath* on Feb. 23, 1856, as "On Feb. 28." It was issued in Montreal by John Lovell, 1855, 23 cm., 110 pp., 2 folding maps; and also by B. Dawson & Co., 21 cm., 86 pp., frontispiece (folding map).

19 ALEXANDER MORRIS *Canada and Her Resources.* 8vo. Maps. 1/6 sewed, 5/0 cloth   Jan. 12 (*Ath* ad)

The *Ath* ad said "This day." This is the first British edition, 119 pp., frontispiece (folding map). It was issued in Montreal, 1855, by John Lovell, 20.3 cm., 156 pp., some copies with maps; and by B. Dawson & Co., 21 cm., 119 pp., frontispiece (folding map). This and the preceding title were issued by Low in 1 vol. in 1856, 22.5 cm., printed in Montreal (see the preceding title).

20 ANONYMOUS *The Commerce and Finance of Australia.* 1/0   Feb. 23 (*Ath* ad)

The ad said "Now ready." This is the first edition, 1856, 51 pp., from the *Banker's Magazine*, with considerable additions.

21 MARY SHERWOOD (MARY MARTHA BUTT, later SHERWOOD) *The Nun.* [New edition.] 12mo. 2/0 boards, 2/6 cloth   Feb. 28 (*Ath*)

This was advertised in the *Ath* on Feb. 23 as "On Feb. 28." It is 1856, with 202 (282) pp. Low issued a new edition (1856), 279 pp., frontispiece, a 2/0 yellowback, listed by *PC* as published Dec. 13–31, 1856. The first edition was issued by R. B. Seeley & Burnside; etc., London, 1833, 17 cm., anonymous, 326 pp., 6/0 boards, listed in the *Ath* on Dec. 7, 1833. There was a new edition, 18mo, 4/6, listed by the *Edinburgh Review* as published Oct. 1838–Jan. 1839; and there was a sixth edition at 3/6 cloth, listed in the *Literary Gazette* on Dec. 6, 1851. Simpkin, Marshall, London; etc., issued it in 1859 in the *Run and Read Library* as No. 56, 1/6 boards, 2/6 cloth, about Dec. 24, 1859; reissued by Ward & Lock, London, in 1864, 2/0 boards, listed in the *Reader* on Nov. 5, 1864.

The first American edition, from the London edition, was issued by Moore & Baker, Princeton, 1834, 19 cm., anonymous, 326 pp., listed in the *North American Review* (quarterly) for Oct. 1834. I think it was also issued by J. Whitham, Philadelphia, 1835, 322 pp.

22 ANONYMOUS *Correspondence Between the Governments of Great Britain and the United States of America upon the Enlistment Question.* 8vo. 1/0   Mar. 29 (*Ath* ad)

The ad said "Now ready." It is probably the first edition but I cannot trace it.

23 JOSEPH CUNDALL *The Photographic Primer.* Second edition. Fcp 8vo. 1/0 sewed Apr. 26 (*Ath* ad)

This is Sampson Low; Photographic Institution, London, 1856, with 30 pp. The first edition was issued by the Photographic Institution, London, 1854, 16.5 cm., 30 pp., frontispiece.

24 ROBERT HOWLETT *On the Various Methods of Printing Photographic Pictures upon Paper.* 12 mo. 1/0 sewed Apr. 26 (*Ath* ad)

This is the first edition, 1856, 18 cm., 32 pp.

25 HARRIET B. STOWE *Dred.* 12 mo. 2/6 boards Aug. 23 (*Ath*)

This is my copy, Low, London; Thomas Constable, Edinburgh, 1856, 17.3 cm., 524 pp. (appendix on pp. 498–524), with a preface (Aug. 21, 1856). It is in unglazed red-maroon boards, printed in white, identical on front and back, dark green endpapers, with publisher's ads, paged (1)–12 at the back. Sadleir had two copies, one in cream pictorial boards, printed in black, with dark green endpapers, and the other in white boards, printed all over in red-maroon, with lettering in reverse, and dark green endpapers. *BAL* gives the cream, pictorial boards issue and also gives a nonpictorial boards copy, printed in red and brown, with green endpapers. At least we may assume that this issue had green endpapers! It was listed in the *Spect* also, on Sept. 13. The first edition was issued by Low, 2 vols., 1856, 19.5 cm., 12/0 in rose-pink cloth with yellow endpapers, and with a preface (Aug. 21, 1856). There is a known presentation copy inscribed Aug. 23, 1856. It was deposited on Aug. 22 and listed in the *Ath* on Aug. 23. Low also issued it in 1 vol., 1856, Cr 8vo, 6/0 in rose cloth, with yellow endpapers, listed in the *Ath* also on Aug. 23, 1856. Low issued the 100th thousand, new edition, 12mo,

3/0 cloth, listed by *PC* as published Sept. 15–30, 1856. Low, London: Thomas Constable & Co., Edinburgh, issued a new edition in 1857, 245 pp., 1/6 in printed paper boards, listed in the *Ath* on Nov. 29, 1856, and by *PC* as published Jan. 1–14, 1857. Low issued the 160th thousand at 1/6, advertised in the *Ath* on Sept. 5, 1857; and issued it, 1875, as a 1/0 yellowback, listed in the *Spect* on Mar. 20; and issued it, 1878, new edition, 12mo, 446 pp., 2/0 sewed, 3/6 cloth, in the *Rose Library* No. 32, listed in the *Spect* on Mar. 16.

It was issued by Tauchnitz, Leipzig, 2 vols., 1856, listed in the *Allgemeine Bibliographie* on Sept. 25 and Oct. 2. It was issued in Canada by E. Pickup, Montreal, 1856, 452 pp.

The first American edition was issued by Phillips, Sampson & Co., Boston, 2 vols., 1856, 19.5 cm., $1.75 muslin, without the preface. It has been variously described as in dark brown cloth, with yellow tinted endpapers; or in black cloth, either with plain endpapers or with ads; and in black-brown cloth, with white endpapers with ads. It was deposited on Oct. 2 and was listed in *APC&LG* on Sept. 6, and reviewed in the *Ind* on Sept. 11.
Also 1890

26 SUSAN B. WARNER *The Hills of the Shatemuc.* 12mo. 2/6 boards; p 8vo, 6/0 cloth Aug. 23 (*Ath*)

This is the first edition, Low, London; Thomas Constable & Co., Edinburgh, 1856, authorized edition, 16.8 cm., 514 pp., illustrated, in printed paper boards and cloth, listed by *PC* as published Sept. 1–15. Low also issued it at 1/6 boards and 3/0 cloth, listed by *PC* as published Sept. 15–30, 1856. The 1/6 had a frontispiece, Fcp 8vo; the 2/6 and 3/0 editions were illustrated; and the 6/0 was p 8vo. It was also issued by George Routledge & Co., London and New York, 1856, anonymous, 1/6 boards, listed in the *Spect* on Oct. 4, and by *PC* as published Sept. 15–

30. It was later issued by Routledge in 1877 as *Hope's Little Hand*. The present title was also issued by C. H. Clarke, London, in 1856, Fcp 8vo, anonymous, 1/o boards, listed in the *Ath* on Sept. 20 and by *PC* as published Sept. 15–30. Ward & Lock, London, issued it in 1890 as *Hope and Rest*. Tauchnitz, Leipzig, issued it in 2 vols., 1856, author's edition, listed in the *Allgemeine Bibliographie* on Sept. 4.

The first American edition was issued by D. Appleton & Co., New York, 1856, 19 cm., anonymous, 516 pp., $1.25, or illustrated, $1.50, in blue, brown, purple, red, or green cloth, with brown, blue, yellow, or green endpapers. It was deposited on Sept. 28 but advertised in the *New York Daily Times* on Sept. 19 as "Tomorrow" and listed in *APC&LG* on Sept. 20. It was issued in a new edition, advertised in the *New York Daily Times* on Oct. 8 as "Now ready."

Sampson Low, Son & Co.
47 Ludgate Hill
1857

27 ANONYMOUS *Common Things Regarding the Bringing up of Our Girls.* 1/0 Mar. 28 (*Ath* ad)

The ad in the *Ath* said "This day." I cannot trace it.

28 ANONYMOUS *Imaginary History of the Next Thirty Years.* 8vo. 1/0 Apr. 18 (*Ath* ad)

The ad in the *Ath* said "Just published." This is the first edition (1857).

29 MARIA S. CUMMINS *Mabel Vaughan.* 1/6 boards, 3/6 cloth Sept. 19 (*Ath*)

This is the first British edition, 1857, 459 pp., frontispiece, 3/6 cloth; and 310 pp., 1/6 in pictorial yellow boards, printed in red and black, with ads on the back in red, and with pale yellow endpapers with ads, the inside front cover ad bearing a date, Sept. 19, 1857. It was edited by Elizabeth C. Gaskell and has her preface, signed E.C.G. The yellowback is Sadleir's copy. It was listed in the *Spect* also, on Sept. 26. It was also issued by George Routledge & Co., London and New York, 1857, by Cummins, Fcp 8vo, 369 pp., 1/6 boards, listed by *PC* as published Nov. 14–30.

The first American edition was issued by John P. Jewett & Co., Boston; etc.; Low, London, 1857, anonymous, 508 pp., listed in *APC&LG* on Sept. 26 and in the *Ind* on Oct. 8. A new edition was issued by Crosby & Nichols, Boston, in 1857, $1.00, advertised in the *Ind* on Oct. 29 as "Now ready," and listed in *Godey's Lady's Book* for Jan. 1858 (and thus probably issued in Oct. or Nov. 1857). The ad in the *Ind* stated that the first edition of 15,000 copies was exhausted and its publishers were embarrassed and couldn't continue, and so new arrangements were made with the authoress.

30 WILLIAM A. BUTLER *Nothing to Wear.* Fcp 8vo. 1/0 sewed Oct. 17 (*Ath*)

This is the first British edition, 1857, 16.5 cm., 58 pp., in verse. Low issued it, 1858, Fcp 8vo, anonymous, 58 pp., with one illustration by Crowquill, advertised in the *Ath* and *Spect* on Aug. 21; and issued the fifth edition, 1858, 1/0, advertised in *PC* on Apr. 1. The first edition was issued by Rudd & Carleton, New York, 1857, 16.5 cm., anonymous, 68 pp., illustrated, from *Harper's Weekly.* It was noticed in the *Knickerbocker* for July, and thus probably issued in May or June. The *U Cat* gives G. P. Putnam & Co., New York (1857), 14 cm., anonymous, 85 pp., with one illustration. See 1858

31 EMILY H. COMYN *Rose Morrison.* 12 mo. 2/0 1857 (*BM*)

This is the first edition, 1857, 96 pp., a tale for children.

Sampson Low, Son & Co.
47 Ludgate Hill
1858

32 THOMAS H. BAYLIS *The Rights, Duties, and Relations of Domestic Servants, etc.* [Second edition.] Fcp 8vo. 1/0 sewed Feb 27–Mar. 13 (*PC*)

The first edition was issued by Low, 1857, 54 pp., 1/0 cloth, by a barrister, advertised in the *Ath* on Sept. 5 as "This day." Low issued the (third edition), Fcp 8vo, 1/0 sewed, listed in the *Ath* on Aug. 4, 1860, and still advertised on Feb. 20, 1864, as "New and forthcoming books." Low issued the fifth edition, 1896, 12 mo, 64 pp., 1/0 limp cloth, advertised in the *Ath* on Jan. 16, 1897, as "Ready"; and issued the sixth edition, 1906, 69 pp.

33 C.S. & M.E.S. *Blighted Pasque-Flowers.* Fcp 8vo. 2/6 boards Apr. 3 (*Ath*)

This is the first edition, 1858, in verse, printed at Oswestry.

34 MARIAN JAMES *Types of Womanhood. In Four Stories.* Fcp 8vo. 2/0 boards May 1 (*Ath*)

This is the first edition, 1858.

35 ELIZABETH S. PHELPS, SR. *The Angel Over the Right Shoulder.* Fcp 8vo. Illustrated. 1/0 sewed Aug. 14 (*Ath*)

This is the first British edition, 1858, 40 pp. Low advertised it in the *Ath* on Jan. 7, 1860, illustrated, 1/0, a New Year's Gift. The first edition was issued in the United States. It was issued by Warren F. Draper,

Andover; etc., 1852, 16 cm., anonymous, 29 pp., frontispiece. It was also issued with what sounds like the same sheets by A.D.F. Randolph, New York, 1852, 16 cm., anonymous, 29 pp., advertised in the *New York Daily Times* on Oct. 28, 1852; and advertised on Jan. 5, 1853, as a new edition, "Just ready," this latter issue dated 1853.

36 WILLIAM A. BUTLER *Two Millions.* Fcp 8vo. 1/0 sewed Aug. 21 (*Ath* ad)

This is the first British edition (1858), 16.5 cm., 96 pp., in verse. Low issued a second edition, no date, 96 pp., *"Two Millions"; and Nothing to Wear* was issued by Ward & Lock, London, 1858, 88 pp., 1/0 boards, listed in the *Ath* on Nov. 27. The first American edition was issued by D. Appleton & Co., New York, 1858, 17 cm., 93 pp., $.50, listed in the *Ind* on Aug. 12 and reviewed in the *Southern Literary Messenger* (monthly) for Sept., and hence probably issued in July or Aug.
See item 39

37 JANE M. PARKER *The Boy Missionary.* 12 mo. 1/6 sewed Oct. 30–Nov. 13 (*PC*)

This is the first British edition, 1858. The first American edition was issued by the General Protestant Episcopal Sunday School Union, New York, 1858, 15.5 cm., 162 pp. Low reissued it in 1870, new edition, 32 mo. 1/0 cloth, listed in the *Spect* on Aug. 13.

38 CHARLES B. TAYLER *The Fools' Pence and Other Narratives of Every-Day Life.* Fcp 8vo. Illustrated. 2/6 cloth Nov. 13 (*Ath*)

This is the first edition, 1859, with designs by A. H. Forrester.

39 WILLIAM A. BUTLER *Nothing to Wear: and Two Millions.* New edition. Fcp 8vo. 1/o boards Nov. 30–Dec. 14 (*PC*)

This is my copy, 1858, 16.6 cm., 109 pp., in pink, glazed pictorial boards, printed in red and black, with the back cover with an all-over collections of coins and with the titles reversed. It has an inscribed date (1858), plain pale yellow endpapers, with 2 pp. of publisher's ads and a catalog paged (1)–12 (Nov. 1858) at the back. The cover design is by Alfred Crowquill. Ward & Lock issued it, 1858, 88 pp., 1/o boards, listed in the *Ath* on Nov. 27. Low issued a new edition, 1881, 12 mo., 143 pp., 1/o sewed, in the *Rose Library*, listed in the *Bks* for Nov. 1880.

See also above and 1857

40 FRANK FOWLER *Southern Lights and Shadows.* Fcp 8vo. 1/6 boards, 2/6 cloth Dec. 25 (*Ath*)

This is the first edition, 1859, 132 pp. Low issued the second edition, Fcp 8vo, 1/6 boards, 2/6 cloth, listed in the *Ath* on Jan. 22, 1859, and by *PC* as published Jan. 31–Feb. 14.

41 HARRIET B. STOWE *Tales and Sketches of New England Life.* 1/o 1858 (*BMO*)

This was first issued by Low, 1855, 17 cm., 328 pp., 1/o limp cloth and with a portrait at 2/6 cloth, *Tales and Sketches of New England Life: Comprising "The May Flower" and Other Miscellaneous Writings*, called the author's cheap edition. It was deposited on May 10 and listed in the *Ath* on Apr. 28 and in *PC* on May 15. It was issued at the same time as the American edition. It was advertised by Low in the *Ath* on Sept. 5, 1857, 1/o. The first American edition was issued by Phillips, Sampson & Co., Boston, 1855, 19 cm., 471 pp., frontispiece (portrait), $1.25, advertised in the *New York Daily Times* on Apr. 9 as "On Apr. 15" and advertised on May 22, 12th thousand, "Now ready." The title was *The May Flower and Miscellaneous Writings*.

The first edition of *The Mayflower* was issued by Harper & Bros., New York, 1843, 16 cm., 324 pp., containing 15 sketches, including "Uncle Tim." It was in green, brown, or purple cloth and was listed in *Wiley & Putnam's Literary News-Letter* for May. Wiley & Putnam, London, imported it, listed in *PC* on Nov. 1, 1843. It was issued by Thomas Nelson, London and Edinburgh, 1849, 14 cm., 240 pp., illustrated, in pictorial cloth, all edges gilt, containing 10 of the original 15 sketches. It was listed in the *Ath* on Dec. 23, 1848, as 32 mo, 1/6; and was listed in *PC* on Feb. 15, 1849; and was listed in the *Ath* on Dec. 30, 1848, 18 mo, 2/o cloth. They reissued it, 1852, 17.5 cm., 220 pp., frontispiece, listed in *PC* on Nov. 13, 1852.

42 ALICE CARY *Alice Cary's Pictures of Country Life.* Fcp 8vo. 1/6 boards May 21 (*Ath*)

This is the first English edition, Low, London; A. Strahan & Co., Edinburgh, 1859, 234 pp. The first edition was issued by Derby & Jackson, New York, 1859, 19 cm., 359 pp., $1.00, advertised in the *New-York Times* on Feb. 26 as "On Mar. 1" and listed in *APC&LG* on Mar. 5.

43 EDWARD HOPLEY *Art, and How to Enjoy It.* Fcp 8vo. 1/0 sewed July 15–30 (*PC*)

This is the first edition, 1859.

44 NATHANIEL P. WILLIS *Paul Fane.* 12mo. 2/6 boards Aug. 31–Sept. 14 (*PC*)

This is 1859, 410 pp. It was reissued at 2/6 boards, listed in *PC* as published Sept. 30–Oct. 14, 1859. The first British edition was issued by Low in 1856, p 8vo, 401 pp., 7/6, Nov. 29–Dec. 13. It was also issued by C. H. Clarke, London, in 1857, no date, Fcp 8vo, 304 pp., 1/6 small format yellowback, with front and back covers identical. It was listed by PC as published advertised in the *Ath* on Dec. 20, 1856, and listed by *PC* as published Jan. 14–31, 1857. The first American edition was issued by Charles Scribner & Co., New York; etc., 1857, 18.5 cm., 402 pp., $1.25, advertised in the *New York Daily Times* on Nov. 18, 1856, as "On Nov. 22." They is-

sued the 5th thousand at $1.25, advertised in *Harper's Weekly* on Jan. 3, 1857, as "Just published."

45 SAMUEL A. BARD (EPHRAIM G. SQUIER) *Waikna; or, Adventures on the Mosquito Shore.* 12 mo. 1/6 boards Aug. 31–Sept. 14 (*PC*)

This is probably the third edition. The first British edition was issued by Low, 1855, 21 cm., 366 pp., illustrated, 1 map, 7/6, listed in the *Ath* and *Spect* on Aug. 25. It has an added illustrated title page with Harper & Bros., New York, imprint. Low issued a new edition, 1856, 12mo, 188 pp., 1/0 limp cloth, advertised in the *Ath* on May 31 and listed by *PC* as published May 14–31. It was also issued by James Blackwood, London, 1856, 17 cm., 310 pp., illustrated, 1 map, 3/6, advertised in the *Ath* on May 10 as "Just published," with the title *Adventures on the Mosquito Shore*, by Samuel Bard. They reissued it in 1858, new edition, 2/0 boards, listed by *PC* as published Dec. 14–31, 1858.

The first edition was issued by Harper & Bros., New York, 1855, 20 cm., 366 pp., illustrated, 1 map, $1.25 muslin, with an added illustrated title page, advertised in the *New York Daily Times* on July 25 as "Tomorrow morning," with the title *Waikna*. They reissued it in 1855, the same, advertised in the *New York Daily Times* on Oct. 13.

46 ANONYMOUS *The Quakers, or Friends: Their Rise and Decline.* Demy 8vo. 1/o sewed Sept. 17 (*Ath* ad)

This is the first edition, 21 cm., with 60 pp. Low issued a second edition, 1859, the same.

47 HARRIET B. STOWE *The Minister's Wooing.* Cr 8vo. 2/6 boards; Demy 8vo, illustrated, 7/6 Sept. 17 (*Ath*)

These are the first editions, 1859, with a preface (Aug. 25, 1859). The 2/6 issue was first issued 16-parts-in-11, in green wrappers, from Jan. 1 to Nov. 1, 1859; and then issued in 1 vol., 19 cm., 239 pp., in blue pictorial boards, printed in dark red and purple (*BAL* says in pale blue cloth with pale yellow endpapers). It was listed also in *PC* on Oct. 1; and there was a second edition, listed in the *Ath* on Oct. 15, 1859. The 7/6 issue was 21 cm., 362 pp., illustrated by "Phiz," in red cloth with yellow endpapers and a 16-page catalog (July 1859) in most copies. It was first issued 14-parts-in-10, o/6 each in printed blue wrappers, issued Feb.–Nov. 1859. It was listed in *Literary Gazette* also on Sept. 17, and in *PC* on Oct. 1. Low advertised a new edition in 1860, illustrated, 7/6, in the *Spect* on Apr. 28; and issued a new edition in 1864, Cr 8vo, 5/o, listed in the *Reader* on Apr. 9, 1864, as "Just ready." It went out of print until Low issued it in the *American Authors* series No. 3, my copy, 1869, 15.8 cm., 318 pp., with the preface, 1/6 limp glazed green boards decorated and printed in tan, plain white endpapers, series title on the cover, and a publisher's ad on the back cover. It was also issued at 2/o in flexible cloth and was listed in the *Ath* on Feb. 6. Low issued it in his *Rose Library* No. 19, 16mo, 1/o sewed, 2/6 cloth, listed in the *Spect* on Mar. 11, 1876.

The first American edition was issued by Derby & Jackson, New York, 1859, 19.5 cm., 578 pp., without the preface, $1.25, advertised in the *New-York Times* on Oct. 8 as "Next week" and on Oct. 15 as "This day" and listed in *APC&LG* on Oct. 22. They issued the 22nd thousand, advertised in *APC&LG* on Nov. 26, 1859. The first American edition was in black, tan, or purple cloth, yellow or tan endpapers; or purple, blue, tan, or brown cloth, yellow endpapers; or green or brown cloth, snowflake-pattern endpapers in green, all edges gilt. It ran in the *Atlantic Monthly* beginning in Dec. 1858.

48 SAMUEL I. PRIME *The Power of Prayer.* Cr 8vo, 1/o limp; 12mo, 2/o cloth boards 1859

The first edition was issued by Charles Scribner & Co., New York, 1859, 19 cm., 373 pp. The fifth edition was listed in the *New Englander*, New Haven (quarterly), for Feb. 1859. The seventh edition was issued by Scribner, New York: Low, London, 1859, 19 cm., 373 pp. Low advertised it in the *Ath* on Jan. 29, 1859, 12mo, 6/o; and issued it in 1859, 12mo, 3/o, 3/6, listed by *PC* as published Mar. 31–Apr. 14; and issued it at 2/o, 3/6 cloth, listed in *PC* as published Apr. 30–May 14. Low issued it in 1859, also, 12mo, 1/o cloth, 146 pp., listed by *PC* as published Aug. 31–Sept. 14; and it was advertised in the *Ath* on Oct. 29, 1859, as "This day," 12mo, 2/o cloth, and Cr 8vo, 1/o limp cover, the 25th thousand. There were editions also in 1859 in Edinburgh and by Milner, London; and by W. Collins, London.

49 FRANK FOWLER *The Wreck of the Royal Charter.* 12mo. 1/o 1859 (*Eng Cat*)

I cannot trace this.

Sampson Low, Son & Co.
47 Ludgate Hill
1860

50 WILLIAM H. MILBURN **The Rifle, Axe, and Saddle-Bags, and Other Lectures.**
Fcp 8vo. 1/6 boards   Mar. 10 (*Ath*)

This is 1860, 151 pp., with an introduction and life of the author by T. Binney. The first British edition was issued by Low, 1857, 18.5 cm., 244 pp., frontispiece (portrait), colored plates, 4/0, with the introduction and life by Binney, advertised in the *Ath* on Nov. 29, 1856, as "Shortly" and on Dec. 20 as if ready, and listed in the *Spect* on Jan. 3, 1857.

The first American edition was issued by Derby & Jackson, New York; etc., 1857, 19.5 cm., 309 pp., frontispiece (portrait), with an introduction by J. McClintock, advertised in the *New York Daily Times* on Nov. 8, 1856, as "This day"; and on Nov. 26, the third edition, "Now ready," and on Dec. 8, four editions in four weeks. They issued it as *The Pioneer Preacher*, 1857, the same.

51 MARIA S. CUMMINS **El Fureidis.**
Fcp 8vo. 2/6 boards   Aug. 18 (*Ath*)

The first British edition was issued by Low, 2 vols., 1860, 18 cm., 10/6, with a catalog (May 1, 1860) at the back of vol. 2. It was listed in the *Ath* on May 12. Low issued it in 1862, new edition, p 8vo, frontispiece, 5/0, listed in the *Ath* on Nov. 8. The first American edition was issued by Ticknor & Fields, Boston, 1860, 18.5 cm., anonymous, 379 pp., $1.00 muslin, listed in *Godey's Lady's Book* for Aug. and thus probably issued in May or June. The 7th thousand was advertised in the *New-York Times* on May 19, $1.00 muslin.

52 HENRY W. BEECHER **Life Thoughts.**
2/0   1860 (*Eng Cat*)

This contains both series. The first American edition of the first series was issued by Phillips, Sampson & Co., Boston, 1858, 19 cm., 299 pp., edited and with the preface signed by Edna D. Proctor. It was advertised in the *New-York Times* on Dec. 11, 1858, as "On Dec. 8." The first British edition of the first series was issued by Alexander Strahan, Edinburgh, 1858, 17 cm., 184 pp., edited by Proctor. Strahan reissued it in 1859, the same. The first American edition of the second series was *Notes from Plymouth Pulpit*, issued by Derby & Jackson, New York, 1859, 12mo, 310 pp., edited by Augusta Moore, listed in *Godey's Lady's Book* for Mar. and hence probably issued in Dec. 1858 or Jan. 1859. They issued the third edition (8th thousand), advertised in the *New-York Times* on Jan. 12, 1859, as "Ready." I think it was also issued in Britain by Strahan, as he issued both series in 1 vol., 1859, 14th thousand, 12mo, 2/0 sewed, listed in the *Ath* on May 7. W. Collins, London, issued both series in 1 vol. in 1860, 2/0. Harper & Bros., New York, issued it, 1865, 12mo, 374 pp., $2.00 with bevelled edges, revised and greatly enlarged, advertised in the *New-York Times* on Dec. 23, 1865, as "Just published."

Sampson Low, Son & Marston
47 Ludgate Hill
1861

Edward Marston's name was added to the style in April.

53 R. B. (ROBERT BLACK) *A Memoir of Abraham Lincoln.* Fcp 8vo, 1/0 sewed; 12mo, 3/6 cloth Feb. 9 (*Ath*)

This is the first edition, 1861, 17.5 cm., 126 pp., frontispiece, at least for the 3/6 issue. It was reprinted from the *Times*.

54 ANONYMOUS *The Twelve Great Battles of England.* 12mo. Frontispiece (folding map). 2/6 boards Mar. 30 (*Ath*)

This is the first edition, my copy, Sampson Low, Son & Co., 1861, 17.5 cm., 223 pp., with an appendix on pp. (217)–223. It is in unglazed pictorial boards, printed identically on front and back in red, green, and black, with plain, pale yellow endpapers. There is a preface dated 1861 and an inscribed date of 1861. A 16-page catalog on small paper (Jan. 1861) is at the back.

55 ANONYMOUS *Banks and Banking in Australia.* Fcp 8vo. 0/6 sewed Apr. 20 (*Spect*)

This is the first edition, 1861, 31 pp.

56 HARRIET B. STOWE *The Pearl of Orr's Island. Part 1.* 12mo. 1/6 boards Apr. 20 (*Ath*)

This is the first edition of part 1, 1861, the first 17 chapters, 157 pp. It was also issued at the same time with a frontispiece, 3/6, in blue cloth with yellow endpapers. There is a preface (Apr. 1861). It was deposited on June 4, and the yellowback issue was also listed in *PC* on May 1. Part 2 was issued by Low, 1862, 12mo, 194 pp., with the final 27 chapters, 2/0 boards, with a preface (Apr. 1862), listed in the *Ath* on May 10 and in *PC* on May 15. Low also issued it complete in 1 vol., 1862, 19.5 cm., 352 pp., frontispiece, 5/0, either with or without the preface (Apr. 1862). It is in purple cloth with cream endpapers and with a 16-page catalog (Jan. 1862) at the back. It was deposited on Apr. 19, advertised in the *Ath* on Apr. 19 as "This day," and listed there on Apr. 26.

The first American edition was issued by Ticknor & Fields, Boston, 1862, 21 cm., 437 pp., without the preface, $1.25, in green or purple cloth with brown endpapers and a 16-page catalog (May 1862) at the back. There was a first printing of 2,000 copies, advertised in the *New-York Times* on May 3 as "This day" and deposited on May 1. A second printing of 1,012 copies was bound on May 6 and 7, 1862. The fourth edition was advertised in *APC&LG* for May 1862 as already published; the fifth edition was advertised in the *New-York Times* on May 16, 1862, $1.25; and the tenth edition was issued, 1866, 437 pp. It ran in the *Ind*, part 1 beginning the first week in 1861, and part 2 beginning in Dec. 1861.

Low issued a new and cheaper edition,

1875, 16mo, 1/0 sewed, 2/6 cloth, in the *Rose Library* No. 18, listed in the *Ath* on Nov. 27; and reissued it in the *Rose Library*, new edition, in 1878, 16mo, 2/0 sewed, listed in the *Bks* for Dec. 1878. Low issued it at 3/6, listed in the *Spect* on Jan. 19, 1878.

57 JOHN H. DUNNE **From Calcutta to Pekin.** 12mo. 2/0 boards   Apr. (*Bks*)

This is the first edition, 1861, 159 pp., one plain, one portrait.

58 COUNT A. E. DE GASPARIN **The Uprising of a Great People.** 12mo. 1/0   Aug. 24 (*Ath* ad)

The ad in the *Ath* said "Now ready." This is the first British edition, abridged from the French, with appendices. The first edition was *Les Etats-Unis en 1861; Un Grand Peuple qui se Rèleve*, Paris, 1861, 21.5 cm., 414 pp. The first American edition was issued by Charles Scribner & Co., New York, 1861,

17 cm., 263 pp., $.75, translated by Mary L. Booth, advertised in the *New-York Times* on June 26 as "This day." They issued a second edition in 1861, $.75, advertised in the same on July 17 as "This day." They issued a new edition, 1862, 19 cm., 298 pp., in the Booth translation, $.75, to conform to the new Paris edition, advertised in the *New-York Times* on Jan. 30, 1862, as "On Jan. 30."

59 WILLIAM PATTON **The American Crisis.** 12mo. 0/6   Aug. 24 (*Ath* ad)

The ad said "Now ready." This is the first British edition, 1861, 18 cm., 40 pp. There was an issue with this title issued by Walsh, Chicago, 1861, 22 cm., 28 pp., by Americus.

60 W.H.G. KINGSTON **Jack Buntline.** Fcp 8vo. Frontispiece. 2/0 cloth Oct. 5 (*Ath*)

This is the first edition, 1861.

Sampson Low, Son & Marston
47 Ludgate Hill
1862

61 ANONYMOUS *A Plain Guide to the International Exhibition. The Wonders of the Exhibition.* o/6   June 1 (*Ath*)

An ad in the *Ath* on May 24 said "On June 1." It is the first edition, 1862, 64 pp.

62 THOMAS HARE *Usque ad Coelum.* Fcp 8vo. 1/o   Aug. 23 (*Ath* ad)

The ad in the *Ath* said "This day." This is the first edition, 1862.

63 GEORGE W. BACON *Bacon's Guide to American Politics.* Cr 8vo. 1/o   1862 (*Eng Cat*)

This is the first edition, Sampson Low; Bacon & Co., London, 1863, 19 cm., 94 pp., tables. Low issued a new edition, 1864, 12mo, folding map, 1/o, given by the *BM* as the (third edition) with 100 pp. The *U Cat* gives 1864, 18 cm., 93 pp., frontispiece (folding map). Low issued the fourth edition, 1867, 17.5 cm., 101 pp., frontispiece (folding map).

Sampson Low, Son & Marston
47 Ludgate Hill
1863

Low advertised in the Spect *on Dec. 5, 1863, that they were moving to 14 Ludgate Hill. An ad in the* Ath *on Dec. 19 advised that Low had moved to 14 Ludgate Hill.*

64 HARRIET B. STOWE *A Reply to the Affectionate and Christian Address of Many Thousands of Women of Great Britain and Ireland, etc.* Fcp 8vo. 1/0 boards   Jan. 10 (*Ath*)

This is the first edition, 1863, 17 cm., 63 pp., in buff boards printed in black, yellow endpapers, with a 16-page catalog (Oct. 1862) at the back. Low issued another edition, 1863, also, Low; etc., London, 1863, 16.8 cm., 24 pp., 0/2 each; 10/0 per 100; 80/0 per 1,000. It had a cover title with printed self-wrappers, advertised in *PC* on Jan. 17, 1863. This reply first appeared in the *Atlantic Monthly*. A rejoinder was issued by Emily Faithful's Victoria Press in London, a pamphlet, reviewed in the *Atlantic Monthly* for Apr. 1863.

65 EDMUND KIRKE (JAMES R. GILMORE) *My Southern Friends.* 12mo. 1/6 boards, 2/6 cloth   July 11 (*Ath*)

This is the first British edition, 1863, 18 cm., 196 pp. In the United States it was is-sued by G. W. Carleton, New York, 1863, 19 cm., 308 pp., $.75 paper, $1.00 cloth, noticed in *Godey's Lady's Book* for July and thus probably issued in Apr. or May. It was listed in the *Knickerbocker* for June. It was also issued by the Tribune Association, New York, 1863, 18 cm., 308 pp. Low also issued it in 1864, Fcp 8vo, 1/6, advertised in the *Ath* on Oct. 29, 1864.

66 THOMAS MILLER *Little Blue Hood.* Fcp 8vo. Illustrated. 2/0 boards, 2/6 cloth Nov. 2 (*Spect*)

This is the first edition, 1863, 132 pp. The first American edition was issued by J. G. Gregory, New York, 1864, 18 cm., 95 pp., one colored plate, with the cover illus-trated in colors.

Sampson Low, Son & Marston
47 Ludgate Hill
1864

67 WILKIE COLLINS *The Woman in White.* 12mo. 2/6 boards Sept. 24 (*Ath*)

This has 494 pp. It ran in *All the Year Round,* Nov. 26, 1859–Aug. 25, 1860. The first book edition was issued by Low, 3 vols., 1860, 19.8 cm., 31/6 in violet cloth with pale yellow endpapers, and with a catalog (Aug. 1, 1860) at the back of vol. 3, and with a preface (Aug. 3, 1860). It was listed in the *Ath* on Aug. 11 and by *PC* as published Aug. 14–31. Low issued a new edition, 3 vols., 1860, identical to the first edition but with "New edition" on the title page and with the catalog (Nov. 1, 1860). They issued the third edition, 3 vols., 1860, in violet cloth, with four pp. of W. H. Smith ads in each vol. He issued the fifth edition, 3 vols., 1860. They issued the first 1-vol. edition, 1861, new edition, 18.8 cm., 494 pp., frontispiece (portrait) and added engraved title page, 6/0 in magenta cloth with cream endpapers, or in green cloth. Some copies have a 16-page catalog (Nov. 1861), and all copies have a new preface (Feb. 1861). It was advertised in the *Spect* on Apr. 27 as "This day." Low reissued it in 1863, new edition, 6/0, advertised in the *Spect* on May 16 as "This day." It was issued by Smith, Elder & Co., London, 1865, 494 pp., 2/6 boards, a new edition, advertised in the *Ath* on Sept. 23 as "Just published." They also issued it in green cloth, 1865, with a new title page but still with the Low engraved title page. They reissued it at 2/0 boards in 1871 and 1873, my copies.

The first American appearance was as a serial in *Harper's Weekly,* Nov. 26, 1859–Aug. 4, 1860, $.05 a week. The first American book edition was issued by Harper & Bros., New York, 1860, 8vo, 260 pp. in double columns, illustrated by John McLenan, $1.00 muslin, in black with brown endpapers, or in brown; and $.75 in buff wrappers. There are 2 pp. of ads in front (Aug. 1860). It was advertised in the *New-York Times* on Aug. 30 as "This day" and advertised and listed in the *Ind* on Sept. 6.

68 THOMAS MILLER *Goody Platts, and Her Two Cats.* Fcp 8vo. Frontispiece. 1/0 Nov. (*Bks*)

This is the first edition, 1864, 17 cm., 78 pp., with a colored frontispiece in scarlet, blue, and yellow, by Walter Crane, with 2 pp. of ads at the back. It is in words of one and two syllables.

The imprint was 14 Ludgate Hill on July 9, 1864, and had become Milton House, Ludgate Hill, by July 1, 1865.

69 CHRISTOPHER CROWFIELD (HARRIET B. STOWE) *House and Home Papers.* Fcp 8vo. 1/0 boards   Feb. 11 (*Ath*)

This is the first English edition, 1865, 160 pp. One hundred copies of the American edition were shipped to Low on Jan. 28, 1865, and this imported edition was listed in *PC* on Mar. 1, 1865. In the United States it ran in the *Atlantic Monthly* beginning in Jan. 1864, and the first book edition was issued by Ticknor & Fields, Boston, 1865, 18.5 cm., 333 pp., plain, $1.50 in purple or blue cloth with brown endpapers, or in blue cloth with a different stamping, with brown endpapers. Records show that 5,086 copies were printed and bound Dec. 28, 1864–Mar. 23, 1866. One hundred copies were shipped to England on Jan. 28, 1865. It was advertised in the *New-York Times* on Dec. 31, 1864 as "This day" and listed in *ALG&PC* on Jan. 16, 1865.

70 WILKIE COLLINS *The Queen of Hearts.* [New edition.] 12mo. 2/6 boards   Mar. 4 (*Ath*)

This has 344 pp., the Glover & Greene copy, containing ten tales embodied in the main narrative. Eight of the tales had been previously published in *Household Words*, *Harper's New Monthly Magazine*, etc. The first edition was issued by Hurst & Black-ett, London, 3 vols., 1859, 19.5 cm., 31/6 in sage-green cloth with ivory (pale yellow) endpapers. There is a dedication (Oct. 1859) and a 16-page catalog at the back of vol. 1. Low issued it, 1862, new edition, 18.5 cm., 344 pp., frontispiece, in mauve cloth with brown endpapers, probably at 5/0. There are 2 pp. of ads (Jan. 1862). Low reissued it in 1863, new edition, frontispiece, 5/0, advertised in the *Spect* on May 16 as "This day." It was issued by Smith, Elder & Co., London, 1865, new edition, 2/6 pictorial boards, listed in the *Reader* on Nov. 25, 1865. Sadleir's copy has Smith, Elder on the title page and Low on the covers. It was reissued at 2/0 boards in 1871 and 1874, and in cloth at 2/6 in 1872. Bernhard Tauchnitz, Leipzig, issued *A Plot in Private Life and Other Tales*, 1859, containing five of the tales.

The first American edition was issued by Harper & Bros., New York, 1859, 19.5 cm., 472 pp., $1.00 in green cloth with brown endpapers. It has the dedication (Oct. 1859) and 8 pp. of ads at the back. It was listed in *APC&LG* on Nov. 26.

71 (JAMES PAYN) *Lost Sir Massingberd.* Third edition. 12mo. 2/6 boards   Mar. 4 (*Ath*)

This is 1865, 328 pp., in orange pictorial boards. Low issued the fourth edition,

1878, 12mo, 2/0 boards, listed in the *Spect* on June 1. This ran in *Chambers's Journal* beginning on Jan. 2, 1864, and completed in 1864. The first book edition was issued by Low, 2 vols., 1864, 19 cm., anonymous, 16/0, listed in the *Ath* on Apr. 23. Low issued the second edition, 1864, 2 vols., anonymous, advertised in the *Spect* on May 28 as "On May 30."

The first American edition was issued by T. B. Peterson & Bros., Philadelphia (1870), anonymous, 334 pp., $1.75, listed in the *Nation* on Mar. 24 and in the *Ind* on Apr. 14.

72 ANONYMOUS *Free Colonization and Trade.* Square 18mo. 1/0 Mar. 25 (*Ath* ad)

The ad said "This day." It is probably the first edition, with an introduction by B. Thomas M'Combie. I cannot trace it.

73 WILKIE COLLINS *Antonina.* New edition. 12mo. 2/6 boards May 13 (*Reader*)

This is 1865, 420 pp., with a 16-page catalog (Jan. 1865). Smith, Elder & Co., London also issued this, 1865, 2/6 boards, and there was a listing in the *Ath* on May 6 with no publisher given. Low sold the rights to Collins's novels to Smith, Elder in 1865, and it is possible that copies will turn up with Smith, Elder on the title page and Low on the covers. The first edition was issued by Bentley, London, 3 vols., 1850, 21 cm., 31/6 in white (cream) cloth with cream (yellow) endpapers, printed with Bentley ads. There are 2 pp. of ads at the back of vol. 3. It was listed in the *Ath* on Mar. 2 and by *PC* as published Feb. 27–Mar. 14. Bentley issued the second edition, 3 vols., 1850, revised and corrected, advertised in the *Spect* on July 27 as "On July 30." Low issued a new edition, 1861, 18.5 cm., 420 pp., in purple cloth with cream endpapers, probably at 5/0. It has a preface (Nov. 1860), an added illustrated

title page, and 4 pp. of ads and a 16-page catalog (Nov. 1, 1860) at the back. Low issued a new edition, 1863, with 1 illustration by John Gilbert, 5/0, advertised in the *Spect* on May 16 as "This day." Smith, Elder & Co., London, issued a new edition, 1871, 12mo, 2/0 boards, listed in the *Ath* on July 1; and they issued a new edition, 1872, my copy, 12mo, 2/0 boards, 17.5 cm., 420 pp., in yellow pictorial boards, printed in red, blue, and black with plain white endpapers, with a publisher's ad on the back. They also issued it at 2/6 cloth, 12mo, 1872, listed by *PC* as published Nov. 1–15.

The first American edition was issued by Harper & Bros., New York, 1850, 22.5 cm., 160 pp. in double columns, *Library of Select Novels* No. 141, $.37½ in tan paper wrappers, with ads on the back and inside covers. It was listed in *Lit W* as published Apr. 27–May 11.

74 (MALCOLM R.L. MEASON) *The Bubbles of Finance: Joint-Stock Companies, etc.* Fcp 8vo. 2/6 boards July 15 (*Ath*)

This is the first edition, 1865, 17 cm., 261 pp., by A City Man.

75 DUTTON COOK (EDWARD DUTTON COOK) *Paul Foster's Daughter.* [New edition.] 12mo. 2/6 boards. Sept. 2 (*Ath*)

The first edition was issued by Hurst & Blackett, London, 3 vols., 1861, 19.5 cm., 31/6, listed in the *Ath* on July 6. It was reissued in 1866, the same, listed in the *Reader* on June 2.

76 HENRY HOLL *The King's Mail.* New edition, revised. 12mo. 2/6 boards Sept. 32 (*Ath*)

This is (1865), with 359 pp. and a new preface by the author, a 16-page catalog (Jan. 1865) at the back, and publisher's ads on the back cover. Low issued it, the same, at 3/6 cloth, listed in the *Reader* on Nov. 25, 1865. The first edition was issued by Low, 3 vols. (1863), 21 cm., 31/6 in grass-green cloth with cream endpapers, and with a preface (May 1, 1863) and a 16-page catalog (May 1863) at the back of vol. 3. It was listed in the *Ath* on May 30.

77 (ADELINE WHITNEY) *Faith Gartney's Girlhood.* 12mo. 2/6 boards, 3/6 cloth Sept. 23 (*Ath*)

This or the S. O. Beeton edition was the first British edition. It was listed also in the *Reader* on Oct. 7 and advertised in the *Spect* on Sept. 16. The 3/6 had colored illustrations. Low issued it, 1866, new edition, 12mo, anonymous, 355 pp., 1/6 pictorial boards, listed in the *Reader* on Dec. 23, 1865. S. O. Beeton, London, issued it in 1865, Fcp 8vo, 254 pp., 1/o sewed, listed in the *Reader* on Dec. 9, 1865. It was also issued by Ward, Lock & Tyler, London, at 1/o sewed, listed in the *Bks* for May 1867.

The first edition was issued by A. K. Loring, Boston; etc., 1863, 19 cm., anonymous, 348 pp., by A.D.T.W., $1.25, in plum cloth with yellow endpapers, all edges trimmed. It was listed in the *Ind* on July 9.

I have a copy, 1871, new edition, 16 cm., anonymous, 355 pp., in flexible brown boards, decorated in yellow and black, cut flush, 1/6 in *Low's Copyright Series of American Authors.* It has plain white endpapers and 8 pp. of publisher's ads at the back. The words "Every work in this series is either English copyright or published by arrangement with the author" appear on the front cover. It was also issued at the same time at 3/6 cloth, and the 1/6 was listed in the *Ath* on Dec. 3, 1870.

78 (ADELINE WHITNEY) *The Gayworthys.* New edition. 12mo. 1/6 boards Nov. 11 (*Ath*)

This is my copy, 1866, 17.5 cm., 400 pp., in white pictorial boards, printed in red, blue, yellow, and black, with plain white endpapers and a publisher's ad on the back cover. There is a prefatory note and "To the English Reader," the latter signed A.D.T.W. The first British edition was issued by Low, 2 vols., 1865, p 8vo, anonymous, 16/o, listed in the *Ath* on June 24. Low issued a new edition, 2 vols., 16/o, listed in the *Reader* on Nov. 11, 1865. They issued it in 1 vol. in 1865, 399 pp., 3/6 cloth; and issued the third edition in 1865, Fcp 8vo, in colored pictorial boards, 1/6, advertised in the *Spect* on Dec. 9, 1865, as "This day." They issued it in 1873, 16mo, 1/6 limp boards and 2/o flexible cloth, listed in the *Ath* on Oct. 4; and issued it in 1891, 12mo, 2/o, listed in *PC* on Oct. 31. S. O. Beeton, London, issued it, 1866, 17 cm., anonymous, 359 pp., 1/o sewed, listed in the *Reader* on Nov. 18, 1865. Ward, Lock & Tyler, London, issued it in 1867, 1/o sewed, and issued it at 2/o boards in Aug. 1870.

The first edition was issued by A. K. Loring, Boston, 1865, 19.5 cm., anonymous, 399 pp., $1.75, advertised in the *New-York Times* on June 10 as "Today." Loring, Boston; Low, London, issued the fourth edition (copyright 1865), 19 cm., anonymous, 399 pp.

79 HARRIET B. STOWE. *Little Foxes.* Author's edition, revised. 12mo. 1/o boards Nov. 18 (*Ath*)

This is Bell & Daldy; Low, London, 1866, 17.5 cm., 133 pp., in yellow boards, by Stowe. It was also listed in the *PC* on Dec. 8, 1865. They also issued it, author's edition, revised, 1866, 19.5 cm., 188 pp., by Stowe, 3/6 in terra-cotta cloth with black endpapers, with 4 pp. of ads. It was listed in the *Ath* on Nov. 11 and in *PC* on Dec. 8, 1865, and deposited on Jan. 19, 1866.

In the United States it ran in the *Atlantic Monthly*, Feb.–Sept. 1865, and the first American book edition was issued by Ticknor & Fields, Boston, 1866, 18.5 cm., by Christopher Crowfield, 287 pp., $1.75 in green, purple, brown, or terra-cotta cloth, with brown endpapers and three different blind stampings. It was advertised in *ALG&PC* on Dec. 1, 1865, as "Just published," listed in the *Nation* on Dec. 21, and deposited on Dec. 8. Records show that 3,515 copies were bound Dec. 5, 1865–Sept. 3, 1866.

80 OLIVER W. HOLMES *The Autocrat of the Breakfast-Table.* 12mo. 1/0 sewed Nov. (*Ath*)

This is Alexander Strahan; Low, London, 1865, 17.5 cm., 200 pp., in blue wrappers, advertised by Low in the *Ath* on Oct. 28, 1865, as "Next week" and listed by the *Bks* as published by Strahan in Nov. or Dec. 1865. Strahan; Low also issued it, Fcp 8vo, illustrated, 6/0 cloth, listed in the *Spect* on Dec. 16, 1865. It ran in the *Atlantic Monthly*, Nov. 1857–Oct. 1858, and the first book edition was issued by Phillips, Sampson & Co., Boston, 1858, 19 cm., anonymous, 373 pp., illustrated, $1.00. Opinions differ as to the first issue of the first edition, giving either bright green or bright red cloth. Later issues of the first edition were in brown, plum, or blue-green cloth. It

was advertised in the *New-York Times* on Nov. 18 as "This day" and listed in *APC&LG* on Nov. 20 and in the *Ind* on Nov. 25, 1858. They issued a large paper edition, 1859, 22 cm., in rust or maroon cloth; and they issued it with the addition of the Low imprint, 1858, the same as above, in tan cloth.

Low imported it in American sheets and used a different title page, omitting the engraved title page. It was 1858, 19 cm., anonymous, 373 pp., illustrated, with a 12-page catalog (Nov. 1858) at the back. It was in tan cloth with terra-cotta endpapers, 6/0, advertised by Low in the *Ath* on Dec. 11, 1858, as "New American books just received."

The first edition entirely set up and printed abroad was issued by Alexander Strahan, Edinburgh; Hamilton, Adams, London, 1859, 17.5 cm., 302 pp., 3/6 in maroon cloth, with 2 pp. of ads. It was listed in the *Ath* on Nov. 27, 1858, and advertised there on Nov. 20 as "On Nov. 24." Strahan issued it with the added Low imprint, 1861, 19 cm., 200 pp., by Holmes.

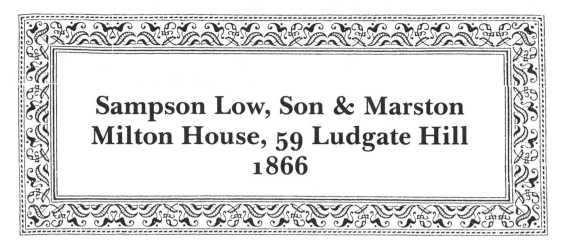

Sampson Low, Son & Marston
Milton House, 59 Ludgate Hill
1866

81 ELIZABETH GASKELL *My Lady Ludlow, and Other Tales.* [New edition.] 12mo. 2/6 boards   Feb. 17 (*Reader*)

This has 318 pp. *My Lady Ludlow* ran in *Household Words* in 14 weekly parts, June 10–Sept. 25, 1858. It was contained in *Round the Sofa*, with five other tales, in the first book edition, issued by Low, 2 vols., 1859, 21 cm., anonymous, 21/0 in orange-red cloth with yellow endpapers, edges uncut. It has a 12-page catalog (Mar. 1859) at the back of vol. 2 and was listed in the *Ath* on Mar. 12. Low issued the second edition in 2 vols., 1859, advertised in the *Ath* on Jan. 14, 1860, as published in 1859. There was a 2-vols.-in-1 remainder issue in dark green cloth. The first 1-vol. edition was issued by Low, 1861, Cr 8vo, 318 pp., frontispiece by John Gilbert, 5/0 in dark green cloth, with a 16-page catalog (July 1861) at the back. It carried the title *My Lady Ludlow, and Other Tales Included in "Round the Sofa"* and was listed in the *Ath* on July 6.

The first edition of *My Lady Ludlow* was issued by Harper & Bros., New York, 1858, 8vo, 77 pp., *Library of Select Novels* No. 209, $.12, listed in *Godey's Lady's Book* for Jan. 1859 and thus probably issued in Oct. or Nov. 1858.

82 JOHN SAUNDERS *Abel Drake's Wife.* [Fifth edition.] 12mo. 2/6 boards Apr. 21 (*Reader*)

This has 312 pp. The first edition was issued by Lockwood & Co., London, 1862, p 8vo, 338 pp., 10/6, listed in the *Ath* on Mar. 29. They issued the second edition, 1862, 19.5 cm., 338 pp., 10/6, advertised in the *Spect* on June 14 as "Now ready"; and issued the third edition in 1863, p 8vo, 6/0, advertised in the *Spect* on Mar. 28 as "Just ready." Low issued the fourth edition in 1863, Cr 8vo, 312 pp., *Favourite Library of Popular Books* No. 14, 5/0, listed in the *Reader* on Nov. 14 as "Just ready."

The first American edition was issued by Harper & Bros., New York, 1862, 8vo, 162 pp., *Library of Select Novels* No. 221, $.25, listed in *APC&LG* on July 1 and advertised in *Harpers Weekly* on July 5 as "Just published."

83 WILLIAM J. STEWART *Footsteps Behind Him.* [New edition.] 12mo. 2/6 boards Apr. 21 (*Reader*)

This has 394 pp. The first edition was issued by Low, 3 vols., 1862. They issued it in 1 vol. in 1863, 5/0.

84 WILLIAM MOY THOMAS *When the Snow Falls.* [New edition.] 12mo. 2/6 boards May 12 (*Ath*)

This has 323 pp. The first edition was issued by Low, 2 vols., 1859, 20.5 cm., 21/0, listed in the *Ath* on Nov. 12. They issued it in 1 vol. in 1861, new edition, p 8vo, frontispiece, 5/0, listed in the *Ath* on Dec. 14, 1861.

85 (MALCOLM R.L. MEASON) **The Profits of Panics.** 12mo. 1/o boards   July 14 (*Ath*)

This is the first edition, 1866, 17.5 cm., 108 pp. It was imported by Scribner & Welford, New York, and issued in 1866, 16mo, anonymous, $.50 boards, advertised in the *Nation* on Aug. 25.

86 JOHN MACGREGOR **Description of the New Rob Roy Canoe.** Illustrated. 1/o Sept. 15 (*Reader*)

This is the first edition (1866).

87 PATRICK BARRY **Over the Atlantic and Great Western Railway.** 12mo. Folding map. 1/o boards   Sept. 15 (*Reader*)

This is the first edition, 1866, 146 pp.

88 WALTER THORNBURY **Cross Country.** 12mo. 2/6 boards   Nov. or Dec. (*Bks*)

The first edition was issued by Low, 1861, 19 cm., 337 pp., illustrated, 5/o, listed in the *Ath* on Sept. 21.

Sampson Low, Son & Marston
Milton House, 59 Ludgate Hill
1867

89 BERTHOLD AUERBACH *On the Heights.*
3 vols., 16mo. 1/6 sewed, 2/0 flexible cloth
each Mar. 9 (*Ath*)

English Editions of German Authors No. 1. In
a Feb. 9 ad in the *Ath* Low announced that
they had just completed arrangements
with Tauchnitz of Leipzig for exclusive
publication in Great Britain and the colonies of *German Authors*, copyright in England. These had the Low imprint added
for the Low editions and had the Leypoldt
& Holt imprint added for the New York issue. The first edition was *Auf der Höhe*,
Stuttgart, 3 vols., 1865, 18 cm., issued in
England by D. Nutt. The present edition is
1867, authorized edition, 16 cm., translated by F. E. Bunnett.

In the United States it was issued by
Roberts Bros., Boston, third edition,
1868, 18 cm., 544 pp., $2.00 cloth, trans-
lated by Bunnett. It was advertised in the
New-York Times on Mar. 20 as "On Mar. 21"
and advertised on Mar. 25 as "Just ready."
It was listed in *Lippincott's Magazine* for
May. They issued the 7th edition, $2.00, in
1868, advertised in the *Nation* on Oct. 29
as "Now ready." Apparently Leypoldt &
Holt, New York, had visions of issuing it as
they advertised it as No. 1 of the Tauchnitz
issue of *German Authors*, in the *Nation* on
May 16, 1867, 3 vols., 16mo, $2.25 paper.
There must have been a slip-up as it wasn't
listed in the *Nation* until Nov. 26, 1868! It
was listed in *Putnam's Monthly* as published
in 1868. It was in the Bunnett translation.

90 FRITZ REUTER (HEINRICH L.C.F.
REUTER) *In the Year '13.* 16mo.
Authorized edition. 1/6 sewed,
2/0 flexible cloth July 20 (*Ath*)

German Authors No. 2. This is 1867, 16 cm.,
299 pp., translated from the Platt-
Deutsch, *Ut de Franzosentid*, by C. L. Lewes.
It was the second story in *Olle Kamellen*, issued at Wismar, 1860, 341 pp., containing
two stories. Here again we have Leypoldt
& Holt asserting squatter's rights by advertising in the *Nation* on Aug. 1, 1867, No. 2
of *German Authors*, 299 pp., authorized
edition, translated by C. L. Lewes, $.75 pa-
per; and it was reviewed there on Aug. 15
(probably a review of the English edition).
I think, however, that it wasn't issued until
Mar. 1868. It was advertised in the *New-
York Times* on Mar. 11, 1868, 16mo, $.75
paper, $1.00 flexible cloth; and listed in
Lippincott's Magazine for May 1868 as
dated 1868; and noticed in the *New Englander*, a New Haven quarterly, in Apr.
1868 as published in 1868; and listed in
Putnam's Monthly as published in 1868.

92 DUTTON COOK (EDWARD DUTTON
COOK) *"Hobson's Choice."* [New edition.]
12mo. 2/0 boards Aug. 31 (*Ath*)

This is 1867. The first edition was issued
by Low, 1867, p 8vo, 319 pp., 8/0, listed in
the *Ath* on Nov. 17, 1866.

92 JOHANN W. VON GOETHE **Faust. First part.** 12mo. 1/6 sewed, 2/0 flexible cloth Aug.?

German Authors No. 3. This is 1867, 295 pp. translated by John Anster. *Faust: Ein Fragment* was issued in Leipzig (1790), and part 1 was issued in Tübingen, 1808. It was issued in London by Thomas Boosey in 1821, 8vo, 6/0, in Oct.; and by John Murray, London, 1823, 8vo, 8/6, translated by F. L. Gower, in June. The Anster translation was issued in London, 1835, 12mo, 5/0 cloth, listed in the *Westminster Review* (quarterly) for Jan. 1835.

It was issued in the United States by Daniel Bixby, Lowell, Mass., 1840, 18mo, 317 pp., translated by A. Hayward, the first American from the third London edition. The present edition was issued by Leypoldt & Holt, New York, in 1867, 16mo, $1.25, bevelled edges, translated by Anster, advertised in the *Nation* on Oct. 10, 1867, probably prematurely, and advertised on Dec. 5 as "On Dec. 1."

93 FRIEDRICH DE LA MOTTE-FOUQUÉ **Undine and Other Tales.** 16mo. 1/6 sewed, 2/0 flexible cloth　Sept. 28 (*Ath*)

German Authors No. 4. This is 1867, 361 pp., translated by F. E. Bunnett. It contains also "The Two Captains," "Aslaugas's Knight," and "Sintram." It was issued by Leypoldt & Holt, New York, in 1867, 16mo, $1.25, bevelled edges, advertised in the *Nation* on Oct. 10 as a recent issue but advertised on Dec. 5 as "On Dec. 5." The first edition of *Undine* was in Berlin, 1811, anonymous, 189 pp. It was issued in Great Britain by Bell, Edinburgh; Simpkin, Marshall, London, 1818, 20 cm., anonymous, 205 pp., 5/6 in blue-gray paper boards with paper spine and white endpapers. It was translated by George Soane and listed in the *Quarterly Review* as published Apr. –June 1818. *Undine and Other Tales* was issued in Philadelphia by E. Lit-

tell, 1824, 18 cm., 170 pp., the first American edition, listed in the *North American Review* (quarterly) for Apr.

The Two Captains is a translation of *Die Beiden Hauptleute* and was issued in translation by Nutt, London, 1845. It was in *Natalia: Aslaugas's Knight and Other Tales*, issued by Jordan & Wiley, Boston, noticed in the *Merchant's Magazine* for Feb. 1846.

Aslaugas's Knight was issued as *German Romance* vol. 1, 1827, translated by Thomas Carlyle; and *Aslauga and Her Knight* was issued by Hamilton, Adams, London, 1843, 16mo, 84 pp., 1/6, listed in the *Gentleman's Magazine* for Jan. 1844.

Sintram und Seine Gefährten was issued in Germany, 1814. It was issued as *Sintram and His Companions* by C. & J. Ollier, London; etc., 1820, 19 cm., 267 pp., 5/6 boards, translated by J. C. Hare. It was listed in the *Edinburgh Review* as published May–Aug. 1820. It was issued in New York by Wiley & Putnam, listed in the *American Review* (monthly) for May 1845.

Low issued *Undine and The Two Captains*, 1875, Leipzig printed, 162 pp., illustrated, translated by F. E. Bunnett, in the *Rose Library* No. 9, 1/0 sewed listed in the *Ath* on Jan. 23; and 2/6 cloth, listed thereon Feb. 6, 1875.

94 PAUL HEYSE **L'Arrabiata and Other Tales.** Authorized edition. 16mo. 1/6 sewed, 2/0 flexible cloth　Oct.?

German Authors No. 5. This is 1867, 274 pp., containing four stories, translated from the German by M. Wilson. The *U Cat* gives *L'Arrabiata*, Berlin (1853?), sixth edition, 55 pp. In the United States it was issued by Leypoldt & Holt, New York, in 1867, advertised in the *Nation* on Oct. 31 as a recent *German Authors* title.

95 HARRIET B. STOWE **Queer Little People.** 1/0 boards, 1/6 cloth　Nov. 16 (*Ath*)

This is the first British edition, Low; Bell & Daldy, London, 1867, 121 pp. It was also listed in the *PC* on Dec. 10 and advertised in the *Spect* on Dec. 21. It was reissued, 1868. The first edition was issued by Ticknor & Fields, Boston, 1867, 19.5 cm., 185 pp., illustrated, $1.50 in green, purple, or blue cloth, with brown endpapers. It was listed in *ALG&PC* (fortnightly) on Nov. 15, and a Harvard copy was received on Oct. 25. Nine of the ten pieces were previously issued by Nimmo, Edinburgh, in *Stories About Our Dogs* (1865) and in *Daisy's First Winter, etc.* (1867). Records show 2,508 copies were printed and bound Oct. 22–Nov. 8. There was a second printing of 1,060 copies on Jan. 2, 1868.

96 JOHANN H.D. ZSCHOKKE ***The Princess of Brunswick-Wolfenbüttel, and Other Tales.*** 16mo. 1/6 sewed, 2/0 flexible cloth Nov. 23 (*Spect*)

German Authors No. 6. This is 1867, 16 cm., 323 pp., containing three pieces, translated by M. A. Faber. *Die Prinzessin von Wolfenbüttel* was issued in Zurich, 1804, anonymously. The title story appeared as the tenth and last story in *Vignetten*, Basel, 1801. It was translated into French in 1806, and Henry Colburn, London, issued *Christina*, 2 vols.,1808, a translation of a French version. *Tales by Zschokke* was issued by Leypoldt & Holt, New York, in 1867, 16mo, $1.25 bevelled boards, advertised in the *Nation* on Dec. 12 and in the *New-York Times* on Dec. 14, 1867.

An ad in the Ath *on Apr. 4, 1868, stated that Low would move on Apr. 6 to the Crown Buildings, 188 Fleet Street.*

97 HARRIET B. STOWE *The Chimney-Corner.* 12mo. 1/o boards, 3/6 cloth Feb. 29 (*Spect*)

This is 1868, Low, and Bell & Daldy, 17 cm., 194 pp., printed boards, also listed in *PC* on Mar. 15. The 3/6 was in green or red cloth, bevelled covers and brown endpapers, all edges gilt, with a 24-page catalog (May 1868), listed in the *Ath* and *Spect* on Mar. 14 and in *PC* on Apr. 1, 1868. The catalog dated May 1868 is given by *BAL* and must refer to a later binding up. Actually Low thought of issuing this in 1866 shortly after it ended in the *Atlantic Monthly*, where it ran Jan. 1865–Sept. 1866, and they advertised it in the *Spect* on Nov. 10, 1866!

The first American edition was issued by Ticknor & Fields, Boston, 1868, 18.5 cm., 311 pp., by Christopher Crowfield, in green or purple cloth with brown endpapers. They printed 2,434 copies and bound them up, Feb. 17–Mar. 9, 1868. It was deposited on Mar. 12 and listed in *ALG&PC* on Apr. 1. The *Atlantic Monthly* serial contained also *Little Foxes*, which does not appear in this book edition.

98 CUTHBERT BEDE (EDWARD BRADLEY) *The White Wife; with Other Stories.* Fcp 8vo. Illustrated. 2/6 boards May 23 (*Ath*)

This is 1868, 252 pp., three plates. The first edition was issued by Low 1865

(1864), 18.5 cm., 252 pp., illustrated by Bede, 6/o, blue cloth and dark brown endpapers, listed in the *Ath* on Nov. 12, 1864.

99 (F. W. ROBINSON) *Female Life in Prison.* Cheap edition. 12mo. 2/6 boards May 23 (*Spect*)

This is 1868, with "Low's Popular Series" on the cover. This was the name given to their 2/6 yellowbacks. The first edition was issued by Hurst & Blackett, London, 2 vols., 1862, p 8vo, 21/o, by A Prison Matron, listed in the *Ath* on June 7. Low issued the third edition, revised, 1863 (1862), 18.5 cm.; and issued a new edition, revised (the fourth), 1864, Cr 8vo, 325 pp., 5/o cloth, in the *Favourite Library of Popular Books* No. 15. The latter was listed in the *Reader* on Nov. 7, 1863, as "Just ready" and advertised in the *Spect* on Dec. 5, 1863.

100 (ANNE J. ROBERTSON) *Myself and My Relatives.* 12mo. 2/6 boards May 23 (*Spect*)

The first edition was issued by Low, 1863 (1862), Cr 8vo, 359 pp., 5/o, listed in the *Ath* on Dec. 13, 1862.

101 ELIHU BURRITT *Jonas Webb, His Life, Labours, and Worth.* Fcp 8vo. Portrait. 1/o sewed May 30 (*Ath*)

This is 1868, 48 pp. The first edition was *A Walk From London to John O'Groats*, issued by Low, 1864, 19.5 cm., 420 pp., illustrated, 12/0, advertised in the *Spect* on Dec. 5, 1863, as "Just ready." It was issued in the United States by Charles Scribner, New York, 1864, printed in London, 420 pp., illustrated. Low issued a second edition of *A Walk . . .*, 1864, 19 cm., portrait, listed in the *Ath* on Apr. 16.

102 GOTTHOLD E. LESSING *Nathan the Wise and Emilia Galotti.* 16mo, 1/6 sewed, 2/0 flexible cloth   July 11 (*Spect*)

German Authors No. 7. This is 1868, 16.5 cm., 298 pp., the first title translated by W. Taylor, and the second by C. L. Lewes. The first edition of *Nathan der Weise*, a dramatic poem, was issued in Berlin, 1779, 276 pp. It was issued in London by J. Fielding, 1781, 103 pp., translated by R. E. Raspie, etc. *Nathan the Wise* was issued by Trübner & Co., London; Leypoldt & Holt, New York, 1868, translated by Ellen Frothingham, noticed in the *Westminster Review* (quarterly) on Oct. 1, 1868; and it was issued by Leypoldt & Holt, New York, 1868, 16mo, $1.75 in bevelled boards, advertised in the *New-York Times* on Dec. 14, 1867, and advertised in the *Nation* on Dec. 12. Leypoldt & Holt issued a second edition, $1.75, advertised in the *Nation* on Mar. 12, 1868.

The second title was in *Trauerspiele*, Berlin, 1772, and was issued by C. F. Voss, Berlin, 1772, 16 cm., 152 pp. It was issued in England by Vernor & Hood, London, 1800, 16 cm., 75 pp., translated by Benjamin Thompson. It was issued in Philadelphia, etc., by Bradford & Inskeep, 1810.

103 (MARIA S. CUMMINS) *Haunted Hearts.* New edition. 16mo. 1/6 stiff cover, 2/0 cloth   Oct. 1 (*Ath*)

Copyright Editions of American Authors No. 1. An ad in the *Ath* on Sept. 19 said "On Oct. 1." The ad also stated that it was the book for which the battle for copyright of American works in England had been fought and won. By a recent judgment the

English copyright is established and the property therein secured to Low. An editorial note in *Notes & Queries* on Sept. 19, 1868, stated that the present title was at last announced after four years' suspension during successive actions in various chancery and appeals courts. The present edition is 1868, 16.5 cm., 342 pp. This new series was at times called *Cheap Editions of American Authors*, and at times *Copyright Cheap Editions of American Authors* (hereafter, simply *American Authors*). The first English edition was issued by Low, 2 vols., 1864, p 8vo, anonymous, 16/0, listed in the *Ath* and in the *Reader* on May 28. It was advertised in the *Reader* on Oct. 8, 1864, 2 vols., 16/0, as "This day." It was also issued by Routledge, Warne & Routledge, London and New York, 1864, Fcp 8vo, anonymous, 425 pp., 2/0 boards and in cloth, listed in both the *Ath* and *Reader* on June 18. This Routledge issue apparently started the copyright embroglio. Wolff had a copy of the Routledge cloth issue, in green with buff endpapers, and with ads paged 89–92, and unpaged at the back.

The first American edition was issued by J. E. Tilton & Co., Boston, 1864, 20 cm., anonymous, 554 pp., $2.00, advertised in the *New-York Times* on May 14 as "On May 25" and on May 25 as "Today." A new edition was advertised there on June 5 as "Today"; and a new edition was advertised there again on Oct. 5. It was reissued at $2.00 in 1865.

104 OLIVER W. HOLMES *The Guardian Angel.* New edition. 16mo. 1/6 limp boards, 2/0 cloth   Dec. 5 (*Ath*)

American Authors No. 2. This is 1869, 16.3 cm., 301 pp., in orange, printed, flexible boards, with 2 pp. of ads at the back. The first English edition was issued by Low, 2 vols., 1867, 19.5 cm., 16/0, listed in *PC* on Nov. 1 and in the *Ath* on Nov. 2. Low issued the second edition, 2 vols., Cr 8vo, 16/0, listed in the *Spect* on Feb. 22, 1868. Ward, Lock & Tyler, London, issued it in 1868, small format, 2/0 boards, listed in the *Spect* on May 2 and by the *Bks* as published in May, and given by the *BM*. Low went to chancery court to get an injunction against it since the last six chapters had been published first in Montreal. The court felt that it could not grant the injunction, but the vice-chancellor did so, and thus Ward, Lock & Tyler were prohibited from publishing the last six chapters! I've never seen it in any of their lists or ads.

The first American appearance was in the *Atlantic Monthly*, where it ran Jan.–Dec. 1867. I think it also ran in the *Weekly Tribune*, New York, as it was advertised by it as in an issue for Dec. 4, 1867. The first American book edition was issued by Ticknor & Fields, Boston, 1867, 18.5 cm., 420 pp., $2.00 in green, brick, blue, or purple cloth, the latter two bindings being on presentation copies in the Berg collection. It was advertised in the *New-York Times* on Nov. 5, 1867, as "This day" and listed in the *Ind* on Nov. 7. They issued a second edition, 1868, 18.5 cm., from the same type.

Low issued it in the *Rose Library* No. 22, 1876, 16mo, 301 pp., 1/0 sewed, renumbered No. 27 before Apr. 1877. It was listed in the *Spect* on Apr. 29. They issued it also, 1889, new edition, 12mo, 2/0 boards, 2/6 cloth, *Standard Novels* No. 5; and reissued it in *Standard Novels*, 1896, my copy, new edition, 18 cm., 301 pp., in pale blue pictorial boards, printed in red and black, with the series title on the front cover and spine, commercial ads on the blue endpapers and back cover, and with 2 pp. of publisher's ads at the back.

105 FRIEDRICH W. HACKLANDER *Behind the Counter.* Authorized edition. 16mo. 1/6 sewed, 2/0 flexible cloth   Dec. 12 (*Spect*)

German Authors No. 8. This is 1868, 15.5 cm., 367 pp., translated by Mary Howitt. The *U Cat* gives also Tauchnitz, Leipzig, 1867, 16mo, translated by Howitt. The first edition was *Handel und Wandel*, Berlin, 2 vols., 1850.

106 (JOHN R. HOULDING) *Australian Tales, and Sketches from Real Life.* p 8vo. 2/0   1868 (*Eng Cat*)

The first edition was issued by Low, 1868, 19 cm., 416 pp., 5/0, advertised in the *Ath* on Feb. 8 as "New books." Most of the pieces had appeared in the *Sydney Mail*. Low advertised it in the *Ath* on Apr. 2, 1870, as *Rural and City Life: Australian Tales and Sketches*, p 8vo, 6/0, as "This day." It was by Old Boomerang.

107 (P. R.) *A Few Hints as to Proving Wills, etc., Without Professional Assistance.* Fcp 8vo. 1/0 sewed   1868?

The first edition was issued by Low, 1866, Fcp 8vo, 32 pp., 1/0 cloth sewed, listed in the *Reader* on Apr. 7, by a probate court official. Low issued the fourth edition, enlarged, 1873, 64 pp., 1/0 sewed, listed in the *Ath* on Apr. 5; and issued a new edition in 1884, 16mo, 1/0 sewed; reissued, the same in 1885, both given by the *Eng Cat*. Low issued the ninth edition . . . , revised up to date, 1889, 16mo, 1/0 sewed, given by the *BM*; and issued the 13th edition in Sept. 1903, 12mo, 68 pp., 1/0 limp, given by the *Eng Cat*; and issued the 14th edition in Oct. 1905, the same.

Sampson Low, Son & Marston
Crown Buildings, 188 Fleet Street
1869

108 WILHELM HAUFF **Three Tales.** 16mo. 1/6 sewed, 2/o flexible cloth   Apr. 10 (*Spect*)

German Authors No. 9. This is 16mo, 326 pp., translated by M. A. Faber. It contains "The Beggar Girl of the Pont des Arts" (Die Bettlerin vom Pont des Arts), "The Cold Heart" (Das Kalte Herz), and "The Emperor's Picture" (Das Bild des Kaisers). The first story was issued as "Josephine; or, The Beggar of the Pont des Arts" in *Clarke's Home Library,* London (1844). The second title was issued in *The Juvenile Englishman's Library,* vol. 4, 1844. The *U Cat* gives "The Beggar-Girl of the Pont-des-Arts" (Morris & Willis, New York, 1844), pp. 10–25, in the *Minion Library.*

109 BAYARD TAYLOR **Views Afoot.** Revised by the author. 16mo. 1/6 limp boards, 2/o flexible cloth   Apr. 17 (*Ath* ad)

American Authors No. 4. This was also listed by the *Bks* as published in Apr. It is 1869, 16.5 cm., 318 pp., with the series title on the cover, and a prefatory note (Feb. 1869). The first edition was issued by Wiley & Putnam, New York, 2 vols., 1846, 19.5 cm., with a preface by N. P. Willis, in printed tan paper wrappers, with "Wiley & Putnam's Library of American Books Nos. 23 and 24" on the cover. It was deposited on Dec. 2, 1846, and listed in the *United States Magazine* (monthly) for Jan. 1847, and there is a known copy with an inscribed date (Dec. 15, 1846). It was imported by Wiley & Putnam, London, 2 vols., 16mo, and issued at 7/6, listed in the *Ath* on Jan. 30, 1847, and in *PC* on Feb. 1. Wiley & Putnam, New York, also issued it 2 vols.-in-1, 1846, 19.5 cm., in slate-gray cloth with cream endpapers. G. P. Putnam, New York and London, issued the eighth edition, 1848, $1.25 cloth, with an added prefatory note (Aug. 1848) and an added chapter 49. It was advertised in *Lit W* on Oct. 14 as "This week," and there is a presentation copy inscribed (Sept. 11, 1848). It was imported by Chapman, London, listed in the *Ath* on Nov. 11, 1848, and in *PC* on Nov. 15. Putnam issued the 11th edition, enlarged, 12mo, $1.25 cloth, advertised in *Lit W* on May 4, 1850, as "This week." G. P. Putnam & Co., New York, Low, London, issued it, 1856, 20th edition, revised, 18 cm., 490 pp., with a new chapter 1 and a new preface, advertised in *ALG&PC* on Dec. 22 as "Now ready" and listed Dec. 29, 1856. Low reissued it in *American Authors,* 1874, given by the *U Cat.*

110 MARIE NATHUSIUS **Joachim v. Kamern: Diary of a Poor Young Lady.** 16mo. 1/6 sewed, 2/o flexible cloth May 22 (*Spect*)

German Authors No. 10. This is 1869, 15.5 cm., 333 pp., translated by Miss Thompson. *Joachim von Kamern* was first issued at Halle, 1854, and there was a second edition, Halle, 2 vols., 1856–57. The present edition was called *German Authors* No. 12 by Tauchnitz, Leipzig, 1869. The first edition of the second title was *Tagebuch einer Armen Frauleins*, and the second edition was issued at Halle, 1853, 160 pp. Bentley, London, issued it as *Step by Step*, 1860; and Trübner & Co., London, issued it as *The Diary of a Poor Young Gentlewoman*, 1860, Fcp 8vo, anonymous, 224 pp., 3/6 cloth, translated by Anna Childs, listed in the *Spect* on May 12. *Diary of a Poor Young Lady* was also issued in London, 1869, translated by Emily Ritzerow, ed., with a preface by J. H. Bryant.

111   ELIZABETH S. PHELPS, later WARD
The Gates Ajar. 32mo. 1/0 cloth
May 29 (*Spect*)

Minion Series No. 1. This is the first British edition, 1869. The *Eng Cat* gives 32mo, 1/0, 0/9, 0/6, 0/4, issued by Low in 1869–70. The 0/4 sewed was listed in the *Bks* for May 1870. Low issued the fourth edition (1870), 16mo, 174 pp., illustrated, 14/0, advertised in the *Ath* on Jan. 8, 1870. It was also issued by J. Burns, London, 1869, listed in *PC* on Nov. 1. It was also issued by Ward, Lock & Tyler, London (1870), 12mo, 155 pp., 1/0 sewed, *Lily Series* No. 4, listed in the *Spect* on Jan. 29; and reissued, 20th thousand, no date, with 30 pp. of ads and with ads on the endpapers, in glazed colored wrappers in brown and green. It was also issued by George Routledge & Sons, London and New York, as follows: Fcp 8vo, 248 pp., illustrated, 3/6, listed in the *Spect* on Mar. 5, 1870, and in the *Ath* on Mar. 15; 1/0 illustrated, 192 pp., 0/6 cloth, one illustration, 144 pp., 0/4 sewed, 144 pp., one illustration, all three listed in the *Bks* for May 1870; 2/0 cloth, 150 pp., illustrated, listed in the *Spect* on June 11, 1870.

The first edition was issued by Fields, Osgood & Co., Boston, 1869, 18.5 cm., 248 pp., $1.50 cloth, green, purple, or terra-cotta, with brown endpapers. Records show 1,506 copies were bound Nov. 13 and 14, 1868, and 1,020 copies were bound Dec. 30, 1868–Jan. 2, 1869. It was deposited Nov. 17, 1868, and advertised in the *New-York Times* on Nov. 18 as "This day" and listed in the *Nation* on Nov. 19. The 20th thousand, $1.50, was advertised on May 12, 1869; and the 50th thousand, $1.50, was advertised Mar. 19, 1870, both in the *New-York Times*. This was one of the best-selling books of the nineteenth century, but not surpassing *Uncle Tom's Cabin* however.

112   JOSIAH G. HOLLAND   *Kathrina.*
16mo. 1/6 limp boards, 2/0 flexible cloth
June 5 (*Spect*)

American Authors No. 5. This is the first British edition, 1869, 16 cm., 287 pp.; reissued, 1874, the same. It is a poem. The first edition was issued by Charles Scribner & Co., New York, 1867, 19.5 cm., 287 pp., $1.50 and $2.50, advertised in the *New-York Times* on Sept. 14 as "On Sept. 21" and on Sept. 21 as "This day." It was listed in the *Ind* on Sept. 26. The 20th thousand was advertised in the *Nation* on Nov. 14, 1867, as "Now ready"; and the 40th thousand was advertised there on Dec. 13, 1868, $1.50 and $2.50, as "Just ready."

113   MARY E. DODGE   *Hans Brinker; or, The Silver Skates.* New edition, revised, 16mo, 1/6 limp boards, 2/0 flexible cloth
July 31 (*Ath*)

American Authors No. 6. This probably has 303 pp. Low issued the first British edition, 1867, 12mo, illustrated, 3/6, with a preface by W.H.G. Kingston, with the title *Silver Skates*. It was listed in the *Ath* on Sept. 14; and reissued in 1869, 3/6, listed in the *Spect* on Feb. 13. Low issued a new edition, revised by the author, 1875, 19 cm., 391 pp., illustrated, 7/6 in decorated green cloth, listed in the *Spect* on Oct. 30. Low issued it in the *Rose Library* in 1876, 1/0 sewed, 2/6 cloth, listed in the *Spect* on Apr. 29; and also reissued it in *American*

Authors, 1876, revised by the author, 17 cm., 303 pp. They issued it in 1880, imperial square, illustrated, 5/o, listed in the *Spect* on Feb. 28.

The first edition was issued by James O'Kane, New York, 1866, 19 cm., 347 pp., frontispiece and four full-page illustrations. It was issued in several colors of cloth with yellow endpapers, with 2 or 4 pp. of ads at the back. It was listed in the *Nation* on Jan. 18, 1866. They issued a third edition in 1867.

114 FERDINAND FREILIGRATH *Poems.* From the German of Ferdinand Freiligrath. Copyright edition. 16mo. 1/6 sewed, 2/o flexible cloth   Oct. 9 (*Spect*)

German Authors No. 11. This is 1869, 15.5 cm., 241 pp., edited by the author's daughter. It was reissued, 1871, the same, the second copyright edition, enlarged, 16 cm., 260 pp. The first edition was *Gedichte*, issued at Stuttgart & Tübingen, 1838, 17 cm., 446 pp.

115 E.N.G. *Infant Life....* 18cm., 1/o   Oct. 9 (*Spect*)

This is the first edition, 1869, 54 pp., with an introduction by E. Wilson.

116 GEORGE WASHINGTON *Washington's Words to Intending English Emigrants to America.* 12mo. 1/o   Oct. 30 (*Spect*)

This is 1870, with an introduction and appendix by Elihu Burritt.

117 FATHER HYACINTHE (CHARLES J.M. LOYSON) *Peace.* 8vo. 1/o   Nov. 13 (*Spect*)

The second edition was issued in Paris, 1869, *La Paix*, 8vo, 30 pp.

118 ELIZABETH S. PHELPS, later WARD *Men, Women, and Ghosts.* 16mo. 1/6 boards, 2/o cloth   Nov. 13 (*Ath*)

American Authors No. 7. This is the first British edition, 1869, 16 cm., 276 pp., in printed blue boards for the 1/6 issue. The first edition was issued by Fields, Osgood & Co., Boston; etc., 1869, 18.5 cm., 334 pp., $1.50 in green, purple, or terra-cotta cloth with brown endpapers. It contains ten pieces. Records show 3,000 copies were bound May 7–11; a second printing of 3,600 copies was bound May 11–17. It was deposited on May 11, advertised in the *New-York Times* on May 12, and listed in the *Nation* on May 20.

119 PAUL HEYSE *Gabriel.* 16mo. 1/6 sewed, 2/o flexible cloth   1869?

German Authors No. 12. This may have been issued in early 1870, but probably before Feb. 5, 1870, as No. 13 in the series was listed then in the *Ath*. "Vetter Gabriel" was one of the stories in *Moralische Novellen*, issued in Berlin, 1869, 15 cm., 411 pp. It contained also "Die Beiden Schwestern," "Am Todten See," and others.

Sampson Low, Son & Marston
Crown Buildings, 188 Fleet Street
1870

120 PAUL HEYSE *The Dead Lake, and Other Tales.* Authorized edition. 16mo. 1/6 sewed, 2/0 flexible cloth   Feb. 5 (*Ath*)

German Authors No. 13. This is 1870, 16 cm., 312 pp., containing four pieces, translated by Mary Wilson. "Am Todten See" was one of the Stories in *Moralische Novellen*, issued in Berlin, 1869, 15 cm., 411 pp. (See Item 119 in 1869.)

121 SARAH F. SMILEY *Who Is He?* 32mo. 1/0 cloth   Feb. 5 (*Spect*)

Minion Series. This is 1870. The first edition was issued by J. B. Lippincott & Co., Philadelphia, 1868, 17.5 cm., 102 pp. The first British edition was F. B. Kitto, London, 1869, 17 cm., 104 pp.

122 EDWARD H. HALL *The Great West.* [New edition.] Map. 1/0 sewed   Feb. (*Bks*)

This was also advertised by Low in the *Ath* on July 9, 1870, revised edition, map, 1/0 sewed. Low first issued it, 1867, 17.5 cm., 127 pp., with the map. The first edition was issued by the Tribune Office, New York, 1864, 18.5 cm., 89 pp., frontispiece (folding map); and was issued by D. Appleton & Co., New York, 1865, 16mo, 198 pp., with the folding map; they also issued it (1866?), 17.5 cm., 181 pp., with the map. This was variously described as a railroad, steamboat, and stage guide; as a handbook for travellers, miners, and emigrants; as an emigrant's, settler's, and traveller's guide to California, Oregon, Nebraska, etc.; and as a handbook to the Western, Northwestern, and Pacific states and territories.

123 RALPH W. EMERSON *Society and Solitude. Twelve Chapters.* 16mo. 1/6 limp boards, 2/0 flexible cloth   Mar. 5 (*Ath*)

American Authors No. 8. This is the first British edition, 1870, 16 cm., 284 pp., given by the *BM* and the *U Cat*. Brussel gives it as having 124 pp.! All are in reference to the *American Authors* edition. Brussel describes the 2/0 issue as in blue cloth with buff endpapers, and states that it was received by the *BM* on Mar. 3, 1870. It was also listed in the *Spect* on Mar. 5, 1870. The first American edition was issued by Fields, Osgood & Co., Boston, 1870, 18 cm., 300 pp., deposited on Mar. 10, advertised in the *Nation* on Mar. 10, noticed in the *Ind* on Mar. 17, and listed in *ALG&PC* (fortnightly) on Mar. 15.

124 ROBERT BLACK *The Blackbird of Baden, and Other Stories.* [New edition.] 2/0 boards   Mar. 12 (*Ath* ad)

The first edition was issued by Low, 1869, 19 cm., 297 pp., 6/0, listed in the *Ath* on May 1.

125 KARL F. GUTZKOW *Through Night to Light.* 16mo. 1/6 sewed, 2/0 flexible cloth   Apr. 9 (*Ath*)

German Authors No. 14. This is 1870, 15.5 cm., 312 pp., translated by Mrs. Faber.

The first edition was issued at Stuttgart, 1870, where it was issued as vol. 1 of the 2-vol. issue of *Lebensbilder*. The *U Cat* gives it as *Durch Nacht zum Licht*, 20 cm., 318 pp., but gives no mention of the 2-vol. issue. *Through Light to Night* (*sic*) by Spielhagen, a different work, was listed in *Harper's New Monthly Magazine* for Feb. 1870, as issued by Leypoldt & Holt, New York. Spielhagen was the author of *Durch Nacht zum Licht*, issued as part 2 of *Problematische Naturen*, the third edition of which was issued in 3 vols., in Berlin, 1866, 17 cm.

126 ELIZABETH S. PHELPS, later WARD *Hedged In.* 16mo. 1/6 boards, 2/0 cloth
Apr. 16 (*Ath*)

American Authors No. 9. Low issued the first British edition, 1870, 17.5 cm., 292 pp., 3/6 cloth, with 16 pp. of ads at the back. It was supposed to be published simultaneously in London and Boston by arrangement with the author. It was listed in the *Ath* on Mar. 13 and in *PC* on Apr. 1. Low reissued it, 1871, 297 pp. The first American edition was issued by Fields, Osgood & Co., Boston, 1870, 18.5 cm., 295 pp., $1.50 in brown, green, purple, or terra-cotta cloth with brown endpapers. There was a first printing of 6,000 copies, bound Mar. 2–5. There were ten printings of 15,162 copies with the imprint 1870. It was deposited on Mar. 4, advertised in the *New-York Times* on Mar. 5 as "This day," and listed in *ALG&PC* (fortnightly) on Mar. 15. They issued the ninth edition, advertised in the *New-York Times* on Mar. 19, 1870.

127 (ELIZABETH PRENTISS) *The Little Preacher.* 32mo. 1/0 cloth   May 7 (*Spect*)
Minion Series. This is the first British edition, 1870. The first edition was issued by A.D.F. Randolph, New York, 1869, anonymous, 223 pp., frontispiece.

128 LOUISA M. ALCOTT *An Old-Fashioned Girl.* 16mo. 1/6 boards, 2/0 cloth
June 25 (*Ath*)

American Authors No. 10. This is 1870, 16 cm., 314 pp. The first six chapters ran in *Merry's Museum*, July–Dec. 1869. The first British book edition was issued by Low, 1870, Fcp 8vo, 314 pp., 3/6 cloth, listed in the *Ath* and *Spect* on Apr. 2 and in *PC* on Apr. 15. Ward, Lock & Tyler issued it in 1871, 12mo, 1/0, listed in the *Spect* on Feb. 4. Low advertised in *PC* on Feb. 15, 1871, that the Ward, Lock edition had been withdrawn as an infringement of copyright. *BAL* states that no ads or listing of the Ward, Lock issue has been found, but I've found the present listing. Low reissued it in this series in 1872, the same, listed in the *Ath* on May 11; and reissued it, the same, 1874, 13th edition, listed in the *Bks* for Aug. Low issued it in 1888, new edition, 2/0. Low issued it in the *Rose Library* No. 6, 1874, 314 pp., 1/0 sewed, 2/6 cloth, listed in the *Ath* on Oct. 24.

The first edition was issued by Roberts Bros., Boston, 1870, 17 cm., 378 pp., with a double frontispiece and two illustrations, $1.50 in several colored cloths with brown or white endpapers. There are publisher's ads, paged (1)–8 (Mar. 1870) at the back. It was deposited on Apr. 20 and advertised in the *New-York Times* on Mar. 19 as "On Apr. 1" and on Apr. 2 as "This day." It was listed in the *Christian Union* on Apr. 9. The 30th thousand was advertised in the *New-York Times* on May 26; and the 34th thousand was advertised in the *Nation*, $1.50, on Aug. 4.

129 JOHN MACGREGOR *A Thousand Miles in the Rob Roy Canoe.* Sixth edition.
12mo. Illustrated, folding map.
2/6 boards   July 23 (*Spect*)

This is my copy, 1870, 17.6 cm., 255 pp., with an appendix on pp. (239)–255, and page (256) with publisher's ads. There is a preface (July 1870), a frontispiece and textual illustrations, with the folding map inserted before the appendix, and a publisher's catalog paged (1)–16 (Nov. 1869) at the back. It is in yellow pictorial boards, printed in red, blue, and black with plain pale yellow endpapers, with a publisher's ad on the back cover. The first edition was issued by Low, 1866, 18 cm., 318 pp., illustrated, 5/0, listed in the *Ath* on Jan. 20. Low issued the second and third editions, 1866, the same, the second listed in the *Reader* on Apr. 21, and the third advertised in the *Spect* on May 12 as "Now ready." Low issued the tenth edition, 1878, a yellowback, illustrated, with the folding map; and he issued a new edition in 1879, 3/6, listed in the *Spect* on Aug. 16. Low issued the 13th edition, 1881; and the 18th edition, in 1891, p 8vo, 2/6, given by the *Eng Cat* as issued in Oct. The fifth edition had a joint imprint with Roberts Bros., Boston, 1867, 18 cm., 318 pp., illustrated, with the folding map, sold in the United States for $2.50, advertised in the *New-York Times* on Sept. 17 as "Ready." Roberts Bros. issued it in 1871, printed in England, listed in *ALG&PC* on Jan. 15, 1871.

130 VICTOR HUGO *Toilers of the Sea.*
12mo. 2/6 boards   Aug. 6 (*Ath* ad)

This was advertised in the *Ath* on July 23, 2/6 boards, "In a few days"; and advertised in the *Spect* on July 30, 2/6 boards, "Just ready." It was listed in the *Ath* and *Spect* on Aug. 13, 12mo, 2/0; and listed in the *Ath* and *Spect* on Sept. 10, 2/6, the former giving it as limp cloth. Low issued the first British edition, 1866, 3 vols., 19.5 cm., 24/0, authorized translation by Moy Thomas, with ads (Mar. 20, 1866) and a 16-page catalog (Feb. 1, 1866) at the back of vol. 3. It was issued simultaneously in London and Paris. It was listed in the *Ath* on Mar. 31 and advertised in the *Spect* on Mar. 24 as "This week." Low issued the second and third editions, 3 vols., 1866, 24/0, the second edition advertised in the *Spect* on May 12 as "Now ready"; and the third edition was advertised there on June

30 as "This day" and listed in the *Reader* on June 30. Low issued it in 1 vol. in 1867, new edition, Cr 8vo, two illustrations by Doré, 6/0, listed in the *Spect* on Jan. 5, 1867; and issued it, 1869, 8vo, illustrated, 10/6, listed in the *Spect* on Oct. 9. Low reissued the present edition, 1872, eighth edition, 402 pp., 2/0 boards, listed in the *Ath* on June 22. Sadleir had a copy of this 2/0 yellowback, 1875, tenth edition, in cream pictorial boards, large format. Low reissued the 2/0 yellowback in 1885, advertised in the *Ath* on May 30.

The first edition was *Les Travailleurs de la Mer*, issued in Bruxelles and Paris, 3 vols., 1866, 23 cm. The Bruxelles edition was reviewed in the *Ath* on Mar. 24 and in the *Spect* on Mar. 31. The Bruxelles edition was issued in New York by F.W. Christern; A. Lacroix et Cie., Bruxelles, 1866, 8vo, $2.00, listed in the *Nation* on Mar. 28.

In the United States, it ran in the *Semi-Monthly Tribune*, New York, for about 8 weeks, beginning on May 5, 1866. The first American edition in English was issued by Harper & Bros., New York, 1866, 24 cm., 155 pp., frontispiece (portrait), $.75 paper, advertised in the *New-York Times* on Apr. 10 as "This day" and listed in the *Nation* on Apr. 19 and in the *ALG&PC* (fortnightly) on Apr. 16. The 9th thousand was advertised in the *New-York Times* on Apr. 13; and Harpers reissued it also, the same, listed in the *Nation* for July 12, 1866.

131 PHINEAS T. BARNUM *Struggles and Triumphs.* [New edition.] Illustrated.
2/6 boards   Sept. 3 (*Ath*)

The first British edition was issued by Low, 1869, 8vo, 780 pp., illustrated, 12/0, listed in the *Ath* on Nov. 6. It was listed in the *Spect* on Jan. 22, 1870, 10/6, possibly a second edition. Barnum must have added a few pages almost every year as it was reissued almost every year from 1871 to 1889, mainly by Buffalo publishers, and always called an update. The first Ameri-

can edition was issued by J. B. Burr & Co., Hartford, 1869, 22 cm., 780 pp., illustrated, listed in the *Ind* on Oct. 21, and in the *ALG&PC* (fortnightly) on Nov. 1.
See 1854

132 JAMES GILL ***The Emigrant's Guide to the South African Diamond Fields.*** 12mo. o/6   Oct. 29 (*Ath* ad)

This is the first edition, 1870, 18 cm., 16 pp., frontispiece (map).

Sampson Low, Marston, Low & Searle
Crown Buildings, 188 Fleet Street
1871

The new style for the company first appeared in PC *on Aug. 15.*

133 OLIVER W. HOLMES *Mechanism in Thought and Morals.* 16mo. 1/6 Jan. 28 (*Ath* ad)

The ad in the *Ath* said "This day," 1/6 cloth. It is the first British edition, 1871, 16 cm., 124 pp., in purple cloth. Low issued the second edition in 1876, 12mo, 1/6, listed in the *Spect* on Jan. 29; and issued the third edition, 1888, 124 pp. The first American edition was issued by James R. Osgood & Co., Boston, 1871, 17.5 cm., 101 pp., $1.00 in green cloth, an address given before the Phi Beta Kappa Society of Harvard on June 29, 1870, listed in the *Nation* on Feb. 16. Osgood issued the second edition, 1871, in plum cloth; and Houghton, Osgood & Co., Boston, issued the fifth edition, 1879.

134 GEORG EBERS *An Egyptian Princess.* 2 vols. Authorized edition. 16mo. 1/6 sewed, 2/0 flexible cloth each Feb. 25 (*Ath*)

German Authors No. 15. This is 1870, 71, 16 cm., translated by Eleanor Grove, the first edition in English. The first edition was *Eine Aegyptische Königstochter*, issued at Stuttgart, 3 vols., 1864. The first American edition was *The Daughter of an Egyptian King*, issued by J. B. Lippincott & Co., Philadelphia, 1871, 19 cm., 368 pp., translated by Henry Reed, and reissued 1878, 80, 81, etc.

135 HARRIET B. STOWE *Old Town Folks.* 16mo. 2/6 boards, 3/0 limp cloth Apr. 29 (*Ath*)

American Authors No. 12. The first American edition was issued by Fields, Osgood & Co., Boston, 1869, 19.5 cm., 608 pp., $2.00 in green or plum cloth; and in red, blue, or terra-cotta cloth with brown endpapers. It has 2 pp. of ads (May 1, 1869) at the back of vol. 3. The first printing of 10,000 copies was bound May 7–15; and there were 12 printings of 32,320 copies in 1869. It was deposited on May 13 and advertised in the *New-York Times* on May 8 as "On May 15" and on May 15 as "This day." There is a known presentation copy with an inscribed date of June 1. The 15th thousand, $2.00, was advertised in the *New-York Times* on June 10 as "Now ready."

It was issued by Tauchnitz, Leipzig, 2 vols., 1869, copyright edition, listed in the *Allgemeine Bibliographie* on June 24. It was issued in Canada by Dawson Bros., Montreal; etc., 1869, 547 pp.

The first British edition was issued by Low, 3 vols., 1869, 19.5 cm., 31/6 in purple cloth with cream endpapers. It was deposited on May 13 and listed in the *Ath* on May 15. Low issued the second and third editions in 3 vols., 1869, the first advertised in the *Spect* on June 5 as "This day" and the second advertised there on Aug. 14 as "This day." Low issued a new edition (the fourth), 1870, 12mo, 554 pp., 6/0, listed in the *Ath* on Dec. 18, 1869; and issued it, 12mo, 3/6, listed in the *Spect* on Dec. 23, 1871; and issued it in 1896, 2/0, listed in *PC* on June 13.

136 JAMES R. LOWELL *My Study Windows.* Second edition. 16mo. 1/6 limp boards, 2/0 flexible cloth   May 6 (*Ath*)

American Authors No. 13. This is 1871, 16 cm., 318 pp. The first British edition was issued by Low, 1871, Cr 8vo, 318 pp., 9/0, printed from 200 sets of sheets sent to Low by Osgood, from the second American printing. This first edition was listed in the *Ath* on Mar. 11. Low issued it (1876) in the *Rose Library* No. 20, 16.5 cm., 318 pp., 1/0 sewed, 2/6 cloth, the fifth edition, listed in the *Spect* on Mar. 11. It was re-numbered to No. 26 before Apr. 1877. Low reissued it in the *Rose Library*, no date, eighth edition.

The first American edition was issued by James R. Osgood & Co., Boston, 1871, 18.5 cm., 433 pp., $2.00, advertised in the *New-York Times* on Jan. 28 as "This day" and listed in the *Nation* on Feb. 9.

137 ANONYMOUS *Smoking and Drinking.* Cr 8vo, 0/6 sewed   July 8 (*Ath* ad)

The ad in the *Ath* said "Ready." This is the first edition, 1871, with a chapter on to-bacco by B. W. Richardson. The book is by Medicus.

138 (JOHN CUMMING) *Bee-Keeping.* Second edition. 12mo. Illustrated. 2/6 boards   July 22 (*Ath* ad)

This is 1871, 17.5 cm., 224 pp., by the Times' Bee-Master. It has a new preface. The first edition was issued by Low, 1864, 18 cm., 224 pp., illustrated, 5/0, listed in the *Ath* on Oct. 8. Low advertised the 3rd thousand, illustrated, 5/0, on Apr. 7, 1866.

139 CHARLES D. WARNER *My Summer in a Garden.* 16mo. 1/6 limp boards, 2/0 flexible cloth   Aug. 5 (*Ath*)

American Authors No. 14. This is the first British edition, 1871, 16 cm., 249 pp., with an introduction by H. W. Beecher. Low is-sued it, 1876, 16mo, 1/0 sewed, as *Rose Library* No. 21, renumbered No. 28 before Apr. 1877. It was listed in the *Spect* on Apr. 29. Low issued it at 2/0 in 1890, and at 2/6 in 1894. Ward, Lock & Tyler, London, is-sued it as *Pusley* (1873), 1/0 sewed, listed in the *Ath* on Jan. 25. Low complained in a letter to the *Ath* on June 7, 1873, about Ward, Lock's reaping the advantage of Low's publication, which Low had paid for, although Low was helpless as the work was not copyrighted. It was issued by Ad-ams, Stevenson & Co., Toronto, 1871, 18 cm., 86 pp.

The first edition was issued by Fields, Osgood & Co., Boston, 1871, 18 cm., 183 pp., $1.00 in green, purple or terra-cotta cloth. It is a series of articles written for the *Hartford Evening Press*. Records show 1,540 copies were bound by Nov. 23, 1870, and 1,020 copies in a second printing were bound Dec. 20–23, 1870. It was adver-tised in the *New-York Times* on Nov. 28, 1870, as "This day" and listed in the *Nation* on Dec. 1. They issued it at $3.00, listed in the *Nation* on Jan. 25, 1872; and issued a new edition, $1.50, advertised in the *New-York Times* on Nov. 17, 1877.

140 JEAN PAUL RICHTER *Flower, Fruit, and Thorn Pieces.* 2 vols. 16mo. 1/6 sewed, 2/0 flexible cloth each Sept. 23 (*Ath*)

German Authors No. 16. This is 1871, 16 cm., translated by E. H. Noel. The first edition was *Blumen, Frucht, und Dornen Stücke*, issued in Berlin, 3 vols., 1796–97, 17.5 cm. The first British edition was is-sued by William Smith, London, 2 vols., 1845, 16.5 cm., translated by E. H. Noel, listed in the *Spect* on Dec. 7, 1844. In the

United States it was issued by J. Munroe & Co., Boston, 2 vols., 1845, 17.5 cm., translated by Noel, and reviewed in *Graham's American Monthly Magazine* for June 1845.

141 ANONYMOUS ***The St. James's Christmas Box.*** Illustrated. 1/0 sewed Oct.?

This was advertised in the *Ath* on Sept. 23 as "Early in Oct." It is the Christmas number of *St. James's Magazine*.

Sampson Low, Marston, Low & Searle
Crown Buildings, 188 Fleet Street
1872

142 CHARLES MACKESON, ed. *Low's Handbook to the Charities of London.* 12mo. 1/o sewed Jan. 20 (*Ath* ad)

The ad in the *Ath* said "Just ready." This began the annual issue of this title. I have not found when it first appeared but later Low ads indicate that it began in 1839. It was issued in 1850, Fcp 8vo, edited by Sampson Low, Jr., 474 pp., frontispiece, 10/6, listed in the *Spect* on June 22. The 1854 issue was 2/6 sewed, listed in the *Spect* on Jan. 24, 1854. Low acted as editor through the 1867 issue, which was 1/o sewed, 1/6 limp cloth, listed in the *Spect* on Apr. 27. The 1870 edition was edited by Charles Mackeson, 198 pp., 5/o, issued about Oct. 1, and with an appendix issued separately at 1/o limp cloth. It appeared annually at 1/o sewed, 1/6 cloth until 1877, when, I think, it began to appear passim. There were editions in 1880, 1882, 1886–87, 1890, 1892, 1896–97, 1902, and 1904. Mackeson was the editor, ending probably with the 1882 edition. By the 1896–97 edition the editor was H. R. Dumville. The 1902 issue had 288 pp., and the 1904 issue had 244 pp.

143 ANONYMOUS *A Few Lines on the Hunter, the Charger, and the Roadster.* Fcp 8vo. 1/o limp boards Jan. 27(*Spect*)

This is the first edition, 1872, with 64 pp., by Woodman.

144 JAMES DYEHARD, ed. *The Queer Things of the Service.* Cr 8vo. Illustrated. 2/6 boards Jan. 27 (*Ath*)

This is the first edition, 1872, with 88 pp.

145 HARRIET B. STOWE *Pink and White Tyranny.* [New edition.] 16mo. 1/6 limp boards, 2/o flexible cloth Feb. 10 (*Ath*)

American Authors No. 15. The first British edition was issued by Low, 1871, 17.5 cm., 3/6 cloth, brown or red, gray endpapers, all edges gilt, with a 16-page catalog (Sept. 1870) at the back. It was deposited on July 27 and listed in the *Ath* on June 24 and in *PC* on July 1.

In the United States it ran in *Old and New* (Boston), Aug. 1870–Aug. 1871, and the first American book edition was issued by Roberts Bros., Boston, 1871, 18 cm., 331 pp., illustrated, $1.50 in blue, green, terra-cotta, or purple cloth with brown endpapers. There is in some copies an 8-page catalog (Summer 1871), and in other copies 4 pp. of ads plus the catalog (Holiday books for 1871–72). It was advertised in the *New-York Times* on June 21 as "On July 1" and advertised in the *Nation* on June 22 as "On July 1." They issued the 15th thousand (third edition), advertised as "On July 20"; and issued a new edition, 16mo, $1.25 cloth and $.50 paper, listed in the *Nation* on Apr. 2, 1885. It was issued in Canada by W. E. Tunis, Clifton, 1871.

146 (WILLIAM S. LINDSAY) *The Log of My Leisure Hours.* Second edition. p 8vo. Frontispiece. 2/0 boards   Feb. 10 (*Ath*)

This is 1872, with 309 pp. The first edition was issued by Low, 3 vols., 1868, 19.5 cm., 24/0, by An Old Sailor, listed in the *Ath* on Oct. 24. Low issued it, 1871, frontispiece, 6/0, advertised in the *Ath* on Jan. 7, 1871.

147 JOSEPH V. VON SCHEFFEL *Ekkehard.* 2 vols. Authorized edition. 16mo. 1/6 sewed, 2/0 flexible cloth each   Apr. 13 (*Spect*)

German Authors No. 17. This is 1872, 16.5 cm., translated by Sofie Delffs. The first edition was issued in Frankfurt, 1855, 463 pp. William S. Gottsberger, New York, issued it in 2 vols. in 1890, $.80 paper and $1.50 cloth, advertised in the *New-York Times* on Apr. 12 as "This day."

148 JOHN MACGREGOR *The Rob Roy on the Baltic.* [New edition.] 12mo. 2/6 boards   Apr. 23 (*Spect*)

This has 274 pp. The first edition was issued by Low, 1867, 312 pp., illustrated, maps, music, 5/0, listed in the *Ath* on Dec. 15, 1866. The second edition was issued by Low, London; Roberts Bros., Boston, 1867, 12mo, 316 pp., illustrated, maps, 5/0, listed in the *Spect* on Nov. 2, 1867. The present edition may have been the third edition, 2/6, advertised in the *Ath* on Nov. 23, 1872. Low issued it in 1874, 12mo, 2/6, listed in the *Spect* on June 20; and issued the fifth edition, 12mo, 3/6, listed in the *Spect* on Aug. 16, 1879; and issued the ninth edition, p 8vo, 2/6, in Oct. 1892, given by the *Eng. Cat.*

In the United States it was issued by Roberts Bros., Boston, 1867, second edition, 16mo, 316 pp., illustrated, $2.50 cloth, advertised in the *New-York Times* on Oct. 3 as "This day" and advertised in the *Nation* on Sept. 19 as "In a few days." They issued the third edition, with a preface dated 1872, 18 cm., 263 pp., illustrated, maps, music.

149 ROBERT G. HALIBURTON *A Review of British Diplomacy and Its Fruits.* 8vo. 1/0 sewed   May 18 (*Ath* ad)

The ad in the *Ath* said "Now ready." This is the first edition, 1872, a 32-page pamphlet, reprinted from *St. James's Magazine* and the *United Empire Review.*

150 ADELINE WHITNEY *We Girls.* 16mo. 1/6 limp boards, 2/0 flexible cloth Sept. 28 (*Ath*)

American Authors No. 16. This has 272 pp. The first edition was issued by Low, 1871, 12mo, 3/6 cloth, listed in the *Ath* on Nov. 19, 1870. Low issued it in 1888, new edition, p 8vo, 2/0. In the United States it ran in *Our Young Folks* (Fields, Osgood), Jan.–Dec. 1870. The first American book edition was issued by Fields, Osgood & Co., Boston, 1870, 19 cm., 215 pp., illustrated, $1.50, advertised in the *New-York Times* on Dec. 3, 1870, as "This day," and listed in the *Nation* on Dec. 22 and in *ALG&PC* (fortnightly) on Jan. 2, 1871.

151 EMMA M. PEARSON & LOUISA MACLAUGHLIN *Under the Red Cross.* 8vo. 2/0 sewed   Sept. (*Bks*)

This is the first edition, 1872, a series of papers reprinted from the *St. James's Magazine.*

152 LOUISA M. ALCOTT *Little Men.* [New edition.] 16mo. 1/6 limp boards, 2/0 flexible cloth   Oct. 12 (*Ath*)

American Authors No. 17. This has 328 pp. The first edition was issued by Low, 1871, 12mo, 332 pp., 3/6 cloth, listed in the *Ath* on May 20 and advertised there on May 13 as "On May 15." It was received at the *BM* on May 15. It was copyright in England, as Alcott was in England when it was published. Low reissued it in *American Authors* in 1873, listed in the *Ath* on Mar. 15; and issued it in the *Rose Library* No. 5, 1874, 16mo, 332 pp., 1/0 sewed, 2/6 cloth, listed in the *Ath* on Oct. 24; and they reissued it in the *Rose Library* in 1875, new edition, 332 pp., 1/0 sewed, listed in the *Spect* on Mar. 20; and issued it at 2/6 cloth, listed in the *Ath* on Nov. 20, 1875.

The first American edition was issued by Roberts Bros., Boston, 1871, 17.5 cm., 376 pp., four illustrations, $1.50 in plum or green cloth. It was deposited on June 12 and advertised in the *New-York Times* on May 20 as "On June 1"; and advertised on June 2 as "Postponed until June 5"; and advertised on June 6 as "Ready." It was listed in *ALG&PC* (fortnightly) on June 15. They issued the 38th thousand, advertised in the *New-York Times* on July 12, 1871.

153 E. MARLITT (EUGENIR JOHN) *The Princess of the Moor.* 2 vols. 16mo. 1/6 sewed, 2/0 flexible cloth each Oct. 19 (*Ath*)

German Authors No. 18. This is 1872, 16 cm., the first British edition. The first edition was issued in Leipzig, 2 vols., 1872, *Das Haideprinzesschen*. The first American edition was issued by J. B. Lippincott & Co., Philadelphia, 1872, 12mo, 408 pp., translated by Mrs. A. L. Wister, *The Little Moorland Princess*. It was listed in *PW* on Feb. 8 and in the *Ind* on Feb. 22. They issued the fourth edition in 1872, 12mo, $1.25, listed in the *Nation* on July 4.

154 LOUISA M. ALCOTT *Little Women.* [New edition.] 16mo. 1/6 limp boards, 2/0 flexible cloth Oct. 26 (*Ath*)

American Authors No. 18. This has 222 pp. It was reduced to 1/0 boards, 1/6 cloth, listed in the *Bks* for Nov. 1874. The first edition was issued by Roberts Bros., Boston, 1868, 17.5 cm., 341 pp., four illustrations, $1.50, deposited on Oct. 3, advertised in the *New-York Times* on Sept. 30 as "Just published" and listed in the *Nation* on Oct. 8. This was part 1 of what has come to be called *Little Women*. The following item gives part 2. Both parts at $3.00, the 14th

thousand, were advertised in the *Nation* on May 27, 1869; and the 17th thousand was advertised there on July 22, and the 23rd thousand on Aug. 7 as "Now ready."

The first British edition was issued by Low, 1869 (1868), 17 cm., 341 pp., illustrated, 3/6 in brown cloth, listed in the *Ath* on Dec. 12, 1868. This was part 1. Low issued it in the *Rose Library* No. 2 in 1874, 1/0 sewed, 2/6 cloth, listed in the *Ath* on Oct. 24. Low issued both parts in 1876, 2/6, listed in the *Spect* on Mar. 11; and issued both parts in 1880, 4to, illustrated, 18/0, listed in the *Spect* on Nov. 27.

155 LOUISA M. ALCOTT *Little Women Wedded.* [New edition.] 16mo. 1/6 limp boards, 2/0 flexible cloth Oct. 26 (*Ath*)

American Authors No. 19. This is part 2 of *Little Women*, 242 pp. The first edition was issued by Roberts Bros., Boston, 1869, 17 cm., 358 pp., four illustrations, $1.50, *Little Women, part 2*. It was advertised in the *New-York Times* on Apr. 12 as "On Apr. 16" and listed in the *Nation* on Apr. 8. The second issue of the first edition was in brick or plum cloth. They issued the second edition of part 1 and the first edition of part 2 in 1 vol. in 1869, 12mo, illustrated, 350 pp., at the same time as the first edition of part 2.

The first British edition was issued by Low, 1869, Fcp 8vo, illustrated, 3/6 cloth, advertised in the *Ath* on May 22 as "Ready" and listed on June 12. Low issued both parts in 1 vol. in 1870, 12mo, 3/6, listed in the *Spect* on Sept. 17; and also in 1871, 464 pp. Low issued the fourth edition, 464 pp., in 1871. It was issued in the *Rose Library* No. 3, 1/0 sewed, 2/6 cloth, listed in the *Ath* on Oct. 24, 1874.

156 EDWARD H. BICKERSTETH *The Master's Home-Call.* 32mo. 1/0 cloth Nov. 9 (*Spect*)

This is the first edition, 86 pp., containing memorials of Alice F. Bickersteth by her father. Low issued the third edition, 1872, 86 pp.; and advertised the 23rd thousand in the *Ath* on Apr. 4, 1885, 1/0. It was issued in the United States by Robert Carter & Bros., New York, 1873, 14 cm., 86 pp., advertised in the *New-York Times* on Dec. 14, 1872, $.50; and listed in *Godey's Lady's Book* for Mar. 1873 and thus probably issued in Dec. 1872 or Jan. 1873.

157 GODFREY MAYNARD **Spray from the Water of the Eisenbrunnen.** 12mo.
2/0 boards   Nov. 23 (*Spect*)
This is the first edition, 1872, 160 pp.

158 CHARLES D. WARNER **Backlog Studies.** 16mo. 1/6 limp boards, 2/0 flexible cloth   Dec. 7 (*Ath*)
American Authors No. 20. This is the first British edition, 1872, 262 pp. Ward, Lock & Tyler, London, issued it in 1873 at 1/0 sewed, 1/6, listed in the *Ath* on May 10. Warner wrote to the *Ath* on May 10, 1873, stating that this work had been published simultaneously in Boston and by Low, who paid the author. It consisted of eleven papers. He stated that he had now received a book from Ward, Lock & Tyler with the same title and with his name as author but it was not the same book. It contained, he continued, only seven of the papers (the other four were protected by copyright) and had added a portion of his address delivered on a college anniversary, which had no connection with the vol. whatsoever. He expressed his appreciation of the delicacy Ward, Lock & Tyler must have felt in preparing the volume (S. O. Beeton was responsible). The added portion was "A Summary of Culture," slightly abridged from Warner's address at Hamilton College on June 26, 1872. The seven parts printed by Ward, Lock were in *Scribner's Monthly* in July 1871 and in Feb.–July 1872. Nothing deterred, Ward, Lock & Tyler issued it in 1 vol. along with "My Summer in a Garden," no date, 2/0 boards, in 1875.

The first American edition was issued by James R. Osgood & Co., Boston, 1873, 18 cm., 281 pp., illustrated, $2.00 in blue, green, brick, or orange cloth, with brown or blue endpapers. There were 21 illustrations by A. Hoppin. I think it must have been issued also in small 4to at $3.00 although not so given by *BAL*. It was so advertised in both the *Nation* and *New-York Times*. *BAL* states that 3,000 copies were bound Dec. 17, 1872–Jan. 11, 1873, and a second printing of 1,000 copies was made on Jan. 5, 1873, no sizes being given. The small 4to at $3.00 was advertised in the *New-York Times* on Dec. 19, 1872, as "This day" and was listed in *PW* on Dec. 12. They issued a new edition in 1877, illustrated, $1.50, advertised in the *New-York Times* on Nov. 17.

159 ANONYMOUS **The St. James's Magazine Christmas Box.** 1872. 8vo.
1/0 sewed   Dec. 7 (*Ath*)

160 W. R. RICHARDSON **From London Bridge to Lombardy by a Macadamised Route.** p 8vo. 2/6 boards   1872
This was listed by *PC* as published Aug. 2–15, with 222 pp. The first edition was issued by Low, 1869, 21 cm., 202 pp., frontispiece, illustrations, map.

Sampson Low, Marston, Low & Searle
Crown Buildings, 188 Fleet Street
1873

161 RICHARD B. JOHNSON **Very Far West Indeed.** Fourth and cheaper edition.
2/0 boards   Feb. 22 (*Spect*)

The *Spect* listing and an *Ath* ad called this the fourth edition, as does the *Eng Cat*. The *U Cat*, however, lists the fourth and cheaper edition, 1872, 18 cm., 280 pp., and lists a fifth edition, 1873. The first edition was issued by Low, 1872, p 8vo, 280 pp., 10/6, advertised in the *Ath* on May 4 as "This day." The second edition was the same, advertised on June 22, and the third edition was the same, 1872, 10/6, advertised in the *Spect* on Sept. 7 as "On Sept. 9."

162 TIMOTHY TITCOMB (J. G. HOLLAND) **Titcomb's Letters to Young People. . . .** Fiftieth edition. 16mo. 1/6 limp boards, 2/0 flexible cloth   Apr. 5 (*Ath*)

American Authors No. 21. This is 1873. Low issued it in 1874 in the *Rose Library* No. 8, 1/0 sewed, 2/6 cloth, listed in the *Ath* on Dec. 26, 1874. The first edition was issued by Charles Scribner & Co., New York, 1858, 19 cm., 251 pp., by Timothy Titcomb, listed in *APC&LG* on July 23 and in the *Ind* on Aug. 5. It was distributed in London by Low, listed in the *Ath* on Aug. 28, 1858.

163 ADELINE WHITNEY **Hitherto.** 16mo. 2/6 boards, 3/6 cloth   May 17 (*Ath*)

American Authors No. 22. Low issued this in the *Rose Library*, 1876, Nos. 28 and 29, 16mo, 1/0 sewed, 2/6 cloth each, listed in

the *Ath* on Aug. 5; and reissued it in the *Rose Library* in 2 vols., Nos. 23 and 24, in 1883, 1/0 sewed each, advertised in the *Ath* on Dec. 29, 1883. It carried the Nos. 27 and 28 in an ad in the *Ath* on Aug. 15, 1885. The first edition was issued by Low, 3 vols., 1869, Cr 8vo, 31/6, advertised in the *Ath* on Nov. 6 as "On Nov. 15" and listed on Nov. 13. Low issued a second edition in 1 vol., frontispiece, 6/0, advertised in the *Spect* on Mar. 11, 1871, as "This day."

The first American edition was issued by A. K. Loring, Boston (copyright 1869), 19.5 cm., 473 pp., listed in *ALG&PC* (fortnightly) on Dec. 1, 1869, and in the *Nation* on Dec. 2.

164 WILL CARLETON **Farm Ballads.** 16mo. 1/0 limp boards, 2/0 flexible cloth   July 5 (*Ath*)

American Authors No. 23. This is my copy, 1873, 15.7 cm., 184 pp., with "Other Poems" on pp. (121)–184. It is in terracotta limp boards, decorated and printed in yellow and black, identical on front and back but with author and title on the front and an ad in its place on the back. The front cover has "Low's Copyright Series of American Authors," and the title page has "Low's Copyright and Cheap Editions of American Books." It is cut flush with plain white endpapers. This is apparently a later binding of the 1873 sheets, as the imprint on the front cover was not used until 1876. Low issued it in the *Rose Library*,

1880, 16mo, 184 pp., 1/0 sewed, listed in the *Bks* for Nov. 1879. From this title on in the *Rose Library* the numbering system went awry and numbers were not assigned or, if they were, they were changed shortly thereafter. Low issued it, 1890, 17 cm., 184 pp., 0/6 sewed, 0/9 cloth back, advertised in the *Ath* on Nov. 23, 1889; and issued it at 3/6 in 1884.

The first British edition was issued by George Routledge & Sons, London and New York (1873), 16.2 cm., 120 pp., my copy, in yellow pictorial boards, printed in red, blue, and black, with publisher's ads on the endpapers and back cover. It was listed in the *Ath* and *Spect* on June 7.

The first edition was issued by Harper & Bros., New York, 1873, 23 cm., 108 pp., $1.50 and $2.00 cloth. It was listed in the *Ind* on May 8 and in *PW* on May 10. They reissued it in 1892, new edition, square 8vo, $2.00 cloth, advertised in the *New-York Times* on June 14.

See 1893

165 THOMAS CARLISLE
The Unprofessional Vagabond.
12mo. Illustrated. 1/0 boards
July 19 (*Ath*)

This is the first edition, 1873, my copy, 17 cm., 64 pp., frontispiece and three full-page sketches by the author's brother, John Carlisle. It is in white pictorial boards, printed in red, green, and black with a catalog paged (1)–32 (Oct. 1872) at the back. It has plain white endpapers and publisher's ads on the back cover. The sketches of four different characters were made with the author as model, made up and garbed for the various characters. It is reprinted from the *Globe* with additions and some deletions.

166 ADELINE WHITNEY *The Other Girls.*
16mo. 2/0 boards, 2/6 cloth   Oct. 4 (*Ath*)
American Authors No. 24. The first British edition was issued by Low (1873), p 8vo,

3/6 cloth, advertised in the *Ath* on Apr. 26 as "On May 1" and listed on May 10. Low issued it in 1888, new edition 12mo, 2/0. The first American edition was issued by James R. Osgood & Co., Boston, 1873, 18.5 cm., 463 pp., illustrated, $2.00, listed by *Lit W* as published in Apr., and listed in *PW* on May 3 and in the *Ind* on May 8.

167 JOHANN W. VON GOETHE *Wilhelm Meister's Apprenticeship.* 2 vols. 16mo.
1/0 sewed, 2/0 flexible cloth each
Oct. 25 (*Ath*)

German Authors No. 19. This is 1873, translated by Eleanor Grove. The first edition was *Wilhelm Meisters Lehrjahre*, Berlin, 4 vols., 1795, 96, 16 cm. The first British edition was issued by Oliver & Boyd, Edinburgh; etc., 3 vols., 1824, 17.5 cm., translated by Thomas Carlyle. It was issued in the United States by Wells & Lilly, Boston, 3 vols., 1828, 18 cm.

168 ELIZABETH S. PHELPS, later WARD
What to Wear? Copyright edition. 12mo.
1/0 boards   Nov. 29 (*Ath*)

This is the first British edition, 1874, with an introductory chapter with alterations for English readers by Perceval Keane. The ads and listings give it variously at 1/0 sewed and 1/0 boards. The first edition was issued by James R. Osgood & Co., Boston, 1873, 17.5 cm., 92 pp., in printed green wrappers, $.50. It was also issued in green, purple, or blue cloth with brown endpapers. Records show 1,530 copies were printed, and 1,025 were bound in paper and 498 in cloth, on June 11 and 12. A second printing of 1,040 copies were bound June 19 and 20, 634 in paper and 399 in cloth. It was listed in *PW* on May 31 and in the *Nation* on June 23. The first four sections were reprinted from the *Ind*.

169 ANONYMOUS *St. James's Christmas Box.* 1873. 8vo. 1/0 sewed   Dec. 13 (*Ath*)

Sampson Low, Marston, Low & Searle
Crown Buildings, 188 Fleet Street
1874

170 JAMES B. STEPHENS *Godolphin Arabian.* 12mo. 2/0 sewed Jan. 17 (*Ath*)

This is in verse by Stephens, based on a French prose tale of Eugène Sue. It was issued in Australia by Watson, Brisbane, 1873, 17 cm., 141 pp. The Sue work was *Deleytar. Arabian Godolphin. Kardiki*, issued in Paris, 1839. The present title was issued by Chapman & Hall, London, 1845, from the French. It was issued in the United States by E. Winchester, New York, 1845, New World Press, 8vo, 32 pp., illustrated, in printed wrappers, in double columns.

171 ROBERT KEMPT *The Anglo-Scottish Year-Book 1874.* 12mo. 1/0 Apr. 25 (*Spect*)

This was advertised in the *Ath* on Apr. 18 as "This day," which gave the price as 1/0 limp cloth. An ad on Apr. 25 gave the price as 1/0 sewed, 1/6 limp cloth. Low seems to have had a problem in coordinating their production and advertising departments. This is a new annual and apparently had only one other issue, that in 1875 for the 1875–76 annual, listed in the *Spect* on June 19, 1875.

172 PAUL HEYSE *Barbarossa, and Other Tales.* Authorized edition. 16mo. 1/6 sewed, 2/0 flexible cloth July 4 (*Ath*)

German Authors No. 20. This is 16 cm., 302 pp., translated by L.C.S., and contains six stories. These *German Author* titles are frustrating to trace as they are frequently concocted from short stories, amassed from here and there.

173 JULES SANDEAU (L. S. JULES SANDEAU) *Seagull Rock.* 12mo. Illustrated. 1/0 sewed, 2/6 cloth Oct. 24 (*Ath*)

Rose Library No. 1. This is 1874, starting a new series. The 1/0 is in stiff wrappers, glazed and printed in colors. I think the 2/6 issue preceded the 1/0 sewed issue. The 1/0 was listed in the *Ath* on Oct. 24, and in the *Spect* on Oct. 31, whereas the 2/6 was listed in the *Spect* on Oct. 10. It is translated by Robert Black, from the French *La Roche aux Mouettes*, issued in Paris (1871), 204 pp. Low issued the first British edition, 1872, p 8vo, 249 pp., illustrated, 7/6 cloth, listed in the *Ath* on Oct. 19. Low issued a new edition in 1890, 12mo, illustrated, 2/0. In the United States, Scribner, Welford & Armstrong, New York, advertised it in the *Nation* on Dec. 12, 1871, royal 16mo, $3.00 cloth. It was issued by Scribner, Welford & Armstrong, New York, 1873, illustrated, in the Black translation; and they advertised the *Rose Library*, Nos. 1–6, in the *New-York Times* on Oct. 9, 1875, 16mo, illustrated, $.50 in a stiff illuminated cover, and p 8vo, $1.25 in cloth.

174 MADAME DE STOLZ (COMTESSE FANNY DE BEGON) *The House on Wheels.*
Illustrated. 1/o sewed, 2/6 cloth
Oct. 24 (*Ath*)

Rose Library No. 4. This is the first British edition, 1874, translated by Nancy D'Anvers (Nancy R. E. Meugens Bell). The first edition was *La Maison Roulante*, issued in Paris, 1869, 287 pp. The first American edition was issued by Lee & Shepard, Boston, 1871, 19 cm., 304 pp., illustrated, translated by Miss E. F. Adams. It was advertised in the *New-York Times* on Oct. 24, 1870, $1.25 and $1.50 cloth, as "This day" and listed in *Old and New* (Boston), a monthly, for Dec. 1870. It was issued by Scribner, Welford & Armstrong, New York, 1874, 16mo, 182 pp., illustrated, translated by D'Anvers. It is probably in the *Rose Library* (see the advertisement in the preceding item).

175 J. G. HOLLAND *The Mistress of the Manse.* 1/o sewed, 2/6 cloth Oct. 24 (*Ath*)

Rose Library No. 7. This is the first British edition, 1874, also advertised in *PC* on Oct. 2 as "Now ready." The 2/6 issue was deposited on Oct. 1, and the 1/o issue on Nov. 3. The first American edition was issued by Scribner, Armstrong, New York, 1874, 19.5 cm., 245 pp., $1.50 cloth, listed in *PW* on Oct. 17 and in the *Ind* on Oct. 22. They issued the 13th thousand, $1.50 cloth, advertised in the *New-York Times* on Oct. 17, 1874, as "This day," and advertised the 20th thousand there on Dec. 19, 1874, $1.50 and $2.50 cloth. They issued it in small 4to, illustrated, $5.00 cloth, advertised in the same on Nov. 16, 1876, and listed in the *Nation* on Dec. 7.

176 FLORENCE MARRYAT, ed. *Chrismas Number of London Society.* 1/o Dec. 5 (*Spect* ad)

The ad in the *Spect* said "Now ready."

Sampson Low, Marston, Low & Searle
Crown Buildings, 188 Fleet Street
1875

177 SAXE HOLM (HELEN HUNT JACKSON)
**Draxy Miller's Dowry, and the Elder's
Wife.** 16mo. 1/0 sewed   Feb. 13 (*Ath*)

Rose Library No. 10. I think that about this
time the cloth issues of the *Rose Library*
were dropped, and the *Half-Crown Series*
began. This latter series was in small p
8vo, illustrated, 2/6 cloth, and the present
title in the series was advertised in the *Ath*
on Mar. 13, 1875, as "Ready." A Jan. 1876
Low catalog gave the *Rose Library* at 1/0
sewed only and gave 12 titles in the *Half-
Crown Series*. The present title is the first
British edition, 1875, containing the two
tales of the title. Low issued a new edition
in Feb. 1890, 12mo, 2/0.

In the United States the first title ran in
Scribner's Monthly in May and June 1872;
and the second title ran there in Apr. and
May 1873. The first book edition was issued as *Saxe Holm's Stories*, by Scribner,
Armstrong & Co., New York, 1874, 12mo,
350 pp., $1.50 in green cloth, containing
the present two stories and four others. It
was advertised in the *New-York Times* on
Nov. 22, 1873, as "This day" and listed in
the *Nation* on Jan. 8, 1874.

178 MADAME JULIE GOURAUD (LOUISE
D'AULNAY) **The Four Gold Pieces.** 16mo.
Illustrated. 1/0 sewed   Mar. 27 (*Ath*)

Rose Library No. 11. The *Half-Crown Series*
edition was advertised in the *Ath* on Mar.
13 as "Now ready." This is the first British
edition, 1875, translated by M.M. The

first edition was *Les Quatre Pièces d'Or*,
Paris, 1873. It was issued in New York, illustrated, in 1875.

179 LOUISA M. ALCOTT **Work.** Third
edition. 16mo. 1/0 sewed   Mar. 27 (*Ath*)

Rose Library No. 12. This is 1875, 218 pp.,
part 1 of *Work*. The first British edition of
the complete work was issued by Low, 2
vols., 1873, 19.5 cm., 21/0, advertised in
the *Spect* on May 31 as "On June 2" and
listed there and in the *Ath* on June 7. Low
issued the second edition in 1 vol., 1873,
443 pp.; and reissued it in 1874, new edition, Cr 8vo, illustrated, 6/0, listed in the
Ath on May 2; and reissued, no date, in
1888, new edition, 12mo, 2/0 in green
cloth with the separate paging, 218 and
226. For part 2 see the next item.

The first American edition was issued
by Roberts Bros., Boston, 1873, with both
parts, 18 cm., 443 pp., illustrated with
many small vignettes, probably issued in
June as it was listed in *Godey's Lady's Book*
for Sept. and in the *New Englander* (New
Haven), a quarterly, for July. The complete work ran in *Christian Union*, Dec.
1872–June 1873.

180 LOUISA M. ALCOTT **Beginning Again.**
16mo. 1/0 sewed   Mar. 27 (*Ath*)

Rose Library No. 13. This is 1875, 226 pp.,
the first separate edition of part 2 of *Work*.
See the preceding title.

181 (CAROLINE W. LAWRENCE) *On the Rock: A Memoir of Alice B. Whitall.* [New edition.] 12mo. 2/0 cloth May 29 (*Ath*)

The first British edition was issued by Low, 1872 (1871), 12mo, anonymous, 3/6, listed in the *Ath* on Dec. 9, 1871. The first edition was issued by G. Maclean, Philadelphia, no date, 12mo, anonymous, 312 pp., frontispiece (portrait), which the *U Cat* gives as (1870) in two locations.

182 WILLIAM GORLACH *Prince Bismarck.* Authorized edition. 16mo. Portrait. 1/6 sewed, 2/0 flexible cloth   July 3 (*Spect*)

German Authors No. 21. This is the first British edition, 1875, 16 cm., 233 pp., translated by Miss M. E. von Glehn. At this time this Tauchnitz series of *German Authors* was issued in the United States by Henry Holt, New York. The first edition was *Fürst Bismarck*, issued at Stuttgart, 2 vols., 1873–75.

183 X. B. SAINTINE (JOSEPH X. BONIFACE) *Picciola.* 16mo. Illustrated. 1/0 sewed July 17 (*Ath*)

Rose Library No. 14. This is 1875, 189 pp. It was issued in the *Half-Crown Series*, small p 8vo, illustrated, in cloth, at about the same time as the present issue. The first British edition was issued by Colburn, London, 2 vols., 1837, 21 cm., 16/0, translated by Catherine Gore?, advertised in the *Spect* on Feb. 18 as "On Feb. 21" and on Feb. 25 as "This day." Frederick Warne, London, issued it (1870), Fcp 8vo, 258 pp., illustrated, 2/6 cloth, in a different translation, listed in the *Ath* on Sept. 10.

The first American edition was issued by Carey, Lea & Blanchard, Philadelphia, 1838, 19.5 cm., 204 pp., in the Colburn translation. It was noticed in the *Christian Examiner* (bi-monthly), for Jan. 1839, and reviewed in the *New York Review* (quarterly), in Jan. 1839. It was probably issued very close to Oct. 29, 1838, when it was ad-

vertised in the *Globe*, a Washington daily, by a bookseller in Washington. They reissued it, 1839, second edition, 251 pp. It ran in the *Select Circulating Library*, a Philadelphia weekly, founded in Oct. 1832.

The first edition was issued in Paris, 1836, 22.5 cm., 419 pp., frontispiece (portrait).

184 Z.M.A. FLEURIOT *Robert's Holidays.* 16mo. Illustrated. 1/0 sewed   Sept. 4 (*Ath*)

Rose Library No. 15. This is the first British edition, 1875, 182 pp., translated by Nancy D'Anvers (Nancy R. E. Meugens, later Bell). It was issued in the *Half-Crown Series*, advertised in the *Ath* on Dec. 18. The first edition was *En Conge*, Paris, 1874.

185 MADAME JULIE GOURAUD (LOUISE D'AULNAY) *The Two Children of St. Domingo.* 16mo. Illustrated. 1/0 sewed Nov. 20 (*Ath*)

Rose Library No. 16. This is the first British edition, 1875. The *Half-Crown Series* was advertised in the *Ath* on Dec. 18. The first edition was *Les Deux Enfants de Saint-Dominique*, Paris, 1874.

186 LOUISA M. ALCOTT *Aunt Jo's Scrap-Bag. Vol. 1. My Boys, etc.* 16mo. 1/0 sewed   Nov. 27 (*Spect*)

Rose Library No. 17. The *Half-Crown Series* was listed in the *Ath* on Nov. 20. The first British edition was issued by Low, 1871, 272 pp., 3/6 cloth, with a 32-page catalog (Oct. 1871) at the back. It was deposited on Dec. 21, 1871, and listed in the *Ath* on Dec. 23. Low issued it, 12mo, 5/0, listed in the *Spect* on Sept. 18, 1886; and issued it in 1889, 2/0, 2/6.

The first edition was issued by Roberts Bros., Boston, 1872, 16 cm., 215 pp., illustrated with a double frontispiece, advertised in the *New-York Times* on Nov. 17, 1871, as "In a few days," $1.00, and advertised in *Harper's Weekly* on Nov. 25 as

"Ready Dec. 1." This contains three new tales; the other eleven appeared in *Merry's Museum* (1868, 69) and in the *Youth's Companion* (1868). *Aunt Jo's Scrap-Bag* is a 6-vol. work, and it was issued by Roberts Bros, 1872–82. They reissued the present title in 1886, 30th thousand, 16mo. portrait, $1.50, listed in the *Nation* on Oct. 7.

187 FLORENCE MARRYAT, ed. *Christmas Number of London Society.* 1/0 Dec. 11 (*Spect* ad)

188 SAMUEL R. VAN CAMPEN *Holland's "Silver Feast."* 8vo. 2/0 1875 (*Eng Cat*)

This is the first edition, in two parts, English and Dutch, 1875. The Dutch translation was printed in Amsterdam.

189 WILLIAM DAVIES *A Fine Old English Gentleman.* [New edition.] 8vo. 2/0 1875 (*Eng Cat*)

This is the life of Lord Collingwood, and the first edition was issued by Low, 1875, 19 cm., 263 pp., frontispiece (portrait), 6/0, advertised in the *Ath* on Oct. 9 as "Now ready."

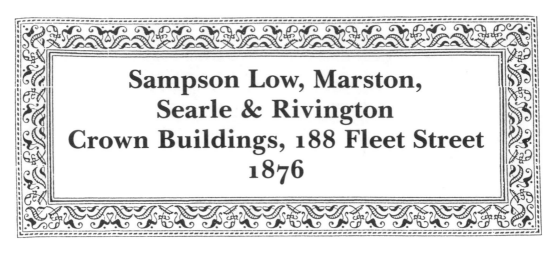

Sampson Low, senior, retired in 1875, and an ad in the Spect *on July 1, 1876, gave the imprint as above.*

190 JULES VERNE *The Adventures of Three Englishmen and Three Russians in South Africa.* Author's illustrated edition. 12mo. 1/o limp boards   Feb. 5 (*Acad*)

This and the following six titles by Verne were all advertised in the *Ath* on Jan. 29 as "Ready." I have a copy, 1876, 18.1 cm., 191 pp., but apparently bound up after July 1, 1876, as the imprint on the cover and title page is the new one with Rivington added. It has a frontispiece and eight full-page illustrations, translated by Ellen E. Frewer, pictorial gray limp boards, cut flush, printed in black and white, with a catalog (Apr. 1877), paged (1)–24 at the back and commercial ads on the endpapers and back cover. These Verne titles were all issued at 1/o only and were so given in a Sept. 1876 Low catalog. They were 1/o and 2/o in the Apr. 1877 catalog. This and the following six Verne titles are uniformly bound but with an appropriate picture on their covers. The first British edition was issued by Low, 1873, *Meridiana*, Cr 8vo, 238 pp., illustrated, 7/6 cloth, listed in the *Ath* on Oct. 26, 1872, and by *PC* as published Nov. 16–30, 1872. Low issued a new edition in 1879, 3/6, listed in the *Spect* on Sept. 20. In a July 1, 1876, ad for Verne's works, Low quoted J. Hetzel of Paris, Verne's publishers, stating that Low alone has the authorized translation and that all other translations are unauthorized.

The first edition was *Aventures de Trois Russes et de Trois Anglais dans l'Afrique Australe*, Paris, 1872. It was issued in French by F. W. Christern, New York, 1873, in paper, listed in the *Nation* on Nov. 7, 1872.

The first American edition was issued by Scribner, Welford & Armstrong, New York, 1873, listed in *PW* on Nov. 14, 1872. Scribner, Armstrong & Co., New York, issued it in 1874, 12mo, $.75 cloth, advertised in the *New-York Times* on June 2, 1874, as "Now ready." In this ad it was stated that this was the only authorized text and with the only complete illustrations, by direct arrangements with the French and English publishers. It continued by stating that an unauthorized edition had been issued by a rival publisher, with 57 pp. in an abridged translation of the original and with the remaining 133 pp. taken from the Scribner translation, and that it has only 20 illustrations as compared to our 48. This evil rival apparently was Henry L. Shepard, Boston, who issued it, 1874, about May 30, as *Adventures in the Land of the Behemoth*, advertised as the

copyright edition and stating that the Scribner edition was not copyrighted. It ran in Low's *St. James's Magazine* in 1872 and 1873.
See 1890

191 JULES VERNE *Five Weeks in a Balloon.* Author's illustrated edition.

12mo. 1/0 limp boards   Feb. 5 (*Acad*)

Low issued the second (English) edition, 1874, Cr 8vo, illustrated, 7/6 cloth, listed in the *Ath* on Apr. 11. The first edition was issued in Paris (1863), 354 pp., *Cinq Semaines en Ballon*. The first edition in English was issued by D. Appleton & Co., New York, 1869, listed in *ALG&PC* on Mar. 1 and in the *Nation* on Mar. 4. The first English edition was issued by Chapman & Hall, London, 1870, illustrated, 7/6, listed in the *Ath* on May 14.
See 1890

192 JULES VERNE *A Floating City.*

Authorized illustrated edition. 12mo. 1/0 limp boards   Feb. 5 (*Acad*)

This is my copy, 1876, 18 cm., 208 pp., frontispiece and eight full-page illustrations, with a vignette on the title page. It is in gray limp boards, pictorially printed in black and white, with a catalog paged (1)–16 (Jan. 1876) at the back. It has plain endpapers and a commercial ad on the back. By July 1 it was being advertised as at 2/0 cloth also. Low issued it, 1882, in green cloth with all edges gilt. The first edition was *Une Ville Flottante*, Paris (1871). The first British edition was issued by Low, *A Floating City and the Blockade Runners*, 1874, Cr 8vo, illustrated, 7/6, advertised in the *Ath* on Sept. 12 as "Just ready" and listed on Sept. 26.

The first American edition was with the Low title, issued by Scribner, Armstrong & Co., New York, 1874, square Cr 8vo, illustrated, $3.00, from the same plates as used by Low. It was advertised in the *New-York Times* on Aug. 29 as "On Sept. 2," and on

Sept. 2 as "This day." It was listed in *PW* on Sept. 5 and in the *Nation* on Sept. 17. They issued a new edition in 1882, 8vo, $2.00, advertised in the *New-York Times*, Sept. 20.
See 1890

193 JULES VERNE *The Blockade Runners.*

Author's illustrated edition. 12mo. 1/0 limp boards   Feb. 5 (*Acad*)

By July 1 this was being advertised as at 2/0 cloth also. The first edition was *Les Forceurs de Blocus*, Paris, 1871 or before. For British and American editions see the preceding item.
See 1890

194 JULES VERNE *From the Earth to the Moon Direct in 97 Hours 20 Minutes.*

Author's illustrated edition. 12mo. 1/0 limp boards   Feb. 5 (*Acad*)

This is my copy, 1876, 18 cm., 168 pp., seven full-page illustrations, in gray, pictorial limp boards, printed in white and black. It has a catalog paged (1)–16 (Sept 1876) at the back, and commercial ads on the inside and back covers, and on the free endpaper at the back. It is translated by Louis Mercier and Eleanor E. King, and by July 1 was advertised at 2/0 cloth also. The first British edition was issued by Low, *From the Earth to the Moon . . . ; and a Trip Round It*, 1873, Cr 8vo, illustrated, 10/6, translated by Mercier and King and listed in the *Ath* on Oct. 11. Low issued the third edition, 1874, Cr 8vo, 10/6, listed in the *Spect* on May 2 and in the *Ath* on May 9.

The first edition was *De la Terre a la Lune, Trajet Direct en 97 Heures*, issued serially in Paris, Sept. 14–Oct. 14, 1865. The first edition in English was issued by the Newark Printing and Publishing Co., Newark, 1869, translated by J. K. Hoyt. Scribner, Armstrong & Co., New York, issued it, 1874, with the Low title and using the same plates, $3.00, listed in *PW* on Nov. 22, 1873, in the *Ind* on Dec. 9, and in the *Nation* on Jan. 8, 1874. It was adver-tised in the *New-York Times* on Nov. 29, 1873, as "Next week" and on Dec. 4 as "This day." It was issued by the Baltimore Gun Club, King & Baird, Philadelphia (1874), with the Scribner, Armstrong title, translated by E. Roth, 442 pp., illustrated, in decorated green cloth.

See 1890

195 JULES VERNE ***Round the Moon.***
Author's edition, with illustrations. 12mo. 1/0 limp boards   Feb. 5 (*Acad*)

This is the first separate British edition, my copy, 1876, 18.3 cm., 192 pp., nine full-page illustrations, in gray pictorial limp boards, cut flush and printed in white and black, with plain white endpa-pers. The title on the cover is *Around the Moon.* There is a 16-page catalog, paged (1)–16 (Jan. 1876) at the back and a com-mercial ad on the back cover. By July 1 it was being advertised as at 2/0 cloth also. The translation is by Mercier and King. Low reissued it, the same, 1881.

   The first edition was *Autour de la Lune,* issued serially in Paris, Nov. 4–Dec. 9, 1869, and issued in book form, 1870. It was issued in New York by the Catholic Publication Society, 1876, *All Around the Moon,* about June 3, translated by E. Roth. For further details on British and Ameri-can issues, see the preceding title.

See 1890

196 JULES VERNE ***Twenty Thousand Leagues Under the Seas.*** 2 vols. Author's edition, with illustrations. 12mo. 1/0 limp boards each; 3/6 cloth in 1 vol.   Feb. 5 (*Acad*)

This is my set, 1876, 18.2 cm., with the title on the covers reading *Twenty Thousand Leagues Under the Sea.* The two vols. are identical except for paging and illustra-tions. Vol. 1 has 142 pp. with frontispiece and four full-page illustrations; and vol. 2 has pp. (145)–302 and frontispiece and

three full-page illustrations. Both vols. have a 16-page catalog paged (1)–16 (Jan. 1876) at the back. The first edition in En-glish was issued by Low, 1873, 19.5 cm., 303 pp., illustrated, 10/6 in green pictorial cloth, translated by Louis Mercier, listed in the *Ath* on Oct. 19, 1872, and by *PC* as published Nov. 1–15. There were at least six editions, illustrated, at 10/6, the fifth being listed in the *Ath* on July 11, 1874, and another such being listed on Apr. 22, 1876. The first edition was *Vingt Mille Lieues sous les Mers,* Paris, 2 vols., 1869–70, illustrated. It ran serially, Mar. 20, 1869–June 20, 1870.

   The first American edition was issued by James R. Osgood & Co., Boston, 1872, 20.5 cm., 303 pp., illustrated, using the same plates as the Low edition. It was ad-vertised in *Lit W* on Dec. 1, 1872, and listed in *PW* on Dec. 5. They reissued it, 1874. It was issued also by George M. Smith & Co., Boston, 1873 (the Osgood edition).

See 1890

197 EDWARD H. BICKERSTETH
The Clergyman in His Home.
12mo. 1/0   Feb. 12 (*Ath* ad)

This is the first edition, 1876, 31 pp., an address delivered on Dec. 16, 1875. It was issued in the United States by Dutton & Co., New York, 1876, 24mo, 32pp.

198 HARRIET B. STOWE ***My Wife and I.***
16mo. 2/0 sewed, 3/6 cloth   Apr. 29 (*Spect*)

Rose Library No. 23. Before Apr. 1877 this was renumbered to No. 24. Low issued it in 1888, new edition, 12mo, 423 pp., 2/0. Low issued the first British edition, 1871, 12mo, 6/0 in red cloth, with a 32-page cat-alog (Oct. 1871) at the back. It was listed in the *Ath* on Nov. 18 and in *PC* on Dec. 18. It ran in the *Christian Union.* The first edition was issued by J. B. Ford & Co., New York, 1871, 19 cm., 474 pp., illustrated, $1.75 in green, purple, terra-cotta, or blue cloth, with gray endpapers. It has 7 pp. of ads and was listed in the *Ind* on Nov. 2 and in *ALG&PC* (fortnightly) on Nov. 1. Ford issued it, 1872, with slight revisions; and issued the 41st thousand, new edition, in 1873, 12mo, illustrated, $1.75 cloth, advertised in the *Nation* on Oct. 16 as "Just out." Fords, Howard & Hulbert, New York, issued it in 1879, illustrated, $1.50 cloth, advertised in the *New-York Times* on Oct. 5 as ready; and they issued it in 1881, 16mo, 474 pp. In Canada it was issued by the Canadian News and Publishing Co., Toronto, 1872, 304 pp.

199 HARRIET B. STOWE *We and Our Neighbors*. 16mo. 2/o sewed, 3/6 cloth Apr. 29 (*Spect*)

Rose Library No. 24. Before Apr. 1877 the number was changed to No. 23. The first edition was issued by Low, 1875, 17 cm., 390 pp., 6/o in terra-cotta or red cloth with brown endpapers and all edges gilt. It has a 40-page catalog (Feb. 1875) at the back. It was deposited on Mar. 31 and listed in the *Ath* on Apr. 10 and in *PC* on Apr. 16. An *Ath* ad on Apr. 3 said "Now ready." Low issued a cheaper edition in 1876, the present edition.

The first American edition was issued by J. B. Ford & Co., New York (1875), 19 cm., 480 pp., illustrated, $1.75 in terra-cotta, green, or blue cloth, with yellow endpapers. It was listed in the *Ind* on Apr. 29 and in *PW* on May 1. It was also issued with the added imprint of Jansen, McClurg & Co., Chicago. It ran in the *Christian Union*. Fords, Howard & Hulbert, New York, issued it in 1879, illustrated, $1.50 cloth, advertised in the *New-York Times* on Oct. 5 as ready; and they issued it in 1881, 480 pp. In Canada it was issued by Belford Bros., Toronto, 18 cm., 392 pp., illustrated, which the *U Cat* gives as 1875, and which *BAL* states was advertised in the *Toronto Weekly Mail* on Oct. 6, 1876, as "Recent."

200 HARRIET B. STOWE *Captain Kidd's Money, and Other Stories*. 16mo. 1/o sewed, 2/6 cloth Apr. 29 (*Spect*)

Rose Library No. 25. This number was changed to No. 22 before Apr. 1877. The title story was one of eleven stories in Sam Lawson's *Oldtown Fireside Stories*, issued by James R. Osgood & Co., Boston, 1872, 20 cm., 199 pp., illustrated, in salmon, green, or terra-cotta cloth with brown endpapers, received at the Boston Athenaeum on Dec. 18, 1871, and listed in *ALG&PC* on Jan. 1, 1872. They reissued it as *Sam Lawson's Oldtown Fireside Stories*, 1872, 18 cm., 216 pp., illustrated, with an added story, about Aug. 8, in printed paper wrappers and in printed paper boards with a leather spine. The first edition was *Oldtown Fireside Stories*, issued by Low, 1871, 17.5 cm., 289 pp., no plates, 3/6 in blue cloth with cream endpapers, listed in the *Ath* on Dec. 23 and in *PC* on Dec. 30.

201 HARRIET B. STOWE *The Ghost in the Mill, and Other Stories*. 16mo. 1/o sewed, 2/6 cloth Apr. 29 (*Spect*)

Rose Library No. 26. The number was changed to No. 21 before Apr. 1877. The title story is one of eleven stories in *Sam Lawson's Oldtown Fireside Stories* (see the preceding title). The present edition (1876), 16.5 cm., 159 pp., is probably the first separate edition. It is illustrated and contains four stories.

202 HARRIET B. STOWE *Betty's Bright Idea; Also Deacon Pitkin's Farm and the First Christmas of New England*. 16mo. 1/o sewed, 2/6 cloth Apr. 29 (*Spect*)

Rose Library No. 27. The number was changed to No. 20 before Apr. 1877. *Betty's Bright Idea: and Other Stories* was issued by the Scottish Temperance League, Glasgow, 1876; and by the National Temperance Society and Publication House, New York, 18.5 cm., 90 pp., in wrappers, which the *U Cat* gives as (1875). Houlston, London, issued the present title, 1876; and James Clarke, London, issued *Deacon Pitkin's Farm, and Christ's Christmas Presents*, 1875, 102 pp.

Wright gives the first edition as the present title, issued by J. B. Ford & Co., New York, 1876, 19.5 cm., 121 pp., illustrated, in an illuminated paper cover, $.30, and $.75 in cloth. It was advertised in the *New-York Times* on Dec. 15, 1875, as "Today" and listed in the *Nation* on Dec. 23.

203 WILHELMINE VON HILLERN
The Vulture Maiden. Authorized edition. 16mo. 1/7 sewed, 2/0 flexible cloth   Apr. 29 (*Ath*)

German Authors No. 22. This is 1876, 279 pp., translated by C. Bell and E. F. Poynter, advertised by Low as the only authorized English translation. The first British edition was *Elsa and Her Vulture*, issued by Longmans, London, 1876, Cr 8vo, 272 pp., 2/0 boards, 2/6 cloth, listed in the *Ath* and *Spect* on Mar. 18, translated by Lady Grace Wallace. I have the 2/0 copy in pictorial yellow boards, with a preface (Mar. 1876). The first edition was *Die Geier-Wally*, issued in Berlin, 2 vols., 1875.

The first edition in English was issued by D. Appleton & Co., New York, 1876, 16 cm., 237 pp., $.50 paper, in the *Handy-volume Series*; and 23.5 cm., 78 pp., $1.25 cloth in the *Library of Choice Novels* No. 49. The paper edition was advertised in the *New-York Times* on Nov. 20, 1875, as "This day" and listed in the *Nation* on Dec. 2; and an ad there on Dec. 22, 1875, gave $1.25 cloth with red edges as "This day." It was reissued in 1876, listed in *Godey's Lady's Book* for July (thus probably issued in Apr. or May). They reissued it in 1879, 237 pp., $.30 paper, listed in the *Nation* on June 19; and issued a new edition in 1886, 12mo, $.25 paper, advertised in the *New-York Times* on Jan. 23 as "This day."

204 JULES VERNE **Around the World in Eighty Days.** Author's illustrated edition. 12mo. 1/0 limp boards, 2/0 cloth   May 6 (*Ath*)

This is my copy, 1876, 18.1 cm., 192 pp., translated by George M. Towle and Nancy D'Anvers. It has a frontispiece and six full-page illustrations, clothed in the usual gray pictorial limp boards. It has commercial ads on the endpapers and back cover, and has a 16-page catalog, paged (1)–16 (Apr. 1876). The first edition was *Le Tour du Monde en Quatre-Vingts Jours*, issued in Paris (1873), 18 cm., 312 pp. It ran as a serial in *Le Temps*, Nov. 6–Dec. 22, 1872. The first edition in English was issued by James R. Osgood & Co., Boston, 1873, *The Tour of the World in 80 Days*, translated by Towle, $1.50, listed in the *Nation* on July 3 and in *PW* on July 5. They reissued it about Dec. 18, 1873. It was also issued by Porter & Coates, Philadelphia, 1873, from the Osgood plates, *Around the World in 80 Days*. The first British edition was issued by Low, 1874, square Cr 8vo, 18.5 cm., 315 pp., illustrated, 7/6, from the Osgood plates, with a 32-page catalog (Oct. 1872) at the back. It was listed in the *Ath* on Nov. 15, 1873. Low issued it in 1879, new edition, Cr 8vo, 3/6, listed in the *Spect* on Oct. 4; and they issued it in 1899, 8vo, illustrated, o/6 sewed, listed in the *Bks* from June.
See 1890

205 JULES VERNE **Dr. Ox's Experiment, and Master Zacharius.** 12mo. Illustrated. 1/0 limp boards, 2/0 cloth   May 6 (*Ath*)

The first edition in book form was issued by Hetzel, Paris, 1874, *Le Docteur Ox; Maître Zacharius; Un Hivernage dans les Glaces; Un Drame dans les Airs (Quarantieme Ascension Français au Mont Blanc, par P. Verne). Une Fantaisie du Docteur Ox* ran as a serial, Mar.–May 1872; *Maître Zacharius* ran in 1854; *Un Hivernage dans les Glaces* ran in 1855; and *Un Drame dans les Airs* ran in

1851. The first edition in English was issued by James R. Osgood & Co., Boston, 1874, *Doctor Ox and Other Stories*, authorized edition, translated by G. M. Towle. It contains all the material of the first edition and was listed in *PW* on July 11 and by *Lit W* as published in July. They reissued it, 12mo, illustrated, $3.00, advertised in the *New-York Times* on Dec. 9, 1874, as "This day." It was also issued by William F. Gill & Co., Boston, 1874, *From the Clouds to the Mountains*, translated by A. L. Alger, containing all the material of the first edition, and listed in *PW* on July 23 and by *Lit W* as published in July.

The first British edition was issued by Low, 1874, *Dr. Ox's Experiment; Master Zacharius; a Drama in the Air; a Winter Amid the Ice*, Cr 8vo, illustrated, 7/6, listed in the *Ath* on Oct. 24. It contains the Paul Verne piece also.
See 1890

206 JULES VERNE *A Winter Amid the Ice, and Other Stories.* 12mo. Illustrated. 1/0 limp boards, 2/0 cloth   May 6 (*Ath*)
This contains the remainder of the first Low edition, the part not contained in the preceding title. (See the preceding title)
See 1890

207 JULES VERNE *Martin Paz, the Indian Patriot.* 12mo. Illustrated. 1/0 limp boards, 2/0 cloth   May 6 (*Ath*)
This is one of the two stories issued by Low, 1875, in 1 vol. The second story, *The Survivors of the Chancellor*, was issued by Low in 1878 in the same format as the present edition, advertised in the *Spect* on Aug. 24. Low issued both stories in 1 vol., 3/6 cloth, listed in the *Spect* on Aug. 31, 1878. They were translated by Ellen E. Frewer. *Martin Paz* appeared in Paris in a periodical in July and Aug., 1852, and was contained in *Le Chancellor, Journal du Passager J. R. Kazallon; Martin Paz*, issued in Paris by Hetzel, 1875. *Le Chancellor* ran se-

rially in *Le Temps*, Paris, Dec. 17, 1874–Jan. 24, 1875, and was issued by Hetzel, Paris (1875). The first edition in English of the two titles was issued by James R. Osgood & Co., Boston, 1875, *The Wreck of the Chancellor; and Martin Paz*, listed in *PW* on May 1, and by *Lit W* as published in Apr. It was translated by Ellen E. Frewer. They issued *The Survivors of the Chancellor*, 1876, advertised in *Lit W* on Jan. 1, 1876.

The first British edition of the two titles was issued by Low, 1875, *The Survivors of the Chancellor, Diary of J. R. Kazallon, Passenger; Martin Paz*, Cr 8vo, illustrated, 7/6, from the Osgood plates. It was listed in the *Spect* on Oct. 30 and in the *Ath* on Nov. 13, 1875. Low issued *The Survivors of the Chancellor . . . , 1880*, square Cr 8vo, frontispiece and title vignette, in pictorial green cloth. *The Wreck of the Chancellor* was issued by Porter & Coates, Philadelphia (1876). The first Canadian edition, *The Wreck of the Chancellor*, was issued by Belford Bros., Toronto, 1875, 8vo, 242 pp., in brownish purple cloth.
See 1890

208 ANONYMOUS *London Society Holiday Number.* Illustrated. 1/0   June 20 (*Spect*)
An ad in the *Spect* on June 17 said "On June 20."

209 FLORENCE MARRYAT, ed. *Christmas Number of London Society.* 1/0   Nov. 4 (*Spect*)

210 (JOHN HABBERTON) *Helen's Babies.* 16mo. 1/0 sewed, 2/6 cloth   Dec. 9 (*Ath* ad)
Rose Library No. 30. The ad in the *Ath* said "Now ready." It was also advertised in the *Spect* on Dec. 16 as "Now ready." It is probably the first British edition. Low claimed it was the only English edition with the sanction of the author, and in which he participated financially. It was also issued by Frederick Warne, London, at 2/0

boards, listed in the *Ath* on Dec. 30, 1876; and by Ward, Lock & Tyler, London, at 1/0 sewed, advertised in the *Ath* on Jan. 6, 1877, as "Just ready"; and by George Routledge & Sons, London and New York (1877), my copy, 16.6 cm., anonymous, 160 pp., 1/0 in yellow pictorial boards, printed in red and black, advertised in the *Ath* on Feb. 3, 1877. Eric Quayle in *Early Children's Books* states that it was issued by David Bryce & Son, Glasgow, 1877, in Dec. 1876, but I've found no confirmation of this. Actually at least twelve British houses issued it in 1876 or 1877.

The first edition was issued by A. K. Loring & Co., Boston (copyright 1876), 17.5 cm., anonymous, 206 pp., $.50 in gray paper wrappers, printed in black, with publisher's ads on pp. (207–208), and on the back and inside covers. It was listed in the *Nation* and *Ind* on July 27.

211 HENRI CARNUSCHI *Bi-Metallic Money.* p 8vo. 1/0   1876 (*Eng Cat*)
This is 1876, 21.5 cm., 48 pp. Low also issued a second edition, 1876, with 48 pp. It originally appeared as *La Monnaie Bimetallique* in *Le Siecle* for Nov.–Dec. 1875, and was issued in Paris, 1876, 23 cm., 62 pp. In the United States it was issued by the office of the *Banker's Magazine*, New York, 1876, 16 pp.

212 (JOHN HABBERTON) *The Barton Experiment.* 16mo. 1/0 sewed, 2/6 cloth Feb. 3 (*Spect*)

Rose Library No. 31. This is 1877, 126 pp., claimed by Low to be the only issue in England with the sanction of the author and in which he participated financially. It was listed in the *Acad* also on Feb. 3. It was also issued by George Routledge & Sons, London and New York (1877), Fcp 8vo, anonymous, 157 pp., 1/0 boards, advertised in the *Ath* on Feb. 3. It was also issued by Ward, Lock & Tyler, London (1877), anonymous, 162 pp., 1/0 sewed, advertised in the *Ath* on Feb. 3, 1877.

The first edition was issued by G. P. Putnam's Sons, New York, 1877, 18 cm., anonymous, 202 pp., advertised in the *New-York Times* on Nov. 25, 1876, $.50 paper, $1.00 cloth, as "Next week," and on Dec. 8 as "This day." It was listed in *PW* on Dec. 2, 1876. They advertised the 20th thousand there on Dec. 20, 1876; and advertised the 30th thousand, square 16mo, $.50 paper, $1.00 cloth, there, on June 9, 1877.

213 GEORG EBERS *Uarda.* 2 vols., 16mo. 1/6 sewed. 2/0 flexible cloth each May 26 (*Ath*)

German Authors No. 23. This is the first edition in English, 1877, translated by Clara Bell, and advertised by Low as the only English copyright edition. The first edition was issued at Stuttgart, 3 vols., 1877. The first American edition was issued by William S. Gottsberger, New York, 2 vols., 1880, my set, 15.6 cm., in buff wrappers, printed in black, with a red border, translated by Clara Bell. There is a preface (Sept. 22, 1876). The paper issue was $.30 each, and the cloth issue was $.75 each. It was advertised in the *New-York Times* on Jan. 17, 1880, as "This day" and listed in the *Ind* on Jan. 29. It was also issued by George Munro, New York (1880), my copy, 32 cm., 84 pp. in double columns, $.20 paper, translated by Clara Bell, with wrapper date Mar. 16, 1880, *Seaside Library* No. 712, and issued very close to that date, as No. 711 was advertised in the *New-York Times* on Mar. 12 as "Out today." There are 4 pp. of publisher's ads at the back indicated an issue of Aug. 1881.

214 JULES VERNE *The Fur Country.* 2 vols., Illustrated. 1/0 limp boards each Oct. 6 (*Ath*)

The first edition was *Le Pays des Fourrures*, Hetzel, Paris, 2 vols., 1873, after it ran as a serial, Sept. 20, 1872–Dec. 15, 1873. The first edition in English was issued by Low, 1874 (1873), 19.5 cm., 234 pp., illustrated, 10/6, translated by Nancy D'Anvers, listed in the *Ath* on Oct. 25, 1873. Low issued it in 1 vol. in 1877, illustrated, all edges gilt, in pink-gray cloth; and issued an authorized and illustrated edition in 1878, 12mo, 1/0 sewed, 1/6 cloth, advertised in the *Ath* on Aug. 3.

The first American edition was issued by James R. Osgood & Co., Boston, 1873, from the Low plates, listed in *PW* on Nov. 29, 1873, and by *Lit W* as published in Nov. Lovell, Adam & Co., New York, issued it, 1876, 8vo, 334 pp., with 100 full-page illustrations, in gray cloth.

See 1890

215 FLORENCE MARRYAT, ed. ***Christmas Number of London Society.*** Illustrated. 1/0   Dec. 1 (*Spect* ad)

The ad said "Now ready."

216 (WALTER BESANT & JAMES RICE) ***Such a Good Man!*** 8vo. Illustrated. 1/0 sewed Dec. 15 (*Ath* ad)

The ad said "Now ready." This is the first edition (1877), 128 pp., a Christmas story. It was one of four stories in *'Twas in Trafalgar's Bay*, issued by Chatto & Windus, London, 1879, Cr 8vo, 343 pp., 6/0, advertised in the *TWEd* on Mar. 14.

Sampson Low, Marston, Searle & Rivington
Crown Buildings, 188 Fleet Street
1878

217 AMOS E. DOLBEAR *The Telephone.*
18mo. Illustrated. 1/o sewed Jan. 12
(*Ath* ad)

The ad said "Now ready." This is the first British edition, 1878, 15 cm., 127 pp., from the American plates. Low issued a new edition, illustrated, 130 pp., 1/o sewed, advertised in the *Ath* on Feb. 16, 1878. The first edition was issued by Lee & Shepard, Boston; etc., 1877, 15 cm., 127 pp., illustrated.

218 ANONYMOUS *My Holiday: Where Shall I Spend It?* 8vo. 1/o May 25
(*Ath* ad)

The ad said "Now ready." This is the first edition, 1878.

219 HARRIET B. STOWE *Uncle Tom's Cabin.* 16mo. 1/o sewed, 2/6 cloth
Aug. 3 (*Ath* ad)

One might be forgiven for thinking this is in the *Rose Library*, and, indeed, the ad in the *Ath* gave it as such, No. 34, but I don't believe it should be so considered. No. 34 was *Six to One* (see below), and I have not found a single listing of this as in the *Rose Library*. The first edition was issued by John P. Jewett, Boston; etc., 2 vols., 1852, listed in the *Ind* on Mar. 20. The first British edition is doubtful, but I think it was issued by Henry Vizetelly; C. H. Clarke, London, 1852, 19 cm., 329 pp., illus-

trated, 2/6 cloth, advertised in the *Ath* on Apr. 24 as "On Apr. 30" and on May 15 as "Now ready," verbatim from the tenth American edition. The *PC* for Oct. 15, 1852, announced ten different editions in one fortnight. At least 12 different editions (not reissues) were published in England within the year 1852; and there were 40 editions from 18 houses in England within a year of the first edition. Low was not among them.

220 CHARLES D. WARNER *In the Wilderness.* 16mo. 1/o sewed, 2/6 cloth
Sept. 7 (*Spect*)

Rose Library No. 33. This is the first British edition, 1878. Low issued it in 1890, 12mo, 2/o. Trübner, London, imported the American edition, and it was "On our table" in the *Ath* for Aug. 10, 1878. The first edition was issued by Houghton, Osgood & Co., Boston; etc., 1878, 15 cm., 176 pp., $.75 in terra-cotta, mauve, or green cloth, blue endpapers, red edges. Records show 1,510 copies were bound June 20–July 29, and a second printing of 500 copies was bound Aug. 16–Sept. 13. It was listed in the *Ind* on July 4 and in *PW* on July 6. Houghton, Mifflin & Co., Boston, issued it, 1881, 18mo, $.75 cloth, with two added chapters, advertised in the *New-York Times* on Nov. 27, 1880.

221 PHILIP S. ROBINSON *Cabul or Afghanistan.* Fcp 8vo. Frontispiece (portrait). Folding map. 1/0 sewed Oct. 5 (*Ath* ad)

The ad said "Now ready." This is the first edition, 1878, 17 cm., 91 pp.

222 (EDWARD BELLAMY) *Six to One.* 16mo. 1/0 sewed, 2/6 cloth   Nov. (*Ath* ad)

Rose Library No. 34. The ad said "Now ready." This is the first British edition, 1878, 126 pp. Low reissued it in the *Rose Library*, 1/0, listed in the *Bks* as published in July 1879. The first edition was issued by G. P. Putnam's Sons, New York, 1878, 16mo, anonymous, 176 pp., frontispiece, $.40 paper, $.75 cloth, listed in the *Ind* on Aug. 1. They issued a new and revised edition in 1890, 16mo, $.35 paper, advertised in the *New-York Times* on Feb. 11.

223 MOWBRAY W. MORRIS *The First Afghan War.* 12mo. 1/0   Nov. 16 (*Ath* ad)

The ad said "Now ready." This is the first edition, 1878, 17 cm., 105 pp.

224 (CHARLES F. BLACKBURN) *A Continental Tour of Eight Days for Forty-Four Shillings.* 12mo. 1/0 Nov. 23 (*Ath* ad)

The ad said "Now ready." This is the first edition, 1878, 107 pp., by A Journey-Man.

225 JULES VERNE *The Mysterious Island.* 3 vols. Illustrated. 12mo. 1/0 limp boards, each   1878?

The first edition was *L'Ile Mysterieuse.* Part 1, *Les Naufrages de L'Air,* Paris, 1874; part 2, *L'Abandonne,* Paris, 1875; part 3, *Le Secret de L'Isle,* Paris, 1875. It ran serially Jan. 1, 1874–Dec. 15, 1875. The first edition in English of part 1 was either *Wrecked in the Air,* issued by Scribner, Armstrong & Co., New York; or Henry L. Shepard, Boston, *Shipwrecked in the Air,* 1874. The first was an authorized edition, 8vo, 48 illustrations, $.30 paper, $.60 cloth, advertised in

the *New-York Times* on Oct. 30 as "This day" and listed in *PW* on Nov. 7, 1874. The second issue was listed in *PW* on Oct. 31 and advertised in *Lit W* on Nov. 1 as "Ready." It was also issued by Hurd & Houghton, New York, in 1874, authorized edition, listed in the *Ind* on Nov. 12, 1874, *The Mysterious Island.* Part 1 ran in *Scribner's Monthly,* Apr. 1874–Jan. 1875; part 2 ran Feb. 1875–June 1875, and in Sept. and Oct., 1875; part 3, condensed, ran in Mar. and Apr. 1876.

The first edition in English of parts 2 and 3 was issued by Low. They issued the three parts, 1875, square Cr 8vo, illustrated, 7/6 each, translated by W.H.G. Kingston. Part 1, *Dropped from the Clouds,* was listed in the *Ath* on Sept. 4; part 2, *Abandoned,* was listed Sept. 4; and part 3, *The Secret of the Island,* was listed Nov. 6. Low issued the second British edition, 3 vols., 1876, the same, in pictorial green cloth. They issued the 3 vols., 3/6 cloth each, listed in the *Ath* on Feb. 1, 1879; and issued them at 2/0 each, Cr 8vo, listed in the *Spect* on May 15, 1880; and issued the 3 vols., 8vo, illustrated, 0/6 sewed each, *The Mysterious Island,* listed in the *Bks* for May 1899. It ran in Low's *St. James's Magazine.*

Scribner, Armstrong & Co., New York, issued it in 3 vols., from the Low plates, 1875, Cr 8vo, illustrated, $2.00 each. Part 1 was advertised in the *New-York Times* on Nov. 6, 1875, as "Now ready" and listed in *PW* on Nov. 13; part 2, advertised on Nov. 27 as "Now ready" and listed in *PW* on Dec. 4; part 3 advertised on Dec. 4 as "Shortly" and on Dec. 11 as if ready, and listed in *PW* on Dec. 18. They issued it in 1 vol. in 1876, new and cheaper edition, 8vo, 145 full-page illustrations, $3.00 cloth, advertised in the *New-York Times* on Mar. 18, 1876; and possibly reissued it, as it was listed in the *Nation* on May 4, 1876. Henry L. Shepard, Boston, also issued it in 3 vols., 1875.

See 1890

226 ANONYMOUS ***Bonn to Metz per Bicycle in Six Days.*** 24mo. 2/0 1878 (*Eng Cat*)

This is the first edition. I cannot trace it.

227 RICHARD GLOVER ***Cyprus.*** Cr 8vo. 0/6 1878 (*BM*)

This is the first edition, 1878.

228 ANONYMOUS ***Three Months in the Paying Ward of a London Hospital. By a Lady.*** 12mo. 0/6 1878 (*Eng Cat*)

This is the first edition, 1879, 40 pp., with a preface signed "R."

229 FRITZ REUTER (HEINRICH L.C.F. REUTER) ***An Old Story of My Farming Days.*** 3 vols., 16mo. 1/6 sewed, 2/0 flexible cloth each 1878 (*BM*)

German Authors No. 25. This is 1878, authorized edition, 16.5 cm., a translation of *Ut Mine Stromtid* by M. W. Macdowall. Low issued it (1878), 3 vols., copyright edition, 20 cm., 31/6, translated by Macdowall and Leipzig printed. It was advertised in the *TWEd* on Nov. 29 as "Ready" and advertised in the *Spect* on Nov. 20 as "Ready." Low issued it in 1880 in 3 vols., 18mo, 6/0, listed in the *Spect* on Mar. 20. The first edition was as vols. 3–5 of *Olle Kamellen: Ut Mine Stromtid*, issued at Wismar, 1863–64.

In the United States it ran in *Littell's Living Age*, as *Seed Time and Harvest*, beginning in Jan. 1871. It was issued by J. B. Lippincott & Co., Philadelphia, as *Seed Time and Harvest* in 1871, 8vo, $1.00 paper, $1.50 cloth, advertised in the *New-York Times* on Sept. 30 as "Just issued." They issued a new edition in 1878, 8vo, $.75 paper, $1.25 cloth, listed in the *Nation* on Apr. 4. It was also issued by George Munro, New York, 2 vols., (1886), *An Old Story of My Farming Days*, 18 cm., $.20 each in buff wrappers, decorated and printed in red and black, *Seaside Library Pocket Edition* No. 750, with wrapper date of Apr. 19, 1886. It was advertised in the *New-York Times* on May 1 as a late issue. It is my set.

230 ELEANOR E. ORLEBAR *Food for the People.* 12mo. 1/0 limp boards Mar. 15 (*Acad*)

This is the first edition, 1879.

231 (EDWARD MARSTON) *Copyright, National and International.* Demy 8vo. 2/0 sewed Mar. 15 (*Ath*)

This is the first edition, 1879, 21 cm., 47 pp., with a prefatory note signed E. M. (Edward Marston).

232 GEORG EBERS *Homo Sum.* 2 vols., 16mo. 1/6 sewed, 2/0 flexible cloth each July 5 (*Ath*)

German Authors No. 24. The *U Cat* and the *BM* both give this as 1878, and that is where it should be according to the number in the series. However, both the *Ath* and the *Spect* list it on July 5, 1879. It is translated by Clara Bell. The first British edition was issued by Low, 2 vols., 1878, copyright edition, Cr 8vo, 21/0, translated by Clara Bell, advertised in the (*Ath*) on May 25 as "Now ready." The first edition was issued in Stuttgart and Leipzig, 1878, 19.5 cm., 376 pp.

In the United States the first edition was issued by William S. Gottsberger, New York, 1880, authorized edition, 16.5 cm., 299 pp., $.40 paper, $.75 cloth, translated by Bell, listed in the *Nation* on June 3 and advertised in the *New-York Times* on May

15 as "This day." The Gottsberger edition barely beat out one by George Munro, New York, 1880, 32.5 cm., 40 pp., translated by Bell, *Seaside Library* No. 765, $.10 paper, advertised in the *New-York Times* on June 12 as a late issue and probably issued very close to June 12.

233 STANDISH O'GRADY *Early Bardic Literature, Ireland.* 12mo. 1/0 July 5 (*Ath* ad)

The ad said, "Now ready." This is the first separate edition, 1879, 18 cm., 88pp., with a cover title. It is the introduction to vol. 2 of the author's *History of Ireland*. Low reissued it in 1881, 1/0, advertised in the *Spect* on July 9.

234 EDWARD H. BICKERSTETH *The Master's Will.* 24mo. 1/0 sewed 1879 (*BM*)

This is the first edition, 1879, 30 pp., a sermon.

235 (HARRIET BICKERSTETH, later COOK) *Family Prayers for Working Men.* 18mo. 1/0 sewed 1879 (*BM*)

This is the first edition , 1879, 48 pp., with an introduction by Edward H. Bickersteth.

236 BOYD M.M. RANKING *A Summer Month in Normandy.* 8vo, 1/0 1879 (*BM*)

This is the first edition, 1879, 96 pp.

Sampson Low, Marston, Searle & Rivington
Crown Buildings, 188 Fleet Street
1880

237 ANONYMOUS *Wealth or Weal?*
8vo. 1/0 sewed   Feb. 14 (*Ath* ad)

This is the first edition, 1880, 24 pp.

238 ANONYMOUS *Back Again; or, Five Years of Liberal Rule, 1880–85.* 8 vo. 0/6 sewed   Mar. 20 (*Ath* ad)

This has 32 pp. I can't trace it except for its listing in the *Eng Cat.*

239 GEORG EBERS *The Sisters.* 2 vols. 16mo. 1/6 sewed, 2/0 flexible cloth each Mar. 20 (*Spect*)

German Authors No. 26. This is 1880, translated by Clara Bell. This is the first British edition. The first edition was issued by Vallberger, Stuttgart, 1880, 432 pp., reviewed in the *Spect* on May 1, 1880, *Die Schwestern.*

In the United States it was issued by William S. Gottsberger, New York, 1880, authorized edition, 16.5 cm., 352 pp., translated by Bell, $.40 paper, $.75 cloth, listed in the *Nation* on June 24 and in *Godey's Lady's Book* for Aug. (thus probably issued in May or June). It was also issued by D. Appleton & Co., New York and London, 1880, 18.5 cm., 371 pp., translated by Bell; and by George Munro, New York, 1880, 32.5 cm., 47 pp., *Seaside Library* No. 880, my copy, with a cover date of Dec. 3, 1880, and listed in *PW* on Dec. 11.

240 (HENRY DUNCKLEY) *I and My Property.* Cr 8vo. 1/6 cloth   May 8 (*Spect*)

This is the first book edition, 1880, 19 cm., 87 pp., by Verax, partly reprinted from *Fraser's Magazine.*

241 WILHELMINE VON HILLERN *The Hour Will Come.* 2 vols., 16mo. 1/6 sewed, 2/0 flexible cloth each   June 12 (*Ath*)

German Authors No. 27. This is translated by Clara Bell. The first edition was *Und Sie Kommt Doch*, Berlin, 3 vols., 1879. Tauchnitz, Leipzig, issued it, 1879, 2 vols., 16 cm., translated by Clara Bell; and a duplicate was issued by Low, 2 vols., 1879, advertised in the *Ath* on Mar. 8. It was issued in New York by William S. Gottsberger, 1880, 16.5 cm., 273 pp., translated by Bell, listed in the *Nation* on Nov. 4.

242 JOHN MACGREGOR *The Voyage Alone in the Yawl "Rob Roy."* Fourth edition. 12mo. Illustrated. Maps. 2/6 boards June 12 (*Ath* ad)

This is probably Low, London; Roberts Bros., Boston, 1880, 17.5 cm., 328 pp. The first edition was issued by Low, 1867, 12mo, 335 pp., illustrated, map, 5/0, listed in the *Ath* on Dec. 14, 1867. The same was still advertised in the *Spect* on July 30, 1870. They issued the second edition, with the Roberts Bros. imprint added, 1868. Low issued a new edition, enlarged and thoroughly revised, in 1878, Cr 8vo, 5/0, advertised in the *Ath* on Nov. 9; and issued the sixth edition in 1893, p 8vo, 2/6, in Oct., given by the *Eng Cat.*

In the United States, Roberts Bros., Boston, issued it in 1868, illustrated, $2.50, advertised in the *Nation* on Apr. 30 as "Just published" and advertised in the *New-York Times* on Apr. 23 as "Just published." They issued the fifth edition, 1880, illustrated, with maps; and issued it in 1887 with the other two "Rob Roy" titles, in 1 vol., new edition, 16mo, $2.00 cloth, advertised in the *New-York Times* on Nov. 24, 1887.

243 BERTHOLD AUERBACH *Brigitta.* Copyright edition. 16mo. 1/6 sewed, 2/0 flexible cloth   Sept. 11 (*Ath*)

German Authors No. 28. This is 1880, 16 cm., 286 pp., translated by Clara Bell. The first edition was issued at Stuttgart, 1880, 18.5 cm., 235 pp. The present edition is the first British edition. In the United States it was issued by Henry Holt & Co., New York, 1880, 16 cm., 244 pp., *Leisure Hour Series* No. 116, $1.00, advertised in

the *New-York Times* on Oct. 2 as "Just ready" and listed in the *Nation* on Oct. 7. It was also issued by George Munro, New York, 1880, 32.5 cm., 22 pp., my copy, $.10 paper, *Seaside Library* No. 841, with a cover date of Sept. 30. It was advertised in the *New-York Times* on Oct. 14 as a late issue, and listed in *PW* on Oct. 10, translated by Clara Bell.

244 ANONYMOUS *The Highland Handbook.* 12mo. 0/6   1880 (*BM*)

This is the first edition, 1880. It includes a list of shooting and fishing, etc., with time tables, June–July 1880.

245 PAUL DELAROCHE (HIPPOLYTE DELAROCHE) *Hemicycle of the Palais des Beaux Arts, Paris.* p 8vo. 1/6 1880 (*Eng Cat*)

I cannot trace this.

246 T. H. LEWIS *Manual for Electors.* 12mo. 0/6   1880 (*Eng Cat*)

I think this was the title advertised by Low in the *Ath* on Mar. 20, 1880, at 0/6, *Have I a Vote?*, "Now ready." Otherwise I cannot trace it.

247 J. L. BASHFORD *Elementary Education in Saxony.* Fcp 8vo. 1/0 Jan. 29 (*Spect* ad)

This is the first edition, 1881, 17 cm., 89 pp.

248 JULES VERNE *Michael Strogoff, the Courier of the Czar.* 2 vols. 12mo. Illustrated. 1/0 limp boards each   Mar. 5 (*Ath* ad)

This was also issued in 1 vol., Cr 8vo, 3/6, at the same time. It ran as a serial in Paris, Jan. 1–Dec. 15, 1876, *Michael Strogoff—Moscow—Irkoutsk*; and Hetzel, Paris, issued it in 2 vols., 1876, part 2 being *Un Drame au Mexique*. It ran in Low's *London Society* beginning in Mar. 1876, and Low issued it with the present title, 1877 (1876), p 8vo, illustrated, 10/6, translated by W.H.G. Kingston. It contains also *The Mutineers* and *A Romance of Mexico* and was listed in the *Ath* on Dec. 16, 1876, the first British book edition. Low issued a new edition in 1879, 8vo, 5/0, listed in the *Spect* on Nov. 29, 1879.

In the United States it was issued by Scribner, Armstrong & Co., New York, 1877, Cr 8vo, illustrated, $3.00, revised by Julius Chambers. It was advertised in the *New-York Times* on Jan. 13, 1877, as "On Jan. 18", and listed in *PW* on Jan. 20 and in the *Nation* on Jan. 25. They issued the second edition, the same, advertised in the *New-York Times* on Jan. 24, 1877, as "Now ready," and issued the third edition, the same, advertised there on Feb. 17, 1877. They issued a new edition, revised, in 1881, $2.00, listed in the *Ind* on Oct. 13 and in the *Nation* on Nov. 3. It was also issued by Frank Leslie's Publishing House, New York, 1876, translated by E. G. Walraven. It was also issued by George Munro, New York, 1877, quarto, paper, $.10, *Seaside Library* No. 131, advertised in the *New-York Times* on Nov. 8, 1877, as "Today." Munro issued a large-type edition in 1881, illustrated, $.20 paper, *Seaside Library* No. 1092, advertised in the *New-York Times* on Sept. 23 as "Out today."
See 1890

249 ROBERT GRANT, ed. *The Confessions of a Frivolous Girl.* p 8vo. 1/0 stiff wrappers   Aug. 6 (*Ath* ad)

The ad said "Now ready." The first edition was issued by A. Williams & Co., Boston; etc., 1880, 18 cm., 220 pp., illustrated, reviewed in *Harper's New Monthly Magazine* for Oct. 1880. It was reissued by James R. Osgood & Co., Boston, in 1882, new edition, 16mo, $1.25, advertised in the *New-York Times* on Mar. 25. The first British edition was issued by Low, 1881, Cr 8vo, 192 pp., 6/0, listed in the *Ath* on Dec. 25, 1880, a duplicate with a new title page of the (8th) American edition of 1880.

250 WILL M. CARLETON ***Farm Festivals.***
12mo. 1/o limp boards, 2/6 cloth
Aug. 27 (*Ath* ad)

Rose Library. The first edition was issued by Low, 1881, small 4to, 151 pp., illustrated, 12/o, printed in New York. It was advertised in *PC* on June 15 as "Now ready" and listed in the *Ath* on June 25. The first American edition was issued by Harper & Bros., New York, 1881, 23 cm., 151 pp., frontispiece, illustrations, $2.00 and $2.50 cloth. It has 6 pp. of ads and was advertised in the *New-York Times* on June 24 as "This day," listed in the *Nation* and *Ind* on June 30, and listed in *PW* on July 2. One of the cloth issues was in gray-green, pictorial cloth, with bevelled boards.
See 1893

251 WILLIAM W. HALL ***How to Live Long.***
[Fifth edition.] 12mo. 2/o Oct. 15 (*Spect*)

The first British edition was issued by Low, 1875, 17 cm., 282 pp., 2/o cloth, listed in the *Spect* on Sept. 25. The first American edition was issued by Hurd & Houghton, New York, 1875, 19.5 cm., 316 pp., reissued 1876, 1877, 328 pp. It was issued by Belford Bros., Toronto, 1875, 19 cm., 293 pp.

252 WILLIAM R. BALCH ***Garfield's Words.***
[Copyright.] 12mo. 1/o Oct. 29 (*Spect* ad)
The ad said "Now ready." A 2/6 cloth edition was listed in the *Ath* on Nov. 26. The present edition is the first British edition, 1881, 183 pp. The first American edition was issued Houghton, Mifflin & Co., Boston, 1881, 15 cm., 184 pp., frontispiece (portrait), $1.00, advertised in the *New-York Times* on Oct. 2 as "On Oct. 8" and on Oct. 8 as if ready.

253 NANCY D'ANVERS (NANCY MEUGENS, later BELL) ***Forms of Land and Water.***
12mo. Illustrated. o/6 1881 (*BM*)

Science Ladders No. 1. This is the first edition, 1881, 66 pp. It was reissued by George Philips & Son, London (1881), 66 pp. It was issued in the United States by G. P. Putnam's Sons, New York, 1882, square 16mo, 67 pp., illustrated, listed the *Nation* on July 19, $.50. They reissued *Science Ladders*, six vols., in 1884, square 16mo, illustrated, $.50 boards each; and 6 vols.-in-1, $1.50 cloth, both advertised in the *New-York Times* on Apr. 14 as "Now ready." The six titles are: 1. Forms of Land and Water; 2. A Story of Early Exploration; 3. Vegetable Life; 4. Flowerless Plants; 5. Lower Forms of Water Animals; 6. Lowly Mantle and Armour-Wearers.

254 NANCY D'ANVERS ***Vegetable Life.***
12mo. Illustrated. o/6 1881 (*BM*)

Science Ladders. This is the first edition, 1881, 80 pp. It was reissued by Philips & Son, London (1881), 80 pp. In the United States it was issued by G. P. Putnam's Sons, New York, no date, 78 pp., illustrated, as No. 3 of *Science Ladders*, listed in the *Nation* on July 19, 1882, $.50. They reissued it in 1884 (see the preceding title).

255 NANCY D'ANVERS ***Lowest Forms of Water Animals.*** 12mo. Illustrated. o/6 1881 (*BM*)

Science Ladders. This is the first edition, 1881, 64 pp. It was reissued by Philips & Son, London (1881). Low did not issue any more of the six titles, the remaining three being issued by George Philips & Son, London. The first American edition was issued by G. P. Putnam's Sons, New York, 1882, square 16mo, 59 pp., illustrated, $.50 boards, *Science Ladders* No. 5, listed in the *Nation* on Dec. 7, 1882. They reissued it in 1884 (see item 253 above).

Sampson Low, Marston, Searle & Rivington
Crown Buildings, 188 Fleet Street
1882

256 WILL M. CARLETON *Farm Legends.*
12mo. 1/0 sewed, 2/6 cloth   Feb. 1 (*PC*)
Rose Library. This is the first British edition, 1882, 192 pp., in verse. Low issued all three "Farm" titles in 1 vol., 1885, new edition, 16.5 cm., 3/6, advertised in the *Spect* on Nov. 1, 1884. The first edition of the present title was issued by Harper & Bros., New York (copyright 1875), 23 cm., 131 pp., illustrated, listed in the *Nation* on Dec. 9, 1875. They issued a new and enlarged edition in 1887, square Cr 8vo, illustrated, $2.00 and $2.50 in cloth, advertised in the *New-York Times* on Nov. 22, 1887; and they issued a new edition, the same, advertised in the same on Aug. 23, 1892. In Canada it was issued by Belford Bros., Toronto, 1875, 154 pp., illustrated. See 1893

257 BERTHOLD AUERBACH *Spinoza.*
2 vols. Authorized edition. 16mo.
1/6 sewed, 2/0 flexible cloth each
Feb. 4 (*Spect*)
German Authors No. 29. This is the first British edition, 1882, 16 cm., translated by E. Nicholson. It was advertised in *Notes & Queries* on Feb. 11. The first edition was issued in Stuttgart, 2 vols., 1837. It was issued in the United States by Henry Holt & Co., New York, 1882, 17 cm., 444 pp., *Leisure Hour Series*, $1.00, translated by Nicholson. It was advertised in the *New-York Times* on Mar. 25 as "Today" and listed in the *Nation* on Apr. 6. It was also issued by George Munro, New York (1882), 32.5 cm., 47 pp., $.20 paper, *Seaside Library* No. 1239, advertised in the *New-York Times* on Mar. 29 as a late issue and listed in *PW* on Apr. 8.

258 (EDGAR L. WELCH) *How John Bull Lost London.* 16 mo. 1/0 sewed   Feb. 25 (*Spect*)
This is the first edition, 1882, 127 pp. Low advertised the second edition, the same, on Mar. 4 as "Now ready"; and they advertised the 10th thousand in Apr.; and issued the fourth edition, 1882. The present edition is in white wrappers, printed in red, blue, and black, by "Grip."

259 JULES VERNE *Dick Sands, the Boy Captain.* Author's illustrated edition.
2 vols. 12mo, 1/0 limp boards each; 1 vol. 3/6 cloth   Mar. 25 (*Ath* ad)
The 3/6 is Cr 8vo, frontispiece, illustrated, in green cloth with all edges gilt. The first edition was *Un Capitaine de Quinze Ans*, Hetzel, Paris, 2 vols., 1878. It ran as a serial in Paris, Jan. 1–Dec. 5, 1878. The first edition of the complete work in English was issued by Low, 1879 (1878), p 8vo, illustrated, 10/6, translated by Ellen Frewer, listed in the *Ath* on Dec. 7, 1878. Low issued a new edition in 1880, 8vo, 5/0, listed in the *Spect* on May 15.

The first edition in English of vol. 2 was issued by George Munro, New York, *A Captain at Fifteen*, 2 vols., 1878, $.10 paper each, *Seaside Library* No. 414. The first half was advertised in the *New-York Times* on Oct. 26, 1878, as a late issue, probably issued very close to Oct. 26; and the second half was advertised on Dec. 20, 1878, as "On Dec. 23." It was also issued by Charles Scribner's Sons, New York, 1879, 8vo, 486 pp., illustrated, $3.00, advertised in the *New-York Times* on Dec. 18, 1878, as "On Dec. 21," and on Dec. 21 as "This day." It was listed in *PW* on Dec. 28 and in the *Ind* on Jan. 2, 1879.
See 1890

260 FREDERICK G. BURNABY *A Ride Across the Channel, and Other Adventures in the Air.* 12mo. Folding map. 1/0 sewed   Apr. 8 (*Ath* ad)

The ad said "Now ready." This is the first edition, 1882, 17 cm., 128 pp., Low advertised the 9th thousand on Apr. 15 as "Ready."

261 FANNY STENHOUSE
An Englishwoman in Utah. New and cheaper edition. Cr 8vo. Portraits. Illustrated. 2/6 boards   Apr. 29 (*Spect*)

This is 1882, 19 cm., 404 pp., with a preface by Harriet B. Stowe. The first British edition was issued by Low, 1880, 20 cm., 404 pp., portraits, 10/6, with the Stowe preface. It was listed in the *Ath* on Apr. 3. Low issued it, 1888, a duplicate of the first edition with a new title page, 3/6 cloth, *The Tyranny of Mormonism.* It was issued in the United States as *Tell It All*, by the Queen City Publishing Co., Cincinnati; etc., 1874, 23 cm., 623 pp., portraits, illustrations, with the preface by Stowe, in green cloth. It was also issued by A. D. Worthington, Hartford, 1874, the same.

262 (EDGAR L. WELCH) *The Monster Municipality.* 12mo. 1/0 colored boards Apr. 29 (*Ath* ad)

The ad said "Now ready." This is the first edition, 1882, 128 pp., by "Grip."

263 JULES VERNE *The Child of the Cavern.* Author's illustrated edition. 12mo. 1/0 limp boards, 2/0 cloth Apr. (*Bks*)

This has 174 pp. The first edition was issued by Hetzel, Paris, 1877, *Les Indes-Noires*, 28 cm., 173 pp., illustrated. It ran in *Le Temps*, Mar. 28–Apr. 22, 1877. The first edition in English was issued by George Munro, New York, 1877, 32.5 cm., $.10 paper, *Seaside Library* No. 5, advertised in the *New-York Times* on June 18 as "Now ready," *Black Indies*. It was issued by Porter & Coates, Philadelphia, 1883, *Underground City*, translated by W.H.G. Kingston, listed in *PW* on Oct. 20.

The first British edition was issued by Low, 1877, 20 cm., 247 pp., illustrated, 7/6, translated by Kingston, listed in the *Ath* on Oct. 20. Low issued the second edition, 1878, 7/6, listed in the *Spect* on Feb. 23, 1878.
See 1890

264 ALFRED H. HUTH *On the Employment of Women.* 12mo. 0/6 sewed   May 20 (*Ath* ad)

This is the first edition, 1882, 18 cm., 40 pp.

265 WILLIAM D. HOWELLS
The Undiscovered Country.
Third edition. 1/0 sewed   June (*Bks*)
Rose Library. This is 1882, 256 pp., in decorated rose wrappers. This ran in the *Atlantic Monthly*, Jan.–July 1880, and the first book edition was issued by Houghton, Mifflin & Co., Boston, 1880, 19.5 cm., 419 pp., in blue cloth, reviewed in the *Ath* on Aug. 21 and noticed in *Harper's New Monthly Magazine* for Sept. (thus probably

issued in June or July). It probably had the joint imprint of Trübner, London. The first British edition was issued by Low, 1880, Cr 8vo, 419 pp., 10/6, a duplicate of the first American edition, with a new title page. It was listed in the *Ath* on Sept. 11. Low issued the second edition, 1881, 256 pp., 3/6 cloth in *Low's Select Novelets*. It was also issued by David Douglas, Edinburgh, 2 vols., 1882, 16mo, 1/o sewed, 1/6 boards each, listed by the *Bks* as published in Nov. 1882, author's edition.

266 LUCIEN BIART **The Clients of Doctor Bernagius.** [New edition.] 2 vols., 12mo. 1/o sewed each   June (*Bks*)
Rose Library. This is translated from the French by Mrs. Cashel Hoey. The first edition was *Les Clientes de Docteur Bernagius*, Paris, 1873, 317 pp. The first British edition was Low, 1881, 18 cm., 343 pp., 3/6, *Low's Select Novelets* No. 4, listed in the *Ath* and *Spect* on Oct. 1.

267 EDGAR FAWCETT **A Gentleman of Leisure.** 12mo. 1/o sewed   July 1 (*Ath* ad)
Rose Library. The first edition was issued by Houghton, Mifflin & Co., Boston; Trübner, London, 1881, 15 cm., 323 pp., advertised in the *New-York Times* on June 19, $1.00, and listed in *PW* on June 25. This seems to indicate that Trübner imported it, but I've found no evidence of this. Houghton, Mifflin issued it in their *Riverside Pocket Series* No. 4 in 1886, $.50 cloth, advertised in the *New-York Times* on Sept. 25. The first British edition was issued by Low, 1881, 256 pp., 3/6 cloth, in *Low's Select Novelets*, listed in *PC* on Nov. 15, 1881. It was issued in Canada by Rose-Belford, Toronto, 1881, about Oct. 12.

268 (WILLIAM C. RUSSELL) **My Watch Below.** Cr 8vo. 2/6   July 8 (*Ath*)
This is the first edition, 1882, 248 pp., with a 32-page catalog (Dec. 1881) at the back, by A Seafarer, reprinted from the

Daily Telegraph. It was advertised in the *Ath* on July 1 as 2/6 boards and had been so advertised for six weeks, but the listing on July 8 was 2/6 cloth, and it was so advertised thereafter. The second edition, 2/6 cloth, was advertised in the *Ath* on Mar. 24, 1883, as "Ready." Low issued it in 1885, Cr 8vo, 6/o, by Russell, listed in the *Ath* on May 23; and Low issued a new edition, 1889, 17 cm., 248 pp.; reissued the same in 1891 and 1895.

The first American edition by a few days, was issued by Harper & Bros., New York (1882), 29.5 cm., 62 pp., $.20 paper, by Russell, advertised in the *New-York Times* on Aug. 4 as "This day" and listed in the *Ind* on Aug. 10 and in *PW* on Aug. 12. It was also issued by George Munro, New York (1882), 32.5 cm., 56 pp., $.20 paper, advertised in the *New-York Times* on Aug. 17 as a late issue, and listed in *PW* on Aug. 19.

269 EDWIN DE LEON **Egypt Under Its Khedives.** Cr 8vo. Illustrated. Colored Map. 2/6 boards   July 13 (*Ath*)
An ad in the *Ath* on July 8 said "On July 13." This is an abridged edition, 1882, 243 pp., reissued at 2/6 boards in Sept. 1882. The first edition was *The Khedive's Egypt*, issued by Low, 1877, 22.5 cm., 435 pp., illustrated, 18/o, advertised in the *Ath* on Aug. 11 as "Ready," and listed in the *Spect* on Aug. 11. Low issued the second edition, 1877, the same, listed in the *Spect* on Sept. 22; and issued the third edition, 1877, the same, listed in the *Spect* on Jan. 26, 1878. Low issued a new edition (the fourth), 1879, 22.5 cm., 435 pp., illustrated, 8/6, listed in the *Spect* on May 17.

The first American edition was issued by Harper & Bros., New York, 1878, 19.5 cm., 435 pp., illustrated, $1.50 cloth, advertised in the *New-York Times* on Dec. 1, 1877, as "This day." They issued it in the *Franklin Square Library* in 1882, *Egypt Under*

Its Khedives, 44 pp., illustrated, revised with a new chapter added, listed in the *Nation* on Sept. 7, 1882, $.20.

270 JOHN W. MARTIN *Float Fishing and Spinning in the Nottingham Style.* Cr 8vo. Illustrated. 2/0 boards   Dec. 2 (*Ath*)

This is the first edition, 1882, 19 cm., 154 pp. Low issued the second edition, revised and enlarged, p 8vo, 182 pp., illustrated 2/0, given by the *BM*; and advertised it, the same, in 1890, as 2/6 colored boards.

271 SIR THOMAS B. LENNARD *To Married Women and Women About to Be Married, the Married Women's Property Act, 1882.* Second edition, 0/6 sewed   Dec. (*Bks*)

This is 1883, 47 pp. The first edition was *Married Women's Property Act*, issued by Waterlow & Son, London, 1882, 32 pp. The *BM* gives the second edition as I've given it, but the *U Cat* gives London, 1883, with no indication of edition, and also Waterlow & Son, 1882, second edition, 22 cm., 39 pp!

272 JULES VERNE *Hector Servadac.* Third edition. 2 vols. 12mo. Illustrated. 1/0 sewed each   1882 (*U Cat*)

These are 1882, and Low also issued this title in 1 vol. in 1882, Cr 8vo, 3/6 cloth, listed in the *Spect* on May 27. Low issued the first British edition, 1878 (1877), p 8vo, 370 pp., illustrated, 10/6 in brown pictorial cloth, translated by Ellen Frewer, and listed in the *Ath* on Nov. 17, 1877. This title consists of "To the Sun" as part 1, and "Off on a Comet" as part 2. The *U Cat* gives the second Low edition as 1881, 370 pp., illustrated, but a new edition, 8vo, 5/0, is listed by the *Spect* on May 15, 1880. Thus there seems to be one too many editions! The first edition in book form was issued by J. Hetzel, Paris, 2 vols., 1877. It ran as a serial, Jan. 1–Dec. 15, 1877.

In the United States it was issued by George Munro, New York, 1877, 32.5 cm., 39 pp., $.20 paper, *Seaside Library* No. 43, advertised in the *New-York Times* on Aug. 29 and again on Dec. 12, 1877. It was also issued by Scribner, Armstrong & Co., New York, 1878, 22 cm., 370 pp., illustrated, translated by Frewer, $3.00, with the same plates as used by Low. It was advertised in the *New-York Times* on Dec. 1, 1877, as "Next week," and on Dec. 8 as "This day," and listed in the *Ind* on Dec. 20. They issued a new edition in 1882, 8vo, illustrated, $2.00, advertised in the *New-York Times* on Sept. 20. Part 1, "To the Sun," was issued by Claxton, Remsen & Heffelfinger, Philadelphia, 1878, translated by Edward Roth, listed in the *Nation* on Jan. 3, 1878, and advertised in *Lit W* (monthly) on Jan. 1, 1878. They issued part 2, "Off on a Comet," 1878, listed by *Lit W* as published in May, and listed in the *Ind* on June 6, 1878, translated by Roth.
See 1890

273 A. C. HUGHES *The Channel Tunnel.* Cr 8vo. 0/6   1882 (*Eng Cat*)

I cannot trace this.

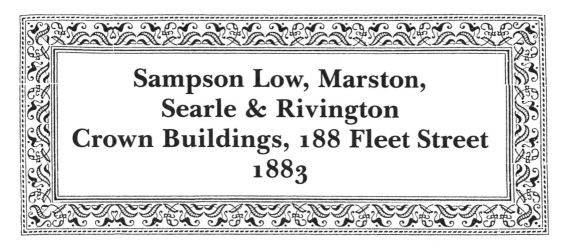

Sampson Low, Marston, Searle & Rivington
Crown Buildings, 188 Fleet Street
1883

274 EDWARD H. BICKERSTETH
Evangelical Churchmanship and Eclecticism. 8vo. 1/0 Jan. 20 (*Ath* ad)

The ad said "Now ready." This is No. 1 of "Thoughts for To-Day" to be published once a month for twelve issues. It is the first edition, 1883, 36 pp.

275 LOUISA M. ALCOTT *Eight Cousins.* [New edition.] 12mo. Illustrated. 2/0 sewed Feb. (*Bks*)

Rose Library. The first edition was issued by Roberts Bros., Boston, 1875, 17.5 cm., 290 pp., illustrated, $1.50, advertised in the *New-York Times* on Sept. 30, and listed in *PW* on Sept. 25 and in the *Ind* on Oct. 14. They issued the 15th thousand, advertised in the *New-York Times* on Oct. 11, the same. In England it ran in *St. Nicholas*, Jan.–Oct. 1875, illustrated, and the first British book edition was issued by Low, 1875, 12mo, 290 pp., illustrated, 5/0, listed in the *Ath* on Oct. 2.

276 LOUISA M. ALCOTT *Rose in Bloom.* [Third edition.] 12mo. 2/0 sewed Feb. (*Bks*)

Rose Library. This is a sequel to *Eight Cousins.* The first American edition was issued by Roberts Bros., Boston, 1876, 17.5 cm., 375 pp., with an added vignette title page, $1.50, advertised in the *New-York Times* on Nov. 29 as "This day" and listed in the *Ind*

on Nov. 30. They issued a new edition, advertised in the *New-York Times* on Feb. 15, 1877, as "Just ready," and issued the 18th edition, advertised there on Feb.27, 1877. The first British edition was issued by Low, 1877 (1876), 12mo, 375 pp., 3/6 cloth, advertised in the *Ath* on Nov. 18, 1876, as "Ready," and listed on Nov. 25.

277 LOUISA M. ALCOTT *Silver Pitchers, and Other Stories.* [New edition.] 12mo. 1/0 sewed, 2/0 cloth Feb. (*Bks*)

Rose Library. The title story ran in the *Youth's Companion*, May 6–June 10, 1875, and the first American book edition was *Silver Pitchers: and Independence*, issued by Roberts Bros., Boston, 1876, 18 cm., 307 pp., $1.25, containing two new pieces and seven others from various periodicals in 1872–75. It was advertised in the *New-York Times* on June 8, and listed in the *Ind* and in the *Nation* on June 15. They advertised in the *New-York Times* on June 17 that the second edition was exhausted and that the third edition would be out in a few days. The first British edition was issued by Low, 1876, with the present title, Cr 8vo, 307 pp., 10/6, advertised in the *Ath* on May 27 as "Now ready", and listed June 3. They issued the second edition in 1876, Cr 8vo, 3/6, listed in the *Ath* on Dec. 16, 1876.

278 LOUISA M. ALCOTT *Under the Lilacs.*
[Third edition.] 12mo. Illustrated. 2/o
sewed Feb. (*Bks*)

Rose Library. This ran in *St. Nicholas*, Dec.
1877–Oct. 1878, and the first book edition
was issued by Roberts Bros., Boston, 1878,
27 cm., 305 pp., illustrated, listed in *PW*
on Oct. 19 and in the *Ind* on Oct. 24. In England it was issued in eleven monthly
parts, Oct. 1877–Sept. 1878, and the first
British book edition was issued by Low,
1878, Cr 8vo, 374 pp., illustrated, 5/o
cloth, advertised as ready and listed in the
Ath on Nov. 2, 1878. Low issued the second
edition in 1879, 12mo, 5/o, listed in the
Spect on Feb. 8.

279 CHARLES M. CLAY (CHARLOTTE M.
CLARK) *Baby Rue.* [New edition.] 12mo.
1/o sewed Feb. (*Bks*)

Rose Library. The first British edition was
issued by Low (1881), 318 pp., 3/6 cloth,
Select Novelets No. 2, listed in the *Ath* on
July 23. It was advertised in the *Ath* on
Dec. 29, 1883, as *Rose Library* No. 21; and
it was advertised as No. 25 on Aug. 15,
1885. The first American edition was issued by Roberts Bros., Boston, 1881, 17
cm., anonymous, 318 pp., $1.00, reviewed
in the *Nation* on July 28 and thus probably
issued in July.

280 (CONSTANCE C. HARRISON) *The Story
of Helen of Troy.* [New edition.] 12mo.
1/o sewed Feb. (*Bks*)

Rose Library. On Dec. 29, 1883, this was advertised as No. 22; and it was advertised as
No. 26 on Aug. 15, 1885. The first British
edition was issued by Low, 1881, anonymous, 206 pp., 3/6 cloth, *Select Novelets* No.
3, reviewed in the *Ath* on Aug. 27. The first
American edition was issued by Harper &
Bros., New York, 1881, 17.5 cm., anonymous, 202 pp.

281 LOUISA M. ALCOTT *Jack and Jill.*
New edition. 12mo. Illustrated. 2/o
sewed Mar. 10 (*Ath*)

Rose Library. This is 1883, 379 pp. The first
British edition was issued by Low, 1881
(1880), 12mo, 379 pp., illustrated, 5/o
cloth, listed in the *Spect* and *Ath* on Oct. 2,
1880. In the United States it ran in *St.
Nicholas*, Dec. 1879–Oct. 1880, and the
first American book edition was issued by
Roberts Bros., Boston, 1880, 17.5 cm.,
325 pp., four illustrations, $1.50 cloth, ad-
vertised in the *New-York Times* on Oct. 11,
and listed in *PW* on Oct. 16

282 LOUISA M. ALCOTT *Jimmy's Cruise in
the "Pinafore," etc.* [New edition.] 12mo.
Illustrated. 2/o sewed Mar. 10 (*Ath*)

Rose Library. This is No. 5 of *Aunt Jo's Scrap-
Bag.* Roberts Bros., Boston, issued six titles in this series, 1872–82. The first British edition was issued by Low, 1879, 17.5
cm., 208 pp., illustrated, 3/6, listed in the
Ath on Oct. 25 and in *PC* on Nov. 3. Low issued the second edition, 12mo, 3/6, listed
in the *Spect* on Dec. 27, 1879. The first
American edition was issued by Roberts
Bros., Boston, 1879, 17 cm., 208 pp.,
$1.00 cloth, with a double vignette frontis-
piece and 16 pp. of publisher's ads at the
back. It contains 13 short stories, six of
which are new and the other seven reprinted from various periodicals where
they appeared 1873–1879. It was advertised in the *New-York Times* on Oct. 17 as
"This day" and listed in *PW* on Oct. 18.

283 WILLIAM C. RUSSELL *The Wreck of
the "Grosvenor."* [Fifth edition.] 4to.
0/6 sewed Apr. 28 (*Ath* ad)

The ad said "Now ready." The first edition
was issued by Low, 3 vols., 1877, 19.5 cm.,
anonymous, 31/6 in green cloth, advertised and reviewed in the *Ath* on Nov. 24.
Low issued the second edition in 3 vols.,
advertised in the *TWEd* on Mar. 29, 1878,
as "Ready"; and they issued the third edi-

tion, 1878, 18 cm., 6/o, listed in the *Spect* on Aug. 21; and they issued the fourth edition, 1882, 17.5 cm., 382 pp., by Russell. Low issued new editions with 382 pp., 1888, 1891; and they issued an edition in 1893, Cr 8vo, portrait, 2/6, advertised in the *Spect* on Sept. 30 as "Ready." Low issued it as *Sixpenny Editions* No. 2, 8vo, 128 pp., o/6 sewed, listed in *PC* on Nov. 20, 1897; and reissued it, the same, in Oct. 1904, given by the *Eng Cat.*

In the United States it was issued by Harper & Bros., New York (1878), 23 cm., anonymous, 120 pp. in double columns, *Library of Select Novels* No. 607, $.30 paper, listed in *PW* on Mar. 9 and in the *Ind* on Mar. 14. They issued it in the *Franklin Square Library*, 4to, $.15 paper, listed in the *Nation* on Apr. 12, 1883. It was also issued by George Munro, New York, 1878, 32.5 cm., paper, *Seaside Library* No. 280, probably in Mar. Munro reissued it in large type, $.20, as *Seaside Library* No. 1339, advertised in the *New-York Times* on July 14, 1882, as a late issue.

284 ALEXANDER M. SULLIVAN, SR.
A "Nutshell" History of Ireland.
24mo. o/6 Aug. 4 (*Ath* ad)
The ad said "Now ready." This is the first edition, 1883, 64 pp.

285 REGINALD F.D. PALGRAVE
The Chairman's Handbook. Fifth and enlarged edition. 12mo. 2/o Aug. 4 (*Ath* ad)
The ad said "Now ready." This is 1883, 103 pp. Low issued it many times, passim, 110 pp., 2/o cloth, including the tenth edition, revised, 1894, and the 14th edition, 1903, 17.5 cm. The first edition was issued by Knight, London (1877), 1/6 limp cloth, listed in the *Ath* on May 19. They issued the second edition (1877), and the third and revised edition (1878).

286 JULES VERNE *The Begum's Fortune.*
[New edition.] 12mo. Illustrated. 1/o sewed, 2/o cloth Sept. (*Bks*)
The first edition was issued by J. Hetzel, Paris, 1879, *Les Cinq Cents Millions de la Be-´gum*, 28.5 cm., 185 pp., illustrated. It ran in a French periodical, Jan. 1–Sept. 15, 1879. In England it ran in the *Leisure Hour* of the Religious Tract Society, beginning in July 1879. The first book edition in English was issued by Low, 1880 (1879), Cr 8vo, 272 pp., illustrated, 7/6, translated by W.H.G. Kingston, and containing also *The Mutineers of the Bounty*. It was listed in the *Ath* on Oct. 25, 1879. Low issued it in 1883, 18 cm., 272 pp., illustrated, 3/6 in green pictorial cloth, with a 32-page catalog (Nov. 1882) at the back, advertised in the *Ath* on Mar. 3; and issued a new edition in 1887, 20 cm., illustrated.

In the United States it was issued by J. B. Lippincott & Co., Philadelphia, 1879, 12mo, 272 pp., translated by Kingston, *The Begum's Fortune*, listed in *PW* on Nov. 29. It was also issued by George Munro, New York, 1879, 32.5 cm., $.10 paper, *Seaside Library* No. 634, probably issued in late Oct. or early Nov. 1879, *The 500 Millions of the Begum.*
See 1890

287 JULES VERNE *The Tribulations of a Chinaman in China.* Author's illustrated edition. 12mo, 1/o sewed, 2/o cloth Sept. (*Bks*)
This is 1883, 256 pp. The first edition was issued by J. Hetzel, Paris, 1879, *Les Tribulations d'un Chinois en Chine.* It ran in *Les Temps*, July 2–Aug. 7, 1879. The first edition in English was issued by Lee & Shepard, Boston; etc., 1880 (1879), 18 cm., 271 pp., $.50 paper, $1.00 cloth, translated by Virginia Champlin, advertised in the *New-York Times* on Oct. 18, 1879, as "Just published," and listed in the *Ind* and the *Nation* on Oct. 23, and in *PW* on Oct. 25. They issued it in 1881, square 8vo, 271 pp., illus-

trated, $1.50, listed in the *Nation* on Nov. 17; and issued it, 1889, the latter according to the *U Cat*. It was also issued by George Munro, New York, 1879, my copy, 32.5 cm., 37 pp., paper, with a cover date of Nov. 13, 1879, *Seaside Library* No. 647, probably issued in Nov. 1879. It was also issued by E. P. Dutton, New York, 1881 (1880), from the Low plates, translated by Ellen Frewer, $2.50, listed in *PW* on Oct. 9 and in the *Nation* on Oct. 21, 1880.

The first British edition was issued by Low, 1880, 18 cm., 262 pp., illustrated, 7/6 in gray-blue pictorial cloth, with a 32-page catalog (Apr. 1880) at the back, translated by Frewer. It was listed in the *Ath* and *Spect* on Oct. 2, 1880.

See 1890

288 GEORGE TAYLOR **Klytia.** 2 vols., 18mo. 1/6 sewed, 2/0 flexible cloth each Dec. 1 (*Spect*)

German Authors No. 30. The first edition was issued in Leipzig, 2 vols., 1883. The present edition was translated by S. F. Corkran. In the United States it was issued by George Munro, New York (1884), *Die Deutsche Library* No. 165, 32 cm., 48 pp., with a title vignette, paper. It was also is-

sued by William S. Gottsberger, New York, in 1884, 364 pp., in cloth, translated by Mary Safford, *Clytia*. It was advertised in the *New-York Times* on May 24, 1884, $.50 paper, $.90 cloth, as "This day."

289 THOMAS H. BLAKESLEY **Electricity and the Board of Trade.** 8vo. 0/6 sewed 1883 (*BM*)

This is the first edition, 1883, a 24-page pamphlet.

290 T. F. CASHIN **The Inutility of Bankruptcy Laws.** Cr 8vo. 1/0 1883 (*BM*)

This is the first edition, 1883, 48 pp., with a prefatory dissertation on bankruptcy by Lord Sherbrooke.

291 FRANCIS G. HEATH **Where to Find Ferns.** Cr 8vo. 2/0 1883 (*U Cat*)

This is 1883, 188 pp., with a special chapter on the ferns around London. The first edition was issued by Low, 1881, Cr 8vo, 118 pp., 3/0, advertised in the *Ath* on Aug. 20 as "Just ready." It was also issued by the Society for Promoting Christian Knowledge, London; E. & J. B. Young & Co., New York, 1885, 17 cm., 153 pp., illustrated, in green cloth.

Sampson Low, Marston, Searle & Rivington
Crown Buildings, 188 Fleet Street
1884

292 GREVILLE FENNEL (JOHN G. FENNELL) *The Book of the Roach.* [New edition.] 12mo. 2/0 cloth Jan. 5 (*Ath* ad)

This is 1884, 17 cm., 118 pp. The first edition was issued by Longmans, London, 1870, 12mo, 118 pp., 2/6.

293 GARBOARD STREYKE *The Sea, the River, and the Creek.* 12mo. 1/0 stiff wrappers Mar. 1 (*Ath* ad)

The ad said "Now ready." This is the first edition, 1884, 125 pp., a series of sketches of the eastern coast.

294 EDGAR A. POE *Tales by Edgar Allen Poe.* 12mo. 1/6 sewed, 2/0 flexible cloth Mar. 15 (*Spect*)

This is 1884, a copy of the Tauchnitz edition with a new title page. It was issued by Tauchnitz, Leipzig, 1884, 16 cm., 328 pp., *Collection of British Authors* (*sic*), edited by John H. Ingram. It probably could be sold in Britain because it was by an American author. *The Prose Romances* was issued by William H. Graham, Philadelphia, 1843; and *Tales* was issued by Wiley & Putnam, New York, 1845.

295 EDGAR A. POE *Poems and Essays by Edgar Allen Poe.* 16mo. 1/6 sewed, 2/0 flexible cloth Mar. 15 (*Spect*)

This was issued by Tauchnitz, Leipzig, 1884, 16 cm., 328 pp., edited, with a new memoir by John H. Ingram, *Collection of British Authors.* The present edition is the British issue with a new title page. There were various issues of the poems, in various states of completeness, including *Tammerlane and Other Poems,* 1827; poems issued by E. Bliss, New York, 1831; poems issued by Wiley & Putnam, New York, 1845; *The Poetical Works of Edgar Allen Poe,* issued by Addey & Co., London, 1853, 144 pp., illustrated.

296 ANONYMOUS *Tracks in Norway of Four Pairs of Feet.* 12mo. Map., 2/0 Mar. 15 (*Spect*)

This is the first edition, 1884, compiled by W. H. Macnamara, 18.5 cm., 95 pp.

297 CORNELIUS NICHOLSON *The Work and Workers of the British Association for the Advancement of Science.* 12mo. 1/0 limp cloth June 28 (*Ath* ad)

This is the first edition, 1884, 59 pp.

298 JULES VERNE *The Green Ray.* [New edition.] 12mo. Illustrated. 1/0 limp cloth July 12 (*Ath* ad)

The first edition was *Le Rayon-Vert,* issued by J. Hetzel, Paris, 1882, 3 francs, listed in the *Ath* on Aug. 5. It ran in *Le Temps,* May 17–June 23, 1882. The first edition in English was issued by Low, 1883, Cr 8vo, illustrated, 5/0 cloth, 6/0 cloth with gilt edges, translated by Mary de Hauteville, listed in the *Ath* on Sept. 22. The first American edition was issued by George Munro, New York (1883), 32.5 cm., paper, *Seaside Library* No. 1716, translated by James Cotterell, listed in *PW* on Oct. 20. See 1890

299 ARTHUR READE (ALFRED A. READE) *Tea and Tea Drinking.* 12mo. Illustrated. 1/0 July 12 (*Ath* ad)

The ad said "Now ready," 1/0 coloured wrappers. An ad in *Notes & Queries* on May 24, 1884, gave it as Cr 8vo, illustrated, 1/0 in stiff board covers. It is the first edition, 1884, 154 pp.

300 JULES VERNE *The Steam House.* 2 vols. New edition. 12mo. Illustrated. 1/6 limp boards, 2/0 cloth each   July 12 (*Ath* ad)

Vol. 1 is *The Demon of Cawnpore,* and vol. 2 is *Tigers and Traitors.* The first edition was issued by J. Hetzel, Paris, 2 vols., 1880, *La Maison à Vapeur.* It ran in a periodical, Dec. 1, 1879–Dec. 15, 1880. The first British edition was issued by Low, 2 vols., 1881, Cr 8vo, illustrated, 7/6 each, translated by Agnes D. Kingston. Vol. 1 was listed in the *Ath* and *Spect* on Nov. 20, 1880; and vol. 2 was listed in the *Ath* on Apr. 9, 1881. Low issued vol. 1 in 1883, Cr 8vo, illustrated, 3/6 cloth, advertised in the *Ath* on Mar. 3.

The first edition in English was issued by George Munro, New York, 2 parts, 32.5 cm., 26 pp. each, $.10 paper each, *Seaside Library* No. 818, translated by J. Cotterell. Part 1 was advertised in the *New-York Times* on Aug. 31, 1880, as "Out tomorrow"; and part 2 was advertised Jan. 21, 1881, as "On Jan 24." It was also issued by Charles Scribner's Sons, New York, 2 vols., 1881, 19.5 cm., a folding map in each vol., translated by Agnes Kingston, probably from the Low plates. Vol. 1 was advertised in the *New-York Times* on Feb. 5, 1881, and listed in the *Ind* on Feb. 10 and in *PW* on

Feb. 12; and vol. 2 was advertised in the *New-York Times* on May 13, 1881, as "This day" and listed in the *Ind* on May 19 and in *PW* on May 21.
See 1890

301 FANNY LEWALD, later LEWALD-STAHR *Stella.* 2 vols. Copyright edition. 16mo. 1/6 sewed 2/0 flexible cloth each July 26 (*Ath*)

German Authors No. 31. This is the first British edition, 1884, 16 cm., translated by B. Marshall. The first edition was issued in Germany, 3 vols., 1883. In the United States it was issued by George Munro, New York (1884), 32.5 cm., paper, *Seaside Library* No. 1882, probably in Sept. 1884.

302 (EDWARD MARSTON) *An Amateur Angler's Days in Dove Dale.* 18mo. 1/0 boards, 1/6 limp leather cloth   Sept. 27 (*Ath* ad)

This is the first edition, 1884, 14 cm., 88 pp., with a dedicatory letter and prefatory note signed E. M. The ad said "Now ready." The *BM* gives it I've described it, and also gives another copy, 1884, with a different title page and with the addition of a frontispiece.

303 ELSA D'ESTERRE, later KEELING *Bib and Tucker.* 24mo. 1/0 fancy boards   Sept. 27 (*Ath* ad)

This is the first edition, 1884, 158 pp.

304 SIR WILLIAM T. MARRIOTT *Two Years of British Intervention in Egypt.* 8vo. 0/6 sewed   Oct. 25 (*Ath* ad)

The ad said "Now ready." This is the first edition, 1884, a 35-page pamphlet.

305 PHILIP S. ROBINSON *Chasing a Fortune.* 16mo. 1/0 fancy boards, 1/6 cloth   Nov. 1 (*Spect* ad)

Indian Garden Series No. 1. This is the first edition, 1884, 177 pp., containing five pieces. The title story first appeared in *Home Chimes* on July 5, 1884. This series lasted for only three titles (see 1885, 86).

306 ANDREW CARNEGIE *An American Four-in-Hand in Britain.* 1/o boards Nov. 8 (*Ath* ad)

The ad said "Now ready." This is 1884, 192 pp. The first edition was issued by Charles Scribner's Sons, New York, 1883, 21.5 cm., 338 pp., frontispiece, $2.00, advertised in the *New-York Times* on May 12 as "This day" and listed in the *Nation* on May 17. They also issued it in 1886, 12mo, $.25 paper, listed in the *Nation* on June 14. The first British edition was issued by Low, 1883, 22.5 cm., 338 pp., frontispiece, 10/6, listed in the *Spect* on July 14 and advertised in the *Ath* on July 14 as "Ready."

307 WILLIAM C. RUSSELL *English Channel Ports, etc.* p 8vo. Maps. Plans. 1/o 1884 (*BM*)

This is the first edition, 1884, 116 pp., with ads on pp. 118–123. It is reprinted from the *Daily Telegraph*.

308 WILLIAM STONE *Shall We Annex Egypt?* 8vo. o/6 sewed 1884 (*BM*)

This is the first edition, 1884, a 52-page pamphlet.

Sampson Low, Marston, Searle & Rivington
Crown Buildings, 188 Fleet Street
1885

309 ANONYMOUS *The New Democracy.* 12mo. 1/0 sewed   Feb. 21 (*Ath* ad)
The ad said "Now ready." This is the first edition, 1885, 17 cm., 155 pp., by the author of *Shooting Niagara!* below (item 318).

310 WILLIAM SENIOR (RED SPINNER) *Waterside Sketches.* Cheap edition. 24mo. 1/0 boards   Feb. 28 (*Ath* ad)
Waterside Shilling Series No. 1. This is 1885, 14 cm., 195 pp. This was an aborted series, as I've never seen a No. 2. The first edition was issued by Grant, London, 1875, 18.5 cm., frontispiece, 3/6, most of the chapters being reprinted from the *Gentleman's Magazine*. It was listed in the *Ath* on Mar. 27, 1875, Cr 8vo, 2/0 boards, with no publisher given.

311 ANONYMOUS *Bechuanaland.* Demy 8vo. 1/0 sewed   Mar. 7 (*Ath* ad)
The ad said "Now ready." This is the first edition, 1885, 89 pp., by a member of the Cape legislature.

312 FRANK POWER *Letters from Khartoum.* 12mo. 1/0 boards   Apr. 4 (*Ath* ad)
The ad said "Now ready." This is the first edition, 1885, 17.5 cm., 119 pp. The second edition was advertised on Apr. 11 as "Now ready"; there was a third edition, 1885, 17.5 cm., 119 pp., edited by Arnold Power.

313 ANTHONY TROLLOPE *Thompson Hall.* 16mo. Illustrated. 1/0 stiff wrappers   July 1–15 (*PC*)
This is the first British edition in separate form, my copy, 1885, 16 cm., 127 pp., gray stiff wrappers, pictorially printed on the front in brown and dark blue, with plain white endpapers and a commercial ad on the back cover. It has the original eight vignettes that were in its appearance in *The Graphic Christmas Number* of 1876, appearing here as textual illustrations. It was contained in *Why Frau Frohmann Raised Her Prices, and Other Stories*, issued by William Isbister, London, 1882.

The first edition in separate form was issued by Harper & Bros., New York, 1877, 12 cm., 91 pp., *Harper's Half-Hour Series* (No. 3), in buff wrappers, printed in red and black, $.20. It has a frontispiece and seven full-page illustrations, "Thompson Hall" on the cover, and "Christmas at Thompson Hall" on the title page. There are publisher's ads on 4 pp. at the back and on the back cover. In a description of this new series at the front, it states that this title will be No. 1, but it was advertised in the *New-York Times* on Mar. 24, 1877 as No. 3.

314 PHILIP S. ROBINSON **Tigers at Large.**
16mo. 1/0 fancy boards, 1/6 cloth　Aug. 1
(*Ath* ad)

Indian Garden Series No. 2. This has 176 pp. and is possibly a reissue, as it was first advertised in the *Spect* on Nov. 1, 1884, 1/0 fancy boards.

315 JULES VERNE **Godfrey Morgan.**
12mo. Illustrated. 1/0 limp boards, 2/0 cloth　Aug. 14 (*Ath* ad)

The first edition was *L'Ecole des Robinsons*, issued by J. Hetzel, Paris, 1882. It ran serially in a periodical, Jan. 1–Dec. 1, 1882. It ran for four weeks, Sept. 29–Oct. 19, complete, unabridged, in *Redpath's Magazine*, translated by Curtin. The first book edition in English was issued by George Munro, New York, 1883, 32.5 cm., $.10 paper, *Seaside Library* No. 1519, advertised in the *New-York Times* on Jan. 19, 1883, as a late issue, *Robinson's School*. It was also issued by Charles Scribner's Sons, New York, 1883, 19 cm., 272 pp., illustrated, $2.00, advertised in the *New-York Times* on Sept. 15 as "This day" and listed in the *Ind* on Sept. 20 and in *PW* on Oct. 6. It was from the Low plates of 1883.

The first British edition was issued by Low, 1883, Cr 8vo, illustrated, 7/6, translated by W. J. Gordon, listed in the *Ath* on Mar. 10. Low issued it in 1885, 3/6 cloth, listed in the *Ath* on June 27.
See 1890

316 JULES VERNE **The Giant Raft.**
[New edition.] 2 vols. 12mo. Illustrated. 1/0 limp boards, 2/0 cloth each
Aug. 14 (*Ath* ad)

These are 1885, 244 pp and 254 pp., translated by W. J. Gordon. The first edition was *La Jangada; Huit Cents Lieues sur l'Amazone*, issued by J. Hetzel, Paris, 2 vols., 1881. It ran in a periodical, Jan. 1–Dec. 1, 1881. It includes a story by Paul Verne. Vol. 1 was review in the *Ath* on July 2, 1881, 3 francs, 50; and vol. 2 was listed

Nov. 19, 1881, 3 francs. The first British edition was issued by Low, 2 vols., Cr 8vo, illustrated, 7/6 cloth each, translated by Gordon. Vol. 1 was *Eight Hundred Leagues on the Amazon*, 1881, listed in the *Ath* on Nov. 12; and vol. 2 was *The Cryptogram*, 1882, with a map, listed in the *Ath* and *Spect* on May 13. Low issued it in 2 vols. 3/6 cloth each, listed in the *Ath* on June 13, 1885.

In the United States it was issued by Charles Scribner's Sons, New York, 2 vols., 19 cm., folding maps, 244 and 254 pp., from the Low plates. Vol. 1 was advertised in the *New-York Times* on Nov. 24, 1881, as "This day," $1.50, and listed in the *Ind* and the *Nation* on Dec. 1, 1881, and in *PW* on Dec. 17; vol. 2 was advertised in the *New-York Times* on Sept. 20, 1882, as "This day," $1.50, listed in the *Ind* on Sept. 28 and *PW* on Sept. 30, 1882. *The Jangada* was issued by George Munro, New York, *Seaside Library* No. 1043, part 1, listed in *PW* on Aug. 6, 1881; and part 2, *The Cryptogram*, pp. 170–260, listed in *PW* on Oct. 28, 1882. It was translated by J. Cotterell. It was also issued by John W. Lovell, New York, 2 vols. (1882), *Lovell's Library* Nos. 34 and 35. My copy of vol. 2 had a wrapper date of Oct. 7, 1882. It was also issued by M. A. Donohue, Chicago, 2 vols., 1882.
See 1890

317 HARRISON W. WEIR, illustrator
Animal Stories, Old and New. 4to.
Illustrated. 5/0 boards　Oct. 16 (ad *TWEd*)

This is the first edition (1885), 25.5 cm., illustrations partly colored, in glazed pictorial boards, printed in red, orange, blue, green, and black. The *U Cat* gives it as with a joint imprint of E. P. Dutton, New York.

318 ANONYMOUS **"Shooting Niagara!"**
12mo. 1/0 sewed　Oct. 31 (*Ath* ad)

The ad said "Ready." This is the first edition, 1885, 190 pp., by the author of *The New Democracy* above (item 309).

319 ANONYMOUS ***Thoughts on Ireland.***
24mo. 0/6 stiff wrappers   Dec. 26
(*Ath* ad)

This is also given by the *Eng Cat*, but otherwise I cannot trace it. It is by an Irish landlord.

320 CHARLES C. CAPEL ***Trout Culture.***
Second edition. Cr 8vo. Illustrated.
2/0   1885 (*BM*)

This is Low, London; H. & C. Treacher, Brighton, 1885, 18.5 cm., 89 pp. The first edition was issued by Hardwicke & Bogue, London, 1877 (1876), 16.5 cm., 93 pp.

321 HENRY LASSALLE, ed. ***Selection from Crowded Out, or Not Being Hung for Want of Space, at the Royal Academy, 1885.*** 8vo. Illustrated. 1/0   1885 (*BM*)

This is the first edition, 1885, 22 cm., 74 pp.

322 ANONYMOUS ***Gleanings from the Muddle.*** 12mo. 1/0   1885 (*BM*)

This is the first edition, 1885, 70 pp., by Zeb, a Devon conservative.

323 HENRY LASSALLE, ed. ***The Royal Academy Illustrated, 1885.*** 1/0   1885 (*BM*)

This was issued by Low for 1884 and 1885, and no more were issued.

324 WILLIAM C. RUSSELL ***A Forecastle View of the Shipping Commission.*** 12mo. 0/3 sewed   1885 (*BM*)

This is the first edition, a 24-page pamphlet, reprinted from the *Contemporary Review*.

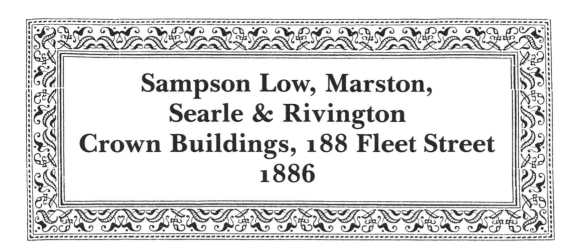

Sampson Low, Marston, Searle & Rivington
Crown Buildings, 188 Fleet Street
1886

325 MALCOLM R.L. MEASON *Sir William's Speculations.* p 8vo. 1/0 sewed May 1 (*Ath* ad)

The ad said "Now ready." This is the first edition, 1886, 120 pp.

326 JAMES BONWICK *The British Colonies and Their Resources.* 4 vols. Maps. 1/0 each; 4 vols.-in-1, 5/0 May 29 (*Ath* ad)

This is the first edition, 19 cm. The 1-vol. edition has a total of 466 pp., with the separate pagination of the four vols.

327 PHILIP S. ROBINSON *The Valley of the Teetotum Trees.* 16mo. 1/0 boards, 1/6 cloth June 5 (*Ath* ad)

The Indian Garden Series No. 3. This is the first book edition, 1886, 159 pp. It was in *Home Chimes*, Jan. 2, 1884, as *The Valley of the Twizzling Trees.*

328 CLAUDE BOSANQUET *Jehoshaphat.* 18mo. 1/0 sewed June 26 (*Ath* ad)

The ad said "New books." This is the first edition, 1886, 146 pp.

329 JOHN P. SANDLANDS *How to Develop General Vocal Power, etc.* p 8vo. 1/0 cloth Sept. 4 (*Ath* ad)

The ad said "New books." This is the first edition, 1886, 72 pp. Low issued the sixth edition, 1907, 72 pp.

330 FREDERICK E. HULME *Wisdom Chips Gathered Together by Frederick E. Hulme.* 18mo. 1/6 Oct. 30 (*Spect*)

This is the first edition, 1886, 143 pp. The *BM* gives it as 18mo, and the *Spect* gives it as 32mo. I suspect it is closer to the 32mo, the *BM* not making very fine distinctions among sizes.

331 FRANK R. STOCKTON *The Casting Away of Mrs. Lecks and Mrs. Aleshine.* 12mo. 1/0 limp boards Nov. 15 (*PC*)

This was advertised in the *Ath* on Nov. 13 as "Ready," and it was listed in the *Spect* on Nov. 27 at 2/0 cloth. This is my copy, 1886, the first British edition, 17.3 cm., 130 pp., in cream pictorial limp boards, printed in red, blue, and black, with plain white endpapers, and with a commercial ad on the back cover. I have a second copy, the same except for a slip inserted at the back advertising *The Dusantes*, 1/0, "Now ready." This latter title was issued in Mar. 1888.

The first American edition was issued by the Century Co., New York (1886), 19.5 cm., 130 pp. It is my copy, in cream paper covers, printed and decorated in gold, with *The Century Series* on the front cover, and publisher's ads on the inside covers. My copy is uncut and unopened, $.50. It was also issued in plum cloth, $1.00. It was advertised in the *New-York Times* on Nov. 30, 1886, third edition in the press, and the first edition was advertised in *PW* on Oct. 16 as "On Oct. 20" and listed there on Oct. 30, and listed in the *Ind* on Oct. 28. It ran in the *Century Magazine*, Aug.–Oct. 1886. Low issued it with *The Dusantes* in 1 vol., in 1888, 12mo, 2/6 cloth, advertised in the *Ath* on May 5; and issued it, the same, 2/0 boards, 2/6 cloth, in their *Standard Novels* No. 9, 1890, listed in the *Ath* on Jan. 18, 1890.

332   MARTIN F. TUPPER *Jubilate!* 12mo. 1/0 sewed   Dec. 4 (*Ath* ad)

The ad said "Now ready." This is the first edition (1886), 40 pp., a poem in honor of Queen Victoria.

333   A. B. BARTLETT *The Comic Angler.* 17mo. Illustrated. 0/6   1886 (*Eng Cat*)

The first edition was issued by A. E. Bartlett, Kalamazoo, Michigan (1884), by an old fisherman, 15 cm., 39 pp., illustrated, with a cover title, "The Comic Angler," and title on the title page, "The Ludicrous Experiences of a Humorous Angler After a Trout, etc."

334   ANONYMOUS *Bribery and Corruption; the Comic Companion to the Corrupt Practices Act.* 4to. 1/0   1886 (*Eng Cat*)

I cannot trace this.

335   ANONYMOUS *Dame Britannica and Her Troublesome Family.* 12mo. 0/6 sewed   1886 (*BM*)

This is the first edition, 1886, a 32-page pamphlet, a satire on Gladstone's third administration.

336   ANDREW CARNEGIE *Triumphant Democracy.* [New edition.] Cr 8vo. 1/0, 1/6   1886 (*Eng Cat*)

This possibly has 1887 on the title page. The first edition was issued by Charles Scribner's Sons, New York, 1886, 2 cm., 512 pp., table, $2.00, advertised in the *New-York Times* on Apr. 17 as "Today" and listed in the *Nation* on Apr. 29. The sixth edition was advertised in the *New-York Times* on June 5, 1886, $2.00, and in the *Nation* on June 10. They issued the eighth edition in 1888, $.50 paper, $1.50 cloth, advertised in the *Nation* on Jan. 19, 1888; and they issued it in 1893, 8vo, 561 pp., $3.00, noticed in *Review of Reviews* for Dec. 1893; and issued it in 1894, $3.00, revised edition, listed in the *Nation* on Nov. 16, 1894.

The first British edition was issued by Low (1886), 18.5 cm., 365 pp., folding frontispiece (table), listed in the *Ath* on May 8 and in the *Spect* on May 8. Low issued the second edition in 1886, noticed in the *Westminster Review* (quarterly) for Jan. 1887; and they issued it, 1888, 18.5 cm., 365 pp., with the folding frontispiece.

337   ANONYMOUS *Facts Disentangled from Fiction for Candidates and Constituents.* 12mo. 1/0   1886 (*BM*)

This is the first edition, 1886, 91 pp., by "Zeb."

338   JOHN B. GREENE *Notes on Ireland.* p 8vo. 1/0   1886 (*BM*)

This is the first book edition, 1886, 108 pp., with an introduction by Goldwin Smith, reprinted from the *Morning Post*.

339   BRAM STOKER *A Glimpse of America.* 8vo. 1/0   1886 (*BM*)

This is the first edition, 1886, 22 cm., 48 pp., a lecture given at the London Institution on Dec. 28, 1885.

Low advertised in the Ath *on Aug. 6 that the firm had removed to St. Dunstan's House, Fetter Lane, Fleet Street.*

340 ROBERT B. MARSTON, ed. *The Sportsman's Illustrated Almanac for 1887.* 4to. Portraits. Illustrated. 1/0 sewed   Jan. 15 (*Ath* ad)
The ad said "Ready." This is (1887), 78 pp., illustrated by W. Foster.

341 OLIVER W. HOLMES *A Mortal Antipathy.* [New edition.] Fcp 8vo. 1/0 sewed, 2/0 cloth   Jan. 27 (*Ath* ad)
The first American edition was issued by Houghton, Mifflin & Co., Boston and New York, 1885, 20 cm., 307 pp., $1.50, advertised in the *New-York Times* on Nov. 25 and listed in the *Ind* on Dec. 3, 1885. The first British edition was issued by Low, 1886, 19.5 cm., 307 pp., 8/6 half-parchment, listed in the *Ath* on Dec. 12, 1885. Low issued a new edition in 1887, Fcp 8vo, 1/0 sewed, 2/0 cloth, advertised in *Notes & Queries* on Feb. 12. Low issued the sixth edition, 1894, 288 pp., 1/0 boards, 2/0 cloth, advertised in the *Ath* on Oct. 20.

342 HENRY C. PENNELL *Modern Improvements in Fishing Tackle and Fish Hooks.* Cr 8vo. Illustrated. 2/0 cloth   Apr. 9 (*Ath* ad)
The ad said "Ready." This is the first edition (1887), 19 cm., 194 pp.

343 JULES VERNE *Kéraban the Inflexible.* 2 vols. 12mo. Illustrated. 1/0 limp boards, 2/0 cloth each   July 23 (*Ath* ad)
The first edition was issued by J. Hetzel, Paris, 2 vols., 1883, *Kéraban-le-Têtu.* It ran in a French periodical, Jan. 1–Oct. 15, 1883. The first edition in English was issued by George Munro, New York, *The Headstrong Turk*, 2 parts, 32.5 cm., $.10 paper each, *Seaside Library* No. 1677, translated by Cotterell, advertised in the *New-York Times* on Apr. 12, 1884, as a late issue. It ran in *Redpath's Weekly* as *Kéraban-le-Têtu*, copyright translation, from advance sheets, advertised in the *New-York Times* on Oct. 1, 1883, as "Out today."
  In England it ran in Routledge's *Every Boy's Annual* as *Kéraban the Inflexible*, no-

ticed in the *Spect* on Nov. 21, 1885. The first British book edition was issued by Low, 2 vols., 19 cm., illustrated, 7/6 each. Vol. 1, *Captain of the Guidara*, 1884, listed in the *Ath* and *Spect* on Nov. 1, 1884; and Vol. 2, *Scarpante the Spy*, 1885, listed in the *Ath* on Mar. 28. Low issued it in 2 vols., 1/0 each, in 1887, noticed in the *Ath* on Aug. 6 and in the *Spect* on Aug. 13; and issued it again in 2 vols. in 1888, 1/0 sewed, 2/0 cloth each, advertised in the *Ath* on Aug. 25.
See 1890

344   CAPTAIN SAMUEL SAMUELS *From the Forecastle to the Cabin.* Cheap edition. p 8vo. Illustrated. 1/0   July 23 (*Ath* ad)
The ad said "Recent." This is 1887, 19 cm., 192 pp. The first British edition was issued by Low, 1887, p 8vo, 320 pp., illustrated, 8/6, listed in the *Spect* on Mar. 26. Low issued a new edition in 1888 according to the *Eng Cat*, p 8vo, 1/0, 2/0. The first American edition was issued by Harper & Bros., New York, 1887, 19 cm., 308 pp., illustrated, probably issued in Mar., as it was listed in the *Atlantic Monthly* for May and reviewed in *Harper's New Monthly Magazine* for July.

345   (EDWARD MARSTON) *Fresh Woods and Pastures New.* 12mo. 1/6 boards, 5/0   Sept. 24 (*Spect*)
This is the first edition, 1887. The 5/0 was a large paper edition. It was by E. M. The *U Cat* gives the second edition, 1888, issued by Low, 12mo, 136 pp., 1/0 sewed. The first American edition was issued by A.D.F. Randolph, New York, 1887, anonymous, 136 pp.

346   HUGH CALLAN *Wanderings on Wheel and on Foot Through Europe.* p 8vo. 1/6 fancy boards   Oct. 8 (*Spect*)
This is the first edition, 1887, 208 pp.

347   WILL M. CARLETON *City Ballads.* 12mo. 1/0 limp boards   Oct. 22 (*Ath* ad) *Rose Library*. The ad said "Now ready." This is 1887, 183 pp. The first edition was issued by Harper & Bros., New York (1885), 23 cm., 180 pp., illustrated, $2.00 in pictorial gray-green cloth, bevelled boards, and $2.50 with gilt edges. It has 4 pp. of ads and was deposited on Aug. 25, and listed in *PW* on Aug. 29. They issued a new edition, 8vo, illustrated, $2.00 and $2.50, advertised in the *New-York Times* on Sept. 20, 1892.
    The first British edition was issued by Low, 1886 (1885), Roy 8vo, 12/6 cloth, a duplicate of the Harper edition but with a new title page. It was advertised in *PC* on Oct. 1, 1885, as "In a few days" and listed in the *Spect* on Oct. 10. It was issued in Canada by the Rose Publishing Co., Toronto, 1886, 19 cm., 235 pp., illustrated, in red cloth.
See 1893

348   JOHN PARKIN *The Volcanic Origin of Epidemics.* Popular edition. p 8vo. Two folding maps. 2/0 cloth   Nov. 12 (*Ath* ad)
The ad said "Now ready." This is 1887, 146 pp. The first edition was *On the Remote Cause of Epidemic Diseases . . .* , issued in London in two parts, which the *BM* gives as 1841–45. The *British Catalogue* gives Hatchard, London, 2 parts, 8vo, 9/0, 1841–54, and the *U Cat* gives J. Hatchard & Son, London, 1841, 23.5 cm., 198 pp.

349   JOHN PARKIN *Are Epidemics Contagious?* Popular edition. p 8vo. 2/0 cloth   Nov. 12 (*Ath* ad)
The ad said "Now ready." This is 1887, 146 pp. See the preceding item.

350   LUCY VALLANCE *Paul's Birthday.* [New edition.] 8vo. 1/6 sewed   1887?
The first edition was issued by Low, 1886, 4to, 74 pp., illustrated, 3/6 cloth.

351 ANONYMOUS *A London Sparrow at the Colinderies.* 12mo. 1/0 1887 (*BM*)

This is the first edition, 1887, by E.V.B., 59 pp.

352 PATRICK H.W. ROSS *Federation and the British Colonies.* 8vo. 1/0 1887 (*BM*)

This is the first edition, 32 pp., with a preface dated 1887.

353 RICHARD D. BLACKMORE *Clara Vaughan.* Cheap edition. 12mo. 2/0 boards 1887

This is a yellowback, 1887, with the words "Issued for the British Colonies and Dependencies Only." The first edition was issued by Macmillan & Co., London and Cambridge, 3 vols., 1864, p 8vo, anonymous, 31/6, listed in the *Ath* on Mar. 12. Sadleir had a presentation copy inscribed Feb. 25, 1864, in dark-blue morocco cloth, chocolate endpapers, with 2 pp. of ads at the back of vol. 3. Macmillan issued the second edition, the same, 1864. Low issued a revised edition, 1872, p 8vo, 390 pp., 6/0 cloth, listed in the *Spect* on Feb. 3. They reissued it many times, with 390 pp., including the sixth edition, 1880, with a 32-page catalog (Jan. 1881); and the 11th edition, 1888. Low issued the first yellowback, 1889, 12th edition, 12mo, 390 pp., 2/0 boards, 2/6 cloth, *Standard Novels* No. 4, Wolff's copy in pictorial boards. They issued the 13th edition, 1892, and reissued it in 1893, 94, and 95. They issued it as *Sixpenny Editions*, sewed, 8vo, in 1901, in July, given by the *Eng Cat*.

The first American edition was issued by J. B. Lippincott & Co., Philadelphia, 1872, imported, listed in *PW* on Sept. 26. Harper & Bros., New York, issued it, 1880, 28.5 cm., 89 pp., $.15 paper, *Franklin Square Library* No. 120, dated May 7, 1880. It was listed in *Harper's New Monthly Magazine* for July, and thus probably issued in Apr. or May.

The company became a limited company in 1888, certainly by Mar. 15.

354 ANONYMOUS ***The Story of the Life of William Shakespeare and His Work.***
Cr 8vo. 2/0 boards   Feb. 11 (*Ath* ad)

The ad said "New books, new and cheaper edition." The *U Cat* gives Low, 1888, 20 cm., 146 pp., illustrated, with the preface signed J. C. This may have been the first edition. I can find no other possible first edition.

355 H. M. UPTON ***Profitable Dairy Farming.*** p 8vo. 2/0 boards   Feb. 25 (*Ath*)

This is the first edition, 1888, 203 pp., tables. I think there was a reissue, no date, the same.

356 FRANK R. STOCKTON ***The Dusantes.***
12mo. 1/0 limp boards   Mar. 15 (*PC*)

An *Ath* ad on Mar. 10 said "Now ready." This is the first British edition, my copy, 1888, with "Limited" in the imprint, 17 cm., 150 pp., in white pictorial limp boards, printed in red, blue, and black, cut flush and printed in England. There are commercial ads on the front endpapers and on the back cover, and publisher's ads on the back endpapers. It is a sequel to *The Casting Away of Mrs. Lecks. . . .* Low issued it along with the latter title in 1 vol. in 1888, 12mo, 2/6 cloth, advertised in the *Ath* on May 5; and issued it in 1 vol., 1890, 12mo,

2/0 boards, 2/6 cloth, *Standard Novels* No. 9, listed in the *Ath* on Jan. 18, 1890.

In the United States it ran in the *Century Magazine,* Dec. 1887–Feb. 1888, and the first book edition was issued by the Century Co., New York (1888), 20.5 cm., 150 pp., in green cloth or printed cream wrappers. The cloth copy was deposited on Feb. 10, and both were listed in *PW* on Feb. 25. It was advertised in the *New-York Times* on Feb. 19, $.50 paper, $.75 cloth, *Century Series* No. 3, "Now ready."

357 MISS M. A. CHREIMAN ***Physical Culture for Women.*** 1/0   July 7 (*Ath* ad)

The ad said "New books." The *BM* gives Low, 1888, 37 pp., and both it and the *U Cat* give Low, 1888, 16mo, 52 pp.

358 HONNOR MORTEN ***Sketches of Hospital Life.*** 12mo. 1/0 sewed
July 14 (*Ath* ad)

The ad said "Now ready." This is the first edition, 1888, 74 pp., reprinted from various periodicals.

359 ALEXANDER B. MACDOWALL ***Curve Pictures of London for the Social Reformer.***
12mo. Diagrams. 1/0   Aug. 25 (*Ath* ad)

This is the first edition, 1888, 18 cm., 49 pp.

360 RICHARD D. BLACKMORE **Mary Anerley.** New edition. 12mo. 2/o boards 1888

This was Wolff's copy, 1888, in white pictorial boards, issued for the British Colonies and Dependencies only. It has variations in design to distinguish it from the first yellowback issued by Low in 1890. It ran in *Fraser's Magazine*, July 1879–Sept. 1880, and the first book edition was issued by Low, 3 vols., 1880, 19.5 cm., 31/6 in blue cloth with cream endpapers. It has a 32-page catalog (Apr. 1880) at the back of vol. 3. It was listed in the *Ath* on May 8. They issued a second edition, 3 vols., advertised in the *Spect* on July 3, 1880. Low issued it in 1 vol., 1881, Cr 8vo, 442 pp., 6/o cloth, listed in the *Spect* on Nov. 13, 1880. The first Low yellowback was issued, 1890, my copy, new and cheaper edition, 171. cm., 442 pp., 2/o boards, 2/6 cloth, *Standard Novels* No. 16, the 2/o issue in pale blue pictorial boards, printed in red and black, with the series title on the front and spine, and the No. 21 on the front, and with ads on the blue endpapers and on the back cover. It was listed in the *Ath* on May 31. Apparently the numbering of the series was changed after 1890, and, in fact, my copy has dates of 1889 in the ads on the endpapers. Wolff had a copy of the yellowback, 1891, new and cheaper edition. Low issued it, 2/6 cloth, 8vo, in 1894, advertised in the *TWEd* on Apr. 20; and issued it in *Sixpenny Editions*, sewed, in 1903, in Mar. according to the *Eng Cat*.

In the United States it ran in *Harper's New Monthly Magazine*, Aug. 1879–Aug. 1880, and the first American book edition was issued by Harper & Bros., New York (1880), 29.5 cm., 88 pp., $.15 paper, *Franklin Square Library* No. 123; and 12mo, 516 pp., library edition, $1.00 cloth. The paper issue was advertised in the *New-York Times* on May 28, 1880, as "This day," and the cloth issue was advertised on July 2 as

"This day." The paper issue was listed in *PW* and *Lit W* on June 5 and in the *Ind* on June 10. It was also issued by George Munro, New York, 1880, 32.5 cm., $.20 paper, *Seaside Library* No. 754, advertised in the *New-York Times* on June 12 as a late issue, and probably issued close to that date.

361 JULES VERNE **The Vanished Diamond.** 12mo. Illustrated. 1/o limp boards, 2/o cloth 1888

This is my copy, 1888, with "Limited" in the imprint on the front cover but not on the title page. It is 18.2 cm., 179 pp., frontispiece and seven full-page illustrations, with a vignette title page. It is clothed in pale blue pictorial limp boards cut flush, and printed in black and white. A page of publisher's ads appears at the front and back, and there are ads on the endpapers and back cover. The first edition was *L'Etoile du Sud: Le Pays du Diamants*, which ran serially in a French periodical, Jan. 1–Dec. 15, 1884, and was issued by J. Hetzel, Paris, 1884, 27.5 cm., 242 pp., illustrations, map; and 18 cm., 336 pp. The first edition in English was issued by George Munro, New York (1885), 17.5 cm., 136 pp., $.20 paper, my copy, *Seaside Library Pocket Edition* No. 368, in buff wrappers, decorated and printed in red and black. It was probably issued in Mar. 1885, but the wrapper date is not legible. The title is *The Southern Star*.

The first British edition was issued by Low, 1885, 18 cm., 263 pp., illustrated, 7/6 in green pictorial cloth, with a 32-page catalog (Oct. 1885) at the back. It was listed in the *Ath* on Oct. 17. Low issued it in 1887, illustrated, 3/6 cloth, listed in the *Ath* on Nov. 5, 1887; and they issued it in 1896, listed in the *TWEd* for July 24.
See 1890

362 FRANK R. STOCKTON **The Hundredth Man.** New and cheaper edition. 2/o boards 1888

This is a known copy, 1888, a yellowback. It ran in the *Century Magazine* beginning in

Nov. 1886, and the first American edition was issued by the Century Co., New York (1887), 20 cm., 432 pp. in blue-black cloth, printed in gold, in two different decorative patterns, or in black cloth printed in orange with still a different decorative pattern. They issued third and fourth editions, the same, in 1887. The first British edition was issued by Low, 1887, 19 cm., 432 pp., 6/o, listed in the *Ath* on Oct. 22. The American edition was deposited on Oct. 8.

363 GERTRUDE JERDON *Keyhold Country.* [New edition.] 2/o 1888 (*Eng Cat*)

The first edition was issued by Low, 1885, p 8vo, 133 pp., illustrated, 5/o. It was issued in the United States by Roberts Bros., Boston, 1886, illustrated.

364 YÜAN WEI *Chinese Account of the Opium War.* Cr 8vo. 2/o 1888 (*Eng Cat*)

The first edition was issued by Kelly & Walsh, Shanghai, 1888, 22 cm., 82 pp., a translation by Edward H. Parker of the last two chapters of *Shêng Wu-Ki*, abridged, the *Pagoda Library* No. 1.

365 PHILIP S. ROBINSON *In My Indian Garden.* [New edition.] 12mo. 2/o 1888 (*Eng Cat*)

The first edition was issued by Low, 1878, 17 cm., 211 pp., with a preface by Edwin Arnold, 3/6 limp cloth, listed in the *Ath* on Mar. 23. Low issued the second edition, 1878, 3/6, about May 4; they issued the third edition, 3/6, about Aug. 10, 1878; and issued the fourth edition, 1882.

366 PHILIP S. ROBINSON *Under the Punkah.* [New edition.] 12mo. 2/o 1888 (*Eng Cat*)

The first edition was issued by Low, 1881, 12mo, 255 pp., 5/o, listed in the *Ath* on Mar. 12. It consists of seventeen miscellaneous pieces in prose.

367 LEW WALLACE (LEWIS WALLACE) *Ben-Hur.* [New edition.] p 8vo. 2/o 1888 (*Eng Cat*)

The first edition was issued by Harper & Bros., New York, 1880, 17.5 cm., 552 pp., $1.50 in powder-blue cloth with gray endpapers, in an edition of 2,500 copies. It was deposited on Oct. 22, advertised in the *New-York Times* on Nov. 12 as "This day," and listed in the *Ind* on Nov. 18. There is a known copy with an inscribed date, Nov. 17, 1880. Harpers issued the 110th thousand, the same advertised in the *New-York Times* on Aug. 27, 1886, as "Now ready." Editorial matter in the *New York Times Book Review* for Jan. 13, 1900, stated that Harper's *Ben-Hur* was now in its 92nd edition and had sold 680,000 copies.

The first British edition was issued by Low, 1881, 17.5 cm., 552 pp., 6/o in red cloth, with a 32-page catalog at the back. It was listed in the *Ath* on Feb. 26 and in *PC* on Mar. 1. Harper records show that Harpers agreed on Nov. 9, 1880, to furnish plates for the English edition. Low issued a new edition in 1881, the same, advertised in the *Spect* on Mar. 12. Frederick Warne, London, issued it (1884), 16mo, 458 pp., 1/6 sewed, and 2/o in blue cloth in gold and black; and reissued it in 1887, 2/o cloth, 458 pp. These are given by the *Eng Cat.* It was also issued by Ward, Lock & Co., London and New York (1887), 18 cm., 422 pp., 1/o sewed, 1/6 and 2/o cloth (olive and red), given by the *Eng Cat.*

368 JULES VERNE *The Archipelago on Fire.* 12mo. Illustrated. 1/o limp boards, 2/o cloth 1888 (*Eng Cat*)

The first French book edition was issued by J. Hetzel, Paris, 1884, *L'Archipel en Feu*, in two different issues, one, 27.5 cm., 198 pp., illustrated, two maps; and the other, 18 cm., 305 pp. One of them was listed in the *Ath* on Aug. 23, 1884, 3 francs, and the other was listed Oct. 4, 5 francs. It ran in *Le Temps*, June 29–Aug. 3, 1884. The first edition in English was issued by George Munro, New York. Munro issued it, 1885, 32.5 cm., 28 pp., paper, listed in *PW* on Mar. 14, *Seaside Library* No. 1980; and issued it (1885), 18.5 cm., 102 pp., wrappers, *Seaside Library Pocket Edition* No. 395, probably in Mar. or Apr.

The first British edition was issued by Low, 1886, Cr 8vo, 198 pp., illustrated, 7/6, advertised in the *Spect* on Oct. 3, 1885, and listed in the *Ath* on Nov. 28. Low issued it in 1887, illustrated, 3/6 cloth, listed in the *Ath* on Nov. 5, 1887.

See 1890

Sampson Low, Marston, Searle & Rivington, Ltd. St. Dunstan's House, Fetter Lane 1889

369 JOHN H.L. ZILLMANN *Past and Present Australian Life.* p 8vo. 2/0 boards   July 13 (*Spect*)

This is the first edition, 1889, 19 cm., 206 pp.

370 GEORGE L. MÉLIO *Manual of Swedish Drill.* Cr 8vo. Illustrated. 1/6 boards July 20 (*Ath* ad)

This is the first edition, 1889, 79 pp., compiled and arranged by Mélio. In the United States it was issued by the Excelsio Publishing House, New York, 1889, 51 pp., illustrated. Low issued the second edition, illustrated, probably at 1/6 boards, 1894, 81 pp., given by the *BM*.

371 RICHARD D. BLACKMORE *Lorna Doone.* Thirtieth edition. 12mo. 2/0 boards, 2/6 cloth   Aug. 3 (*Ath* ad)

Standard Novels No. 1. The ad said "Now ready." This began a new issue of this series, now in yellowback form, the original series being started in 1881, at 6/0 cloth each. This is my copy, 1889, 17.5 cm., 517 pp., in pale blue pictorial boards, printed in red and black with the series title on the front and spine. It has a preface, undated, and a preface to the sixth edition (Jan. 1873), blue endpapers with commercial ads, 3 pp. of ads at the back, and a commercial ad on the back cover. I have another copy of the 2/0 boards issue, 39th

edition, the same but with no date (probably 1893), 18.2 cm., with the preface dated (Mar. 1869), and with the same preface to the sixth edition (Jan. 1873). The endpaper ads differ, and there are no ads at the back. One of the endpaper ads contains a date (Feb. 8, 1892). The 36th edition was also the 2/0 boards issue, 1892, and the 38th edition had a portrait, 2/6 cloth, listed in the *TWEd* on Aug. 4, 1893. There were many, many more editions. Low issued it in *Sixpenny Editions of Books by Popular Authors* No. 1, 8vo, 254 pp., sewed, listed in *PC* on Oct. 9, 1897. The sixpenny edition was reissued in June 1902, in Aug. 1904, and in Oct. 1904. The *TLS* for June 20, 1902, said this sixpenny edition was issued in 150,000 copies. Low issued the *Pocket Edition* at 2/0 cloth, 3/0 leather, on India paper, in 1900; and they issued it in 1902, 8vo, 1/0 sewed. I have a copy, no date (after 1920?), 21.5 cm., 245 pp. in double columns, 1/0 in white pictorial wrappers, printed in red and blue. It has "Unabridged Edition" and "Author's Copyright Edition" on the front, and "Copyright" on the title page. There are ads on the inside front and on both sides of the back cover, the ad on the back cover being in purple, yellow, and red.

The first edition was issued by Low, 3 vols., 1869, 18.8 cm., 31/6 in blue cloth with cream endpapers. It has a 16-page catalog (Mar. 1869) at the back of vol. 3. It was listed in the *Ath* on Mar. 13, and Sadleir's presentation copy was inscribed Mar. 20, 1869. Low issued the second edition, 1870, Cr 8vo, frontispiece, 6/0, listed in the *Spect* on Oct. 1; and issued the third edition, the same, advertised in the *Spect* on Apr. 29, 1871, as "This day." The 6/0 edition was reissued as the 12th edition in 1879, and as the 18th edition in 1881.

The first American edition was issued by Harper & Bros, New York, 1874, 22.5 cm., 280 pp., frontispiece, *Library of Select Novels* No. 421, $.75 paper, advertised in the *Nation* on Oct. 15 and listed in *PW* on Oct. 17. Harpers issued it in 1882, *Franklin Square Library* No. 7 (two-columns issue), 8vo, $.25 paper, advertised in the *New-York Times* on Nov. 10 as "This day."

372 THOMAS HARDY *Far from the Madding Crowd.* New and cheaper edition. 12mo. 2/0 boards, 2/6 cloth Aug. 17 (*Ath*)

Standard Novels No. 2. This is my copy, 1889, 17.5 cm., 407 pp., the same as the preceding title in all respects except for the cover picture and the title page. This ran in the *Cornhill*, Jan.–Dec. 1874, anonymously, illustrated. The first British book edition was issued by Smith, Elder & Co., London, 2 vols., 1874, 22 cm., frontispiece and five illustrations in each vol., 21/0 in bright green cloth, with chocolate endpapers; 7,000 copies were printed on Nov. 23, 1874. It was listed in the *Ath* on Nov. 28, 1874. They issued the second edition, 2 vols., the same, 1874, 500 copies, advertised in the *Spect* on Jan. 16, 1875, as "Next week." *BAL* thought it was issued in early Feb. 1875, but the date on the title page is 1874. Smith, Elder issued a new edition, 1877, large Cr 8vo, 407 pp., frontispiece and five illustrations, 7/6 in bright green cloth, with gray-chocolate endpapers. It was advertised in the *Spect* on Mar. 24 and listed on Mar. 31.

Low took over the plates and issued a

new edition, 1882, 407 pp., *Standard Novels*, 6/0, listed in the *Spect* on Feb. 11 and advertised in the *TWEd* on Feb. 17. Low reissued the yellowback, 1892, 2/0 boards; and issued it as No. 1 of a reissue of Hardy's novels, 2/6 cloth, advertised in the *Spect* on June 24, 1893, as "Ready."

In the United States there was a feeding frenzy. It ran in *Every Saturday*, Jan. 31–Oct. 24, 1874, and in Oct. 1874 the magazine was merged into *Littell's Living Age*, where the story finished on June 9, 1875. It ran in the *Eclectic Magazine*, Mar. 1874–Feb. 1875; and it ran in the *New York Tribune*, June 26–Dec. 15, 1874. The first American book edition was issued by Henry Holt & Co., New York, author's edition, 1874, 17 cm., 474 pp., illustrated, $1.25 cloth, *Leisure Hour Series*. The endpaper ads contain a date (Nov., 17, 1874). It was advertised in the *New-York Times* on Nov. 28 as "This day," deposited on Nov. 17, and listed in *PW* on Nov. 28. Harper & Bros., New York, issued it as No. 1 of an issue of Hardy's novels, $1.50, listed in the *Nation* on June 6, 1895.

373 GASTON TISSANDIER *The Eiffel Tower.* p 8vo. Illustrated. Portrait. Plans. 1/0 Aug. 17 (*Ath* ad)

The ad said "Now ready." This is the first British edition, 1889, 20 cm., 96 pp. The first edition was *La Tour Ediffel*, Paris, 1889, 23 cm., 79 pp., frontispiece (portrait). There was a new edition, revised and enlarged, Paris, 1889, 23 cm., 81 pp., illustrated, portrait.

374 CHARLOTTE RIDDELL *The Senior Partner.* New edition. 12mo. 2/0 boards, 2/6 cloth Sept. 7 (*Ath*)

Standard Novels No. 3. This is 1889. This ran in *London Society* beginning in Jan. 1881, and the first book edition was issued by Bentley, London, 3 vols., 1881, 19 cm., in apple-green cloth, advertised in the *Ath* on Dec. 3, 1881, as "Ready." It was issued in Hamburg, Germany, 3 vols., 1882. James Hogg, London, issued it, 1882, 19 cm., 469 pp., 6/0, listed in the *Spect* on Sept. 9, 1882.

In the United States it was issued by Harper & Bros., New York (1882), 29.5 cm., 94 pp., $.20 paper, *Franklin Square Library* No. 223, listed in the *Ind* on Jan. 12, 1882, and in *PW* on Jan. 14, and advertised in the *New-York Times* on Jan. 6 as "This day." It was also issued by George Munro, New York, 1882, 32.5 cm., $.20 paper, *Seaside Library* No. 1160, listed in *PW* on Jan. 21, 1882, and advertised in the *New-York Times* on Jan. 19 as a late issue.

375 RANDOLPH CALDECOTT *Randolph Caldecott's Sketches.* 4to. Illustrated. 2/6 boards   Oct. 19 (*Ath*)

This is the first edition, 1890 (1889), 28 cm., 94 pp., with an introduction by Henry Blackburn.

376 PETER H. EMERSON *English Idyls.* 12mo. 2/0 cloth   Oct. 26 (*Ath* ad)

This is the first edition, 1889, 17 cm., 160 pp. Low issued the second edition, revised, 1889, 160 pp., 2/0 cloth.

377 LUCY B. WALFORD *Her Great Idea, and Other Stories.* 12mo. 2/0 boards, 2/6 cloth   Oct.?

Standard Novels No. 6. The first edition was issued by Henry Holt & Co., New York, 1888, 17 cm., 243 pp., *Leisure Hour Series* No. 219, listed in *PW* on Oct. 6, in the *Ind* on Oct. 11, and in *Lit W* on Oct. 13. The first British edition was issued by Low, 1888, Cr 8vo, 311 pp., 10/6, listed in the *Ath* on Oct. 27 and advertised there on Oct. 13 as "Ready."

378 THOMAS HARDY *The Mayor of Casterbridge.* 12mo. 2/0 boards, 2/6 cloth   Nov.?

Standard Novels No. 7. This ran in the *Graphic*, Jan. 2–May 15, 1886, illustrated, and the first British book edition was is-

sued by Smith, Elder & Co., London, 2 vols., 1886, 19.5 cm., 21/0 in smooth dark blue cloth, with gray-on-white flowered endpapers. There are 2 pp. of ads at the back of vol. 1 and 4 pp. at the back of vol. 2. It was advertised in the *Spect* on Apr. 24 as "On May 10" and listed there and in the *Ath* on May 15. Sadleir had a secondary binding in light sage-green cloth. Records show 758 copies were printed and 650 were bound by Dec. 1886, and 108 quires and 32 bound copies were remaindered to Low for £7, seven. Low issued a new edition, 1887, 18.5 cm., 432 pp., 6/0, in their *Standard Novels*, advertised in the *Spect* on Apr. 30; and they issued a new edition, 1893, listed in the *TWEd* on July 28.

In the United States it ran in *Harper's Weekly*, Jan. 2–May 15, 1886, illustrated. It was issued by Henry Holt & Co., New York, 1886, 16.5 cm., 356 pp., in the *Leisure Hour Series*, $1.00 cloth, and in the *Leisure Moment Series* No. 68, $.30 in gray-green wrappers. I have two copies of the latter, with publisher's ads on the inside covers and back cover, with the series title on the front. They are identical except that a leaf of publisher's ads precedes the title page in one copy and follows it in the other. It was advertised in the *New-York Times* on May 17, advertised in the *Nation* on May 20 as "Just published," and listed in *PW* on May 29. It was also issued by George Munro, New York (1886), 18.5 cm., 302 pp. in wrappers, *Seaside Library Pocket Edition* No. 79, listed in *PW* on May 29. It was also issued by John W. Lovell, New York (1886), 18.5 cm., 288 pp., in wrappers, *Lovell's Library* No. 749, listed in *PW* on June 12. It was also issued by Norman Munro, New York, (1886), *Munro's Library* No. 570, listed in *PW* on June 12. Harpers didn't issue it until June 1895, Cr 8vo, frontispiece, $1.50 cloth.

379 MARY E. HAWEIS *Beautiful Houses.* Third edition. 12mo. 1/0 boards   Dec. 7 (*Ath* ad)

This is 1889, 17 cm., 115 pp. The first edition was issued by Low, 1882, 18 cm., 115 pp., frontispiece, 4/0 parchment, advertised in the *Ath* on June 10 as "Ready." Low issued the second edition, 1882, 12mo, 115 pp., frontispiece, in mock vellum. The first American edition was issued by Scribner, Welford & Co., New York, 1882, 18 cm., 115 pp., illustrated, $1.50 parchment, advertised in the *New-York Times* on July 8.

380 SIR HENRY M. STANLEY *The Story of Emin's Rescue as Told in H. M. Stanley's Letters.* Cr 8vo. Map. 1/0 boards Dec. 28 (*Ath* ad)

The ad said "Now ready." This is the first edition, 1890, 190 pp., edited by J. S. Keltie. Low issued the second edition, the same, advertised in *Notes & Queries* on Mar. 15, 1890. The first American edition was issued by Harper & Bros., New York, 1890, 20.5 cm., frontispiece (double map), portrait, edited by Keltie, listed in *Lippincott's Monthly Magazine* for Apr. 1890, and thus probably issued in Feb. or Mar.

381 BITHIA M. CROKER *Some One Else.* [New edition.] 12mo. 2/0 boards, 2/6 cloth Dec.?

Standard Novels No. 8. The first edition was issued by Low, 3 vols., 1885, Cr 8vo, 31/6 in brown cloth with pale yellow endpapers. There is a 32-page catalog (Oct. 1884) at the back of vol. 3. It was advertised in *Notes & Queries* on Jan. 10 as "On Jan. 15" and advertised in the *Ath* on Jan. 17 as "Ready." Low issued the second edition, 1886, Cr 8vo, 6/0, in their *Standard Novels*, listed in the *Spect* on Apr. 24.

The first American edition was issued by Harper & Bros., New York, 29.5 cm., 61 pp., $.20 paper, *Franklin Square Library* No. 455. It is my copy, with a wrapper date (Mar. 7, 1885). It was listed in *PW* on Mar. 7 and in the *Ind* on Mar. 12. It was also issued by George Munro, New York (1885), *Seaside Library* No. 1990, 32.5 cm.; and *Seaside Library Pocket Edition* No. 412, 18.5 cm., both in paper and both listed in *PW* on Apr. 4, 1885.

382 JULES VERNE *Mathias Sandorf.* 12mo. Illustrated 1889

The *Eng Cat* gives this as 2 vols., 1/0 each, and the *U Cat* gives it as 2 vols.-in-1, 1889. It ran in *Le Temps*, June 16–Sept. 30, 1885, and was issued by J. Hetzel, Paris, 3 vols., 1885, with either 18 cm., in pink wrappers, or 22 cm., 552 pp., illustrated. Vol. 1 was listed in the *Ath* on Aug. 8; vol. 2 on Aug. 22; and vol. 3 on Oct. 31, each at 3 francs. F. W. Christern, New York, issued it in French, vol. 1 listed in the *Nation* on Sept. 17, 1885. The first edition in English was issued by George Munro, New York (1885), 32.5 cm., 3 vols.-in-1, paper, *Seaside Library* No. 2039, probably issued in Sept. or Oct. 1885. Munro also issued it in *Seaside Library Pocket Edition* No. 578, in 2 parts, illustrated, $.10 each, part 1 advertised in the *New-York Times* on Oct. 17, 1885, as a late issue, and vol. 2 advertised on Oct. 17 as "Out today."

The first British edition was issued by Low, 1886, Demy 8vo, illustrated, 10/6, advertised in the *Spect* on Oct. 2 and listed there and in the *Ath* on Oct. 9. Low issued it in 1888, Cr 8vo, 5/0, listed in the *Ath* on Nov. 10.

383 J. BICKERDYKE (CHARLES H. COOK) *An Irish Midsummer-Night's Dream.* 12mo. Illustrated. 1/0, 1/6 1889 (*BM*)

This is (1889), illustrated by E. M. Cox, 83 pp. The first edition was issued by W. Swan Sonnenschein & Co., London, 1884, p 8vo, 83 pp., 1/6.

384 CARL BRUMM *Bismarck: His Deeds and His Aims.* 8vo. 1/0 1889 (*BM*)

This is the first edition (1889), 51 pp., a reply to "The Bismarck Dynasty" in the *Contemporary Review.*

385 ANONYMOUS *Bruntie's Diary. A Tour Round the World.* 12mo. 1/6 1889 (*BM*)

This is the first edition, 1889, 17 cm., 128 pp., by C.E.B.

386 (GEORGE NUGENT-BANKES) *A Day of My Life.* 1/0 1889 (*U Cat*)

This is 1889, 183 pp., by An Eton Boy. The first edition was issued by Low, 1877, 16 cm., 177 pp., 2/6 limp cloth, by An Eton Boy, about Feb. 5. Low issued a second edition, 1877, about Apr. 7, 16 cm., 183 pp., 2/6, and a third edition, 1877, about May 19, 2/6; and the 7th thousand was issued, 1879, 16 cm., 183 pp., 2/6.

Sampson Low, Marston, Searle & Rivington, Ltd. St. Dunstan's House, Fetter Lane 1890

In many cases the imprint was Sampson Low & Co., Ltd.

387 ANONYMOUS *Sporting Celebrities.*
4to. Portraits. 1/0 Jan. (*Eng Cat*)
This is the first issue of an abortive periodical, of which only three numbers were issued, Jan.–Mar. 1890, 31 cm.

388 GEORG EBERS *Joshua.* 2 vols.
Copyright edition. 16mo. 1/6 sewed,
2/0 flexible cloth each Feb. 1 (*Spect*)
German Authors No. 32. This is the first British edition, 1890, 16 cm., translated by Clara and Margaret Bell. The first edition was issued at Stuttgart, 1889, 426 pp. In the United States it was issued by W. S. Gottsberger, New York, 1890, 16 cm., 371 pp., translated by Mary Safford, $.40 paper, $.75 cloth, listed in the *Nation* on Feb. 2. It was also issued by John W. Lovell, New York, 18.5 cm., 267 pp., "Lovell's Series of Foreign Literature No. 1" on the cover, called the only authorized edition, listed in *PW* on Jan. 4, 1890, in *Public Opinion* on Jan. 19, and in the *Nation* on Feb. 20, 1890, $.50.

389 GEORGE MACDONALD *Adela Cathcart.* New and cheaper edition.
12mo. 2/0 boards, 2/6 cloth Feb. 8 (*Ath*)
Standard Novels No. 10. This is 1890, 412 pp. The first edition was issued by Hurst & Blackett, London, 3 vols., 1864, 19.5 cm.,

31/6 in brown cloth, listed in the *Ath* on Apr. 2. Low issued it in 1 vol., 1882, revised edition, Cr 8vo, 412 pp., 6/0, listed in the *Spect* on July 1. Low issued a new and cheaper edition, 1894, 2/0 boards, 2/6 cloth, in Feb. according to the *Eng Cat*.

It was issued in the United States by A. K. Loring, Boston, 1871, 20 cm., 423 pp., frontispiece (portrait), advertised in the *New-York Times* on May 23, $1.75, and listed in the *Nation* on May 25. It was also issued by George Routledge, New York, in the 1870s, 18.5 cm., 423 pp., frontispiece. George Munro, New York, issued it as *Seaside Library* No. 1439 (1882), 4to, $.20 paper, advertised in the *New-York Times* on Nov. 16, 1882, as a late issue.

390 WILLIAM SENIOR ("RED SPINNER")
Near and Far. New and cheaper edition.
12mo. 2/0 boards, 2/6 cloth Feb. 15 (*Ad*)
This is my copy, 1890, 17.7 cm., 304 pp., in yellow pictorial boards, printed in red and black. The ad in *Notes & Queries* was on Feb. 15, and it is given by the *Eng Cat* as issued in Feb. It consists of articles reprinted in mostly extended and recast form from various periodicals (*Gentleman's Magazine*, *Bell's Life*, etc.). There are commercial ads on the blue endpapers and in red and black on the back cover.

The *U Cat* gives this as having the cover title "Sport and Colonial Life," which, if true, must have applied to the 2/6 cloth issue. The first edition was issued by Low, 1888, 19.5 cm., 304 pp., 6/0, listed in the *Ath* on Mar. 31.

391 RICHARD D. BLACKMORE *Cripps, the Carrier.* New and cheaper edition. 12mo. 2/0 boards, 2/6 cloth Mar. 1 (*Ath*)

Standard Novels No. 11. This is my copy, 1890, 17.5 cm., 419 pp., in pale blue pictorial boards, printed in red and black, with the series title on the front and spine. The number 12 occurs on the front cover and inconspicuously in the lower left corner of the title page, and I have found no reason for it. There is a page of ads at the back giving the *Standard Novels* unnumbered but still giving the present title as eleventh in the list. There are commercial ads on the blue endpapers and on the back cover. The first edition was issued by Low, 3 vols., 1876, 19 cm., 31/6 in olive-green cloth with cream endpapers. Sadleir's copy was a presentation copy (May 17, 1876), and it was listed in the *Ath* on June 3. Low issued the second edition, 3 vols., 1876, the same, advertised in the *Spect* on July 1 as "Now ready"; and issued the third edition, 1877, 18 cm., 419 pp., 6/0, with a 24-page catalog (Oct. 1876), listed in the *Spect* on Dec. 16, 1876. Low issued the fourth edition, 1883; and issued a new edition, 1892, 12mo, 2/0 boards (Wolff's copy); and issued it in 1894, Cr 8vo, 2/6 cloth, advertised in the *TWEd* on Feb. 9. Low issued it in *Sixpenny Editions* in 1903, sewed, 21.6 cm., 188 pp., listed in the *TLS* on May 1.

The first American edition was issued by Harper & Bros., New York, 1876, 23 cm., 165 pp. in double columns, frontispiece and full-page illustrations, in buff wrappers, printed in black, $.75. It is my copy, with 10 pp. of publisher's ads at the back and 4 pp. at the front, with ads on the inside and back covers. It was advertised in the *New-York Times* on July 25 as "This

day" and listed in *Literary News* as published in July. It is in the series *Library of Select Novels* No. 464. It was also issued by Donnelley, Loyd, Chicago, no date, 31.5 cm., my copy, with a cover title, *Lakeside Library* No. 209, $.15 paper. There is an illustration on the front, and it is paged (499)–545 in triple columns. There are publisher's ads on the verso of page 545 stating tht the type in the *Lakeside Library* issues is so large and clear that readers will not ruin their eyesight! I've never seen type so small! It was probably issued in 1879.

392 RUDYARD KIPLING *Soldiers Three.* 8vo. 1/0 sewed Mar. 8 (*Ath ad*)

This is the first British edition, issued by Low, 1890, probably the fourth edition, 21.2 cm., 93 pp., in gray wrappers, pictorially printed on the front in black. It has "A. H. Wheeler & Co.'s Indian Railway Library No. 1" on the front. The first edition was issued by the Pioneer Press, Allahabad (India), 1888, 22 cm., 97 pp., in wrappers, greenish-gray. It contains seven stories, six of which were reprinted from the *Week's News*. The second edition was issued by A. H. Wheeler & Co., Allahabad, 1889, 22 cm., 97 pp. It was also issued by W. Thacker & Co., London; Thacker, Spink & Co., Calcutta, 2/6, advertised in the *TWEd* on Nov. 1, 1889. A. H. Wheeler & Co. issued the third edition, 1890, 22 cm., 93 pp. with a cover imprint of Sampson Low, London; Bromfield, New York. Low issued it at 1/0 sewed, 93 pp. passim, the eleventh edition being 1894. I have a copy, Low, 1891, ninth edition, 21.1 cm., (94) pp., 1/0 sewed, in pictorial gray wrappers, printed in black with "Indian Railway Library No. 1" on the front. A poem, "L'Envoie," is on page (94), and there are commercial ads on the inside and back covers, press notices on a page at the front and back, and a page of A. H. Wheeler & Co. ads at the back.

In the United States, *Soldiers Three; and*

Other Stories was issued by John W. Lovell, New York (1890), authorized edition, 12mo, *International Series* No. 98, $.50 yellow wrappers, printed in red and black, ads on the inside and back covers, and dated on the cover, May 29, 1890; and tan cloth, $1.00. It contains also "Only a Subaltern" on pp. 177–207 and "In Black and White" on pp. 209–409. There is a prefatory note by Kipling authorizing Lovell to state that all Lovell editions have been overlooked by him. It was advertised in the *New-York Times* on July 12 and advertised in *Dial* for July as "Recent." *Indian Tales* was issued by the United States Book Co., New York, in 1890, 12mo, 771 pp., $1.50 cloth. It contains "Plain Tales from the Hills," "Soldiers Three and Other Stories," "The Story of the Gadsbys," and "Phantom 'Rickshaw." It was advertised in the *New-York Times* on Oct. 4 and listed in the *Nation* on Oct. 16, 1890. It was also issued by George Munro (John W. Lovell), New York (1890), *Seaside Library Pocket Edition* No. 1443, listed in *PW* on Aug. 17, 1890. It was also issued by J. S. Ogilvie, New York, (1890), *Fireside Series* No. 114, containing also "The Story of the Gadsbys."

393 STUART C. CUMBERLAND (CHARLES GARNER) *The Vasty Deep.* [New edition.] 12mo. 2/o boards, 2/6 cloth   Mar. 22 (*Ath*)

Standard Novels No. 12. The first edition was issued by Low, 2 vols., 1889, 19 cm., 21/o in smooth mauve cloth with gray and white floral endpapers, with a 32-page catalog (Sept. 1888) at the back of both vols. It was advertised in the *Spect* on Mar. 30 as ready.

394 HARRIET B. STOWE *Dred.* New edition. 12mo. 2/o boards, 2/6 cloth Mar. 22 (*Ath* ad)

Standard Novels No. 13. The ad said "Now ready." I am satisfied that this title was is-

sued at this time in this series, but my copy is dated 1889 on the title page. This is possible, perhaps, if the title page for an 1889 cloth issue is used for this 1890 boards issue. My copy is a new edition, 17.8 cm., 445 pp., with an appendix on pp. (415)–445. It has a preface (London, Aug. 21, 1856) and is in pale blue pictorial boards, printed in red, green, and black, with commercial ads on the blue endpapers and on the back cover, and with an ad on the verso of the last page of text. The series title appears on the front cover and spine.

Also 1856.

395 WILL M. CARLETON *City Legends.* [New edition.] 12mo. 1/o limp boards Mar. (*Eng Cat*)

Rose Library. Although the *Eng Cat* gives this as Mar. 1890, it was advertised at 1/o boards, Cr 8vo, in the *Spect* on Sept. 28, 1889, and was also advertised in the *TWEd* on Apr. 18, 1890, Cr 8vo, 1/o boards. Low issued the first British edition, 1889, special edition, Roy 8vo, illustrated, 12/6, listed in the *Ath* and *Spect* on Oct. 5 and advertised in the *TWEd* on Oct. 18. Low issued it with *City Ballads* in 1 vol., 2/6 cloth, advertised in the *TWEd* on Apr. 18, 1890.

The first edition was issued by Harper & Bros., New York, 1890, 23 cm., 170 pp., illustrated, $2.00 cloth, etc. It has 4 pp. of ads and is bound in gray-green pictorial cloth, bevelled boards. It was advertised in the *New-York Times* on Sept. 28, 1889, as "This day" and listed in the *Nation* on Oct. 3 and in *PW* on Oct. 5, 1889. They issued a new edition, the same, advertised in the *New-York Times* on July 19, 1892.

See 1893

396 THOMAS HARDY *The Trumpet-Major.* New and cheaper edition. 12mo. 2/o boards, 2/6 cloth Apr. 5 (*Ath*)

Standard Novels No. 14. I am satisfied that this title appeared in this series at this time, and, in fact, there is a known copy dated 1890. My copy, however, is 1889, 18.2 cm., 428 pp., in pale blue pictorial boards, printed in red and black, with the series title and the No. 17 on the front and spine. There are commercial ads on the blue endpapers, and a commercial ad on the back cover contains the date 1889. Low issued the first 1-vol. edition, 1881, cheap edition, p 8vo, 428 pp., 6/o in scarlet cloth with dark gray endpapers. It has a 32-page catalog (Jan. 1881) at the back, and was listed in the *Spect* on Sept. 17. Low issued it in 1893 as No. 2 of a reissue of Hardy, 2/6 cloth, advertised in the *TWEd* on June 16 as "Just ready."

It ran in *Good Words* Jan.–Dec. 1880, illustrated, and the first book edition was issued by Smith, Elder & Co., London, 3 vols., 1880, 19.5 cm., 31/6 in scarlet cloth with cream-white endpapers, listed in the *Ath* on Oct. 30. Records show 1,000 copies were printed, of which 250 quires were remaindered to W. Glaisher, a wholesale book dealer, in 1882. Hardy received £200 from Smith, Elder for this.

In the United States it ran in *Demorest's Monthly Magazine* (New York), Jan. 1880–Jan. 1881, advance sheets being secured for $500. It also ran in George Munro's *Fortnightly Review*, Jan.–Dec. 1880. Munro also issued it as *Seaside Library* No. 890, 32.5 cm., 54 pp., $.20 paper, my copy, dated Dec. 7, 1880. It was deposited Dec. 17, 1880, advertised in the *New-York Times* on Dec. 11 as "Out today," and listed in *PW* on Dec. 18. It was also issued by Henry Holt & Co., New York, 1880, 17 cm., 366 pp., *Leisure Hour Series* No. 118, $1.00 in mustard yellow cloth, printed and decorated in black. It was deposited Dec. 13, 1880, advertised in the *New-York Times* on Dec. 4, and listed in *PW* on Dec. 11. Harper & Bros., New York, didn't issue it until 1896, Cr 8vo, frontispiece, $1.50 cloth, listed in the *Nation* on Feb. 27.

397 CHARLOTTE RIDDELL **Daisies and Buttercups.** New and cheaper edition. 12mo. 2/o boards, 2/6 cloth   Apr. 19 (*Ath* ad)

Standard Novels No. 15. This is my copy, no date, 17.4 cm., 480 pp., in pale blue pictorial boards, printed in red and black, with a dedication (1882). It has commercial ads on the blue endpapers and on the back cover, and the series title appears on the front and spine. Low issued it, 1883, 19 cm., 480 pp., probably at 6/o. The first edition was issued by Bentley, London, 3 vols., 1882, Cr 8vo, in pinkish-ochre cloth with pale gray flowered endpapers, advertised in the *Ath* on Aug. 26 as "Just ready."

In the United States it was issued by Harper & Bros., New York, (1882), 29.5 cm., 95 pp., $.20 paper, *Franklin Square Library* No. 279, advertised in the *New-York Times* on Nov. 3 as "This day," and listed in the *Ind* on Nov. 9 and in *PW* on Dec. 2, 1882. It was also issued by George Munro, New York, 1882, 32.5 cm., 82 pp., paper, *Seaside Library* No. 1451, issued in Nov. and listed in *PW* on Dec. 2, 1882.

398 RICHARD H. GLOVER **A Handy Guide to Dry-Fly Fishing.** Cr 8vo. Illustrated. 1/o cloth   Apr. (*Eng Cat*)

This is the first edition (1890), 18.5 cm., 34 pp., by Cotwold Isys. Low issued the third edition, revised, 1894, p 8vo, 34 pp., two plates, 1/o, given by the *BM*.

399 EDWARD S. BISHOP **Lectures to Nurses on Antiseptics in Surgery.** Cr 8vo. Illustrated. 2/o boards   May 17 (*Ath* ad)

Nursing Record Series No. 1. It was listed in the *Spect* on Apr. 26. This is the first edition (1890), 65 pp. Low reissued it (1891), Cr 8vo, 65 pp., seven colored plates, 2/o, advertised in the *TWEd* on June 5.

400 FRANK R. STOCKTON *The Stories of the Three Burglars.* 12mo. 1/0 boards June 1 (*PC*)

This is my copy, 1890, the first British edition, 17.7 cm., 159 pp., in white pictorial boards cut flush, printed in red and black with plain white endpapers, with an inscribed date (July 1890). The title on the cover and spine is "Three Burglars," and there is a commercial ad on the back cover in red and black. Glover and Greene give this as having 118 pp.! It was advertised in the *Ath* on May 24, 1890, 1/0 boards, "First edition exhausted on the day of publication. Second edition now ready." The *BM* gives only the second edition, and the *Eng Cat* gives only the second edition as issued in Aug. 1890. It apparently was exhausted so fast that the *BM* didn't get a copy and the *Eng Cat* never heard of it! There is a known copy, second edition, 1890, and the second edition was advertised in the *Spect* on June 28, 1890.

The first edition was issued by Dodd, Mead & Co., New York (1890, copyright 1889), 19 cm., 159 pp., $.50 in printed paper wrappers and $1.00 in blue cloth. There are ads on page (160) and a 16-page catalog at the back. It was advertised in the *New-York Times* on Mar. 29, 1890, as "This day" and listed in the *Ind* on Mar. 27 and in *PW* on Mar. 29. It was advertised in *PW* on Mar. 22 as "New publications." Both Glover and Greene and *BAL* give this incorrectly as (1889).

401 RUDYARD KIPLING *The Story of the Gadsbys.* Third editon. Demy 8vo. 1/0 sewed June (*Eng Cat*)

This is my copy, A. H. Wheeler & Co., Allahabad; Low, London, no date, 21.2 cm., 93 pp., with the only Low imprint on the front. It is in gray wrappers cut flush, with a vignette in black on the front and a different vignette on the back. There is a poem, "L'Envoi," on page (94), and "A. H.

Wheeler & Co.'s Indian Railway Library No. 2" on the front cover. A leaf of Wheeler ads appears at the front and back, with the inside wrappers plain. The *U Cat* gives the third edition as I've given it, but the *BM* gives the third edition as 1890, 100 pp.! The Livingston bibliography gives the first English edition as I've given it but with 86 pp.! It states that Low ordered 10,000 copies to be printed on Mar. 4, 1890. The *U Cat* gives Wheeler; Low (1890), with 85 pp.! The Berg collection gives the first English edition as Wheeler; Low (1890), 21 cm., with no mention of edition or number of pages. The first edition was issued by A. H. Wheeler & Co., Allahabad (1888), 22 cm., 100 pp., with "L'Envoi" on pp. 101 and 102. It is in greenish-gray wrappers, with 4 leaves of ads at the back, and contains eight stories, six of which had appeared in the *Week's News* in 1888. They issued the second edition, 1889, 22 cm., 100 pp. The fourth edition was issued by Wheeler; Low (1891), 22 cm., 93 pp., in gray wrappers, printed in Aberdeen, Scotland. I wonder if the correct bibliography of the Kipling Indian tales will ever be ascertained! I'm certainly not proud of this discussion, nor have I ever seen any better!

I have another copy, Wheeler, Allahabad; Low, London, and only Low on the front, no date, seventh edition, 21.3 cm., 94 pp., 1/0 in pictorial gray wrappers cut flush, printed in black. "L'Envoi" is on page (94), and there are commercial ads on the inside and back covers, with a leaf of ads in front and a page of ads at the back. It was advertised in the *Ath* on Aug. 22, 1891. The fifth edition, the same, was advertised in the *Ath* on July 25, 1891, and in *PC* on May 23.

The first authorized American edition was issued by John W. Lovell, New York (1890), authorized edition, 19 cm., 173 pp., *Westminster Series* No. 4 on the cover, in brick-red wrappers, $.25. It has the wrapper date June 30, 1890, and was advertised in the *New-York Times* on July 26 as books of the week, and listed in *PW* on Aug. 12. Wrapper dates with Lovell are usually largely meaningless. It was also issued by Lovell, Coryell & Co., New York (1891), 12mo, in red cloth, the second authorized American edition. It has a Kipling note on the page following the title, "This edition of my collected writings is issued in America with my cordial sanction." It was also issued by George Munro, New York (1890), 18.5 cm., *Seaside Library Pocket Edition* No. 1499, with wrapper date Aug. 22, 1890, listed in *PW* on Sept. 27. It was contained in *Soldiers Three, etc.*, issued by J. S. Ogilvie, New York (1890), *Fireside Series* No. 114.

402 THOMAS GRAY *An Elegy Written in a Country Churchyard.* Cr 8vo. Illustrated. 1/0 cloth   June (*Eng Cat*)

Choice Series. This began a reissue of this series which ran to 14 vols. at 1/0 and *The Pilgrim's Progress* at 2/0. Low first issued it in this series (1875), 17.5 cm., 26 pp. interleaved, illustrated by Birket Foster, with the series title on the cover. Low published it for Joseph Cundall, 1854, 20.5 cm., 23 leaves printed on one side only, illustrated by Foster; and Low issued it, 1869, 16 cm., illustrated. The first edition was issued by R. Dodsley, London, 1751, 28.5 cm., anonymous, 11 pp., o/6, *An Elegy Wrote in a Country Church Yard.* Dodsley issued the second edition, 1751; and the third edition, corrected, 27 cm., including stanza 30 for the first time.

In the United States it was issued as *A Voice from the Tombs*, Parker, New York, 1762. It was also issued as *The Grave by Robert Blair . . . to which is added An Elegy Written in a Country Church-Yard*, H. Taylor, Philadelphia, 1791, 12mo, (32) pp. The seventh edition of the latter was issued in Boston, 1772, 8vo, 45pp.; and was issued by R. Aitkin, Philadelphia, 1773, 31, (1) pp.

403 THOMAS HARDY *The Hand of Ethelberta.* New and cheaper edition. 12mo. 2/0 boards, 2/6 cloth   July 12 (*Ath*)

Standard Novels No. 17. This is my copy, 1890, 17.5 cm., 412 pp., in pale blue pictorial boards, printed in red and black, with the series title and the No. 33 on the front and spine. There are commercial ads on the blue endpapers and on the back cover. This ran in the *Cornhill Magazine*, July 1875–May 1876, illustrated by George Du Maurier. The first book edition was issued by Smith, Elder & Co., London, 2 vols., 1876, 22 cm., 2 pp. of ads, frontispiece and five illustrations in vol. 1, and 1 page of ads, frontispiece and four illustrations in vol. 2, the illustrations by Du Maurier. It was in bright brown cloth with café-au-lait endpapers, top edges uncut, 21/0, listed in the *Ath* on Apr. 8. Records show 1,000 copies were printed. Smith, Elder issued it, 1877, Cr 8vo, (416) pp., 6 illustrations by Du Maurier, 7/6, in bright green cloth with gray-chocolate endpapers, listed in the *Spect* on June 2. Records show 1,000 copies were printed, and 500 and the moulds were sold to Low in 1882. Low issued a new edition in 1882, p 8vo, six illustrations, 6/0, listed in the *Spect* on Mar. 25. Low issued a new and cheaper edition, 1888, 18 cm., 412 pp.; reissued the yellowback, 2/0 boards, 1892, Sadleir's copy, new and cheaper edition; and they issued a new and cheaper edition in 1893, listed in the *TWEd* on Sept. 15.

In the United States it ran in the *New-York Times* Sunday edition, June 20, 1875–Apr. 9, 1876. I think Purdy nodded when he gave this serial run as in the *New York Tribune* Sunday edition. The first American book edition was issued by Henry Holt & Co., New York, 1876, 17 cm., 423 pp., *Leisure Hour Series* No. 62, $1.25 cloth, an authorized edition. It was advertised in the *New-York Times* on May 13 as "Just ready," deposited May 9, and listed in *PW* on May 6. Harper & Bros., New York, issued it in 1896, Cr 8vo, frontispiece, $1.25, listed in the *Nation* on Mar. 19.

404 ROBERT P. ASHE *Two Kings of Uganda; or, Life by the Shores of Victoria Nyanza.* New and cheaper edition. Cr 8vo. Illustrated. Folding map. 1/0 boards   July 19 (*Ath* ad)

The ad said "New books." This is 1890, 19 cm., 291 pp. The first edition was issued by Low, 1889, 19.5 cm., 354 pp., illustrated, folding map, advertised in the *TWEd* on July 12, 6/0, "Now ready"; and they reissued it in 1897, Cr 8vo, illustrated, 2/6 cloth, advertised in the *TWEd* on Apr. 2.

405 HARRISON W. WEIR *The Poetry of Nature.* Cr 8vo. Illustrated. 1/0 cloth July (*Eng Cat*)

Choice Series. These were chosen and illustrated by Weir. Low first issued it in this series (1875), 72 pp., illustrated, 2/6 cloth. I am uncertain as to the first edition. The *U Cat* gives Cassell, Petter & Galpin, London (1859?), 18 cm., 72 pp. illustrated; and it also gives Low (1859?), 72 pp. The *BM* and the *U Cat* give Low 1861 (1860), 23 cm., 111 pp., illustrated, interleaved with blank pages, 12/0. The *Eng Cat* gives only Low in 1860, square 8vo, 12/0, selected and illustrated by Weir. Low advertised it in the *Ath* on Jan. 2, 1864, small 4to, illustrated, 12/0, 21/0 morocco, as "New books." Low issued it, 1868, small 4to, 71 pp., illustrated, 5/0, 6/0 morocco, advertised in the *Ath* on Nov. 9, 1867, as "This day." In the United States it was issued by D. Appleton & Co., New York, 1861, the same as the 1861 Low issue.

406 THOMAS HARDY *The Return of the Native.* New edition. 12mo. 2/0 boards, 2/6 cloth   Aug. 9 (*Ath*)

Standard Novels No. 18. This is 1890, 17.5 cm., 412 pp., in pale blue pictorial boards,

with the No. 82 on the front. Low first issued it, 1884, Cr 8vo, 6/0, *Standard Novels*, listed in the *Spect* on May 3; and issued a new edition, 1893, 17.5 cm., 412 pp., 2/6, listed in the *TWEd* on Aug. 18. It ran in *Belgravia*, Jan.–Dec. 1878, with 12 illustrations by Arthur Hopkins, never used again! The first book edition was issued by Smith, Elder & Co., London, 3 vols., 1878, 19.5 cm., frontispiece (map), in brown cloth with cream-white endpapers, top edges uncut. Records show 1,000 copies were printed and 100 quires were remaindered to W. Glaisher, London, a wholesale book dealer, in 1882. There are 2 pp. of ads in vol. 2, and it was advertised in the *Spect* on Oct. 26 as "On Nov. 1" and in the *Ath* on Nov. 2 as "This day." It was received in the *BM* in Dec. C. Kegan Paul & Co., London, issued a new edition, 1880, 19.5 cm., 412 pp., frontispiece, with a 32-page catalog, 6/0, advertised in the *TWEd* on Jan. 9, 1880.

The first appearance in the United States was in *Harper's New Monthly Magazine*, where it ran Feb. 1878–Jan. 1879. The first American book edition was issued by Henry Holt & Co;, New York, 1878, 17 cm., 465 pp., frontispiece (map), *Leisure Hours Series* No. 103. $1.00 cloth. It was advertised in the *New-York Times* on Dec. 4, 1878, as "Today" and listed in the *Ind* and the *Nation* on Dec. 26, and in *PW* on Dec. 28, 1878. Carroll Wilson had copies with ads on the endpapers of Sept. 18 in one copy, and Oct. 28, 1878, in another copy, but he states that the usual date was Dec. 10 or later. Harpers issued it in 1895, Cr 8vo, in a library edition, frontispiece, $1.50 cloth, advertised in the *Nation* on Oct. 24.

407 RUDYARD KIPLING *In Black and White.* Demy 8vo. 1/0 sewed   Aug. 9 (*Ath* ad)

The ad said "Ready." This is the first British edition (1890), 21 cm., 94 pp., in pale green wrappers, pictorially printed in black, with both Wheeler, Allahabad, and Low on the title page and only Low on the front. The Livingston bibliography says Low ordered 10,000 copies to be printed on June 12, 1890. Low advertised the second edition in the *Spect* on Sept. 27, 1890; and the third edition in the *Ath* on Oct. 4, 1890, these Low editions apparently referring to British editions. Low issued the sixth edition in 1891, Demy 8vo, 1/o sewed, printed at Aberdeen, advertised in the *Ath* on July 25. I have a copy, eighth edition, no date, Wheeler and Low on the title page and only Low on the front, 21.7 cm., 96 pp., in pictorial gray wrappers, printed in black, 1/o, with an inscribed date (July 1892). There are commercial ads on the inside and back covers, and a dedication on pp. (95) and 96.

The first edition was issued by A. H. Wheeler & Co., Allahabad (1888), 22 cm., 106 pp., in buff pictorial wrappers, with *Indian Railway Library* No. 3 on the front. There are 4 leaves of ads and a 2-page dedication at the back, and a leaf of ads at the front. It contains eight pieces, seven of which are from the *Week's News*, 1888. The *Week's News*, Nos. 1–36, Jan. 7–Sept. 15, 1888, was issued by the Pioneer Press, Allahabad. The present title was advertised in the *TWEd* on Nov. 1, 1889, 2/6, by W. Thacker & Co., London; Thacker, Spink & Co., Calcutta.

The first American edition was issued by John W. Lovell, New York, *Soldiers Three and Other Stories* (1890), authorized edition, *International Series* No. 98, with wrapper date May 29, 1890. It contains also *Only a Subaltern* and *In Black and White* and was listed in *Dial* for July as "Recent."

408 THOMAS HARDY *A Laodicean.*
New edition. 12mo. 2/o boards,
2/6 cloth   Aug. 30 (*Ath*)
Standard Novels No. 19. This is 1890, 17.5 cm., 374 pp., Wolff's copy. This ran in the European edition of *Harper's New Monthly*

Magazine, Dec. 1880–Dec. 1881, with 13 illustrations by George Du Maurier. The first British book edition was issued by Low, 3 vols., 1881, 19.5 cm., 31/6 in slate-gray cloth with cream-white endpapers, with a 32-page catalog (Dec. 1881) at the back of vol. 3 in some copies. It was advertised in the *Spect* on Dec. 3, 1881, as "Next week" and advertised in the *Ath* on Dec. 10 as "Ready." Purdy says it was remaindered to Mudie by 1882. Low issued it, 1882, new edition, Cr 8vo, 374 pp., 6/o

o, listed in the *Spect* on Nov. 11, 1882. Low issued a new edition, 1892; and issued it, 1893, Cr 8vo, 374 pp., 2/6, advertised in the *Spect* on Sept. 30 as ready.

Harpers also ran it in the American edition of their *New Monthly Magazine*, Jan. 1881–Jan. 1882, with 13 illustrations by Du Maurier. It was issued by Harper & Bros., New York (1881), my copy, 29.5 cm., 71 pp., *Franklin Square Library* No. 215, $.20 paper, with the title leaf dated Nov. 25, 1881, and with a statement on the caption title that it is published by arrangement with Henry Holt & Co. It was advertised in the *New-York Times* on Nov. 25 as "This day at 11 o'clock," deposited on Nov. 26, and listed in the *Ind* on Dec. 1, in the *Nation* on Dec. 8, and in *PW* on Dec. 10. It was also issued by Henry Holt & Co., New York, 1881, 17.5 cm., 432 pp., eight illustrations by Du Maurier, *Leisure Hour Series* No. 131, $1.00 cloth, advertised in the *New-York Times* on Nov. 25, 1881, and listed in the *Ind* on Dec. 1, in the *Nation* on Dec. 8, and in *PW* on Dec. 17. They issued it in 1896, Cr 8vo, frontispiece, $1.50, listed in the *Nation* on Apr. 2. It was also issued by George Munro, New York, 1881, 32.5 cm., $.20 paper, *Seaside Library* No. 1147, with cover date, Dec. 1, 1881, advertised in the *New-York Times* on Dec. 15 as a late issue, and listed in *PW* on Dec. 10, 1881.

409 RUDYARD KIPLING *Wee Willie Winkie and Other Stories.* [Second edition.] 8vo. 1/0 sewed   Sept. 27 (*Spect* ad)

This probably refers to the second British edition, also advertised in the *Ath* on Oct. 4. It is in pale green pictorial wrappers printed in black, with Wheeler and Low on the title page and only Low on the front. The first edition was issued by A. H. Wheeler & Co., Allahabad (1888), 22 cm., 104 pp., *Wee Willie Winkie and Other Child Stories*, *Indian Railway Library* No. 6, in greenish-gray wrappers, with 4 leaves of ads at the back and a leaf at the front. It contains four pieces, including *The Drums of Fore and Aft.* Three of the pieces were in the *Week's News* in 1888. Wheeler issued the second edition, 1889, 22 cm., 104 pp, in wrappers. The first British edition was issued by Low (1890), 21 cm., 96 pp., in pictorial wrappers, printed in Aberdeen. Low placed an order for 10,000 copies on June 13, 1890. Low issued the fifth edition in 1891, 21.6 cm., 96 pp., in Feb., given by the *Eng Cat*; and he issued the sixth edition, the same, advertised in the *Ath* on July 25, 1891. I have a copy, eighth edition, no date, 21.6 cm., 96 pp., in pale gray pictorial wrappers, printed in black, "Indian Railway Library No. 6" on the front, with a 1-page Wheeler ad in front and ads on the inside and back covers. It was printed in Aberdeen and has an inscribed date (Aug. 1892). The present title was advertised by W. Thacker & Co., London; Thacker, Spink & Co., Calcutta, in the *TWEd* on Nov. 1, 1889, 2/6.

The first American edition was issued by John W. Lovell, New York, (1890) 391 pp., in tan cloth and in wrappers, the latter dated June 12, 1890, *International Series* No. 103, listed in the *Ind* on Aug. 14 and in the *Nation* on Aug. 21, *The Phantom 'Rickshaw and Other Tales*, which included the *Wee Willie Winkie* stories. It was also issued by Rand McNally & Co., Chicago and New York, 1891, listed in *PW* on May 2 and in *Lit W* on May 9.

410 BROWNLOW FFORDE (ARTHUR B. FFORDE) *The Subaltern, the Policeman, and the Little Girl.* 8vo Illustrated. 1/0 sewed   Sept. 27 (*Spect* ad)

Shilling Novels No. 1. This is the first British edition, 1890, 100 pp., *Indian Railway Library* No. 10. The first edition was issued by A. H. Wheeler & Co., Allahbad. Low reissued the present edition in Oct., the same.

411 BROWNLOW FFORDE (ARTHUR B. FFORDE) *"The Trotter"* 8vo. Illustrated. 1/0 sewed   Sept. 27 (*Spect* ad)

Shilling Novels No. 2. This is the first British edition, 1890, 94 pp. The first edition was issued by A. H. Wheeler & Co., Allahabad, *Indian Railway Library* No. 12. Low reissued the present edition in Oct., the same.

412 RUDYARD KIPLING *Under the Deodars.* 8vo. 1/0 sewed   Oct. 18 (*Ath*)

This is the first British edition (1890), with Wheeler and Low on the title page and only Low on the front, 23 cm., 96 pp., in pale green wrappers, pictorially printed in black, printed in Aberdeen. Livingston's bibliography states that Low ordered 10,000 copies to be printed on July 30, 1890. Low issued it again in Nov., the same, probably the second (British) edition. Low issued the fourth edition in 1891, Demy 8vo, 1/0 sewed, advertised in the *Ath* on July 25; and they issued the sixth edition, my copy, no date, 21.7 cm., 96 pp., in pictorial gray wrappers, printed in black, with "Indian Railway Library No. 4" on the front. It has an inscribed date (Aug. 1892), and has commercial ads on the inside and back covers, Wheeler & Low on the title page, only Low on the front.

The first edition was issued by A. H. Wheeler & Co., Allahabad (1888), 22 cm., 106 pp., in greenish-gray pictorial wrappers, with "Indian Railway Library No. 4" on the front. There are 4 leaves of ads at the back and 1 leaf at the front, and it has six stories, five of which appeared in the *Week's News* in 1888. Wheeler issued the second edition (1889). It was advertised by Thacker & Co., London; Thacker, Spink & Co., Calcutta, in the *TWEd* on Nov. 1, 1889, 2/6.

In the United States it was issued by the United States Book Co., New York, no date, authorized edition, 18.5 cm., 86, 51 pp., *Westminster Series* No. 23 in terra-cotta wrappers, dated on the cover, Nov. 3, 1890, $.25, containing also "Departmental Ditties." It was advertised in the *New-York Times* on Jan. 31, 1891, as "Recent" and listed in *PW* on Jan. 3, and in the *Ind* on Jan. 15. It was also issued by the International Book Co., New York (1891), *Surprise Series* No. 150, with wrapper date June 25, 1891. *The Story of the Gadsbys and Under the Deodars* was issued by Lovell, Coryell & Co., New York (1891), authorized edition, 323 pp.

413 EDWARD MARSTON *How Stanley Wrote "In Darkest Africa."* Illustrated.
1/o Oct. (*Eng Cat*)

This is 1890, 80 pp., partly reprinted from *Scribner's Magazine*, with additions. The first edition was issued by Low in 1890, large paper, 5/o half-bound, listed in the *Ath* on Sept. 27

414 FRANK R. STOCKTON *The Schooner "Merry Chanter."* p 8vo. Illustrated.
2/6 boards Nov. 1 (*Ath*)

This is 1890, 20 cm., 192 pp. Low advertised *The Merry Chanter* (1890), a duplicate of the present edition, in the *Ath* on Oct. 4 and in the *Spect* on Sept. 27, 2/6 boards. What the purpose of this gambit was I can't imagine. Low issued a new edition in

1893, p 8vo, 1/o boards, listed in *PC* on Jan. 21, 1893, *The Schooner "Merry Chanter."*

This ran in the *Century Magazine* (New York), Nov. 1889–Mar. 1890, and the first book edition was issued by the Century Co., New York (1890), 20 cm., 192 pp., illustrated, $.50 in printed cream wrappers and in cloth, *The Merry Chanter.* The cloth issue was deposited on May 23 and listed in the *Ind* on May 29 and in *Public Opinion* on May 31. The paper issue was listed in *PW* on July 12 and in the *Nation* on July 31, 1890, and a known copy of the paper issue has an inscribed date, June 1890.

415 THOMAS HARDY *A Pair of Blue Eyes.*
12mo. 2/o boards, 2/6 cloth Nov. 15 (*Ath*)

Standard Novels No. 20. This is 1890, 17.5 cm., 309 pp. Low first issued it in 1884, p 8vo, 6/o, listed in the *Spect* on May 3. They reissued it, 1892, Sadleir's copy, new and cheaper edition, 12mo, 2/o boards; and issued it in 1893, 2/6, listed in the *TWEd* on July 21. It ran in *Tinsley's Magazine*, Sept. 1872–July 1873, illustrated, anonymously, and the first book edition was issued by Tinsley Bros., London, 3 vols., 1873, 19.5 cm., 31/6 in green cloth with cream-white endpapers, with Chapman & Hall ads, top edges uncut. There is a 16-page catalog (Mar. 1873) in some copies at the back of vol. 3. It was listed in the *Ath* on May 31. Sadleir had a secondary issue in bright blue cloth with pale yellow endpapers with Chapman & Hall ads, Tinsley on the spine. There was a remainder issue in blue cloth, plain yellow endpapers, no imprint on the spine. It was issued by Henry S. King, London, 1877, 19.5 cm., 369 pp., one plate, 6/o, listed in the *Spect* on Aug. 4. It was issued by C. Kegan Paul & Co., London, 1880, the same.

In the United States it ran in the *New*

York Tribune (semi-weekly), Sept. 26–Dec. 16, 1873, and the first American book edition was issued by Holt & Williams, New York, 1873, 17 cm., 390 pp., *Leisure Hour Series* No. 23, $1.25 cloth, with endpaper ads dated July 26. It was listed in the *Nation* on July 31 and in *PW* on Aug. 2. Weber states that endpapers ads bearing a date of Aug. 5 or later have the imprint Henry Holt & Co. Wolff's copy is Henry Holt & Co., 1873, in smooth white cloth, with white endpapers with ads in red. Harper & Bros., New York, issued it in 1895, Cr 8vo, $1.50 cloth, listed in the *Nation* on Aug. 1.

416 RUDYARD KIPLING *The Phantom 'Rickshaw and Other Tales.* Demy 8vo. 1/o sewed   Dec. (*Eng Cat*)

This is the first British edition (1890), with both Wheeler and Low on the title page and only Low on the front, 21.5 cm., 104 pp. in gray-green wrappers, pictorially printed in black, with a plain back cover, and with the title on the front cover, *The Phantom 'Rickshaw and Other Eerie Tales.* Livingston states that Low ordered 10,000 copies to be printed in Aberdeen on Sept. 22, 1890. Low issued the second (British) edition in 1891, advertised in *PC* on May 23; and issued the third edition in 1891, Demy 8vo, 1/o sewed, advertised in the *Ath* on July 25. I have a copy, no date, with Wheeler and Low on the title page and only Low on the front, the fifth edition, 21.6 cm., 104 pp., 1/o in greenish-gray pictorial wrappers, printed in black, with "Indian Railway Tales No. 5" on the front cover, and commercial ads on the inside and back covers; the titles are as for the present edition, and there is an inscribed date, July 1892.

The first edition was issued by A. H. Wheeler & Co., Allahabad, (1888), 22 cm., 114 pp., *Indian Railway Library* No. 5, in greenish-gray pictorial wrappers, with the titles as for the present edition. There are four leaves of ads at the back and a leaf at the front. It contains four pieces, one of which is from the *Week's News* of Feb. 25, 1888, and two are from *Quartette*, 1885. Wheeler issued the second edition (1889), the same, with a leaf of ads at the back.

In the United States the authorized edition was issued by John W. Lovell, New York (1890), 19 cm., 391 pp., $.50 paper, $1.00 cloth, with the wrappers issue having *International Series* No. 103 on the cover, and wrapper date June 12, 1890. It contains also *Wee Willie Winkie*. It was advertised in the *New-York Times* on July 19 and listed in the *Ind* on Aug. 14 and in the *Nation* on Aug. 21. The pirates descended on this title. It was issued by Rand McNally, Chicago and New York (1890), 20 cm., 211 pp., listed in *PW* on Nov. 15, 1890, and in *Lit W* on Dec. 20. It was also issued by J. S. Ogilvie & Co., New York, 1890, my copy, 224 pp., with wrapper date of Aug. 1890, *Fireside Series* No. 115. It was also issued by George Munro (United States Book Co.) (1890), *Seaside Library Pocket Edition* No. 1479, listed in *PW* on Sept. 6. It was also issued by M. J. Ivers, New York (1890), 18 cm., 207 pp. The United States Book Co., New York, issued *Indian Tales* (1890), authorized edition, 8vo, 771 pp., in red or blue cloth, gilt top, containing all six Kipling Indian tales and two other stories. The latter was advertised in the *New-York Times* on Oct. 4, $1.50 vellum cloth.

417 SARAH A. TOOLEY *Life of Harriet Beecher Stowe, Told for Boys and Girls.* Cr 8vo. 2/o   Dec. (*Eng Cat*)

This was advertised in the *Ath* on Dec. 20, 1890, Cr 8vo, 5/o as "New books." This 5/o issue was the first edition, 1891, 19 cm., 268 pp. Low reissued it in 1891, new edition, Cr 8vo, 2/o, listed in *PC* on Oct. 31.

418 JULES VERNE *Works.* 40 vols. 1/o sewed each   Jan.–Dec. (*Eng Cat*)

This reissue consists of all the Verne titles previously given in this bibliography. In addition I've found the following reissues: *Five Weeks in a Balloon*, new edition, Cr 8vo 2/6, in Mar. 1895, given by the *Eng Cat*; *The Child of the Cavern*, 1892, fifth edition, 174 pp., illustrated, given by the *U Cat*; *The Vanished Diamond*, 1896, new and cheaper edition, 19 cm., 263 pp., illustrated, given by the *U Cat*; *The Archipelago on Fire*, no date, new and cheaper edition, 19 cm., 198 pp., illustrated, given by the *U Cat*; *The Cryptogram*, part 2 of *The Giant Raft*, was listed in *PC* on Feb. 20, 1897, Cr 8vo, 254 pp., illustrated, 2/6; and *Godfrey Morgan* was offered by a dealer, 1892, slim 8vo, frontispiece and six plates, in red cloth blocked in blue and black.

419 T. HERBERT **Salads and Sandwiches.** p 8vo. 1/0 1890 (*Eng Cat*)

This is the first edition, 1890, 31 pp. Low issued a new edition, in 1891, p 8vo, 0/6 boards, listed in *PC* on July 4.

420 OLIVER GOLDSMITH **The Deserted Village.** Cr 8vo. Illustrated. 1/0 cloth 1890 (*Eng Cat*)

Choice Series. Low issued this in this series (1875), 18 cm., 43 pp., interleaved, illustrated by the Etching Club. He issued it for Joseph Cundall, 1855, 20.5 cm., 46 pp., interleaved, illustrated by the Etching Club, the illustrations being from an 1841 edition. Low reissued it, 1859, 61, 69. The first published edition was issued by W. Griffing, London, 1770, 28.5 cm., 23 pp.,

with a vignette on the title page, issued on May 26 and reviewed in the *Gentleman's Magazine* for June. Apparently the first three issues were trial or privately printed issues, 1770. The second through sixth editions were 1770, and there was a Dublin issue, 1770. In the United States it was issued by William and Thomas Bradford, Philadelphia, 1771, 8vo, 22 pp. It was also issued by William Pritchard, etc., Philadelphia, 1782.

421 OLIVER GOLDSMITH **The Vicar of Wakefield.** Cr 8vo. Illustrated. 1/0 cloth 1890 (*Eng Cat*)

Choice Series. Low issued this in this series (1875), 17.5 cm., 140 pp., illustrated by George Thomas. Low issued it, 1855, illustrated by Thomas, 20 cm., 219 pp.; and reissued it, 1858. The first edition was issued by F. Newbery, London, 2 vols., 1766, 17.4 cm., 5/0 sewed, 6/0 bound, with Goldsmith's signature on the preface. It was issued on Mar. 27; the second edition was issued, the same, on May 31; and the third edition, 2 vols., was issued on Aug. 27. It was issued in Dublin by W. & W. Smith, etc., 1766, 16.3 cm, anonymous. Eugene Swiney of Cork issued it, 1766, probably pirated, 2 vols. 17 cm., anonymous.

The first American edition was issued by William Mentz, Philadelphia, 1772, 2 vols.-in-1, 16.6 cm., 180 pp., anonymous, an exact reprint of the first British edition of 1766. It was also issued by James Humphries, Jr., Philadelphia, 1773.

Sampson Low, Marston, Searle & Rivington, Ltd. St. Dunstan's House, Fetter Land 1891

The imprint was sometimes given as Sampson Low, Marston & Co., Ltd., and at times as Sampson Low & Co., Ltd.

422 ANONYMOUS ***Roughing It After Gold.***
Cr 8vo. 1/6 sewed   Jan. 10 (*Ath* ad)
Shilling Novels No. 3. The ad said "Ready." I'm pretty sure that the price is 1/6 and thus it seems odd to call it a shilling novel! This is the first edition, 1891, 19 cm., 152 pp., by "Rux." Low listed it in their 1902 catalog as the third edition.

423 THOMAS HARDY ***Two on a Tower.***
New and cheaper edition. 12mo. 2/o boards, 2/6 cloth   Jan. 31 (*Ath*)
Standard Novels No. 21. This is 1891, 17.5 cm., 346 pp., in pale blue pictorial boards. Sadleir gives his copy in *Standard Novels* as 1890, and I have seen a copy advertised as 1890. This ran in the English *Atlantic Monthly* (Trübner), May–Dec. 1882, and the first book edition was issued by Low, 3 vols., 1882, 19.5 cm., 31/6 in green cloth with pale yellow endpapers. Records show 1,000 copies were printed, and it was received at the *BM* on Nov. 2, 1882, and listed in the *Ath* and *Spect* on Nov. 4. Low issued the second edition, actually a second impression, revised, 3 vols., 1883, with a 32-page catalog (Nov. 1882) at the back of vol. 2. It was in green cloth or in a variant plum cloth. Low issued the third edition, 1883, 18 cm., 346 pp., 6/o, with some mi-

nor changes, listed in the *Spect* on Apr. 28. Low issued it in 1893 in *Standard Novels*, 2/6 cloth, advertised in *Notes & Queries* on Sept. 30 as "Next week." Trübner issued it in 8 parts, 1882, 24 cm. in blue paper wrappers, offsets of the *Atlantic Monthly* installments, part 1 received at the *BM* on Mar. 31, 2/o, and part 5 received Aug. 28, 1/o. Purdy had no evidence that they were ever advertised or sold, but they were noticed in the *Spect*, which seems to support their being for sale.

In the United States it ran in the *Atlantic Monthly*, May–Dec. 1882. It was issued by John W. Lovell, New York (1882), 18 cm., 284 pp., *Lovell's Library* No. 43, with wrapper date Nov. 14, 1882. Carroll Wilson, placing undue confidence in the wrapper date, thought this was the first American edition. It was also issued by Henry Holt & Co., New York, 1882, 17 cm., 366 pp., *Leisure Hour Series* No. 142, $1.00 cloth, advertised in the *New-York Times* on Nov. 15 as "Published today" and listed in the *Ind* and the *Nation* on Nov. 23, and in *PW* on Dec. 9. It was also issued by George Munro, New York, 1882, 32.5 cm., 45 pp., $.20 paper, *Seaside Library* No. 1459. It has a cover date of Dec. 12, 1882, and was advertised in the *New-York Times* on Nov. 23

as "Out today" and listed in *PW* on Dec. 9. Harper & Bros., New York, issued it in 1895, new edition, Cr 8vo, frontispiece, $1.50, listed in the *Nation* on Sept. 5.

424 JAMES MORTIMER, ed. *The Chess Players Pocket-Book, etc.* Seventh edition. 16mo. 1/0 boards   Mar. 14 (*Ath* ad)

The ad said "Ready." This is 1891, 74 pp., and Low issued the 14th edition, 1902, 74 pp. The first edition was issued by Wyman & Sons, London (Preface 1888), 14 cm., 73 pp. They issued the second through sixth editions from 1888 to 1890, 74 pp. In the United States it was issued by Dick & Fitzgerald, New York, no date, fifth edition, 15.5 cm., 74 pp.

425 JAMES W. HYDE *A Hundred Years by Post.* p 8vo. Illustrated. 1/0 sewed Mar. 14 (*Ath* ad)

The ad said "Ready." This is the first edition, 1891, 144 pp.

426 JULES VERNE *The Clipper of the Clouds.* New and cheaper edition. 12mo. Illustrated. 1/0 sewed, 2/0 cloth   Mar. 21 (*PC*)

The 2/0 issue is in red pictorial cloth and was listed in *PC* on May 2. The first edition was *Robur-le-Conquesant*, issued by J. Hetzel, Paris, 1886, either 28.5 cm., 220 pp., illustrated; or 19 cm., 318 pp. It ran as a serial in a French periodical, June 29–Aug. 18, 1886. The first British edition was issued by Low, 1887, Cr 8vo, 234 pp., illustrated, 7/6, listed in the *Ath* on Oct. 15 and advertised in the *Spect* on Oct. 1 as "Now ready." The first edition in English was issued by George Munro, New York (1887), 18.5 cm., 181 pp., *Seaside Library Pocket Edition* No. 976, *Robur the Conqueror*, listed in *PW* on June 11, 1887.

427 JULES VERNE *The Lottery Ticket.* 12mo. Illustrated. 1/0 sewed, 2/0 cloth Mar. 21 (*PC*)

The 2/0 issue was listed in *PC* on May 9. Low issued the first British edition, 1887,

Cr 8vo, 219 pp., illustrated, 7/6, listed in the *Ath* on Nov. 20, 1886. The first edition was *Un Billet de Loterie*, issued by J. Hetzel, Paris, 1886, 27.5 cm., 198 pp., map, listed in the *Ath* on Nov. 13, 3 francs, printed wrappers. It ran in a French periodical, Jan. 1–Nov. 1, 1886. The first edition in English was issued by George Munro, New York (1886), 2 parts, *Seaside Library Pocket Edition* No. 833, $.10 each, in wrappers, translated by Laura Kendall, *Ticket No. "9672,"* issued in Aug. 1886, for part 1, at least.

428 GEORGE MACDONALD *Guild Court.* 12mo. 2/0 boards, 2/6 cloth   Apr. 25 (*Ath*)

Standard Novels No. 22. It has perhaps been noticed that several of the novels in this series, given here as 1891, have, in fact, 1890 on the title page. The present title is another instance of this. It was advertised in the *Ath* and the *Spect* on Apr. 26, 1890, 2/0 boards, 2/6 cloth. I place it here, however, as it was listed in the *Ath* as here given; listed in *PC* on May 2, 1891; advertised in the *Academy* on May 23, 1891; and given by the *Eng Cat* as issued in May 1891. I think it possible that these 1891 titles were using the title pages of a previous issue of 1890. Low first issued this in 1881, new edition, Cr 8vo, 6/0, listed in the *Spect* on July 16; and they issued it in 1893, listed in the *TWEd* on Dec. 29, 1893. The first edition was issued by Hurst & Blackett, London, 3 vols., 1868 (1867), 18.5 cm., 31/6 in tan cloth with slate purple endpapers, with a 16-page catalog at the back of vol. 3. It was listed in the *Spect* on Nov. 9, 1867, and in the *Ath* on Nov. 16.

In the United States it was issued by Harper & Bros., New York, 1868, 8vo, 148 pp., $.50 paper, advertised in the *Nation* on Dec. 19, 1867, and advertised in the *New-York Times* on Jan. 17, 1868, as "This day." I think it possible that it was issued by

George Routledge & Sons, New York and London, in New York (1868), as it is so given by the *U Cat*.

429 PHINLAY GLENELG *The Devil and the Doctor.* Cr 8vo. 1/o sewed   May 23 (*PC*) *Shilling Novels* No. 4. This is the first edition, 1891, 188 pp.

430 RACHEL WILLIAMS, later NORRIS & ALICE FISHER *Norris's Nursing Notes.* Cr 8vo. Illustrated. 2/o boards   May 30 (*Ath* ad)

Nursing Record Series No. 2. This is (1891), 184 pp. The ad said "Just ready." This is the second edition of *Hints for Hospital Nurses*, first issued by McLachlan & Stewart, Edinburgh; Simpkin, Marshall, London, 1877, 12mo, 174 pp., 1 plate, 2/6. *The Nursing Record* was started as a weekly by Low, about Apr. 7, 1888, o/2 per issue.

431 ARTHUR J. HARRIES & H.N. LAWRENCE *A Manual of Practical Electro-Therapeutics.* Cr 8vo. Illustrated. 1/6 boards   May 30 (*Ath* ad)

Nursing Record Series No. 3. This is the first edition (1891).

432 GEORGE H. SHEPHERD *A Short History of the British School of Painting.* [Third edition.] 8vo. 5/o, 1/o   May (*Eng Cat*)

The *BM* gives Low, 1891, second edition, 160 pp.; and the *U Cat* gives Low, 1891, fifth edition, 22 cm., 160 pp. The first edition was issued by Low, 1881 (1880), 19.5 cm., 194 pp.

433 RICHARD D. BLACKMORE *Christowell.* New and cheaper edition. 12 mo. 2/o boards, 2/6 cloth   June 20 (*Ath*)

Standard Novels No. 23. My copy is in pale blue pictorial boards, printed in red and black, title page missing, 18 cm., 410 pp., with the series title on the front and spine

and the No. 15 on the front. There are commercial ads on the blue endpapers and on the back cover. There is a known copy, 1891, the same as mine with the No. 15 on both the front cover and spine. This ran in *Good Words* beginning in Jan. 1881, and the first British edition was issued by Low, 3 vols., 1882 (1881), 19 cm., 31/6 in maroon cloth with cream endpapers. Wolff had a presentation copy (Nov. 29, 1881). It was advertised in the *Spect* on Nov. 19, 1881, as "On Nov. 23" and was listed there and in the *Ath* on Nov. 26, 1881. Low issued it in 1882, Cr 8vo, 6/o, listed in the *Spect* on Sept. 30; and they issued a new and cheaper edition, 1893, 18.5 cm., 410 pp., illustrated, listed in the *TWEd* on Dec. 29, 1893. Low issued it in 1902 in *Sixpenny Editions*, 22 cm., 191 pp., sewed, listed in the *TLS* on Nov. 14, 1902.

In the United States it ran in *Harper's Weekly* in 1881 and was issued by Harper & Bros., New York (1881), 29.5 cm., 84 pp., $.20 paper, *Franklin Square Library* No. 213, advertised in the *New-York Times* on Nov. 12 as "This day" and listed in the *Ind* on Nov. 24 and in *PW* on Dec. 10. It was also issued by George Munro, New York, 1881, 32.5 cm., *Seaside Library* No. 1131, $.20 paper, advertised in the *New-York Times* on Dec. 15, 1881, as a late issue, and listed in *PW* on Dec. 3. It was also issued by J. S. Ogilvie & Co., New York (1881), *People's Edition* No. 129, my copy, with wrapper date Nov. 28, 1881, and listed in *PW* on Dec. 3.

434 LUCY FITCH *Massage for Beginners.* Cr 8vo. 1/o boards   June 20 (*Ath* ad) *Nursing Record Series* No. 4. This is the first edition (1891), 31 pp.

435 SEBASTIAN & FRANK EVANS *The Upper Ten.* Cr 8vo. 1/o sewed July 4 (*PC*) *Shilling Novels* No. 5. This is the first edition thus, 1891, 92 pp., adapted from *Le Monde ou l'on S'Ennuie* by E. Pailleron, a comedy in three acts, issued in Paris, 1881.

436 MATILDA BETHAM-EDWARDS
A Dream of Millions and Other Tales.
Cr 8vo. 1/o sewed   Sept. 26 (*Spect* ad)
Shilling Novels No. 6. The ad said "Ready."
This is the first edition, 1891, 128 pp. It
was reissued in *Shilling Novels* in May 1892.

437 ANONYMOUS *The Penny Postage
Jubilee, etc.* Cr 8vo. Portrait. Illustrated.
1/o colored cover   Oct. 3 (*Ath* ad)
The *Eng Cat* gives this as issued in Sept. It
is the first edition, but is not in the *BM* or
the *U Cat*. It is by "Phil."

438 WILLIAM P. THORNTON *Heads, and
What They Tell Us.* Cr 8vo. Portraits.
Illustrated. 1/o cloth   Oct. 3 (*Ath* ad)
This is the first edition, 1891, 66 pp. The
third thousand was 1892, 12mo, 115 pp.,
illustrated, 1/o, given by the *BM*. Low issued *Phrenology or Heads and What They Tell
Us*, 1894, fourth edition, 12mo, 120 pp.,
illustrated, 1/o, listed in *PC* on Dec. 1,
1894. The same was issued, 1896, 19 cm.,
120 pp., illustrated, 1/o, given by the *U
Cat*; and the fifth edition was issued in
1915 or 1916.

439 EDWARD P. ROE *Nature's Serial
Story.* [new edition.] p 8vo. 2/o   Oct. 31
(*PC*)
The first American edition was issued by
Harper & Bros., New York, 1885 (1884),
23.5 cm., 430 pp., illustrated, 2 pp. of ads,
$5.00 in green cloth with brown endpa-
pers. It was deposited on Nov. 13 and advertised in the *New-York Times* on Nov. 13
as "This day," and listed in *Lit W* on Nov.
29. It ran in *Harper's New Monthly Magazine*, Dec. 1883–Dec. 1884. It was also issued by Dodd, Mead & Co., New York, in
1886, new edition, 12mo, 486 pp., illustrated, $1.50, advertised in the *New-York
Times* on Sept. 15 as "This day."
The first British edition was issued by
Low, 1885 (1884), 4to, 430 pp., illustrated,

24/o, listed in the *Spect* on Nov. 15, 1884,
and in the *Ath* on Nov. 22. Low issued it in
1889, Cr 8vo, illustrated, 3/6, advertised
in the *Ath* on May 4.

440 WILLIAM L. ALDEN *Trying to Find
Europe. By Jimmy Brown.* [New edition.]
p 8vo. 2/o   Oct. (*Eng Cat*)
The first edition was issued by Low, 1889,
19 cm., 167 pp., illustrated, 2/6 cloth, edited (or rather written) by Alden, advertised in the *Ath* on Nov. 23, 1889.

441 VEVA KARSLAND *Women and Their
Work.* Cr 8vo. 1/o boards   Nov. 28 (*PC*)
This is the first edition, 1891, 166 pp.

442 ANONYMOUS *Bobby.* Cr 8vo.
1/o sewed   Nov. 28 (*PC*)
Shilling Novels No. 7. This is the first edition, 1891, 122 pp., a Christmas Eve story
by "Vesper."

443 RUDYARD KIPLING *The City of
Dreadful Night, and Other Places.*
Demy 8vo. 1/o sewed   Nov. 28 (*PC*)
This is the first British edition, my copy,
with A. H. Wheeler & Co., Allahabad;
Low, London, on the title page and only
Low on the front, 21.5 cm., 96 pp., in pic-
torial gray wrappers, printed in black.
The title on the front is "The City of
Dreadful Night," and there is a slip in-
serted at the front stating permission to
use the title; commercial ads are on the inside and back covers, with "Indian Railway
Library No. 14" on the front cover. It has
four main heads containing 15 chapters.
The first edition was issued by A. H.
Wheeler & Co., Allahabad, 1890, 8vo, 99
pp., brown cloth, in an edition of 3,000
copies, suppressed by Kipling, with possibly only three copies preserved. It contained 18 stories and sketches from the
Civil and Military Gazette and from the *Pioneer*. It had the title "The City of Dreadful

Night and Other Sketches." Wheeler issued the second edition, 1891, 22 cm., 108 pp., *The City of Dreadful Night and Other Places*, in gray-green wrappers, with five leaves of ads at the back and two at the front, containing a statement by Kipling, "Suppressed by me." The contents were the same as for the present edition, 11 sketches being from *Pioneer*.

In the United States it was issued by R. F. Fenno & Co., New York, 1899, 16 cm., 90 pp. The title story only was issued by Alexander Grosset & Co., New York, 1899, 19.5 cm., 92 pp., illustrated by C. D. Farrand, in yellow cloth, untrimmed. It was also issued by J. S. Ogilvie & Co., New York, 1899, the *Sunnyside Series*, in wrappers, *The City of Dreadful Night and Other Stories*.

444 JOSEPH GREGO **Royal Navy Exhibition.** Demy 8vo. Illustrated, 1/0 Nov. (*Eng. Cat*)

The *BM* gives W. P. Griffith & Sons, London (1891), 96 pp., with historical notes by Grego, and it gives also Low (1891) 82 pp., illustrated. Both it and the *U Cat* give Low (1891), 21.5 cm., 96 pp., illustrated.

445 FERGUS HUME **A Creature of the Night.** Cr 8vo. 1/0 sewed   Dec. 19 (*PC*)

Shilling Novels No. 8. This is the first edition, 1891, 19.5 cm., 156 pp. An ad in the *Ath* on Dec. 19 said the first edition was exhausted on the day of publication and the second edition would be ready shortly. The second edition came out about Dec. 26. The first American edition was issued by Lovell, Coryell & Co., New York (1892), *Westminster Series* No. 57, $.25 paper, listed in *PW* on Aug. 13. The *U Cat* gives John W. Lovell, New York (copyright 1891), 19 cm., 208 pp., but I cannot verify this, and it seems highly unlikely since the No. in *Lovell's Library* would have to be after No. 1484, and I think the series did not run this high.

446 PETER H. EMERSON **East Coast Yarns.** Cr 8vo. 1/0 sewed   Dec. 26 (*PC*)

Shilling Novels No. 9. This is the first edition, 1891, 118 pp.

447 WILLIAM C. RUSSELL *Mrs. Dines' Jewels.* 12mo. 2/0 boards, 2/6 cloth Jan. 16 (*Ath*)

This is the first British edition, 1892, 18 cm., 258 pp. I've given the *Ath* listing for the 2/0 issue. The 2/6 was advertised in the *Ath* on Dec. 19, 1891, as "On Dec. 21." In the United States it was issued by Cassell Publishing Co., New York, 1891, *Cassell's Christmas Annual* for 1891. It was also issued by Harper & Bros., New York, 1892, my copy, 20.1 cm., 160 pp., frontispiece and seven full-page illustrations, *Franklin Square Library* No. 715, $.50 in light blue wrappers, printed in dark blue, cut flush, with publisher's ads on the inside covers and on 4 pp. at the back. The No. 715 is on the front cover and the spine, and the front cover is dated Jan. 1892. It was listed in the *Nation* on Jan. 14, 1892, in *PW* on Jan. 16, and in the *Ind* on Jan. 21. The present issue at 2/6 was in Wolff's collection, in dark blue with white endpapers. However, Sadleir's copy was in smooth scarlet cloth with ads on the pale blue endpapers. It was listed in the *TWEd* on Jan. 29, 1892. Low reissued it in 1895, listed in the *TWEd* on Feb. 22.

448 ANONYMOUS *Nuggets of the Gough and Albert Gold Fields.* 8vo. Reduced to 0/6 Jan. (*Eng Cat*)

I cannot trace this.

449 ANONYMOUS *Through the Mill.* Cr 8vo. 1/0 sewed Feb. 13 (*PC*)

Shilling Novels No. 10. This is the first edition, 1892, 19 cm., 136 pp., by "Rux." The third edition was advertised in the *Ath* on Feb. 13 as ready.

450 MATILDA BETHAM-EDWARDS *Half-Way.* 12mo. 2/0 boards, 2/6 cloth Feb. 27 (*Ath*)

Standard Novels No. 24. The first British edition was issued by Low, 2 vols., 1886 (1885). They issued a new edition, 1889, Cr 8vo, 6/0 cloth, in *Standard Novels*, advertised in *Notes & Queries* on Apr. 20. The first American edition was issued by Harper & Bros., New York, 1885, 17.5 cm., 287 pp., *Handy Series* No. 41, with a cover title. It was also issued by George Munro, New York (1886), 18 cm., 191 pp., *Seaside Library Pocket Edition* No. 668, listed in *PW* on Feb. 6. The Harper issue was advertised in the *New-York Times* on Dec. 19, 1885, as "Latest issues."

451 RICHARD CADBURY *Cocoa: All About It.* 12mo. Illustrated. 1/0 boards Mar. 12 (*PC*)

The first edition was issued by Low, 1892 (1891), 18.5 cm., 114 pp., folding frontispiece, eight colored plates and other illustrations, with 10 pp. of ads, in brown cloth, by "Historicus." Low also issued it, 1896, 21.5 cm., 99 pp., illustrations, partly colored, 2/6 cloth.

452 ANONYMOUS *Pensions for All at Sixty and an Eight Hours Day.* 12mo. 0/6 sewed, 1/0 parchment Mar. 19 (*Ath* ad)
This is the first edition, 1892, 45 pp., by the chairman of a Yorkshire school board.

453 ANONYMOUS *The Visitors' Book.* Demy 8vo. 1/0 sewed Apr. 2 (*PC*)

Shilling Novels No. 11. This is the first edition, 1892, my copy, 21.5 cm., 96 pp., in pictorial gray-green wrappers, printed in black, uniform with the Kipling tales. There is a publisher's ad on the inside back cover and commercial ads on the inside front and back covers. It is edited by "Ignotus" and consists of studies and sketches in a Swiss hotel.

454 ANONYMOUS *Married by Proxy.* Demy 8vo. 1/0 sewed Apr. 2 (*PC*)
Shilling Novels No. 12. This is the first edition, 1892, 96 pp., uniform with the preceding item.

455 RICHARD D. BLACKMORE *Alice Lorraine.* New and cheaper edition. 12mo. 2/0 boards, 2/6 cloth Apr. 9 (*Ath*)
Standard Novels No. 25. This is my copy, 1891, 18.1 cm., 393 pp., in pale blue pictorial boards, printed in red, green, and black, with the series title on the front and spine. There are commercial ads on the blue endpapers and on the back cover. As was noticed above, several of these *Standard Novel* issues have the date of the preceding year on the title page. That is the case here also, as Wolff's copy of the present title in 1892. The first edition was issued by Low, 3 vols., 1875, 19 cm., 31/6 in royal blue cloth with cream endpapers. There is a 40-page catalog (Feb. 1875) at the back of vol. 1. It was advertised in the

Ath on Apr. 17 as "On Apr. 20," and on Apr. 24 as "Ready." Low issued the fourth edition, 3 vols., in 1875, 31/6, advertised in the *Spect* on June 5 as "Now ready"; and they issued it in 1876, Cr 8vo, 6/0, cloth in *Standard Novels*, listed in the *Spect* on Apr. 29; and they issued the sixth edition, revised, 1877, 17.5 cm., 393 pp.; and they issued the seventh edition, revised, 1883, the same. Low issued it in *Sixpenny Editions*, 21.5 cm., 192 pp., sewed, listed in the *TLS* on Nov. 14, 1902. It ran in *Blackwood's Magazine*, Mar. 1874–Apr. 1875.

The first American edition was issued by Harper & Bros., New York, 1875, 23 cm., 212 pp., $.75 paper, *Library of Select Novels* No. 440, advertised in the *New-York Times* on May 1 as "This day" and listed in the *Ind* on May 6 and in *PW* on May 8.

456 GEORGE S. LAYARD *His Golf-Madness and Other "Queer Stories."* Demy 8vo. 1/0 sewed May 14 (*PC*)
Shilling Novels No. 13. This is the first edition, 1892, 96 pp., reprinted from *Truth*, and is uniform with the Kipling tales.

457 MARGARET OLIPHANT *Innocent.* [New edition.] 12mo. 2/0 boards, 2/6 cloth May 21 (*Ath*)
Standard Novels No. 26. The first edition was issued by Low, 3 vols., 1873, 18.5 cm., 31/6, listed in the *Ath* on June 7. Low issued the third edition, 3 vols., in 1873, 31/6, advertised in the *Spect* on Aug. 2; issued the fourth edition, 1874, Cr 8vo, eight illustrations, 6/0, advertised in the *Spect* on May 30 as "Now ready"; and issued a new edition, 1890.

The first American edition was issued by Harper & Bros., New York, 1873, 23.5 cm., 186 pp., illustrated, $.75 paper, listed in *PW* on July 26 and in the *Ind* on July 31.

458 SIR CHARLES G. DUFFY *A Fair Constitution for Ireland.* [Second edition.] Roy 8vo. 1/0 sewed   June 4 (*Spect* ad)

The ad was Low, London; James Duffy & Co., Dublin. This is also in the *Eng Cat*, but otherwise I cannot trace it.

459 T. HOLMAN *Life in the Royal Navy.* Third edition. Demy 8vo. Illustrated. 1/0 sewed   June 11 (*PC*)

Shilling Novels No. 14. This is 1892, 152 pp. The first edition was issued by Chamberlain, London, in Sept. 1891, Cr 8vo, illustrated, 1/0, by A Ranker.

460 T. HOLMAN *Salt Yarns.* Demy 8vo. 1/0 sewed   June 11 (*PC*)

Shilling Novels No. 15. This is the first edition, 1892, 133 pp.

461 ETHEL M. HEWITT *The Effacement of Oriel Penhaligon.* Demy 8vo. 1/0 sewed June 25 (*PC*)

Shilling Novels No. 16. This is the first edition, 1892, 96 pp.

462 WILLIAM HUGHES *Dark Africa and the Way Out.* Cr 8vo. Illustrated. 2/0 cloth   June 25 (*Spect*)

This is the first edition, 1892, 19 cm., 155 pp., portraits, plates, maps.

463 JAMES BAKER *Our Foreign Competitors: Their Life and Labour.* 12mo. 1/0 sewed   June (*Eng Cat*)

This is the first edition, 1892, 112 pp. It was advertised in the *Ath* on Dec. 16, 1893, the same, as "New books."

464 WILLIAM A. GIBBS *Prelude to the Idylls of the Queen.* 1/0 sewed, 3/0 cloth, 5/0 parchment   July 29 (*TWEd*)

The *Eng Cat* gives Cr 8vo, 1/0, issued in May 1892, and gives 3/6, issued in 1893. The present edition is 1892, Cr 8vo, 28 pp.

465 WILLIAM A. GIBBS *Home Rule!* Cr 8vo. 0/6 sewed   Aug. 20 (*PC*)

This is the popular edition, 1892, 26 pp. The listing in *TWEd* was also popular edition, and the *PC* listing said new edition. I have not discovered the first edition if, indeed, there was such.

466 THEODORE REUNERT *Kimberley South Africa and International Exhibition.* 8vo. 2/0 sewed   Sept. 3 (*Ath*)

This was issued by Reunert's Diamond Mines of South Africa, the first edition, 1892, 64 pp.

467 WILLIAM CARLETON *City Festivals.* 1/0 boards   Oct. 15 (*Ath* ad)

This is 1892, 192 pp., in verse. The first British edition was issued by Low, 1892, Roy 8vo, 164 pp., illustrated, 12/6, printed in New York. It was listed in the *Ath* and *Spect* on Oct. 8. The first edition was issued by Harper & Bros., New York, 1892, 28 cm., 164 pp., illustrated, $2.00 in gray-green pictorial cloth, bevelled boards, or $2.50 with gilt edges. It has 4 pp. of ads and was advertised in the *New-York Times* on July 15 and listed in *PW* on July 9. They issued a new edition, the same, advertised in the *New-York Times* on Nov. 8, 1892.

See 1893

468 EDWARD MARSTON *Days in Clover.* 16 mo. 1/0 boards   Nov. 12 (*PC*)

This is 1892, 120 pp., by The Amateur Angler, with the preface signed E.M. I'm uncertain as to the first edition. The present edition was advertised in the *Ath* on Oct. 15. There was a cloth edition, advertised in the *Spect* on Sept. 24, illustrated, 5/0, but given by the *Eng Cat* as 2/6, issued in Nov.

469 LOUISA M. ALCOTT *Recollections of My Childhood's Days.* [New edition.] 12 mo. 2/0   Nov. 26 (*PC*)

The first edition was issued by Low, 1890, Cr 8vo, 258 pp., 3/6, advertised in the *Ath* on Oct. 18.

470 DENZIL VANE (FANNY DU TERTRE)
The Lynn's Court Mystery. Demy 8vo.
1/0 sewed 1892 (*Eng Cat*)
Shilling Novels No. 17. This is the first edition (1892), 139 pp. This is given as issued in 1892 by the *Eng Cat*, and it was listed by the *Bookman* in Jan. 1893. An ad in the *Ath* on Dec. 12, 1891 (*sic*), giving the book as "Ready" thus appears incomprehensible.

Sampson Low, Marston, Searle & Rivington, Ltd.
St. Dunstan's House, Fetter Lane
1893

The imprint is frequently given as Sampson Low, Marston & Co., Ltd.

471 SIR JOHN E. EARDLEY-WILMOT *A Famous Fox-Hunter. Reminiscences of the Late Assheton Smith, Esq.* Fifth and cheaper edition. Cr 8vo. Portrait. Illustrated. 2/0 boards, 2/6 cloth Jan. 21 (*PC*)

This is 1893, 212 pp., with a preface by Eardley-Wilmot. The first edition was *Reminiscences of the Late Thomas Assheton Smith, Esq. . . . by Sir John E. Eardley-Wilmot, Bart.*, issued by John Murray, London, 1860, 22.5 cm., 301 pp., portrait, illustrations, diagrams. The *U Cat* gives Chatto & Windus, London, no date, a new and revised edition (the third), 20 cm., 212 pp., illustrated. This would have been after 1873.

472 G. VAN HARE *Fifty Years of a Showman's Life.* New and cheaper edition. Cr 8vo. Frontispiece (portrait). Illustrated. 2/0 boards, 2/6 cloth Jan. 28 (*Spect* ad)

This is 1893, 18 cm., 418 pp. The first edition was issued by W. H. Allen & Co., London, 1888, 19.5 cm., 418 pp., frontispiece and illustrations, 7/6.

473 KATHERINE ST. HILL *The Grammar of Palmistry.* [New edition.] 12mo. Illustrated. 1/0 cloth Feb. 4 (*PC*)

Low also issued the 31st edition, 1901, 16.5 cm., 124 pp. The first edition was is-

sued by G. Redway, London, 1889 (1888), 100 pp., illustrated. It was issued in the United States by H. Altemus, Philadelphia, 1893, 18 cm., 124 pp., illustrated; and they also issued it, no date, 16.5 cm., 118 pp., illustrated.

474 CHARLES W. SMITH *Original Theories Upon and Remedies for Depression in Trade, Land, Agriculture, and Silver.* 12mo. 2/0 Feb. 11 (*Spect*)

This is the first edition, 1893, 17.5 cm., 74 pp.

475 DENZIL VANE (FANNY DU TERTRE) *From the Dead.* [New edition.] 12mo. 2/0 boards, 2/6 cloth Feb. 18 (*Ath*)

Standard Novels No. 27. The 2/0 boards issue was listed as I've given it, and it was listed in *PC* on Apr. 22, 2/0 boards, 2/6 cloth. The first edition was issued by Low, 2 vols., 1888, 19.5 cm., 21/0, listed in the *Ath* on Oct. 27.

476 WILLIAM M. CARLETON *Poems.* Six Vols. Fcp 8vo. 1/0 each; 8/0 in a box Mar. (*Eng Cat*)

These are all six of the previously given Carleton poems.

477 CHARLES E. PASCOE *London's World Fair for 1893.* Roy 8vo. Illustrated.
1/0 sewed   Apr. 22 (*Ath* ad)
This is the first edition, 1893, 104 pp., illustrated by Fred Pegram.

478 RICHARD D. BLACKMORE **Erema.**
New edition. 12mo. 2/0 boards, 2/6 cloth   Apr. 22 (*PC*)
Standard Novels No. 28. This is Wolff's copy, 1893, in pictorial boards. The first book edition was issued by Smith, Elder & Co., London, 3 vols., 1877, 19.5 cm., 31/6 in slate cloth with primrose endpapers. Sadleir's copy was a presentation copy (Sept. 29, 1877). There are 2 pp. of ads at the back of vols. 2 and 3. It was listed in the *Ath* on Sept. 29. It ran in the *Cornhill Magazine*, Nov. 1876–Nov. 1877. They issued second and third editions, 3 vols., advertised in the *Spect* on Oct. 20 and Nov. 3 respectively, as "Now ready." They issued it in 1878, Cr 8vo, eight illustrations, 6/0, listed in the *Spect* on May 18. Low issued it, 1880, new edition, 18 cm., 437 pp., illustrated, 6/0, listed in the *Spect* on Dec. 27, 1879. It may have been reissued in 1880, as it was listed in the *Spect* also on Mar. 6, 1880. Low reissued it, new editions, 1883, 1894, and 1895, all with 437 pp. In the United States it was issued by Harper & Bros., New York, 1877, 8vo, illustrated, *Library of Select Novels* No. 596, $.50 paper, listed in the *Ind* on Nov. 1, in *PW* on Nov. 3, and in the *Nation* on Nov. 15. It was also issued by George Munro, New York, 1877, 32.5 cm., $.10 paper, *Seaside Library* No. 126, advertised in the *New-York Times* on Nov. 5 as "Out today." It ran in *Harper's New Monthly Magazine*, Dec. 1876–Nov. 1877.

479 GEORG EBERS *Per Aspera.* 2 vols.
Copyright edition. 16mo. 1/6 sewed, 2/0 flexible cloth each   May 20 (*Ath*)
German Authors No. 33. This has 1892 on the title page according to both the *BM* and the *U Cat*. It is 16.5 cm., translated by Clara Bell. The first edition was issued at Stuttgart, 2 vols., 1892. The first British edition was issued by Low in 1892, 2 vols., translated by Clara Bell, 21/0, listed in the *Ath* and *Spect* on July 2.

The first American edition was issued by D. Appleton & Co., New York, 2 vols., in 1892, *A Thorny Path*, 16mo, translated by Bell, $1.50 cloth, advertised in the *New-York Times* on June 25 and listed in the *Nation* on July 14.

480 JULES VERNE *The Flight to France.*
Cr 8vo. Illustrated. 1/0 limp boards, 2/0 cloth   June 3 (*PC*)
This is 1893, 18.5 cm., 179 pp. It first appeared in *Le Temps*, Aug. 31–Sept. 30, 1877, *Le Chemin de France*; and J. Hetzel, Paris, issued it in 1887, 18.5 cm., 324 pp., in printed olive-green wrappers, with a 32-page catalog, and also, 28.5 cm., 220 pp., plates (partly colored), and maps. One of these was listed in the *Ath* on Oct. 8, 1887, 3 francs. It was issued in French by F. W. Christern, New York, with the joint imprint of J. Hetzel, listed in the *Nation* on Dec. 15, 1887. The first edition in English was issued by Low, 1888, 18.5 cm., 231 pp., 34 full-page illustrations, 7/6 in blue pictorial cloth, with a 32-page catalog (Apr. 1888). It was listed in the *Ath* on Nov. 3.

In the United States it was issued by Frank F. Lovell, New York (1888); and by George Munro, New York (1889), 12mo, 158 pp., *Seaside Library Pocket Edition* No. 1168, listed in *PW* on Apr. 6, 1889.

481 JULES VERNE *North Against South.* 2 vols. Cr 8vo. Illustrated. 1/0 limp boards, 2/0 cloth each   June 3 (*PC*)
This first appeared in a Paris periodical, Jan. 1–Dec. 1, 1887, and the first book edition was issued by J. Hetzel, Paris, in 1887, *Nord Contre Sud*, in 2 parts, 18 mo; or in 1 vol., 28.5 cm., 416 pp., illustrated, map. One of these two editions was listed in the *Ath* on June 4, 1887, 3 francs. It was issued

by Christern, New York, in French, with the joint imprint of J. Hetzel, listed in the *Nation* on July 14, 1887. The first British edition was issued by Low in 2 parts, 1888 (1887), 18.5 cm., 154 pp., illustrated, 7/6, *I: Burbank the Northerner; II: Texar the Southerner*. It was listed in the *Ath* on Dec. 17, 1887. Low reissued *Burbank the Northerner*, 1891, 18 cm., illustrated.

The first edition in English was issued by George Munro, New York, (1887), *Part I, Texar's Vengeance*, 12mo, *Seaside Library Pocket Edition* No. 1011, $.20 paper, translated by Laura Kendall, listed in the *Nation* on Aug. 18 and in *PW* on Aug. 20, 1887. It was also issued by Rand, McNally & Co., Chicago and New York, *Texar's Revenge*, 1887, both parts, $1.25, listed in the *Nation* on Dec. 1, 1887.

482 FERGUS HUME **The Chinese Jar.**
Demy 8vo. 1/0 sewed   July 1 (*PC*)
Shilling Novels No. 18. This is the first edition, 1893, 156 pp. Glover and Greene had only the second edition, 1893, 156 pp., in red wrappers printed in black, and the *BM* gives only the second edition, 1893.

483 PETER H. EMERSON **Signor Lippa, Burnt-Cork Artiste.** Demy 8vo. 1/0 sewed   July 8 (*PC*)
Shilling Novels No. 19. This is the first edition, 1893, 106 pp.

484 RICHARD D. BLACKMORE **Cradock Nowell.** New and cheaper edition. 12mo. 2/0 boards, 2/6 cloth   Sept. 9 (*Ath*)
Standard Novels No. 29. This was Sadleir's copy, in pale blue pictorial boards, 1893, 461 pp. The first edition was issued by Chapman & Hall, London, 3 vols., 1866, 20.5 cm., 31/6 in apple-green cloth with cream endpapers. Sadleir's copy was a presentation copy (Sept. 11, 1866). It was listed in the *Ath* on Sept. 1. Sadleir stated that there was a secondary binding in

beach-leaf brown cloth with no spine imprint. It ran in *Macmillan's Magazine*, May 1865–Aug. 1866. The first Low edition was 1873, diligently revised and reshapen, Cr 8vo, 461 pp., 6/0, listed in the *Spect* on Jan. 11, 1873. Low issued the fifth edition, 1880, 18.5 cm., 461 pp., frontispiece; and issued the 11th edition, 1887, the same; and issued a new and cheaper edition, 1888, 461 pp. They issued a popular edition in *Sixpenny Editions*, sewed, 8vo, listed in The *TLS* on Sept. 12, 1902.

The first American edition was issued by Harper & Bros., New York, 1866, 8vo, 218 pp. $.75 paper, advertised in the *New-York Times* on Dec. 28, 1866, as "This day" and in *Harper's Weekly* on Jan. 12, 1867, as "Recent."

485 VARIOUS **Stories of New York. Stories of the Railway. Stories of the South.** 3 vols. Roy 32mo. Illustrated. 1/6 parchment paper, 2/0 half-bound each   Sept. 30 (*PC*)
These are 1893, the paper editions enclosed in a transparent wrapper fastened with a gold seal. The first editions were issued by Charles Scribner's Sons, New York, 1893, 3 vols., 13 cm., 214 pp., five stories; 195 pp., four stories; 222 pp., four stories, respectively. These were illustrated, edges uncut, $.50 paper, $.75 cloth each. The first two were advertised in the *New-York Times* on May 13, 1893, and the third was advertised on June 24. They were listed in the *Nation* on May 25, June 1, and in Oct. 1893, respectively. Bentley, London, issued these 3 vols. plus three more, 6 vols., super Roy 32mo, uncut edges, 1/6 sewed, 2/0 cloth each, advertised in *Notes & Queries* on Jan. 6, 1894, but perhaps issued earlier. I have a copy of *Stories of the Railway*, issued by Charles Scribner's Sons, New York, 1893, 12.8 cm., 195 pp., illustrated, in white wrappers cut flush, all edges uncut, printed in blue and black with a vignette in rust on the front

and repeated on the title page and a vignette in blue on the back. There are 2 pp. of ads at the back.

486 GEORGE T. TEMPLE *Notes on a Winter's Cruise in the West Indies.*
Small 4to. 1/0 Oct. (*Eng Cat*)

This was reissued in Dec. 1894. Aside from the *Eng Cat* I cannot trace it.

487 E. ROTHESAY MILLER *Princess Splendor, the Wood-Cutter's Daughter.*
12 mo. Illustrated. 2/0 sewed
Nov. 4 (*Ath*)

This is an extra number of *Japanese Fairy Tales,* issued by T. Hasegawa, Tokio (*sic*), 1895, translated (or rather written) by E. R. Miller, illustrated, second edition. He apparently issued the first edition without a date, earlier, 14 cm., (188) pp., colored plates, printed on one side of double leaves, folded in Japanese style.

488 WILLIAM G. CORDINGLEY *Cordingley's Guide to the Stock Exchange.*
18mo. 2/0 cloth Dec. 23 (*Ath*)

This is the first edition (1893), 130 pp. The second through 13th editions were issued by Effingham Wilson, London, 1901–31.

Sampson Low, Marston, Searle & Rivington, Ltd. St. Dunstan's House, Fetter Lane 1894

489 VARIOUS *Stories of Italy. Stories of the Army. Stories of the Sea.* 3 vols. Roy 32 mo. Illustrated. 1/6 sewed, 2/0 cloth each   Feb. 10 (*PC*)

These are stories from *Scribner's Magazine*, bound with uncut edges. The first book editions were issued by Charles Scribner's Sons, New York, 1893, 13 cm., illustrated, four stories each: 208 pp.; 186 pp.; 256 pp. respectively, $.50 paper, $.75 cloth each. They were advertised in the *New-York Times* on Sept. 14 as "Today"; on Oct. 3; and on Aug. 5 as "Today," respectively. They were also offered 6 vols. in a box, $3.00 paper, $4.50 cloth (see item 485, 1893).

In England they were also advertised by Bentley, London, in *Notes & Queries* on Jan. 6, 1894, super Roy 32 mo, 6 vols., uncut edges, 1/6 sewed, 2/0 cloth each, but perhaps issued earlier.

490 WILLIAM J. CONYBEARE *School Chronology.* [New edition.] 16mo. 1/0   Apr. (*Eng Cat*)

This is a new edition by Edward Conybeare. The *U Cat* gives this as 1894, small 4to, 28 pp. The first edition was issued by Longmans, London, 1845, oblong 12mo, 23 pp., with a preface signed W.J.C.

491 MRS. FREWEN LORD *Tales from Westminster Abbey. Told to Children.* Cr 8vo. Portrait. Plans, 1/0 boards   Apr. 28 (*Spect* ad)

These are told to children, retold by Mrs. Lord from Dean Stanley's *Memorials of Westminster Abbey* and from her recollections of his stories. The *U Cat* gives this as the second edition, 1894, 96 pp. The first edition was issued by Low, 1893, 19 cm., 109 pp., portrait, plate, plan, 2/6. Low issued the third edition, 1896, 98 pp., reissued 1905 and 1912. Stanley's work was first issued by James Murray, London, 1868, 23 cm., 564 pp., illustrated, reissued many times.

492 ARTHUR LLOYD *The Higher Buddhism.* Cr 8vo. 1/6   May 12 (*Spect*)

The first edition was issued in Tokyo, 1893, 19 cm., 39 pp.

493 FREDERICK H. AMPHLETT *The Lower and Mid Thames.* p 8vo. Illustrated. Map. 1/0   May (*Eng Cat*)

This is the first edition (1894), 128 pp.

494 MRS. FREWEN LORD *Tales from St. Paul's Cathedral. Told to Children.* Cr 8vo. Plan. 1/0 boards   Sept. 29 (*Spect* ad)

The ad said "In Oct," but the *Eng Cat* gives it as issued in Dec. I think the first edition was issued in 1894, probably at 2/6. The *U Cat* gives the second edition, no date, 18.5 cm., 108 pp., frontispiece, two plans.

495 ARTHUR A. BEALE *Feeding and Management in Infancy.* 12mo. 0/6, 1/0   Dec. (*Eng Cat*)

Aside from the *Eng Cat* I cannot trace this.

496 HENRY P. ROBINSON **Letters on Landscape Photography.** 1/0 Dec. (*Eng Cat*)

The first British edition was from Piper & Carter, London, 1888, 18 cm., 66 pp., *Photographic Handy-Books* No. 9. The first American edition was issued by Scovill Manufacturing Co, New York, 1888, revised by the author, 23.5 cm., 94 pp., illustrated, reprinted from the *Photographic Times*.

497 ELIZABETH BURNABY, later MAIN *Hints on Snow Photography.* 8vo. Illustrated. 1/6 boards Jan. 12 (*Spect*)

This is the first edition (1895), 14 pp., 14 plates.

498 WILLIAM DE W. ABNEY *Instantaneous Photography.* Cr 8vo. Illustrated. 1/0 sewed Sept. 28 (*Ath* ad)

This was listed in the *TWEd* on Oct. 11. This is the first British edition, 1895, 18.5 cm., 95 pp., with "Photographic Primer No. 2" on the cover. It is partly reprinted from *Photographic Work.* The first American edition was issued by Scovill & Adams Co., New York, 1895, 95 pp., illustrated.

499 JOSEPH CUNDALL *A Brief History of Wood-Engraving.* . . . Cr 8vo. Illustrated. 2/6 boards Oct. 19 (*Ath*)

This is the first edition, 1895, 19.5 cm., 132 pp.

500 ANONYMOUS *Sampson Low's Annual. 1896.* Folio. Illustrated. 1/0 Nov. 2 (*Spect* ad)

This was the beginning of this annual. It has stories by William C. Russell, Richard D. Blackmore, et al. It has two colored plates.

501 ROBERT L. JEFFERSON *Awheel to Moscow and Back.* p 8vo. Illustrated. 2/0 boards, 2/6 cloth Nov. 9 (*Spect*)

This is the first edition, 1895, 172 pp., with a preface by A. R. Savile.

502 ERNEST PHILLIPS *How to Become a Journalist.* p 8vo. 2/0 boards, 2/6 cloth Nov. 16 (*Ath*)

This is the first edition (1895), 20.5 cm., 150 pp., introduction by R. H. Dunbar, reprinted from the *Reporters' Journal.*

503 HONNOR MORTEN *How to Treat Accidents and Illnesses.* p 8vo. Illustrated. 2/0 boards, 2/6 cloth Nov. 30 (*Spect* ad)

This is the first edition (1895), 147 pp. There was a second edition, no date, 20.5 cm., 146 pp.

Sampson Low, Marston, Searle & Rivington, Ltd.
St. Dunstan's House, Fetter Lane
1896

504 EDWARD MARSTON *By Meadow and Stream.* Illustrated. 1/0 boards, 2/6, 6/0 Mar. 14 (*Spect*)

This is the first edition, 1896, 134 pp., by The Amateur Angler. Much of it had appeared in the *Fishing Gazette*. The 1/0 and 2/6 issues were 18mo, and the 6/0 issue was a limited edition of 250 copies, signed E.M., with the plates being mounted India proofs, 19 cm.

505 JUSTIN MCCARTHY & SIR JOHN ROBINSON *The "Daily News" Jubilee.* Cr 8vo. Illustrated. 1/0 sewed, 2/6, 10/6 cloth Mar. 21 (*PC*)

This is the first edition, 1896, 167 pp., portraits. The 10/6 was a signed and numbered edition, Demy 8vo.

506 WALTER W. READ *Annals of Cricket.* p 8vo. Frontispiece (portrait). Illustrated. 2/6 picture boards, 10/6 June 20 (*Ath* ad)

This is the first edition, 1896, 268 pp., with an introduction by John Shuter. The third edition, p 8vo, illustrated, 1/0, probably in picture boards but possibly sewed, was issued in 1897, 284 pp., listed in *PC* on June 19. Low's ads and listings are inconsistent as to the binding.

507 GUSTAV RUHLAND *The Ruin of the World's Agriculture and Trade.* Roy 8vo. 2/0 sewed Aug. (*Eng Cat*)

This is the first edition, 24.5 cm., 66 pp., with a preface by Charles W. Smith.

508 H. J. PERKINS *Notes on British Guiana and Its Gold Industry.* Second edition. 8vo. Maps. 1/6 sewed Oct. (*Eng Cat*)

This is (1968), 40 pp. The first edition was issued by Waterlow, London, 1895, 8vo, 1/0, in Mar. This second edition is enlarged.

509 JOZEF POPOWSKI *England and the Triple Alliance.* Roy 8vo. 1/0 sewed Dec. (*Eng Cat*)

This is the first British edition, 1896, 24.5 cm., 39 pp. translated from the German by G. G. Bagster. It was listed in the *TWEd* on Dec. 11.

Sampson Low, Marston, Searle & Rivington, Ltd.
St. Dunstan's House, Fetter Lane
1897

510 ANONYMOUS *Infant Diet and Sterilized Milk.* Cr 8vo. o/6 sewed, 1/o   Feb. (*Eng Cat*)

This is the first edition, 1896, 46 pp., by a physician.

511 ALFRED CLARK *A Dark Place of the Earth.* [New edition.] 12mo. 2/o boards, 2/6 cloth   Mar. 27 (*PC*)

The first edition was issued by Low, 1891, Cr 8vo, 340 pp., 6/o, listed in the *Ath* on Nov. 7.

512 ROBERT B. MARSTON *War, Famine, and Our Food Supply.* Cr 8vo. Illustrated. 2/o sewed, 2/6 cloth   Apr. 3 (*Ath*)

This is the first edition, 1897, 19 cm., 215 pp., colored folding frontispiece, plates.

513 MRS. FREWEN LORD *Tales from Canterbury Cathedral. Told to Children.* Cr 8vo. Plan. 1/o boards   Apr. 24 (*Spect* ad)

This is the first edition, 1897, 125 pp.

514 GILARMI A. FARINI *How to Grow Begonias.* p 8vo. Illustrated. 2/o boards, 2/6 cloth   May 8 (*Spect*)

This is the first edition (1897), 20 cm., 135 pp.

515 LORD CHESTERFIELD (PHILIP DORMER STANHOPE) *Letters, Sentences, and Maxims, by Lord Chesterfield.* [New edition.] 12mo. 1/6   May 8 (*PC*)

This has 252 total pp. The first edition was issued by Low, 1870, 16mo, 224 pp., in the *Bayard Series*, advertised in the *Ath* on Dec. 4, 1869, 2/6 cloth. It had an essay by C. A. Sainte-Beuve and prefatory remarks by J.H.F. (James H. Friswell). It consists of selections from his letters to his son. The first London edition of the latter was *Letters Written by the Late Right Honourable Philip Dormer Stanhope . . . to His Son . . .* , J. Dodsley, London, 2 vols., 1774, 30 cm., frontispiece (portrait), 42/o boards, entered at Stationers' Hall on Apr. 6. Dodsley issued the second through fifth editions, 1774, 8vo, 8vo, 4to, 8vo; 4, 4, 2, 2 vols. respectively. The first Dublin edition was issued by G. Faulkner, Dublin, 2 vols, 1774, Demy 8vo, frontispiece, 10/6 in blue paper on Apr. 30, and a few days later at 13/o, bound. It was also issued by E. Lynch, et al., Dublin 2 vols., 1774, 21.6 cm., frontispiece. Low issued the present title, 1873, 15 cm., 224 pp., with a portrait on the title page and with the Sainte-Beuve essay; and issued the third edition, 1875, the same; and the fourth edition, 1878, the same.

In the United States the present title was issued by Scribner, Welford & Co.,

New York, 1870, 348 pp., with the essay
and a prefatory note by Charles Sayle.
The first complete American edition of
the letters was issued by G. Long, New
York, 3 vols., 1813; and the second complete American edition was issued by
Hickman & Hazzard, Philadelphia; etc., 3
vols., 1821. Other editions were issued by
John Kingston, Baltimore, 2 vols., 1813;
and by Benjamin Warner, Philadelphia,
1818, 258 pp.

516 E. WALFORD *The Story of the
Chevalier Bayard.* [New edition.]
12mo. 1/6 May 8 (*PC*)
This probably has 255 pp. Low issued
"*Spotless and Fearless*," 1868, 255 pp., from
the French of the Loyal Servant (J. de
Mailles), M. de Berville, et al. They also issued it as *The Story of the Chevalier Bayard*,
1868, 15.5 cm., 255 pp., *Bayard Series* No.
1, edited by James H. Friswell, listed in the
Ath on Oct. 19, 1867, 2/6 cloth. Low issued
the fifth edition, 1875, 15.5 cm., 255 pp.;
and the seventh edition (189-?), the same.

The present title was issued in the
United States by Scribner, Welford & Co.,
New York, 1869, 15.5 cm., 255 pp., which
the *BM* gives as the third edition.

517 FRANCIS B. CROFTON *For Closer
Union.* Cr 8vo. 1/6 sewed July 31 (*PC*)
This has 76 total pages. I think the first
edition was issued by A. & W. Mackinley,
Halifax, 1897, 20 cm., 57 pp., reprinted
from various periodicals.

518 NATHANIEL E. YORKE-DAVIES
Homburg and Its Waters. Cr 8vo.
1/6 cloth Aug. 14 (*PC*)
This is the first edition, 1897, 90 pp., consisting of articles on obesity, gout, etc.

519 CHARLES W. SMITH *Agricultural and
Trade Depression.* Folio. 2/0 sewed
Sept. 3 (*TWEd*)
This is the first edition, 1897, 56 pp., a re-
ply to the final report of the British Royal
Commission on Agriculture.

Sampson Low & Co., Ltd.
St. Dunstan's House, Fetter Lane
1898

The imprint almost constantly used now was as given.

520 WILLIAM C. RUSSELL
John Holdsworth: Chief Mate.
8vo. o/6 sewed   Mar. (*Bks*)

Sixpenny Editions No. 3. The first edition was issued by Low, 3 vols., 1875, Cr 8vo, anonymous, 31/6, listed in the *Spect* on Oct. 23. They issued the second edition, 3 vols., 1875, 31/6, advertised in the *Spect* on Jan. 8, 1876. They issued the third and cheaper edition, 1880, Wolff's copy, Cr 8vo, 382 pp., 6/o in scarlet cloth, bevelled boards, with dark brown endpapers. There are 2 pp. of ads and a 32-page catalog (Sept. 1883) (*sic*) at the back, and pp. 381 and 382 give an account of the novel's origin. It was listed in the *Spect* on Nov. 6, 1880. Low reissued it, sixth and cheaper edition, 1889, 17.5 cm., 382 pp., Wolff's copy, with 2 pp. of ads and a 32-page catalog (Sept. 1888) at the back.

In the United States it was issued by Harper & Bros., New York (1884), 29.5 cm., 53 pp., *Franklin Square Library* No. 379, $.20 paper, my copy, with a date on the front page of May 23. It was advertised in the *New-York Times* on May 24 as "This day" and listed in the *Ind* on May 29 and in *PW* on May 31. It was also issued by George Munro, New York (1884), 32.5 cm., *Seaside Library* No. 1840, $.20 paper, advertised in the *New-York Times* on June 5, 1884, as a late issue; Munro also issued it

as *Seaside Library Pocket Edition* No. 209, 18 cm., paper, in Aug. It was also issued by John W. Lovell, New York (1884), *Lovell's Library* No. 399, $.20 paper, probably in June.

521 WILLIAM C. RUSSELL *The Frozen Pirate.* Popular edition. 8vo. o/6 sewed Apr. 16 (*Acad*)

Sixpenny Editions No. 4. The first British edition was issued by Low, 2 vols., 1887, 19.5 cm., 12/o in smooth navy blue cloth with dark gray and white foliage-patterned endpapers. It was advertised in the *Spect* on Nov. 26 as "Now ready" and listed in the *Ath* and *Spect* on Dec. 3, 1887. Low issued a new and cheaper edition, 1888, 20.5 cm., 389 pp., frontispiece and six illustrations, 6/o, Wolff's copy, in smooth blue-green cloth, bevelled boards, all edges gilt, with tan and white foliage-patterned endpapers, *Standard Novels*. There are three pp. of ads and a 32-page catalog (Oct. 1887) at the back. It was advertised in *Notes & Queries* on Mar. 17 and in the *TWEd* on Apr. 20. Low issued a new and cheaper edition, 1890, 19 cm., 389 pp., and reissued it, 1892. Wolff had a copy, no date, 18.5 cm., 389 pp., frontispiece and six illustrations, in smooth brown cloth, pictorially blocked in black and white, with a 32-page catalog (1894) at the back. Wolff also had a copy, no date, new and cheaper edition, 389 pp, frontispiece and three illustrations, 2 pp. of ads, in dark blue cloth with white endpapers. It ran in *Belgravia* beginning in July 1887. In the United States it was issued by Harper & Bros., New York (1887), 29.5 cm., 56 pp, *Franklin Square Library* No. 607, $.25 paper, advertised in the *New-York Times* on Nov. 8 as "Recent issues" and listed in the *Ind* and *Nation* on Nov. 10 and in *PW* on Nov. 12. It was also issued by John W. Lovell (1887), *Lovell's Library* No. 1087, in wrappers, probably in Oct. or Nov. It was also issued by George Munro, New York, (1887), 18 cm., paper, *Seaside Library Pocket Edition* No. 1044, listed in *PW* on Dec. 24, 1887, but issued somewhat earlier perhaps. It was also issued by Worthington, New York, 1887, 19 cm., 389 pp.

522 WILLIAM BLACK *A Daughter of Heth.*
Popular edition. 8vo. 0/6 sewed June 25 (*Spect* ad)

Sixpenny Editions No. 5. The numbering of this series is mine. The first edition was issued by Low, 3 vols., 1871, 19.5 cm., anonymous, 31/6 in maroon cloth, with a 16-page catalog (Sept. 1879) at the back of vol. 3. It was listed in the *Ath* on May 27. Low issued the eleventh edition revised, 1872, p 8vo, 481 pp., 6/o cloth, listed by *PC* as published July 1–15. Low issued the 16th edition, 1878, Cr 8vo, frontispiece, 6/o in red cloth, with 2 pp. of ads and a 32-page catalog (Oct. 1879) at the back (a known copy). It was listed in the *Spect* on Aug. 24. In 1892 Low began a reissue of Black's novels, completely revised, with No. 1 to be the present title, new preface, portrait, 2/6 cloth, and the ads stated that there would be no yellowback edition. It was advertised in the *TWEd* on Mar. 18, 1892, as "Now ready." Low issued a new and revised edition, 1894, 17.5 cm., 338 pp., frontispiece (portrait); and issued the

19th edition, 1895; and issued a new edition, 1905, 338 pp.

The first American edition was issued by Harper & Bros., New York, 1871, 8vo, anonymous, 136 pp., *Library of Select Novels*, $.50 paper, advertised in the *New-York Times* on Sept. 8 as "This day" and listed in the *Nation* on Sept. 14. They issued a new and revised edition in 1892, listed in the *Nation* on Jan. 28, 1892.

523 WILLIAM C. RUSSELL *A Sea Queen.*
Popular edition. 8vo. 0/6 sewed June (*Bks*)

Sixpenny Editions No. 6. The first British edition was issued by Low, 3 vols., 1883, 19 cm., 31/6 in pale blue cloth with white endpapers, advertised in the *Ath* on Sept. 22 as "On Sept. 26" and on Sept. 29 as "Ready." There was a second edition in 3 vols., of which Wolff had the first and third vols., in the same binding as the first edition and with a 32-page catalog (Sept. 1883) at the back of vol. 3. Low issued it in *Standard Novels*, 1884, 451 pp., 6/o, listed in the *Spect* on Mar. 1; and they issued new and cheaper editions with 451 pp., 1889 and 1894, the latter at 2/6 listed in the *TWEd* on June 13, 1894.

The first edition was issued by Harper & Bros., New York, 1883, 17.5 cm., 451 pp., $1.00, with 12 pp. of ads; and also (1883) in the *Franklin Square Library* No. 314, 29.5 cm., 81 pp., $.20 paper. They were advertised in the *New-York Times* on May 11 as "This day" and listed in the *Ind* on May 17 and in *PW* on May 19. Wolff describes the 12mo edition as in three-quarters bright blue cloth with marbled sides and buff endpapers printed with ads in blue. I can scarcely believe this. It was also issued by George Munro, New York, 1883, 32.5 cm., 75 pp., *Seaside Library* No. 1653, $.20 paper, advertised in the *New-York Times* on May 19 as a late issue. It was also issued by

John W. Lovell, New York (1883), *Lovell's Library* No. 123, listed in *PW* on June 16 and probably issued somewhat earlier.

524 WILLIAM C. RUSSELL *A Sailor's Sweetheart*. Popular edition. 8vo. o/6 sewed   June 25 (*Spect* ad)

Sixpenny Editions No. 7. The first British edition was issued by Low, 3 vols., 1880, 19.5 cm., 31/6, advertised in the *Ath* on Oct. 2 as "Now ready" and advertised on Sept. 18 as "On Oct. 1." It was held up to insure simultaneous issue in America and England. The third edition was in 3 vols., 1881, 31/6 in blue cloth with a 32-page catalog (Jan. 1881) at the back of vol. 3, and with a preface dated 1880, advertised in the *Spect* on Feb. 19 as "Just ready" and listed on Mar. 19. Low issued the fourth edition, 1881, 17.5 cm., 344 pp., 6/o in scarlet cloth with brown endpapers and bevelled boards, with a 32-page catalog (Jan. 1881). There was a new edition listed in the *Spect* on Aug. 13, 1881, Cr 8vo, 6/o. Low issued a new and cheaper edition, 1888, 17.5 cm., 344 pp., reissued, 1896.

In the United States it was issued by Harper & Bros., New York, 1880, 29.5 cm., 81 pp., caption title, *Franklin Square Library* No. 142, $.15 paper, advertised in the *New-York Times* on Oct. 1 as "This day" and listed in the *Ind* on Oct. 7 and in *PW* on Oct. 9. It was also issued by George Munro, New York, 1880, 32.5 cm., 77 pp., *Seaside Library* No, 848, $.20 paper, advertised in the *New-York Times* on Oct. 14 as a late issue. It was also issued by John W. Lovell, New York, *Lovell's Library* No. 835, 18 cm., (320) pp., with 16 pp. of ads at the back, in tan wrappers, printed in red and black, probably issued in Dec. 1886.

525 WILLIAM C. RUSSELL *The Emigrant Ship*. Popular edition. 8vo. o/6 sewed   Aug. 20 (*Acad*)

Sixpenny Editions. The first edition was issued by Low, 3 vols., 1893, 19 cm., 31/6 in smooth gray-blue cloth with pale salmon decorated endpapers (Sadleir's copy) or gray and white decorated endpapers (Wolff's copy). It was advertised in the *Ath* on Oct. 14 as "Now ready" and listed in the *Spect* on Oct. 12. Low issued the second edition, 3 vols., advertised in the *Spect* on Dec. 2, 1893, as "Just ready." Low issued a new and cheaper edition (1894), 19 cm., 400 pp., in smooth red cloth, advertised in the *TWEd* on May 18.

The first American edition was issued by the Cassell Publishing Co., New York (1893), 19.5 cm., 348 pp., listed in the *Ind* and the *Nation* on Dec. 21, 1893. They issued it in 1895, 12mo, $.50 paper, $1.00 cloth, advertised in the *New-York Times* on Mar. 30 as "Just published."

526 WILLIAM C. RUSSELL *An Ocean Free-Lance*. Popular edition. 8vo. o/6 sewed Aug. (*Bks*)

Sixpenny Editions. The first edition was issued by Bentley, London, 3 vols., 1881, 19 cm., in smooth sand-colored cloth with pale yellow endpapers, avertised in the *Ath* on Apr. 2 as "Ready." It has 2 pp. of ads at the back of vol. 2 and 4 pp. at the back of vol. 3. Bentley issued it in their *Favourite Novels*, 1882, 19.5 cm., 460 pp., 6/o in dark green cloth, with 4 pp. of ads (June 20, 1882) at the back. They issued a new edition, 1884, 19.5 cm., 460 pp. Low issued it, 1889, new edition, 19.5 cm., 460 pp., 3/6, listed in the *Ath* on Aug. 10; and reissued it, 1893.

In the United States it was issued by Harper & Bros., New York, 1881, 29.5 cm., 81 pp., *Franklin Square Library* No. 194, $.20 paper, listed in the *Ind* on July 7 and in *PW* on July 9. It was also issued by George Munro, New York, 1881, my copy, 32.5 cm., *Seaside Library* No. 1034, paper, with a date on the front sheet (July 13). It was listed in *PW* on July 30.

527 WILLIAM BLACK *A Princess of Thule.* Popular edition. 8vo. o/6 sewed   Sept. 3 (*Acad*)

Sixpenny Editions. The first edition was issued by Macmillan & Co., London, 3 vols., 1873, Cr 8vo, 31/6, listed in the *Ath* on Nov. 22. They issued the fourth and fifth editions, 3 vols., 31/6, 1874, advertised in the *Spect* on Jan. 17 and Feb. 7, 1874, respectively. Wolff had a copy of the fourth edition in royal blue cloth with brown endpapers, with 2 pp. of ads at the back of vol. 1 and a preface (Nov. 1873). Macmillan issued the sixth edition, 1874, Cr 8vo, 6/o, listed in the Spect on June 27; and issued the tenth edition, 1876, 19.5 cm., 459 pp. They issued it, 1881, in blue cloth, with 2 pp. of ads and a 24-page catalog (Apr. 1882) (a known copy). Low issued it probably in 1879, a new edition, 12mo, 480 pp; and issued a new and revised edition, 1892, 480 pp., No. 3 in a monthly series of a reissue of Black's novels, 2/6 cloth, advertised in the *TWEd* on Mar. 18 as "Just ready." It ran in *Macmillan's Magazine*, Mar.–Dec. 1873.

In the United States it ran in *Lippincott's Magazine*, Mar. 1873–Jan. 1874. It was issued by Harper & Bros., New York, 1874, 22.5 cm., 272 pp., my copy, *Library of Select Novels* No. 404, $.75 paper, advertised in the *New-York Times* on Jan. 24, 1874, as "This day." They also issued it in 1877, 12mo, $1.50 cloth, advertised in the *New-York Times* on Feb. 1.

528 FRANCIS R. WINGATE *Ten Years' Captivity in the Mahdi's Camp 1882–1892.* Popular edition. 8vo. o/6 sewed Sept. 9 (*TWEd*)

Sixpenny Editions. This is my copy, 1898, from the original manuscript of Father Joseph Ohrwalder, 21.3 cm., 128 pp. in double columns, with a preface (July 30, 1892), in pictorial pink wrappers cut flush, printed in black. There is a pub-

lisher's ad on the bottom two-thirds of page 128, and commercial ads are on the inside and back covers. The first edition was issued by Low, 1892, 23 cm., 460 pp., portraits, illustrations, folding maps, 21/o, advertised in the *Ath* on Oct. 22 as "Now ready" and listed in the *Spect* on Oct. 22. Low issued the second edition, 1892, Demy 8vo, 500 pp., 21/o, advertised in the *Spect* on Nov. 5, 1892, as "Now ready." They issued the fourth edition, advertised in the *TWEd* on Nov. 18, 1892, as "Now ready"; and issued the seventh edition, Demy 8vo, illustrations, maps, 500 pp., 21/o, advertised in *Notes & Queries* on Jan. 7, 1893. They issued the eighth edition, the same, advertised in *Notes & Queries* on Feb. 11, 1893; and issued the tenth edition, revised, corrected, and condensed, 1893, 19 cm., 471 pp., illustrated, maps, 6/o, advertised in the *Spect* on Sept. 30, 1893, as "Just ready"; and reissued, 1894 at 2/6 cloth; and reissued 1895 and 1903.

In the United States it was imported by Charles Scribner's Sons, New York, and issued at $6.00, illustrated, listed in the *Literary Digest* on May 27, 1893; and reissued in 1893, at $2.00, listed in the *Outlook* on Nov. 11.

529 GEORGE A. HENTY *Jack Archer.* Popular edition. 8vo. o/6 sewed Oct. 22 (*Acad*)

Sixpenny Editions. The first edition was issued by Low, 1883, 19 cm., 302 pp., illustrated, maps (partly folding), 6/o, listed in the *Ath* on Oct. 20. Low reissued it, 1884; and issued a new and cheaper edition, 1888, 19 cm., 302 pp., illustrated, maps; reissued, the same, 1894. The first American edition was issued by Roberts Bros., Boston, in 1884, square 12mo, illustrated, $1.50 cloth, advertised in the *New-York Times* on Sept. 23 and listed in the *Nation* on Oct. 2.

530 W.H.G. KINGSTON *With Axe and Rifle*. Popular edition. 8vo. o/6 sewed Oct. 22 (*Acad*)

Sixpenny Editions. This is my copy, 1898, 21.5 cm., 113 pp. of text in double columns, with pp. 114–128 being publisher's ads. It is in pictorial pink wrappers, printed in black, with commercial ads on the inside and back covers. The first edition was issued by Low, 1878, 19.5 cm., 382 pp, illustrated, 7/6, listed in the *Ath* on Sept. 28. Low issued it in 1882, square, 5/0, listed in the *Spect* on Jan. 28, 1882; and issued it, no date, probably in 1887, new and cheaper edition, 18.5 cm., 382 pp, illustrated. The first American edition was issued by J. B. Lippincott & Co., Philadelphia, 1878, listed in *PW* on Dec. 14, 1878.

531 WILLIAM BLACK *Macleod of Dare*. Popular edition. 8vo. o/6 sewed   Oct. (*Bks*)

Sixpenny Editions. The first British edition was issued by Macmillan & Co., London, 3 vols., 1878, 19 cm., illustrated, 31/6 in royal blue cloth with dark brown endpapers. There are 2 pp. of ads and a 40-page catalog (June 1878) at the back of vol. 1, and 2 pp. of ads at the back of vol. 3. There is a frontispiece and 3 illustrations in each vol. by twelve different artists! It was listed in the *Ath* on Nov. 2, 1878. It ran in *Good Words*, Jan.–Dec. 1878, illustrated. Macmillan issued it, 1879, 19 cm., 431 pp., illustrated, 6/0, listed in the *Spect* on May 10. The first Low edition was in 1892, new and revised edition, 431 pp., 2/6 cloth, advertised in the *TWEd* on Oct. 14.

In the United States it ran in *Harper's New Monthly Magazine*, Feb. 1878–Jan. 1879, illustrated. Harper & Bros., New York, issued it in three forms: a library edition, 1879, 12mo, 400 pp., illustrated, $1.25 cloth; *Library of Select Novels* No. 614, 1879, 8vo, illustrated, $.60 paper; and *Franklin Square Library* No. 25, 28.5 cm., 68 pp., $.10 paper, caption title, illustrated. All three were advertised in the *New-York Times* on Nov. 1, 1878, as "This day." Harpers issued a new edition, revised by the author, in 1892, p 8vo, $.90 cloth, listed in the *Nation* on Nov. 10. It was also issued by George Munro, New York (1878), 32.5 cm., 74 pp., caption title, $.10 paper, *Seaside Library* No. 417, advertised in the *New-York Times* on Nov. 2, 1878, "Out today," and in the *Ind* on Nov. 21. It was also issued by Donnelley, Gassette & Loyd, Chicago (1878).

532 WILLIAM BLACK *In Silk Attire*. Popular edition. 8vo. o/6 sewed Nov. (*Bks*)

Sixpenny Editions. The first edition was issued by Tinsley Bros., London, 3 vols., 1869, Cr 8vo, 31/6 in plum colored cloth, with 4 pp. of ads at the back of vol. 3. It was listed in the *Ath* on Feb. 13. They issued the second edition, 3 vols., advertised in the *Spect* on Apr. 17, 1869, as "This day." Low issued the third edition, 1872, Cr 8vo, 462 pp., 6/0, listed in the *Spect* on Dec. 16, 1871; and issued a new and revised edition, 1892, 318 pp., No. 4 in the monthly issue of Black's novels, 2/6 cloth, advertised in *Notes & Queries* on Apr. 16.

The first American edition was issued by Harper & Bros., New York, 1869, 8vo, 126 pp., $.50 paper, advertised in the *New-York Times* on Sept. 29 as "This day" and listed in the *Nation* on Sept. 30.

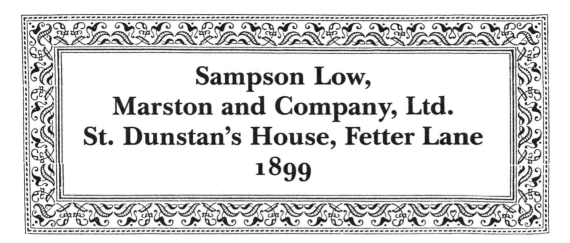

Sampson Low,
Marston and Company, Ltd.
St. Dunstan's House, Fetter Lane
1899

533 HERBERT RUSSELL *The Incubator.*
Cr 8vo. 1/6 Mar. (*Eng Cat*)

This is the first edition (1899), 19.5 cm., 86 pp., a book on poultry hatching.

534 JOSEPH HATTON *Three Recruits.*
Popular edition. 8vo. o/6 sewed
Apr. 1 (*Acad*)

Sixpenny Editions. This is my copy, 1899, 21.6 cm., 157 pp. in double columns, in pink pictorial wrappers, printed in black, with a prefatory note for this edition (1899). There are 3 pp. of publisher's ads at the back and commercial ads on the inside and back covers. The first edition was issued by Hurst & Blackett, London, 3 vols., 1880, 19.5 cm., 31/6, listed in the *Ath* on Mar. 27. Low issued it, 1882, 17.5 cm., 402 pp., 6/0 in red cloth; and issued it in 1895, Cr 8vo, 2/6, advertised in the *Spect* on Jan. 26, 1895. The first American edition was issued by Harper & Bros., New York, 1880, 29.5 cm., 58 pp., caption title, *Franklin Square Library* No. 145, $.15 paper, listed in *PW* on Oct. 23.

535 CHARLES H. SPURGEON *Messages for the Multitude.* Popular edition. 8vo. o/6 sewed   Apr. 29 (*Spect* ad)

Sixpenny Editions. The ad said ready. The first edition was issued by Low, 1892, 19.5 cm., 306 pp., frontispiece (portrait), 3/6, listed in the *Spect* on Apr. 9 but advertised in *Notes & Queries* on Apr. 16 as "On Apr. 26." It is *Preachers of the Age* series No. 10, and it contains ten sermons and two unpublished addresses, a bibliography on pp. (301)–306, and a preface by J. A. Spurgeon. This series went to 22 vols., 3/6 each, 1891–97.

536 SIDNEY K. LEVETT YEATS *The Honour of Savelli.* Popular edition. 8vo. o/6 sewed   Apr. (*Bks*)

Sixpenny Editions. This is my copy, 1899, 21.3 cm., (124) pp. in double columns, in pale blue wrappers printed in black, with 4 pp. of publisher's ads at the back and on the back cover, and commercial ads on the inside covers. There is an undated preface. The first British edition was issued by Low, 1895, Cr 8vo, 373 pp., 6/0, listed in the *Ath* on Jan. 26, 1895. Low issued the second and third editions, the same, advertised in the *TWEd* on Apr. 5 and July 12, 1895, respectively. Low issued a new and cheaper edition (1896), the tenth thousand, Cr 8vo, 373 pp., 2/6, advertised in the *Spect* on Sept. 26 as "Ready." The first American edition was issued by D. Appleton & Co., New York, 1895, 18.5 cm., 314 pp., *Town and Country Library* No. 161, $.50 paper, $1.00 cloth, advertised in the *New-York Times* on Feb. 9. I think they reissued it, the same, in 1897, as it was so advertised in the *New-York Times* on Apr. 21, 1897.

537 WILLIAM BLACK *Madcap Violet.*
Popular edition. 8vo. 0/6 sewed　May
(*Bks*)

Sixpenny Editions. This ran in *Macmillan's Magazine*, Jan.–Dec. 1876, and the first book edition was issued by Macmillan & Co., London, 3 vols., 1876, Cr 8vo, 31/6, listed in the *Ath* on Oct. 28. They issued the second and third editions, 3 vols., Cr 8vo, 31/6, advertised as "Now ready" in the *Spect* on Nov. 11, and Nov. 25, 1876, respectively. Macmillan issued the 4th thousand in 1877, Cr 8vo, 6/0, advertised in the *Spect* on May 19 as "This day," and they issued the 5th thousand in 1877, the same, 402 pp. Low issued it in 1892, new and revised edition, 445 pp., 2/6, listed in the *TWEd* on June 17.

In the United States it ran in Sheldon's *Galaxy*, Jan. 1876–Jan. 1877. It was issued by Harper & Bros., New York, 1877, 20 cm., 429 pp., $1.50 cloth, listed in *PW* on Dec. 23, 1876, and in the *Ind* on Dec. 28. They also issued it in the *Library of Select Novels* No. 478, 1877, my copy, 23 cm., 259 pp. in double columns, in tan wrappers printed in black, $.50. There are 2 leaves of publisher's ads at the front and 4 leaves at the back, and publisher's ads are on the inside and back covers. The back cover advertises the Dec. 1876 issue of *Harper's Magazine*, and the Nos. of the series in front end with No. 487. In Wolff's copy, the ad on back is for the Feb. 1877 issue and the numbers in front end with No. 482! It was listed in *PW* on Feb. 3, 1877. Harpers issued a new edition, revised, in 1892, p 8vo, $.90 cloth, listed in the *Nation* on June 30.

538 WILLIAM BLACK *Three Feathers.*
Popular edition. 8vo. 0/6 sewed　May
(*Eng Cat*)

Sixpenny Editions. This ran in the *Cornhill*, Aug. 1874–June 1875. The first British book edition was issued by Low, 3 vols., 1875, 19 cm., 31/6, advertised in the *Ath* on May 1 as "This day." Wolff had a third edition, 3 vols., 1875, in grass-green cloth with white endpapers, with a dedication leaf (May 1) and a 40-page catalog (Feb. 1873) at the back of vol. 3. Low issued the fourth edition in 3 vols., 1875, Cr 8vo, 31/6, advertised in the *Spect* on June 19, the ad also saying the fifth edition would be out in a few days. Low issued the sixth edition in *Standard Novels*, 1876, Cr 8vo, 408 pp., 6/0 in red cloth, listed in the *Spect* on Apr. 29. The sixth edition was reissued, 1885, the same.

In the United States it ran in *Lippincott's Magazine*, Jan. 1875–June 1875, and the first American book edition was issued by Harper & Bros., New York, 1875, 8vo, 186 pp. in double columns, $1.00 paper, $1.50 cloth, my copy, missing the wrappers. There are a double frontispiece and full-page illustrations and a vignette on the title page, with a leaf of publisher's ads at the front and 4 leaves at the back. It was listed in the *Ind* on May 20 and in *PW* on May 22. Harpers reissued it in 1892, new edition, revised by the author, p 8vo, $.90 cloth, listed in the *Nation* on Aug. 4.

539 WILLIAM BLACK *The Strange Adventures of a Phaeton.* Popular edition. 8vo. 0/6 sewed　June (*Bks*)

Sixpenny Editions. This ran in *Macmillan's Magazine*, Jan.–Nov. 1872, and the first book edition was issued by Macmillan & Co., London, 2 vols., 1872, Cr 8vo, 21/0 in blue cloth with dark brown endpapers, listed in the *Ath* on Oct. 19, 1872. They issued the second and third editions, 1872, the same, advertised as "This day" in the *Spect* on Nov. 2 and Nov. 30, 1872, respectively. They issued the fourth and fifth editions, 1873, the same, advertised in the *Spect* on Jan. 25 and Feb. 15, 1873, respectively. Macmillan issued it, 1874, 22.5 cm., 421 pp., with a frontispiece, eleven illustrations, and a vignette on the title page, 10/6 in blue cloth with dark brown endpapers, Wolff's copy. It was listed in the *Spect* on Oct. 25, 1873. They issued the seventh edition in 1874, Cr 8vo, 6/o, listed in the *Spect* on June 27; and issued the tenth edition, 1875, 18.5 cm., 421 pp., reissued, 1878. Low issued it, 1892, new and revised edition, Cr 8vo, 381 pp., No. 2 of a monthly reissue of Black's novels, 2/6 cloth, advertised in the *TWEd* on Feb. 19, reissued, the same, 1897.

In the United States it ran in *Lippincott's Magazine*, Feb.–Dec. 1872, and the first American book edition was issued by Harper & Bros., New York, 1873, 8vo, 216 pp. in double columns, $.75 paper, *Library of Select Novels* No. 387, advertised in the *New-York Times* on Dec. 14, 1872, as "This day" and listed by *Lit W* as published in Dec. 1872. Harpers also issued it in 12mo, $1.50 cloth, probably about the same time; and issued it in 1893, $.50, listed in the *Nation* on Dec. 14, 1893.

11; and they issued it, 1898, new edition, revised, 428 pp.

In the United States it ran in *Harper's New Monthly Magazine*, May 1882–Apr. 1883, and Harper & Bros., New York, issued it, 1883, 19 cm., 414 pp., illustrated, $1.25 cloth, advertised in the *New-York Times* on Feb. 24 as "This day" and listed in the *Nation* on Mar. 15. They also issued it (1883), 29.5 cm., 81 pp., illustrated, *Franklin Square Library* No. 297, $.20 paper, advertised in the *New-York Times* on Feb. 24 as "This day" and listed in the *Ind* on Mar. 1 and in *PW* on Mar. 3. Harpers issued a new and revised edition in 1893, listed in the *Nation* on Apr. 20. It was also issued by George Munro, New York, (1883), 32.5 cm., 68 pp., *Seaside Library* No. 1556, $.20 paper, advertised in the *New-York Times* on Mar. 2 as "Out today" and listed in *PW* on Mar. 17, 1883.

540 WILLIAM BLACK *Shandon Bells.*
Popular edition. 8vo. o/6 sewed   June
(*Bks*)

Sixpenny Editions. The first British edition was issued by Macmillan & Co., London, 3 vols., 1883, 19.5 cm., 31/6, in blue cloth with dark brown endpapers, and with a 32-page catalog (Oct. 1882) at the back of vol. 1 and 2 pp. of ads at the back of vol. 3. It was listed in the *Ath* on Feb. 17. Macmillan issued it, 1883, Cr 8vo, 6/o, advertised in the *TWEd* on Oct. 5. Low issued it, 1893, new edition, 12mo, 428 pp., in their monthly reissue of Black's novels, 2/6 cloth, advertised in *Notes & Queries* on Mar.

541 HENRY S. WILKINSON *British Policy in South Africa.* Cr 8vo. 1/o sewed Aug. 4 (*TWEd*)

This is the first edition, 1899, 18.5 cm., 114 pp., articles from the *Morning Post*. Low issued the second edition, 1899, the same; and issued the third edition in 1900, Cr 8vo, 1/o boards, advertised in the *Spect* on Feb. 24 as ready.

542 SIR HENRY MEYSEY-THOMPSON *The Transvaal Crisis.* Roy 8vo. o/6 sewed   Aug. (*Eng Cat*)

This is the first edition, 1899, 30 pp., containing also "Real Grievances of the Uitlanders" from *Nineteenth Century Review*.

Sampson Low & Co., Ltd.
St. Dunstan's House, Fetter Lane
1900

The above imprint was used interchangeably with "Sampson Low, Marston and Company, Ltd."

543 F. E. WEATHERLY *Oxford Days.* [Cheap edition.] 12mo. 1/o June (*Eng Cat*)

The first edition was issued by Low, 1879, 16.5 cm., 171 pp., 2/6, by a resident M.A.

544 EDWARD MARSTON *An Old Man's Holidays.* Cr 8vo. Illustrated. 2/o Oct. (*Eng Cat*)

This is probably the first edition, 1900, 19.5 cm. The *U Cat* gives it as a limited edition of 250 copies, by The Amateur Angler, signed E. M. Low issued the second edition, 1901, 17.5 cm., 140 pp., illustrated.

545 THOMAS F. T. DYER *Strange Pages from Family Papers.* [New issue.] Cr 8vo. 1/o sewed Nov. (*Eng Cat*)

The first edition was issued by Low, 1895, 17.5 cm., 319 pp., illustrated, and the present edition probably has 319 pp. also. A duplicate was issued by Dodd, Mead & Co., New York, 1895, with a different title page.

546 ANONYMOUS *India and Imperial Federation.* Cr 8vo. 1/o sewed Nov (*Eng Cat*)

This has 76 total pages, and aside from the *Eng Cat* I cannot trace it.

Sampson Low & Co., Ltd.
St. Dunstan's House, Fetter Lane
1901

The above imprint was used interchangeably with "Sampson Low, Marston and Company, Ltd."

547 THOMAS G. BOWLES *Gibraltor: A National Danger, etc.* Roy 8vo. Illustrated. Map. 1/0 sewed eb. (*Eng Cat*) This is the first edition, 1901, 24.5 cm., 41 pp.

548 JOHN P. SMYTH *The Bible for the Young. Genesis.* 12mo. 1/0 sewed, 1/6 May (*Eng Cat*) This is the first edition. The *BM* says the series consisted of 5 vols., 1901–08; and the *Eng Cat* gives eight titles, all before 1905, in the appendix, but lists only four titles in the text.

549 JOHN P. SMYTH *The Bible for the Young. St. Matthew.* 12mo. 1/0 sewed, 1/6 May (*Eng Cat*) This is the first edition. I list four titles in the series, here and in 1902.

550 WILLIAM T. LYNN *Remarkable Eclipses.* Sixth edition, revised. Fcp 8vo. 0/6 limp Sept. (*Eng Cat*) This is 1901, 17 cm., 56 pp. The first edition was issued by Edward Stanford, London, 1896, 54 pp. Stanford issued the third edition, Fcp 8vo, 0/6 cloth, probably in 1898, and advertised it in *Notes & Queries* on July 2, 1898, and on July 29, 1899; they issued the fourth edition, revised, 54 pp., 0/6 cloth, advertised there on Aug. 5, 1899. Low advertised the 11th edition in the *Ath* on Feb. 20, 1904, 0/6 cloth.

Sampson Low & Co., Ltd.
St. Dunstan's House, Fetter Lane
1902

The above imprint was used interchangeably with "Sampson Low, Marston and Company, Ltd."

551 JOHN LOCKE *How to Bring Up Your Children.* Fcp 8vo. 1/0 Apr. (*Eng Cat*)

This was *Some Thoughts Concerning Education*, edited, with an introduction by E. M., 1902, 115 pp., frontispiece (portrait). The first edition was issued by A. & J. Churchill, London, 1693, 18 cm., anonymous, 262 pp. The third edition, enlarged, was issued, 1695, 16.5 cm., 374 pp., and the fourth edition was 1699. In the United States it was issued by Gray & Bower, Boston, 1830, 18.5 cm., 317 pp.

552 FREDERICK S. ROBERTS *The Rise of Wellington.* Popular edition. 8vo. Plans. 0/6 sewed Apr. 26 (*Spect* ad)

Sixpenny Editions. The ad said "In May." It is 1902, 21.5 cm., 116 pp. The first edition was issued by Low, 1895, the *Pall Mall Magazine Library* No. 2, Cr 8vo, 198 pp., portraits, plans, illustrated, 3/6, listed in the *Ath* on Apr. 27, reprinted from the *Pall Mall Magazine*, 1894, 95. The first American edition was issued by Roberts Bros., Boston, 1895, 19 cm., 198 pp., illustrated, the *Pall Mall Magazine Library.*

553 E. N. HARTNOLL *The British Navy.* Obl 4to. Illustrated. 1/0 sewed June 6 (*TLS*)

This has 38 pp., the first edition, a souvenir of the coronation of King Edward VII,

containing a list of ships, with dimensions, armament, etc.

554 JOHN P. SMYTH *The Bible for the Young. Joshua and the Judges.* 12mo. 1/0 sewed, 1/6 June (*Eng Cat*)

This is the first edition. See 1901.

555 OUIDA (LOUISE DE LA RAMÉE) *The Massarenes.* Popular edition. 8vo. 0/6 sewed Aug. 9 (*Acad*)

Sixpenny Editions. The first edition was issued by Low, 1897, Cr 8vo, 574 pp., 6/0 in smooth olive-green cloth, with a dedication and a notice in front. It was listed in the *Ath* and *PC* on Mar. 27. Low issued the second edition, 1897, advertised in the *TWEd* on Apr. 2 as "Now ready" and stating that the first edition was exhausted on the day of publication. Low issued the third edition, 6/0, advertised in the *TWEd* on Apr. 30 as "Now ready," and issued the fourth edition, 21 cm., 6/0, 574 pp., advertised in the *Spect* on June 2, 1897; and they issued the fifth edition, 1897, the same. Low issued the seventh edition (1898), Cr 8vo, 574 pp., 2/6, advertised in the *Spect* on June 25, 1898, as "Just ready."

The first American edition was issued by R. F. Fenno & Co., etc., New York; Low, London (copyright 1897), 18.5 cm., 298 pp., probably in paper; and 19 cm., 583 pp., $1.25 cloth, advertised in the *New York Times Book Review* on May 1, 1897, as "Out to-day" and listed May 22, and listed in *PW* on May 8 and in the *Nation* on May 20. Fenno issued the seventh edition, $1.25 cloth, advertised in the *Atlantic Monthly* for Mar. 1898.

556 RICHARD D. BLACKMORE
Springhaven. Popular edition. 8vo.
o/6 sewed   Aug. (*Eng Cat*)

Sixpenny Editions. The first British edition was issued by Low, 3 vols., 1887, 19.5 cm., 31/6 in smooth gray-green pictorial cloth with pale yellow endpapers. Sadleir's copy was inscribed Mar. 3, and it was advertised in the *Ath* on Mar. 5 as "Ready." Low issued the second edition, the same, advertised in the *Spect* on Mar. 26 as "Now ready"; they issued the third edition, the same, advertised in *Notes & Queries* on Apr. 9, 1887; and they issued the fourth edition, the same, advertised in the *Spect* on Apr. 30 as "Now ready." Low issued the first illustrated edition, 1888, square Demy 8vo, 22.5 cm., 512 pp., illustrated, 12/0, listed in the *Spect* on Nov. 18, 1887. Sadleir's copy was inscribed (Nov. 25, 1887), and Wolff's copy was inscribed (Dec. 17, 1887). It is in smooth pale green pictorial cloth with dark green and white foliage endpapers, with all edges gilt. Low issued this illustrated edition, the same, at 7/6, advertised in the *TWEd* on Nov. 8, 1889. They issued it in *Standard Novels* in 1890, Cr 8vo, illustrated, 6/0, listed in the *Spect* on May 17; and Low issued a new and cheaper edition, 1894, 18 cm., 479 pp., illustrated.

In the United States it ran in *Harper's New Monthly Magazine*, Apr. 1886–Apr. 1887, but not in Dec. 1886. It was issued by Harper & Bros., New York (1887), 29.5 cm., 138 pp., illustrated, *Franklin Square Library* No. 568, $.25 paper, caption title, advertised in the *New-York Times* on Mar. 5 as "Latest issues," and listed in the *Ind* and the *Nation* on Mar. 10. Harper also issued

it, 1887, 19 cm., 512 pp., illustrated, $1.50 cloth, advertised in the *New-York Times* on Mar. 19 as "This day" and listed in the *Nation* on Mar. 31. It was also issued by George Munro, New York (1887), 18 cm., *Seaside Library Pocket Edition* No. 926, in paper, advertised in the *New-York Times* on Apr. 2, 1887, $.20, "Latest issues."

557 ANONYMOUS *Africanderism, the Old and the Young.* 12mo. 2/0   Sept. 12 (*TWEd* ad)

This is the first edition, 1902, 86 pp., letters to John Bull, by Anglo-Africander.

558 WILLIAM WILLIS *The Shakespeare–Bacon Controversy.* 4to. 3/0 sewed Sept. (*Eng Cat*)

This is the first edition, 1902, 25 cm., 88 pp. plus 73 leaves of appendix, a report of the trial of an issue in Westminster Hall, June 20, 1627, etc.

559 JOHN A. AUSTIN *Manual of First Aid.* New and cheaper edition. 12mo. Illustrated. 2/0   Nov. (*Eng Cat*)

This is (1902), 203 pp. The first edition was issued by Low, 1898, illustrated, 203 pp., reissued, 1904, 18 cm., illustrated, 203 pp., 1/0 boards, in Oct.

560 JOHN P. SMYTH *The Bible for the Young. Moses and the Exodus.* 12mo. Illustrated. Map, 1/0 sewed, 1/6 Nov. (*Eng Cat*)

This is the first edition. See 1901.

561 WILLIAM C. RUSSELL *Jack's Courtship.* Popular edition. 8vo. o/6 sewed   1902?

I list this here as it was in the Low 1902 Spring catalog, but I have not found it elsewhere. The first edition was in the United States where it was issued by Harper & Bros., New York (1884), my copy, 29.5 cm., 132 pp. in double columns,

Franklin Square Library No. 372, $.25 paper, dated Apr. 4, 1884, on the first page of text. There are publisher's ads on the bottom half of page 132 and on a leaf at the back. It was advertised in the *New-York Times* on Apr. 5 as "This day" and listed in the *Nation* on Apr. 10 and in *PW* on Apr. 12. Harpers also issued it in 1884, 16 mo, 476 pp., $.75 half-cloth, advertised in the *New-York Times* on Nov. 1, 1884, as "This day." It was also issued by George Munro, New York, 1884, my copy, 32.5 cm., 110 pp. in triple columns, *Seaside Library* No. 1814, $.20 paper, dated Apr. 15, 1884, on the cover sheet and on the first page of text. The cover sheet has publisher's ads on both sides in the front and on both sides at the back. The numbers in the *Seaside Library* in the ads end with No. 1815. It was advertised in the *New-York Times* on Apr. 5 as "Out to-day" and listed in *PW* on May 17.

In England it ran in *Longman's Magazine*, Nov. 1883–Dec. 1884, and the first British edition was issued by Low, 3 vols., 1884, 19 cm., 31/6 in dark blue cloth with cream endpapers. A 32-page catalog (Oct. 1884) appears at the back of vol. 3. It was advertised in the *Ath* on Oct. 25 as "Just ready." Low issued a new and cheaper edition, 1885, 17.5 cm., 474 pp., 6/o; and issued it, 1887, the same; and issued it, 1889, 3/6. They issued it, 1894, Cr 8vo, 2/6 cloth, advertised in *Notes & Queries* on Feb. 10; and issued a new and cheaper edition, 1905.

562 WILLIAM C. RUSSELL *A Strange Voyage.* Popular edition. 8vo. o/6 sewed 1902?

Sixpenny Editions. I list this here as it was in the Low 1902 Spring catalog, but I have not found it elsewhere. The first edition was issued by Harper & Bros., New York (1885), 29.5 cm., 117 pp. in double columns, *Franklin Square Library* No. 492, $.20 paper, advertised in the *New-York Times* on Oct. 3 as "This day" and listed in the *Ind* on Oct. 8 and in *PW* on Oct. 10. They issued a second edition in 1885, *Franklin Square Library* No. 492, small size, 21.5 cm., $.20 paper. George Munro, New York (1885), also issued it, 18.5 cm., 403 pp., *Seaside Library Pocket Edition* No. 592, $.20 paper, advertised in the *New-York Times* on Oct. 17 as "Late issues" and listed in *PW* on Oct. 24.

In England it ran in *Belgravia* beginning in Jan. 1885, and the first British edition was issued by Low, 3 vols., 1885, Cr 8vo, 31/6 in light blue-gray cloth, with a 32-page catalog (Oct. 1885) at the back of vol. 3. It was advertised in the *Spect* on Oct. 3 as "On Nov. 1" and in the *Ath* on Nov. 7 as "Ready." Low issued it, 1886, 17.5 cm., 452 pp., 6/o, listed in the *Spect* on Oct. 30; and issued it, 1889, 3/6, reissued, 1890 and 1894. Low issued it at 2/o, 1908. Downey & Co., London, issued it, 21.7 cm., 222 total pp., o/6 sewed, listed in the *Bks* for May 1900.

Sampson Low & Co., Ltd.
St. Dunstan's House, Fetter Lane
1903

563 THOMAS G. BOWLES **Gibraltor and the Ministry.** Roy 8vo. Map. 1/0 sewed Feb. (*Eng Cat*)

This is the first edition, 1903, 25 cm., 22 pp.

564 WILLIAM C. RUSSELL **The Two Captains.** Popular edition. 8vo. 0/6 sewed   May 1 (*TLS*)

The first British edition was issued by Low, 18987, 19.5 cm., 423 pp., frontispiece and three full-page illustrations, 6/0 in navy blue cloth with brown and white arabesque-patterned endpapers, top edge gilt. The title page is in red and black. It was listed in the *Ath* and *PC* on Oct. 9 and in the *Spect* on Oct. 16. It was issued by Downey & Co., London, no date, my copy, 21.7 cm., 158 pp. in double columns, 0/6 sewed, in white wrappers cut flush, pictorially printed in dark blue, with commercial ads on the inside and back covers in dark blue. It was listed in the *Bks* for July 1899.

In the United States it was issued by Dodd, Mead & Co., New York, 1897, 19.5 cm., 372 pp., illustrated, $1.50, listed in the *New-York Times* on Oct. 9 and in *PW* on Oct. 9. They issued a second edition, the same, advertised in the *Nation* on Oct. 28, 1897, as "Now ready." It was also issued by Peter F. Collier, New York, probably the first American edition, Wolff's copy, issued as the *Fortnightly Library* Nos. for Mar. 18 and Apr. 1, 1897, 372 pp., continuous pagination, in white wrappers cut flush, decorated and printed in black. There are ads on both sides of the back covers, and the second vol. has 10 pp. of ads at the back.

565 ANONYMOUS **The Truth About the Civilisation in Congoland.** 8vo. Map. 1/0 May 15 (*TWEd*)

This is the first British edition, 23.5 cm., with 180 pp. The first edition was *La Vérité sur la Civilisation au Congo*, issued in Brussels, 1903, map, 204 pp., by a Belgian. It was also issued in Brussels, 1903, in English, by J. Lebèque, 23.5 cm., 180 pp., folding map.

566 ÉDOUARD E. F. DESCAMPS **New Africa.** Demy 8vo. 5/0 sewed   May (*Eng Cat*)

This is the first British edition, 1903, 21.5 cm., 402 pp., printed in Brussels, and translated from the French. Low issued the second edition, 1904, 8vo, 476 pp., with two annexes. The first edition was *L'Afrique Nouvelle*, Paris; Bruxelles, 1903, 22 cm., 626 pp.

567 ROBERT STANLEY **Angling Anecdotes.** Fcp 8vo. Illustrated. 1/0 sewed   Aug. 14 (*TLS*)

This is the first edition (1903), 16 cm., 179 pp. Low issued the second edition (1903), 2/0, in Sept.

568 WILLIAM J. HAMMER **Radium, and Other Radioactive Substances.** 8vo. Illustrated. 1/0 sewed Sept. (*Eng Cat*)

The first edition was issued by D. Van Nostrand Co., New York, 1903, 23.5 cm., 72 pp., illustrated. The *BM* gives it as issued jointly with Low, London, and the *U Cat* gives it as issued jointly with C. Lockwood & Son, London. It is a lecture given on Apr. 17, 1903.

569 EDMONDO DE AMICIS **Heart.** p 8vo. Portrait. 1/4 sewed, 2/0 Oct. (*Eng Cat*)

This is 1903, 21 cm., 301 pp, translated from the Italian by G. S. Godkin. The *Eng Cat* says that it is from the 158th Italian edition. The *BM* gives Low (1895), 301 pp., translated by Godkin; and the *UCat* gives Low, London; Kaiser, Berne, no date, 19.5 cm., 301 pp., translated from the 158th edition by Godkin. The first edition was *Cuore*, issued in Milan, 1886, 338 pp.

In the United States it was issued as *The Heart of a Boy*, by Laird & Lee, Chicago, 1895, 19.5 cm., 290 pp., translated by G. Mantellini, from the 166th Italian edition.

Sampson Low & Co., Ltd.
St. Dunstan's House, Fetter Lane
1904

570 (JOHN JACKSON) *The Advantages of Ambidexterity.* 8vo. 0/6 sewed Sept. (*Eng Cat*)

This was first issued by the Ambidextral Culture Society, London, 1904, 24 cm., 32 pp., with a cover title, and with an introduction signed John Jackson. It is a lecture given on May 4, 1904.

Sampson Low & Co., Ltd.
St. Dunstan's House, Fetter Lane
1905

The firm struggled on until the death of Marston in 1914.

571 W. T. LYNN *Remarkable Comets.* 12th edition, revised. Fcp 8vo. o/6 Feb. 24 (*TLS*)

This is 16.5 cm., 46 pp. It was issued by Edward Stanford, London, 1895, at o/6 cloth, listed in the *TWEd* on Feb. 8. They issued the seventh edition, o/6 cloth, advertised in *Notes & Queries* on Feb. 11, 1899. The first edition was issued by Stanford, 1893, 16.5 cm., 40 pp.; and the second editon was issued by them, 1894, the same; the fifth edition, revised, was 1897, 44 pp. Low issued the tenth edition, revised, 1902, 16 cm., 46 pp., frontispiece; and issued the 13th edition, revised, 1906, 46 pp.

572 JOHN P. SMYTH *How We Got Our Bible.* 17th edition. Cr 8vo. Illustrated. 1/o cloth Nov. 4 (*Spect* ad)

The ad said "Now ready." I think the first edition was issued by S. Bagster & Sons, London, 1885, 19 cm., 127 pp., diagrams. This probably has the joint imprint of John Wiley & Sons, New York. Bagster issued the second edition, probably in 1885; and issued the third edition (1886), both with 127 pp. Low issued a new edition, 1899, 139 pp., with added illustrations; and reissued it, new edition (the 16th), the same, 1903, 19 cm.

Indexes

Name Index for
Frederick Warne & Co.

*Listings are alphabetically by title, followed by item number and **page** number (in boldface).*

Title Index for
Frederick Warne & Co.

*Listings are alphabetically by title, followed by item number and **page** number (in boldface).*

Series Index for
Frederick Warne & Co.

*Listings are alphabetically by title, followed by item number and **page** number (in boldface).*

Columbia Library

Companion Library

Notable Novels

Name Index for
Sampson Low & Co.

*Listings are alphabetically by title, followed by item number and **page** number (in boldface).*

Title Index for
Sampson Low & Co.

*Listings are alphabetically by title, followed by item number and **page** number (in boldface).*

Series Index for
Sampon Low & Co.

*Listings are alphabetically by title, followed by item number
and **page** number (in boldface).*

Standard Novels

Waterside Shilling Series